AF576758

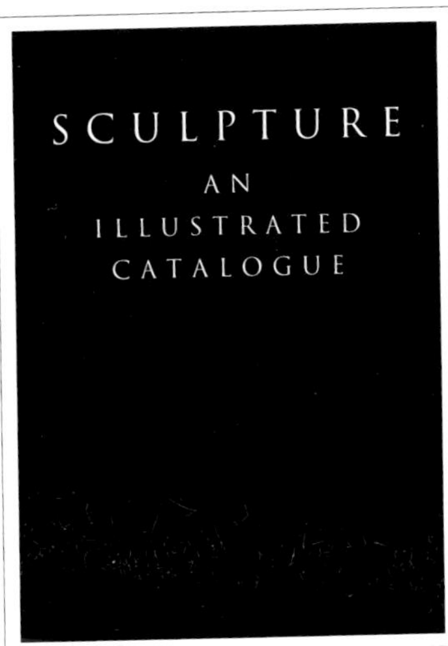
SCULPTURE
AN
ILLUSTRATED
CATALOGUE

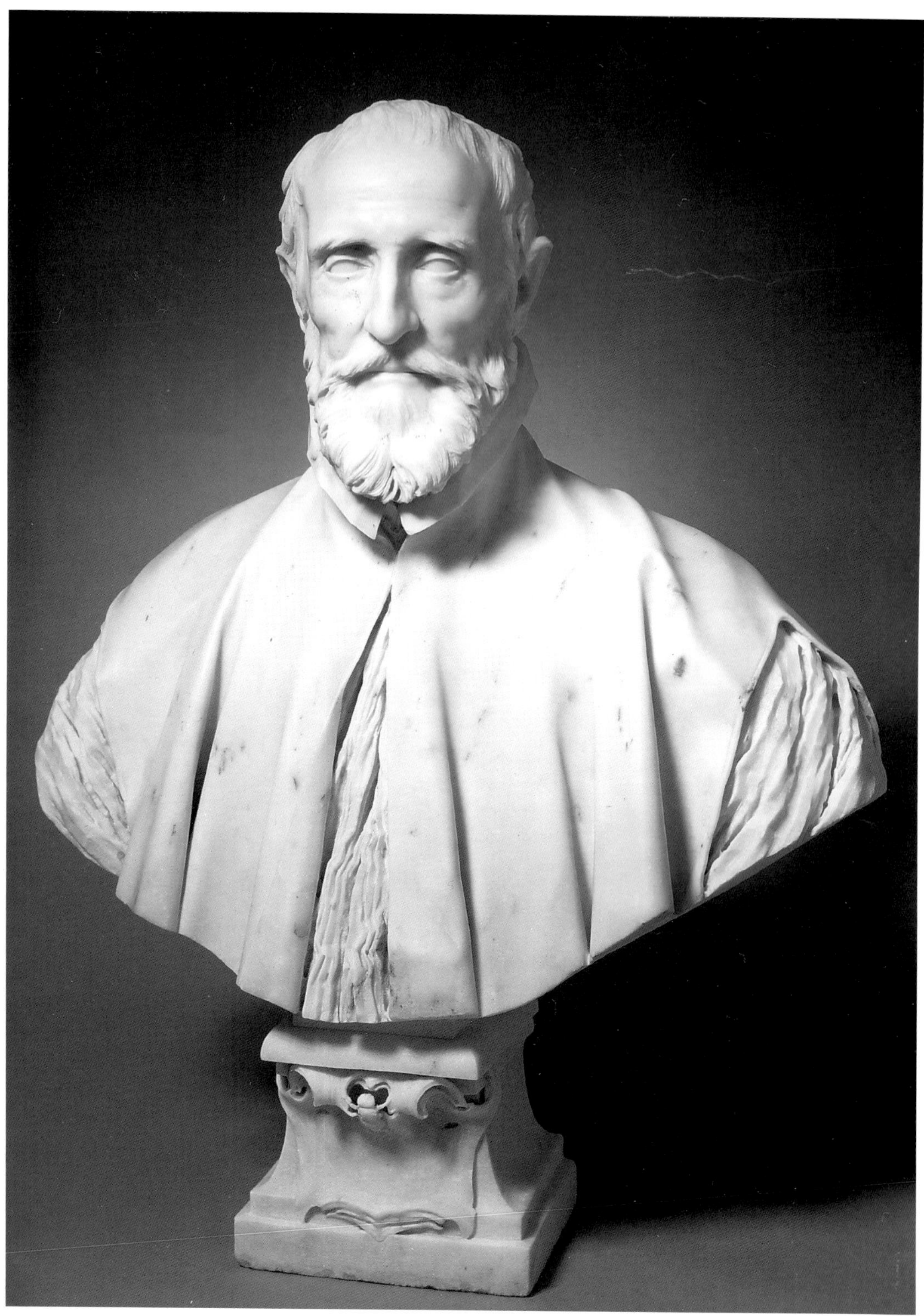

# SCULPTURE
## AN ILLUSTRATED CATALOGUE

NATIONAL GALLERY OF ART

WASHINGTON

This publication was produced by the Editors Office
Editor-in-chief, Frances Smyth
Edited by Julie Warnement with Barclay Gessner

Designed by Tom Suzuki with Constance D. Dillman
Falls Church, Virginia
Cover design by Timothy Cook

Typeset in Sabon with display type in Trajan
Printed by Graphtek
Baltimore, Maryland

| | |
|---|---|
| Cover: | Florentine 15th Century, *Madonna and Child* |
| Frontispiece: | Gian Lorenzo Bernini, *Monsignor Francesco Barberini* |
| p. 6: | Max Ernst, *Capricorn* |
| p. 18: | Benedetto da Rovezzano, *Relief from an Altar or Tabernacle* (detail of) |

Library of Congress Cataloging-in-Publication Data
Sculpture : an illustrated catalogue.
p. cm.
ISBN 0-89468-187-7
1. Sculpture—Washington (D.C.)—Catalogs. 2. National Gallery of Art (U.S.)—Catalogs. I. National Gallery of Art (U.S.)
NB25.W37N387 1994
730'.74'753—dc20 93-29268
CIP

# TABLE OF CONTENTS

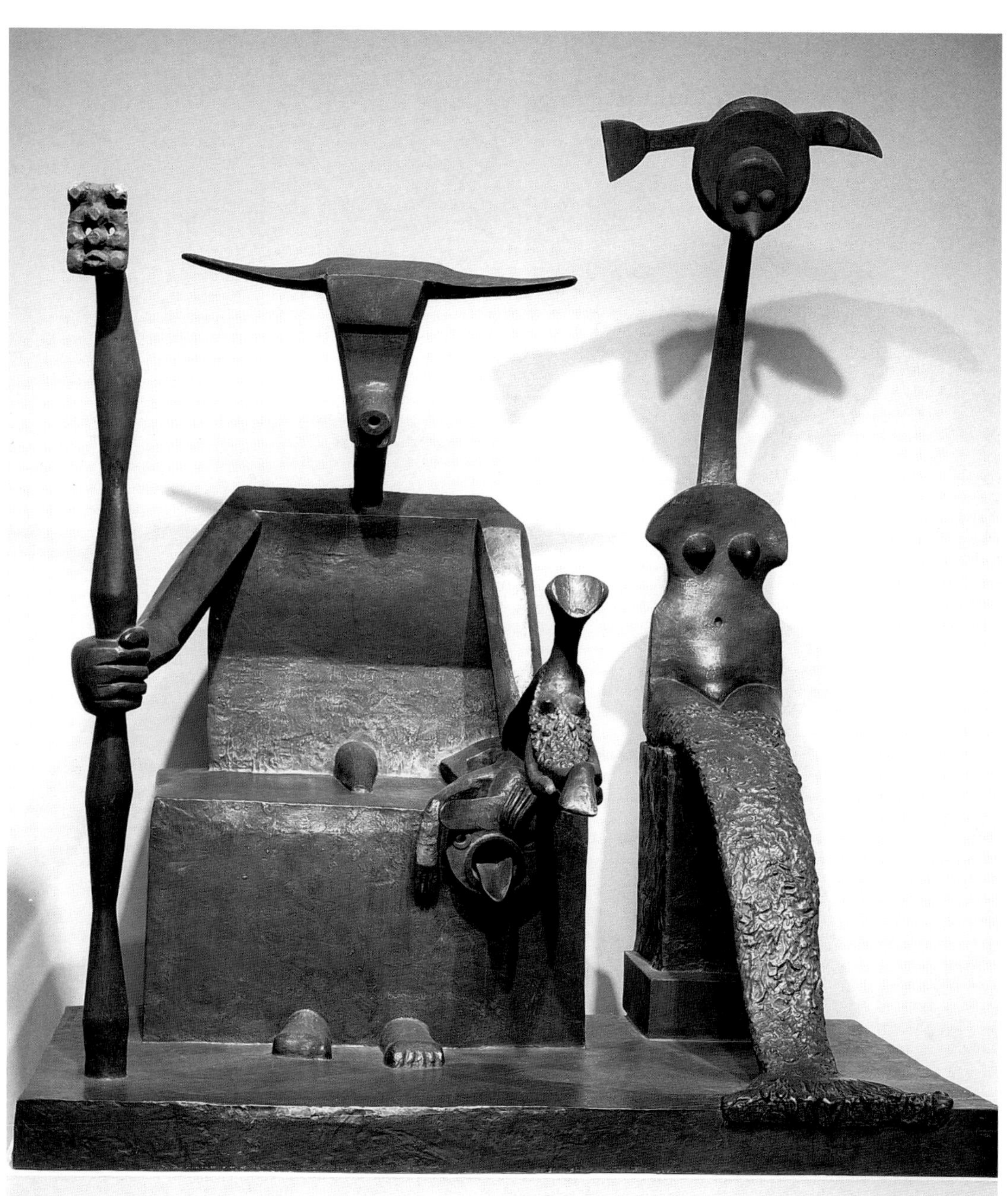

# FOREWORD

This is the first summary catalogue dedicated exclusively to sculpture to be published by the National Gallery of Art. It has been more than a quarter century since publication of the *Summary Catalogue of European Paintings and Sculpture* (Washington 1965), which was followed in 1983 by a more specialized guide to our collection of Renaissance small bronze sculpture and related decorative arts. In the intervening years, our sculpture collection has experienced a remarkable period of growth. Recording our holdings as of May 1991, this compendium of some 725 objects constitutes a comprehensive, illustrated list of the National Gallery's sculpture.

In recent years, the sculpture collection has grown markedly in the areas of French and American sculpture, providing a balanced complement to the National Gallery's traditional areas of strength, particularly in works of the Italian Renaissance. With the opening in 1978 of the East Building, and subsequent major renovations to the ground floor of John Russell Pope's historic West Building, our ability to display these works has also increased. A brief introductory video has been installed at the entrance to the West Building ground floor galleries to help familiarize visitors with the processes and themes of sculpture. This program was made possible with support in part from the Bauman Foundation, in memory of Lionel R. Bauman. Finally and most recently, the Gallery's fiftieth anniversary has occasioned a complete reinstallation of the main floor galleries in the West Building, with the integration of sculpture and paintings.

Since its birth more than fifty years ago, the National Gallery's collection of sculpture has enjoyed the consistent generosity of numerous donors and benefactors, the sources upon which we rely for acquisitions. While the remarkable strength and breadth of the National Gallery's collection derive from many such precious gifts, the continued generosity of our honorary trustee Paul Mellon has remained of essential importance to its development. Support for new sculpture acquisitions from the Collectors Committee, Patrons' Permanent Fund, Ailsa Mellon Bruce Fund, Andrew W. Mellon Fund, and Pepita Milmore Memorial Fund has also enabled us to make many important additions to our holdings, building on strengths and filling in gaps.

While collecting and exhibiting works of art are among their primary functions, museums are also responsible for actively fostering research on their holdings. A thirty-volume systematic catalogue containing scholarly discussion of every object in the National Gallery collection is now in preparation and will be published in stages, as research is completed, during the years to come. Initial results of the authors' research are already reflected in this summary catalogue, which anticipates and complements the systematic catalogue by providing a concise compendium of essential facts on each work of sculpture.

Preparation of the summary catalogue has required the hard work, patience, and meticulous attention to detail of many staff. To all we are grateful. Our special thanks go to Suzannah Fabing, former head of the division of research on collections, for her guidance; to Donald Myers, Mellon assistant curator in the department of sculpture, who provided expert advice throughout the course of this project; to Molly Bourne, who diligently prepared the manuscript; to Frances Smyth and her staff in the editors office, especially Julie Warnement, who expertly edited the manuscript; and to Tom Suzuki for his elegant design.

EARL A. POWELL III
*Director*

# PREFACE

Since the last summary catalogue that included sculpture, the National Gallery of Art's sculpture collection has grown significantly. That publication included both paintings and sculpture, but only works of European origin, the criterion for inclusion of sculpture being a minimum height of eight inches. This catalogue, in contrast, contains sculpture of all nationalities and sizes. Other earlier publications of the sculpture collection include *Masterpieces of Sculpture from the National Gallery of Art* by Charles Seymour, Jr., (Washington, 1949); *Renaissance Bronzes from the Samuel H. Kress Collection* by John Pope-Hennessy (London, 1965); *Sculptures from the Samuel H. Kress Collection, European Schools XIV–XIX Century* by Ulrich Middeldorf (London, 1976); and *Renaissance Small Bronze Sculpture and Associated Decorative Arts at the National Gallery of Art* by Carolyn C. Wilson, with Douglas Lewis (Washington, 1983).

Numerous attribution changes and refinements, which are summarized in tabular form at the end, are reflected in this volume. These have resulted from continuing research for the systematic catalogue of the Gallery's collections, to be published in the coming years. Among the more notable changes, *The David of the Casa Martelli,* long ascribed to Donatello, is now recognized as by Bernardo (or perhaps Antonio) Rossellino. The marble *Relief from an Altar or Tabernacle,* formerly called Florentine school, is now given to Benedetto da Rovezzano. Two marble reliefs, *The Adoration of the Magi* and *The Flight into Egypt,* formerly called Lombard school, are now given jointly to Briosco and Cazzaniga. A monumental marble figure attributed to Pilon and called *Allegory of Victory* is now recognized as *Justice* by Prieur. The marble *Thetis,* which was called school of Bernini, is now called *A Nereid* and attributed to his follower Mazzuoli. Finally, the monumental bronzes known as the Mellon *Venus* and *Bacchus and a Faun*, which were formerly given to Sansovino, are now associated with Francesco Brambilla the Younger.

Since 1965 the sculpture collection has grown by more than eighty percent. Significantly, more than half of this increase is in American sculpture, especially that of the twentieth century. In comparison, in 1965 the Gallery owned only three works of American sculpture, all portraits of Andrew W. Mellon. French sculpture, particularly nineteenth-century bronzes, account for nearly a third of the new works. These deliberate collecting initiatives complement the historical core of the collection: mainly early Italian works that were the prevailing taste of early American collectors.

A number of donors deserve special mention. Paul Mellon has been extraordinarily generous. In 1980, he presented ten works of nineteenth-century French sculpture, including five bronzes by Barye; the impressive bronze *A Horseman in a Storm* by Meissonier; a bronze *Crowing Rooster* by Cain; and three horses by Gericault. One of these is the wax *Flayed Horse I,* from which the two Gericault bronzes were cast, with the artist's name inscribed in the base. Since Gericault made very few pieces of sculpture in his short lifetime, the wax is a signal document for understanding this artist.

In 1983 Mr. Mellon gave twenty-three works of sculpture, including a terra-cotta *Mother and Child* by Dalou; five diminutive terra cottas by Maillol; a large bronze *Torso of a Young Woman* and a stone group of *Two Young Girls* also by Maillol; eight bronzes by Manzù, including six panels associated with his doors for St. Peter's, Rome; a terra cotta by Renoir depicting *Madame Renoir and Son*; *Obus*, a monumental stabile by Calder; and a sensitive marble portrait of *Ailsa Mellon Bruce* by Davidson, whose portraits of *Andrew W. Mellon* were the Gallery's first pieces of American sculpture.

In 1985 Mr. Mellon added Marini's *The Concept of the Rider* and twenty-three works by Degas. These included seventeen of Degas' sixty-nine extant waxes, a gift of profound importance and generosity. The patinated plaster of the celebrated *Dressed Ballet Dancer* and five bronzes were also included. For the Gallery's fiftieth anniversary, ten "Animobiles" by Calder were given. These intimately scaled works of painted, cut, and bent sheet metal depict whimsical animals, most with mobile elements.

Gemini G.E.L. (Graphic Editions Limited) has donated forty works of sculpture from editions, including works given jointly with the artists Kienholz, Lichtenstein, Oldenburg, and Rauschenberg. A Gemini G.E.L. Archive has been established at the National Gallery, which will include an example of every sculpture and print edition that the workshop produces, as well as related preparatory materials. Eight additional works of sculpture from Gemini editions were donated by Mr. and Mrs. Roger P. Sonnabend.

A similar archive of edition sculpture and prints made at Graphicstudio/University of South Florida, Tampa, has brought fifteen works of sculpture to the Gallery; all were jointly donated by the artists Rauschenberg, Dine, Lichtenstein, Chia, and Graves. In addition, Dine independently donated two multi-part edition works of sculpture to the Graphicstudio Archive.

Enid A. Haupt has significantly enriched the twentieth-century holdings by her 1977 gift, which included six important bronzes by Giacometti, plus one work each by Butler, Lassaw, Marini, Moore, Schlemmer, and Trova. Agnes E. Meyer gave five pieces of sculpture in 1967, including Barye's *Tiger Seizing a Gazelle*; two works by Brancusi, the elegant white marble *Bird in Space* of 1925, and a black marble portrait of the donor; another portrait of her, in plaster, by Despiau; and the marble *Sphinx* by Rodin. Mr. and Mrs. Burton Tremaine presented five works of sculpture to the Gallery, by Bell, Arp, Callery, José de Rivera, and Trova. Asbjorn R. Lunde also has given five pieces of sculpture, including a terra-cotta relief by Barye of *The Lion of the Colonne de Juillet* and a magnificent South German sixteenth-century bronze *Striding Stag*, the latter in honor of the Gallery's fiftieth anniversary.

Several important old master purchases were made possible by the Ailsa Mellon Bruce Fund, including a bronze relief of *Peace Establishing Her Reign* attributed to Antonio Lombardo, a Paduan sixteenth-century bronze *Seated Bacchante*, a terra-cotta *Saint Matthew* by Algardi, and the bronze *Pistoia Crucifix* by Tacca. The Ailsa Mellon Bruce Fund has made possible the acquisition of notable modern sculpture as well, including the ceramic *Eve* by Gauguin, Duchamp-Villon's bronze *Torso of a Young Man*, Giacometti's *The Invisible Object (Hands Holding the Void)*, and five works by David Smith.

The Collectors Committee, established in 1975 for funding the art works to be commissioned for the Gallery's East Building, has continued since that date, providing for the acquisition of numerous pieces of twentieth-century sculpture. The works they donated for the opening of the East Building included the huge mobile by Calder, which meanders slowly and majestically around the open space in the building's atrium, an untitled painted aluminum sculpture by Rosati, and the welded steel *National Gallery Ledge Piece* by Caro. Since then the following works of sculpture have entered the Gallery under the

Committee's auspices: *Sentinel I* by David Smith, *Capricorn* by Ernst, *Wandering Rocks* by Tony Smith, *Medici Prince* by Cornell, *The Dancers* by Segal, two works called *Rock Settee* by Burton, *Lever No. 3* by Puryear, *Mirrored Cell* by Samaras, and an untitled bronze by Shapiro.

The Andrew W. Mellon Fund has made possible purchases including five French bronzes: *The Penitent Magdalen* by Legendre; a pair of equestrian portraits of *The Grand Dauphin* and *Louis XIV*, both after Desjardins; *Milo of Croton* after Puget; and the stunning *Gloria Victis!* by Mercié. The fund also allowed purchase of the monumental *Seated Youth* by Lehmbruck.

Seven works of sculpture have been acquired by the Pepita Milmore Memorial Fund: two early Italian bronzes by Severo da Ravenna and Sansovino; the bronze *Diana of the Tower* by Saint-Gaudens; a terracotta *Silenus Crowned by Nymphs* by Clodion; a bronze *Comedy and Tragedy: 'Sic Vita'* by Gilbert; a marble relief, *La Pensée*, by Chapu; and a bronze by Hébert, *Queen Sémiramis Called to Arms*.

The Patrons' Permanent Fund, established in 1981 as an endowment fund for acquisitions, has supported four distinguished sculpture purchases: the dynamic bronze *Ceres Searching for Persephone* by Anguier, the haunting alabaster South Netherlandish fifteenth-century *Pietà*, a superb silver *Flagellator* by Algardi, and a fine *Winged Victory* in bronze by Canova.

Several other acquisitions since the last summary catalogue deserve special mention. The small terra-cotta *Model for "Poetry and Music"* by Clodion was purchased with the Loula D. Lasker Fund in 1976; the large, marble version of this design from the Kress collection has been in the Gallery since 1952. It is a rare luxury for one institution to own two such closely related productions from a single artistic commission. A marble portrait by Jean-Baptiste Lemoyne II, *Jules-David Cromot, Baron du Bourg*, was the gift of Camille de Nuchèze, a direct descendant of the sitter, and her husband, John Hadley Cox. The Gallery's holdings of works by Rodin were significantly increased, including two lifetime plaster busts given by the B. Gerald Cantor Art Foundation, *Jean d'Aire* and *Lady Sackville*.

The number of artists whose sculpture is newly represented in the Gallery's collection since the last sculpture summary catalogue is impressive. Included are: Algardi, Bartholdi, Barye, Brancusi, Calder, Canova, Cornell, David d'Angers, Degas, Giacometti, Gilbert, Manship, Manzù, Moore, Noguchi, Oldenburg, Saint-Gaudens, Segal, and David Smith. Of special note are Algardi's three works of sculpture in different media and types: the silver *Flagellator* figure, the terra-cotta bust of *Saint Matthew,* and a bronze relief of *The Rest on the Flight into Egypt,* the last a joint purchase of the Kaiser Aluminum and Loula D. Lasker funds, and Edward E. MacCrone Charitable Trust.

The opening of the East Building created many possibilities for display of sculpture, especially works whose size is incompatible with the more traditional architecture of the West Building.

In the West Building, renovations to the ground floor, completed in 1983, created additional exhibition space for sculpture: a suite of nineteen galleries is used primarily for Renaissance bronzes and other less-than-life sized sculpture of all periods, while the marble court on the central axis displays baroque portraits. Reinstallation of the main floor galleries for the fiftieth anniversary resulted in a configuration that alternates and sometimes integrates sculpture and painting of the same period and place.

This summary catalogue is the result of careful and painstaking work on the part of many people. In addition to those cited in the Foreword, special thanks are due to Douglas Lewis and Alison Luchs, curators of sculpture and decorative arts, and to Willow Johnson. Jack Cowart, former curator of twentieth-century art, his colleague Marla Prather, and former curators Nan Rosenthal and Jeremy Strick, gave generously of their time for this project, as did Ruth Fine, curator of modern prints and drawings, and her colleagues Mary Lee Corlett, Carlotta Owens, and Charles Ritchie. We are also grateful to Robin Dowden of data processing; Anne Halpern of curatorial records and files; the art handlers, especially Gary Webber; and photographic services, under the leadership of Richard Amt.

Donald Myers
*Mellon Assistant Curator,*
*Sculpture*

# DONORS TO THE SCULPTURE COLLECTION

George Matthew Adams
Avalon Fund
David Baron
Robert M. and Anne T. Bass
Patricia Bauman and John L. Bryant, Jr.
Ferdinand Lammot Belin Fund
Bernard and Audrey Berman
Ruth Blumka
Mrs. Ralph Harman Booth
Margaret Bouton Memorial Fund
Mr. and Mrs. Harry Brooks
The Brown Foundation, Inc.
Ailsa Mellon Bruce Fund
Syma Busiel Fund
Lewis Cabot
The Morris and Gwendolyn Cafritz Foundation
B. Gerald Cantor Art Foundation
Mrs. Calvert Carey
Leo Castelli
Sandro Chia
Mr. and Mrs. Ralph F. Colin
Collectors Committee
Camille de Nuchèze and John Hadley Cox
William Nelson Cromwell Fund
Chester Dale
Jim Dine
Estate of Sir Jacob Epstein
Mr. and Mrs. Sidney M. Feldman
The Fiftieth Anniversary Gift Committee
David Edward Finley
David Edward and Margaret Eustis Finley Fund
Mr. and Mrs. Donald G. Fisher
Angelika Wertheim Frink
Elizabeth Merrill Furness
Mr. and Mrs. John R. Gaines
Gemini G.E.L.
Rose and Charles F. Gibbs
Arnold and Mildred Glimcher
Arnold and Esther Gottlieb Foundation, Inc.
Katharine Graham
Graphicstudio/University of South Florida
Nancy Graves
Mr. and Mrs. Winston F.C. Guest
Mr. and Mrs. Nathan L. Halpern
Enid A. Haupt
The Christian Humann Foundation
Dahlov Ipcar
William B. Jaffe
Rupert L. Joseph
Harry and Margery Kahn
The Children of Mr. and Mrs. Otto H. Kahn
Kaiser Aluminum Fund
Ellsworth Kelly
David Keppel
Edward Kienholz
Robert P. and Arlene R. Kogod
Samuel H. Kress
Samuel H. Kress Foundation
Loula D. Lasker Fund
Mr. and Mrs. Earl M. Latterman
Evelyn and Leonard A. Lauder
Madeleine Chalette Lejwa
Margaret Seligman Lewisohn
Roy Lichtenstein

Lotte Walter Lindt
Seymour Lipton
Asbjorn R. Lunde
Edward E. MacCrone Charitable Trust
A. W. Mellon Educational and Charitable Trust
Andrew W. Mellon Fund
Paul Mellon
Mrs. Houghton P. Metcalf
Agnes E. Meyer
Dieter Erich Meyer
Robert and Jane Meyerhoff
Adolph Caspar Miller Fund
Mr. and Mrs. Myron Miller
Pepita Milmore Memorial Fund
Stanley Mortimer
Raymond D. Nasher
Mr. and Mrs. Morton G. Neumann
Mr. and Mrs. William A. Nitze
Frederick C. Oechsner
Claes Oldenburg
Patrons' Permanent Fund
C. Michael Paul Memorial Fund
Gustave Pimienta
Cynthia Hazen Polsky
Esther W. Putnam
Robert Rauschenberg
The Roberts Foundation
Cornelius Van S. Roosevelt
James Rosati
Alexandre P. Rosenberg
Lessing J. Rosenwald
Mrs. Lessing J. Rosenwald
Lawrence Rubin
William S. Rubin
Mrs. John Barry Ryan
Arthur M. Sackler
Mortimer D. Sackler
Rita Schreiber
Virginia Steele Scott
Mrs. William C. Seitz
Mr. and Mrs. Robert Hilton Simmons
Lucille Ellis Simon
Mrs. John W. Simpson
Benjamin B. Smith
Mr. and Mrs. Roger P. Sonnabend
Lauson H. Stone
Marshall H. Stone
Mrs. Herbert N. Straus
Mrs. Jesse Isidore Straus
W. S. Stuckey, Jr.
The Ruth and Vernon Taylor Foundation
Joseph Ternbach
Mr. and Mrs. Burton Tremaine
Friends of Anne Truitt
University of South Florida Foundation
Untitled Press Inc.
Versailles Foundation, Inc.
Lila Acheson Wallace
Mr. and Mrs. Hans W. Weigert
Barbara Harrison Wescott
Joseph E. Widener
Daniel Wildenstein
Eric M. Wunsch
Z-Bank of Vienna
Dorothy Zimmerman
Tessim Zorach

# NOTES TO THE READER

This catalogue reflects the sculpture holdings of the National Gallery of Art as of May 1991. Decorative arts, plaquettes, medals, coins, and *nielli* are not included and will be treated in other volumes. Entries are arranged alphabetically by artist's surname, or given name when there is no surname, unless the artist is better known by a sobriquet. If the artist is unknown, entries are listed under a nationality or school. Works by the same artist are arranged alphabetically by title—except for portraits, which are alphabetized by the sitter's surname; works with the same attribution and title are arranged by National Gallery accession numbers. Artists known by more than one name and sculpture created by multiple artists are cross referenced.

Current National Gallery accession numbers, which begin with the year in which the work was acquired, are used. Old accession numbers, used prior to 1983, begin with A-, B-, or SA- and are listed in the Concordance of Old and New Accession Numbers at the end of this volume.

Height precedes width, which precedes depth. Dimensions are in meters, followed by inches in parentheses, and represent the maximum measurement in the stated direction, unless noted otherwise. Inches are rounded off to the nearest one-eighth inch; measurements of objects less than eight inches are rounded off to the nearest one-sixteenth inch.

Inscriptions or foundry marks are generally described from the viewer's point of view; if, however, a mark is found on a figure or is described in relation to part of the figure, right and left are given from the figure's perspective. Illegible or reconstructed sections are enclosed within brackets, [ ]. Sections that cannot be transcribed are described in parentheses, ( ). Line breaks are indicated by a diagonal slash, and two or more discrete inscriptions on the same object are separated from one another by a semicolon.

Execution dates refer to the original model; they may be followed by casting, reduction, or enlargement dates, if known. Dates assigned follow this system:

| | |
|---|---|
| 1500: | executed in 1500 |
| c. 1500: | executed sometime around 1500 |
| 1500–1525: | begun in 1500, finished in 1525 |
| 1500/1525: | executed between 1500 and 1525 inclusive |
| c. 1500/1525: | executed between approximately 1500 and 1525 |

## Attribution Terms

**Artist:** a named artist

**Attributed to:** indicates probably by the named artist

**Studio of, Workshop of:** produced in the named artist's workshop or studio, by students or assistants, with possible participation by the named artist; the creative concept is by the named artist and the work was meant to leave the studio as his

**Follower of:** an unknown artist who, working specifically in the style of the named artist, may or may not have been trained by the named artist; possibly contemporaneous, or with an implied time limit of about a generation after the named artist's death

**Circle of:** an unknown contemporary of the named artist, working in a similar style, who could be a follower or an independent master who has contact with the named artist and draws on him or on common sources

**Style of:** indicates a stylistic relationship only, possibly vague; not necessarily contemporaneous

**After:** a copy of any date

**Imitator of:** someone working in the style of the named artist with the intention to deceive

**School:** indicates a geographical distinction only, a town, district, or province, etc., where it is impossible to isolate a specific artist, his studio, or following

**Probably:** indicates some doubt that the work is by an artist of the named school

**Possibly:** indicates less certainty with regard to school than **probably**

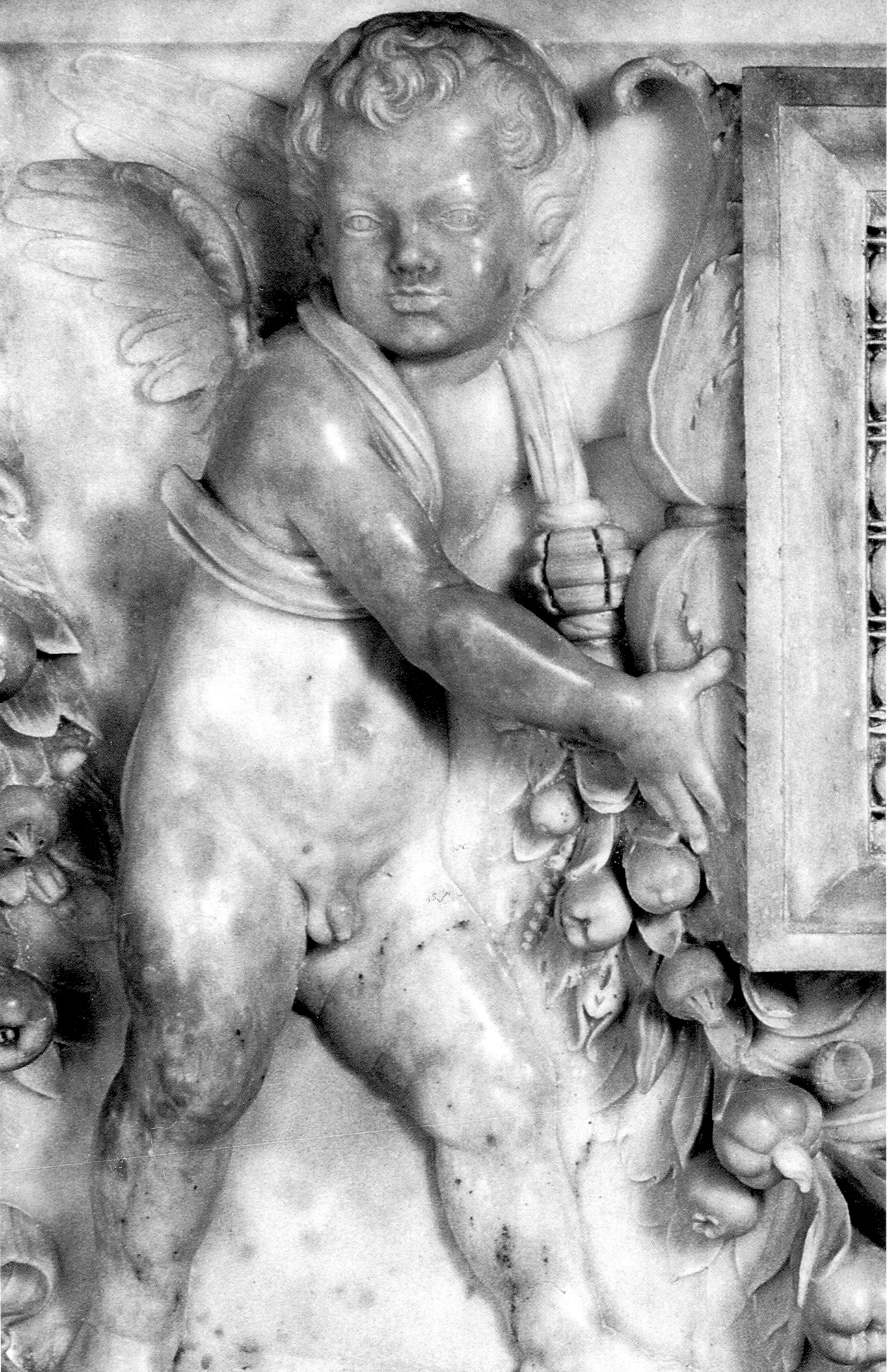

# SCULPTURE

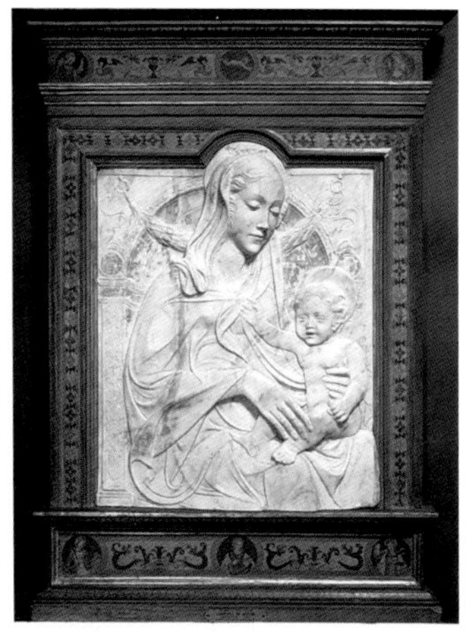

Agostino di Duccio
Florentine, 1418–probably 1481

*Madonna and Child,* 1460/1470
Marble, .720 x .573 (28 1/4 x 22 1/2)
Andrew W. Mellon Collection
1937.1.116

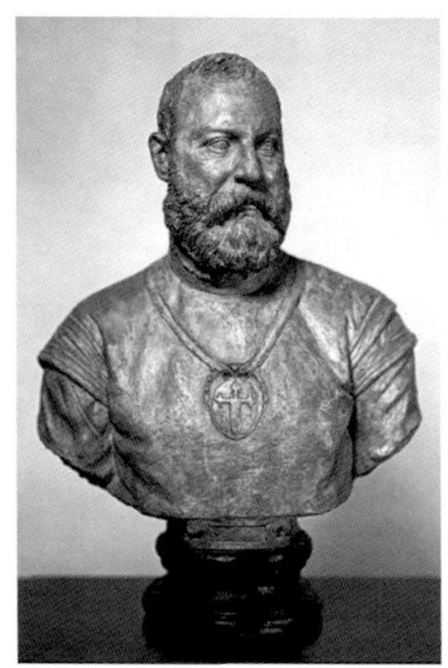

Attributed to Jacopo Albarelli
Venetian, active 1594–1638

*A Knight of Santiago,* c. 1600/1625
Terra cotta, painted, .710 x .532 x .276 (28 x 20 7/8 x 10 7/8)
Samuel H. Kress Collection
1943.4.85

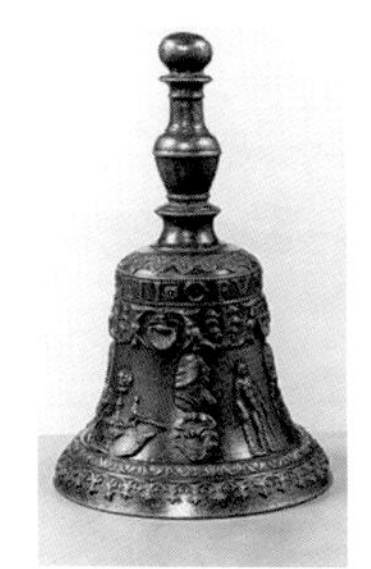

Giovanni I Alberghetti
Ferrarese-Venetian, active 1505–1515

*A Table-Bell with Portrait of Lodovico Maria Sforza, 1451–1508, called Il Moro, 7th Duke of Milan 1494–1508,* possibly c. 1494/1499
Bronze, .152 x .099 (6 x 3 15/16)
Inscribed around top, beneath acanthus strip: OPVSZANINI•ALBERGETI
Samuel H. Kress Collection
1957.14.110

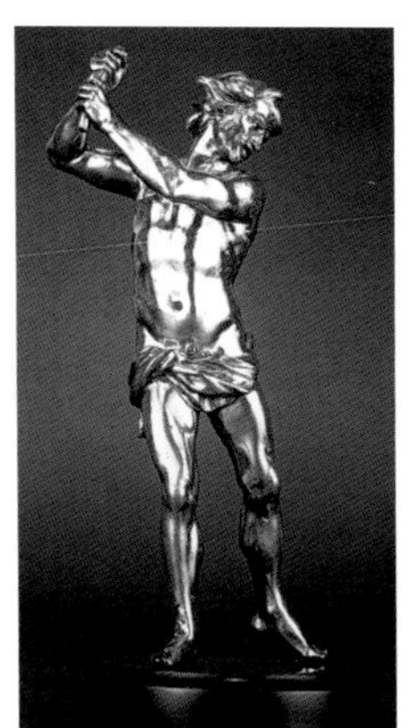

Alessandro Algardi
Bolognese-Roman, 1598–1654

*A Flagellator,* c. 1630s
Silver, .234 x .124 x .073 (9 1/8 x 4 7/8 x 2 7/8)
Patrons' Permanent Fund
1991.124.1

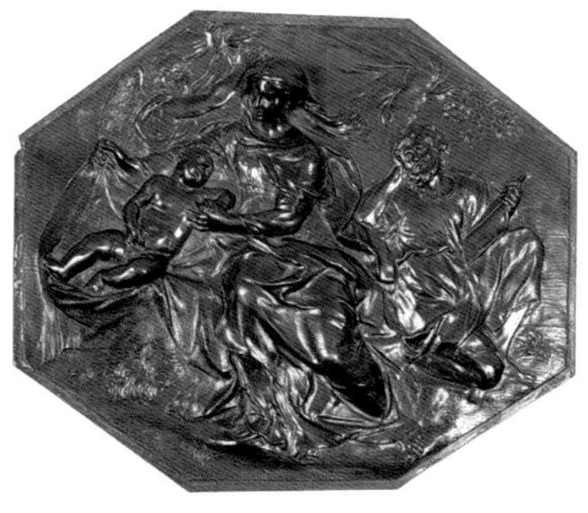

*The Rest on the Flight into Egypt*, c. 1635
Bronze, .298 x .362 ($11\frac{3}{4}$ x $14\frac{1}{4}$)
Kaiser Fund, Loula D. Lasker Fund, and
Edward E. MacCrone Fund
1983.20.1

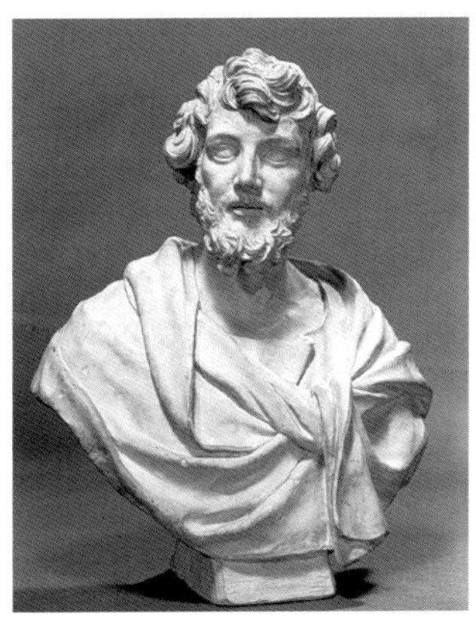

*Saint Matthew*, c. 1640
Terra cotta, .380 x .324 x .198
(15 x $12\frac{3}{4}$ x $7\frac{3}{4}$)
Ailsa Mellon Bruce Fund
1970.7.1

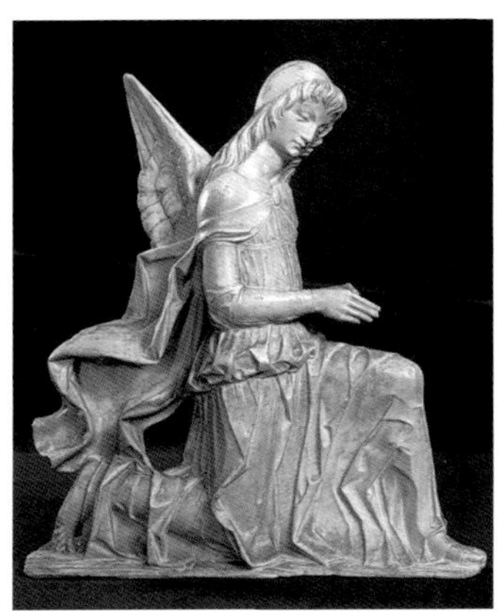

## Giovanni Antonio Amadeo
Lombard, c. 1447–1522

*Kneeling Angel*, 1470/1480
Marble, .465 x .429 x .095
($18\frac{3}{8}$ x $16\frac{7}{8}$ x $3\frac{3}{4}$)
Samuel H. Kress Collection
1939.1.320

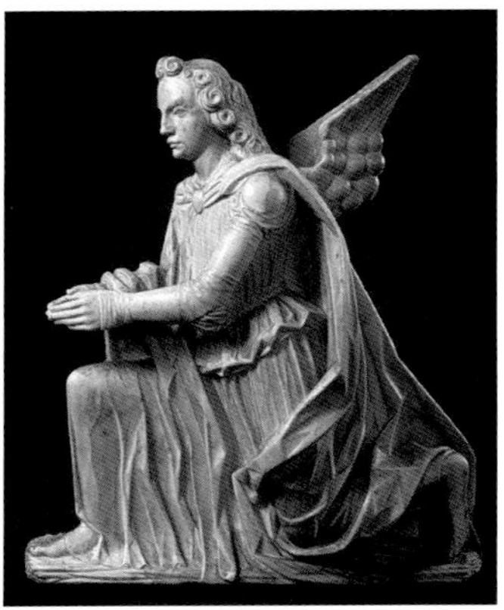

## Workshop of Giovanni Antonio Amadeo
Lombard

*Kneeling Angel*, 1470/1480
Marble, .495 x .451 x .121
($19\frac{1}{2}$ x $17\frac{3}{4}$ x $4\frac{3}{4}$)
Samuel H. Kress Collection
1939.1.321

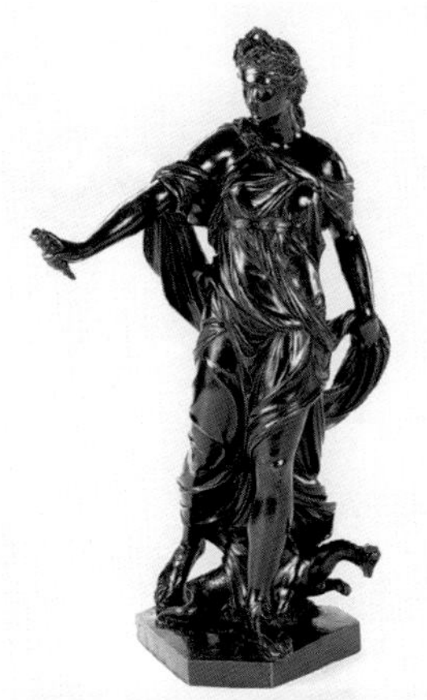

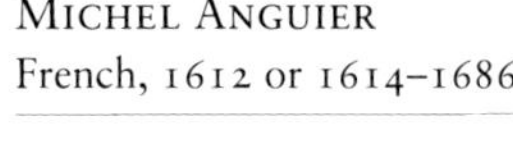

MICHEL ANGUIER
French, 1612 or 1614–1686

*Ceres Searching for Persephone,* 1652, cast probably 1650s/1670s
Bronze, .539 x .279 x .251 ($21^{1}/_{4}$ x 11 x $9^{7}/_{8}$)
Inscribed on top of base next to left foot: 93A
Patrons' Permanent Fund
1989.44.1

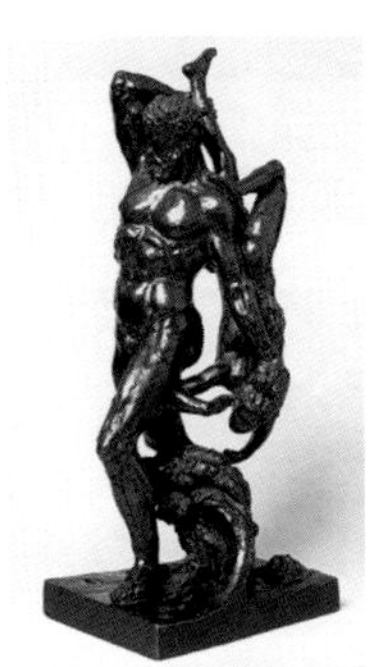

AFTER THE ANTIQUE
19TH/20TH CENTURY
Italian

*Hercules Slaying Lichas*
Bronze, .507 x .171 x .225 (20 x $6^{3}/_{4}$ x $8^{7}/_{8}$)
Gift of Mr. and Mrs. William B. Jaffe
1974.8.1

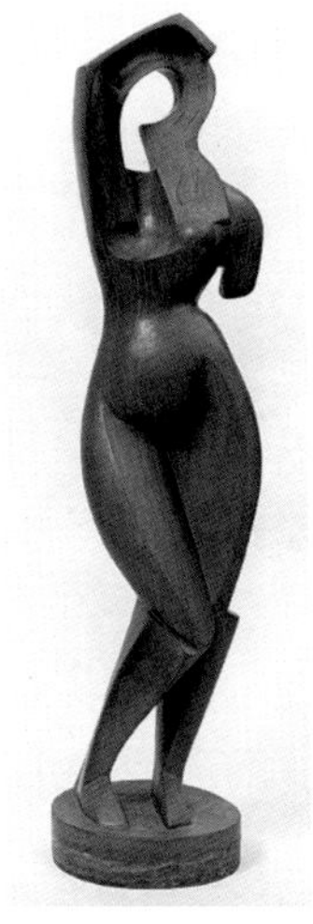

ALEXANDER ARCHIPENKO
American, 1887–1964

*Woman Combing Her Hair,* 1915
Bronze, 1.807 x .470 x .429 ($71^{1}/_{8}$ x $18^{1}/_{2}$ x $16^{7}/_{8}$)
Inscribed on base next to left foot: ARCHIPENKO / 1915 / PARIS A
Ailsa Mellon Bruce Fund
1971.66.10

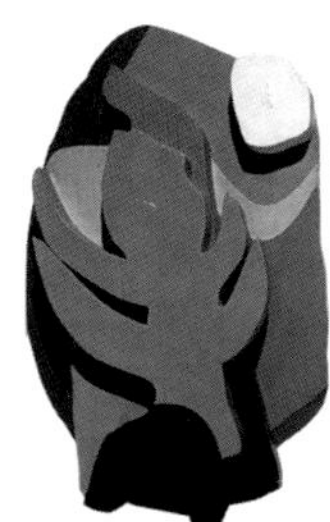

JEAN ARP (HANS ARP)
French (born Alsace-Lorraine), 1886–1966

*The Forest,* 1916
Wood, carved and painted
.327 x .197 x .076 ($12^{7}/_{8}$ x $7^{3}/_{4}$ x 3)
Andrew W. Mellon Fund
1977.20.1

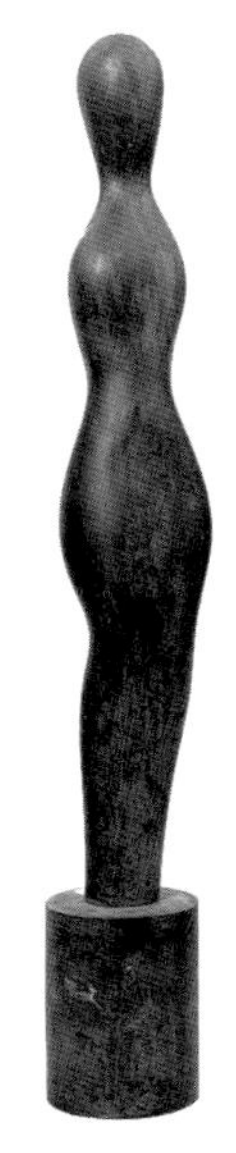

*Grande Sculpture Classique,* 1963/1964
Bronze, 2.385 x .370 x .368
($93^{7}/_{8}$ x $14^{5}/_{8}$ x $14^{1}/_{2}$)
Ailsa Mellon Bruce Fund
1971.66.11

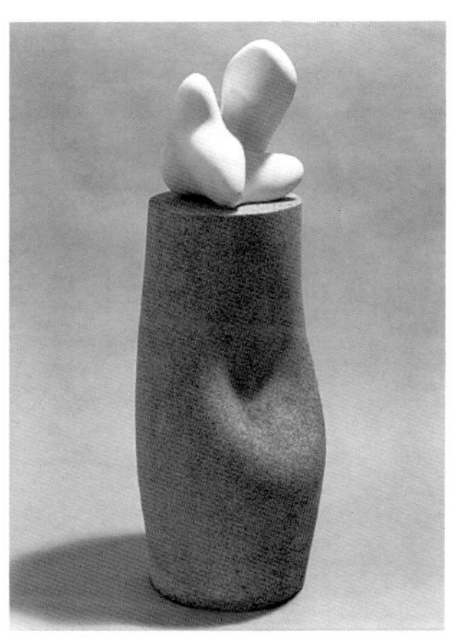

*Mirr,* 1936/1960
Marble, .175 x .219 x .153
(6 $^{7}/_{8}$ x $8^{5}/_{8}$ x 6)
Gift of Mr. and Mrs. Burton Tremaine
1977.75.6

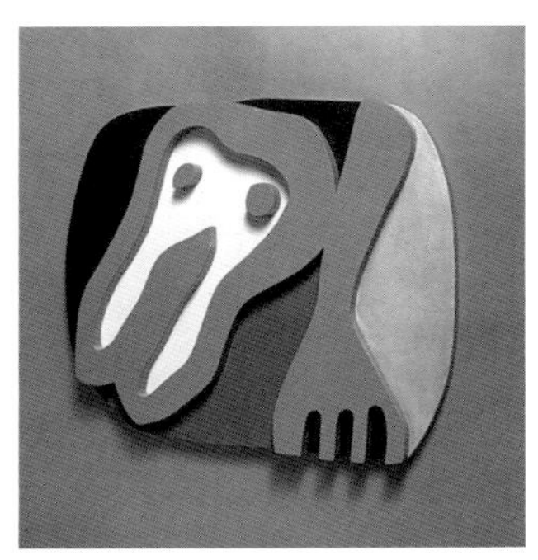

*Shirt Front and Fork,* 1922
Wood, .584 x .700 x .061
(23 x $27^{1}/_{2}$ x $2^{3}/_{8}$)
Ailsa Mellon Bruce Fund
1983.3.1

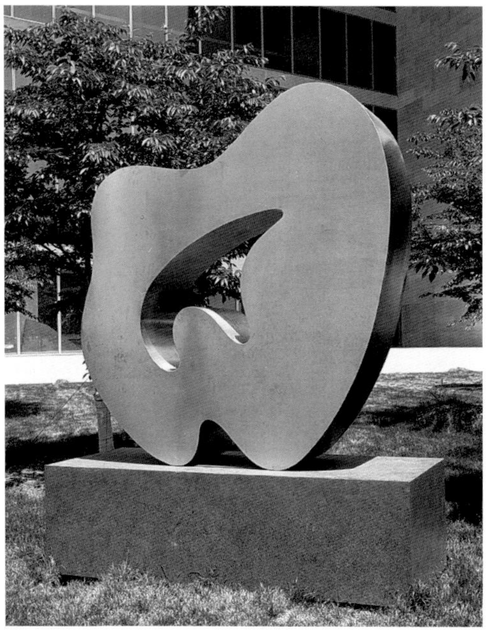

After Jean Arp (Hans Arp)
French

*Oriforme*, 1977
Stainless steel, 2.279 x 2.146 x .600 ($89\frac{3}{4}$ x $84\frac{1}{2}$ x $23\frac{5}{8}$)
Inscribed on outer rim at bottom: ARP / 1 / 1
To the American People in Gratitude–Leon Chalette, Arthur Lejwa and Madeleine Chalette Lejwa
1978.22.1

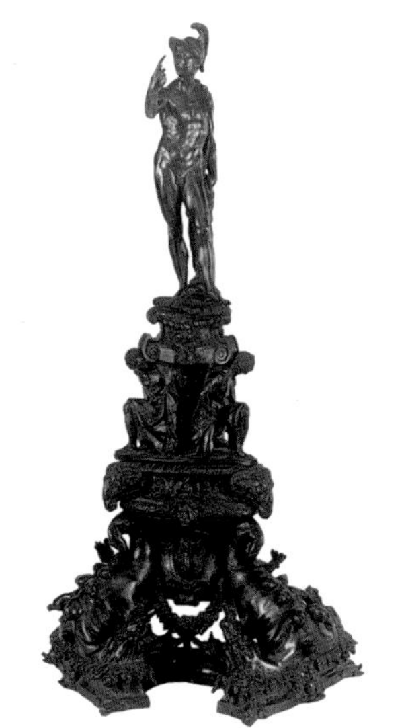

Circle of Tiziano Aspetti
Paduan-Venetian

*Andiron with Figure of Mars*, 1565/1607
Bronze, 1.076 x .558 x .412 ($42\frac{3}{8}$ x 22 x $16\frac{1}{4}$)
Samuel H. Kress Collection
1961.9.100

*See also*: Circle of Girolamo Campagna, *Andiron with Figure of Venus*, 1961.9.101

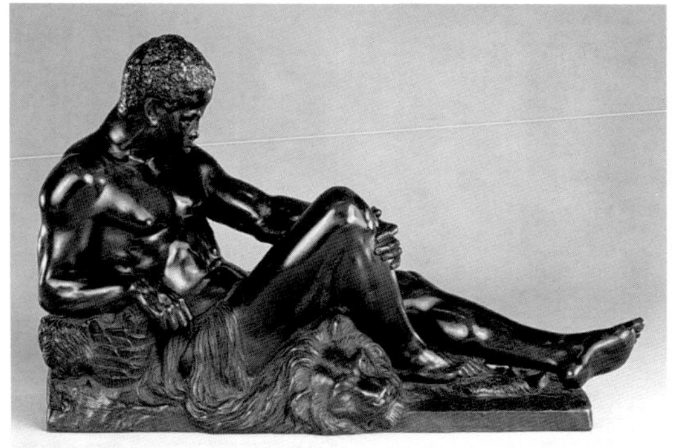

Frédéric-Auguste Bartholdi
French, 1834–1904

*Allegory of Africa*, c. 1863/1865
Bronze, .318 x .520 x .168 ($12\frac{1}{2}$ x 20 x $6\frac{5}{8}$)
Inscribed on top of base at rear right corner, next to extended leg: A BARTHOLDI
Gift of the 50th Anniversary Gift Committee
1991.84.1

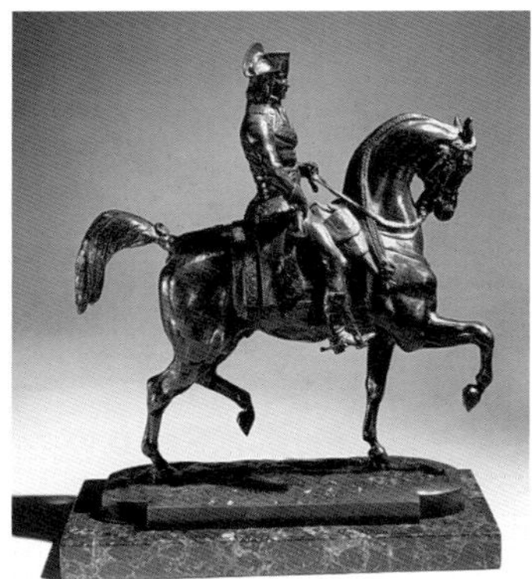

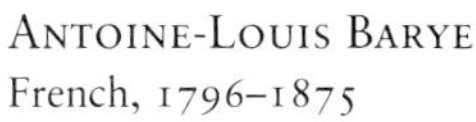

ANTOINE-LOUIS BARYE
French, 1796–1875

*General Bonaparte on Horseback*, c. 1838
Bronze, .357 x .330 x .134
(14 x 13 x $5\frac{1}{4}$)
Inscribed on top of base, behind horse's rear right hoof: BARYE
Collection of Mr. and Mrs. Paul Mellon
1980.44.3

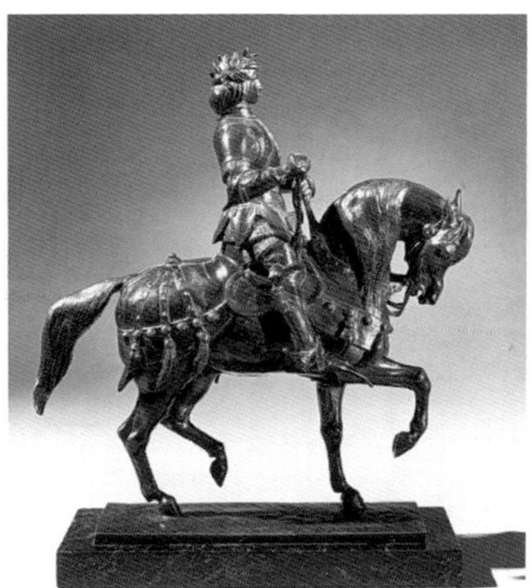

*Charles VII Victorious on Horseback*, 1860
Bronze, .292 x .273 x .108
($11\frac{1}{2}$ x $10\frac{3}{4}$ x $4\frac{1}{4}$)
Inscribed on top of base, near horse's front left hoof: BARYE 1860; in ink inside base: G.A. LUCAS / 21 RUE DE L'ARC DE [TRIOM]PHE; in white paint under base: LUCAS
Collection of Mr. and Mrs. Paul Mellon
1980.44.1

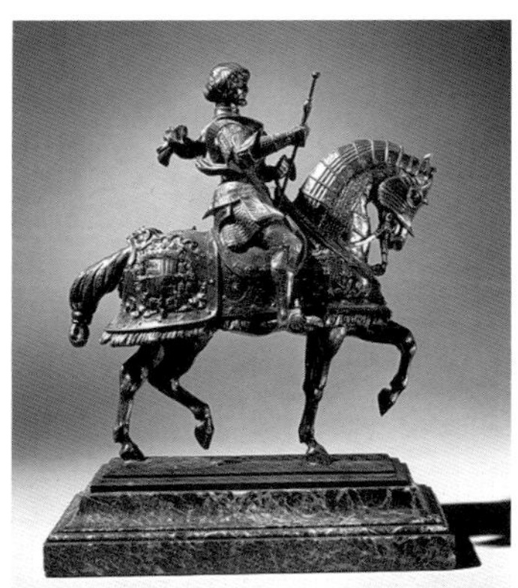

*Gaston de Foix on Horseback*, 1839/1840
Bronze, .335 x .321 x .137
($13\frac{1}{4}$ x $12\frac{5}{8}$ x $5\frac{1}{2}$)
Inscribed on top of base, under horse's raised front left leg: BARYE
Collection of Mr. and Mrs. Paul Mellon
1980.44.2

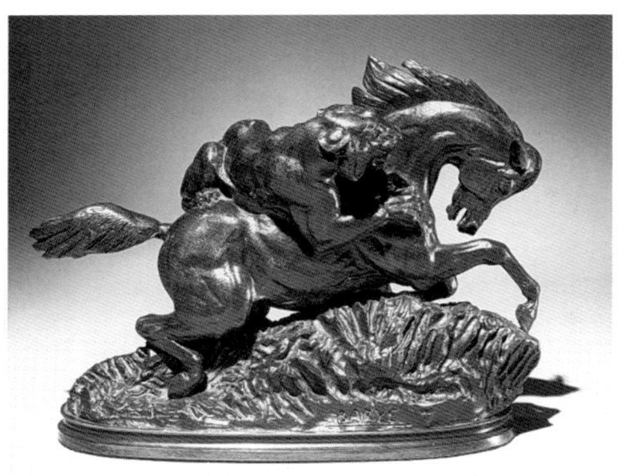

*Horse Attacked by a Tiger*, in or before 1837
Bronze, .261 x .369 x .162
($10\frac{1}{4}$ x $14\frac{1}{2}$ x $6\frac{3}{8}$)
Inscribed on middle of proper right side of base: BARYE
Collection of Mr. and Mrs. Paul Mellon
1980.44.4

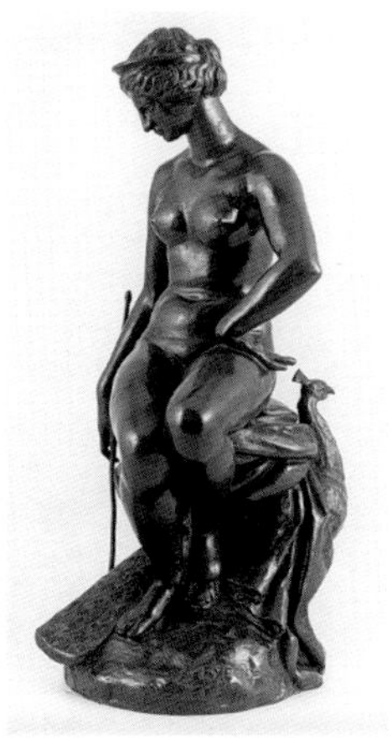

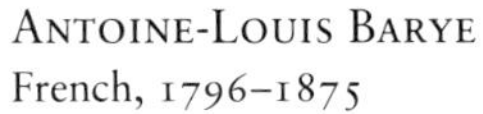

Antoine-Louis Barye
French, 1796–1875

*Juno with Her Peacock*, c. 1840, probably cast by 1855
Bronze, .280 x .380 x .151 (11 x 15 x 6)
Inscribed on base below Juno's left foot: BARYE
Gift of The Brown Foundation, Inc.
1986.61.1

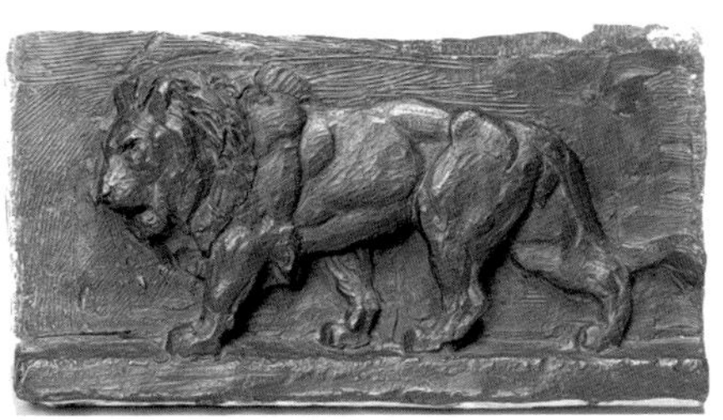

*The Lion of the Colonne de Juillet*, 1836
Terra cotta, tinted, .210 x .405 x .052 ($8^{1}/_{4}$ x 16 x $2^{1}/_{8}$)
Gift of Asbjorn R. Lunde
1984.62.1

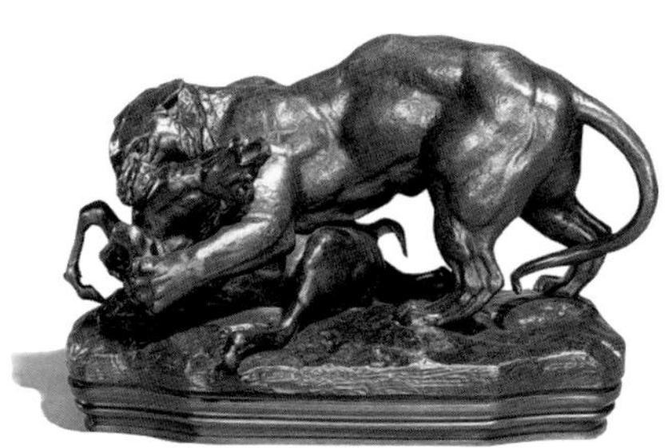

*Tiger Seizing a Gazelle*, 1834
Bronze, .349 x .553 x .229 ($13^{3}/_{4}$ x $21^{3}/_{4}$ x 9)
Inscribed on ground near tiger's front right paw: BARYE
Gift of Eugene and Agnes E. Meyer
1967.13.2

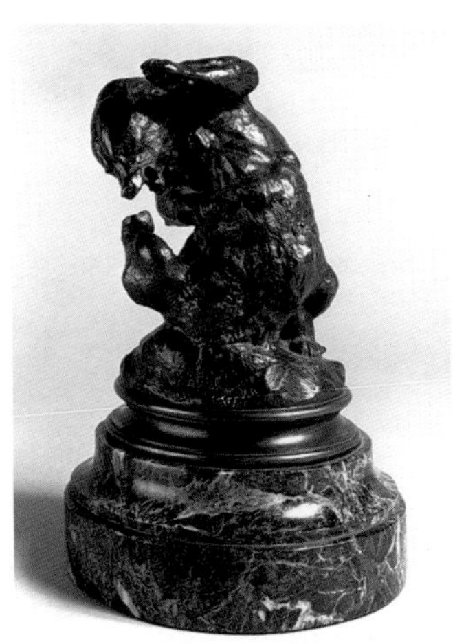

*Two Bears Wrestling*, 1833
Bronze, .220 x .138 x .173 ($8^{5}/_{8}$ x $5^{1}/_{2}$ x $6\ ^{7}/_{8}$)
Inscribed on side of base: BARYE
Collection of Mr. and Mrs. Paul Mellon
1980.44.5

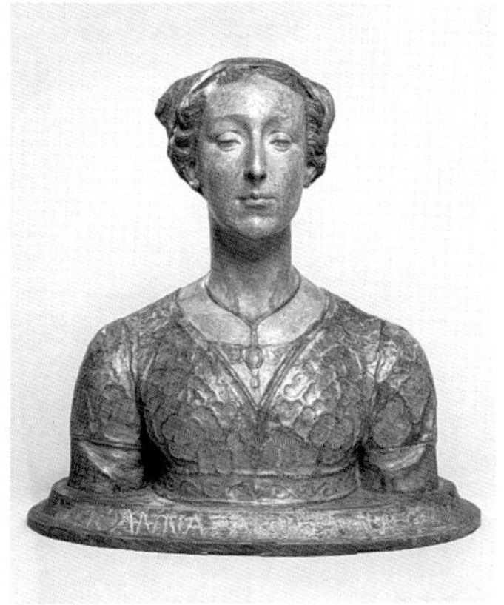


Giovanni Bastianini
Italian, 1830–1868

*Portrait of a Lady, "Giovanna Albizzi,"* c. 1860
Gesso and polychrome over wood and mixed media, .530 x .540 x .308 (20 3/4 x 21 1/4 x 12 1/8)
Falsely dated on front of base: IOANNA ALBIZA MCCCCIX
Andrew W. Mellon Collection
1937.1.129

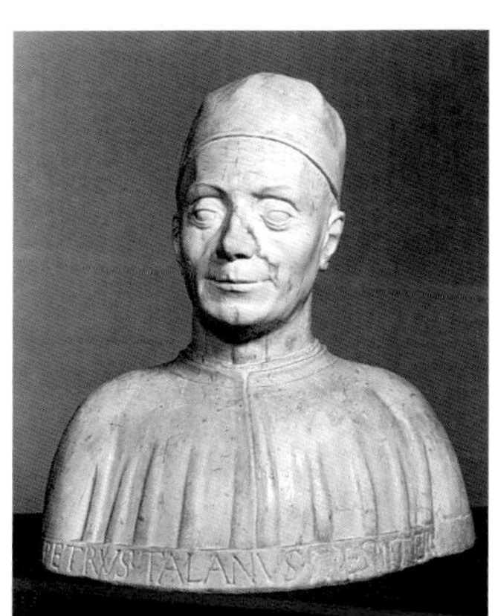


*Pietro Talani*
Marble, .483 x .440 x .237 (19 x 17 1/4 x 9 3/8)
Inscribed across bottom front: PETRVS•TALANVS•PRESBITER
Widener Collection
1942.9.105

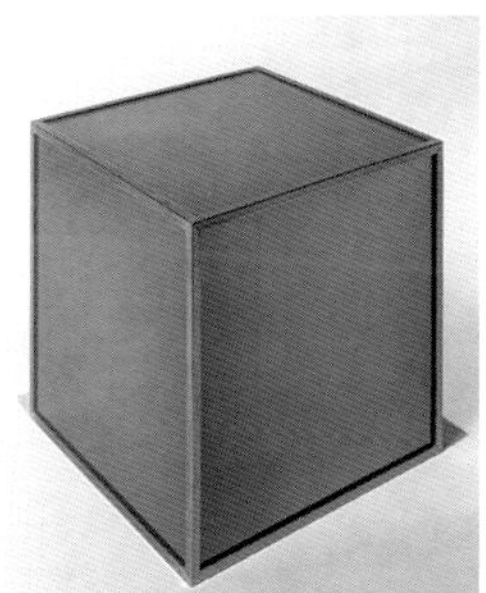

Larry Bell
American, born 1939

*Chrome and Glass Construction,* 1965
Chrome and glass, .311 x .311 x .311 (12 1/4 x 12 1/4 x 12 1/4)
Gift of Mr. and Mrs. Burton Tremaine
1975.100.2

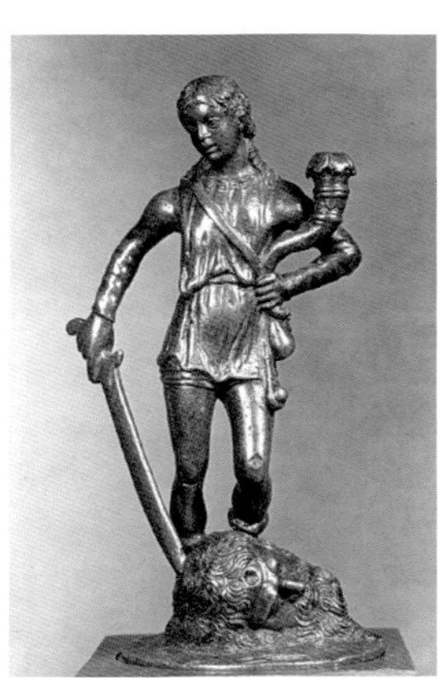

After Bartolomeo Bellano
Italian

*David,* early 16th century
Bronze, .220 x .117 x .060 (8 3/4 x 4 5/8 x 2 3/8)
Widener Collection
1942.9.103

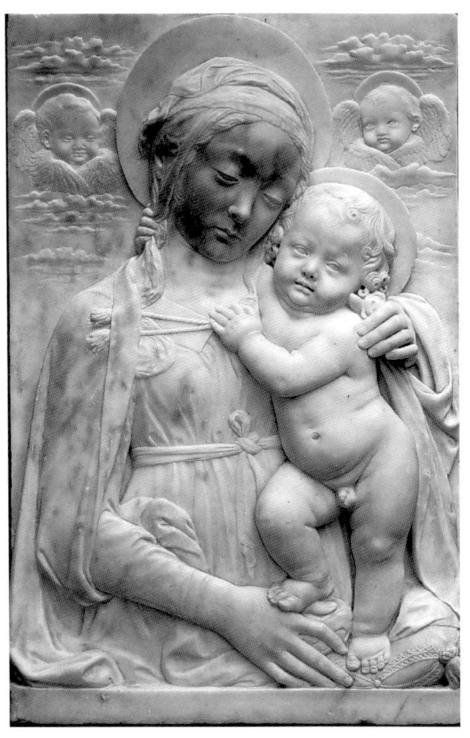

Benedetto da Maiano
Florentine, 1442–1497

*Madonna and Child,* c. 1475
Marble, .583 x .390 x .098
(22 7/8 x 15 1/4 x 3 7/8)
Samuel H. Kress Collection
1960.5.16

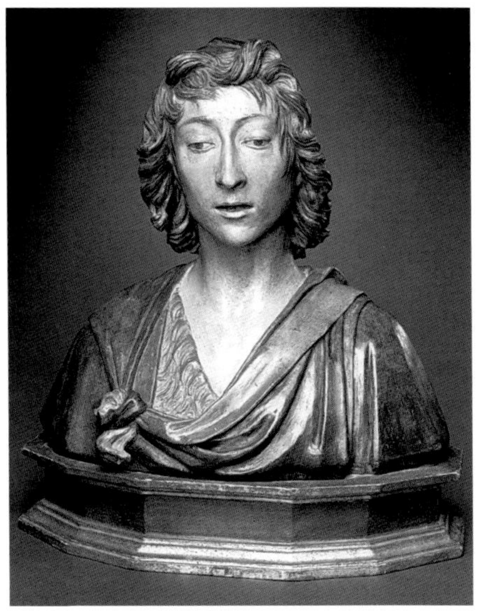

*Saint John the Baptist,* c. 1480
Terra cotta, painted, .489 x .520 x .260
(19 1/4 x 20 1/2 x 10 1/4)
Andrew W. Mellon Collection
1937.1.130

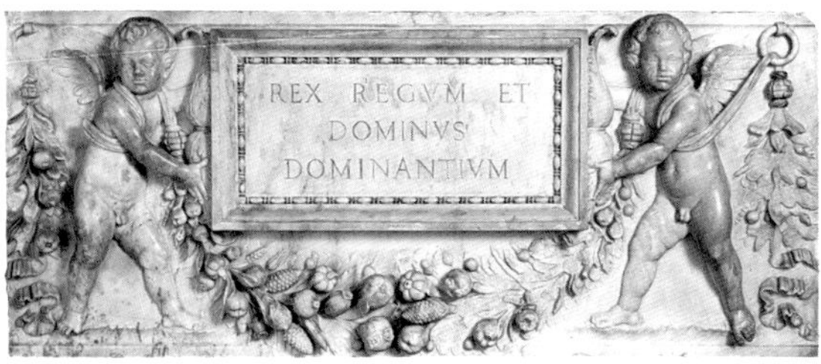


Benedetto da Rovezzano
Florentine, 1474–c. 1554

*Relief from an Altar or Tabernacle,*
c. 1507/1512
Marble, .530 x 1.295 x .077
(20 7/8 x 51 x 3)
Inscribed on tablet at center: REX REGVM ET / DOMINVS / DOMINANTIVM
Widener Collection
1942.9.131

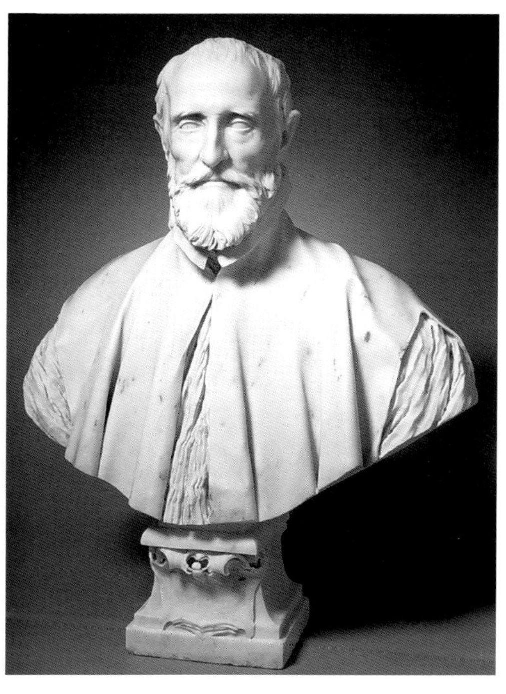

Gian Lorenzo Bernini
Roman, 1598–1680

*Monsignor Francesco Barberini,* c. 1623
Marble, .792 x .661 x .267
($31^1/_8$ x 26 x $10^1/_2$)
Samuel H. Kress Collection
1961.9.102

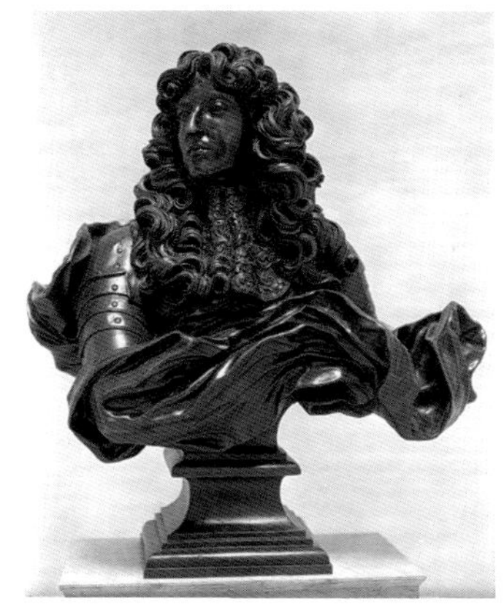

After Gian Lorenzo Bernini
French

*Louis XIV,* c. 1700
Bronze, .842 x 1.000 x .432
($33^1/_8$ x $39^3/_8$ x 17)
Samuel H. Kress Collection
1943.4.87

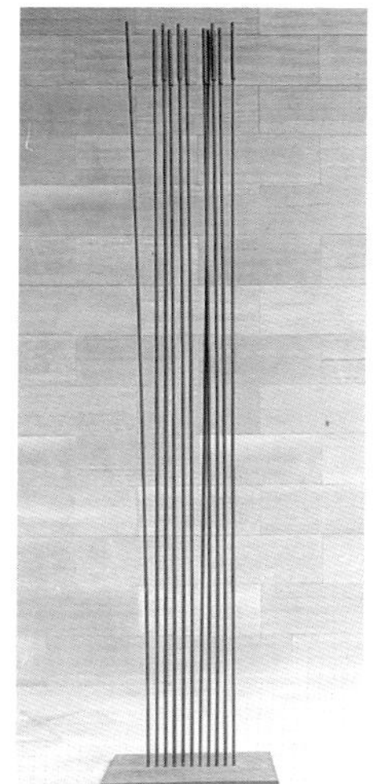

Harry Bertoia
American, 1915–1978

*Tonal Sculpture,* 1977
Beryllium copper with bronze weights, height: 5.385 (212); base only: 1.229 x 1.229 ($48^1/_3$ x $48^1/_3$)
Gift of Bernard and Audrey Berman
1984.103.1

Martin van den Bogaert, called Desjardins
*See* Desjardins

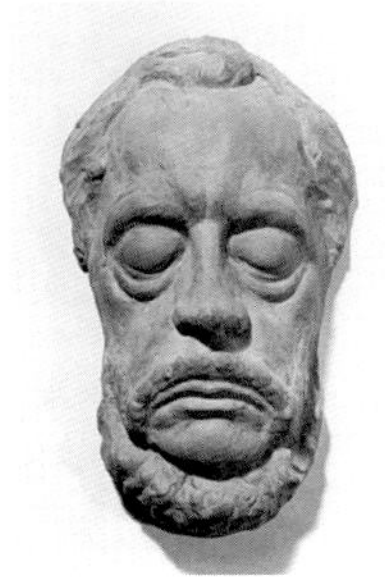

Bernhard A. Böhmer
German, died 1945

*Death Mask of Ernst Barlach ?,* probably 1938
Plaster, .347 x .210 x .114
($13^{5}/_{8}$ x $8^{1}/_{4}$ x $4^{1}/_{2}$)
Gift of Frederick C. Oechsner
1962.7.1

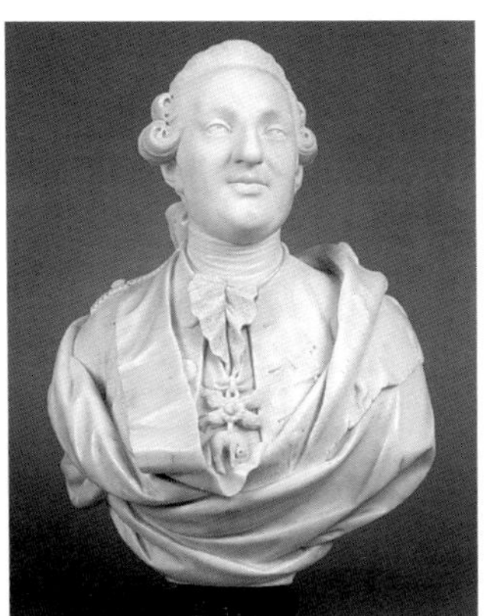

Louis-Simon Boizot
French, 1743–1809

*Louis XVI,* 1777
Marble, .635 x .527 x .372
(25 x $20^{3}/_{4}$ x $14^{5}/_{8}$)
Gift of the Versailles Foundation
1976.28.1

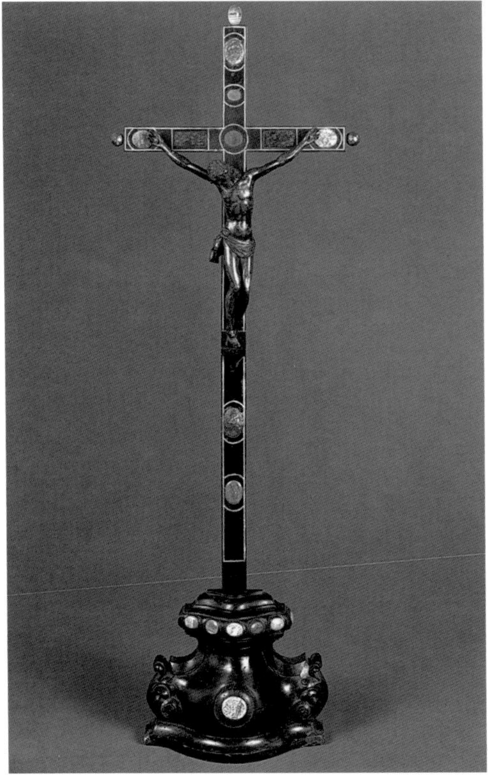

Giovanni Bologna, called Giambologna
Flemish (active in Italy), 1529–1608

*Christ Crucified,* probably before 1588
Bronze, corpus only: .308 x .250 x .076
($12^{1}/_{8}$ x $10^{1}/_{8}$ x 3)
Gift of Mr. and Mrs. John R. Gaines in memory of Clarence F. and Amelia R. Gaines, and Gloria Gaines, and in Honor of the 50th Anniversary of the National Gallery of Art
1991.16.1

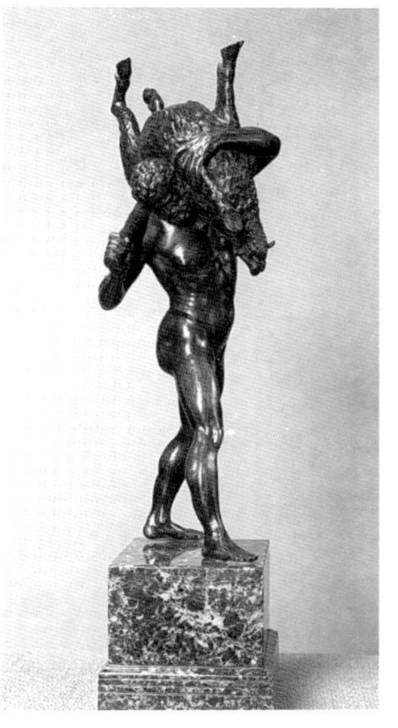

After Giovanni Bologna, called Giambologna
Italian

*Hercules Carrying the Erymanthian Boar*, c. 1575/1675
Bronze, .445 x .170 x .255
(17 1/2 x 6 3/4 x 10)
Widener Collection
1942.9.121

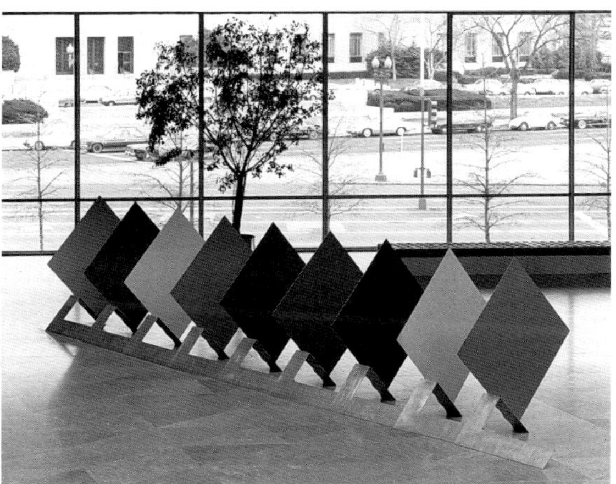

Michael Bolus
British, born 1934

*Sculpture Number 2*, 1969
Aluminum, painted,
1.741 x 1.752 x 1.219 (68 5/8 x 69 x 48)
Gift of Lewis Cabot
1977.65.1

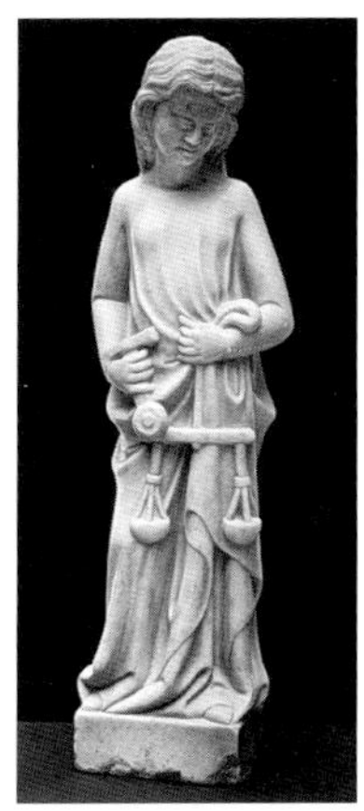

Bonino da Campione
Lombard, active 1357–1397

*Justice*, c. 1357
Marble, .650 x .200 x .139
(25 1/2 x 7 3/4 x 5 1/2)
Samuel H. Kress Collection
1960.5.5

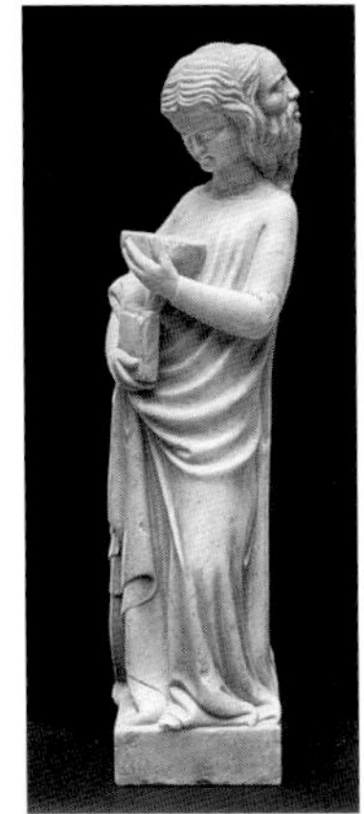

Bonino da Campione
Lombard, active 1357–1397

*Prudence*, c. 1357
Marble, .677 x .191 x .152
(26 5/8 x 7 1/2 x 6)
Samuel H. Kress Collection
1960.5.6

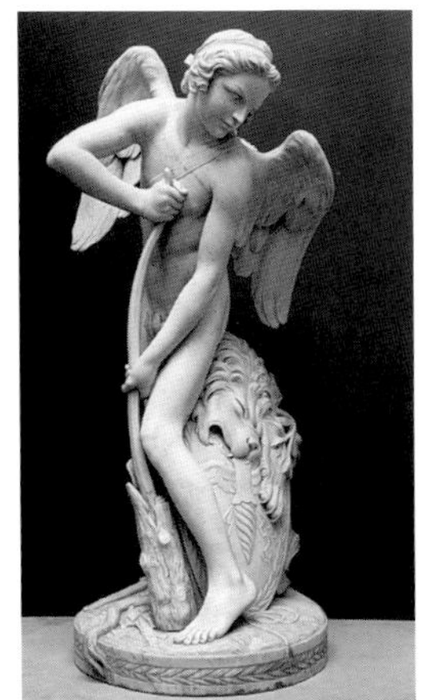

Edmé Bouchardon
French, 1698–1762

*Cupid*, 1744
Marble, height: .739 (29); diameter of base: .345 (13 1/2)
Inscribed on side of base at rear: BOUCHARDON 1744.
Samuel H. Kress Collection
1952.5.93

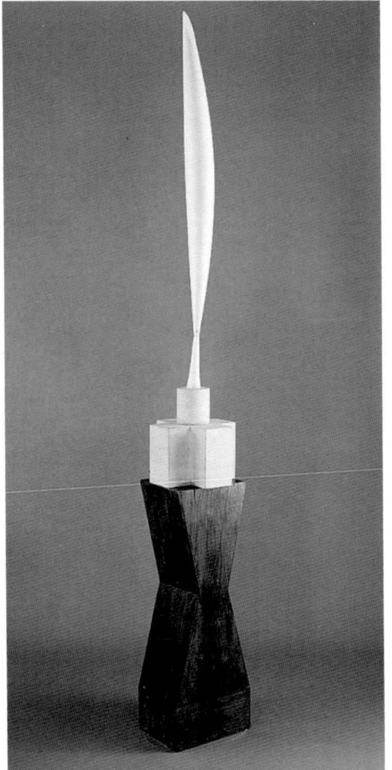

Constantin Brancusi
Romanian, 1876–1957

*Bird in Space*, 1925
Marble, stone, and wood, total height: 3.446 (136 1/2); marble "bird": 1.819 x .137 x .162 (71 5/8 x 5 3/8 x 6 3/8); stone pedestal height: .448 (17 5/8); wood pedestal height: 1.200 (47 1/4)
Gift of Eugene and Agnes E. Meyer
1967.13.3

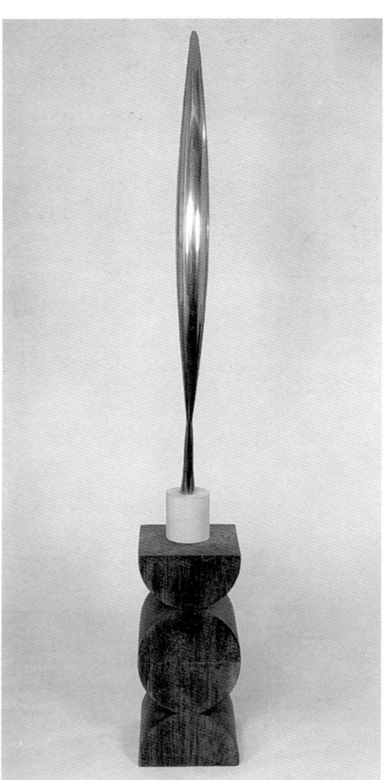

*Bird in Space*, 1927
Bronze, cast stone, and wood, total height: 2.877 ($113^1/_4$); bronze "bird": 1.854 x .136 x .156 (73 x $5^3/_8$ x $6^1/_8$); cast stone base height: .184 ($7^1/_4$); wood base height: .838 (33)
Inscribed on underside of "bird":
C. BRANCUSI 1927
Given in loving memory of her husband, Taft Schreiber, by Rita Schreiber
1989.31.3

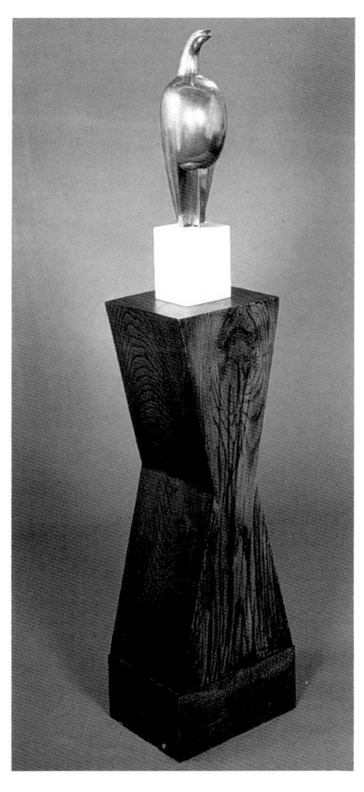

*Maiastra (Bird Before It Flew)*, c. 1911
Bronze, marble, and wood, total height: 1.921 ($75^5/_8$); bronze "bird": .556 x .186 x .187 ($21^7/_8$ x $7^3/_8$ x $7^3/_8$); marble base height: .203 (8); wood base height: 1.162 ($45^3/_4$)
Foundry mark on back at bottom right:
CIRE / C. VALSUANI / PERDUE
Gift of Katharine Graham
1980.75.1

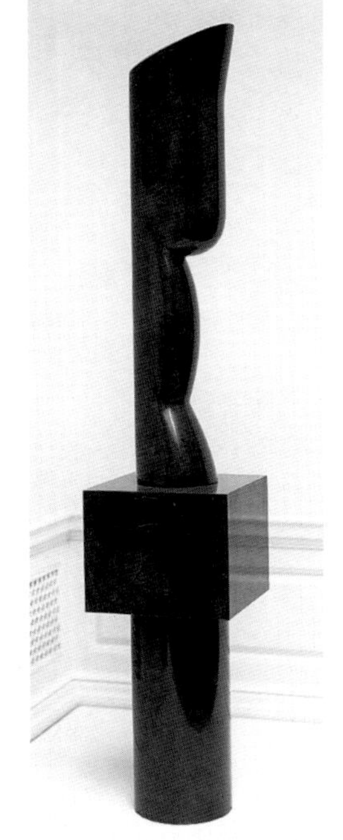

Constantin Brancusi
Romanian, 1876–1957

*Agnes E. Meyer,* 1929
Marble, in three parts, total height: 2.301 (90 5/8); top element: 1.340 x .248 x .327 (52 3/4 x 9 3/4 x 12 7/8); square base height: .349 (13 3/4); round base height: .613 (24 1/8)
Gift of Eugene and Agnes E. Meyer
1967.13.4

Andrea Briosco (Andrea Riccio, called Riccio)
*See* Andrea Riccio

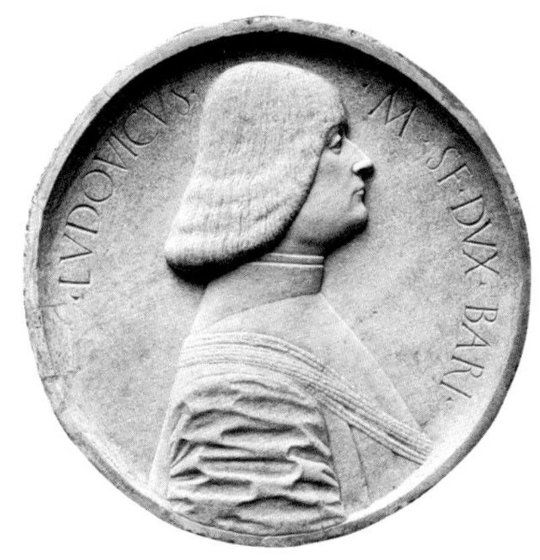


Benedetto Briosco
Lombard, active 1477–1525

*Lodovico Sforza, Duke of Bari,* early 1490s
Marble, diameter: .610 (24)
Inscribed around edge: •LVDOVICVS• •M• SF•DVX•BARI•
Andrew W. Mellon Collection
1937.1.120

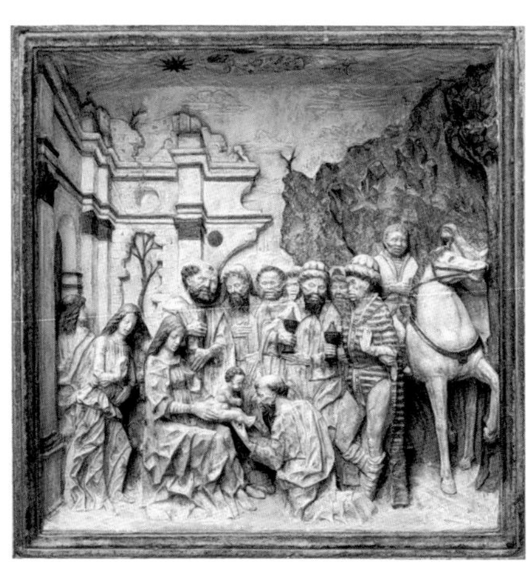

Benedetto Briosco
Lombard, active 1477–1525
and Tommasso Cazzaniga
Milanese, active 1483–1504

*The Adoration of the Magi,* commissioned 1484
Marble, partly gilded, .610 x .610 (24 x 24)
Samuel H. Kress Collection
1952.5.90

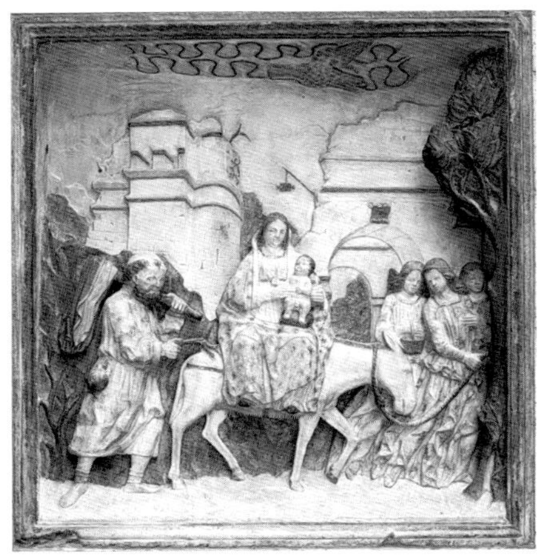

*The Flight into Egypt*, commissioned 1484
Marble, partly gilded, .610 x .610
(24 x 24)
Samuel H. Kress Collection
1952.5.91

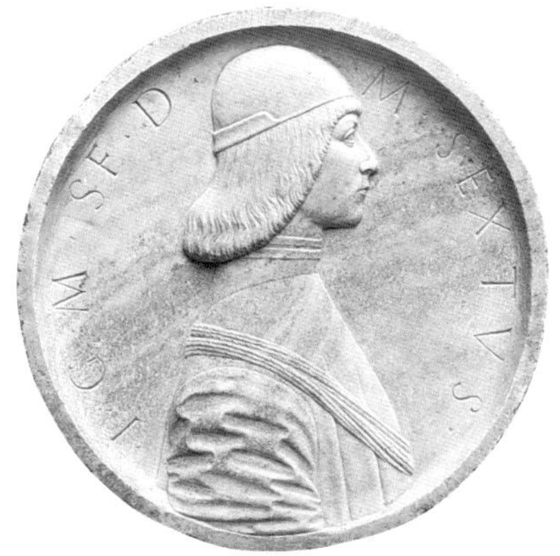


WORKSHOP OF BENEDETTO BRIOSCO
Lombard

*Gian Galeazzo Maria Sforza, Duke of Milan*, early 1490s
Marble, diameter: .620 (24 3/8)
Inscribed around edge: •I•G•M•SF•D• •M• SEXTVS•
Andrew W. Mellon Collection
1937.1.121

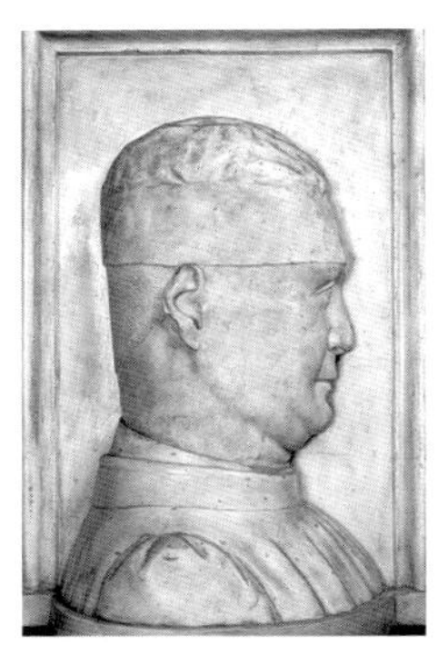

IMITATOR OF BENEDETTO BRIOSCO

*Filippo Maria Visconti*, part pre-1878, part 1930
Marble, .487 x .358 (19 1/8 x 14)
Samuel H. Kress Collection
1943.4.77

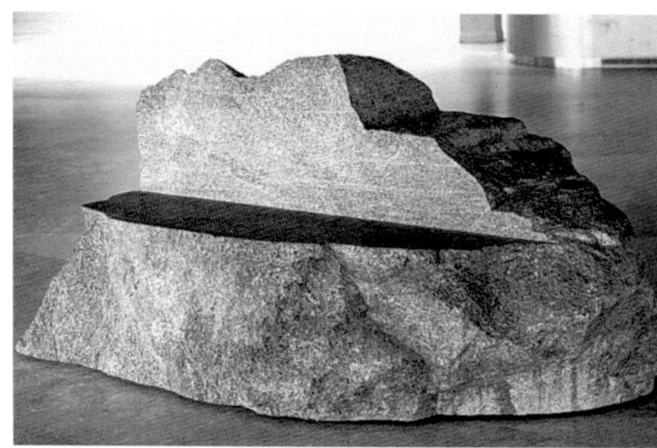

Scott Burton
American, 1939–1989

*Rock Settee,* 1988
Granite (green), .981 x 2.134 x 1.067
(38 5/8 x 84 x 42)
Gift of the Collectors Committee
1988.68.1

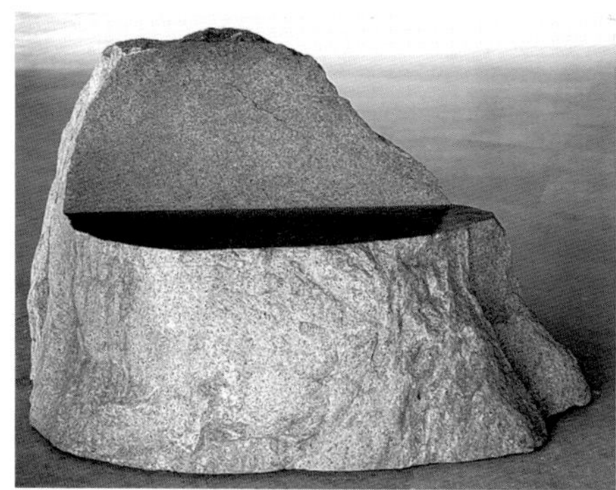

*Rock Settee,* 1988
Granite (pink), .978 x 1.600 x 1.079
(38 1/2 x 63 x 42 1/2)
Gift of the Collectors Committee
1988.68.2

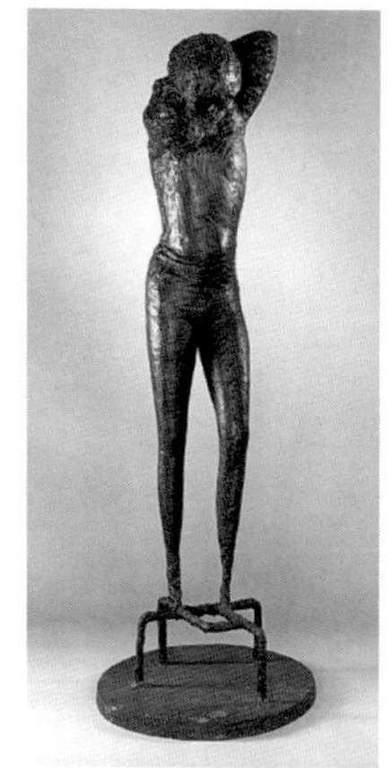

Reginald Butler
British, born 1913

*Girl,* 1957/1958
Bronze, 1.790 x .616 x .616
(70 1/2 x 24 1/4 x 24 1/4)
Inscribed on top of base at back: RB (monogram) 3/8; foundry mark on top of base at back: SUSSE FONDEUR PARIS
Gift of Enid A. Haupt
1977.47.1

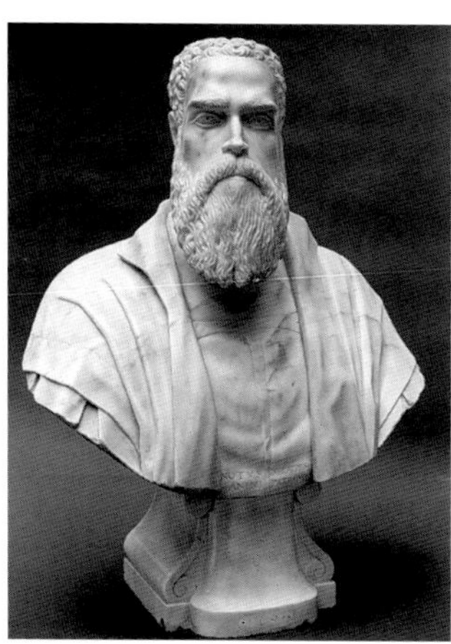

Attributed to
Giovanni Battista Caccini
Florentine, 1556–1612/1613

*Giovanni Capponi,* c. 1590/1600
Marble, .602 x .600 x .257
(23 5/8 x 23 1/2 x 10 1/8)
Inscribed on chest: NOTVS INFRATRES / ANIMI PATERNI
Samuel H. Kress Collection
1943.4.84

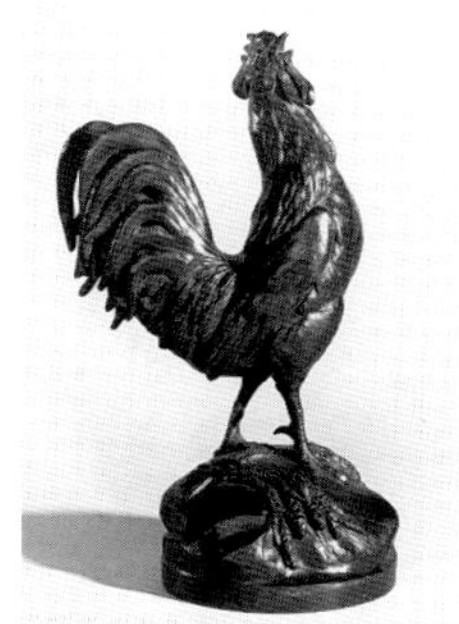

AUGUST-NICOLAS CAIN
French, 1822–1894

*Crowing Rooster,* c. 1860/1894
Bronze, .305 x .135 x .298
(12 x 5 3/8 x 11 3/4)
Inscribed on front of base: CAIN; foundry mark at rear of base: SUSSE FRÈRES EDITEURS / • PARIS •
Collection of Mr. and Mrs. Paul Mellon
1980.44.6

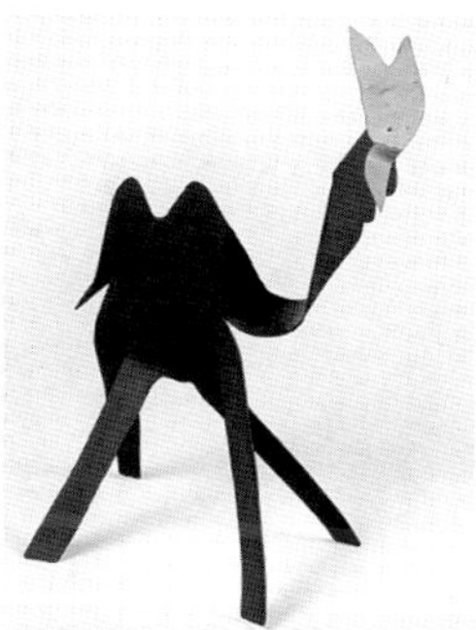

ALEXANDER CALDER
American, 1898–1976

*Black Camel with Blue Head and Red Tongue,* 1971
Sheet metal, painted, height: .537 (21 1/8)
Inscribed on camel's right side: CA (monogram) 71
Gift of Mrs. Paul Mellon, in Honor of the 50th Anniversary of the National Gallery of Art
1991.7.13

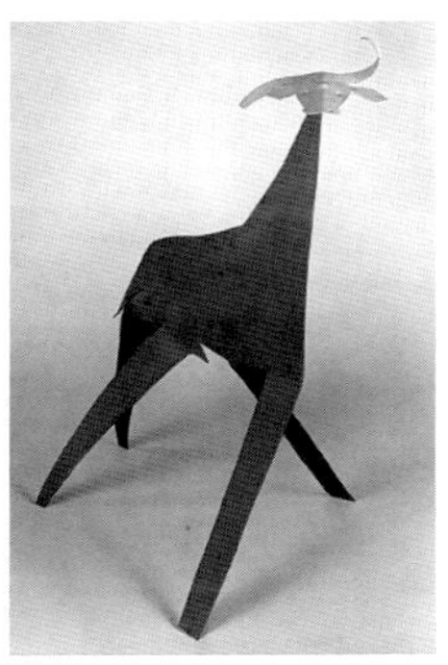

*Blue and Red Bull with Yellow Head,* 1971
Sheet metal, painted, height: .994 (39 1/8)
Inscribed on blue side: CA (monogram) 71
Gift of Mrs. Paul Mellon, in Honor of the 50th Anniversary of the National Gallery of Art
1991.7.12

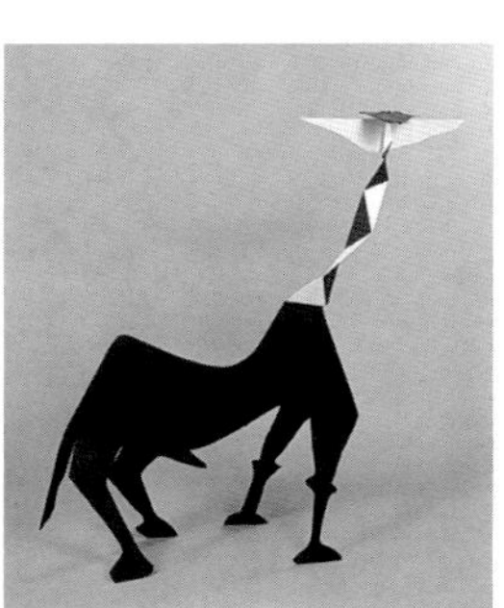

*Crinkly Taureau,* 1970
Sheet metal, painted, height: 1.003 (39 1/2)
Inscribed on right side: CA (monogram) 70
Gift of Mrs. Paul Mellon, in Honor of the 50th Anniversary of the National Gallery of Art
1991.7.6

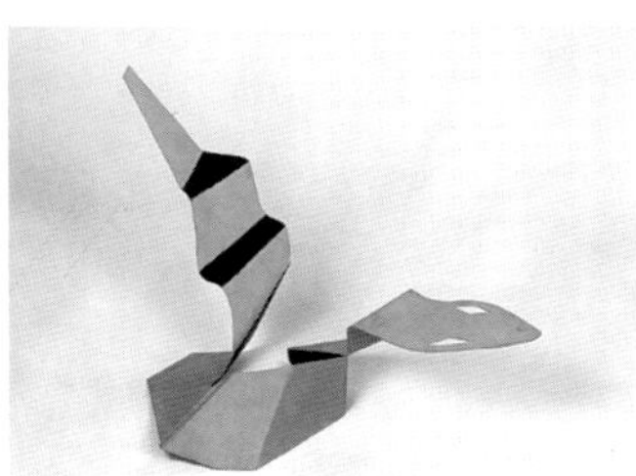

## Alexander Calder
American, 1898–1976

*Crinkly Worm*, 1971
Sheet metal, painted, height: .460 (18 1/8)
Inscribed on red near base of blue and black "tail": CA (monogram) / 71
Gift of Mrs. Paul Mellon, in Honor of the 50th Anniversary of the National Gallery of Art
1991.7.10

*Deux Angles Droits*, 1971
Sheet metal, painted, height: .508 (20)
Inscribed on bottom of base: CA (monogram) 71
Gift of Mrs. Paul Mellon, in Honor of the 50th Anniversary of the National Gallery of Art
1991.7.8

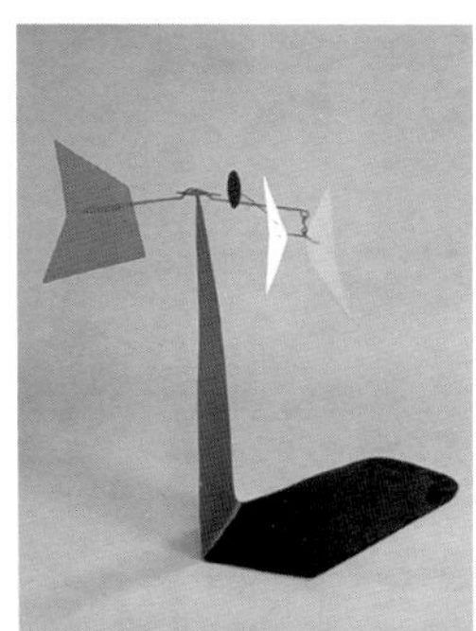

*Les Fleches*, 1976
Sheet metal, painted, height: .638 (25 1/8)
Inscribed on top of black base: CA (monogram) / 76
Gift of Mrs. Paul Mellon, in Honor of the 50th Anniversary of the National Gallery of Art
1991.7.15

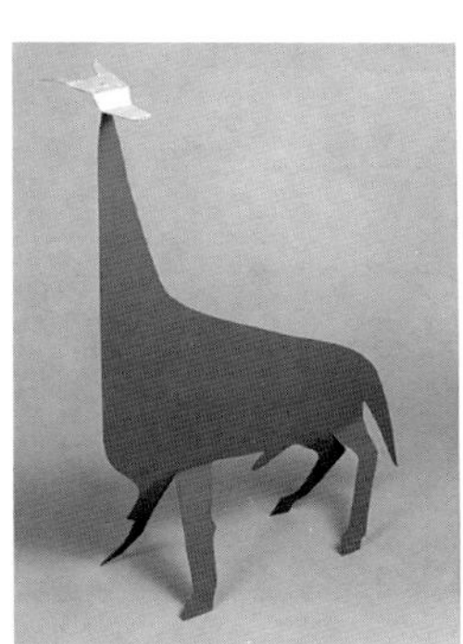

*Horse*, 1970
Sheet metal, painted, height: .975 (38 3/8)
Inscribed on blue side: CA (monogram) 70
Gift of Mrs. Paul Mellon, in Honor of the 50th Anniversary of the National Gallery of Art
1991.7.9

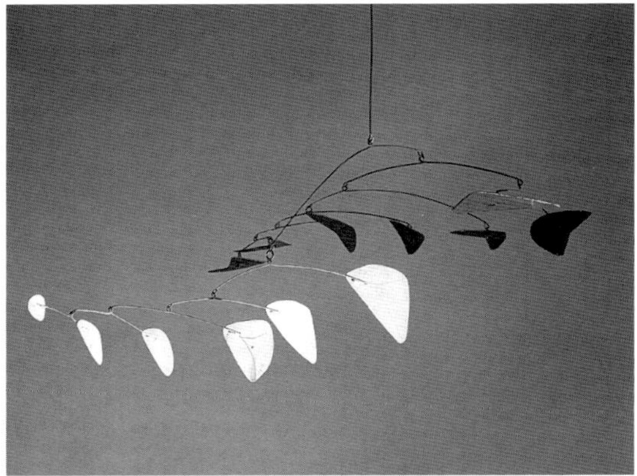

*Model for East Building Mobile,* 1972
Painted aluminum and steel wire
.289 x .692 (11 3/8 x 27 1/4)
Gift of the Collectors Committee
1975.114.1

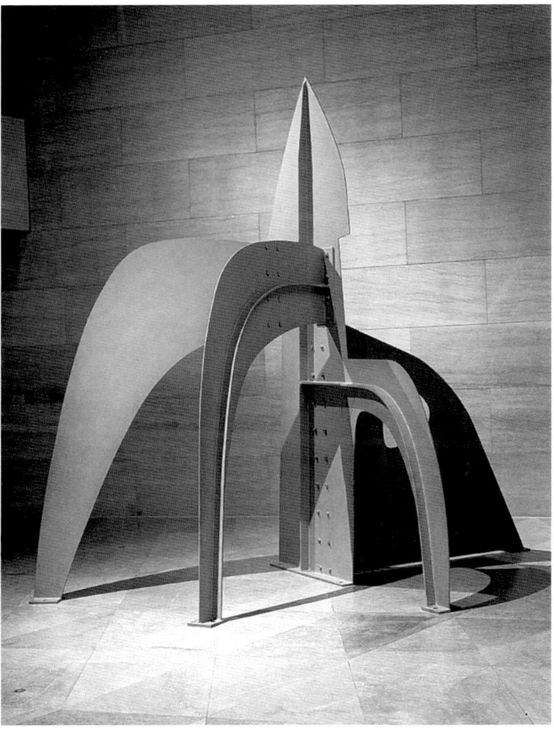

*Obus,* 1972
Steel, painted, 3.618 x 3.859 x 2.276
(142 1/2 x 152 x 89 5/8)
Inscribed on center component below horizontal ridge: CA (monogram) 72
Collection of Mr. and Mrs. Paul Mellon
1983.1.49

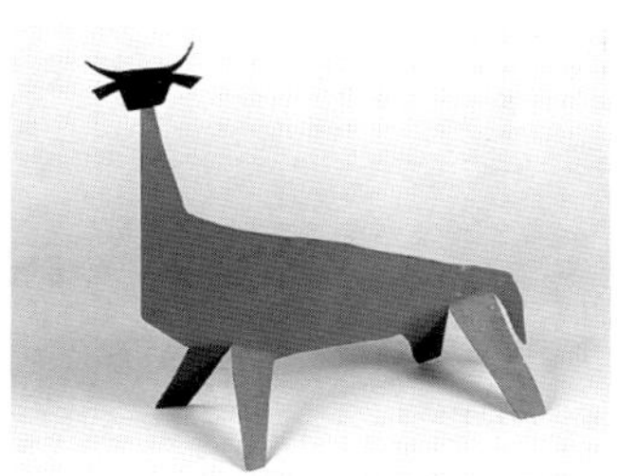

*Red Cow with Black Head,* 1971
Sheet metal, height: .568 (22 3/8)
Inscribed on cow's right side: CA (monogram) 71
Gift of Mrs. Paul Mellon, in Honor of the 50th Anniversary of the National Gallery of Art
1991.7.14

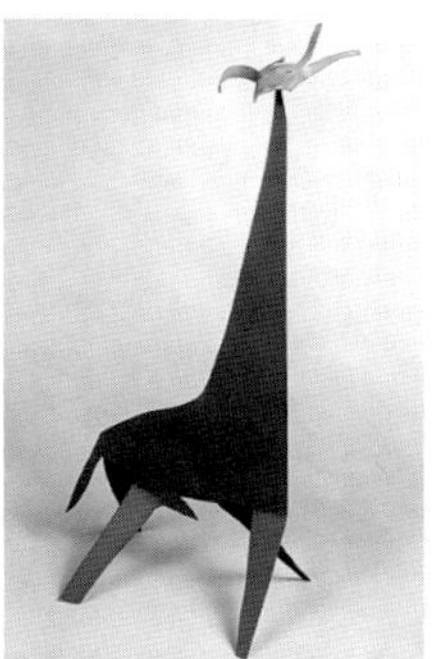

ALEXANDER CALDER
American, 1898–1976

*Red and Yellow Bull with Blue Head,* 1971
Sheet metal, height: 1.019 (40 1/8)
Inscribed on red side: CA (monogram) 71
Gift of Mrs. Paul Mellon, in Honor of the 50th Anniversary of the National Gallery of Art
1991.7.11

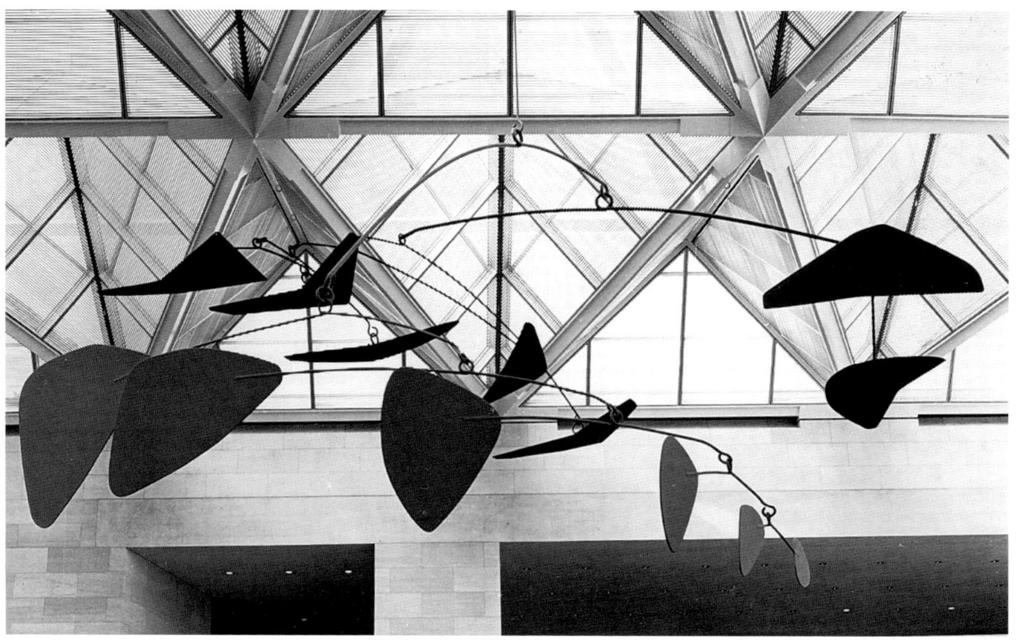

*Untitled,* 1976
Aluminum and steel, 9.103 x 23.155 (29'10 1/2 x 76')
Gift of the Collectors Committee
1977.76.1

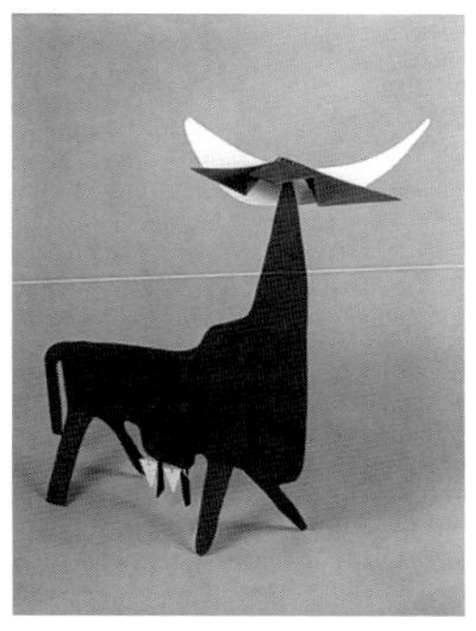

*La Vache,* 1970
Sheet metal, painted, height: .867 (34 1/8)
Inscribed on right side: CA (monogram) / 70
Gift of Mrs. Paul Mellon, in Honor of the 50th Anniversary of the National Gallery of Art
1991.7.7

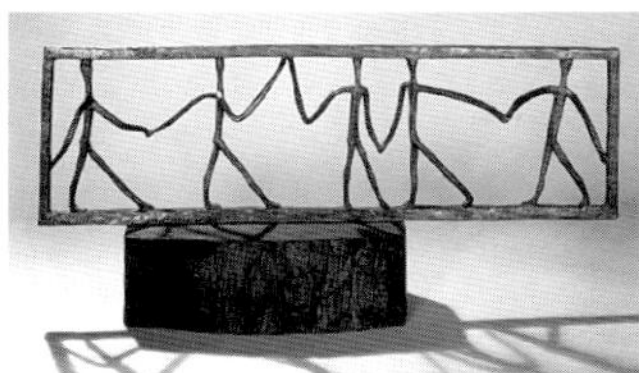

MARY CALLERY
American, 1903–1977

*Amity*, 1947
Bronze, .196 x .660 x .105
($7^3/_4$ x 26 x $4^1/_8$)
Gift of Mr. and Mrs. Burton Tremaine
1977.75.7

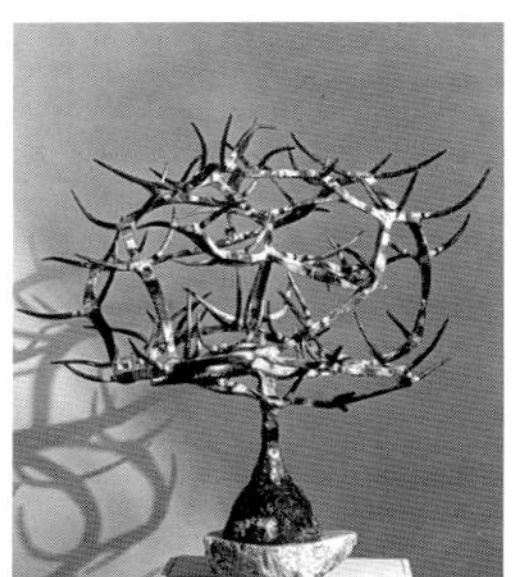

*Epoque de Rennes*, 1960
Bronze, .413 x .486 ($16^1/_4$ x $19^1/_8$)
Inscribed at bottom: CM (monogram)
Collection of Mr. and Mrs. Paul Mellon
1983.1.50

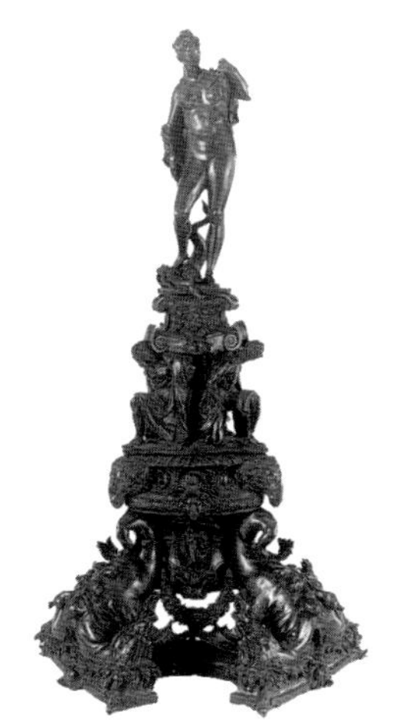

CIRCLE OF GIROLAMO CAMPAGNA
Veronese-Venetian

*Andiron with Figure of Venus*, probably 1549/1625
Bronze, 1.034 x .563 x .402
($40^3/_4$ x $22^1/_8$ x $15^7/_8$)
Samuel H. Kress Collection
1961.9.101

*See also:* CIRCLE OF TIZIANO ASPETTI, *Andiron with Figure of Mars*, 1961.9.100

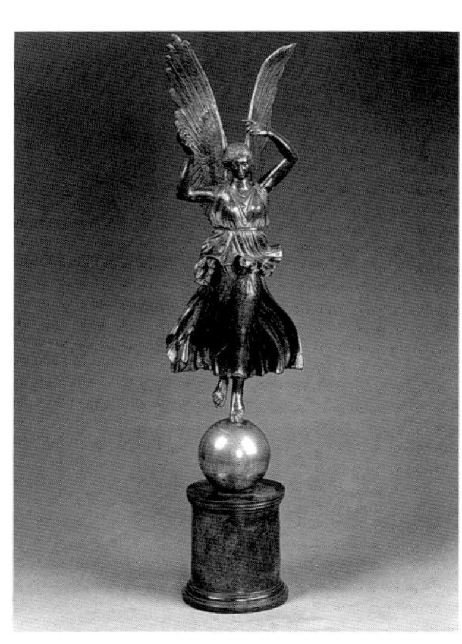

ANTONIO CANOVA
Italian, 1757–1822

*Winged Victory*, c. 1803/1806
Bronze, with base: .766 x .200 x .181
($30^1/_4$ x $7^7/_8$ x $7^1/_8$)
Patrons' Permanent Fund
1991.125.1

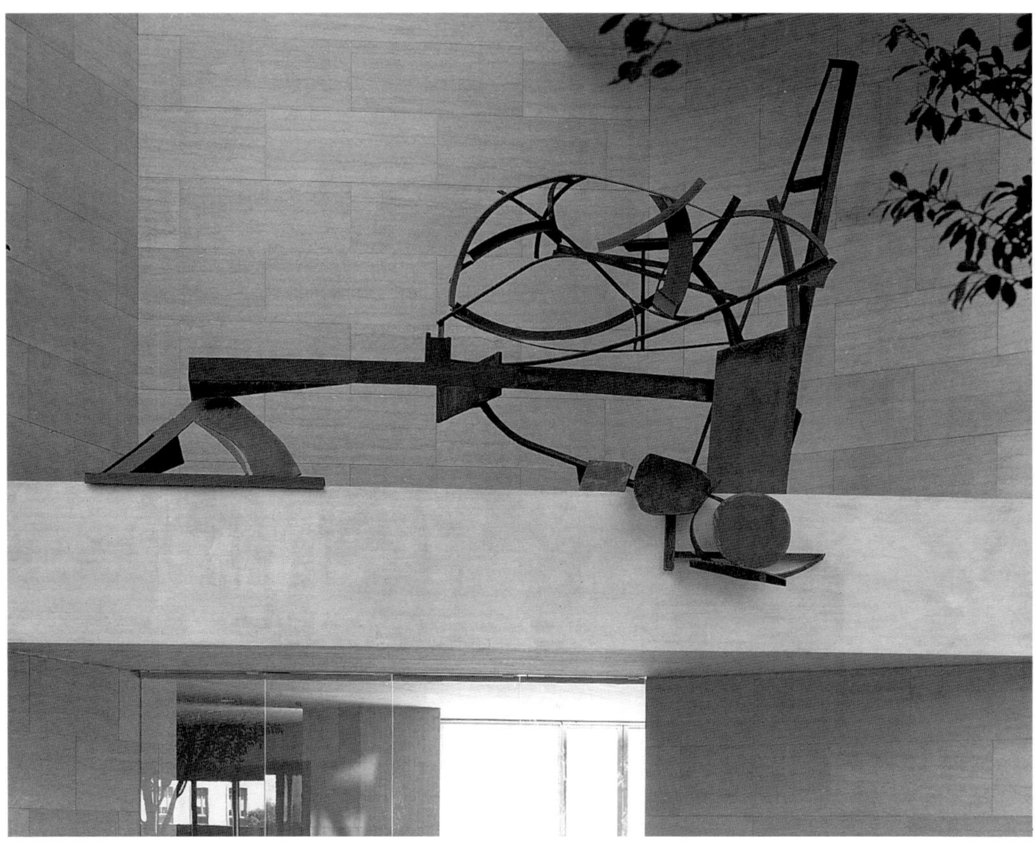

Anthony Caro
British, born 1924

*National Gallery Ledge Piece,* 1978
Welded steel, 4.345 x 6.176 x 2.692 (171 1/8 x 243 1/4 x 106)
Inscribed on reverse of triangular piece at upper right side: TONY C / JANE W / MARK / BILL N / CARLOS / M / 78
Gift of the Collectors Committee
1978.21.1

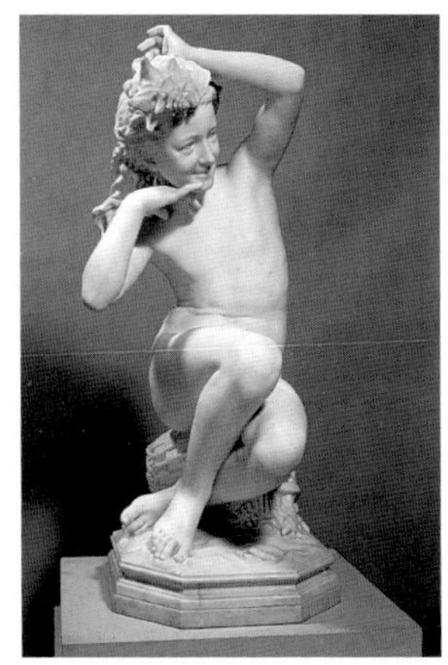

Jean-Baptiste Carpeaux
French, 1827–1875

*Girl with a Shell,* 1863–1867
Marble, including plinth:
1.026 x .515 x .623 (40 1/2 x 20 3/8 x 24 1/2)
Inscribed on top of base next to mouth of basket: JBTE CARPEAUX / PARIS 1867
Samuel H. Kress Collection
1943.4.90

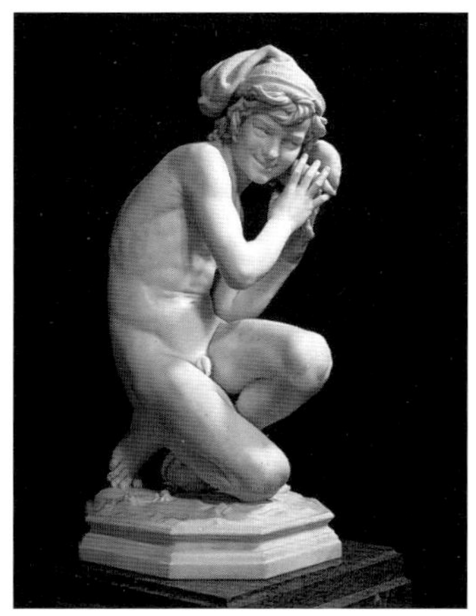

*Neapolitan Fisherboy*, 1857–c. 1861
Marble, .920 x .420 x .470
($36\frac{1}{4}$ x $16\frac{1}{2}$ x $18\frac{3}{8}$)
Inscribed on shell between legs (faint):
[CD] or [(A)] / CARPEAUX / ROMA
18[5 or 6]7
Samuel H. Kress Collection
1943.4.89

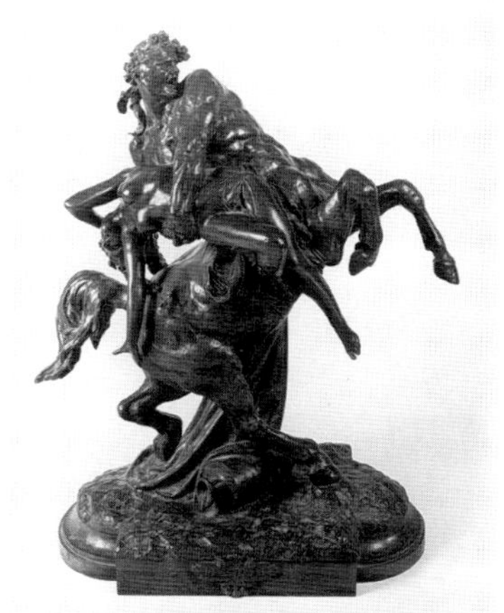

## ALBERT-ERNEST CARRIER-BELLEUSE
French, 1824–1887

*The Abduction of Hippodamia*, model c. 1879
Bronze, including self-base:
.648 x .556 x .292 ($25\frac{1}{2}$ x $21\frac{7}{8}$ x $11\frac{1}{2}$)
Inscribed on ground next to urn: CARRIER-BELLEUSE; embossed on title plaque on base: L'ENLÈVEMENT; foundry mark on edge of base near centaur's rear left hoof: BRONZE GARANTI AU TITRE; on rear edge of base: (two undeciphered symbols)
William Nelson Cromwell Fund
1977.58.1

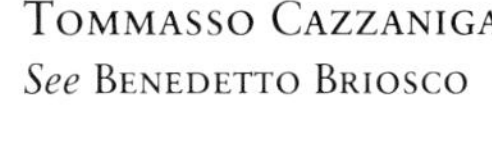

## TOMMASO CAZZANIGA
*See* BENEDETTO BRIOSCO

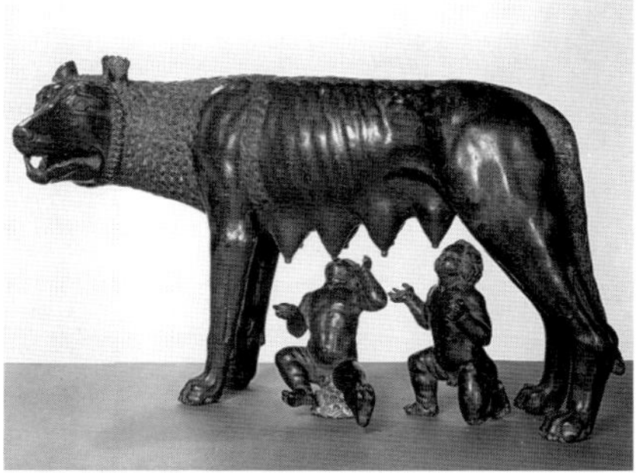

## CENTRAL ITALIAN (ROMAN?) 15TH OR 16TH CENTURY

*The She-Wolf Suckling Romulus and Remus*, late 15th or early 16th century
Bronze, wolf: .380 x .642 x .159
($14\frac{7}{8}$ x $25\frac{1}{4}$ x $6\frac{1}{4}$); height of seated twin: .137 ($5\frac{3}{8}$); height of kneeling twin: .181 ($7\frac{1}{8}$)
Samuel H. Kress Collection
1957.14.8

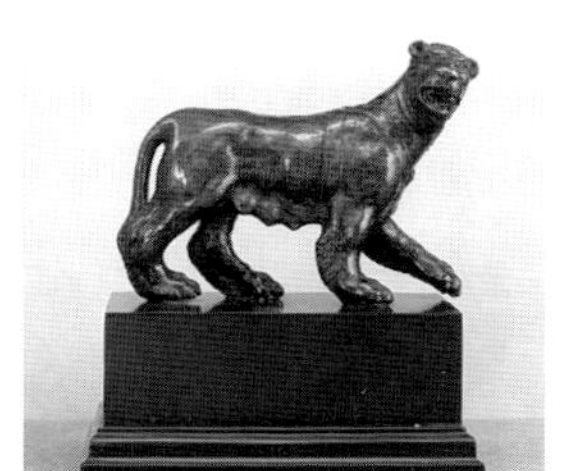

## CENTRAL OR NORTH ITALIAN 16TH CENTURY

*Pacing Female Panther*, c. 1500
Bronze, .100 x .142 x .054
($3\frac{15}{16}$ x $5\frac{5}{8}$ x $2\frac{1}{8}$)
Samuel H. Kress Collection
1957.14.73

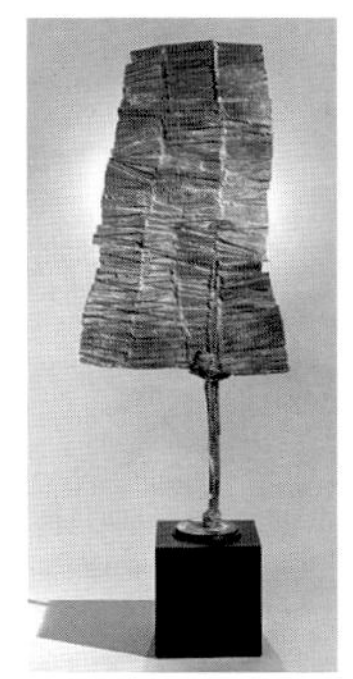

Cesar Baldaccini, called Cesar
French, born 1921

*Homage to Brancusi,* 1957
Bronze, 1.511 x .683 x .228
(59 1/2 x 26 7/8 x 9)
Gift of Mr. and Mrs. Morton G. Neumann
1980.74.1

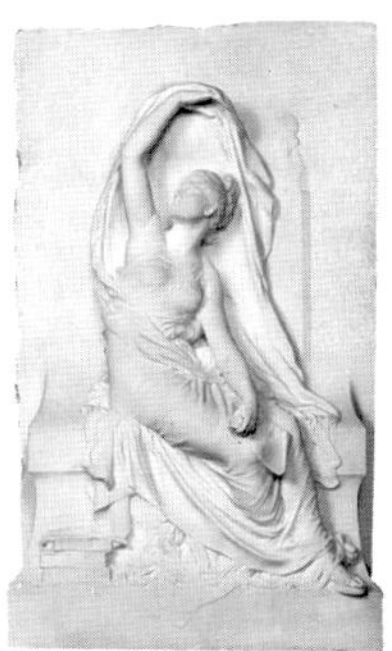

Henri-Michel-Antoine Chapu
French, 1833–1891

*La Pensée,* 1876–1891
Marble, .890 x .535 x .248
(35 x 21 x 9 3/4)
Inscribed at lower left beneath books: H.CHAPU
Pepita Milmore Memorial Fund
1986.27.1

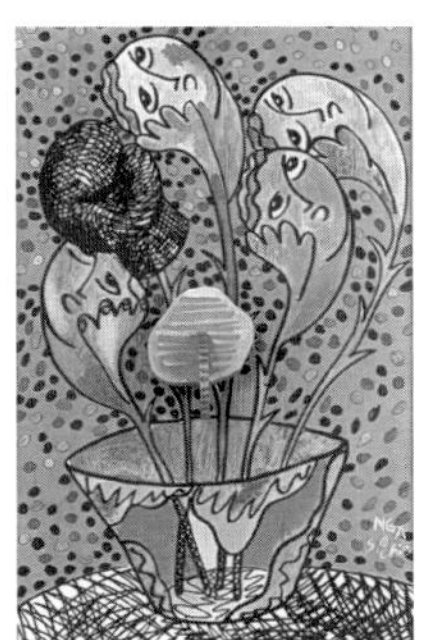

Sandro Chia
Italian, born 1946

*Flowers Fight,* 1987–1989
Wood bas-relief with gold-leaf frame and plywood assemblage, .905 x .606 x .178
(35 5/8 x 23 7/8 x 7)
Inscribed at lower right: NGA / S. CHIA
Gift of Graphicstudio/University of South Florida and the Artist
1989.90.1

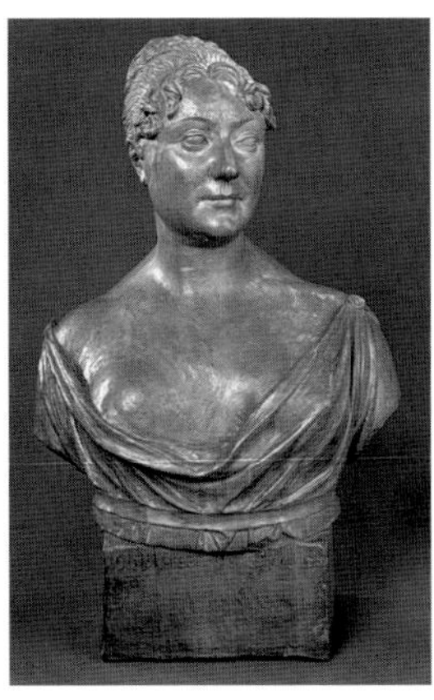

Joseph Chinard
French, 1755–1813

*A Lady,* 1810
Terra cotta, .670 x .394 x .299
(26 3/8 x 15 1/2 x 11 3/4)
Inscribed on front of base: CHINARD DE LYON 1810
Gift of Daniel Wildenstein, in Honor of the 50th Anniversary of the National Gallery of Art
1990.128.1

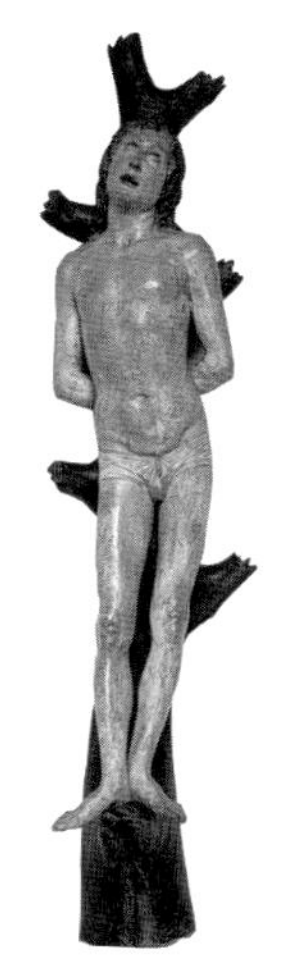

MATTEO CIVITALI
Tuscan, 1436–1501

*Saint Sebastian*, c. 1492
Terra cotta, painted, .653 x .177 x .097
(25 3/4 x 7 x 3 1/4)
Samuel H. Kress Collection
1943.4.76

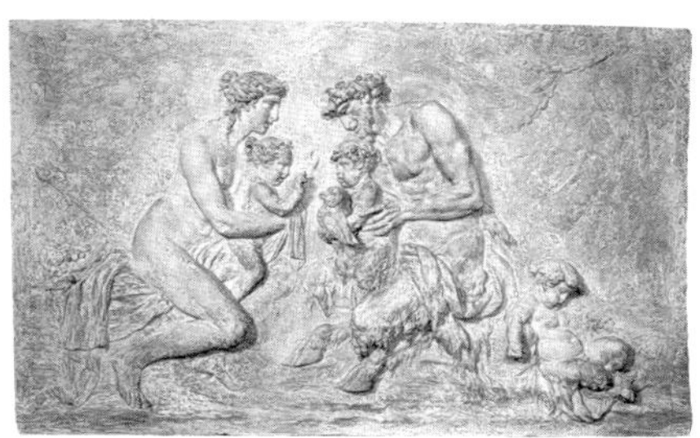

CLAUDE MICHEL, CALLED CLODION
French, 1738–1814

*Faun Family*, c. 1785
Terra cotta, .711 x 1.168 (28 x 46)
Inscribed at lower left: CLODION
Widener Collection
1942.9.109

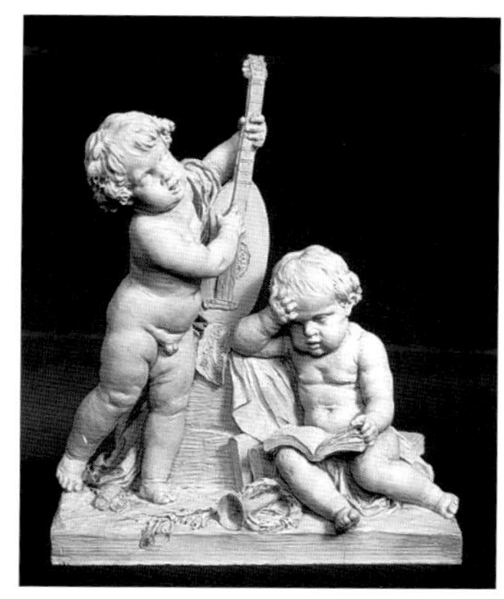

*Model for "Poetry and Music,"* 1774
Terra cotta, .270 x .233 x .156
(10 5/8 x 9 1/4 x 6 1/8)
Inscribed on back: CLODION.
Loula D. Lasker Fund
1976.10.1

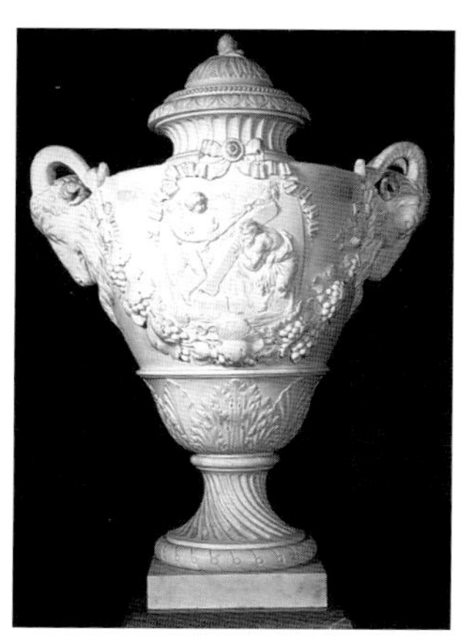

*Monumental Urn*, 1782
Marble, 1.312 x .973 x .727
(51 5/8 x 38 3/8 x 28 5/8)
Inscribed on relief medallion, on base of statue of Pan: CLODION / 1782.
Andrew W. Mellon Collection
1940.2.2

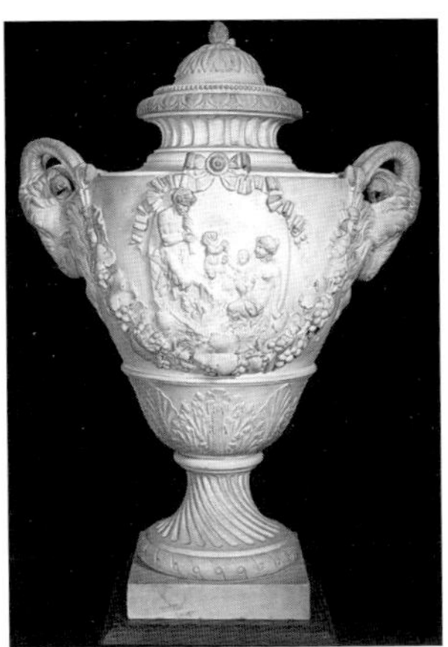

Claude Michel, called Clodion
French, 1738–1814

*Monumental Urn,* 1782
Marble, 1.314 x .965 x .728
(51 3/4 x 38 x 28 3/4)
Andrew W. Mellon Collection
1940.2.3

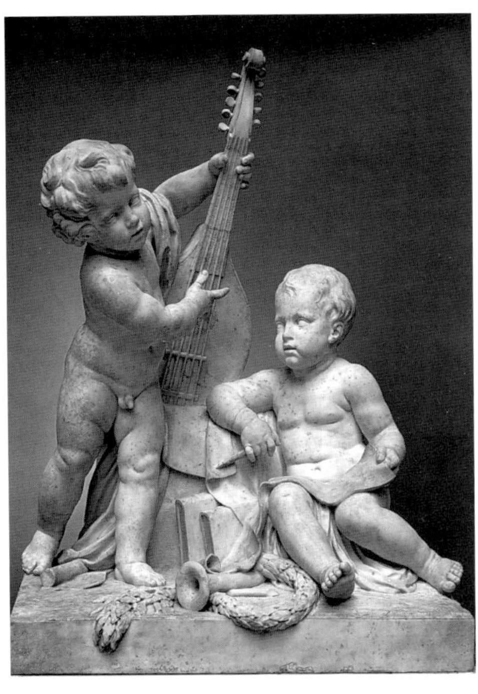

*Poetry and Music,* c. 1771/1774
Marble, 1.175 x .889 x .600
(46 1/4 x 35 x 23 5/8)
Samuel H. Kress Collection
1952.5.98

*See also*: Jean-Pierre-Antoine Tassaert, *Painting and Sculpture,* 1952.5.110

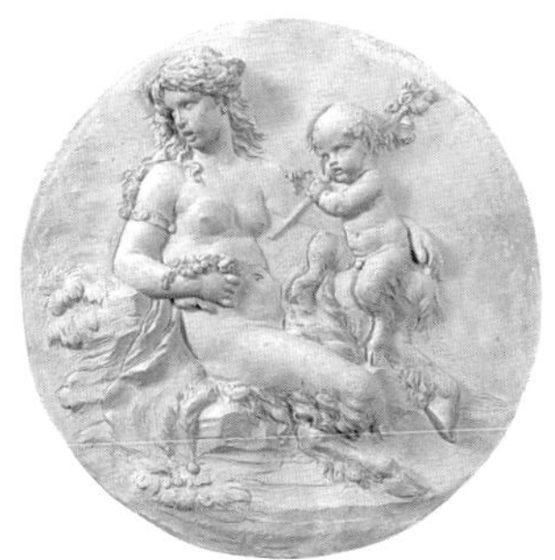

*Satyrs at Play,* c. 1783/1785
Terra cotta, diameter: .290 (11 2/5)
Gift of Mrs. John W. Simpson
1942.5.31

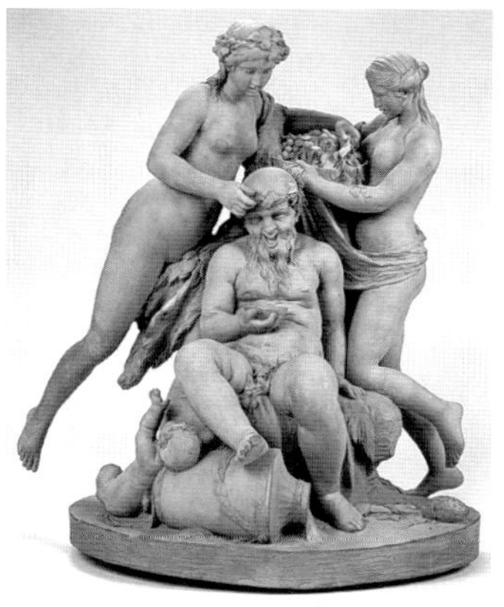

*Silenus Crowned by Nymphs,* 1768
Terra cotta, .420 x .383 x .305
(16 1/2 x 15 1/8 x 12)
Inscribed on rear of rock: CLODION • IN ROMA /• 1768•
Pepita Milmore Memorial Fund
1977.59.1

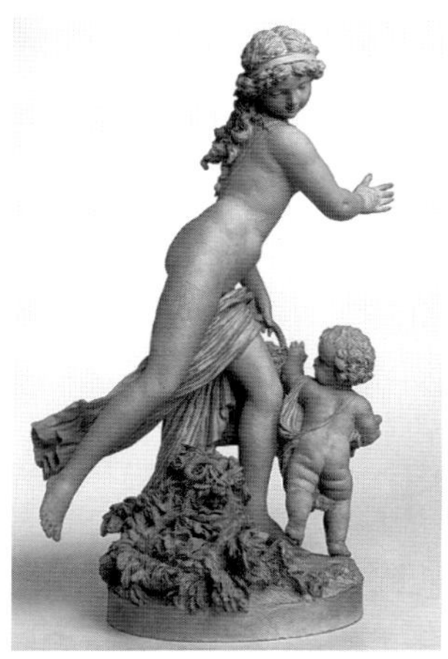

*The Surprise,* 1799
Terra cotta, including self-base:
.368 x .260 x .187 (14 1/2 x 10 1/4 x 7 1/4)
Inscribed on rear of base below drapery:
CLODION. / 1799.
Gift of Irma I. Straus in memory of her husband, Jesse Isidor Straus
1942.12.1

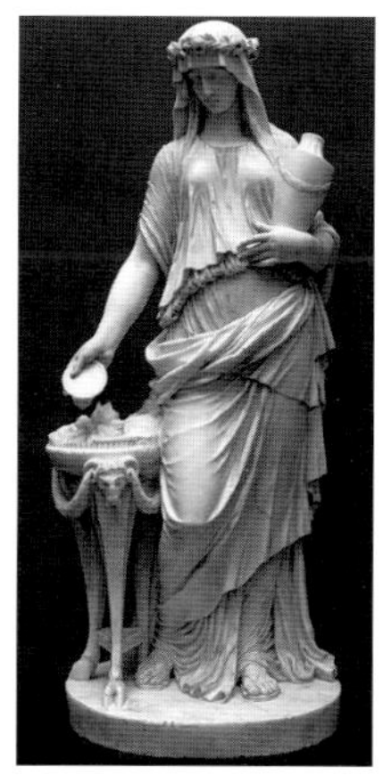

*A Vestal,* 1770
Marble, .955 x .421 x .350
(37 1/2 x 16 1/2 x 13 3/4)
Inscribed on side of base at back:
CLODION. INV. FECIT ROMAE. 1770
Samuel H. Kress Collection
1952.5.99

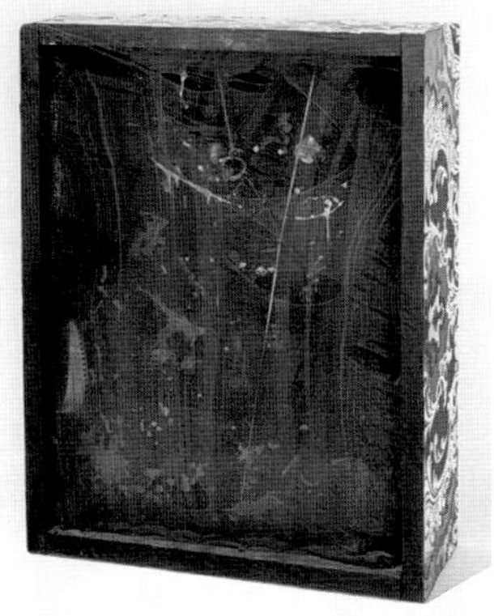

Bruce Conner
American, born 1933

*Camera Obscura*, c. 1962
Mixed media, .461 x .370 x .137
(18¹/₈ x 14¹/₂ x 5³/₈)
Gift of Mrs. William C. Seitz
1982.33.2

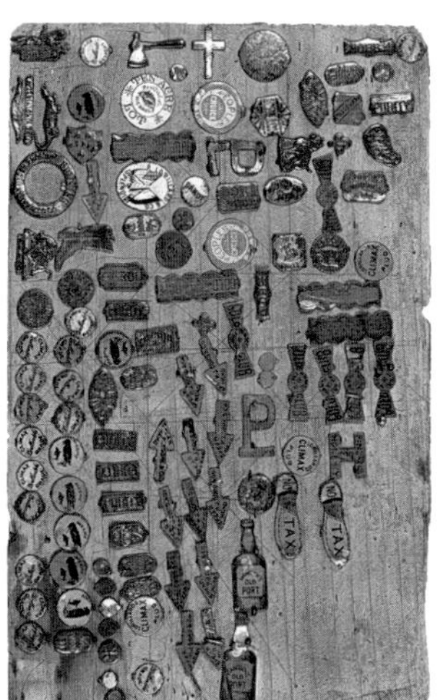

Joseph Cornell
American, 1903–1972

*La Ricordanza*, 1964
Mixed media (metal on wood),
.295 x .187 (11⁵/₈ x 7³/₈)
Inscribed on piece of paper stapled to back, in artist's hand: TO WM. C. SEITZ, ESQ. / EN SOUVENIR AMICALE / JOSEPH CORNELL / 10/24/64 / LA RICORDANZA
Gift of Mrs. William C. Seitz
1982.33.3

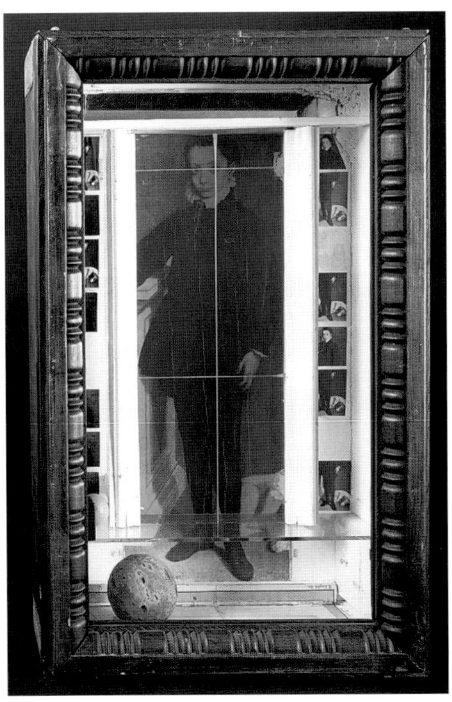

*Untitled (Medici Prince)*, c. 1953
Mixed media, .432 x .270 x .112
(17 x 10⁵/₈ x 4³/₈)
Inscribed on back, in reverse script: JOSEPH CORNELL
Gift of the Collectors Committee
1982.54.1

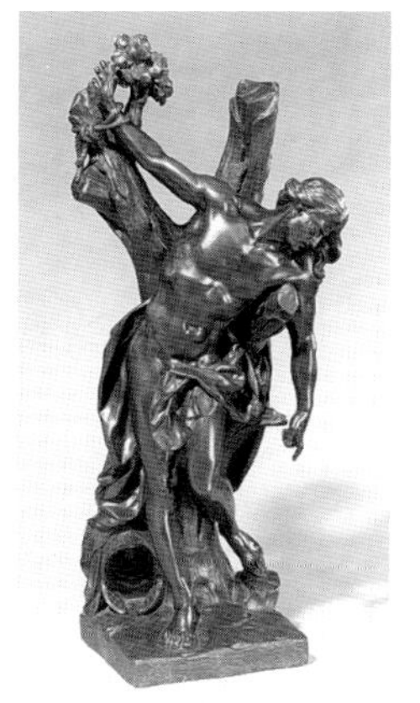

FRANÇOIS COUDRAY
French, c. 1678–1727

*Saint Sebastian,* 1712
Bronze, .905 x .368 x .376
($35^{5}/_{8}$ x $14^{1}/_{2}$ x $14^{7}/_{8}$)
Ailsa Mellon Bruce Fund
1972.24.1

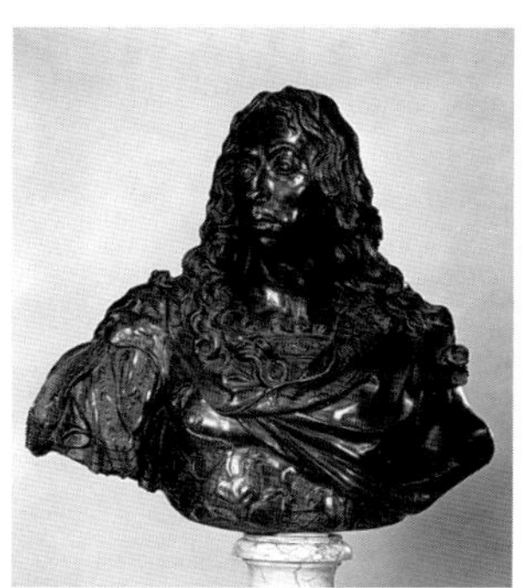

ANTOINE COYSEVOX
French, 1640–1720

*Louis II de Bourbon, Prince de Condé,* 1686
Bronze, .583 x .675 x .349
($22^{7}/_{8}$ x $26^{1}/_{2}$ x $13^{3}/_{4}$)
Inscribed on truncation of right arm:
A. COYZEVOX. F. / 1686
Widener Collection
1942.9.110

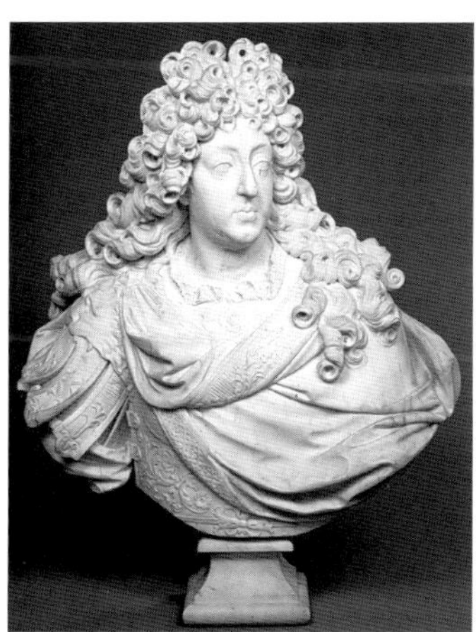

*Louis of France, The Grand Dauphin,* c. 1698–1699
Marble, .790 x .751 x .340
($31^{1}/_{8}$ x $29^{5}/_{8}$ x $13^{3}/_{8}$)
Samuel H. Kress Collection
1960.5.7

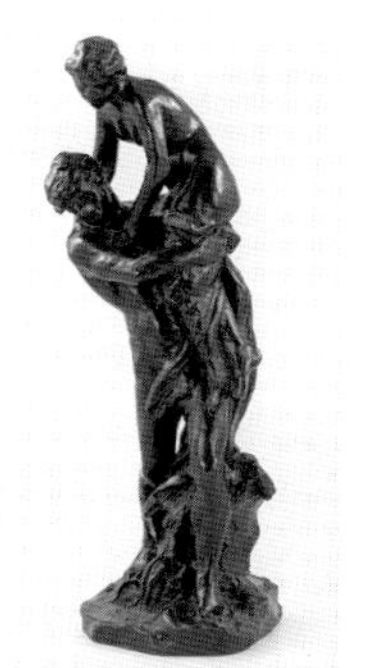

JULES DALOU
French, 1838–1902

*The Espousal (The Passage of the Rhine),* 1892, cast c. 1907
Bronze, .264 x .114 x .124
($10^{3}/_{8}$ x $4^{1}/_{2}$ x $4^{7}/_{8}$)
Inscribed on back of base: DALOU;
foundry mark: CIRE / PERDUE / A.A. HÉBRARD
Gift of Patricia Bauman and John L. Bryant, Jr. in honor of Douglas Lewis and in Honor of the 50th Anniversary of the National Gallery of Art
1990.68.2

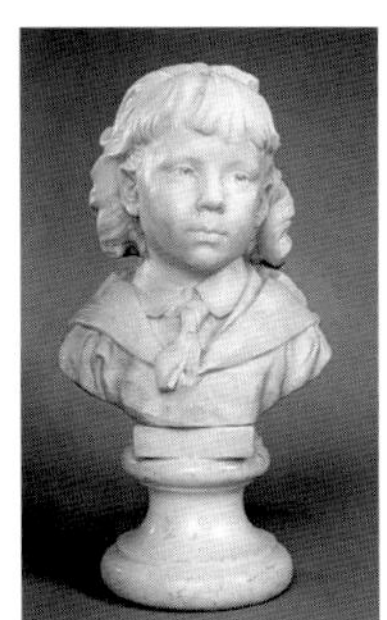

## Jules Dalou
French, 1838–1902

*Head of a Young Boy,* c. 1879
Marble, .476 x .245 x .225
(18 3/4 x 9 5/8 x 8 7/8)
Inscribed on underside of rear of sculpture: DALOU.
Gift of the Iris and B. Gerald Cantor Foundation, in Honor of the 50th Anniversary of the National Gallery of Art
1991.2.1

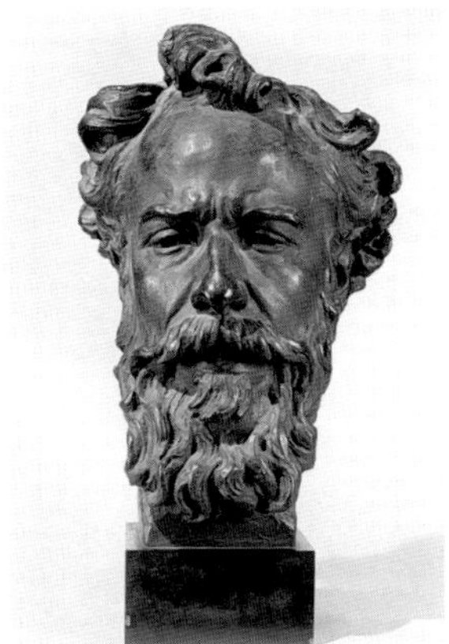

*Alphonse Legros,* c. 1876, cast possibly before 1922
Bronze, .341 x .237 x .237
(13 3/8 x 9 1/4 x 9 1/4)
Gift of George Matthew Adams in memory of his mother, Lydia Havens Adams
1956.14.2

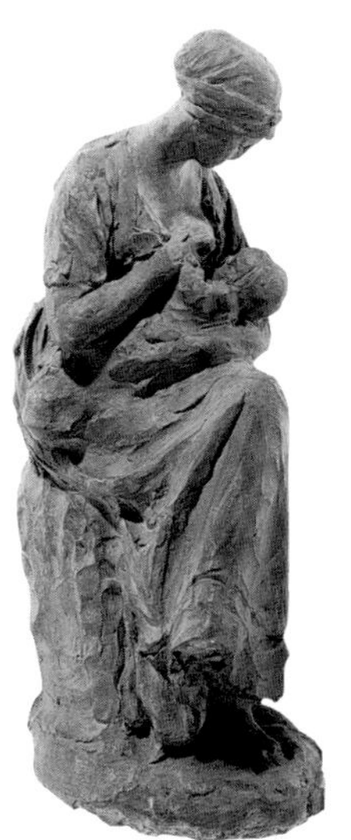

*Mother and Child,* c. 1873
Terra cotta, .292 x .108 x .159
(11 1/2 x 4 1/4 x 6 1/4)
Inscribed on proper left side of base: DALOU
Collection of Mr. and Mrs. Paul Mellon
1983.1.51

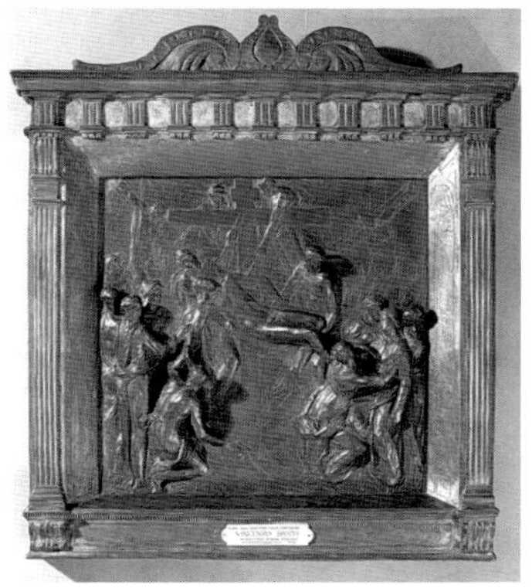

## VINCENZO DANTI
Florentine-Umbrian, 1530–1576

*The Descent from the Cross*, c. 1560
Bronze, without frame: .445 x .471
(17 1/2 x 18 1/2)
Widener Collection
1942.9.111

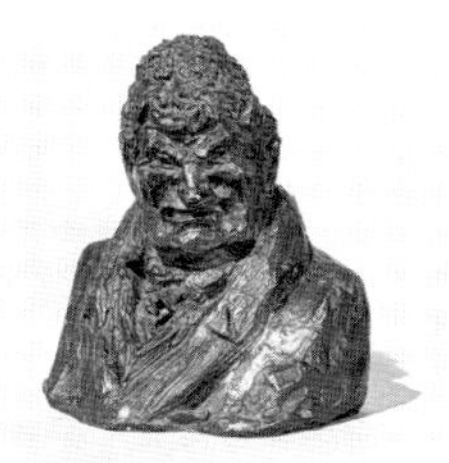

## HONORÉ DAUMIER
French, 1808–1879

*Girod de l'Ain (or Admiral Verhuel?)*, c. 1832/1835, cast 1929–1940
Bronze, .127 x .114 x .089
(5 x 4 1/2 x 3 1/2)
Foundry mark on lower left side: M.L.G.; on bottom rim: 2196–1; inside: 3/30
Rosenwald Collection
1943.3.20

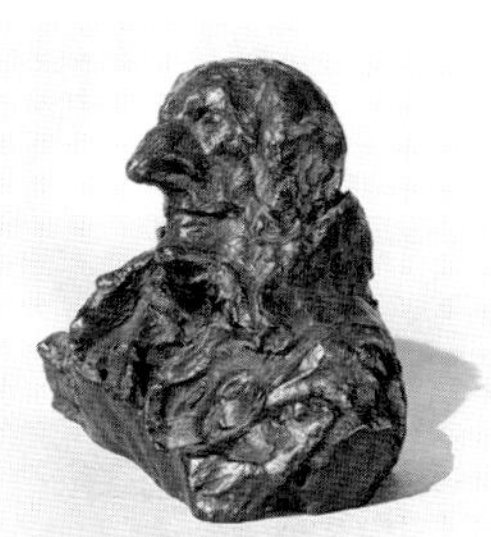

*Antoine-Maurice-Apollinaire, Comte D'Argout*, c. 1832/1835, cast 1929–1950
Bronze, .130 x .159 x .102
(5 1/8 x 6 1/4 x 4)
Foundry mark at lower left rear: M.L.G. / BRONZE; inside: 23/30
Rosenwald Collection
1951.17.5

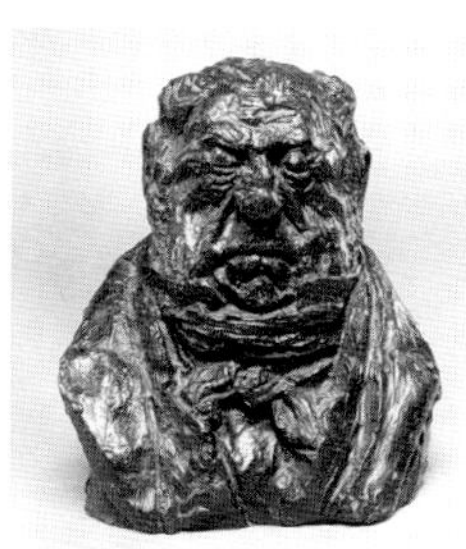

*Claude Baillot*, c. 1832/1835, cast 1929–1940
Bronze, .172 x .159 x .130
(6 3/4 x 6 1/4 x 5 1/8)
Foundry mark on lower right side: M.L.G.; on bottom rim: 2200–1; inside: 3/25
Rosenwald Collection
1943.3.22

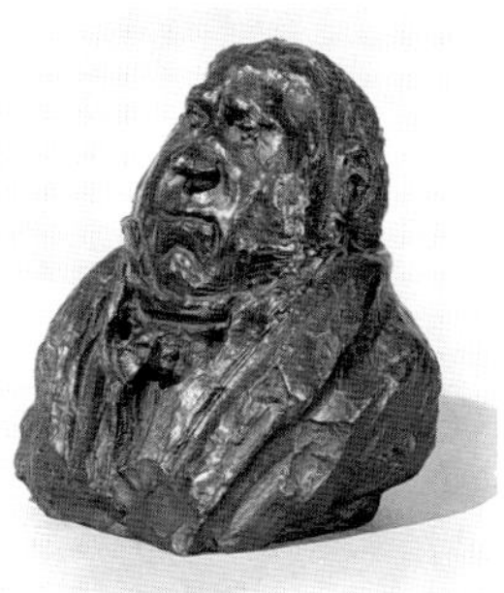

*Félix Barthe*, c. 1832/1835, cast 1929–1930
Bronze, .165 x .146 x .130
(6 1/2 x 5 3/4 x 5 1/8)
Foundry mark on lower left side: M.L.G.; on bottom rim: 3/25 C1; inside: 3/25
Rosenwald Collection
1943.3.5

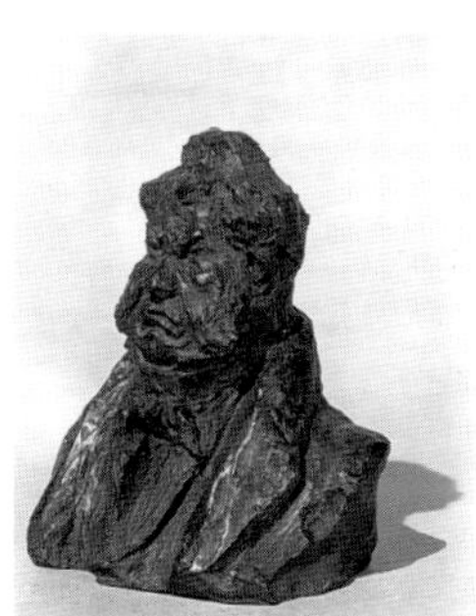

Honoré Daumier
French, 1808–1879

*Laurent Cunin, Called Cunin-Gridaine,* c. 1832/1835, cast 1936–1950
Bronze, .146 x .130 x .098 (5 3/4 x 5 1/8 x 3 7/8)
Foundry mark at lower center rear: M.L.G. / BRONZE; inside: 23/25
Rosenwald Collection
1951.17.7

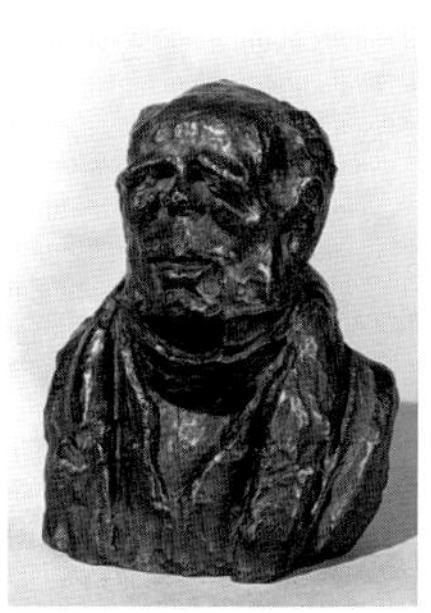

*Benjamin Delessert,* c. 1832/1835, cast 1929–1930
Bronze, .175 x .143 x .102 (6 7/8 x 5 5/8 x 4)
Foundry mark at lower center rear: M.L.G. / BRONZE; inside: 23/25
Rosenwald Collection
1943.3.2

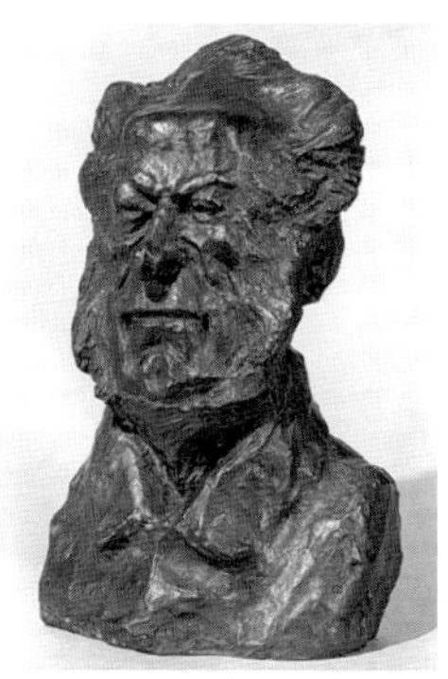

*Jacques-Antoine-Adrien, Baron Delort,* c. 1832/1835, cast 1934–1950
Bronze, .229 x .143 x .102 (9 x 5 5/8 x 4)
Foundry mark at lower right rear: M.L.G. / BRONZE; inside: 23/25
Rosenwald Collection
1951.17.8

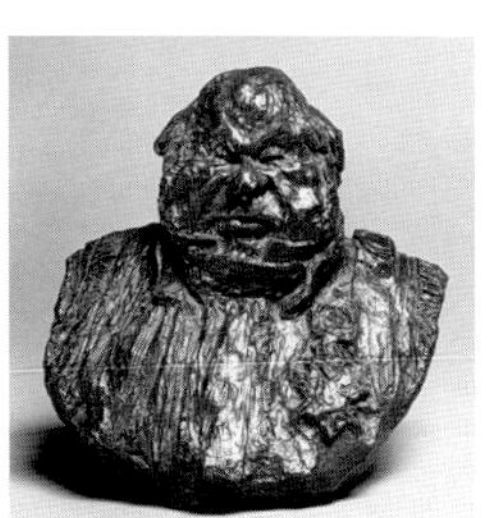

*Hippolyte-Abraham (?) Dubois,* c. 1832/1835, cast 1929–1950
Bronze, .193 x .195 x .143 (7 9/16 x 7 11/16 x 5 5/8)
Foundry mark at lower right rear: M.L.G.; inside: 23/25
Rosenwald Collection
1951.17.4

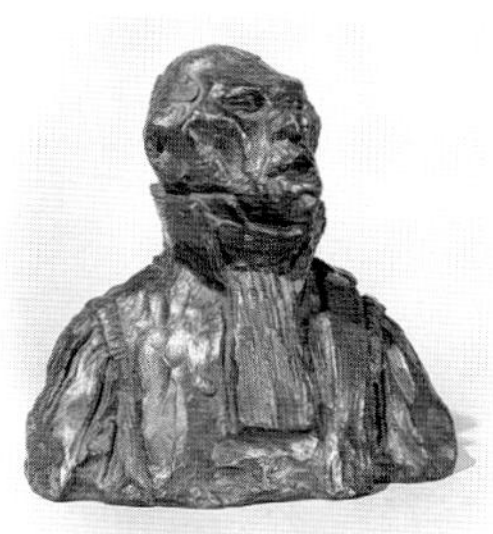

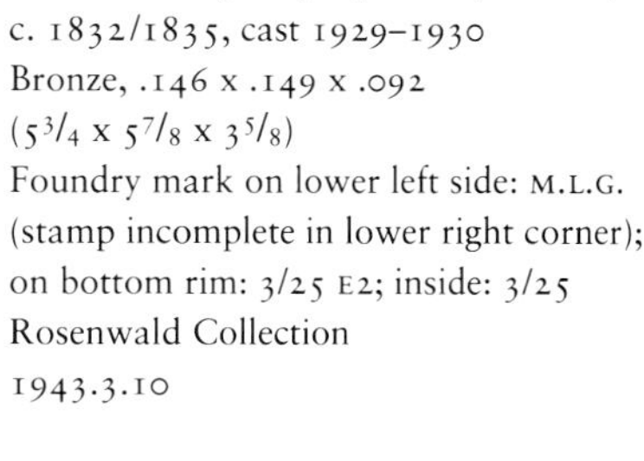

*André-Marie-Jean-Jacques Dupin Âiné,*
c. 1832/1835, cast 1929–1930
Bronze, .146 x .149 x .092
($5^{3}/_{4}$ x $5^{7}/_{8}$ x $3^{5}/_{8}$)
Foundry mark on lower left side: M.L.G.
(stamp incomplete in lower right corner);
on bottom rim: 3/25 E2; inside: 3/25
Rosenwald Collection
1943.3.10

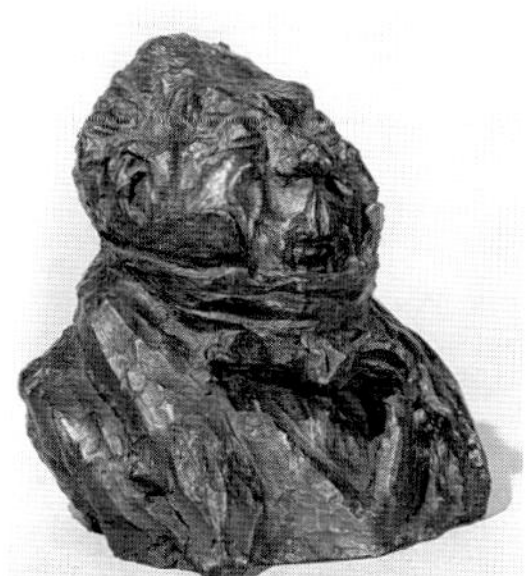

*Charles-Guillaume Etienne,* c. 1832/1835,
cast 1929–1950
Bronze, .162 x .149 x .137
($6^{3}/_{8}$ x $5^{7}/_{8}$ x $5^{3}/_{8}$)
Foundry mark at lower right rear: M.L.G.
/ BRONZE; inside: 23/25
Rosenwald Collection
1951.17.9

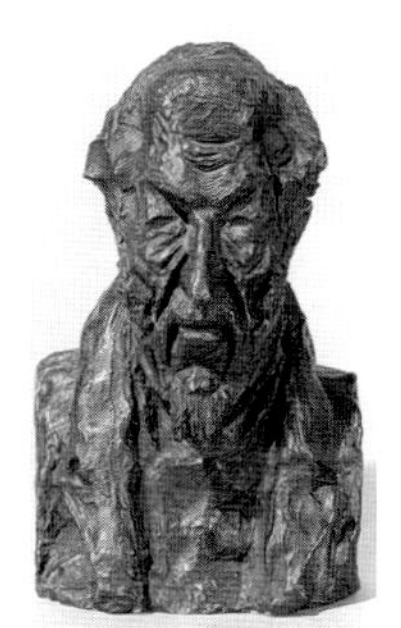

*Alfred-Frédéric-Pierre, Comte de Falloux,*
c. 1832/1835, cast 1929–1940
Bronze, .229 x .140 x .137
(9 x $5^{1}/_{2}$ x $5^{3}/_{8}$)
Foundry mark on lower right side: M.L.G.;
on bottom rim, right: 2202–2;
inside: 3/25
Rosenwald Collection
1943.3.23

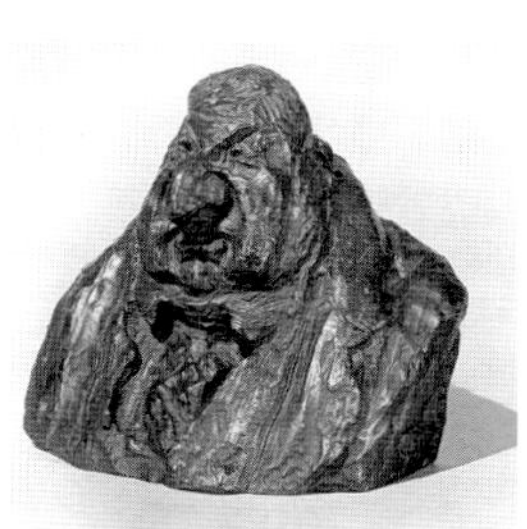

*Jean-Marie Fruchard,* c. 1832/1835,
cast 1929–1930
Bronze, .127 x .145 x .118
($5^{1}/_{8}$ x $5^{3}/_{4}$ x $4^{5}/_{8}$)
Foundry mark on lower left side: M.L.G.;
on bottom rim: 3/25; inside: 3/25
Rosenwald Collection
1943.3.11

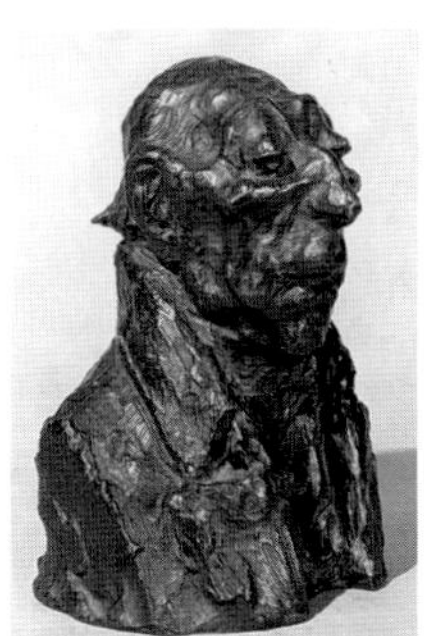

## HONORÉ DAUMIER
French, 1808–1879

*Jean-Claude Fulchiron*, c. 1832/1835, cast 1929–1930
Bronze, .162 x .124 x .111
(6 3/8 x 4 7/8 x 4 3/8)
Foundry mark on lower left side: M.L.G.; on bottom rim: 3/25 F1; inside: 3/25
Rosenwald Collection
1943.3.3

*Charles-Léonard Gallois (?)*, c. 1832/1835, cast 1929–1940
Bronze, .213 x .137 x .108
(8 3/8 x 5 3/8 x 4 1/4)
Foundry mark on lower right side: M.L.G.; on bottom rim: 2199–1; inside: 3/25
Rosenwald Collection
1943.3.21

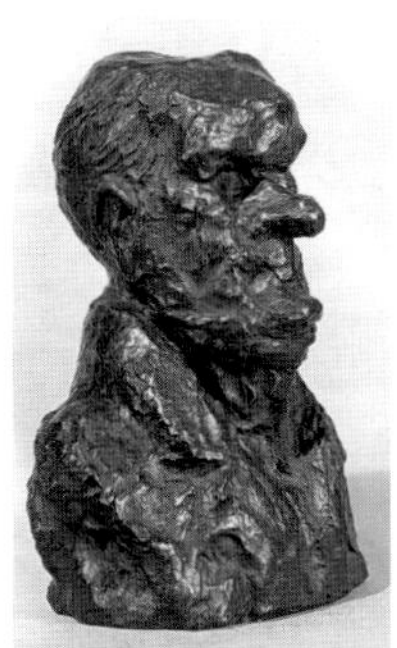

*Auguste-Hippolyte Ganneron*, c. 1832/1835, cast 1929–1930
Bronze, .181 x .130 x .105
(7 1/8 x 5 1/8 x 4 1/8)
Foundry mark on lower left side: M.L.G.; on bottom rim: 3/25 D1; inside: 3/25
Rosenwald Collection
1943.3.7

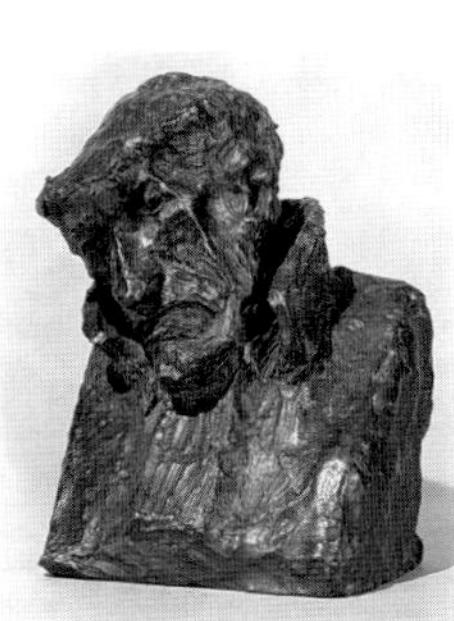

*Joachim-Antoine-Joseph Gaudry*, c. 1832/1835, cast 1929–1950
Bronze, .162 x .127 x .114
(6 3/8 x 5 x 4 1/2)
Foundry mark at lower left rear: M.L.G. / BR; inside: 23/25
Rosenwald Collection
1951.17.10

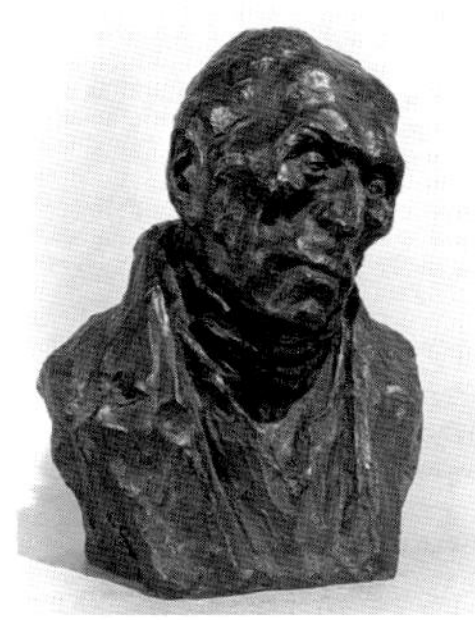

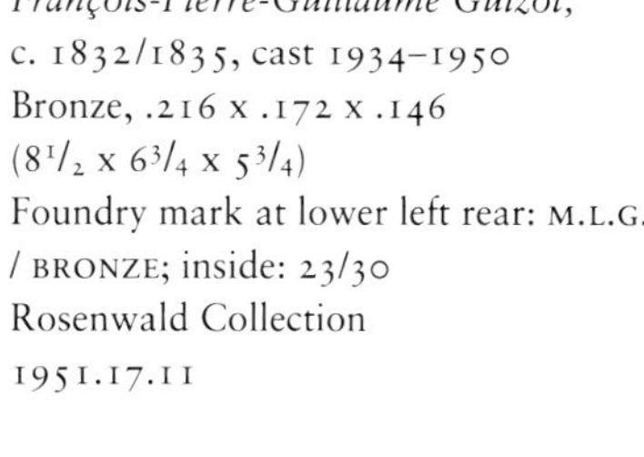

*François-Pierre-Guillaume Guizot,*
c. 1832/1835, cast 1934–1950
Bronze, .216 x .172 x .146
(8 1/2 x 6 3/4 x 5 3/4)
Foundry mark at lower left rear: M.L.G.
/ BRONZE; inside: 23/30
Rosenwald Collection
1951.17.11

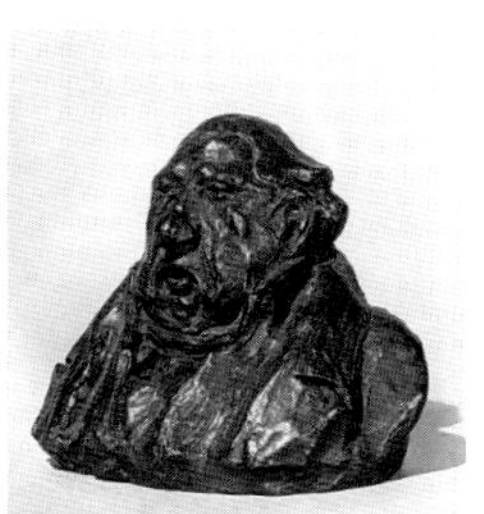

*Père Jean-Marie Harlé,* c. 1832/1835,
cast 1929–1950
Bronze, .121 x .146 x .111
(4 3/4 x 5 3/4 x 4 3/8)
Foundry mark at lower right rear: M.L.G.
/ BRONZE; inside: 23/30
Rosenwald Collection
1951.17.12

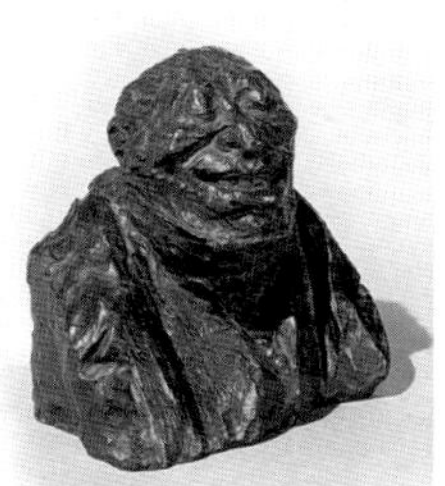

*Auguste-Hilarion, Comte de Kératry,*
c. 1832/1835, cast 1929–1930
Bronze, .121 x .133 x .092
(4 3/4 x 5 1/4 x 3 5/8)
Foundry mark on lower left side: M.L.G.;
on bottom rim: 3/25 B2; inside: 3/25
Rosenwald Collection
1943.3.4

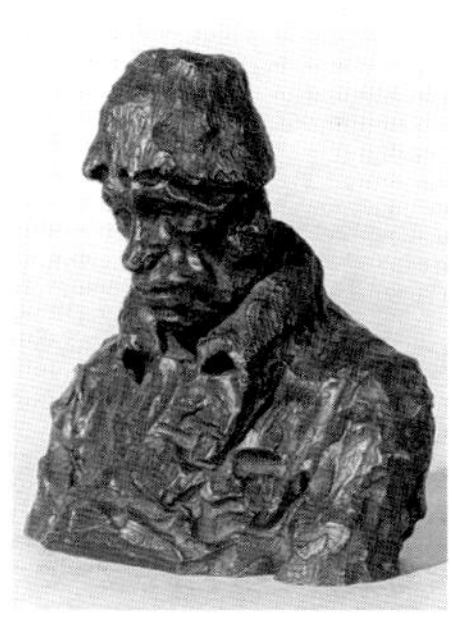

*Charles-Malo-François, Comte de Lameth,*
c. 1832/1835, cast 1929–1940
Bronze, .146 x .143 x .083
(5 3/4 x 5 5/8 x 3 1/4)
Foundry mark at lower left rear: M.L.G.;
on bottom rim: 2198–1; inside: 3/30
Rosenwald Collection
1943.3.18

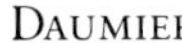


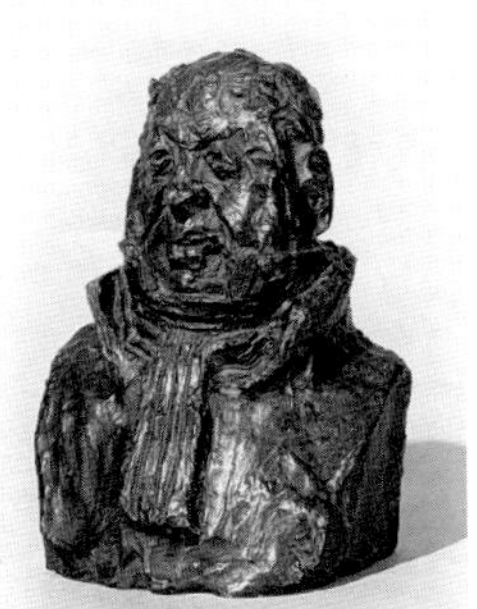

## HONORÉ DAUMIER
French, 1808–1879

*Alexandre (?) Lecomte*, c. 1832/1835, cast 1929–1940
Bronze, .172 x .127 x .121
($6\frac{3}{4}$ x 5 x $4\frac{3}{4}$)
Foundry mark at lower left rear: M.L.G.; on bottom rim: 2195–1; inside: 3/25
Rosenwald Collection
1943.3.16

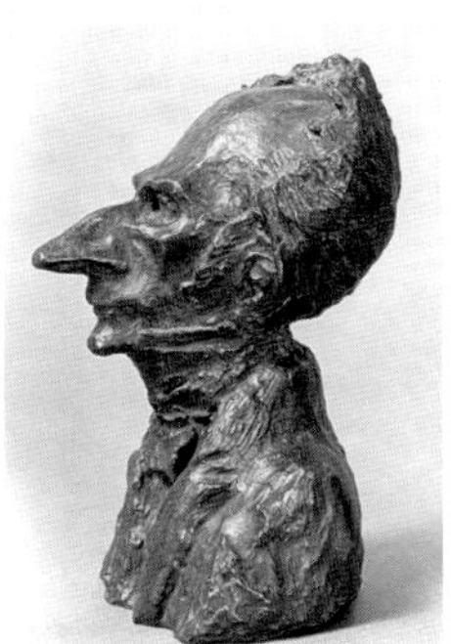

*Jacques Lefebvre*, c. 1832/1835, cast 1934–1950
Bronze, .194 x .118 x .140
($7\frac{5}{8}$ x $4\frac{5}{8}$ x $5\frac{1}{2}$)
Foundry mark at center rear: M.L.G. / BRONZE; inside: 23/25
Rosenwald Collection
1951.17.13

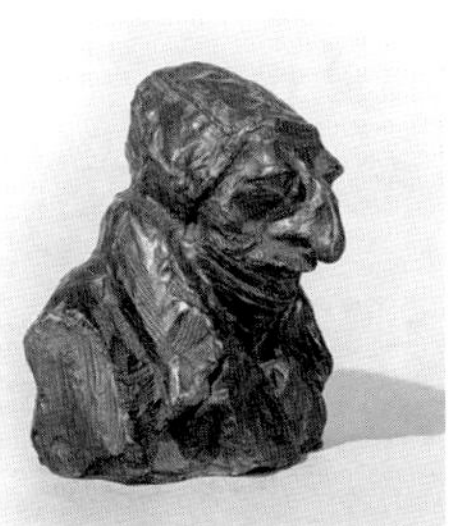

*Pelet de la Lozère (?)*, c. 1832/1835, cast 1929–1930
Bronze, .140 x .127 x .108
($5\frac{1}{2}$ x 5 x $4\frac{1}{4}$)
Foundry mark on lower left side: M.L.G.; on bottom rim: 3/25 F2; inside: 3/25
Rosenwald Collection
1943.3.13

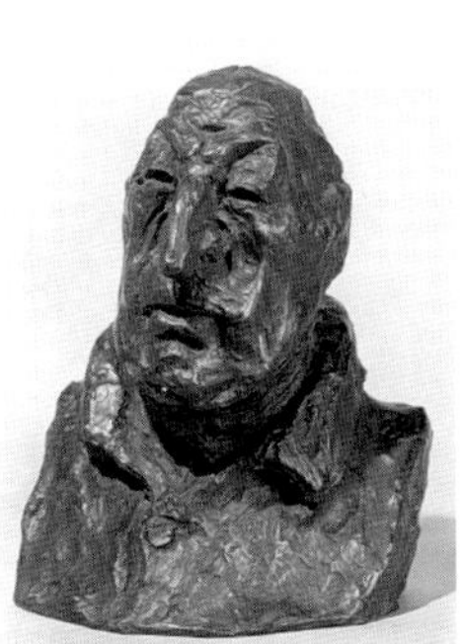

*François-Dominique-Reynaud, Comte de Montlosier*, c. 1832/1835, cast 1934–1950
Bronze, .187 x .143 x .159
($7\frac{3}{8}$ x $5\frac{5}{8}$ x $6\frac{1}{4}$)
Foundry mark at lower right rear: M.L.G. / BRONZE; inside: 23/30
Rosenwald Collection
1951.17.6

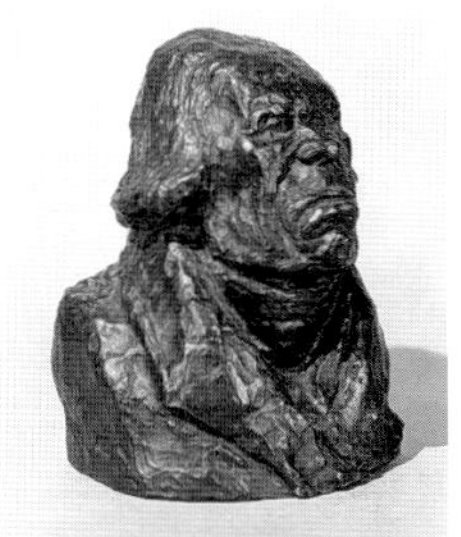

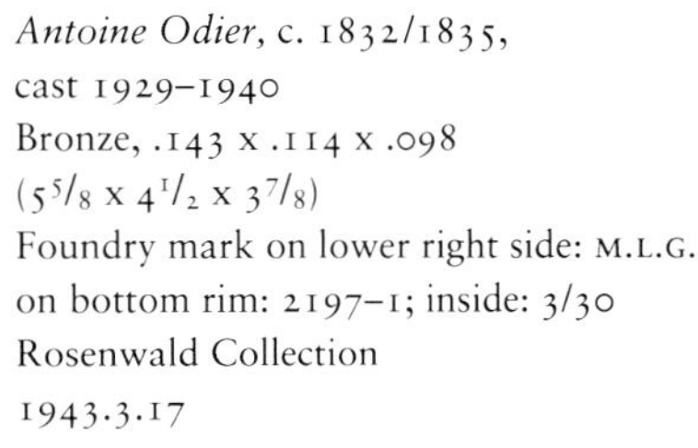

*Antoine Odier*, c. 1832/1835,
cast 1929–1940
Bronze, .143 x .114 x .098
(5 5/8 x 4 1/2 x 3 7/8)
Foundry mark on lower right side: M.L.G.;
on bottom rim: 2197–1; inside: 3/30
Rosenwald Collection
1943.3.17

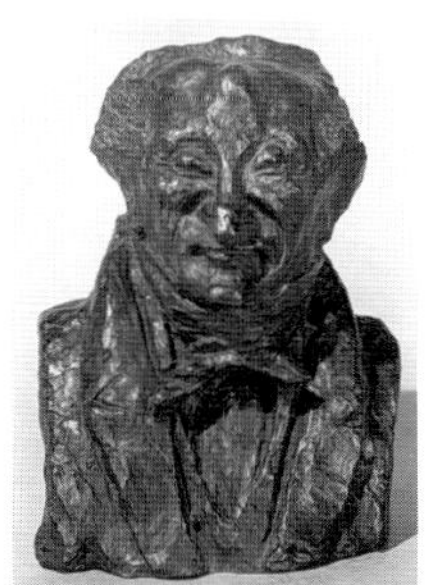

*Alexandre-Simon Pataille*, c. 1832/1835,
cast 1934–1950
Bronze, .168 x .133 x .108
(6 5/8 x 5 1/4 x 4 1/4)
Foundry mark at lower right rear: M.L.G.
/ BRONZE; inside: 23/30
Rosenwald Collection
1951.17.14

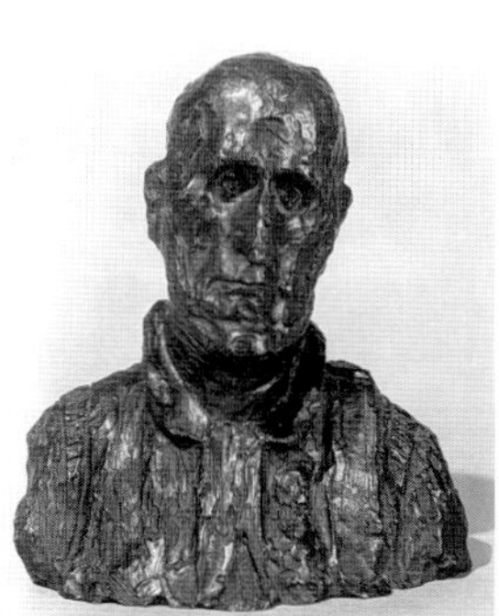

*Jean-Charles Persil*, c. 1832/1835,
cast 1929–1940
Bronze, .191 x .168 x .102
(7 1/2 x 6 5/8 x 4)
Foundry mark at lower left rear: M.L.G.;
on bottom rim: 2194–1; inside: 3/25
Rosenwald Collection
1943.3.15

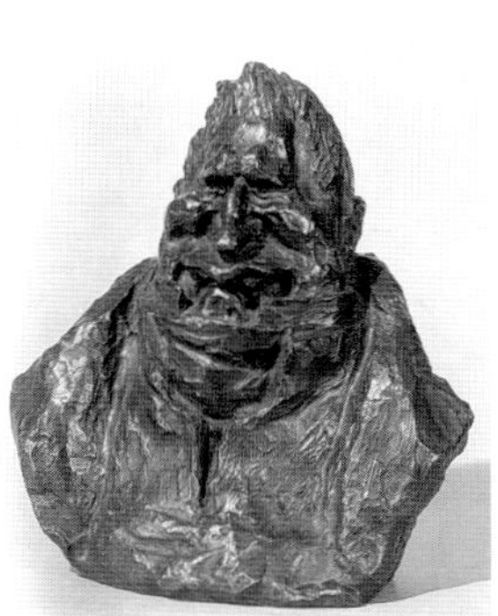

*Joseph, Baron de Podenas*, c. 1832/1835,
cast 1929–1930
Bronze, .206 x .194 x .118
(8 1/8 x 7 5/8 x 4 5/8)
Foundry mark on lower left side: M.L.G.;
on bottom rim: 3/25 A1; inside: 3/25
Rosenwald Collection
1943.3.1

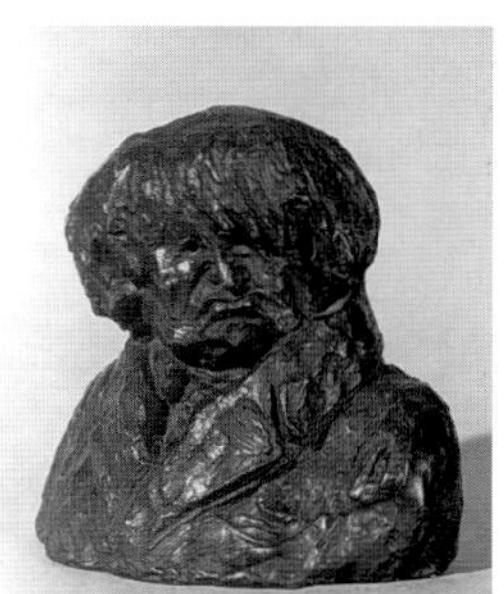

## Honoré Daumier
French, 1808–1879

*Dr. Clément-François-Victor-Gabriel Prunelle,* c. 1832/1835, cast 1929–1930
Bronze, .130 x .149 x .105
($5\frac{1}{8}$ x $5\frac{7}{8}$ x $4\frac{1}{8}$)
Foundry mark on lower left side: M.L.G.; on bottom rim: 3/30 D2; inside: 3/30
Rosenwald Collection
1943.3.8

*Ratapoil,* c. 1850/1851
Bronze, .440 x .170 x .193
($17\frac{1}{4}$ x $6\frac{3}{4}$ x $7\frac{5}{8}$)
Inscribed on top of base, in rear right corner: DAUMIER / 17; foundry mark on rear side of base: SIOT-DECAUVILLE / FONDEUR / PARIS
Rosenwald Collection
1951.17.3

*The Refugees,* c. 1851/1852
Bronze, including border:
.372 x .765 x .068 ($14\frac{5}{8}$ x $30\frac{1}{8}$ x $2\frac{3}{4}$)
Inscribed in lower right corner:
H. DAUMIER; 2 (in circle); foundry mark in lower right corner: SIOT-DECAUVILLE / FONDEUR / PARIS.
Rosenwald Collection
1943.3.25

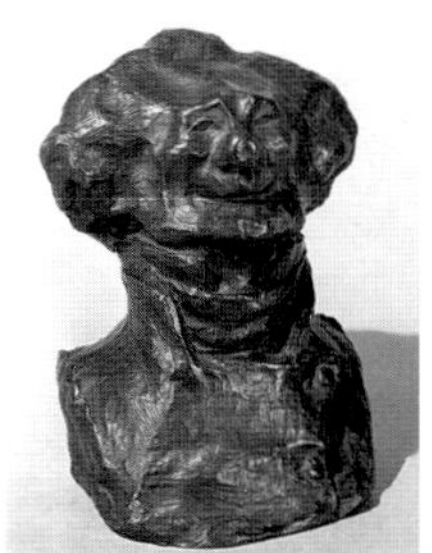

*Le Rieur Edenté (Toothless Laughter, Charles Philipon?),* c. 1832/1835, cast 1929–1930
Bronze, .156 x .137 x .102
($6\frac{1}{8}$ x $5\frac{3}{8}$ x 4)
Foundry mark on lower left side: M.L.G.; on bottom rim: 3/25; inside: 3/25
Rosenwald Collection
1943.3.12

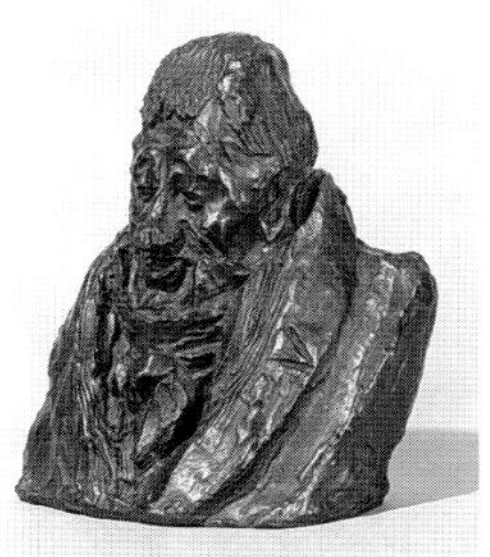

*Pierre-Paul Royer-Collard*, c. 1832/1835, cast 1929–1930
Bronze, .130 x .118 x .089
(5 1/8 x 4 5/8 x 3 1/2)
Foundry mark on lower left side: M.L.G.; on bottom rim: 3/25 C2; inside: 3/25
Rosenwald Collection
1943.3.6

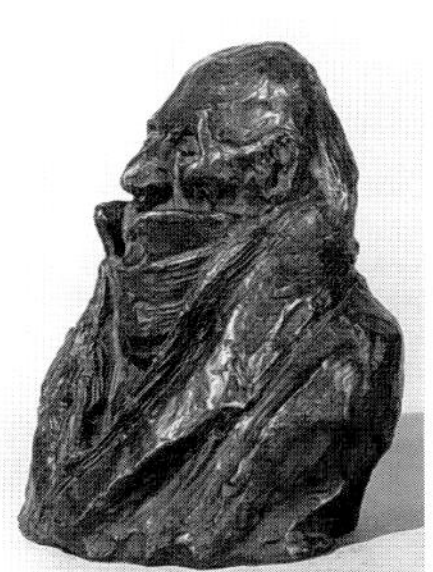

*Horace-François, Comte Sébastiani*, c. 1832/1835, cast 1929–1940
Bronze, .130 x .118 x .102
(5 1/8 x 4 5/8 x 4)
Foundry mark on lower right side: M.L.G.; on bottom rim: 2201–1; inside: 3/25
Rosenwald Collection
1943.3.19

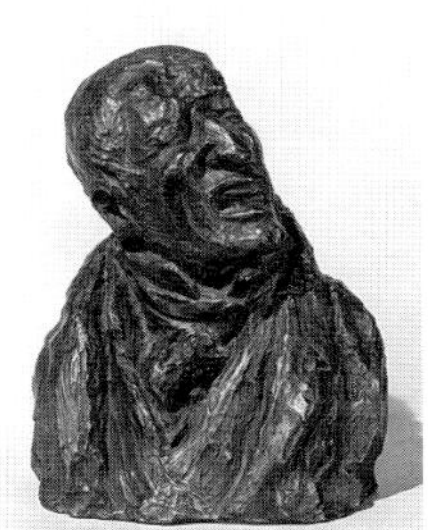

*Nicolas Soult (?)*, c. 1832/1835, cast 1934–1950
Bronze, .149 x .127 x .095
(5 7/8 x 5 x 3 3/4)
Foundry mark at lower rear: M.L.G. / BRONZE; inside: 23/25
Rosenwald Collection
1951.17.15

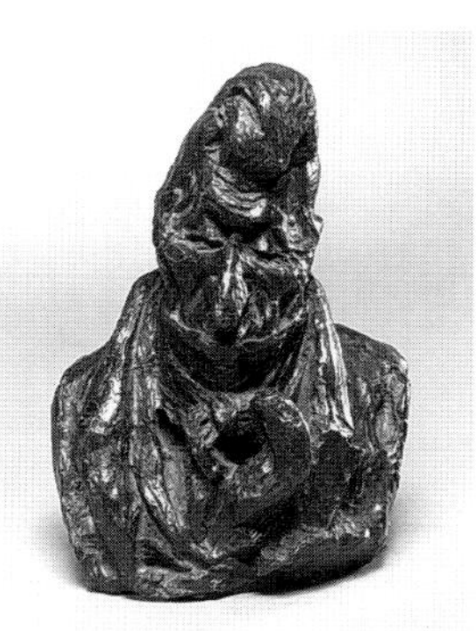

*Jean-Auguste Chevandier de Valdrome*, c. 1832/1835, cast 1929–1940
Bronze, .184 x .143 x .121
(7 1/4 x 5 5/8 x 4 3/4)
Foundry mark on lower left side: M.L.G.; on bottom rim: 2193–1; inside: 3/25
Rosenwald Collection
1943.3.14

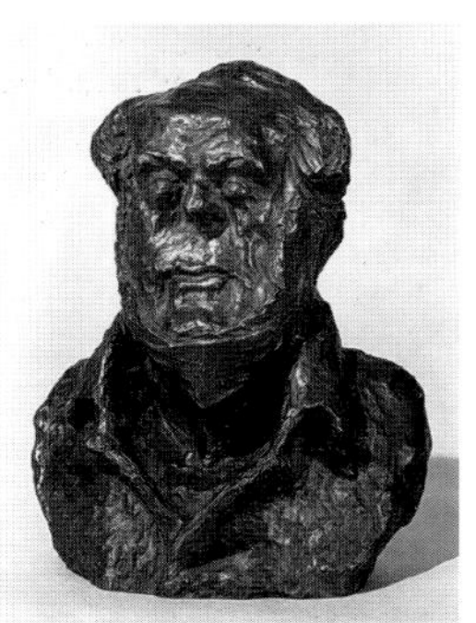

## HONORÉ DAUMIER
French, 1808–1879

*Jean Vatout,* c. 1832/1835, cast 1929–1940
Bronze, .194 x .159 x .102 ($7^{5}/_{8}$ x $6^{1}/_{4}$ x 4)
Foundry mark at lower left rear: M.L.G.; on bottom rim, at back: 2203–1; inside: 3/25
Rosenwald Collection
1943.3.24

*Jean-Pons-Guillaume Viennet,* c. 1832/1835, cast 1929–1930
Bronze, .197 x .159 x .127 ($7^{3}/_{4}$ x $6^{1}/_{4}$ x 5)
Foundry mark on lower left side: M.L.G.; on bottom rim: 3/30 E1; inside: 3/30
Rosenwald Collection
1943.3.9

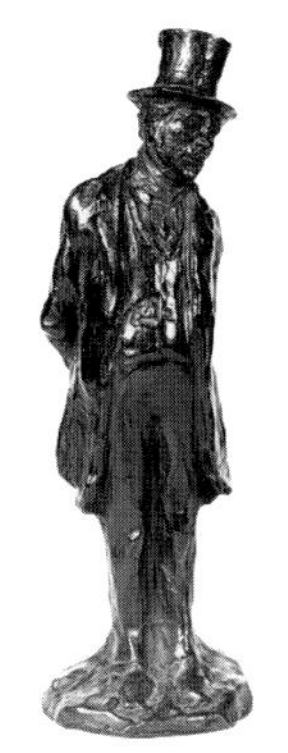

## IMITATOR OF HONORÉ DAUMIER
French

*The Confidant,* late 19th/early 20th century, cast 1930/1957
Bronze, .184 x .060 x .058 ($7^{1}/_{4}$ x $2^{3}/_{8}$ x $2^{5}/_{16}$)
Falsely signed on back of base: H.D; on rim: 20/30; foundry mark on back of base: CIRE / C. VALSUANI / PERDUE
Rosenwald Collection
1958.8.1

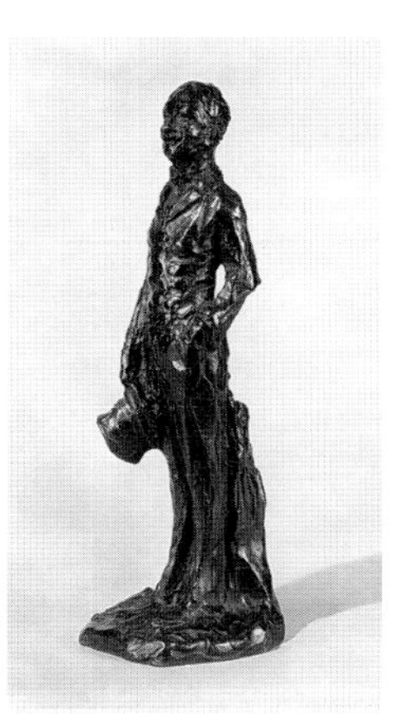

## IMITATOR OF HONORÉ DAUMIER
French

*The Dandy,* late 19th/early 20th century, cast 1930/1952
Bronze, .187 x .068 x .065 ($7^{3}/_{8}$ x $2^{11}/_{16}$ x $2^{9}/_{16}$)
Falsely signed on top of base, left side: H.D.; inside: 6/30; foundry mark on side of base at back: CIRE / C. VALSUANI / PERDUE / BRONZE
Rosenwald Collection
1953.8.2

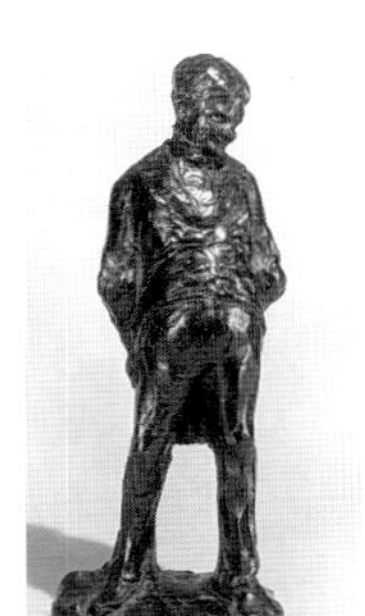

Imitator of Honoré Daumier
French

*The Jolly Good Fellow,* late 19th/early 20th century, cast 1930/1957
Bronze, .162 x .065 x .054
($6^{3}/_{8}$ x $2^{9}/_{16}$ x $2^{1}/_{8}$)
Falsely signed on top of base at back: H.D.; on rim: 11/30; foundry mark on side of base at back: CIRE / C. VALSUANI / PERDUE
Rosenwald Collection
1964.8.1

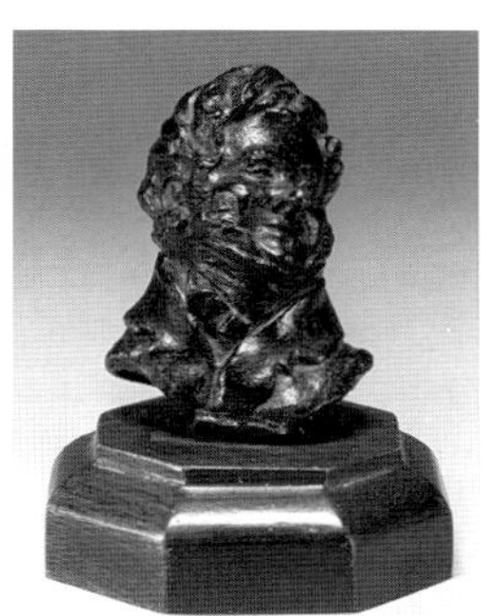

Imitator of Honoré Daumier
French

*The Laughing Man,* late 19th/early 20th century, cast 1944/1950
Bronze, .086 x .061 x .053
($3^{3}/_{8}$ x $2^{3}/_{8}$ x $2^{1}/_{8}$)
Inscribed at center rear of base: HD
Rosenwald Collection
1951.17.1

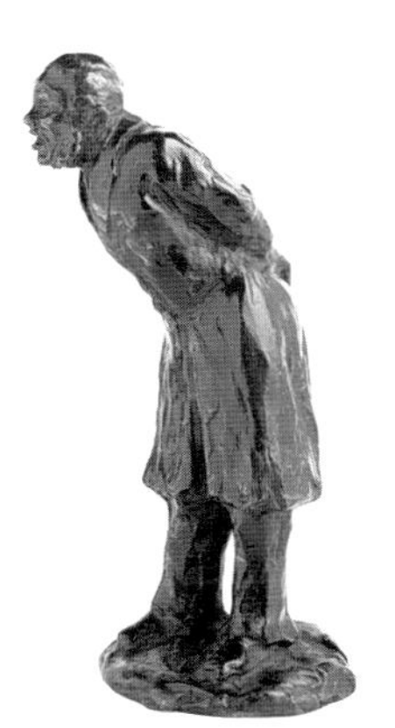

Imitator of Honoré Daumier
French

*The Listener,* late 19th/early 20th century, cast 1930/1957
Bronze, .155 x .069 x .074
($6^{1}/_{8}$ x $2^{11}/_{16}$ x $2^{15}/_{16}$)
Falsely signed on top of base: H.D.; on rim: 11/30; foundry mark on side of base at back: CIRE / C. VALSUANI / PERDUE
Rosenwald Collection
1964.8.2

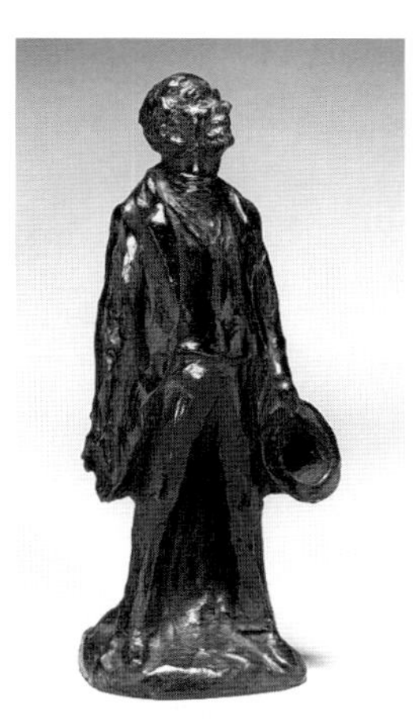

Imitator of Honoré Daumier
French

*The Lover,* late 19th/early 20th century, cast 1930/1953
Bronze, .180 x .083 x .063
($7^{1}/_{16}$ x $3^{1}/_{4}$ x $2^{1}/_{2}$)
Falsely signed on back of base: H.D.; on rim: 20/30; foundry mark on back of base: CIRE / C. VALSUANI / PERDUE
Rosenwald Collection
1954.13.3

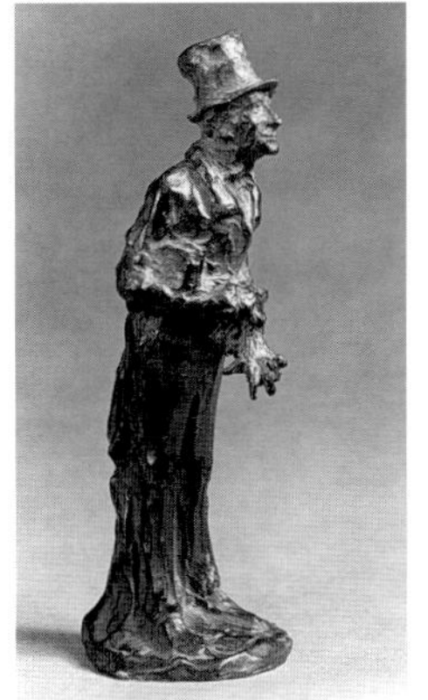

Imitator of Honoré Daumier
French

*The Man of Affairs,* late 19th/early 20th century, cast 1930/1952
Bronze, .195 x .068 x .070
($7^{11}/_{16}$ x $2^{11}/_{16}$ x $2^{3}/_{4}$)
Falsely signed on back of base: H.D.; inside: 6/30; foundry mark on back of base: CIRE / C. VALSUANI / PERDUE / BRONZE
Rosenwald Collection
1953.8.1

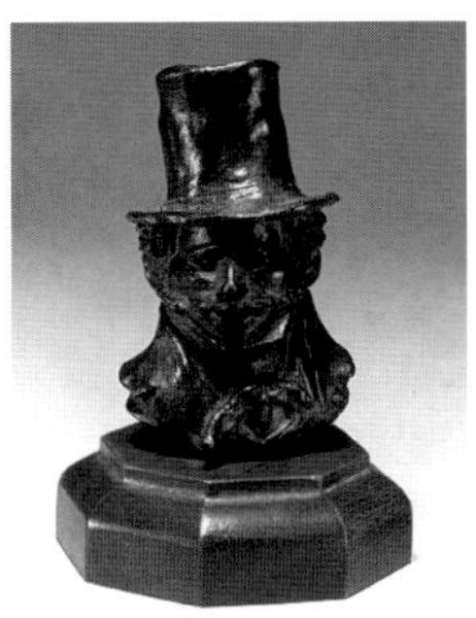

Imitator of Honoré Daumier
French

*Man in a Tall Hat,* late 19th/early 20th century, cast 1944/1950
Bronze, .098 x .064 x .062
($3^{7}/_{8}$ x $2^{1}/_{2}$ x $2^{7}/_{16}$)
Inscribed on rear of collar: H D
Rosenwald Collection
1951.17.2

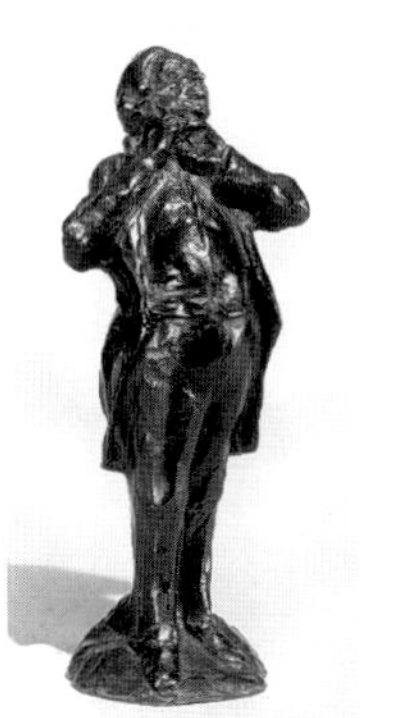

Imitator of Honoré Daumier
French

*The Representative,* late 19th/early 20th century, cast 1930/1957
Bronze, .176 x .072 x .065
($6^{15}/_{16}$ x $2^{13}/_{16}$ x $2^{9}/_{16}$)
Falsely signed on back of base: H.D; inside: 20/30; foundry mark on back of base: CIRE / C. VALSUANI / PERDUE
Rosenwald Collection
1958.8.2

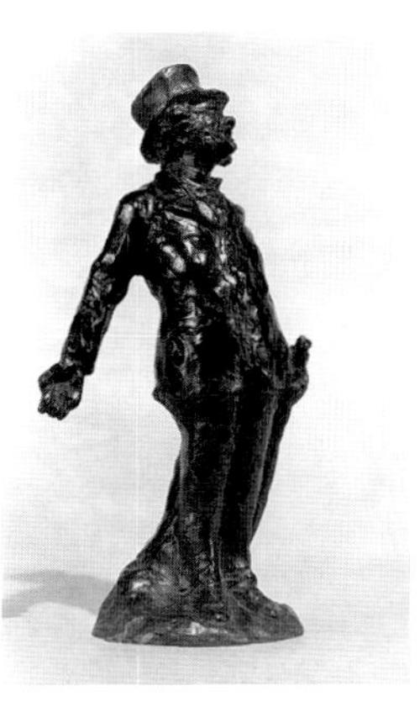

Imitator of Honoré Daumier
French

*The Small Shopkeeper,* late 19th/early 20th century, cast 1930/1957
Bronze, .169 x .078 x .057
($6\ ^{5}/_{8}$ x $3^{1}/_{16}$ x $2^{1}/_{4}$)
Falsely signed on back of base: H.D.; on rim: 11/30; foundry mark on back of base: CIRE / C. VALSUANI / PERDUE
Rosenwald Collection
1961.17.1

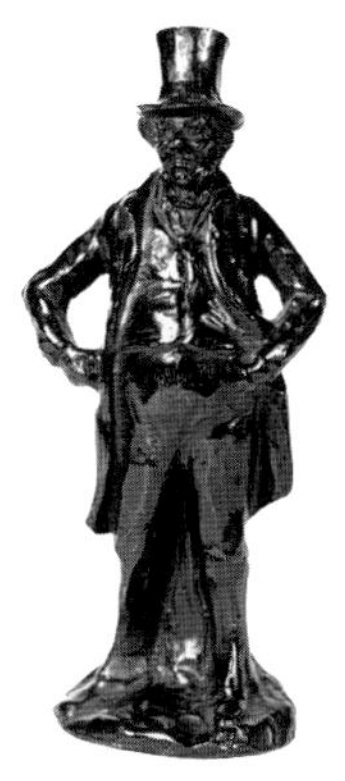

Imitator of Honoré Daumier
French

*The Stroller*, late 19th/early 20th century, cast 1930/1953
Bronze, .188 x .084 x .060
(7 3/8 x 3 5/16 x 2 3/8)
Falsely signed on back of base: H.D.; inside: 20/30; foundry mark on back of base: CIRE / C. VALSUANI / PERDUE
Rosenwald Collection
1954.13.2

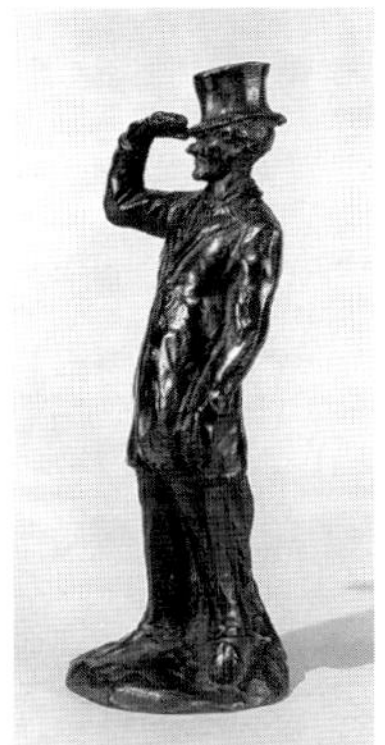

Imitator of Honoré Daumier
French

*The Visitor*, late 19th/early 20th century, cast 1930/1957
Bronze, .170 x .063 x .062
(6 11/16 x 2 1/2 x 2 7/16)
Falsely signed on back of base: H.D.; on rim: 11/30; foundry mark on back of base: CIRE / C. VALSUANI / PERDUE
Rosenwald Collection
1961.17.2

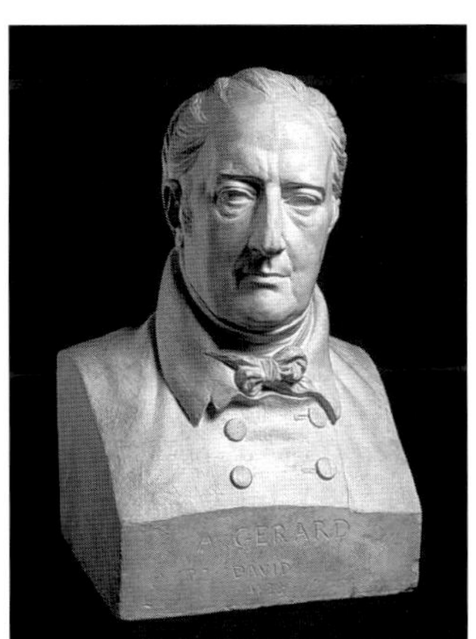

Pierre-Jean David d'Angers
French, 1788–1856

*François-Pascal-Simon, Baron Gérard*, 1838
Plaster, .610 x .397 x .300
(24 x 15 5/8 x 11 7/8)
Inscribed on front: À GERARD / P.J. DAVID / 1838; on truncation of left shoulder: À MADAME GERARD / DAVID
Gift of The Christian Humann Foundation, in Honor of the 50th Anniversary of the National Gallery of Art
1991.95.1

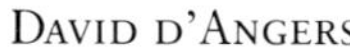


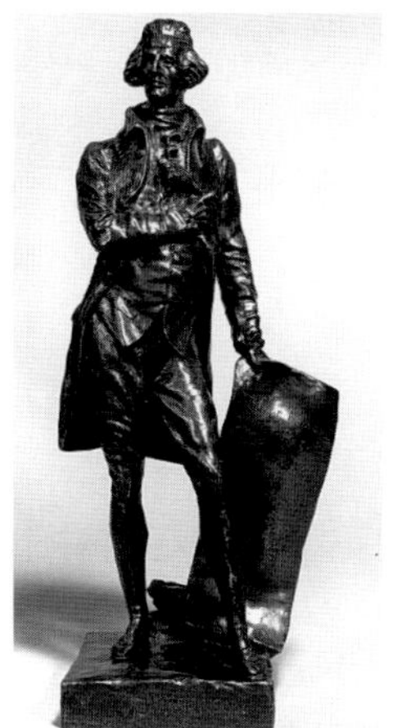

## PIERRE-JEAN DAVID D'ANGERS
French, 1788–1856

*Thomas Jefferson,* 1833–1834, cast after 1892
Bronze, .387 x .167 x .120
(15 1/4 x 6 5/8 x 4 3/4)
Inscribed on front of base: JEFFERSON; on right side of base, under scroll: DAVID; on scroll: TOUT HOMME / A DEUX PATRIES: / LA SIENNE / ET / LA FRANCE; foundry mark on back of base: CIRE PERDUE / LE BLANC BARBEDIENNE / A PARIS / BRONZE
Ferdinand Lammot Belin Fund
1975.11.1

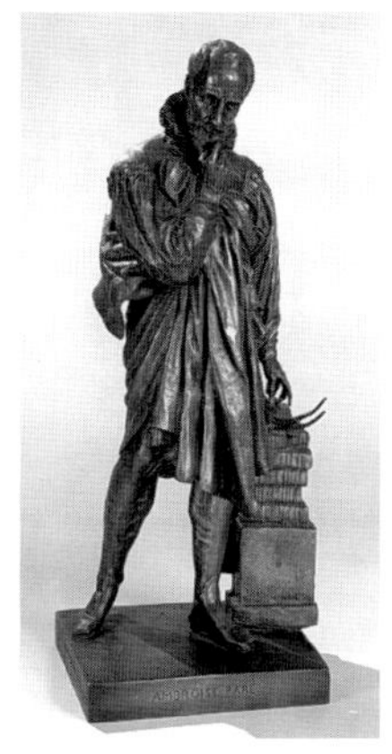

*Ambroise Paré,* 1836–1839, cast after 1840
Bronze, .477 x .207 x .171
(18 3/4 x 8 1/8 x 6 3/4)
Inscribed on front of base: AMBROISE. PARÉ.; on right side of base, under books: P.J. DAVID / 1840; on spines of books: AMB. / PARE; underneath base: 112; foundry mark on left side of base: F. BARBEDIENNE.FONDEUR.; on back of base: RÉDUCTION MÉCHANIQUE. A. COLLAS / BRÉVETÉ
Gift of Mr. and Mrs. Myron Miller
1977.27.1

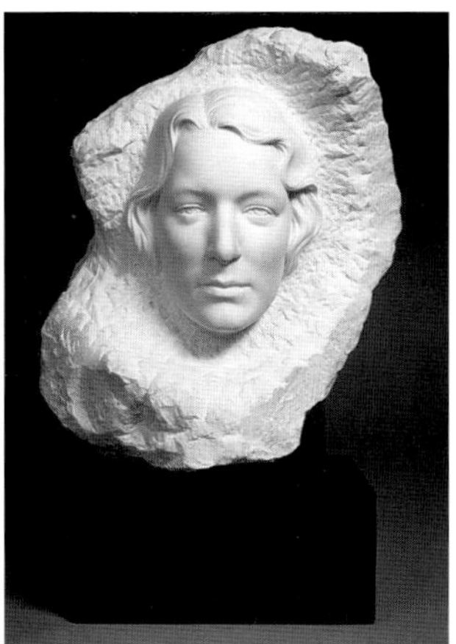

## JO DAVIDSON
American, 1883–1952

*Ailsa Mellon Bruce,* 1927
Marble, .400 x .358 x .237
(15 3/4 x 14 1/8 x 9 3/8)
Inscribed at lower left: JO DAVIDSON / PARIS / 1927
Collection of Mr. and Mrs. Paul Mellon
1983.1.52

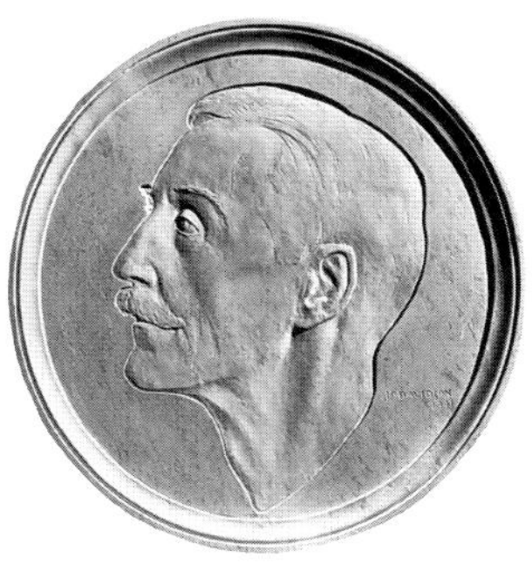

*Andrew W. Mellon,* 1941
Marble, diameter: .559 (22)
Inscribed at lower right: JO DAVIDSON / 1941
Andrew W. Mellon Collection
1941.13.1

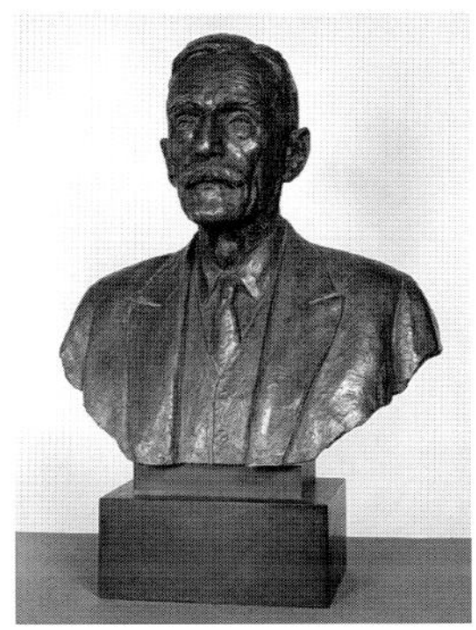

*Andrew W. Mellon,* 1927
Bronze, .546 x .521 x .279 ($21^{1}/_{2}$ x $20^{1}/_{2}$ x 11)
Inscribed on back: JO DAVIDSON•PARIS• 1927; foundry mark on back: CIRE / VALSUANI / PERDUE
Andrew W. Mellon Collection
1942.8.43

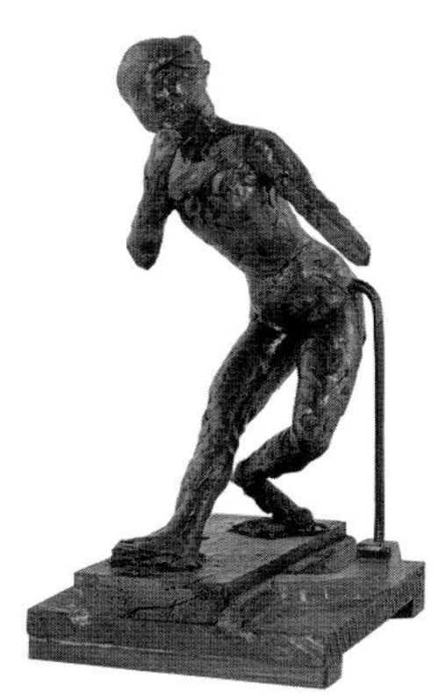

EDGAR DEGAS
French, 1834–1917

*The Bow,* probably c. 1885
Yellow wax and plastilene, height withou base: .333 ($13^{1}/_{8}$)
Inscribed on wax between feet: DEGAS
Collection of Mr. and Mrs. Paul Mellon
1985.64.50

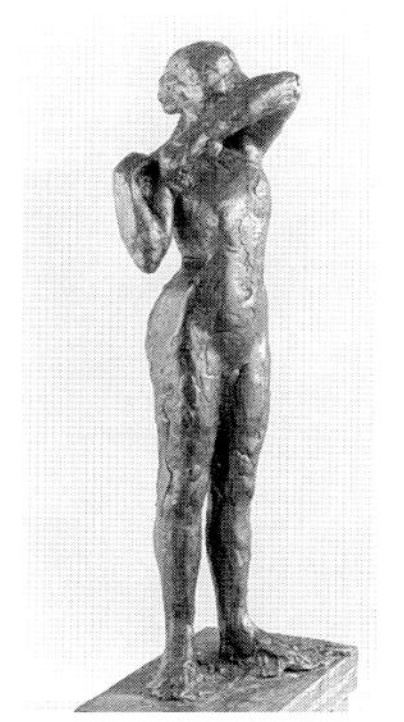

*Dancer Adjusting the Shoulder Strap of Her Bodice,* probably 1882/1895
Yellow brown wax and plastilene, height without base: .349 ($13^{3}/_{4}$)
Inscribed on wax behind heels: DEGAS
Collection of Mr. and Mrs. Paul Mellon
1985.64.47

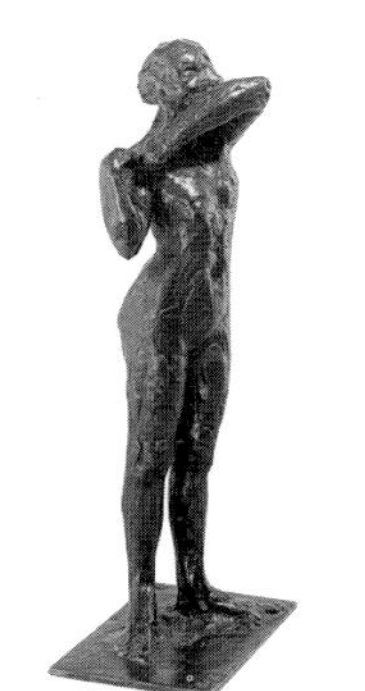

Edgar Degas
French, 1834–1917

*Dancer Adjusting the Shoulder Strap of Her Bodice,* probably 1882/1895, cast 1919–1921
Bronze, .352 x .160 x .104 ($13\frac{7}{8}$ x $6\frac{3}{8}$ x $4\frac{1}{8}$)
Inscribed on top of base in front left corner: DEGAS; foundry marks on top of base in rear right corner: CIRE / PERDUE / A.A. HÉBRARD; 64/Q
Collection of Mr. and Mrs. Paul Mellon
1985.64.64

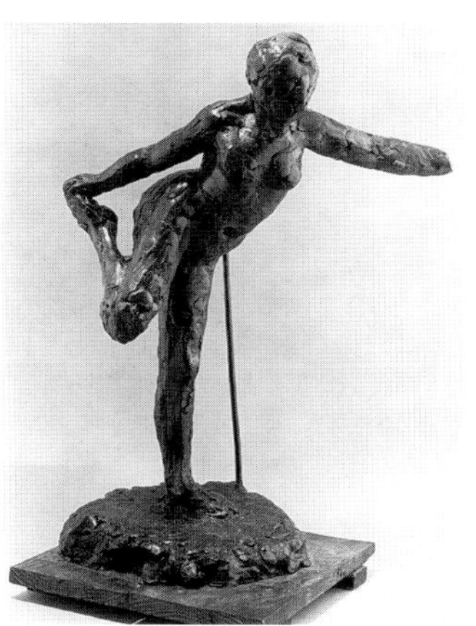

*Dancer Holding Her Right Foot in Her Right Hand,* probably 1900/1910
Brown wax and plastilene, height without base: .495 ($19\frac{1}{2}$)
Inscribed on wax behind left foot: DEGAS
Collection of Mr. and Mrs. Paul Mellon
1985.64.53

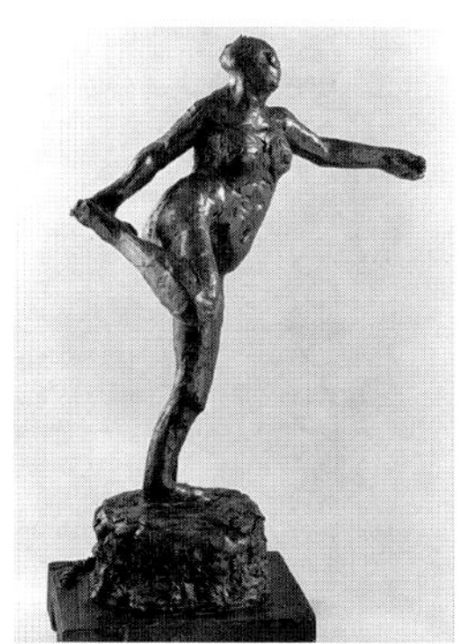

*Dancer Holding Her Right Foot in Her Right Hand,* probably 1900/1910
Brown wax and plastilene, height without base: .524 ($20\frac{5}{8}$)
Inscribed on wax on proper right side of base: DEGAS
Collection of Mr. and Mrs. Paul Mellon
1985.64.56

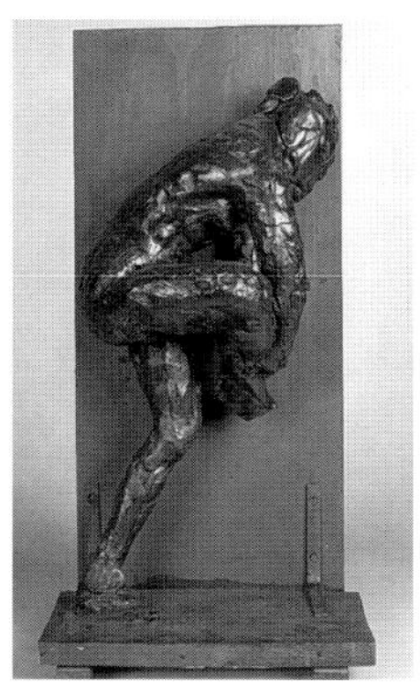

*Dancer Putting on Her Stocking,* probably 1896/1911
Yellow brown wax and plastilene, height without base: .457 (18)
Inscribed on wax beside left foot: DEGAS
Collection of Mr. and Mrs. Paul Mellon
1985.64.52

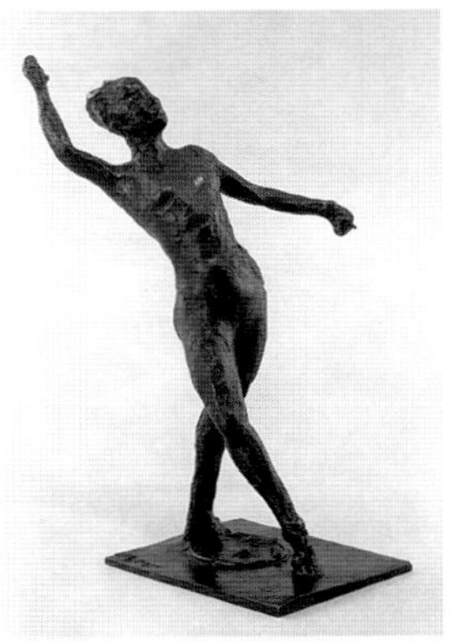

*Dancer with a Tambourine,* probably c. 1885, cast 1919-1921
Bronze, .276 x .166 x .175 ($10^{7}/_{8}$ x $6^{1}/_{2}$ x $6^{7}/_{8}$)
Inscribed on top of base in rear left corner: DEGAS; foundry marks on top of base in rear left corner: HER.12 / D / CIRE / PERDUE / A.A. HÉBRARD
Collection of Mr. and Mrs. Paul Mellon
1985.64.63

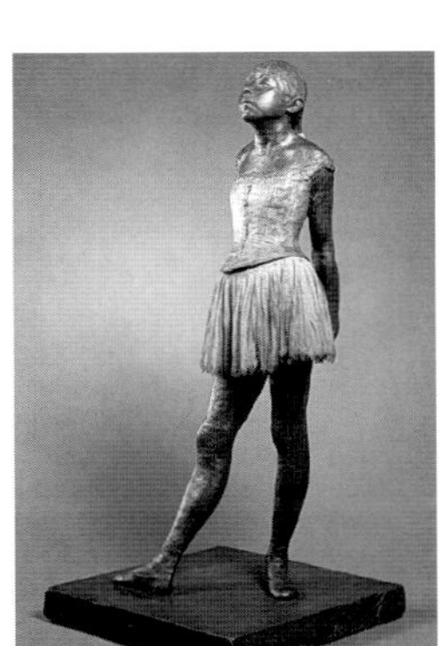

*Dressed Ballet Dancer (Petite Danseuse de Quatorze Ans),* 1880/1881, cast c. 1920–1923
Plaster cast, with base:
1.041 x .483 x .508 ($41^{1}/_{2}$ x $19^{7}/_{8}$ x $20^{1}/_{4}$)
Collection of Mr. and Mrs. Paul Mellon
1985.64.62

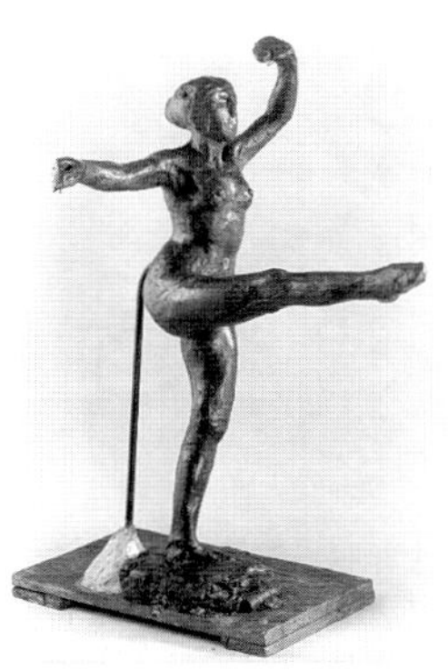

*Fourth Position Front, on the Left Leg,* probably 1885/1890
Yellow brown wax and plastilene, height without base: .568 ($22^{3}/_{8}$)
Inscribed on wax along outside of left foot: DEGAS; carved on top of wood base: 73
Collection of Mr. and Mrs. Paul Mellon
1985.64.49

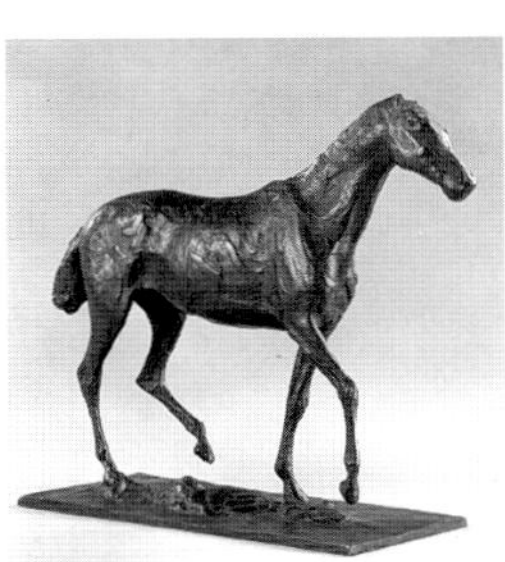

*Horse Walking,* c. 1860/1870, cast 1919–1921
Bronze, .210 x .266 x .098 ($8^{1}/_{4}$ x $10^{1}/_{2}$ x $3^{7}/_{8}$)
Inscribed on top of base in corner closest to rear left hoof: DEGAS; foundry marks on top of base in corner closest to rear right hoof: 10/B; CIRE / PERDUE / A.A. HÉBRARD
Gift of Mrs. Lessing J. Rosenwald
1989.28.2

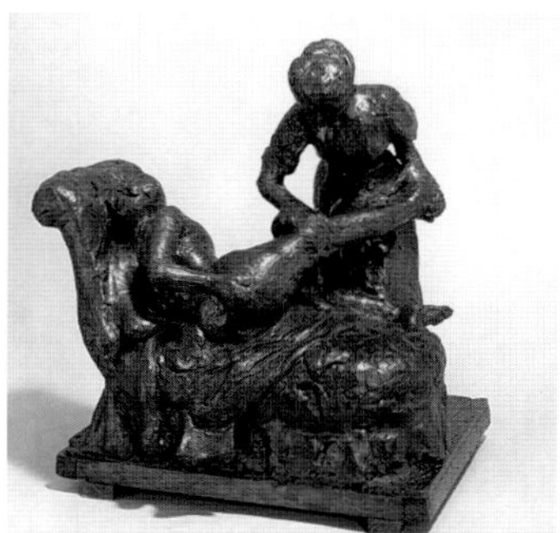

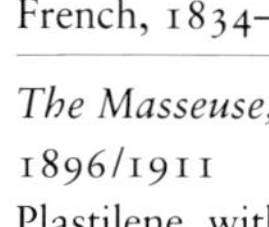

Edgar Degas
French, 1834–1917

*The Masseuse, Group,* probably 1896/1911
Plastilene, without base:
.413 x .381 x .305 (16¼ x 15 x 12)
Collection of Mr. and Mrs. Paul Mellon
1985.64.61

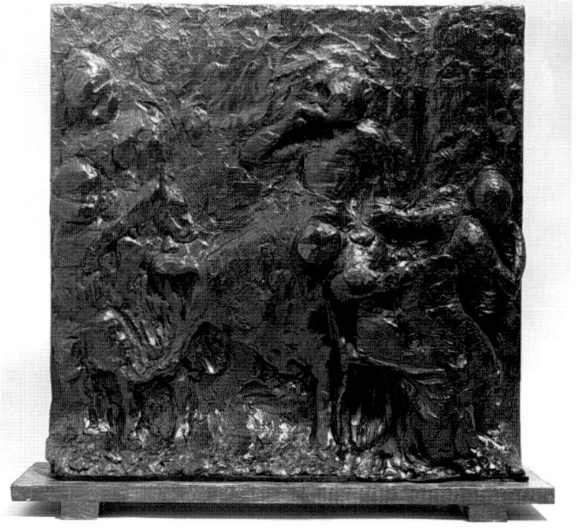

*Picking Apples,* c. 1890
Red wax and plastilene on wood
.451 x .471 (17¾ x 18¾)
Inscribed in lower right corner: DEGAS
Collection of Mr. and Mrs. Paul Mellon
1985.64.45

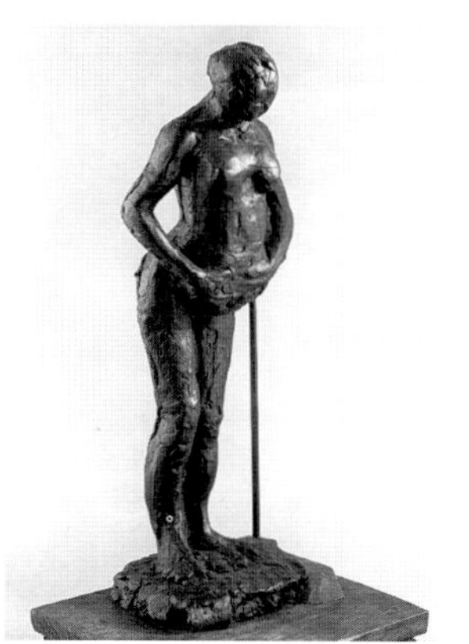

*Pregnant Woman,* probably 1896/1911
Brown wax and plastilene, height without base: .432 (17)
Inscribed on wax beside right foot: DEGAS
Collection of Mr. and Mrs. Paul Mellon
1985.64.54

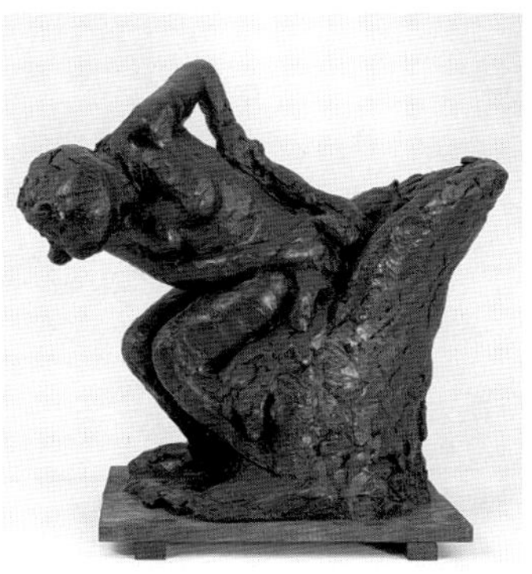

*Seated Woman Wiping Her Left Hip,*
probably 1901/1911
Brown wax, without base:
.444 x .505 x .470 (17 1/2 x 19 7/8 x 18 1/2)
Inscribed on wax near right foot: DEGAS
Collection of Mr. and Mrs. Paul Mellon
1985.64.59

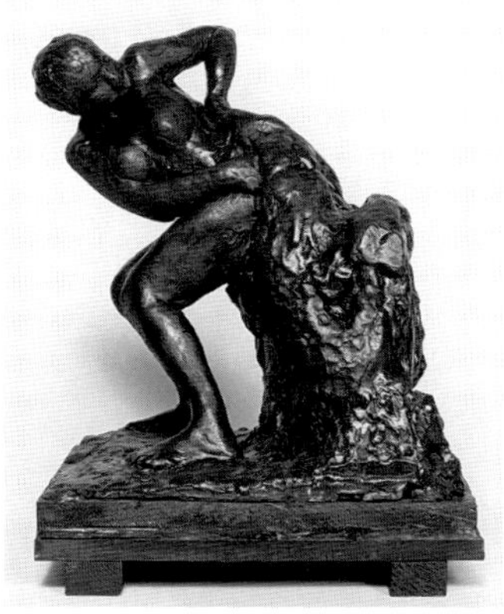

*Seated Woman Wiping Her Left Side,*
probably 1901/1911
Red wax and plastilene, without base:
.349 x .295 x .300 (13 3/4 x 11 5/8 x 11 7/8)
Inscribed on wax near left foot: DEGAS
Collection of Mr. and Mrs. Paul Mellon
1985.64.57

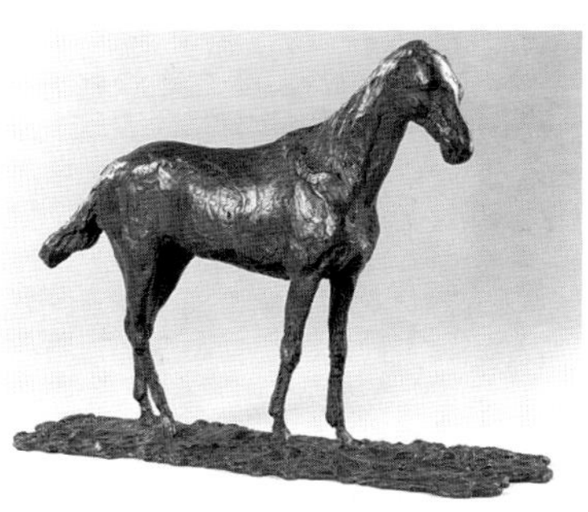

*Study of a Mustang,* c. 1860/1862,
cast 1919–1921
Bronze, .219 x .312 x .116
(8 5/8 x 12 1/4 x 4 5/8)
Inscribed on ground in corner closest to front right hoof: DEGAS; foundry marks on ground in corner closest to rear left hoof: 21/B; CIRE / PERDUE / A.A. HÉBRARD
Gift of Mrs. Lessing J. Rosenwald
1989.28.1

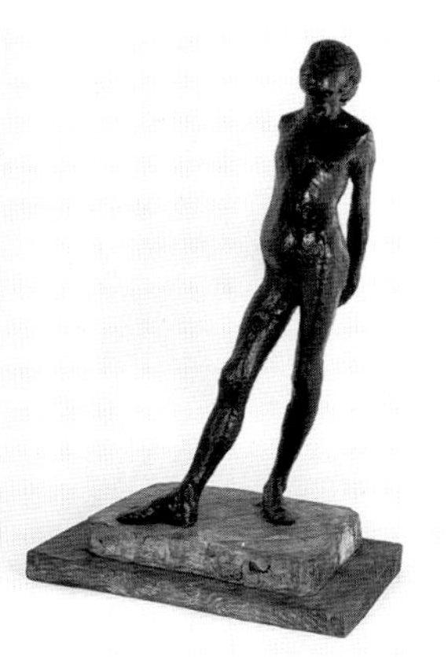

*Study in the Nude for the Dressed Ballet Dancer,* 1878/1879
Red wax and plastilene, without base:
.724 x .295 x .305 (28 1/2 x 11 5/8 x 12)
Collection of Mr. and Mrs. Paul Mellon
1985.64.46

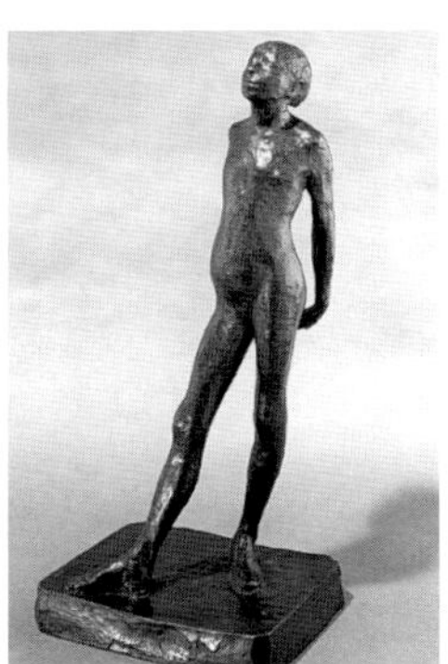

EDGAR DEGAS
French, 1834–1917

*Study in the Nude for the Dressed Ballet Dancer,* 1878/1879, cast 1919–1921
Bronze, with self-base: .727 x .349 x .305 (28 5/8 x 13 3/4 x 12)
Inscribed on top of base in front left corner: DEGAS; foundry marks on side of base in rear right corner: CIRE / PERDUE / A.A. HÉBRARD; 56/O
Collection of Mr. and Mrs. Paul Mellon
1985.64.67

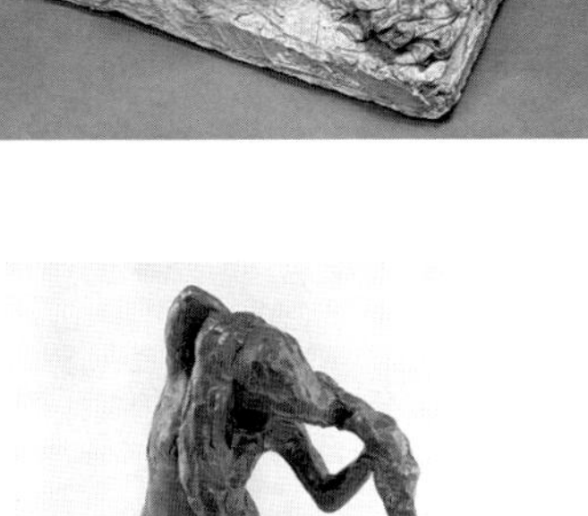

*The Tub,* 1889
Brownish red wax, lead, plaster of Paris, cloth, diameter: .470 (18 1/2)
Collection of Mr. and Mrs. Paul Mellon
1985.64.48

*Woman Arranging Her Hair,* probably 1896/1911, cast 1919–1921
Bronze, .463 x .263 x .170 (18 1/4 x 10 3/8 x 6 3/4)
Inscribed on top of base in front right corner: DEGAS; foundry marks on top of base in rear left corner: 50/M; CIRE / PERDUE / A.A. HÉBRARD
Collection of Mr. and Mrs. Paul Mellon
1985.64.65

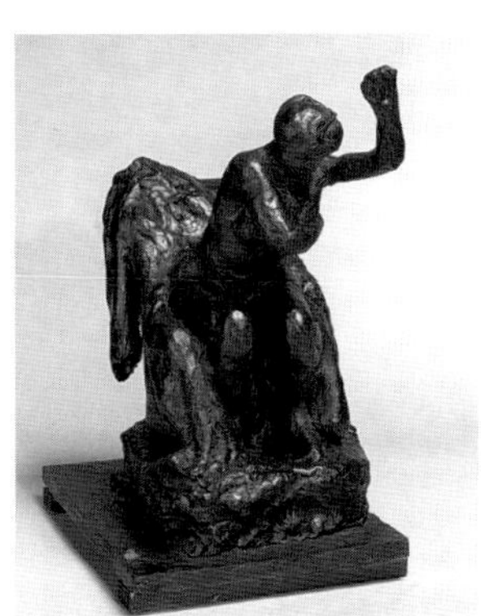

*Woman Seated in an Armchair Wiping Her Left Armpit,* probably 1901/1911
Brown wax and plastilene, height without base: .317 (12 1/2)
Inscribed on wax at proper left back corner of chair: DEGAS
Collection of Mr. and Mrs. Paul Mellon
1985.64.60

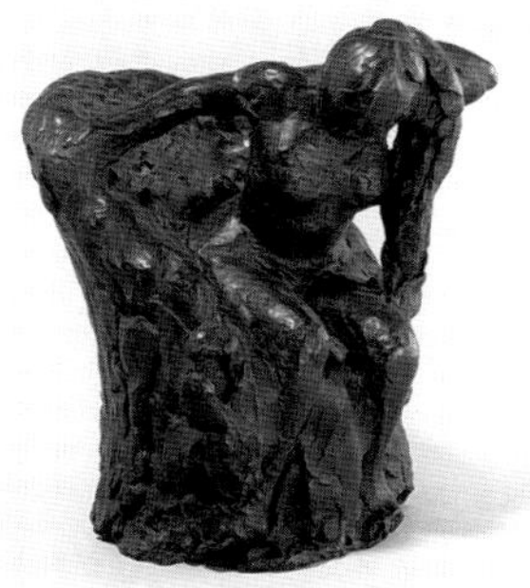

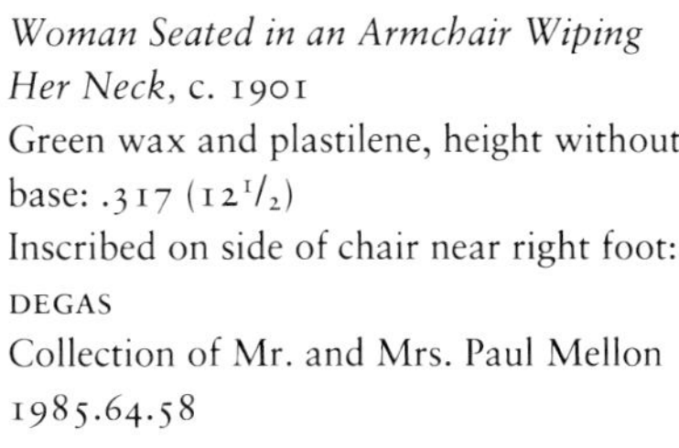

*Woman Seated in an Armchair Wiping Her Neck*, c. 1901
Green wax and plastilene, height without base: .317 ($12^{1}/_{2}$)
Inscribed on side of chair near right foot: DEGAS
Collection of Mr. and Mrs. Paul Mellon
1985.64.58

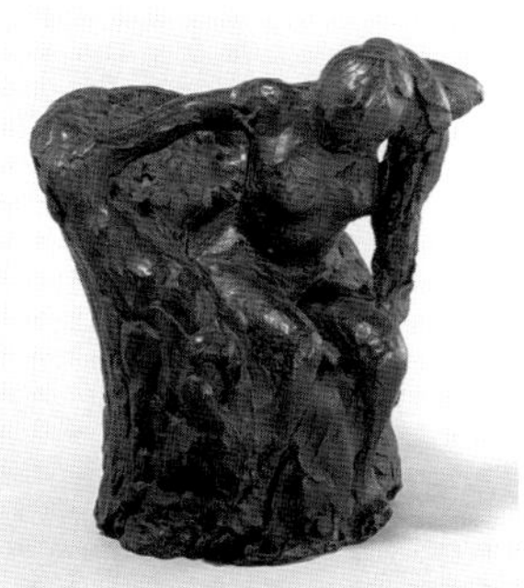

*Woman Seated in an Armchair Wiping Her Neck*, c. 1901, cast 1919–1921
Bronze, .317 x .254 x .289 ($12^{1}/_{2}$ x 10 x $11^{3}/_{8}$)
Inscribed on lower proper left front corner of chair: DEGAS; foundry marks on lower proper right back corner of chair: CIRE / PERDUE / A.A. HÉBRARD; 44/C
Collection of Mr. and Mrs. Paul Mellon
1985.64.66

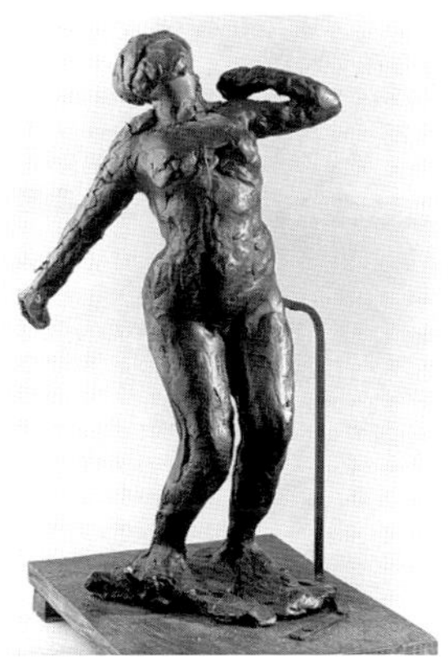

*Woman Stretching*, probably 1896/1911
Red wax and plastilene, height without base: .365 ($14^{3}/_{8}$)
Inscribed on wax beside left foot: DEGAS
Collection of Mr. and Mrs. Paul Mellon
1985.64.55

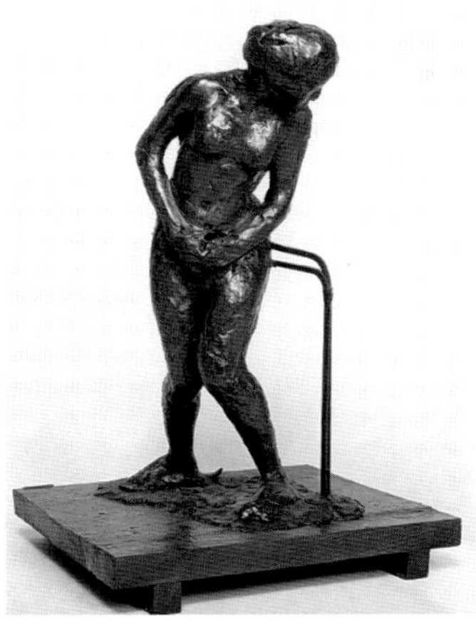

*Woman Taken Unawares*, probably c. 1892
Yellow brown wax and plastilene, height without base: .406 (16)
Inscribed on wax behind left foot: DEGAS
Collection of Mr. and Mrs. Paul Mellon
1985.64.51

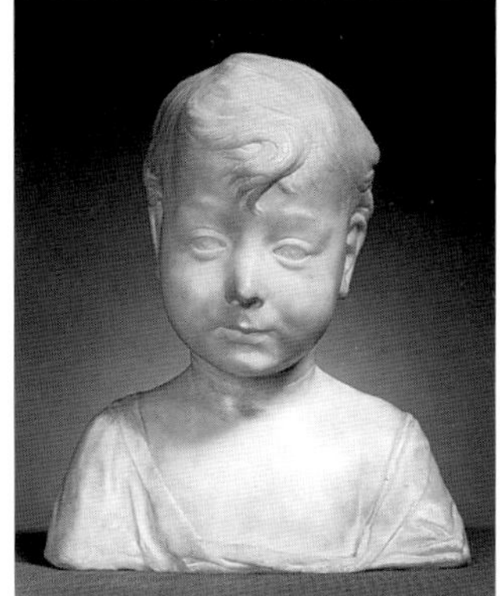

Desiderio da Settignano
Florentine, 1429/1430–1464

*The Christ Child (?)*, c. 1460
Marble, .305 x .265 x .163
(12 x $10^{3}/_{8}$ x $6^{3}/_{8}$)
Samuel H. Kress Collection
1943.4.94

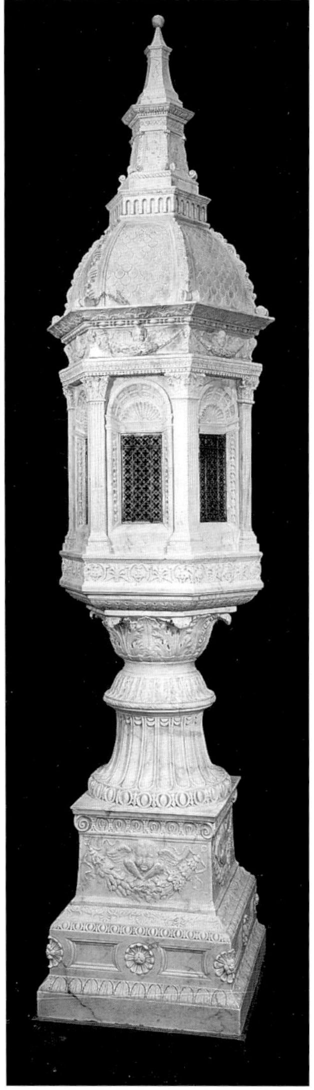

*Ciborium for the Sacrament*, c. 1455
Marble, 3.221 x .808 x .699
($126^{5}/_{8}$ x $31^{3}/_{4}$ x $27^{1}/_{2}$)
Samuel H. Kress Collection
1952.5.100

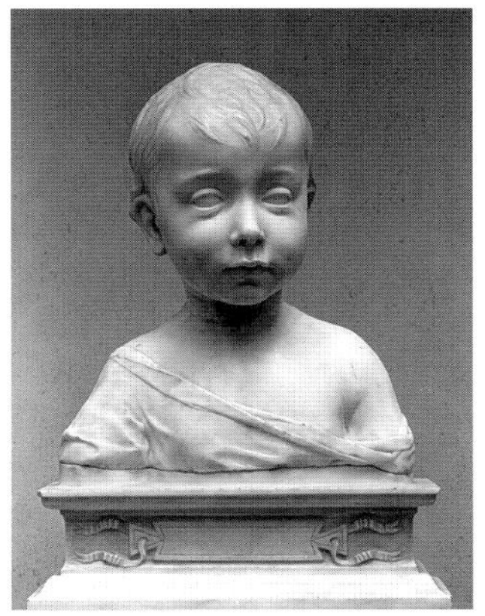

*A Little Boy,* 1455/1460
Marble, .263 x .247 x .150
($10^3/_8$ x $9^3/_4$ x $5^7/_8$)
Andrew W. Mellon Collection
1937.1.113

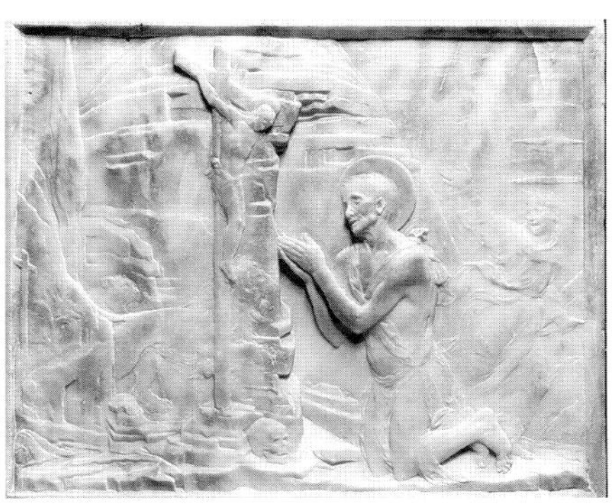

*Saint Jerome in the Desert,* c. 1461
Marble, .427 x .548 ($16^3/_4$ x $21^1/_2$)
Widener Collection
1942.9.113

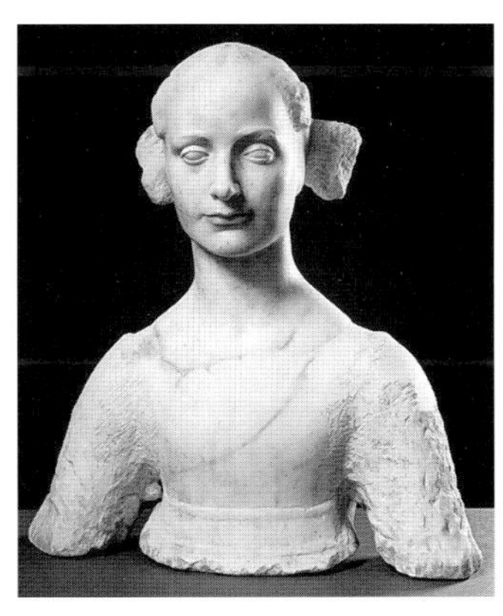

*"Marietta Strozzi,"* c. 1453/1455
Marble, .530 x .488 x .199
($20^7/_8$ x $19^1/_8$ x $7^3/_4$)
Widener Collection
1942.9.112

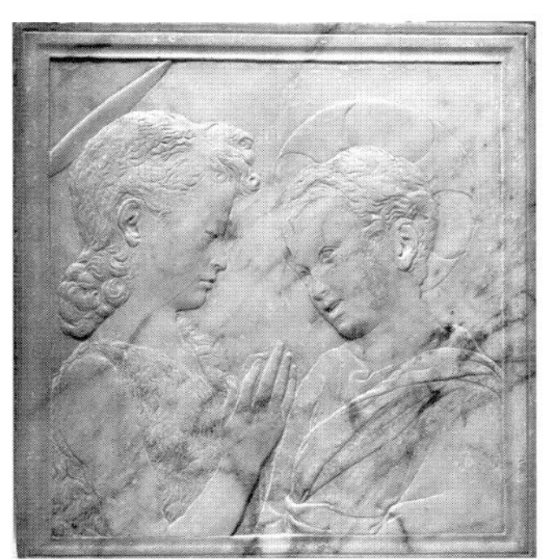

Style of Desiderio da Settignano
Florentine

*Christ with Saint John the Baptist as Children,* second half 15th century
Marble, .402 x .402 ($15^3/_4$ x $15^3/_4$)
Andrew W. Mellon Collection
1937.1.115

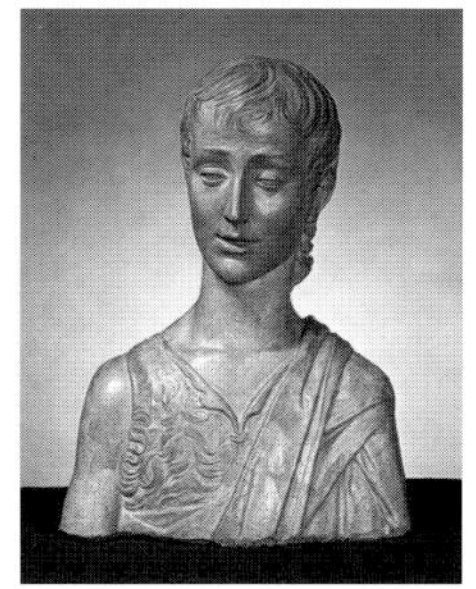

Style of Desiderio da Settignano
Florentine

*Saint John the Baptist,* 15th/19th century
Terra cotta, .505 x .385 x .185
(19 7/8 x 15 1/8 x 7 3/8)
Samuel H. Kress Collection
1943.4.83

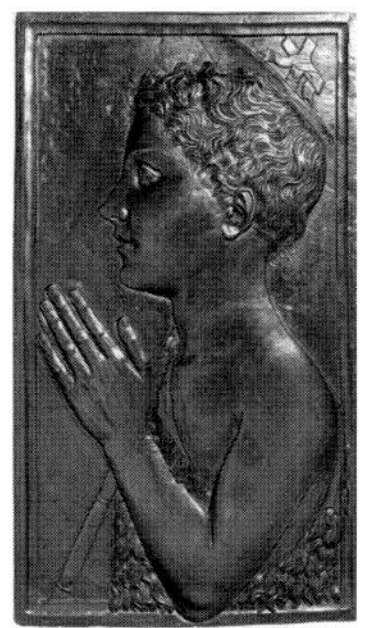

Imitator of
Desiderio da Settignano
Florentine

*Saint John the Baptist,* c. 1850/1875
Bronze, .514 x .299 (20 1/4 x 11 3/4)
Falsely signed at lower left on staff:
DONATELLI OPUS
Samuel H. Kress Collection
1957.14.13

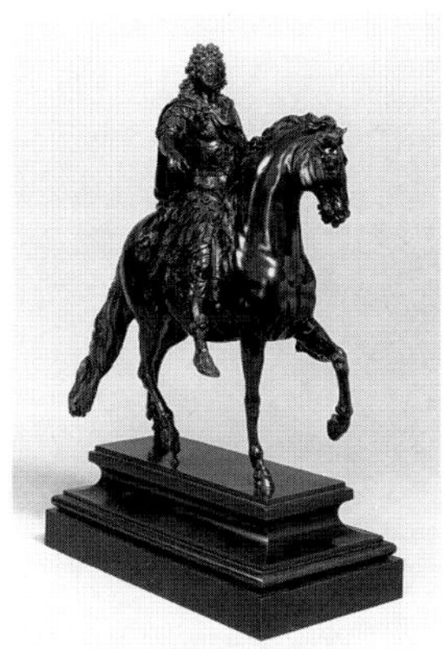

After Martin van den Bogaert, called Desjardins
French

*The Grand Dauphin,* 1688/1699, cast c. 1699 in Paris by Roger Schabol (born Brussels c. 1656)
Bronze, with base: .570 x .213 x .480
(22 3/8 x 8 3/8 x 16 1/2)
Andrew W. Mellon Fund
1971.5.1

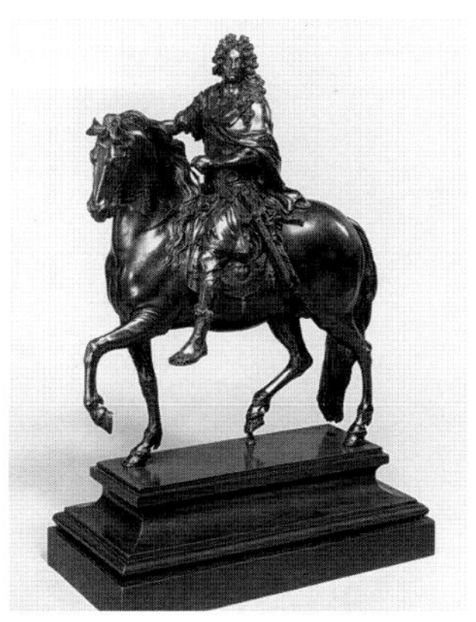

After Martin van den Bogaert, called Desjardins
French

*Louis XIV,* c. 1683/1699, cast c. 1699 in Paris by Roger Schabol (born Brussels c. 1656)
Bronze, with base: .566 x .219 x .400
(22 1/4 x 8 5/8 x 15 3/4)
Andrew W. Mellon Fund
1971.5.2

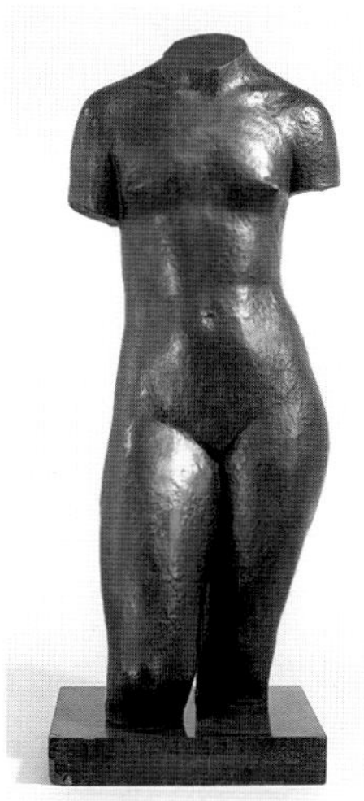

## Charles Despiau
French, 1874–1946

*Adolescent Girl,* 1921 (original model enlarged in 1929 and this cast from enlarged version)
Bronze, 1.254 x .495 x .454
($49^{3}/_{8}$ x $19^{1}/_{2}$ x $17^{7}/_{8}$)
Inscribed on outer side of left leg below knee: C. DESPIAU. / 5/5; foundry mark on truncation of right leg: GEORGES RUDIER. / FONDEUR. PARIS
Collection of Mr. and Mrs. Paul Mellon
1983.1.53

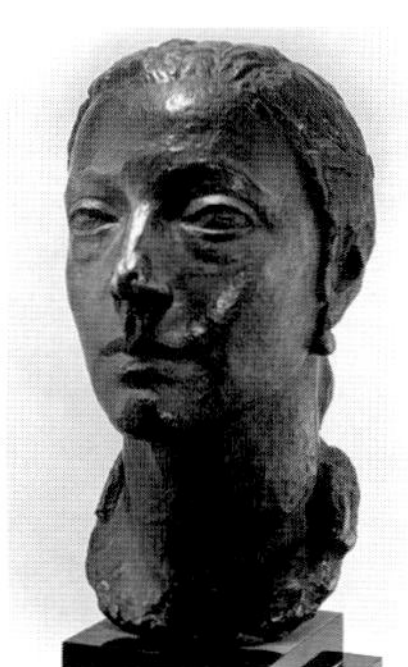

*Maud Dale,* 1931
Bronze, .355 x .182 x .247
(14 x $7^{1}/_{8}$ x 9 $^{3}/_{4}$)
Inscribed on right edge: C. DESPIAU
Chester Dale Collection
1963.10.236

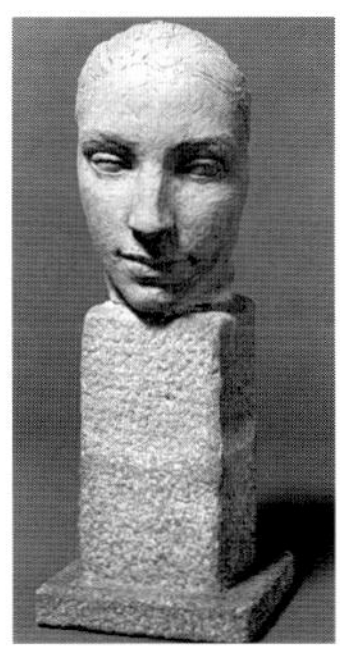

*Head of a Woman,* 1925
Terra cotta, .230 x .126 x .139
(9 x 5 x $5^{1}/_{2}$)
Inscribed on back at bottom: 1925 / C. DESPIAU
Gift of Angelika Wertheim Frink
1969.10.2

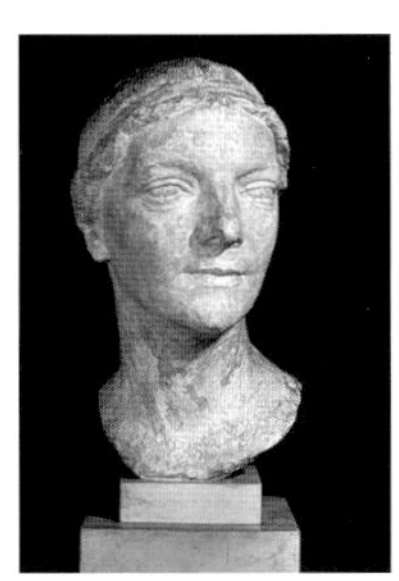

*Agnes E. Meyer,* 1929
Plaster, .382 x .242 x .281
(15 x $9^{1}/_{2}$ x 11)
Inscribed on back of neck: C. DESPIAU
Gift of Eugene and Agnes E. Meyer
1967.13.5

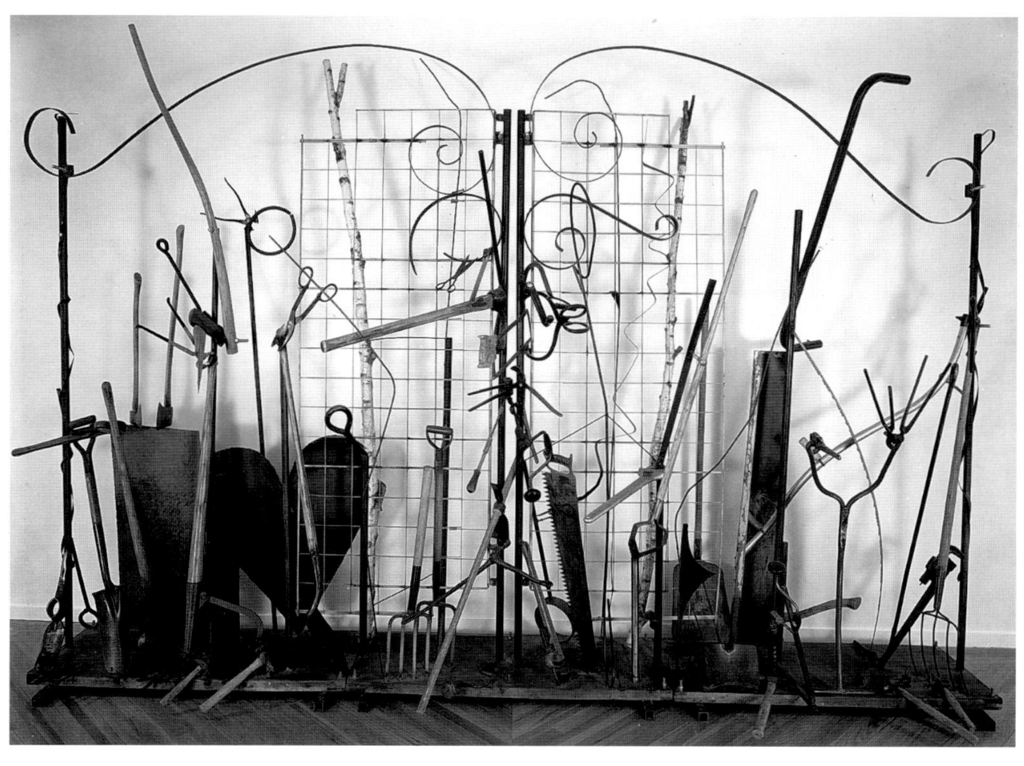

JIM DINE
American, born 1935

*The Gate, Goodbye Vermont,* 1985
Steel, tools, wood
2.832 x 4.318 x 1.588
(111 1/2 x 170 x 62 1/2)
Gift (Partial and Promised) of Mr. and Mrs. Donald G. Fisher, in Honor of the 50th Anniversary of the National Gallery of Art
1991.61.1

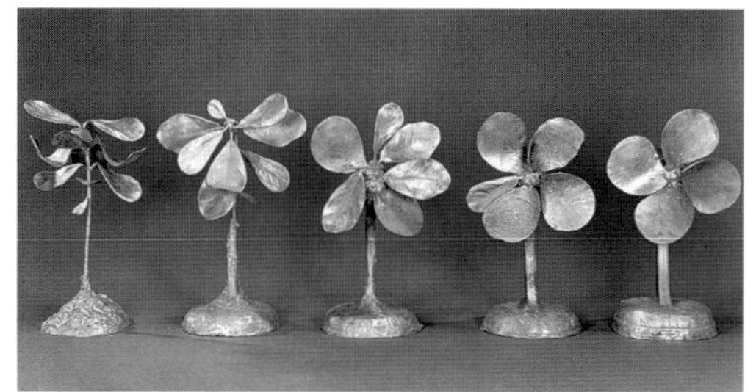

*Metamorphosis of a Plant into a Fan,* 1973–1974
Cast aluminum in five parts, each part approximately: .660 x .406 x .305
(26 x 16 x 12)
Gift of Jim Dine, in Honor of the 50th Anniversary of the National Gallery of Art
1990.130.1–5

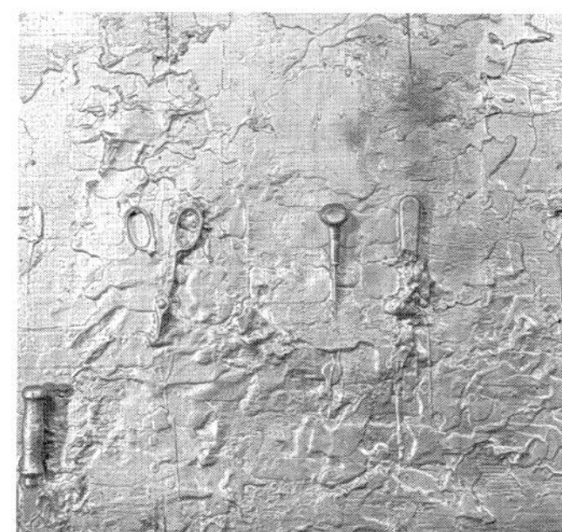
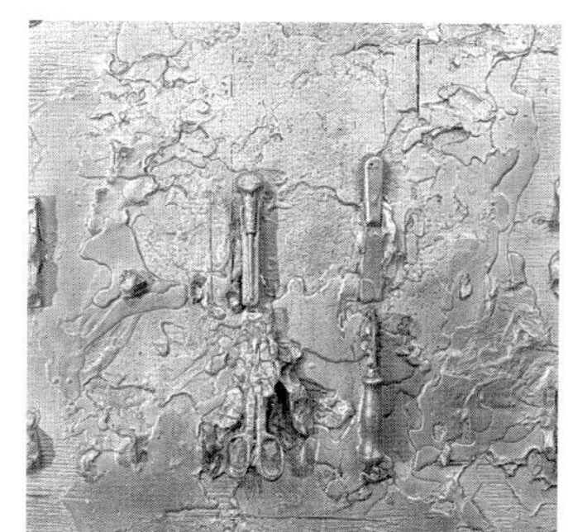
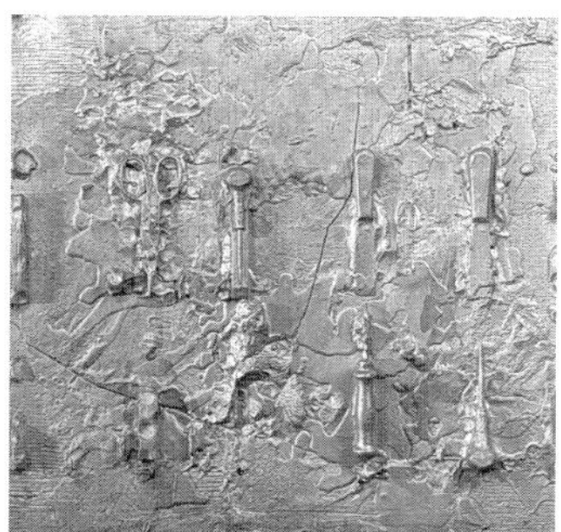
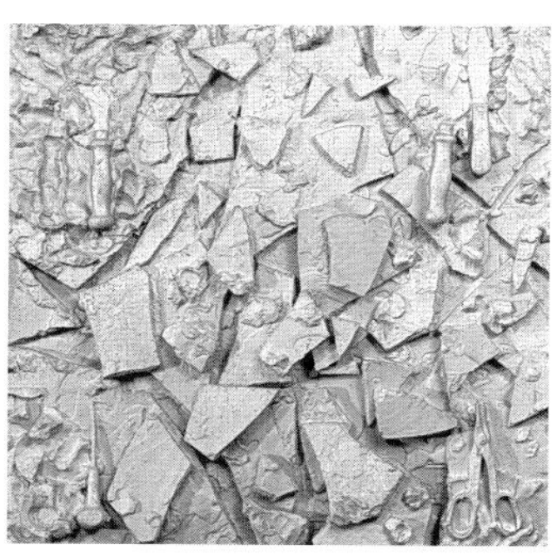

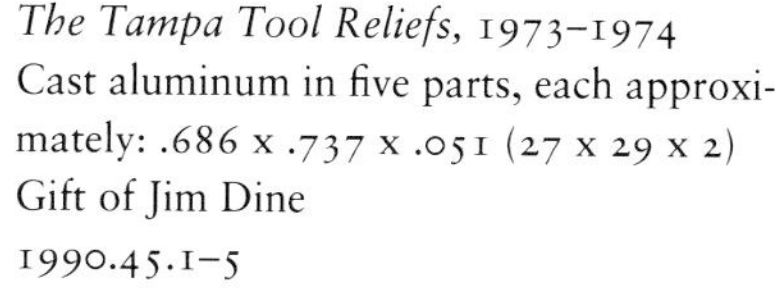

*The Tampa Tool Reliefs,* 1973–1974
Cast aluminum in five parts, each approximately: .686 x .737 x .051 (27 x 29 x 2)
Gift of Jim Dine
1990.45.1–5

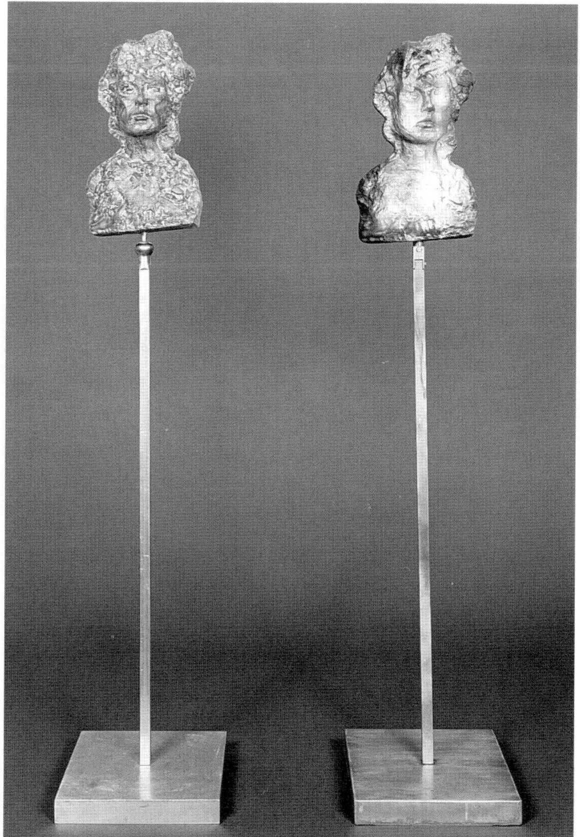

*Untitled Cast Concrete,* 1985
Cast concrete with painted additions
Head: .483 x .305 x .114 (19 x 12 x $4^{1}/_{2}$); stand: 1.283 x .381 x .381 ($50^{1}/_{2}$ x 15 x 15)
Inscribed on verso, lower center: H/C 3/4 / JIM DINE / 1981–5 / FOR N.G.A. / GRAPHIC STUDIO / TAMPA / FLA.
Gift of Graphicstudio/University of South Florida and the Artist
1986.26.27

*Untitled Cast Concrete,* 1985
Cast concrete
Head: .483 x .305 x .114 (19 x 12 x $4^{1}/_{2}$); stand: 1.283 x .381 x .381 ($50^{1}/_{2}$ x 15 x 15)
Inscribed on verso, lower center: 4/4 H/C JIM DINE / TAMPA FLORIDA / FOR N.G.A. / GRAPHIC STUDIO; lower left: 1981–5
Gift of Graphicstudio/University of South Florida and the Artist
1986.26.28

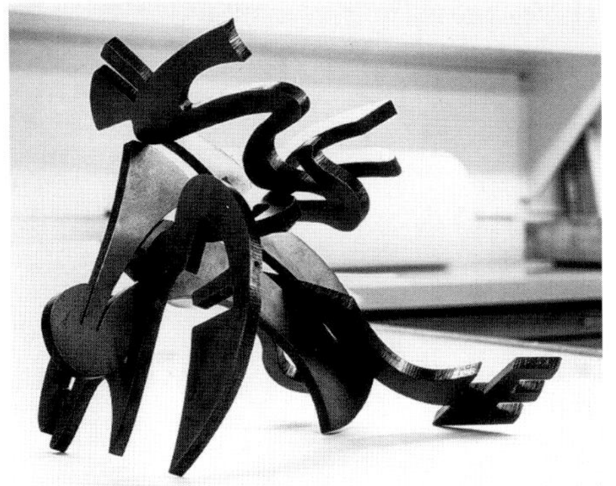

Mark Di Suvero
American, born 1933

*Rising (For Walt Whitman),*
published 1980
Copperplated aluminum in five pieces
closed: .018 x .406 x .483 (5/8 x 16 x 19);
variable when open
Gift of Mr. and Mrs. Roger P. Sonnabend
1986.90.7

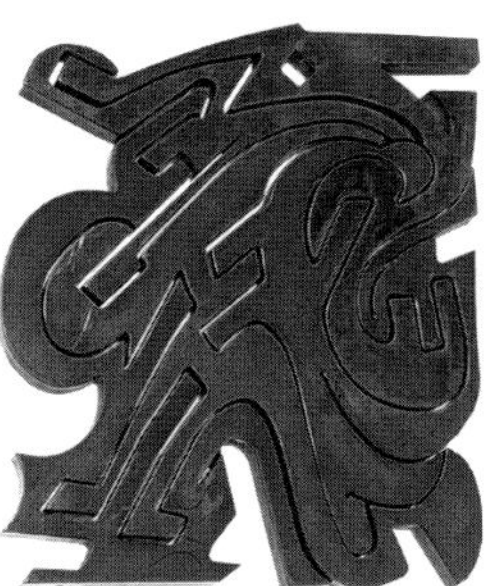

*T'ang,* published 1977
Torch-cut steel plate in five pieces, closed:
.378 x .327 x .015 (14 7/8 x 12 7/8 x 5/8);
variable when open
Inscribed at lower left on face of one
segment: DI S; on bottom: (Gemini chop)
GEMINI II
Gift of Gemini G.E.L.
1981.5.134

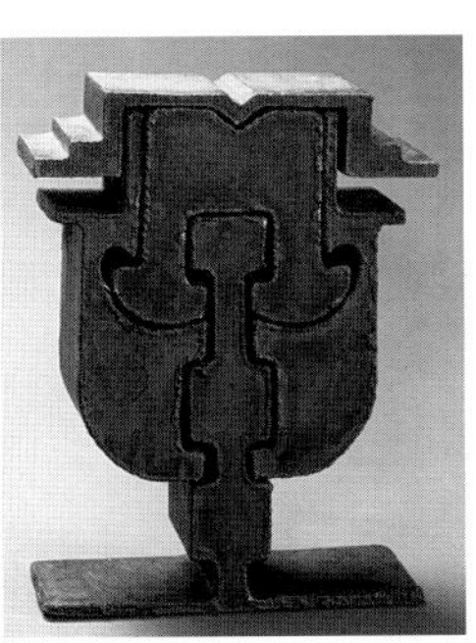

*Untitled,* published 1972
Steel plate, closed: .254 x .203 x .051
(10 x 8 x 2); variable when open
Gift of Mr. and Mrs. Roger P. Sonnabend
1986.90.6

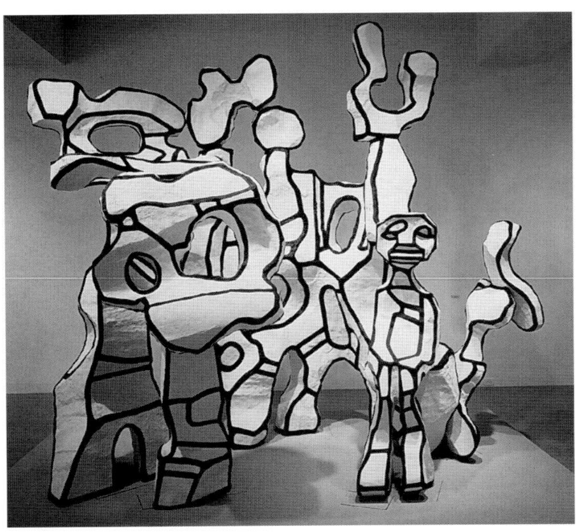

Jean Dubuffet
French, 1901–1985

*Site à l'homme assis,* 1969–1984
Polyester resin, cast and painted
3.048 x 3.658 x 1.880 (120 x 144 x 74)
Inscribed on lower right "leg" of left-most
tree: J.D.84
Gift of Robert M. and Anne T. Bass and
Arnold and Mildred Glimcher, in Honor
of the 50th Anniversary of the National
Gallery of Art
1991.100.1

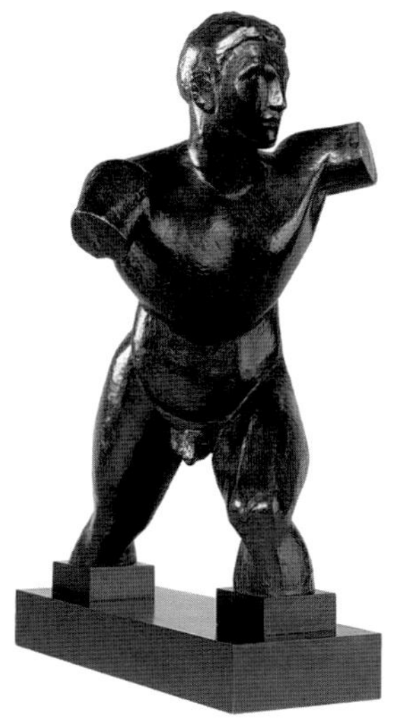

### Raymond Duchamp-Villon
French, 1876–1918

*Torso of a Young Man,* 1910
Bronze, .552 x .339 x .402
(21 3/4 x 13 3/8 x 15 7/8)
Inscribed on outside of left leg below knee: DUCHAMP VILLON / 4/8; on outside of right leg below knee: .GEORGES RUDIER. / .FONDEUR.PARIS. ; ON INSIDE OF RIGHT LEG BELOW KNEE: LOUIS CARRÉ . ÉDITEUR.
Ailsa Mellon Bruce Fund
1971.66.12

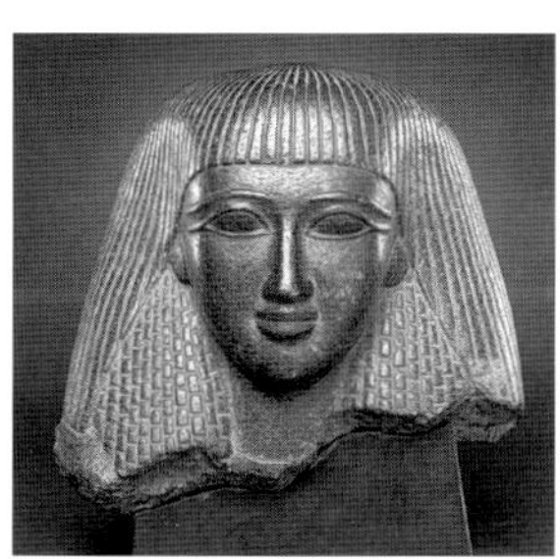

### Possibly Egyptian Ptolemaic Period, 332–30 B.C.

*Male Head*
Black granite, .261 x .149 x .157
(10 1/4 x 5 3/4 x 6 1/8)
Gift of David Keppel
1949.15.1

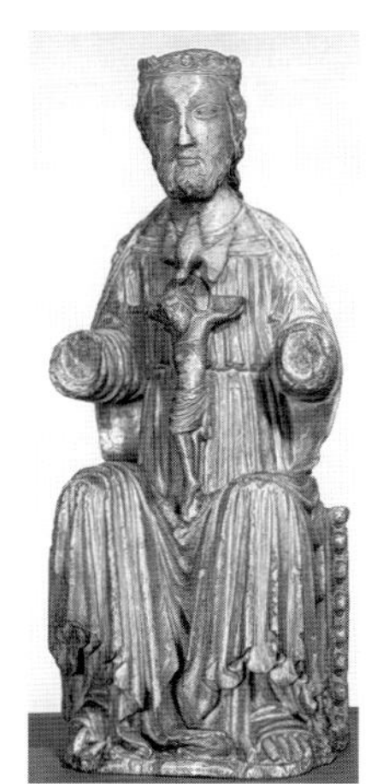

### English or Spanish 14th Century

*The Holy Trinity,* c. 1300/1350
Alabaster with traces of polychromy
.853 x .357 x .292 (33 1/2 x 14 x 11 1/2)
Samuel H. Kress Collection
1953.2.1

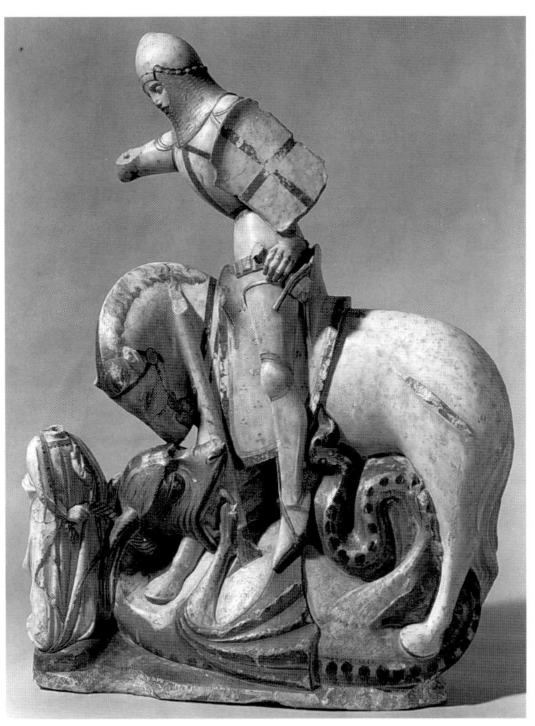

English 14th or 15th Century

*Saint George and the Dragon,*
c. 1370/1420
Alabaster, painted and gilded
.815 x .605 x .205 (32 x 23 3/4 x 8 1/8)
Samuel H. Kress Collection
1953.2.2

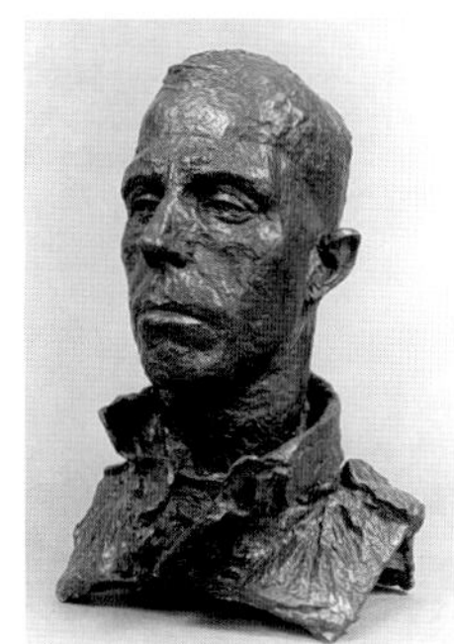

Sir Jacob Epstein
British, 1880–1959

*An American Soldier,* 1917
Bronze, .399 x .268 x .243
(15 5/8 x 10 5/8 x 9 5/8)
Gift of Rupert L. Joseph
1960.2.2

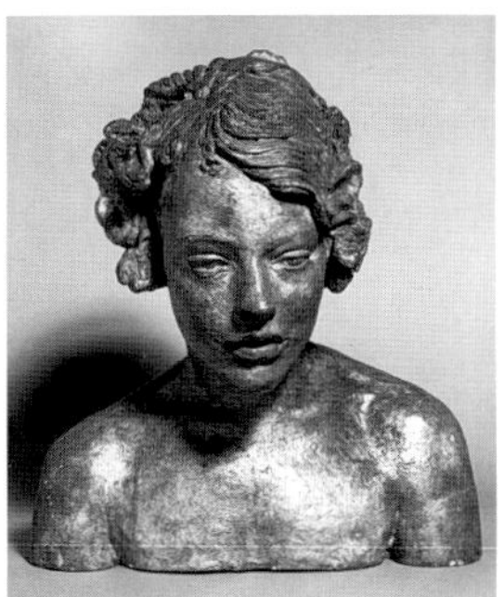

*Meum Lindsell-Stewart,* 1916/1918
Plaster, painted, .435 x .400 x .310
(17 1/8 x 15 1/2 x 12 1/4)
Gift of the Epstein Estate
1975.43.1

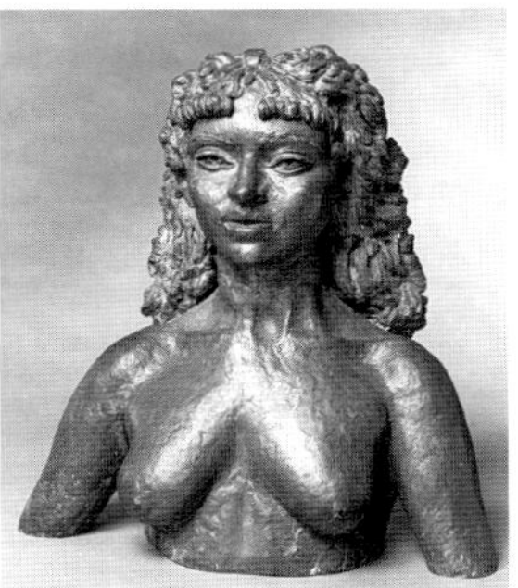

*Princess Menen,* 1949
Bronze, .543 x .533 x .327
(21 3/4 x 21 x 12 7/8)
Gift of Virginia Steele Scott
1973.2.3

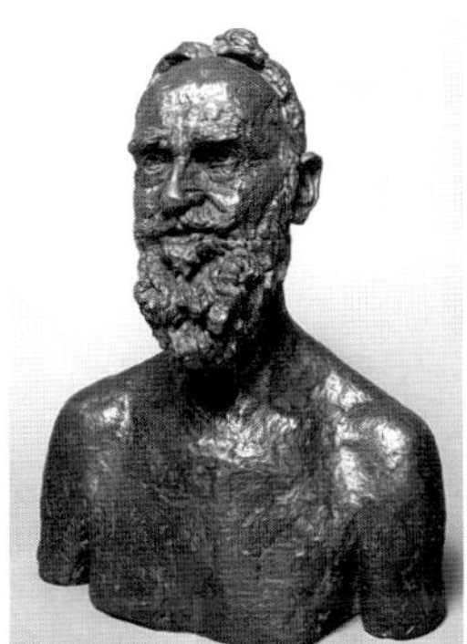

*George Bernard Shaw,* 1934
Bronze, .635 x .495 x .312
(25 x 19 1/2 x 12 1/4)
Anonymous Gift
1982.77.1

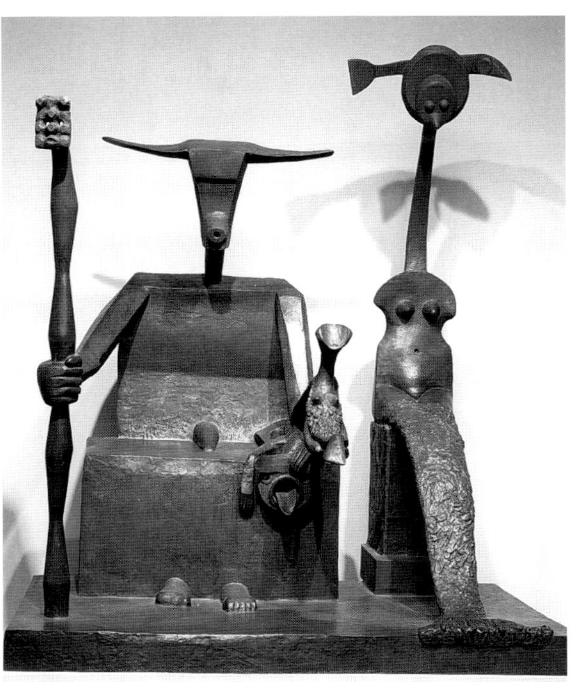

Max Ernst
German, 1891–1976

*Capricorn,* 1948/1975
Bronze, 2.425 x 2.069 x 1.510
(95 1/2 x 81 1/2 x 59 1/2)
Inscribed on left side of base: MAX ERNST / E.A. II/II; on top of base in rear left corner: SUSSE FONDEUR. PARIS
Gift of the Collectors Committee
1979.30.1

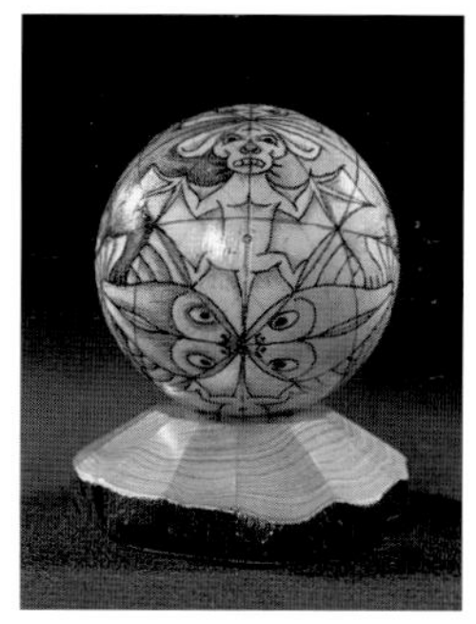

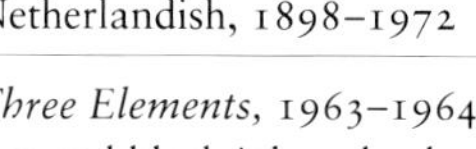

M. C. Escher
Netherlandish, 1898–1972

*Three Elements*, 1963–1964
Pen and black ink and colored pencil on plastic ball, diameter: .114 ($4^{1}/_{2}$)
Cornelius Van S. Roosevelt Collection
1974.28.82

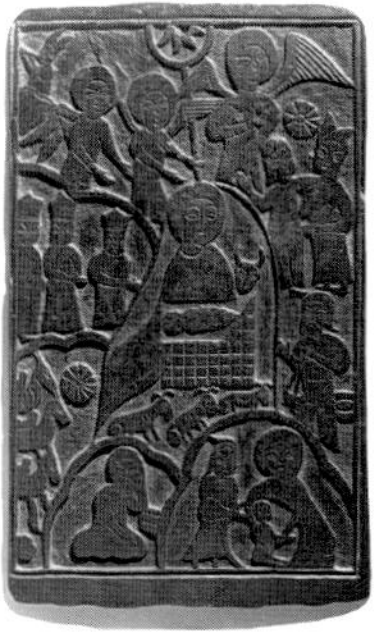

Ethiopian 18th or 19th Century

*The Nativity*
Iron, .204 x .128 (8 x 5)
Rosenwald Collection
1964.8.4

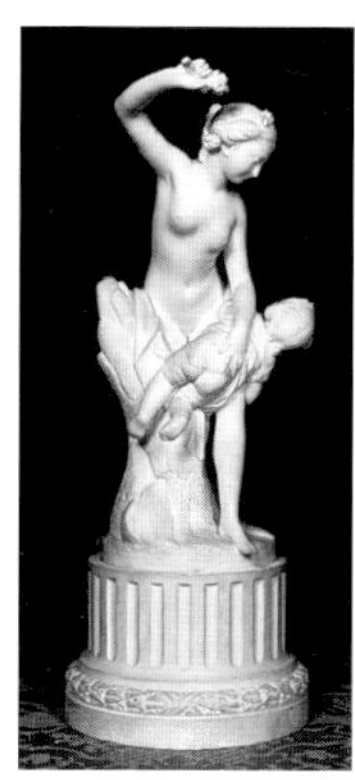

Étienne-Maurice Falconet
French, 1716–1791

*The Punishment of Cupid*
Marble, .364 x .180 x .165
($14^{1}/_{4}$ x 7 x $6^{5}/_{8}$)
Widener Collection
1942.9.116

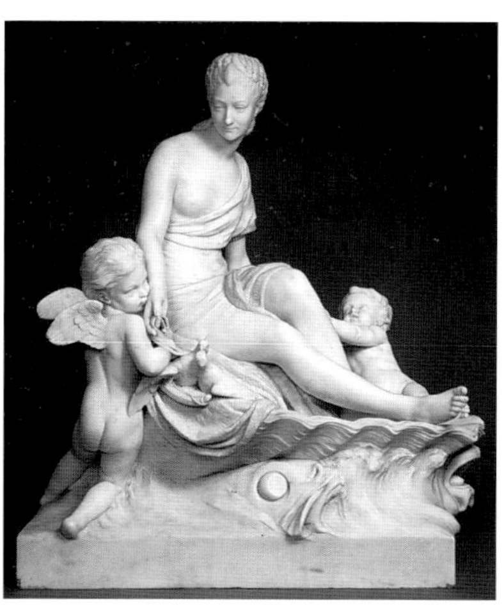

*Venus of the Doves*
Marble, .751 x .713 x .457
($29^{1}/_{2}$ x 28 x 18)
Samuel H. Kress Collection
1952.5.101

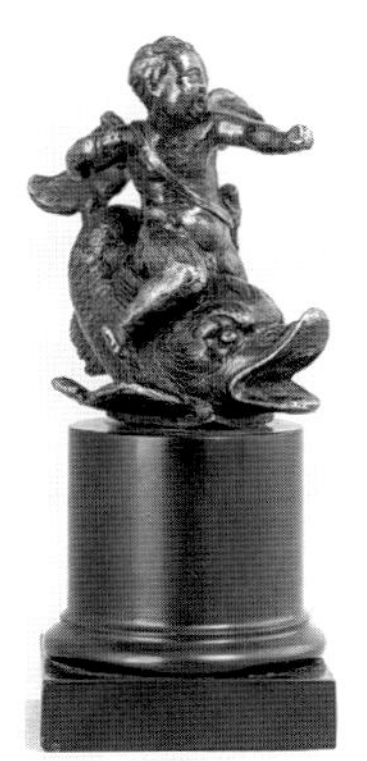

Workshop of Francesco Fanelli
Florentine

*Cupid on a Dolphin*, c. 1635/1660
Bronze, .081 x .051 x .077
($3^{3}/_{16}$ x 2 x $3^{1}/_{16}$)
Samuel H. Kress Collection
1957.14.50

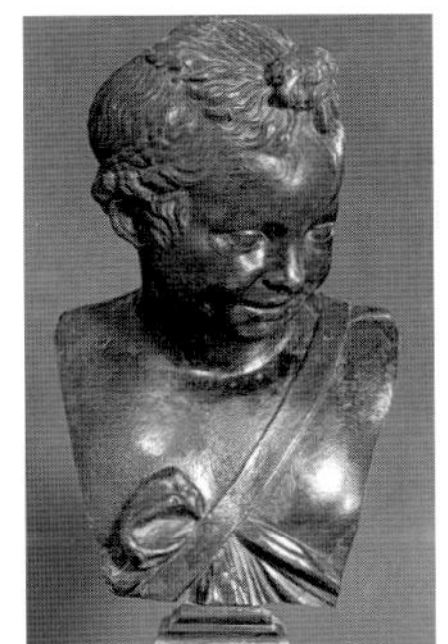

Attributed to Lucas Faydherbe
Flemish, 1617–1697

*Cupid (?)*, c. 1640/1650, cast 18th/19th century
Bronze, .390 x .253 x .253
($15^{1}/_{4}$ x $9^{7}/_{8}$ x $9^{7}/_{8}$)
Widener Collection
1942.9.114

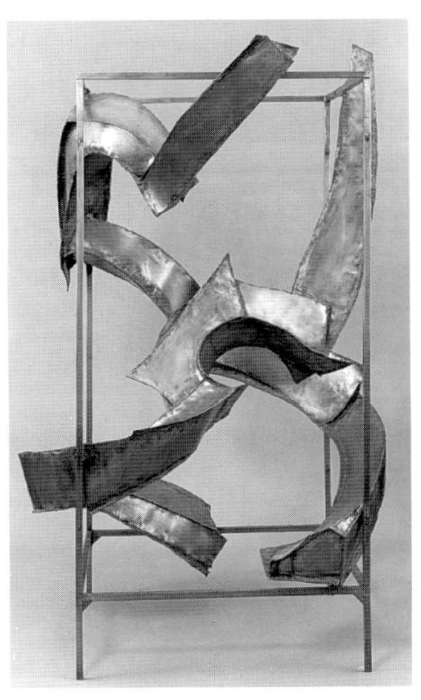

Herbert Ferber
American, 1906–1991

*Homage to Piranesi V*, 1965/1966
Copper, 2.450 x 1.457 x 1.578
($96^{1}/_{2}$ x $57^{3}/_{8}$ x $62^{1}/_{8}$)
Inscribed on copper plate attached to top side of front bottom brass bar: FERBER 66
Gift of William S. Rubin
1977.64.1

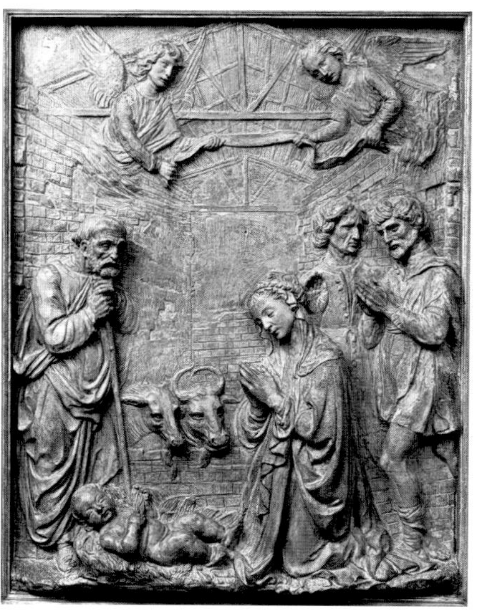

FRANCESCO DI SIMONE FERRUCCI
Florentine, 1437–1493

*The Adoration of the Shepherds*, c. 1475/1485
Terra cotta, .810 x .650 (31 3/4 x 25 3/4)
Samuel H. Kress Collection
1939.1.333

ANSELME FLAMEN
*See* GASPARD MARSY II *and* BENOÎT MASSOU

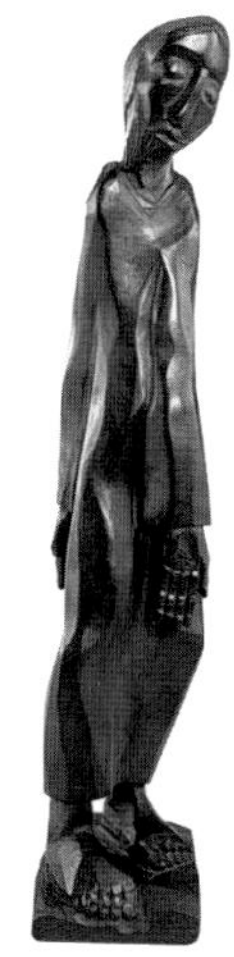

JOHN BERNARD FLANNAGAN
American, 1895–1942

*Christ*, 1925
Wood, .854 x .165 x .216
(33 5/8 x 6 1/2 x 8 1/2)
Given in memory of Frederick Zimmermann by his wife, Dorothy Zimmermann
1985.18.1

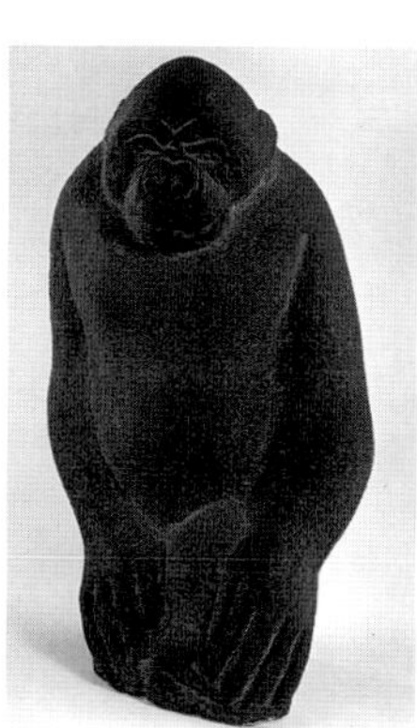

*Gorilla*, 1938
Stone, .354 x .206 x .152
(14 1/8 x 8 1/8 x 6)
Given in memory of Frederick Zimmermann by his wife, Dorothy Zimmermann
1985.18.2

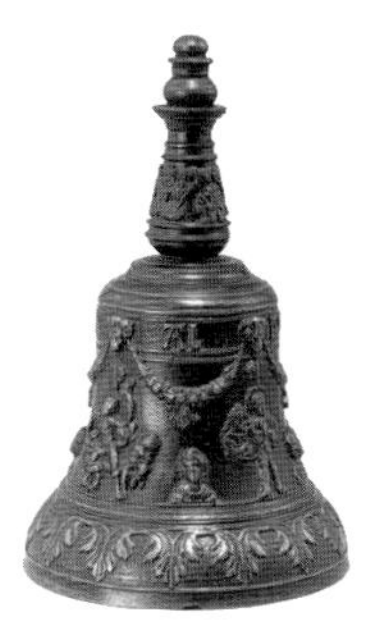

## Flemish 16th Century

*Table-Bell*
Bronze, .158 x .103 ($6\frac{1}{4}$ x $4\frac{1}{8}$)
Inscribed on strip at top: LOEFT GODE VAN AL
Samuel H. Kress Collection
1957.14.118

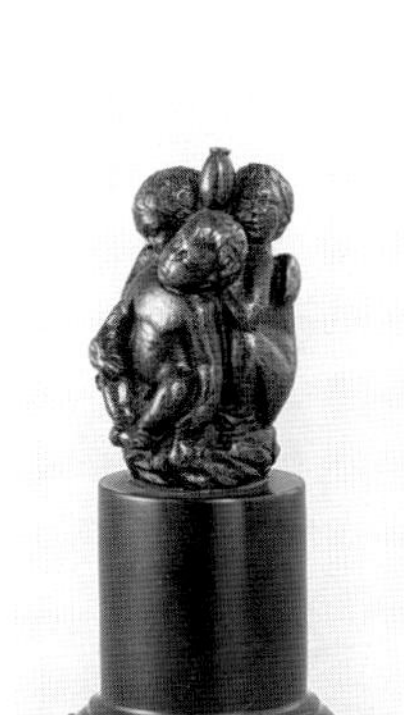

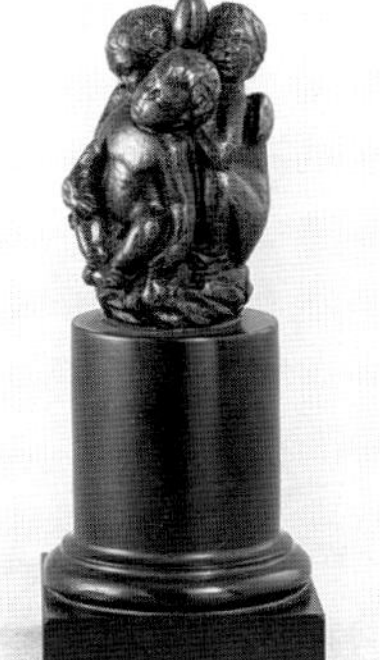

## Flemish 16th Century

*Three Cupids*
Bronze, .064 x .041 x .040
($2\frac{1}{2}$ x $1\frac{5}{8}$ x $1\frac{9}{16}$)
Samuel H. Kress Collection
1957.14.41

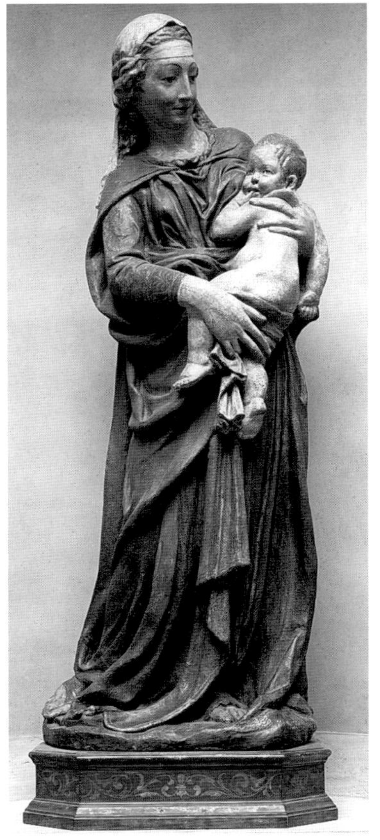

## Florentine 15th Century

*Madonna and Child*, c. 1425
Terra cotta, painted and gilt
1.208 x .472 x .335 ($47\frac{1}{2}$ x $18\frac{1}{2}$ x $13\frac{1}{8}$)
Andrew W. Mellon Collection
1937.1.112

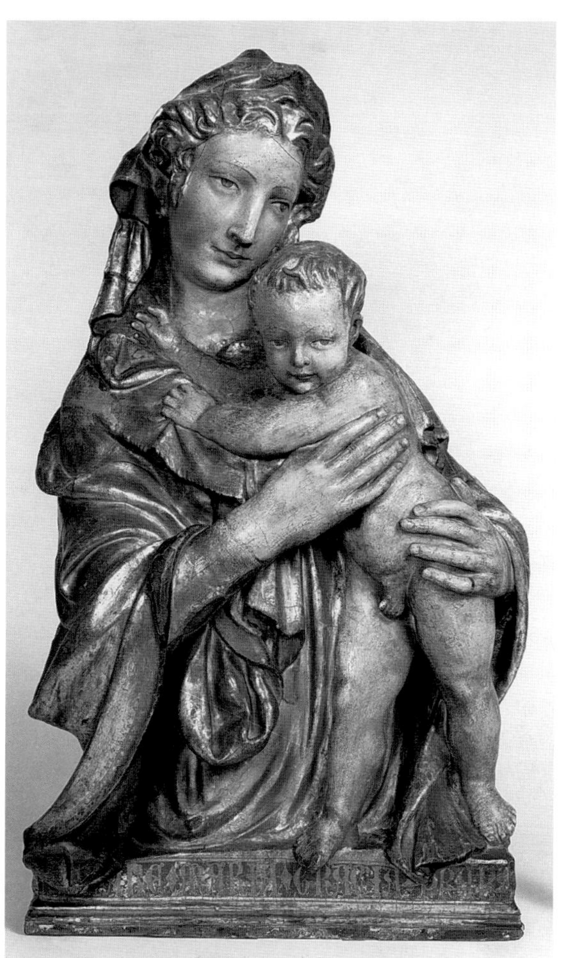

FLORENTINE 15TH CENTURY

*Madonna and Child*, c. 1425
Terra cotta, painted and gilt
1.025 x .622 x .283 (40 3/8 x 24 1/2 x 11 1/8)
Inscribed on front of base: AVE•MARIA•
GRATIA•PRENA [sic]
Samuel H. Kress Collection
1943.4.93

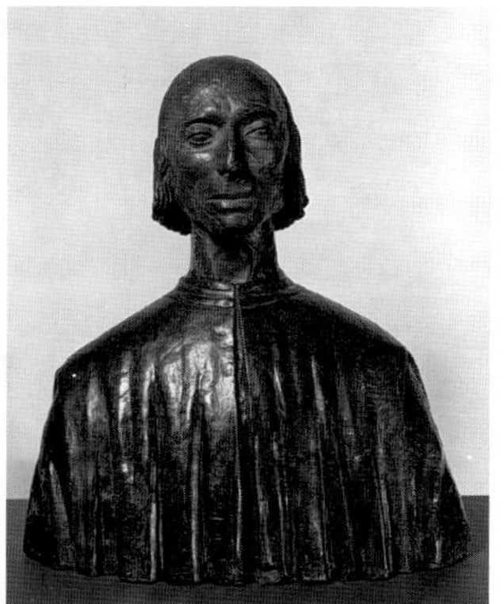

FLORENTINE 15TH CENTURY

*An Old Man*, second half 15th century
Terra cotta, painted, .587 x .543 x .260
(23 1/8 x 21 3/8 x 10 1/4)
Given by the children of Mr. and Mrs.
Otto H. Kahn in memory of their parents
1952.13.1

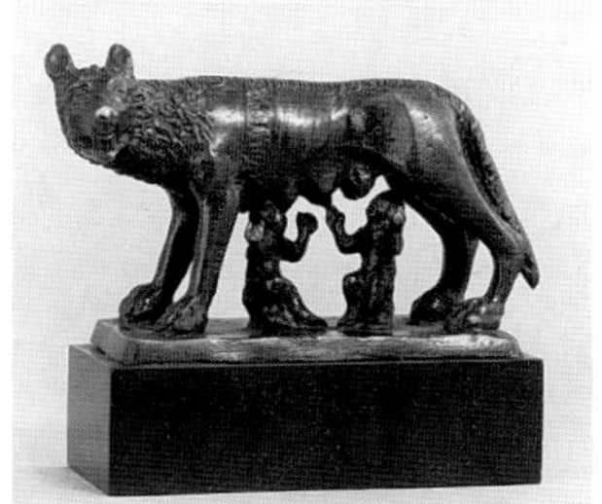

FLORENTINE 15TH CENTURY

*Romulus and Remus Suckled by a She-Wolf*
Bronze, .060 x .103 x .038
(2 3/8 x 4 1/16 x 1 1/2)
Samuel H. Kress Collection
1957.14.72

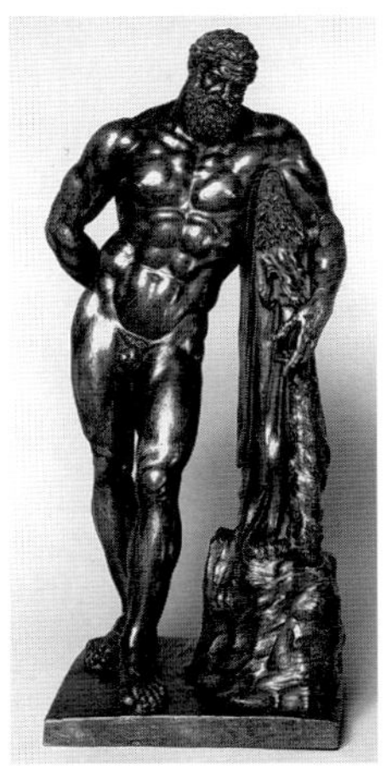

## FLORENTINE 16TH CENTURY

*Farnese Hercules*, c. 1550/1599
Bronze, .568 x .273 x .254
(22 3/8 x 10 3/4 x 10)
Gift of Stanley Mortimer
1960.10.1

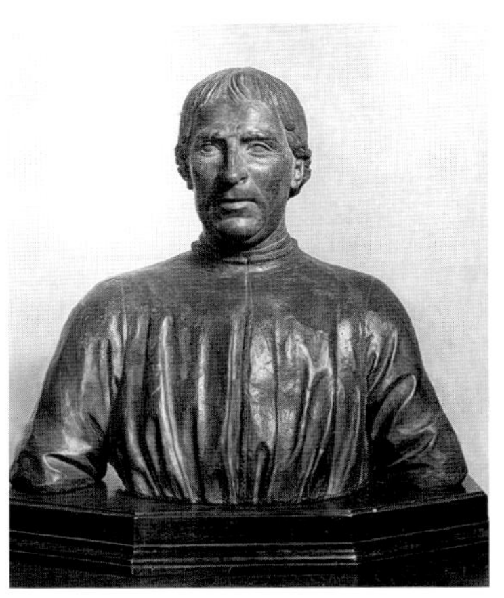

## FLORENTINE 16TH CENTURY

*A Gentleman*, c. 1510/1525
Terra cotta, .570 x .638 x .279
(22 3/8 x 25 1/2 x 11)
Samuel H. Kress Collection
1943.4.75

## FLORENTINE 16TH CENTURY

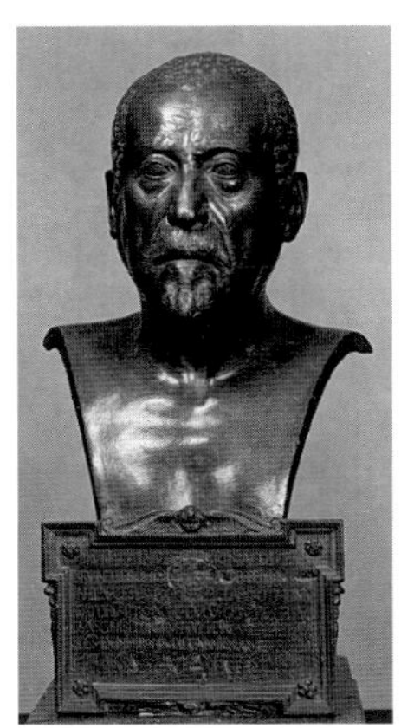

*Brunaccino Rinaldi*
Bronze, .610 x .330 x .200
(24 x 13 x 7 7/8)
Inscribed on tablet on base: •MCC• •LX
/ BRVNACCINVS•RINALDI•DE• /
BRVNELLESCHIS•FLOR•REIPVB•PREAF• /
•LVCĒSES•FX•CLARO•OTHONV̄•/ ĪPATOR
ET•SAXŌĪÆ•DVCV̄•GENERE•ORTVS• / DV:
GHIBELLINORV̄•ROCCIÆ•AC•VILLÆPE-
TRAIÆ• / CŌES•EX•NIPOZANI•VOLOG-
NANIQ•DOMĪĪS•PRÆCLAR /•BRVĀCCĪŌRV̄
FĀĪLIÆ•AGŌMĒ•PRESTĀS• PATRIT•ET•C•
FLOR:NVC̄•CŌDITVS•SAXO•IACET•QVE•
CERĪS•FIE•POTITVS•SVO
Widener Collection
1942.9.118

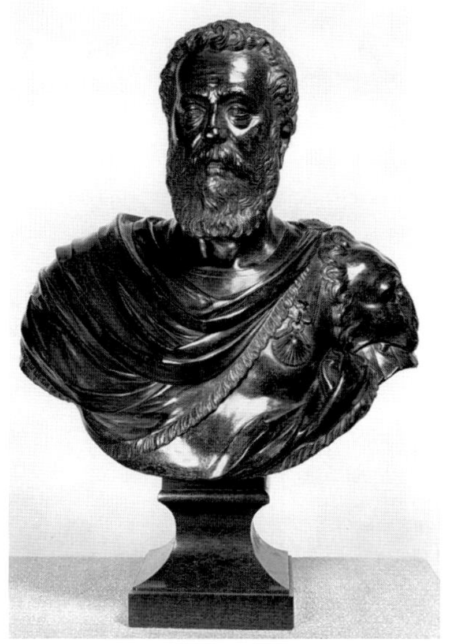

FLORENTINE OR NEAPOLITAN
16TH CENTURY

*Don Pedro Alvarez de Toledo (1484–1553)*, c. 1560/1600
Bronze, .646 x .627 x .394
(25 1/2 x 24 3/4 x 15 1/2)
Gift of Stanley Mortimer
1948.15.1

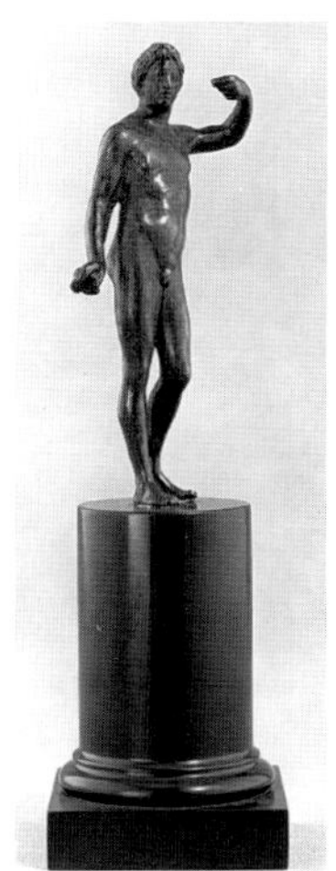

POSSIBLY FLORENTINE
16TH CENTURY

*Male Nude with Raised Left Arm*, second quarter 16th century
Bronze, .114 x .062 x .027
(4 1/2 x 2 7/16 x 1 1/16)
Samuel H. Kress Collection
1957.14.25

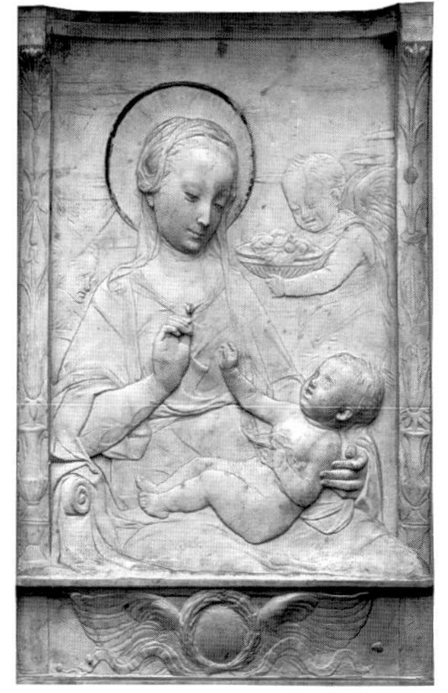

FLORENTINE 19TH CENTURY

*Madonna and Child*, c. 1860
Marble, .700 x .470 (27 1/2 x 18 1/2)
Andrew W. Mellon Collection
1937.1.114

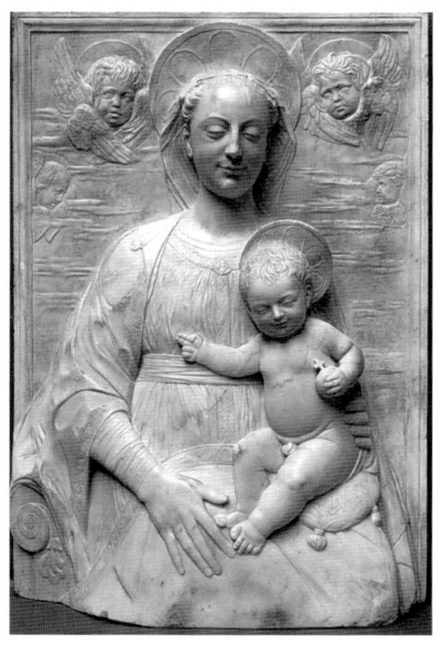

## FLORENTINE 19TH CENTURY, AFTER THE MASTER OF THE MARBLE MADONNAS

*Madonna and Child*, c. 1860/1900
Marble, .881 x .643 x .213
(34 5/8 x 25 1/4 x 8 3/8)
Samuel H. Kress Collection
1960.5.9

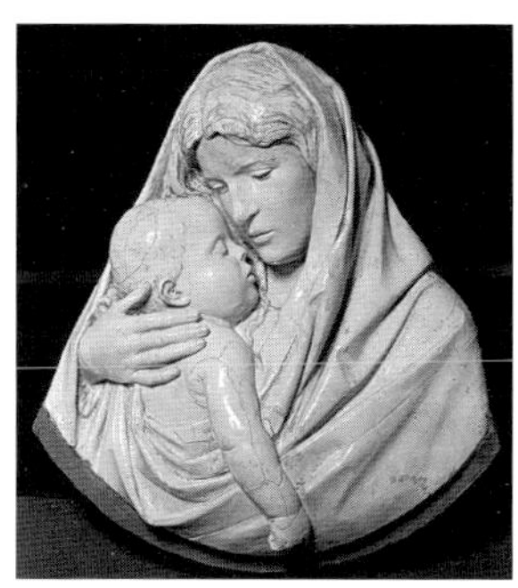

## FLORENTINE 19TH CENTURY

*Madonna with the Sleeping Child*, mid-19th century
Terra cotta, .620 x .566 x .214
(24 3/8 x 22 3/8 x 8 1/2)
Samuel H. Kress Collection
1961.9.96

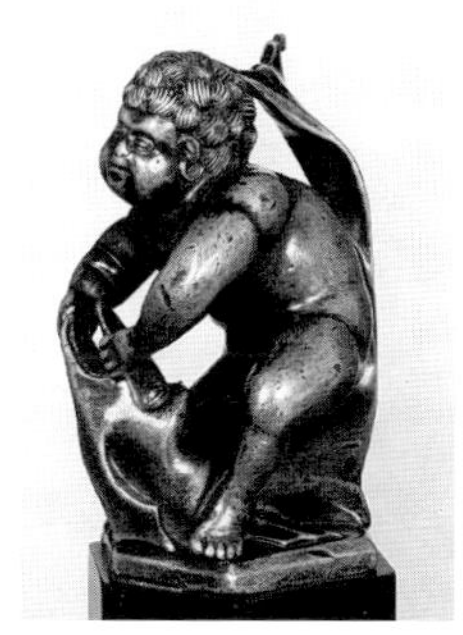

## ATTRIBUTED TO A FOLLOWER OF PETER FLÖTNER
German

*A Child on a Dolphin*, c. 1525/1550
Bronze, .145 x .089 x .096
(5 11/16 x 3 1/2 x 3 3/4)
Samuel H. Kress Collection
1957.14.42

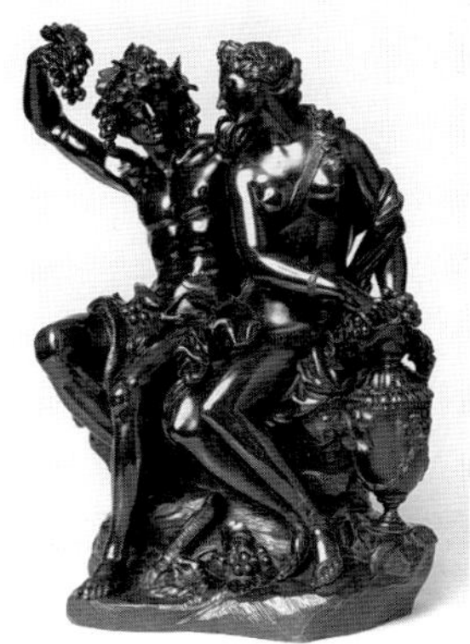

## GIOVANNI BATTISTA FOGGINI
Florentine, 1652–1725

*Bacchus and Ariadne*, 1711/1724
Bronze, .391 x .329 x .239
(15 3/8 x 13 x 9 3/8)
Ailsa Mellon Bruce Fund
1974.18.1

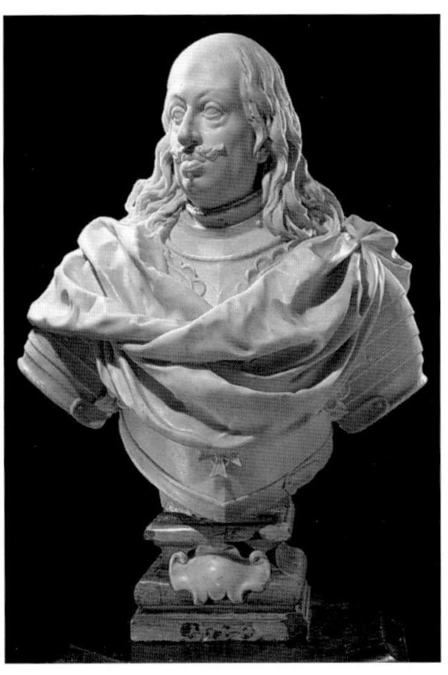

GIOVANNI BATTISTA FOGGINI
Florentine, 1652–1725

*Ferdinando II de' Medici, Grand Duke of Tuscany*, c. 1690
Marble, .795 x .732 x .400
(31 1/4 x 28 3/4 x 15 3/4)
Widener Collection
1942.9.129

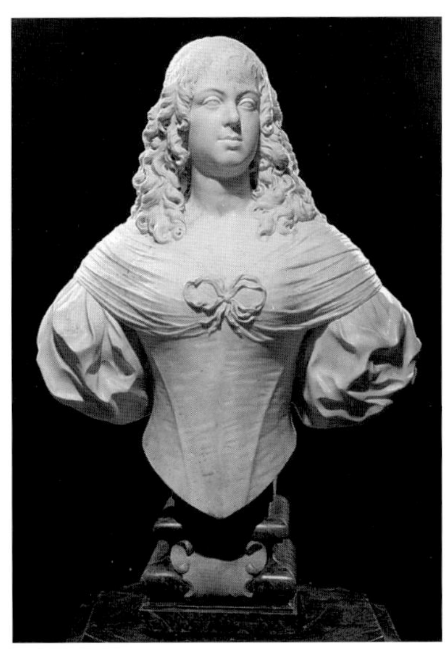

*Vittoria della Rovere, Wife of Ferdinando II*, c. 1690
Marble, .830 x .712 x .340
(32 5/8 x 28 x 13 3/8)
Widener Collection
1942.9.130

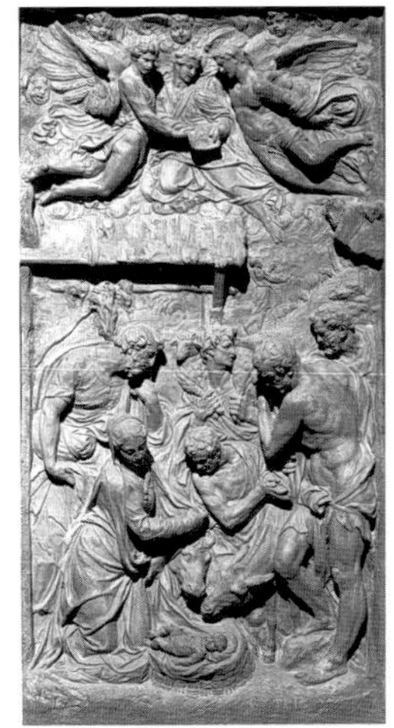

AFTER ANNIBALE FONTANA
Milanese

*The Adoration of the Shepherds*, c. 1625/1675
Terra cotta, 1.090 x .570 (43 x 22 1/2)
Samuel H. Kress Collection
1939.1.319

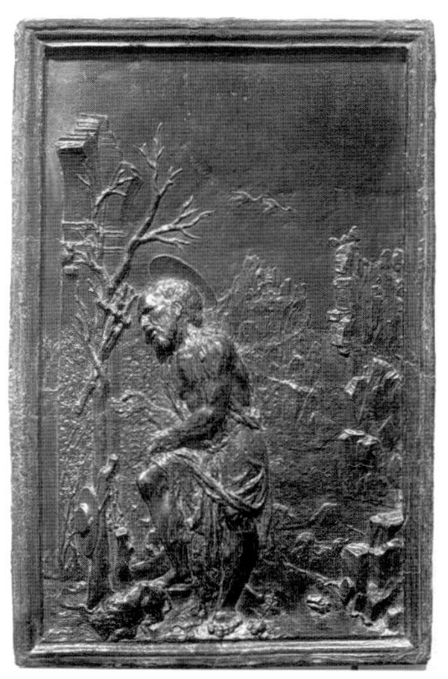

Francesco di Giorgio Martini
Sienese, 1439–1501/1502

*Saint Jerome*, c. 1477
Bronze, .550 x .373 (21 5/8 x 14 3/4)
Samuel H. Kress Collection
1957.14.12

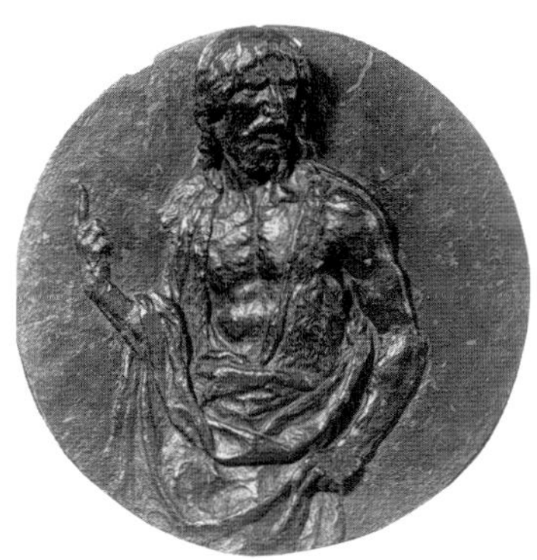

*Saint John the Baptist*, c. 1475/1485
Bronze, diameter: .198 (7 3/4)
Samuel H. Kress Collection
1957.14.248

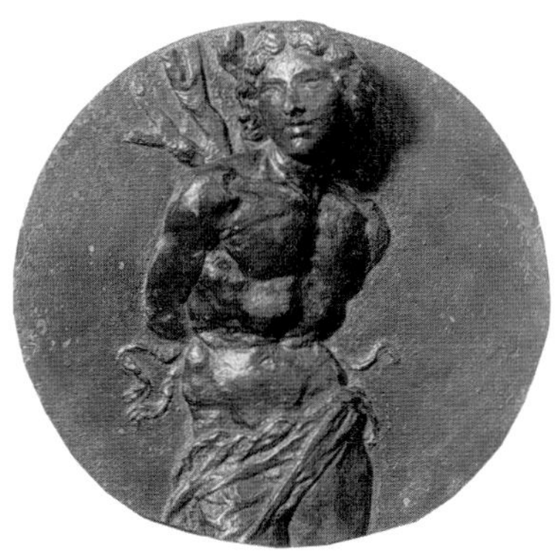

*Saint Sebastian*, c. 1475/1485
Bronze, diameter: .203 (8)
Samuel H. Kress Collection
1957.14.247

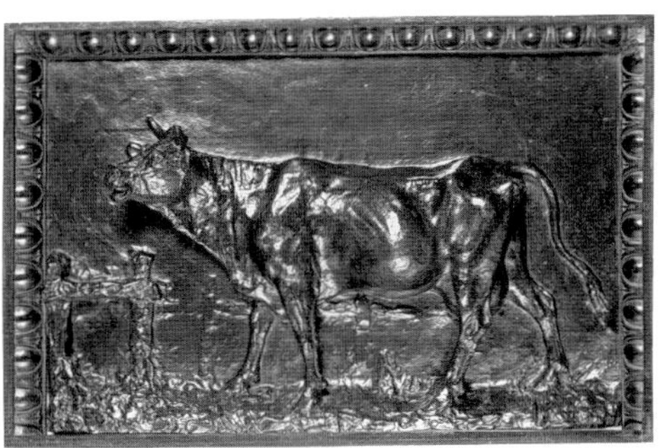

Christophe Fratin
French, c. 1800–1864

*Cow Lowing Over a Fence*, c. 1845/1864
Bronze, with frame: .280 x .440 x .060 (11 x 17 3/8 x 2 3/8); without frame: .253 x .405 x .060 (10 x 16 x 2 3/8)
Inscribed on verso at upper left: N 2
Collection of Mr. and Mrs. Paul Mellon
1983.65.1

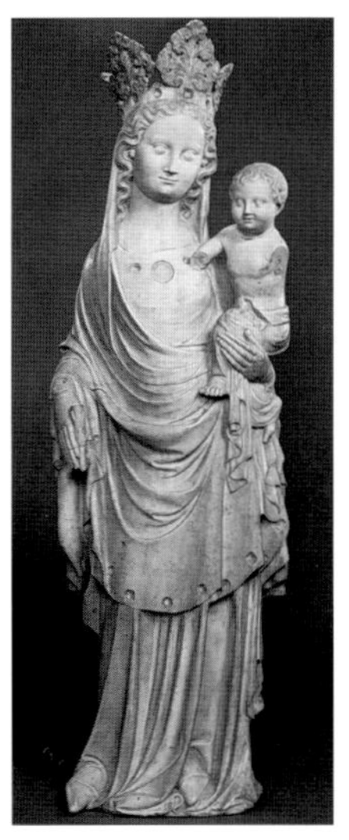

FRENCH 14TH CENTURY

*Virgin and Child,* c. 1325/1350
Marble, 1.008 x .312 x .178
(39 5/8 x 12 1/4 x 7)
Samuel H. Kress Collection
1961.9.99

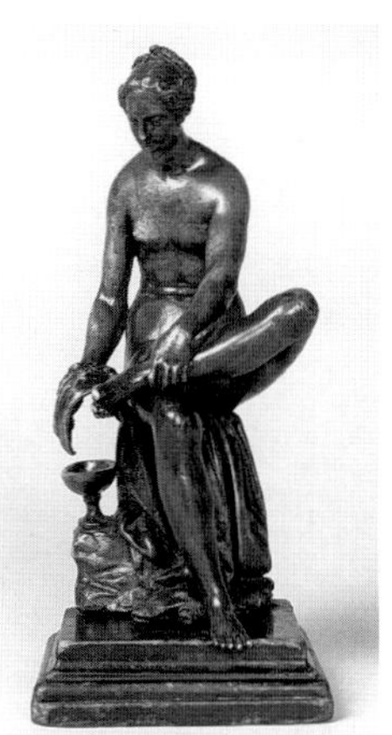

PROBABLY FRENCH (POSSIBLY BARTHÉLEMY PRIEUR)
17TH CENTURY

*Woman Bathing Her Foot,* early 17th century
Bronze, .187 x .079 x .092
(7 3/8 x 3 1/16 x 3 5/8)
Gift of David Edward Finley and Margaret Eustis Finley
1983.66.1

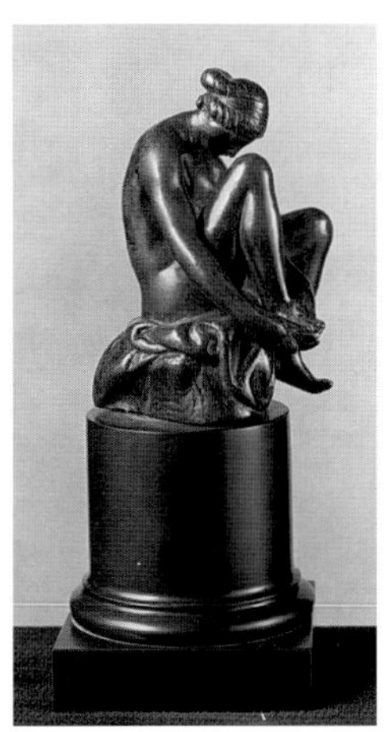

PROBABLY FRENCH (POSSIBLY BARTHÉLEMY PRIEUR)
17TH CENTURY

*Woman Cutting Her Nails,* early 17th century
Bronze, .082 x .051 x .060
(3 2/8 x 2 x 2 3/8)
Samuel H. Kress Collection
1957.14.24

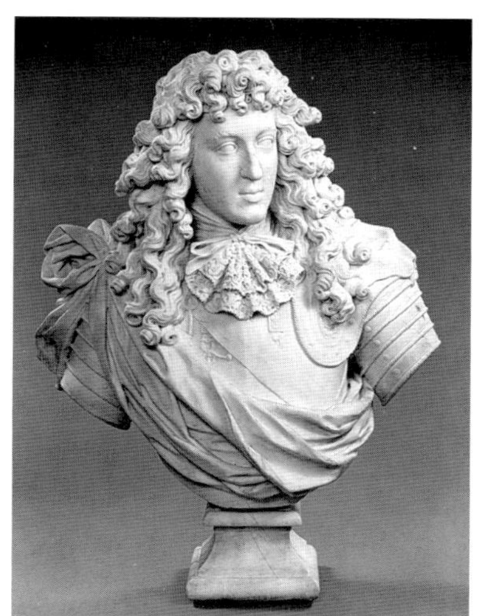

French 18th Century

*Louis, Duc de Bourgogne*
Marble, .750 x .753 x .464
($29^{1}/_{2}$ x $29^{5}/_{8}$ x $18^{1}/_{4}$)
Samuel H. Kress Collection
1960.5.8

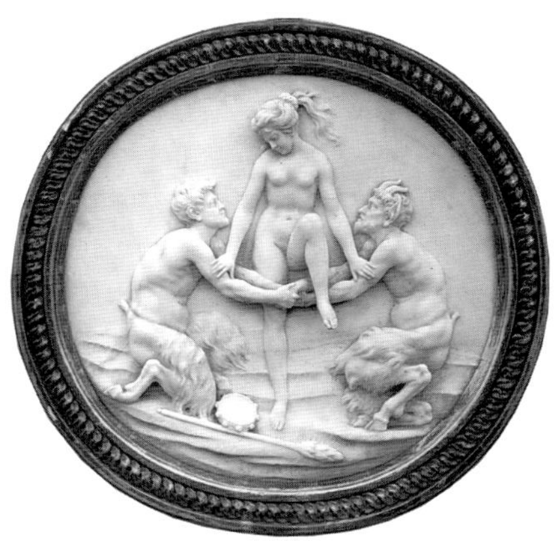

French 19th Century, after Jean-Honoré Fragonard

*Bacchanal*
Marble, .300 x .330 ($11^{3}/_{4}$ x 13)
Widener Collection
1942.9.108

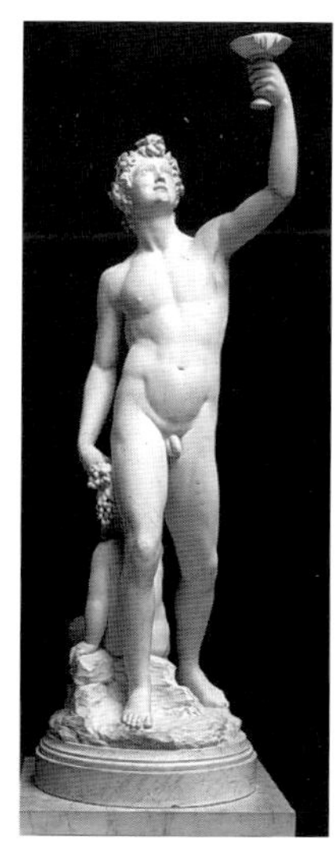

French 19th Century

*Bacchant*
Marble, 1.704 x .560 x .664
(67 x 22 x $26^{1}/_{8}$)
Samuel H. Kress Collection
1952.5.95

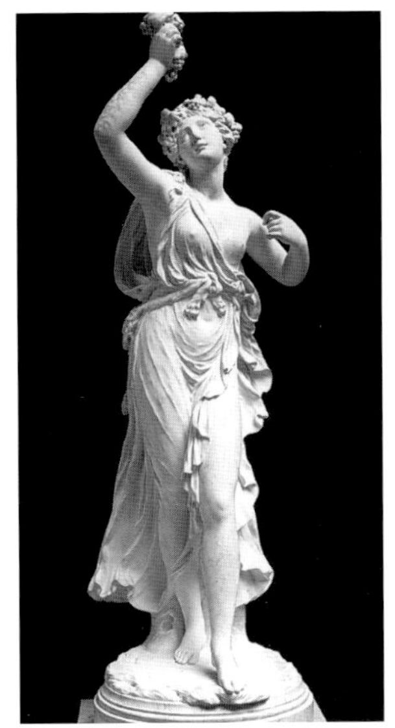

French 19th Century

*Bacchante*
Marble, 1.735 x .586 x .556
(68 1/4 x 23 x 21 7/8)
Samuel H. Kress Collection
1952.5.96

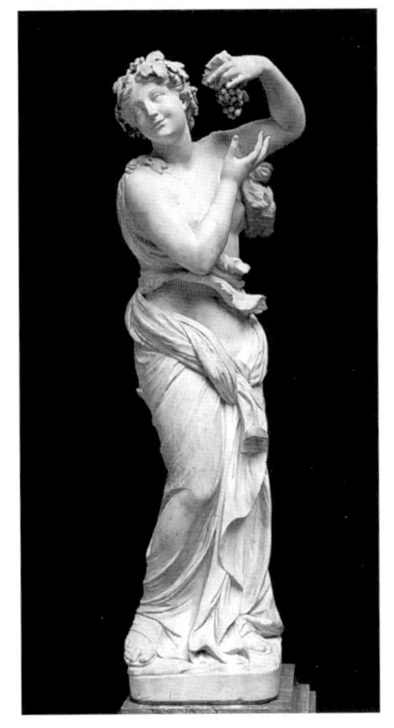

French 19th Century

*Bacchante*
Marble, 1.615 x .450 x .489
(63 1/2 x 17 5/8 x 19 1/4)
Inscribed on plaque on back, screwed to base: BACCHANTE / PROVENANT DE LA PROPRIÉTÉ / DE MADAME ELISABETH / SŒUR DU ROI LOUIS XVI / À VERSAILLES
Samuel H. Kress Collection
1952.5.97

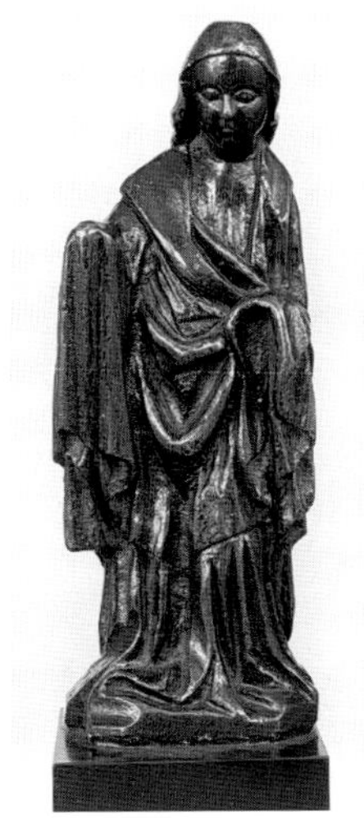

Probably French 19th Century

*The Virgin of the Annunciation*
Bronze, .172 x .067 x .043
(6 3/4 x 2 5/8 x 1 11/16)
Samuel H. Kress Collection
1957.14.30

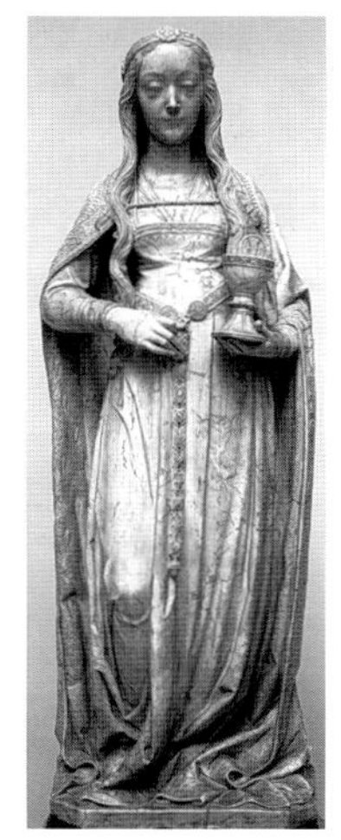

PROBABLY FRENCH OR BELGIAN
19TH CENTURY

*Saint Barbara*, c. 1860/1910
Alabaster, 1.209 x .462 x .362
(47 1/2 x 18 1/8 x 14 1/4)
Samuel H. Kress Collection
1952.5.102

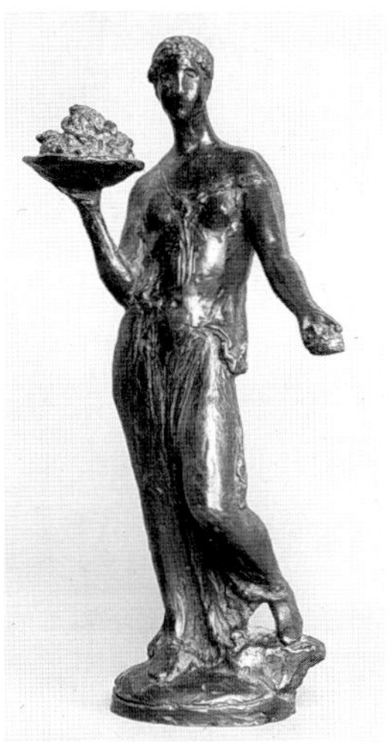

DANIEL CHESTER FRENCH
American, 1850–1931

*Draped Female Figure*, c. 1922/1929, cast 1932
Bronze, .260 x .146 x .105
(10 1/4 x 5 3/4 x 4 1/8)
Inscribed on rear of base: © D.C. FRENCH; foundry mark: QIAV GORHAM CO.
Gift of Mr. and Mrs. Robert Hilton Simmons
1987.69.1

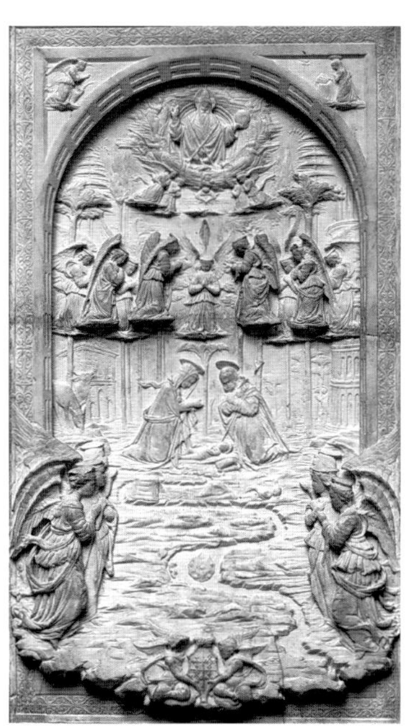

DOMENICO GAGINI
Lombard, active c. 1449–1492

*The Nativity*, c. 1460
Marble, .900 x .520
(35 1/2 x 20 1/2)
Samuel H. Kress Collection
1939.1.328

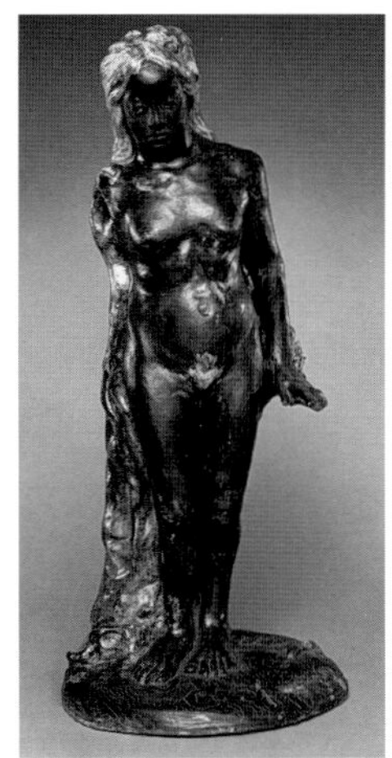

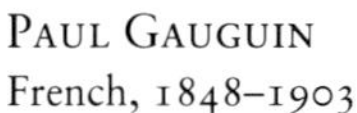

Paul Gauguin
French, 1848–1903

*Eve,* 1890
Ceramic, painted, .606 x .279 x .273
($23^{7}/_{8}$ x 11 x $10^{3}/_{4}$)
Inscribed on base near left foot:
P GAUGUIN
Ailsa Mellon Bruce Fund
1970.30.1

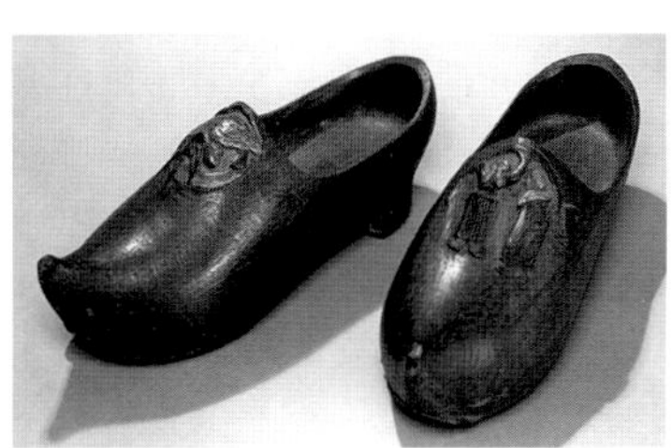

*Pair of Wooden Shoes,* 1889
Wood, polychromed, and leather
left: .129 x .327 x .113
($5^{1}/_{8}$ x $12^{7}/_{8}$ x $4^{1}/_{2}$),
right: .128 x .327 x .112
(5 x $12^{7}/_{8}$ x $4^{3}/_{8}$)
Chester Dale Collection
1963.10.239.b and a

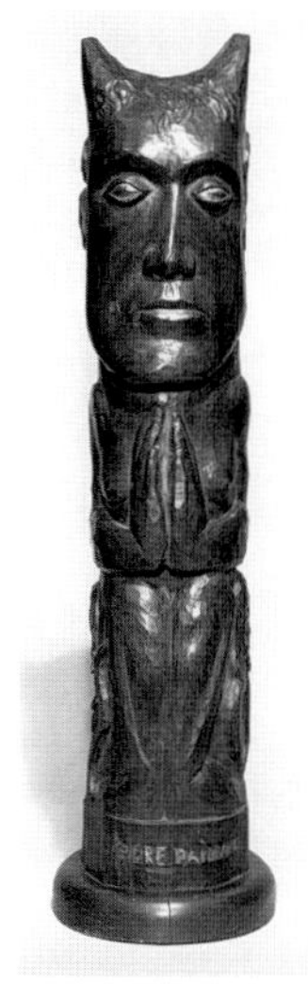

*Père Paillard,* c. 1902
Wood, .679 x .180 x .207
($26^{3}/_{4}$ x $7^{1}/_{8}$ x $8^{1}/_{8}$)
Inscribed on front of base:
PERE PAILLARD PGO.
Chester Dale Collection
1963.10.238

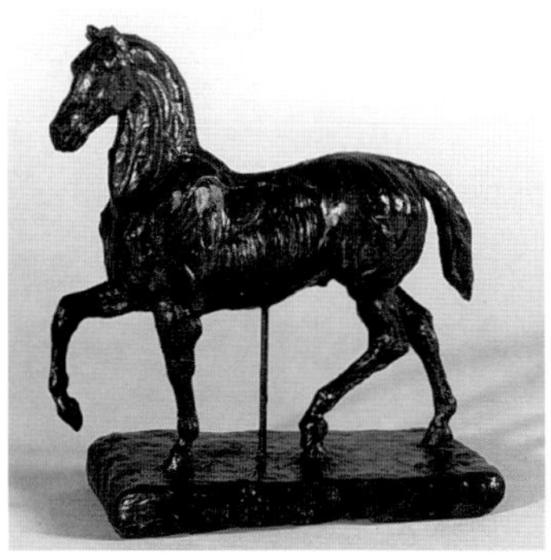

Théodore Gericault
French, 1791–1824

*Flayed Horse I,* c. 1820/1824
Wax, .232 x .217 x .117
($9^{1}/_{8}$ x $8^{1}/_{2}$ x $4^{5}/_{8}$)
Inscribed on top of base, along edge of proper left side: GERICAULT (some letters indistinct); GE
Collection of Mr. and Mrs. Paul Mellon
1980.44.7

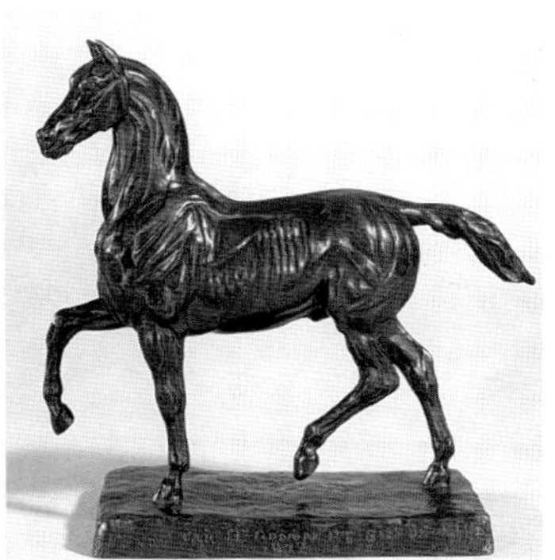

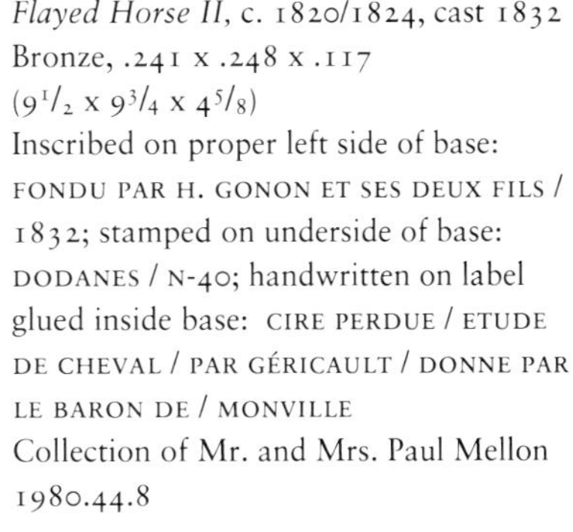

*Flayed Horse II*, c. 1820/1824, cast 1832
Bronze, .241 x .248 x .117
($9^{1}/_{2}$ x $9^{3}/_{4}$ x $4^{5}/_{8}$)
Inscribed on proper left side of base: FONDU PAR H. GONON ET SES DEUX FILS / 1832; stamped on underside of base: DODANES / N-40; handwritten on label glued inside base: CIRE PERDUE / ETUDE DE CHEVAL / PAR GÉRICAULT / DONNE PAR LE BARON DE / MONVILLE
Collection of Mr. and Mrs. Paul Mellon
1980.44.8

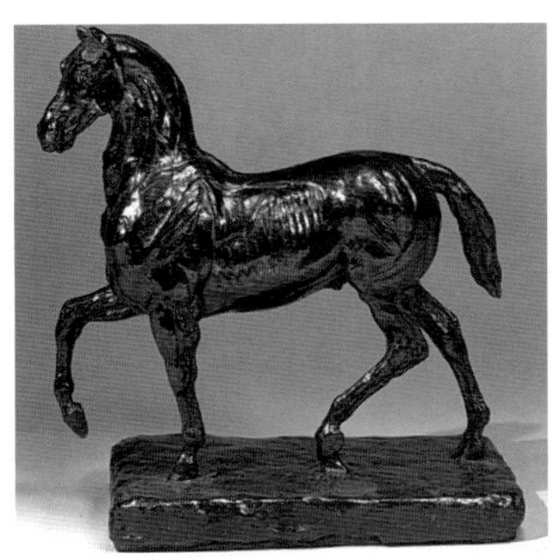

*Flayed Horse III*, c. 1820/1824, cast 1959
Bronze, .232 x .217 x .116
($9^{1}/_{8}$ x $8^{1}/_{2}$ x $4^{5}/_{8}$)
Inscribed on top of base, rear proper right corner: 7/15; foundry mark on rear side of base: CIRE / C. VALSUANI / PERDUE
Collection of Mr. and Mrs. Paul Mellon
1980.44.9

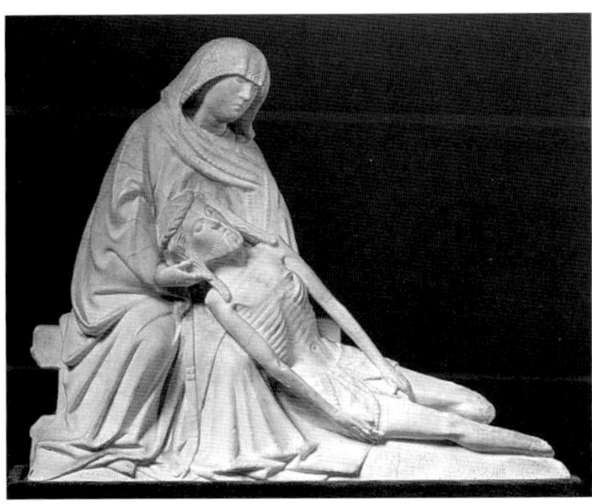

## GERMAN OR NETHERLANDISH 15TH CENTURY

*Pietà*, c. 1450/1500
Alabaster, .299 x .362 x .064
($11^{3}/_{4}$ x $14^{1}/_{4}$ x $2^{1}/_{2}$)
Gift of Mrs. Ralph Harman Booth
1942.11.2

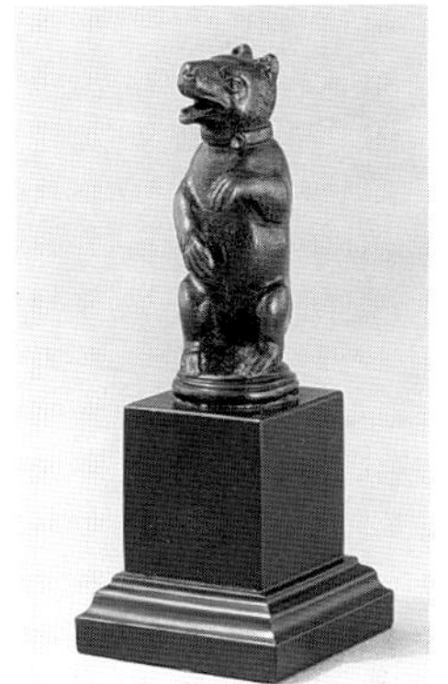

## GERMAN 16TH CENTURY

*A Bear*, second half 16th century
Bronze, .066 x .024 x .026
($2^{9}/_{16}$ x $^{15}/_{16}$ x 1)
Samuel H. Kress Collection
1957.14.81

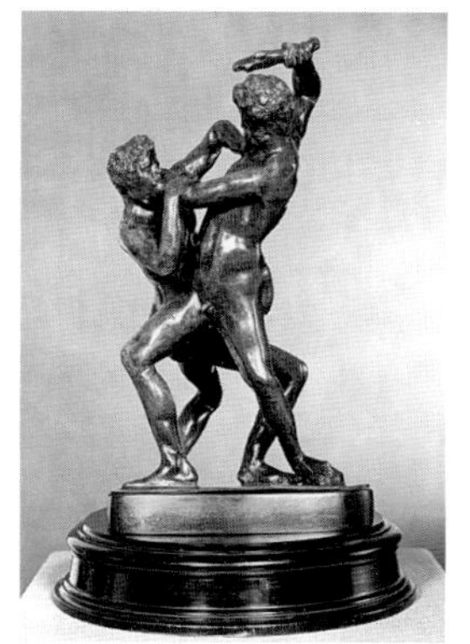

German 16th Century

*Samson Slaying the Philistine,* late 16th century
Bronze, .481 x .200 x .229 (19 x $8^3/_4$ x 9)
Widener Collection
1942.9.102

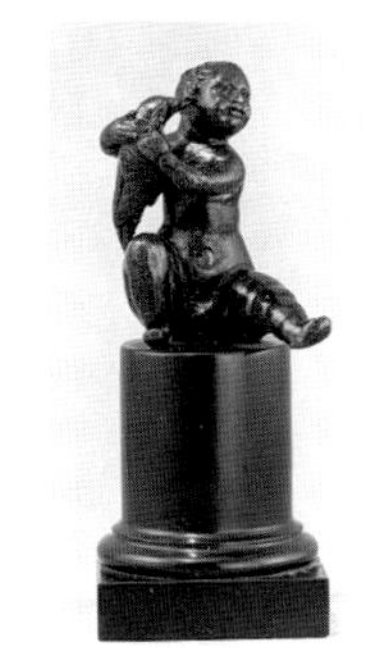

German 16th Century (possibly Nuremberg)

*A Child with a Crow,* first half 16th century
Bronze with traces of gilding
.064 x .037 x .053 ($2^9/_{16}$ x $1^7/_{16}$ x $2^1/_8$)
Samuel H. Kress Collection
1957.14.40

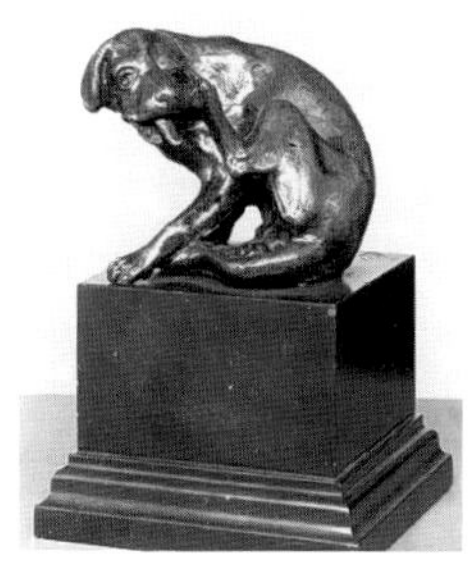

German 16th Century (possibly Nuremberg)

*A Dog Scratching,* second quarter 16th century
Bronze, .059 x .092 x .087
($2^5/_{16}$ x $3^5/_8$ x $3^7/_{16}$)
Samuel H. Kress Collection
1957.14.78

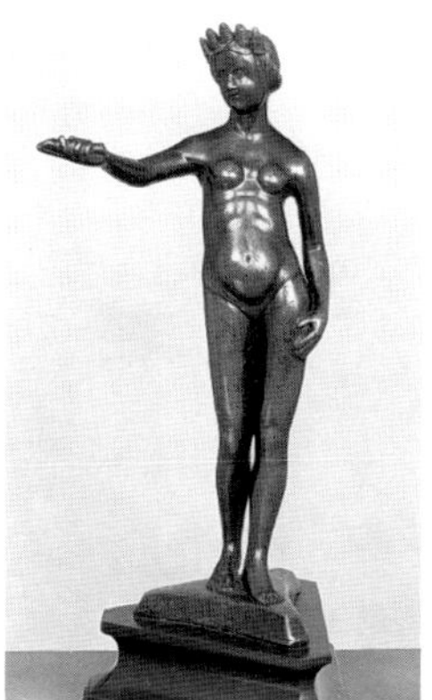

German 16th Century (Southern)

*Venus,* c. 1500
Bronze, parcel gilt, .230 x .113 x .102
($9^1/_8$ x $4^1/_2$ x 4)
Samuel H. Kress Collection
1957.14.31

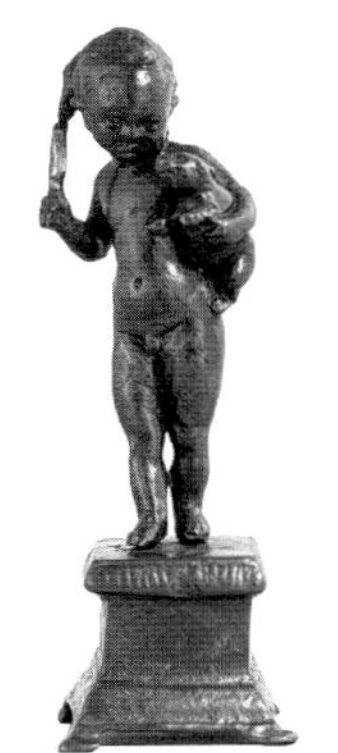

### GERMAN 16TH CENTURY (POSSIBLY SOUTHERN)

*A Child with a Puppy*, first half 16th century
Bronze, .108 x .034 x .026
($4\frac{1}{4}$ x $1\frac{5}{16}$ x $1\frac{1}{16}$)
Samuel H. Kress Collection
1957.14.43

### GERMAN 17TH CENTURY

*A Dancing Faun*, c. 1600
Bronze, .231 x .111 x .108
($9\frac{1}{8}$ x $4\frac{3}{8}$ x $4\frac{1}{4}$)
Widener Collection
1942.9.120

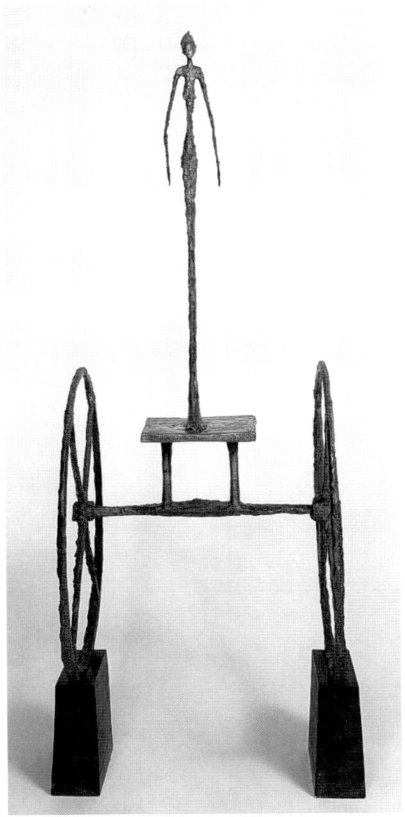

### ALBERTO GIACOMETTI
Swiss, 1901–1966

*The Chariot*, 1950
Bronze with wood base
1.641 x .686 x .670 ($64\frac{5}{8}$ x 27 x $26\frac{3}{8}$)
Inscribed on horizontal plate supporting figure, right edge: A GIACOMETTI; stamped on rear edge of same plate: 6/6; foundry mark on rear edge of same plate: ALEXIS. RUDIER / FONDEUR. PARIS
Gift of Enid A. Haupt
1977.47.2

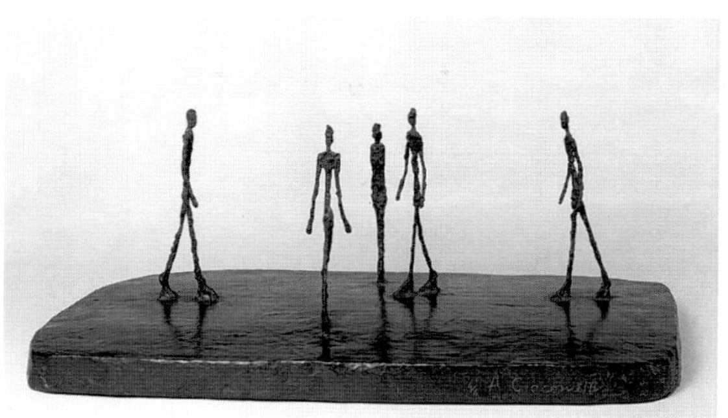

## Alberto Giacometti
Swiss, 1901–1966

*The City Square,* 1948/1949
Bronze, .240 x .647 x .434
($9^{1}/_{2}$ x $25^{1}/_{2}$ x $17^{1}/_{8}$)
Inscribed on edge of base, left back: 4/6 A. GIACOMETTI; foundry mark on base, right front corner: ALEX RUDIER / FONDEUR.PARIS
Gift of Enid A. Haupt
1977.47.3

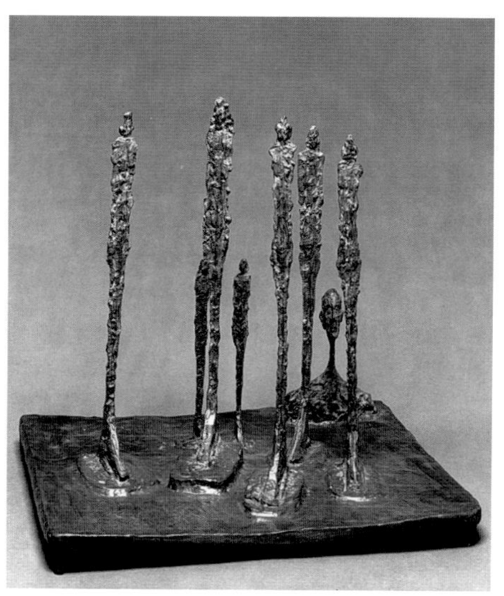

*The Forest,* 1950
Bronze, painted, .558 x .611 x .489
(22 x 24 x $19^{1}/_{4}$)
Inscribed on right edge of base: A. GIACOMETTI; stamped: 6/6; foundry mark on rear edge of base: .ALEXIS RUDIER. / .FONDEUR.PARIS.
Gift of Enid A. Haupt
1977.47.4

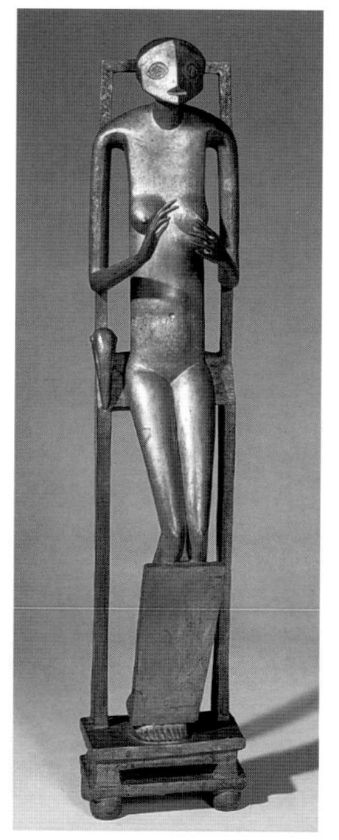

*The Invisible Object (Hands Holding the Void),* 1935
Bronze, 1.530 x .326 x .298
($60^{1}/_{4}$ x $12^{7}/_{8}$ x $11^{3}/_{4}$)
Inscribed on top of bottom base, at rear: ALBERTO GIACOMETTI / 1935; on rear edge of bottom base: 3/6; foundry mark on rear edge of bottom base: ALEXIS.RUDIER / FONDEUR.PARIS
Ailsa Mellon Bruce Fund
1973.27.1

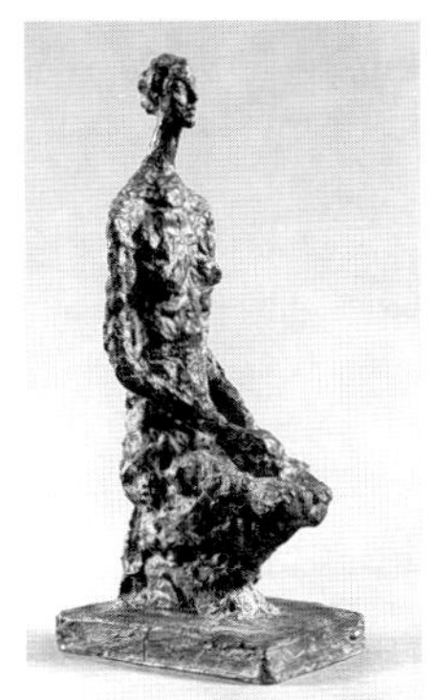

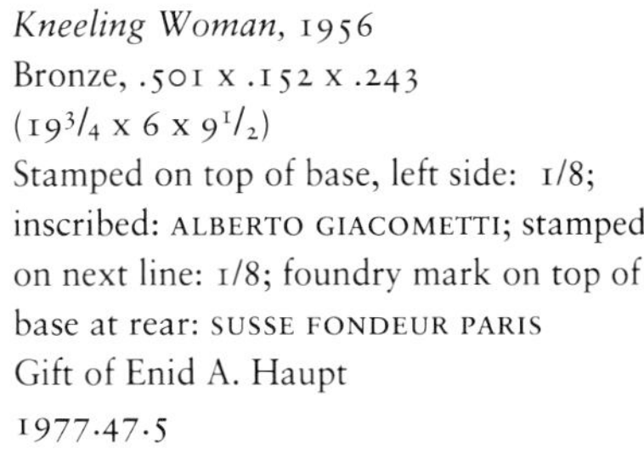

*Kneeling Woman,* 1956
Bronze, .501 x .152 x .243
(19 3/4 x 6 x 9 1/2)
Stamped on top of base, left side: 1/8; inscribed: ALBERTO GIACOMETTI; stamped on next line: 1/8; foundry mark on top of base at rear: SUSSE FONDEUR PARIS
Gift of Enid A. Haupt
1977.47.5

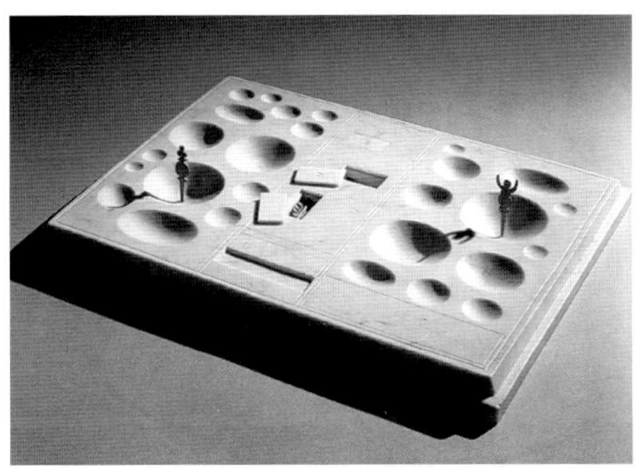

*No More Play,* 1931–1932
Marble, wood, bronze, .041 x .580 x .452
(1 5/8 x 22 7/8 x 17 3/4)
Inscribed on top in corner, in reverse script: ON NE JOUE PLUS
Gift (Partial and Promised) of Raymond D. Nasher, in Honor of the 50th Anniversary of the National Gallery of Art
1991.40.1

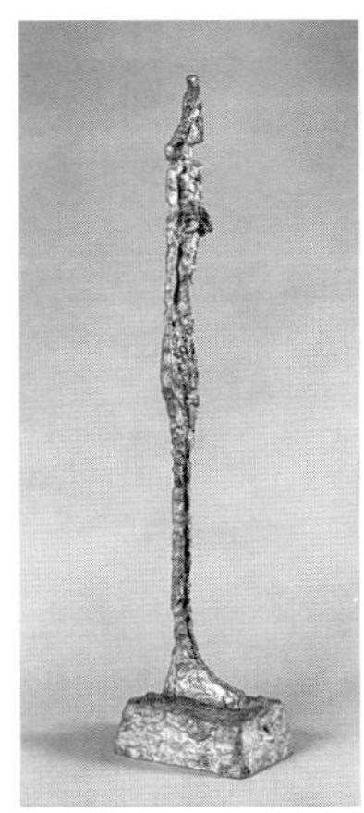

*Standing Woman,* c. 1947
Bronze, 1.181 x .210 x .283
(46 1/2 x 8 1/4 x 11 1/8)
Stamped on top of base, rear right corner: 2/6; inscribed on next line: ALBERTO GIACOMETTI; foundry mark on top of base, rear left corner: SUSSE FONDEUR PARIS
Gift of Enid A. Haupt
1977.47.6

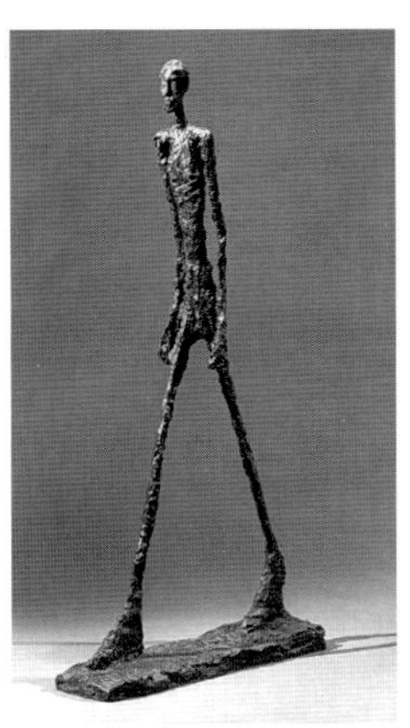

*Walking Man II,* 1960
Bronze, 1.885 x .279 x 1.107
(74 1/4 x 11 x 43 5/8)
Inscribed on top of base, right side: ALBERTO GIACOMETTI / 1/6; foundry mark on top of base, rear: SUSSE FONDEUR PARIS
Gift of Enid A. Haupt
1977.47.7

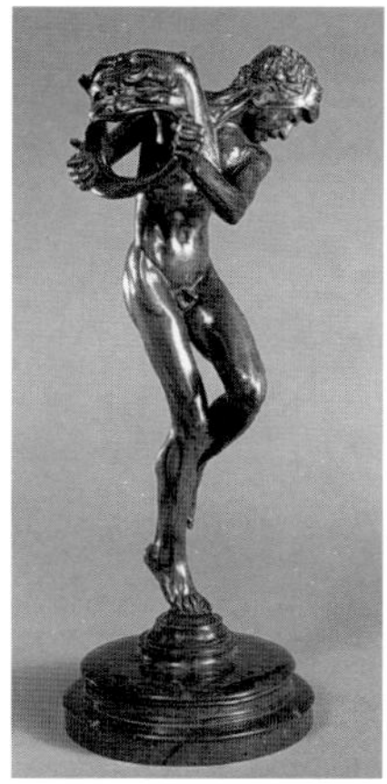

SIR ALFRED GILBERT
British, 1854–1934

*Comedy and Tragedy: 'Sic Vita'*, 1892
Bronze, .345 x .156 x .137
($13^{5}/_{8}$ x $6^{1}/_{8}$ x $5^{3}/_{8}$)
Inscribed on base behind figure's right foot: (artist's initials in a cipher)
Pepita Milmore Memorial Fund
1984.67.1

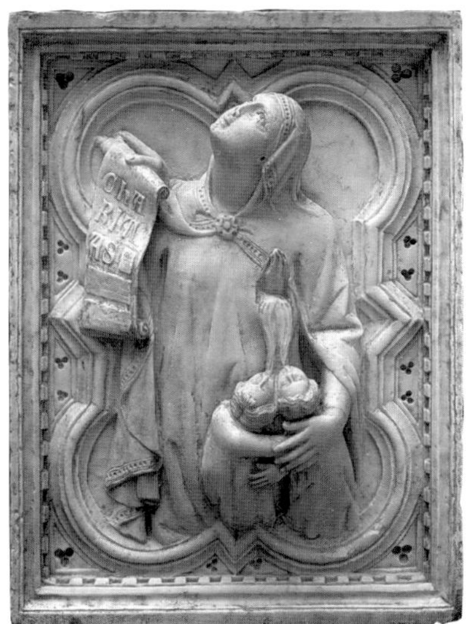

GIOVANNI DI BALDUCCIO
Pisan, active 1318/1319–1349

*Charity*, c. 1330
Marble, .451 x .353 ($17^{3}/_{4}$ x $13^{7}/_{8}$)
Inscribed on scroll: CHA / RIT / AS
Samuel H. Kress Collection
1960.5.4

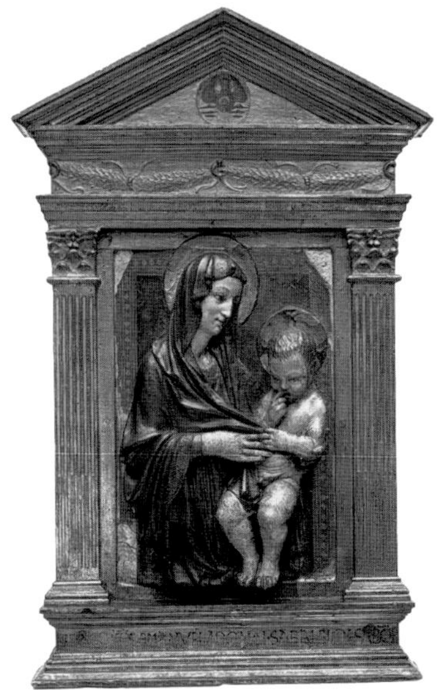

CIRCLE OF GIOVANNI DI TURINO
Sienese

*Madonna and Child*, c. 1430
Terra cotta, painted and gilt, without frame: .667 x .457 ($26^{1}/_{4}$ x 18)
Inscribed on frame across bottom: IESVS• XRS•EMANVEL•ADONAI•SABAI•ELOI• SABOT
Samuel H. Kress Collection
1961.9.103

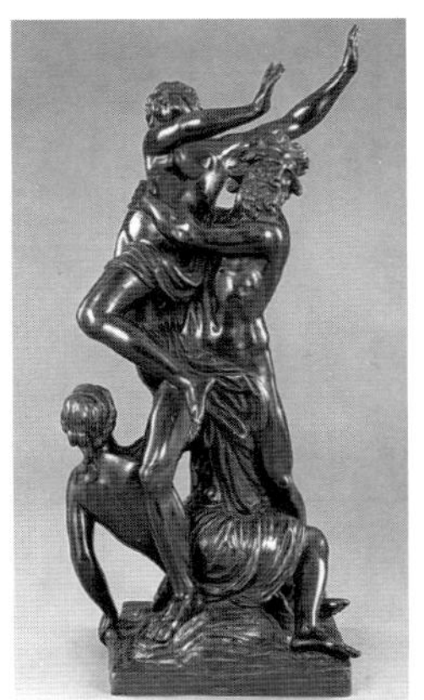

François Girardon
French, 1628–1715

*Pluto and Persephone (Allegory of Fire)*, 1677/1699, bronze reduction made and cast c. 1693–1716
Bronze, .550 x .254 x .229
(21 5/8 x 10 3/4 x 9 3/8)
Gift of Asbjorn R. Lunde
1986.74.1

*See also:* Gaspard Marsy II and Anselme Flamen, *Boreas and Orithyia (Allegory of Air)*, 1986.74.2

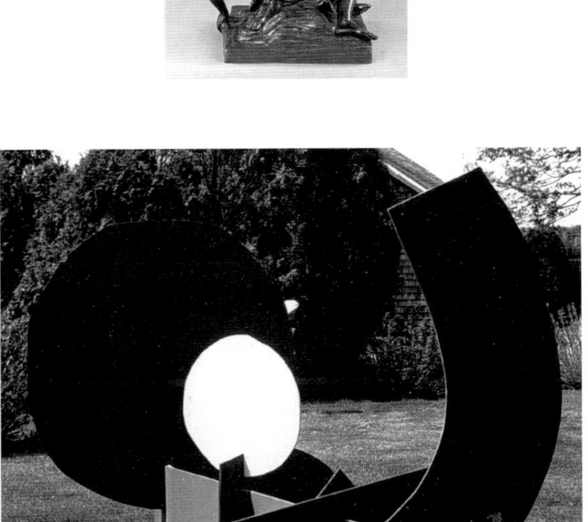

Adolf Gottlieb
American, 1903–1974

*Wall*, 1968
Aluminum, painted
2.080 x 3.086 x 1.905
(81 7/8 x 121 1/2 x 75)
Gift of Adolph and Esther Gottlieb Foundation, Inc.
1990.8.1

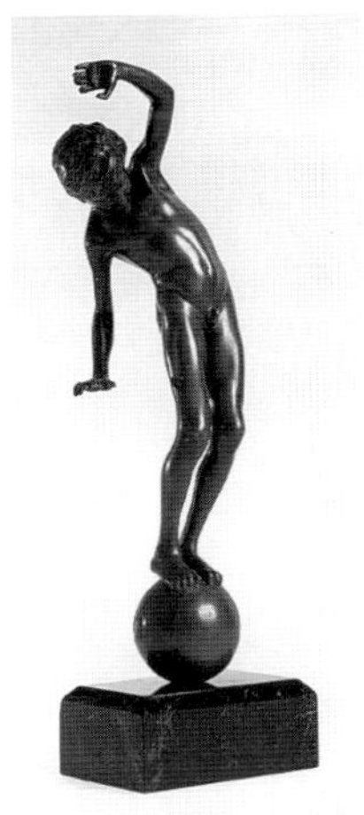

Johannes Götz
German, 1865–1934

*Boy Balancing on a Ball*, 1888
Bronze, .246 x .077 x .073
(9 3/4 x 3 x 2 7/8)
Inscribed on ball, below right foot:
J. GÖTZ / BERLIN
Gift of Dr. Dieter Erich Meyer
1976.3.1

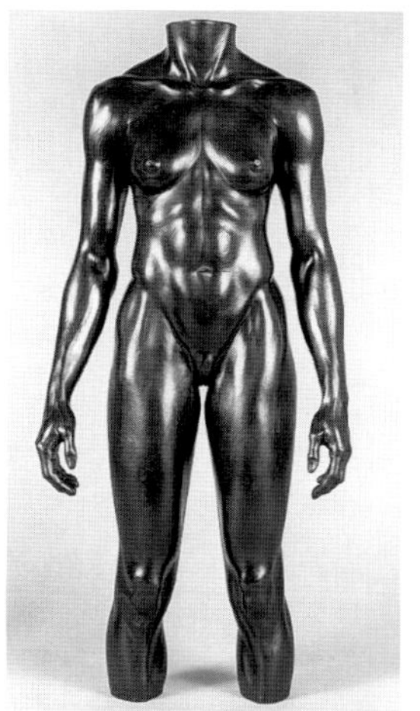

ROBERT GRAHAM
American, born 1938

*Olympic Torso (Female),* 1983
Cast bronze, .673 x .318 x .178
(26 1/2 x 12 1/2 x 7)
Anonymous Gift
1985.30.1

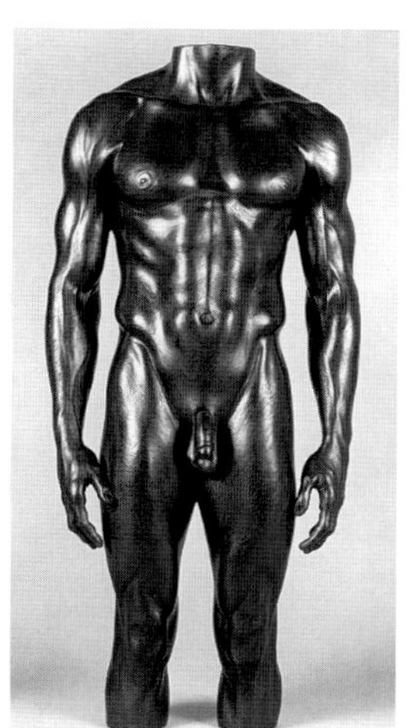

*Olympic Torso (Male),* 1983
Cast bronze, .679 x .330 x .159
(26 3/4 x 13 x 6 1/4)
Gift of Lila Acheson Wallace
1985.37.1

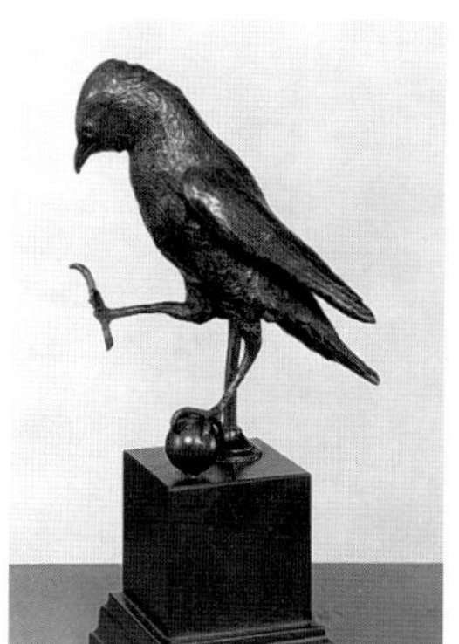

CASPAR GRAS
German, probably 1590–1674

*A Crow*
Bronze, .112 x .047 x .076
(4 3/8 x 1 13/16 x 3)
Samuel H. Kress Collection
1957.14.85

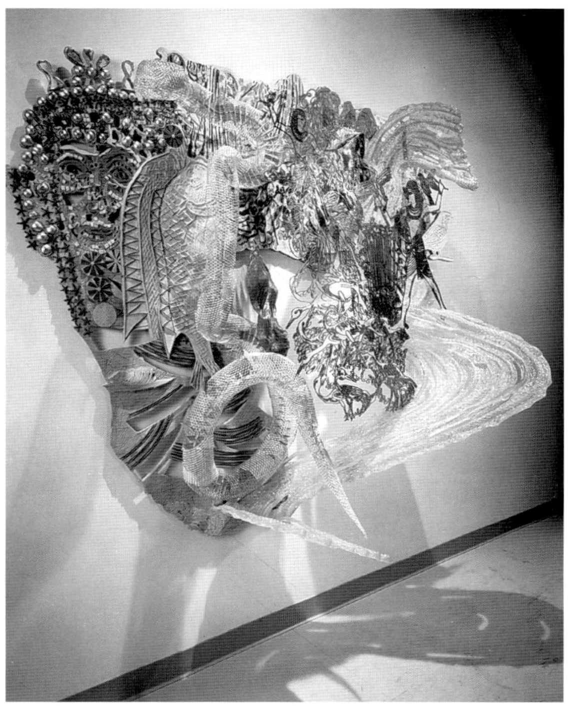

Nancy Graves
American, born 1940

*Canoptic Legerdemain,* 1990
Brushed stainless steel, aluminum mesh, cast resin, cast paper, aluminum panels, cast epoxy, color lithograph
2.159 x 2.413 x .939 (85 x 95 x 37)
Gift of Graphicstudio/University of South Florida and the Artist in Honor of the 50th Anniversary of the National Gallery of Art
1990.72.5

Maquette for 1990.72.5 is Nancy Graves, *Maquette for "Canoptic Legerdemain,"* 1991.75.178

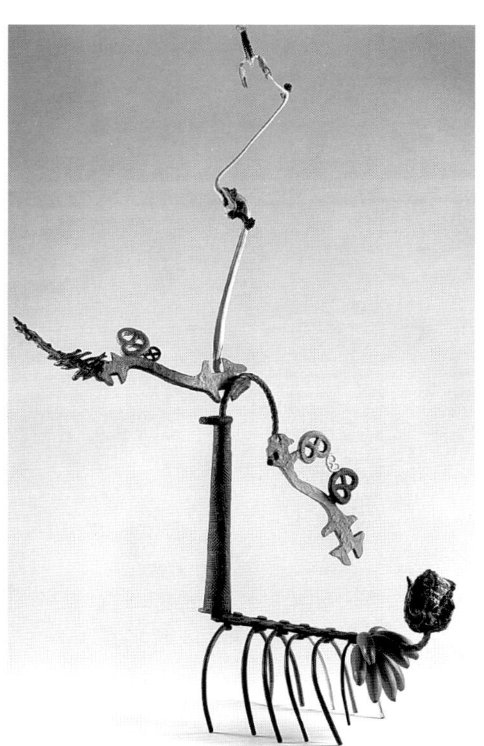

*Spinner,* 1985
Bronze with polychrome patina and glass enamel, 1.346 x .889 x .298 (53 x 35 x 11¾); piece is in two parts
Inscribed on yellow horizontal element: "SPINNER" N.S. GRAVES 8–85
Gift of Lila Acheson Wallace
1986.19.1

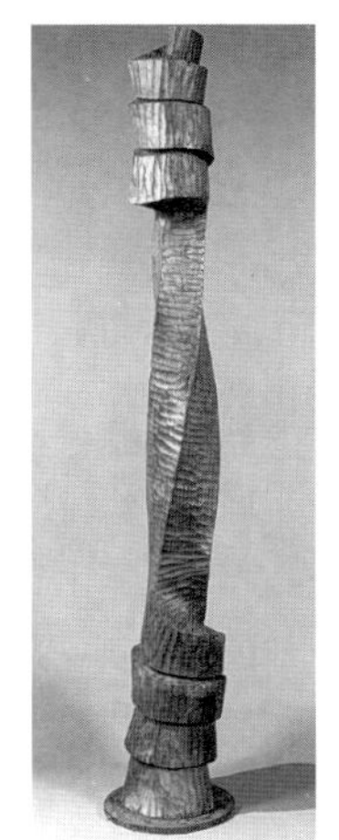

James Garrison Hagan
American, born 1936

*Column IV,* 1974
Wood, 2.385 x .362 x .321
(93 7/8 x 14 1/4 x 12 5/8)
Anonymous Gift
1974.89.1

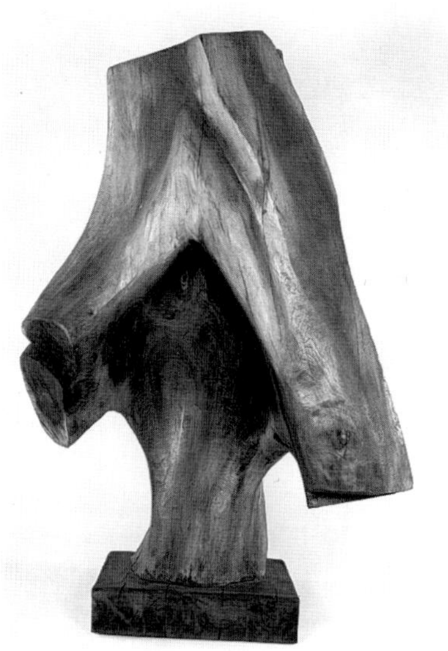

Raoul Hague
American, born 1905

*Schwamengang Hills,* 1968
Wood, 1.676 x 1.143 x .965
(66 x 45 x 38)
Gift of Cynthia Hazen Polsky
1989.30.1

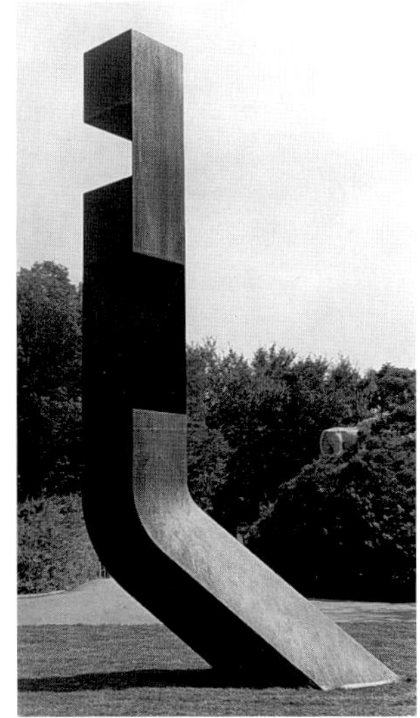

Alfredo Halegua
American, born 1930

*America,* 1970
Cor-ten steel, 7.620 x 3.658 x 1.219
(300 x 144 x 48)
Donated in memory of Andre Lovell Roberts, 1894–1971
1977.28.1

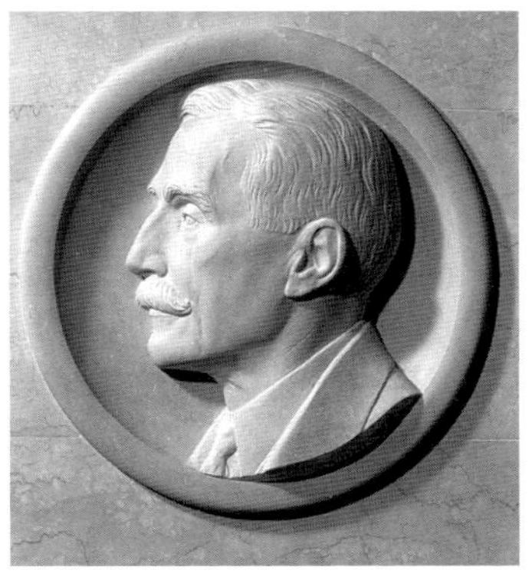

WALKER HANCOCK
American, born 1901

*Andrew W. Mellon,* 1954
Marble, diameter: .559 (22)
Inscribed under left shoulder: WALKER HANCOCK 1954
Andrew W. Mellon Collection
1954.21.1

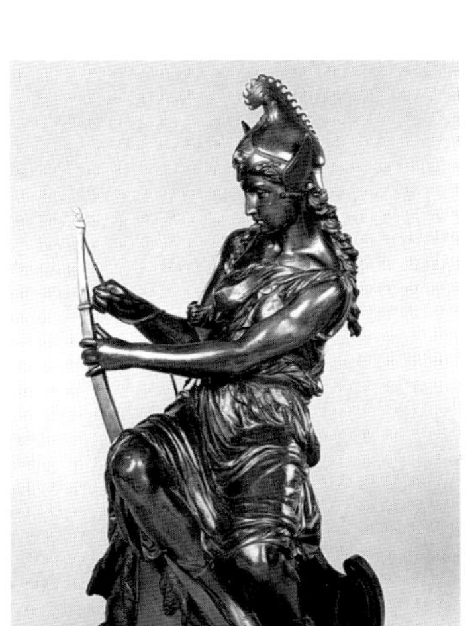

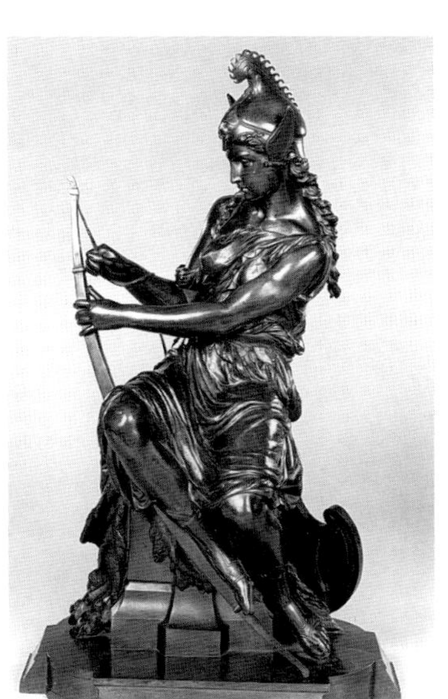

PIERRE-EUGÈNE-EMILE HÉBERT
French, 1828–1893

*Queen Sémiramis Called to Arms,* 1853
Bronze, .653 x .406 x .266 ($25\frac{3}{4}$ x 17 x $10\frac{1}{2}$)
Inscribed on top of base near left foot: EMILE HEBERT
Pepita Milmore Memorial Fund
1987.25.1

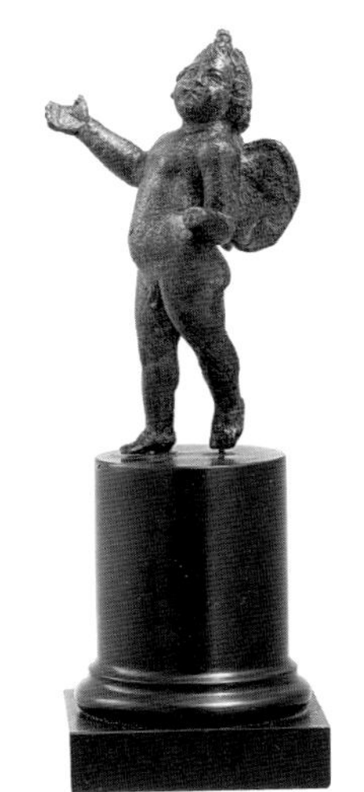

HELLENISTIC OR ROMAN
2D CENTURY B.C.–1ST CENTURY A.D.

*Striding Cupid*
Bronze, .076 x .048 x .032 (3 x $1\frac{7}{8}$ x $1\frac{1}{4}$)
Samuel H. Kress Collection
1957.14.52

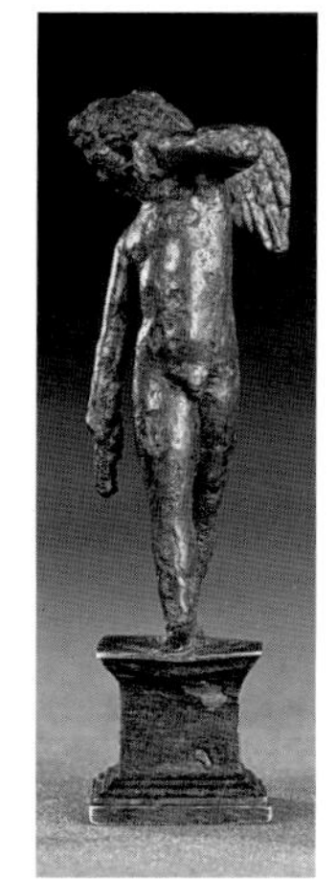

Hellenistic or Roman
2d Century B.C.–1st Century A.D.

*Winged Child Carrying a Torch*
Bronze, with base: .106 x .034 x .035
($4^{3}/_{16}$ x $1^{3}/_{4}$ x $1^{3}/_{8}$)
Samuel H. Kress Collection
1957.14.51

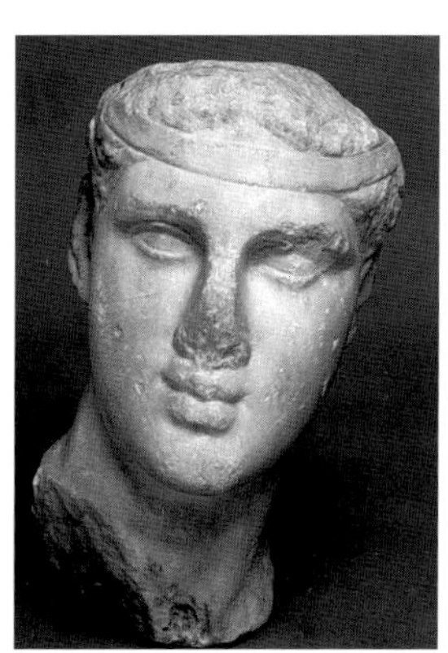

Probably Hellenistic
School, Egypt

*Head of a Youth (Dionysos or a Follower?)*, c. 220/100 B.C.
Marble, .261 x .149 x .157
($10^{1}/_{4}$ x $5^{3}/_{4}$ x $6^{1}/_{8}$)
Gift of Mrs. Ralph Harman Booth
1942.11.1

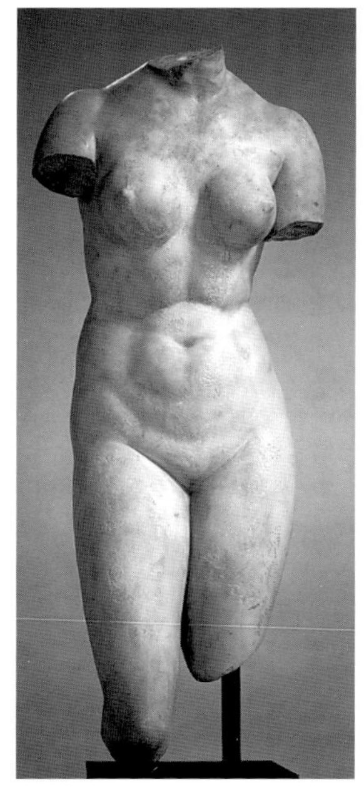

Possibly Hellenistic or Roman
2d Century B.C.–1st Century A.D.

*Torso of Aphrodite*, c. 200 B.C./150 A.D.
Marble, .981 x .426 x .334
($38^{5}/_{8}$ x $16^{3}/_{4}$ x $13^{1}/_{8}$)
Gift of Barbara Harrison Wescott in memory of the Hon. Francis Burton Harrison
1969.9.1

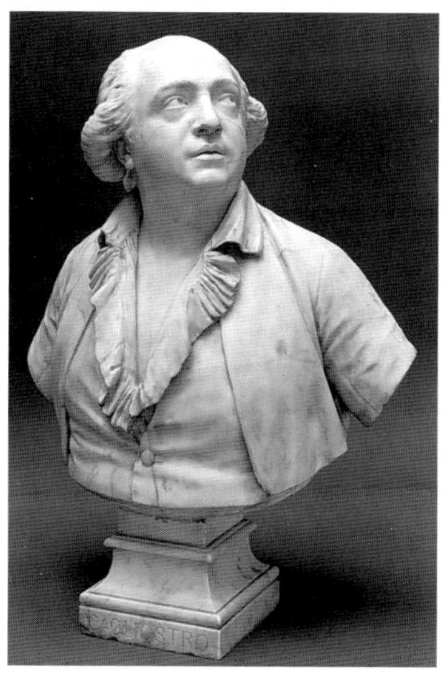

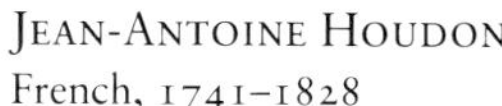

JEAN-ANTOINE HOUDON
French, 1741–1828

*Giuseppe Balsamo, Comte di Cagliostro,* 1786
Marble, .629 x .589 x .343
($24\frac{3}{4}$ x 23 x $13\frac{1}{2}$)
Inscribed on truncated right arm:
HOUDON / F. / 1786.
Samuel H. Kress Collection
1952.5.103

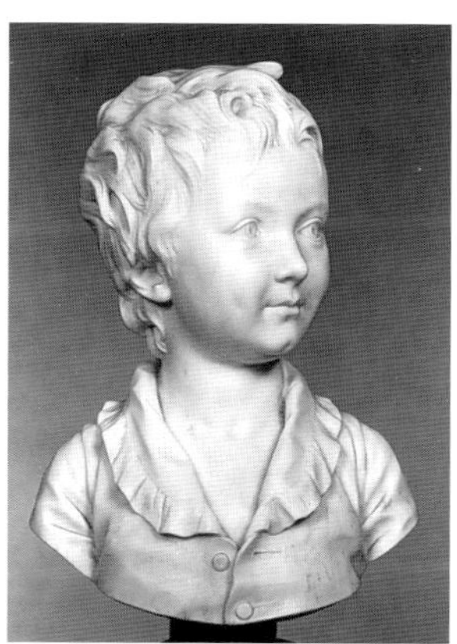

*Alexandre Brongniart,* 1777
Marble, .392 x .287 x .190
($15\frac{3}{8}$ x $11\frac{1}{4}$ x $7\frac{3}{8}$)
Inscribed on rear edge of truncation:
HOUDON, F. AN. 1777
Widener Collection
1942.9.123

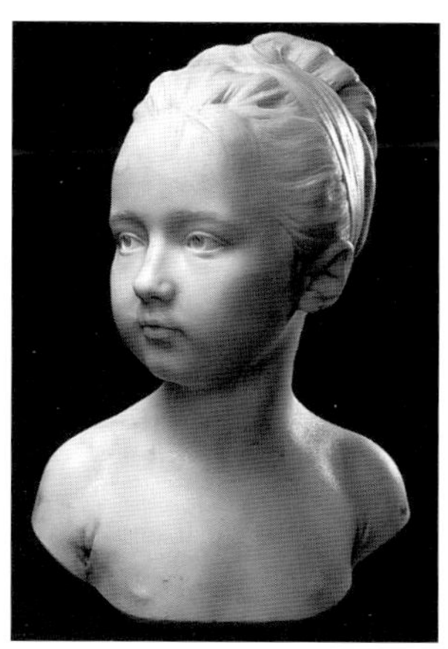

*Louise Brongniart,* 1777
Marble, .377 x .253 x .195
($14\frac{1}{8}$ x $9\frac{7}{8}$ x $7\frac{5}{8}$)
Widener Collection
1942.9.124

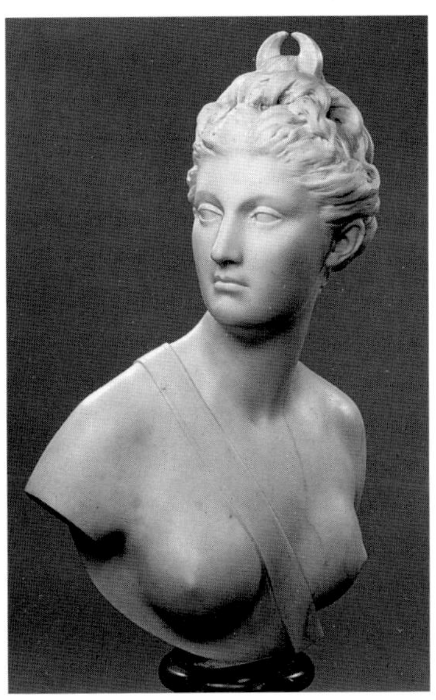

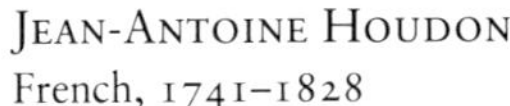

JEAN-ANTOINE HOUDON
French, 1741–1828

*Diana*, 1778
Marble, .630 x .451 x .322
(24 3/4 x 17 3/4 x 12 5/8)
Inscribed on truncated right arm:
HOUDON / FECIT. / 1778.
Gift of Syma Busiel
1957.1.1

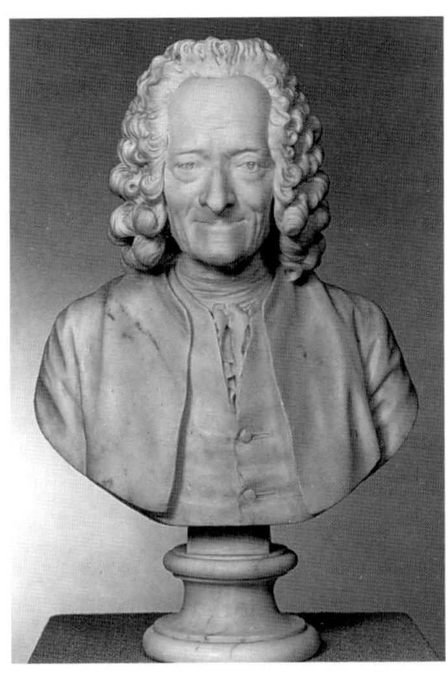

*Voltaire*, 1778
Marble, .527 x .455 x .333
(20 3/4 x 17 7/8 x 13 1/8)
Inscribed on rear edge of truncation:
AROUET DE VOLTAIRE, / NÉ À PARIS EN 1694, ET MORT EN 1778.; on truncated right arm: HOUDON, F. 1778.
Widener Collection
1942.9.127

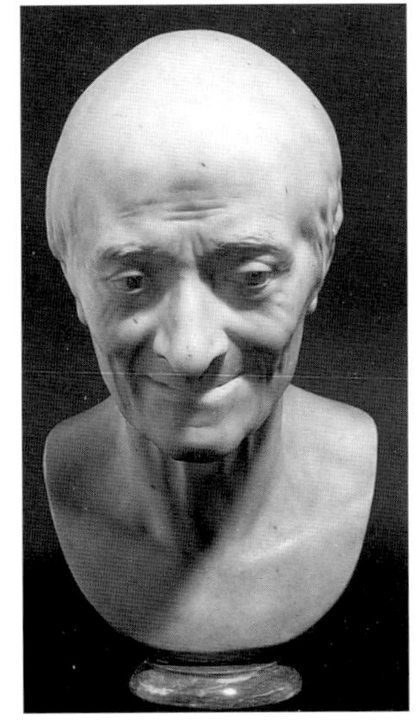

*Voltaire*, 1778
Marble, .366 x .212 x .213
(14 3/8 x 8 3/8 x 8 3/8)
Inscribed on truncation of right shoulder:
HOUDON • 1778 •; inscribed on red wax seal under rear rim: ACADEM. / ROYALE / DE PEINTURE / ET SCULPT. / [H]OUDON / SC.
Chester Dale Collection
1963.10.240

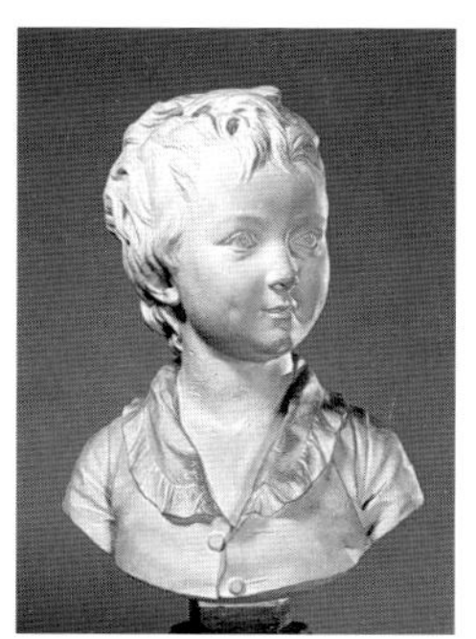

Imitator of
Jean-Antoine Houdon
French

*Alexandre Brongniart,* c. 1910
Terra cotta, .377 x .273 x .180
($14^{7}/_{8}$ x $10^{3}/_{4}$ x $7^{1}/_{8}$)
Falsely signed and dated, on rear edge of truncation: A. HOUDON, F. AN. 1777
Widener Collection
1942.9.125

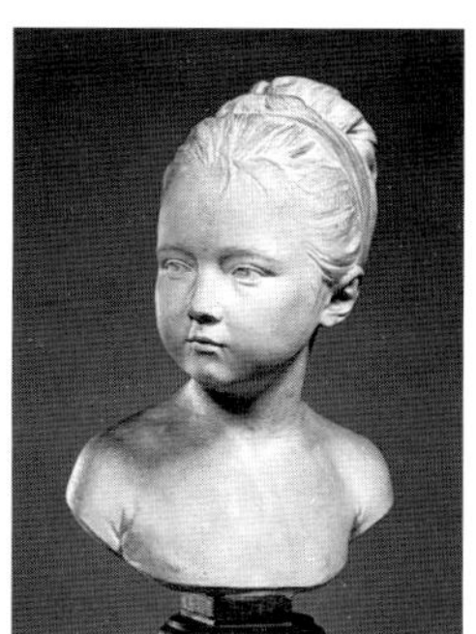

Imitator of
Jean-Antoine Houdon
French

*Louise Brongniart,* c. 1910
Terra cotta, .355 x .240 x .173
(14 x $9^{1}/_{2}$ x $6^{7}/_{8}$)
Widener Collection
1942.9.126

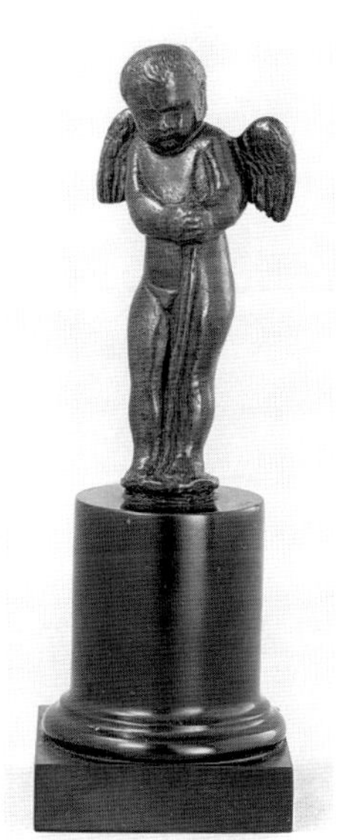

Italian 15th Century

*Cupid,* late 15th century
Bronze, .094 x .046 x .025
($3^{11}/_{16}$ x $1^{13}/_{16}$ x 1)
Samuel H. Kress Collection
1957.14.37

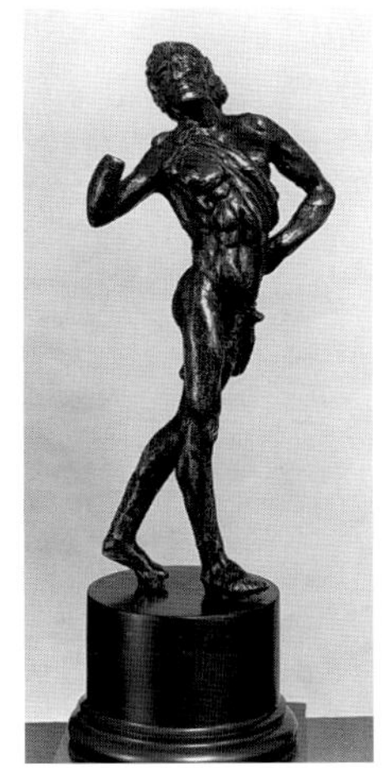

## Probably Italian 15th Century

*A Dancing Faun,* late 15th or 16th century
Bronze, .152 x .084 x .052
(6 x 3 5/16 x 2 1/16); depth is from left heel to right toe
Samuel H. Kress Collection
1957.14.15

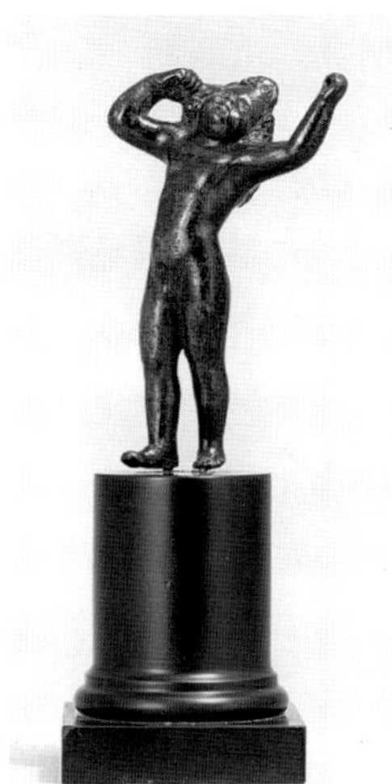

## Italian 15th or 16th Century

*Cupid with Raised Arms,* late 15th or early 16th century
Bronze, .076 x .047 x .027
(3 x 1 7/8 x 1 1/16)
Samuel H. Kress Collection
1957.14.36

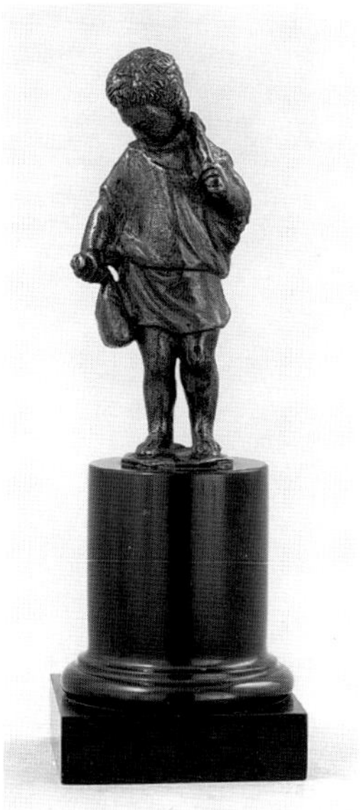

## Italian 16th Century

*A Child Standing,* early 16th century
Bronze, .090 x .042 x .025
(3 9/16 x 1 11/16 x 1)
Samuel H. Kress Collection
1957.14.44

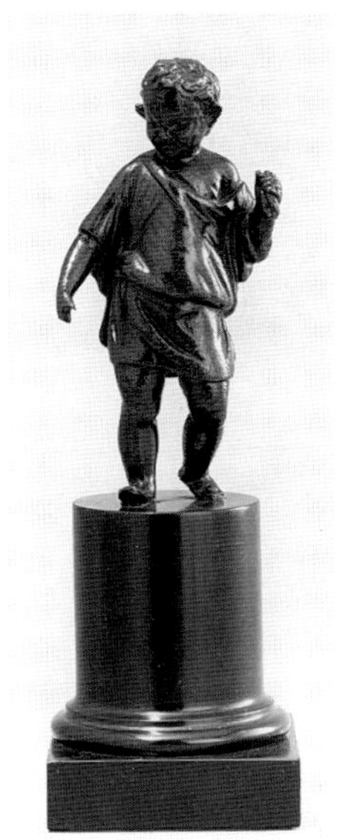

ITALIAN 16TH CENTURY

*A Child Standing*, early 16th century
Bronze, .095 x .049 x .032
($3^3/_4$ x $1^{15}/_{16}$ x $1^5/_{16}$)
Samuel H. Kress Collection
1957.14.46

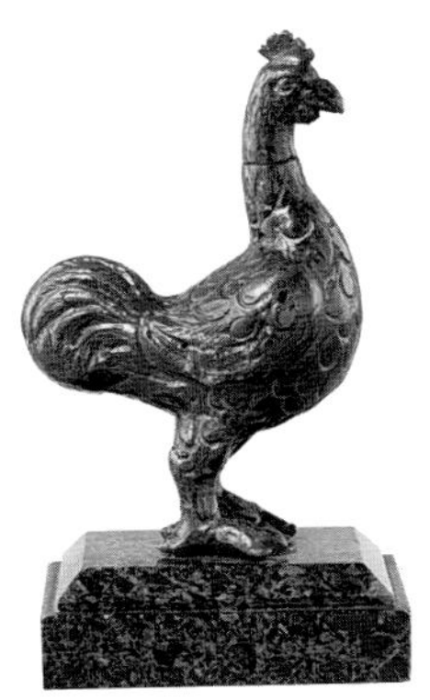

ITALIAN 16TH CENTURY

*A Cock*, first half 16th century
Bronze, .087 x .033 x .061
($3^7/_{16}$ x $1^5/_{16}$ x $2^3/_8$)
Samuel H. Kress Collection
1957.14.83

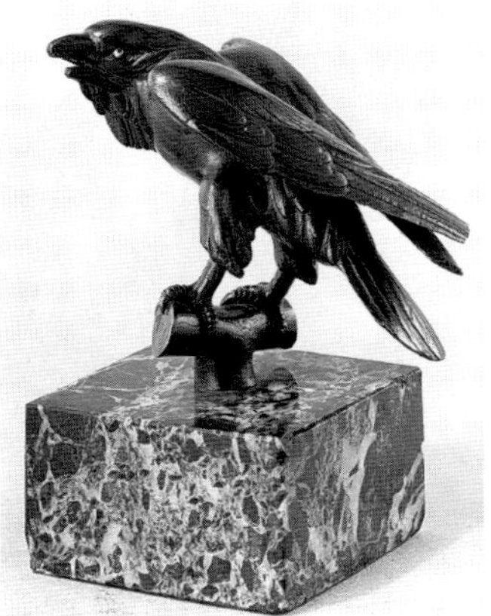

ITALIAN 16TH CENTURY

*A Crow*
Bronze with gilt eyes, .074 x .063 x .095
($2^{15}/_{16}$ x $2^1/_2$ x $3^1/_2$)
Samuel H. Kress Collection
1957.14.84

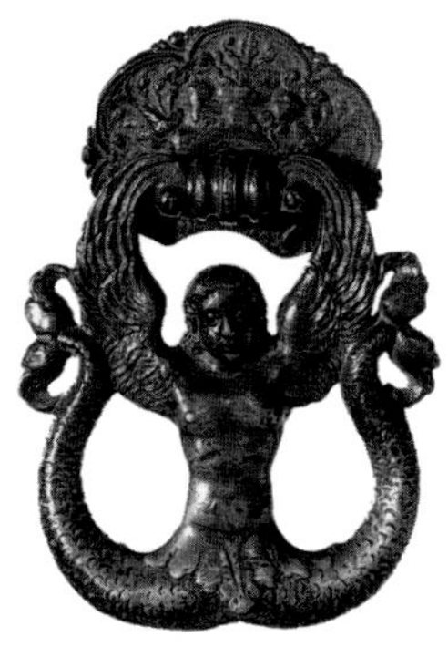

ITALIAN 16TH CENTURY

*Door Knocker*
Bronze, .159 x .110 x .030
(6 1/4 x 4 5/16 x 1 3/16)
Samuel H. Kress Collection
1957.14.120

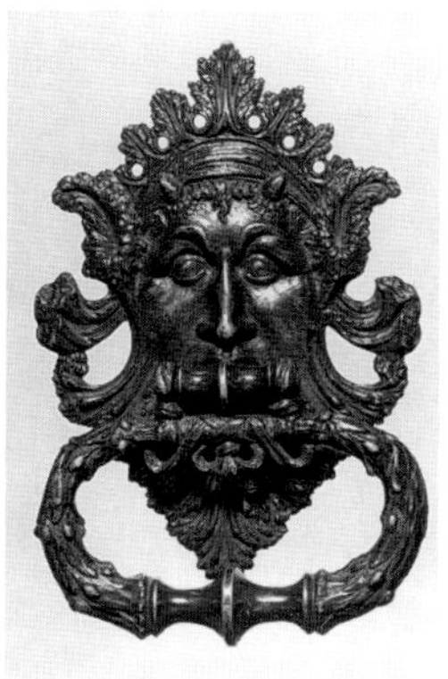

ITALIAN 16TH CENTURY

*Door Knocker*
Bronze, .180 x .120 x .027
(7 1/8 x 4 3/4 x 1 1/16)
Samuel H. Kress Collection
1957.14.121

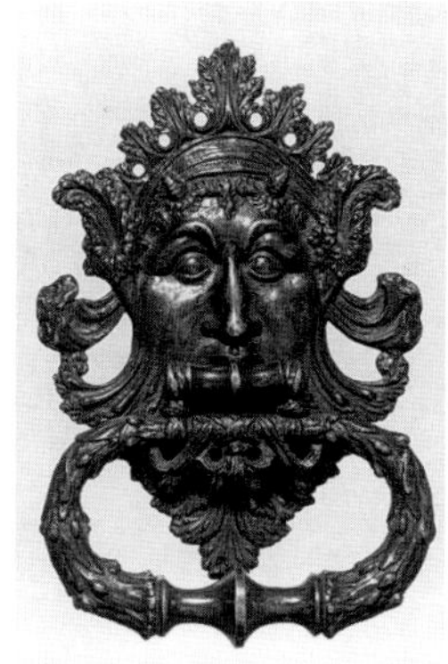

ITALIAN 16TH CENTURY

*Door Knocker*
Bronze, .180 x .120 x .027
(7 1/8 x 4 3/4 x 1 1/16)
Samuel H. Kress Collection
1957.14.122

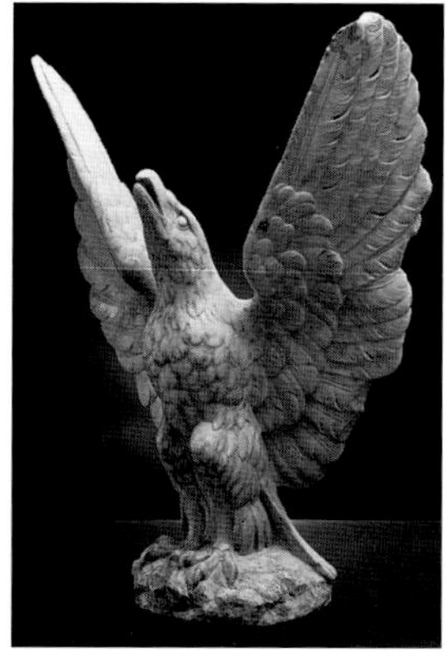

ITALIAN 16TH CENTURY

*Eagle*
Marble, .756 x .620 x .318
(29 3/4 x 24 3/8 x 12 1/2)
Samuel H. Kress Collection
1952.5.89

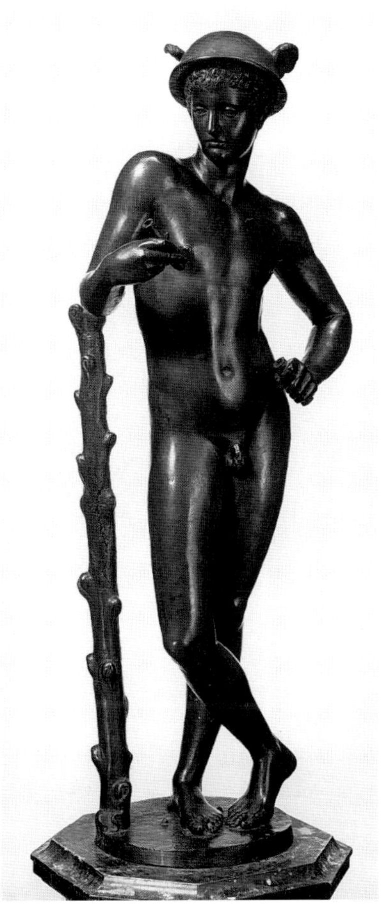

Italian 16th Century

*Mercury*
Bronze, 1.560 x .640 x .407
(61 3/8 x 25 1/4 x 16)
Andrew W. Mellon Fund
1959.7.1

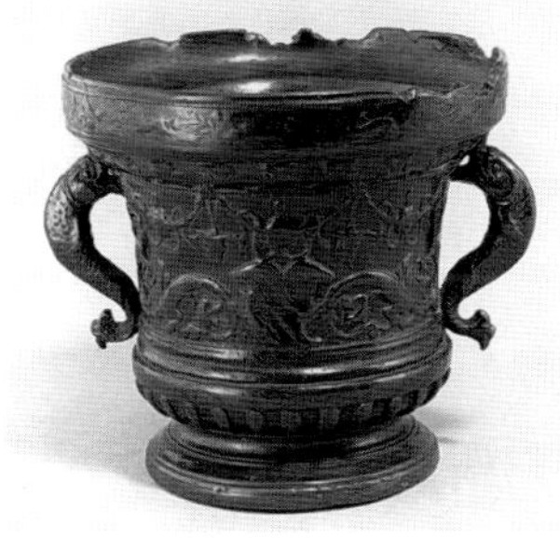

Italian 16th Century

*Mortar,* early 16th century
Bronze, .120 x .159 (4 3/4 x 6 1/4)
Samuel H. Kress Collection
1957.14.98

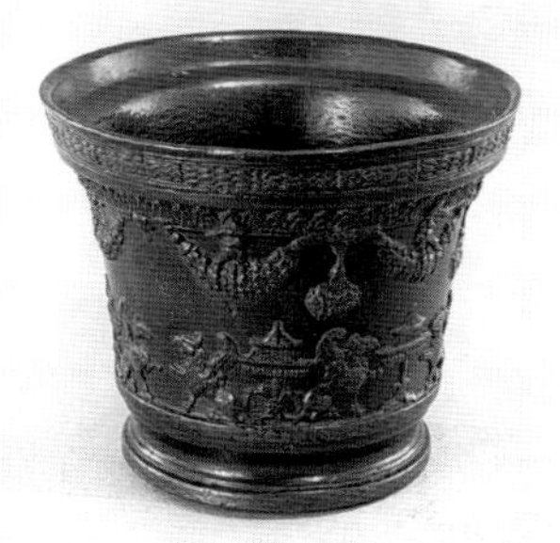

Italian 16th Century

*Mortar,* early 16th century
Bronze, .133 x .177 (5 1/4 x 7)
Samuel H. Kress Collection
1957.14.99

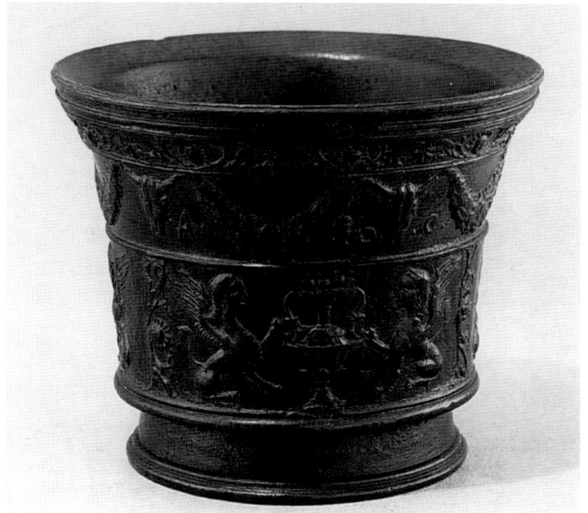

## Italian 16th Century

*Mortar,* early 16th century
Bronze, .102 x .132 (4 x $5^{3}/_{16}$)
Inscribed under belt of garlands: •A• •BO• •C•
Samuel H. Kress Collection
1957.14.101

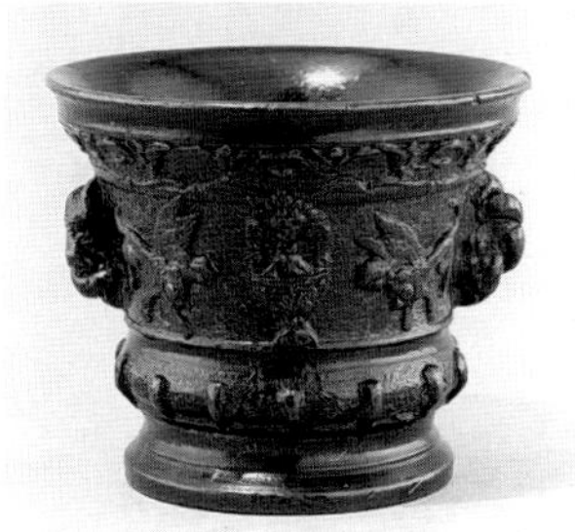

## Italian 16th Century

*Mortar,* early 16th century
Bronze, .095 x .118 ($3^{3}/_{4}$ x $4^{5}/_{8}$)
Samuel H. Kress Collection
1957.14.102

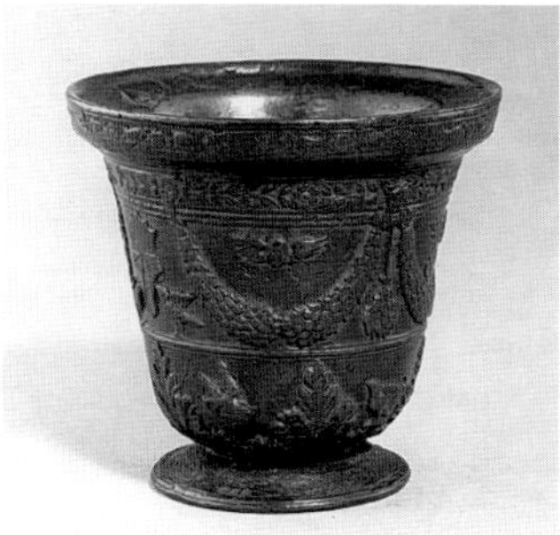

## Italian 16th Century

*Mortar,* early 16th century
Bronze, .085 x .100 ($3^{11}/_{16}$ x $3^{15}/_{16}$)
Samuel H. Kress Collection
1957.14.104

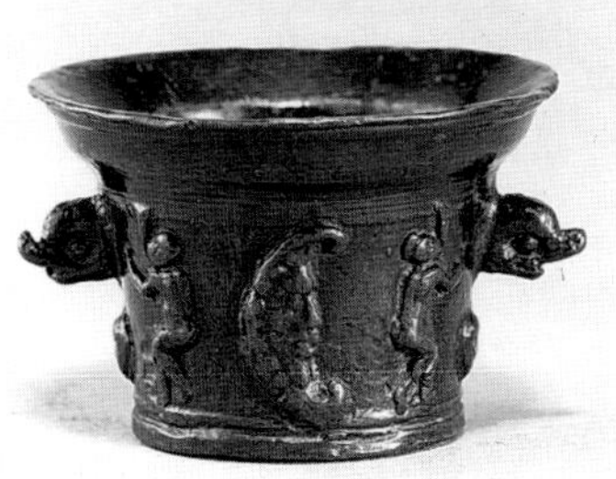

## Italian 16th Century

*Mortar,* early 16th century
Bronze, width given at handles:
.037 x .065 ($1^{7}/_{16}$ x $2^{9}/_{16}$)
Samuel H. Kress Collection
1957.14.105

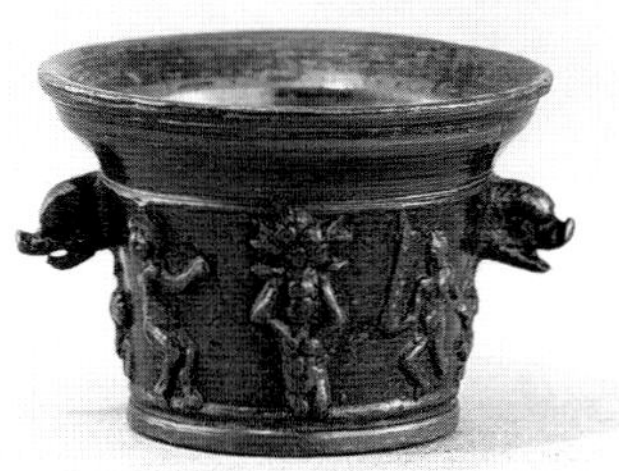

## Italian 16th Century

*Mortar,* early 16th century
Bronze, width given at handles:
.038 x .061 (1 1/2 x 2 7/16)
Samuel H. Kress Collection
1957.14.106

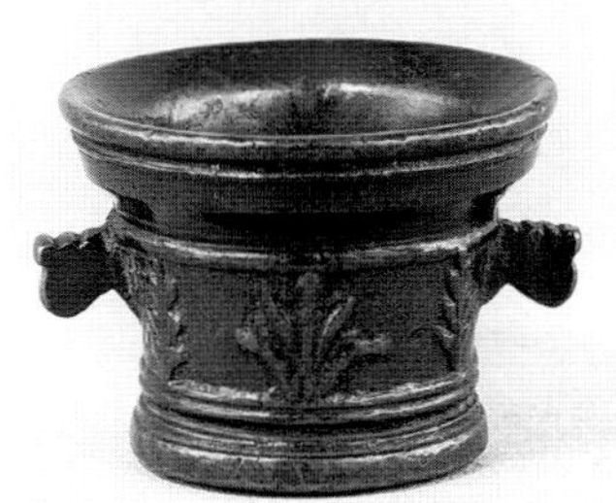

## Italian 16th Century

*Mortar,* early 16th century
Bronze, width given at handles:
.044 x .068 (1 3/4 x 2 11/16)
Samuel H. Kress Collection
1957.14.107

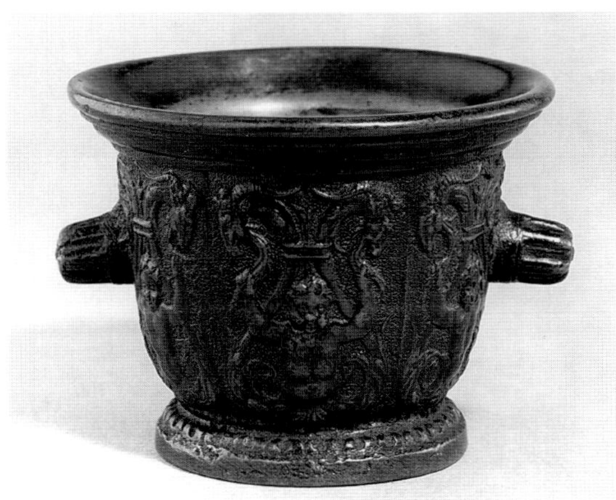

## Italian 16th Century

*Mortar,* mid-16th century
Bronze, .081 x .116 (3 3/16 x 4 9/16)
Samuel H. Kress Collection
1957.14.108

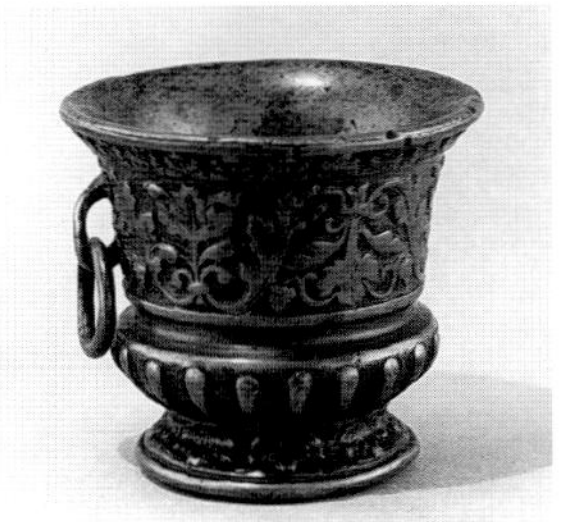

## Italian 16th Century

*Mortar*
Bronze, .085 x .102 (3 3/8 x 4)
Samuel H. Kress Collection
1957.14.109

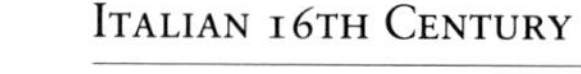

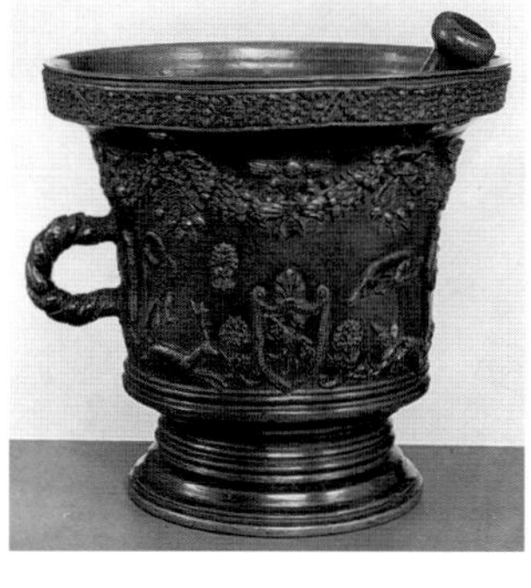

## ITALIAN 16TH CENTURY

*Mortar with Rope-Shaped Handle* and *Pestle,* early 16th century
Bronze, mortar: .153 x .170 ($6 \times 6^{11}/_{16}$),
pestle: .162 x .033 ($6^{3}/_{8} \times 1^{3}/_{8}$)
Samuel H. Kress Collection
1957.14.100.a and b

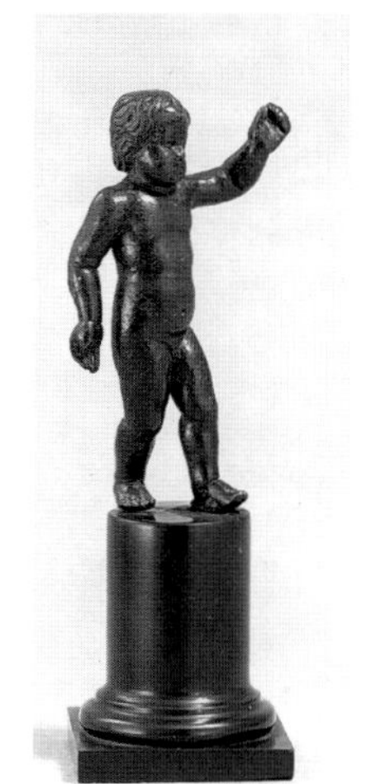

## ITALIAN 16TH CENTURY

*Standing Child with Raised Left Arm,* early 16th century
Bronze, .062 x .034 x .019
($2^{7}/_{16} \times 1^{3}/_{8} \times {}^{3}/_{4}$)
Samuel H. Kress Collection
1957.14.48

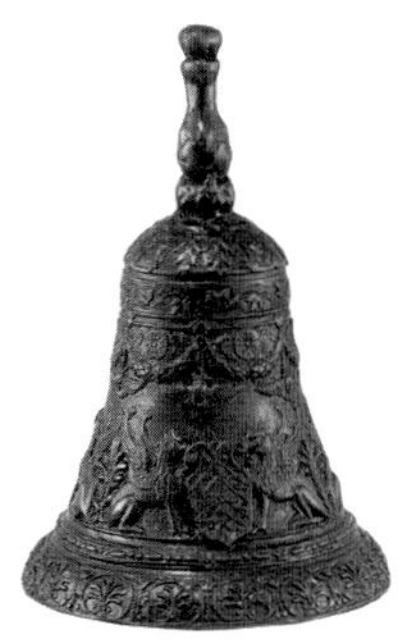

## ITALIAN 16TH CENTURY

*Table-Bell,* first half 16th century
Bronze, .149 x .105 ($5^{7}/_{8} \times 4^{1}/_{8}$)
Inscribed on shield between gryphons:
SVRTEP [reversed] / MASSARO / TVS /
ISINA [reversed]
Samuel H. Kress Collection
1957.14.111

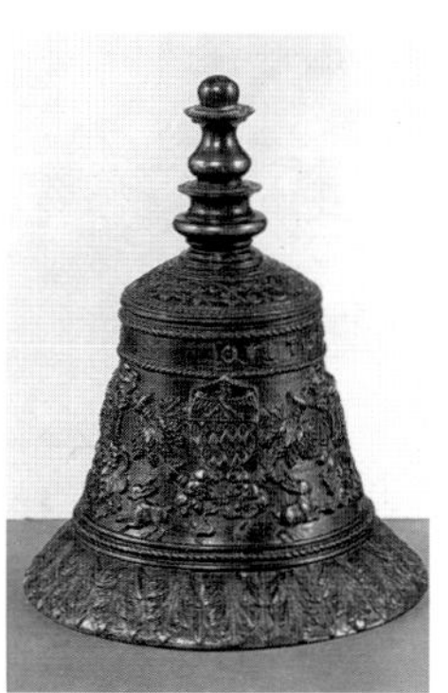

## ITALIAN 16TH CENTURY

*Table-Bell*
Bronze, .128 x .105 ($5^{1}/_{16} \times 4^{3}/_{16}$)
Inscribed below upper frieze of foliage:
QVI TIMET DEVM FACIET BONA
Samuel H. Kress Collection
1957.14.113

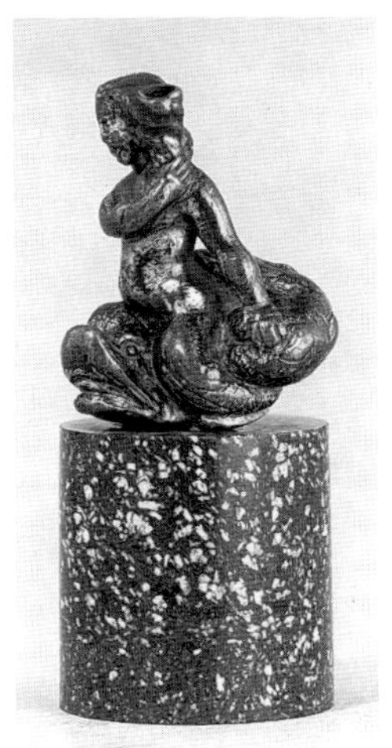

ITALIAN 16TH CENTURY

*A Triton,* early 16th century
Bronze (originally fully gilt)
.046 x .032 x .034 ($1^{13}/_{16}$ x $1^{5}/_{16}$ x $1^{5}/_{16}$)
Samuel H. Kress Collection
1957.14.47

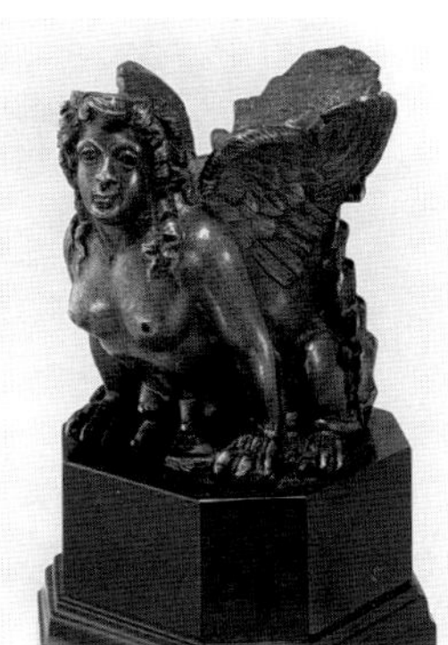

PROBABLY ITALIAN
16TH/19TH CENTURY

*Object with Sphinx Head (Furniture Mount?)*
Bronze with copper inlay, lined in lead
.104 x .091 x .122 ($4^{1}/_{8}$ x $3^{5}/_{8}$ x $4^{13}/_{16}$)
Samuel H. Kress Collection
1957.14.76

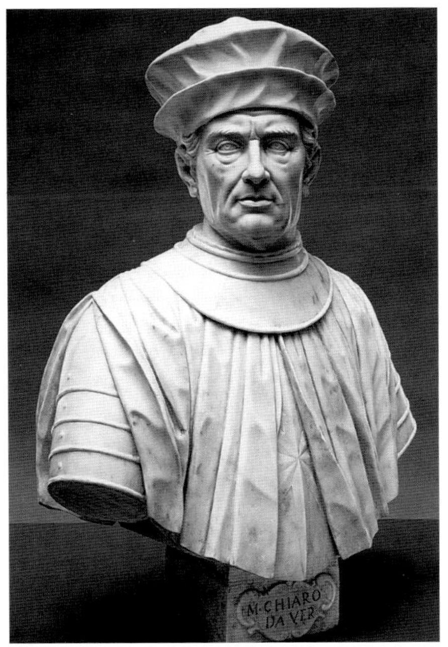


ITALIAN 17TH CENTURY

*Chiaro da Verrazano*
Marble, with base: .914 x .689 x .378 (36 x $27^{1}/_{8}$ x $14^{7}/_{8}$)
Inscribed on front of base: M•CHIARO / DA VER•
Samuel H. Kress Collection
1961.9.104

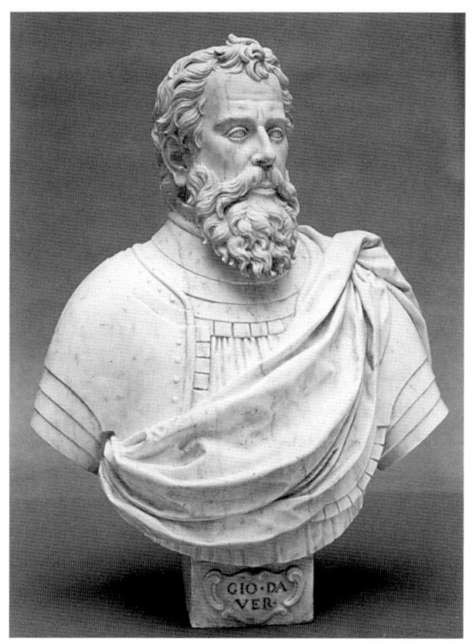


## Italian 17th Century

*Giovanni da Verrazano*
Marble, with base: .886 x .689 x .336
(34 7/8 x 27 1/8 x 13 1/4)
Inscribed on front of base: GIO•DA / VER•
Samuel H. Kress Collection
1961.9.105

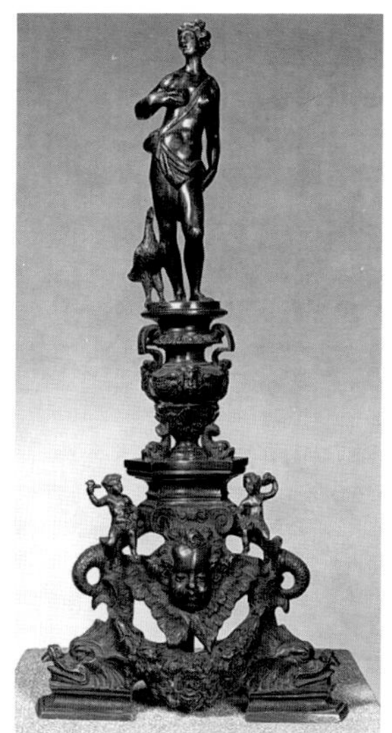

## Italian 17th/19th Century

*Andiron with Figure of Juno*
Bronze, .796 x .376 x .152
(31 1/4 x 14 3/4 x 6)
Widener Collection
1942.9.144

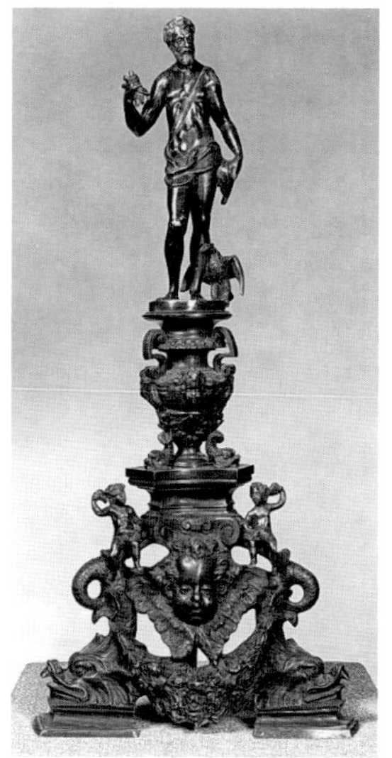

## Italian 17th/19th Century

*Andiron with Figure of Jupiter*
Bronze, .792 x .376 x .152
(31 1/8 x 14 3/4 x 6)
Widener Collection
1942.9.143

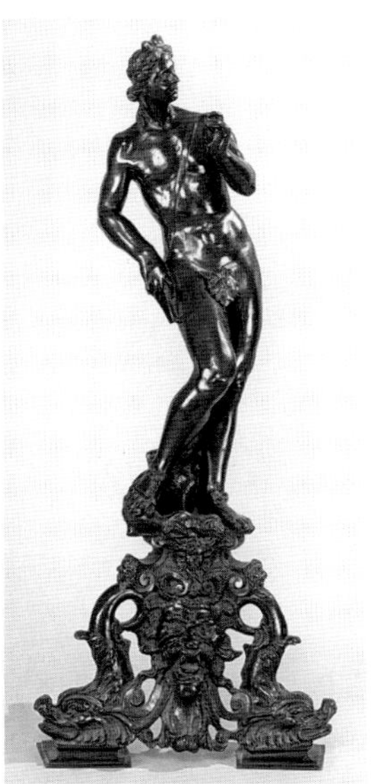

## Italian 18th Century

*Andiron: Apollo with the Serpent*
Bronze, .914 x .400 x .220
(36 x 15 3/4 x 8 5/8)
Widener Collection
1942.9.2520

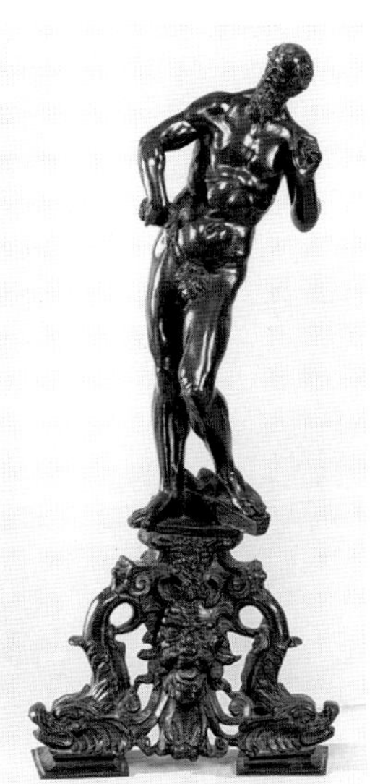

## Italian 18th Century

*Andiron: Vulcan with His Anvil*
Bronze, .914 x .400 x .220
(36 x 15 3/4 x 8 5/8)
Widener Collection
1942.9.2521

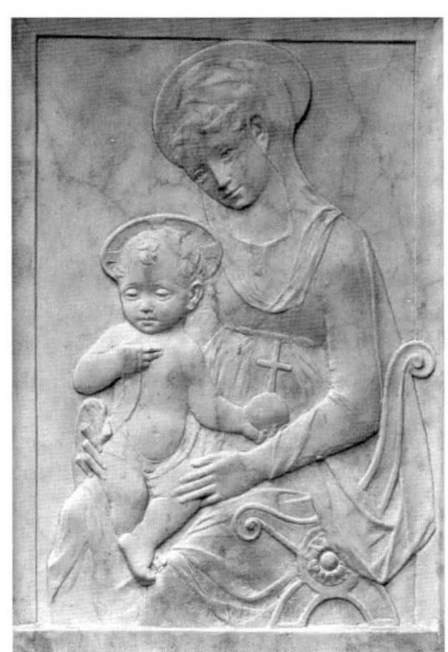

## Italian 19th Century

*Madonna and Child*, mid-19th century
Marble, .410 x .300 (16 1/4 x 11 3/4)
Andrew W. Mellon Collection
1937.1.126

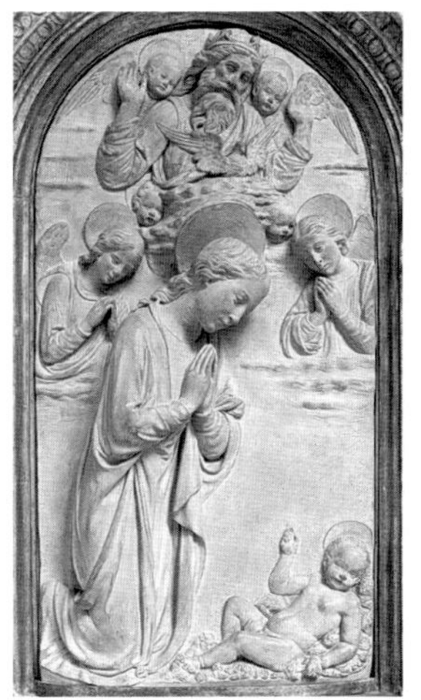

## ITALIAN 19TH CENTURY

*The Virgin in Adoration,*
mid-19th century
Terra cotta, .770 x .410 (30 1/4 x 16 1/4)
Andrew W. Mellon Collection
1937.1.124

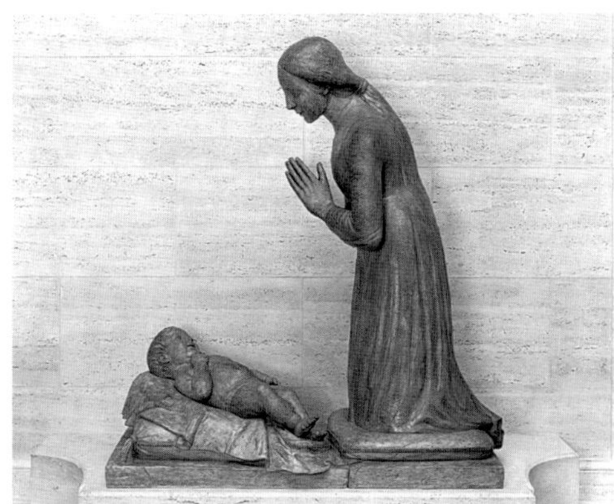

## ITALIAN 20TH CENTURY

*Madonna Adoring the Child,* c. 1900
Terra cotta with traces of polychromy
1.203 x 1.130 x .581
(47 3/8 x 44 1/2 x 22 7/8)
Samuel H. Kress Collection
1943.4.82

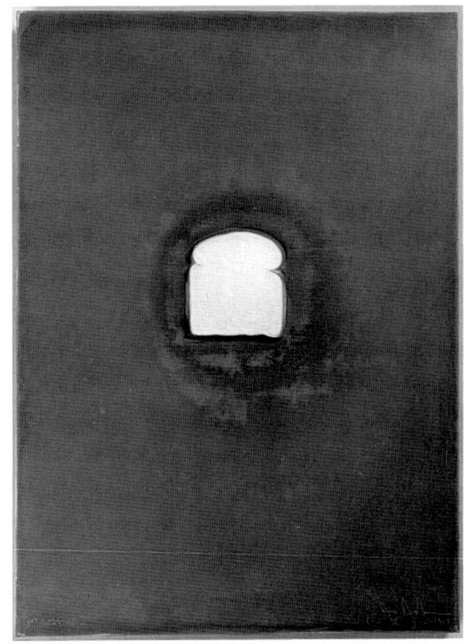

## JASPER JOHNS
American, born 1930

*Bread,* published 1969
Lead relief with laminated, embossed paper, hand-colored in oil, .584 x .432 (23 x 17)
Inscribed at lower right: J JOHNS / 1969; at lower left: (Gemini chop) GEMINI I
Gift of Gemini G.E.L.
1991.74.72

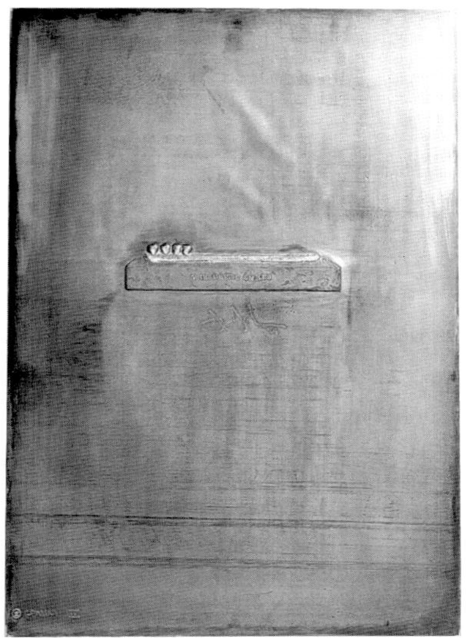

*The Critic Smiles*, published 1969
Sheet lead with cast gold and tin leaf in welded aluminum frame, including frame: .584 x .432 (23 x 17)
Inscribed under toothbrush: THE CRITIC SMILES / J JOHNS '69; at lower left: (Gemini chop) GEMINI III
Gift of Gemini G.E.L.
1985.4.1

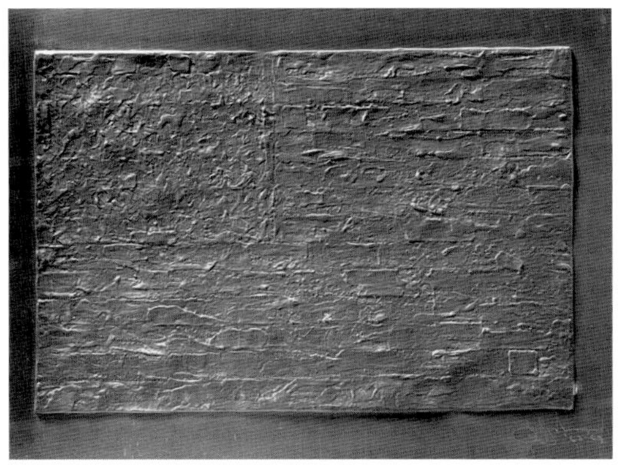

*Flag*, published 1969
Lead relief, .432 x .584 (17 x 23)
Inscribed at lower right: J JOHNS / '60–'69; at lower left: GEMINI I
Gift of Gemini G.E.L.
1981.5.103

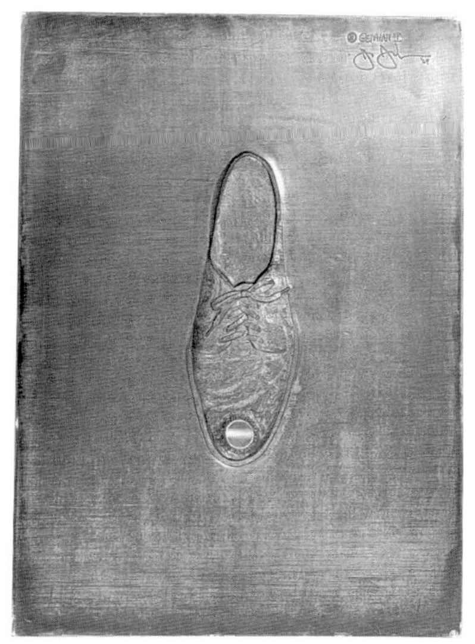

*High School Days*, published 1969
Lead relief with mirror, .584 x .432 (23 x 17)
Inscribed at upper right: (Gemini chop) GEMINI I / J JOHNS / '69; around mirror: HIGH SCHOOL DAYS
Gift of Gemini G.E.L.
1991.74.73

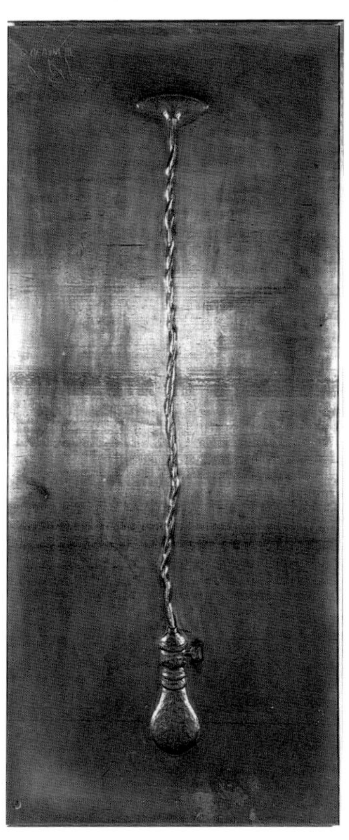

JASPER JOHNS
American, born 1930

*Light Bulb*, published 1969
Lead relief (sheet lead), 1.016 x .435 (40 x 17 1/8)
Inscribed at upper left: (Gemini chop) GEMINI III / J JOHNS / '69
Gift of Gemini G.E.L.
1991.74.74

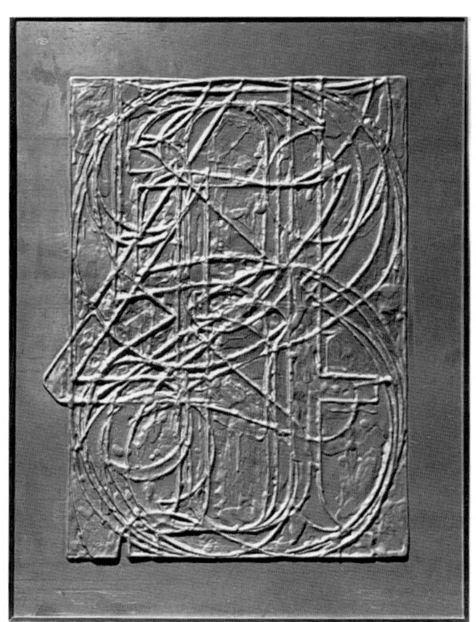

*0 through 9*, published 1970
Lead relief, .762 x .597 (30 x 23 1/2)
Inscribed at lower right: J JOHNS / '70; at lower left: GEMINI III
Gift of Gemini G.E.L.
1981.5.104

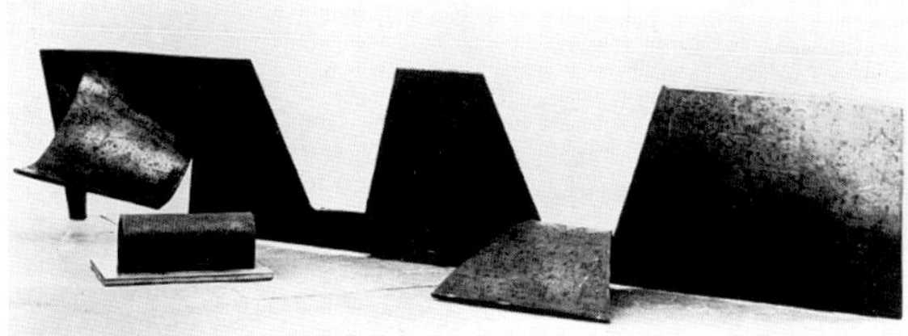

LILA PELL KATZEN
American, born 1932

*Antecedent*, 1975
Steel, 1.829 x 7.620 x 2.438 (72 x 300 x 96)
Gift of Mr. and Mrs. Sidney M. Feldman and Mr. and Mrs. Earl M. Latterman
1975.80.1

## Ellsworth Kelly
American, born 1923

*Dark Red-Violet Panel,* published 1982
Painted aluminum, .762 x .797 x .005 (30 x 31 3/8 x 1/4)
Inscribed on verso, lower center, on metal plate: KELLY DARK RED-VIOLET PANEL NATIONAL / GALLERY / © ELLSWORTH KELLY 1982 PUBLISHED BY GEMINI G.E.L. (Gemini chop) EK81–2069
Gift of Mr. and Mrs. Roger P. Sonnabend
1986.90.18

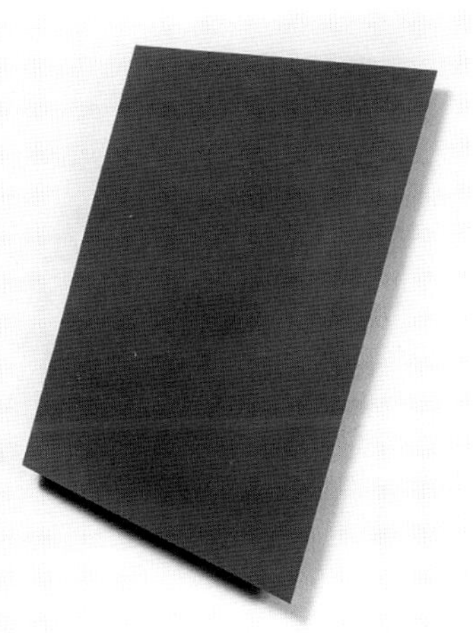

*Light Green Panel,* published 1982
Painted aluminum, 1.070 x .807 x .005 (42 1/8 x 31 3/4 x 1/4)
Inscribed on verso, lower center, on metal plate: KELLY LIGHT GREEN PANEL NATIONAL / GALLERY / © ELLSWORTH KELLY 1982 PUBLISHED BY GEMINI G.E.L. (Gemini chop) EK81–2074
Gift of Mr. and Mrs. Roger P. Sonnabend
1986.90.17

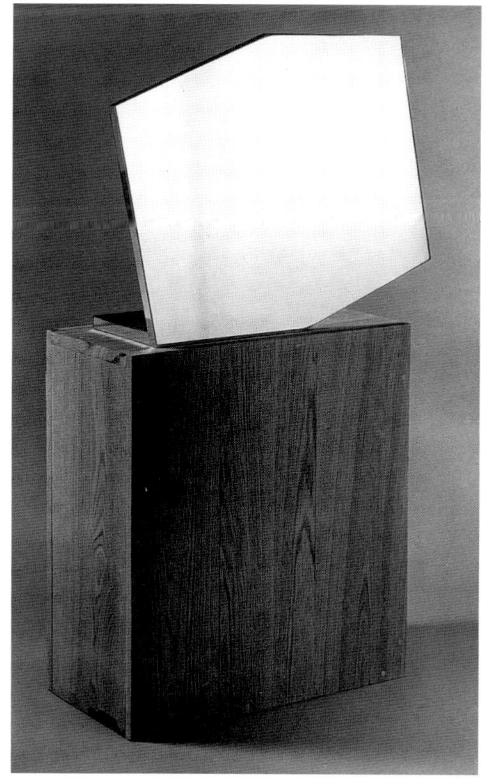

*Mirrored Concorde,* published 1971
Chrome-plated steel with oak base
.579 x .749 x .254 (22 3/4 x 29 1/2 x 10)
Gift of Gemini G.E.L.
1981.5.279

ELLSWORTH KELLY
American, born 1923

*Untitled,* 1988
Bronze, 3.035 x .622 x .025
(119 1/2 x 24 1/4 x 1)
Gift of the Artist, in Honor of the 50th Anniversary of the National Gallery of Art
1989.88.1

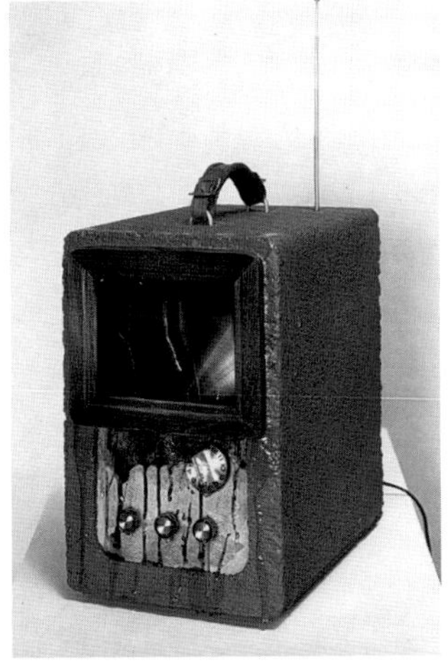

EDWARD KIENHOLZ
American, born 1927

*The Block Head,* published 1981
Concrete/pumice construction block, wooden bevel, Fresnel lens, plastic knobs, leather handle, AM/FM/TV reception transistor radio, internal wooden construction, resin, .318 x .216 x .311
(12 1/2 x 8 1/2 x 12 1/4)
Inscribed on verso on brass plate: KIENHOLZ GEM I; (Gemini chop) GEMINI G.E.L. / THE BLOCK HEAD / ED. K 79–2052 / © COPYRIGHT GEMINI G.E.L. 1979
Gift of Gemini G.E.L. and the Artist
1981.5.273

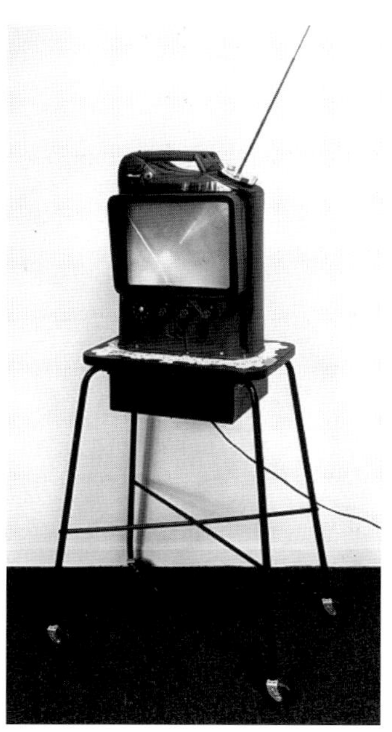

*The Jerry Can Standard,* published 1981
Metal gasoline can with Fresnel lens system and light bulb mounted on formica-metal stand with plastic doily; cassette player and tapes
With antenna extended:
1.715 x .457 x .305 (67 1/2 x 18 x 12)
Inscribed on back on brass plate: (Gemini chop) / GEMINI G.E.L. / MODEL THE JERRY CAN STANDARD / MODEL NO. ED. K. 79–2050 / KIENHOLZ GEM. I / © COPYRIGHT GEMINI G.E.L. 1979
Gift of Gemini G.E.L. and the Artist
1981.5.278

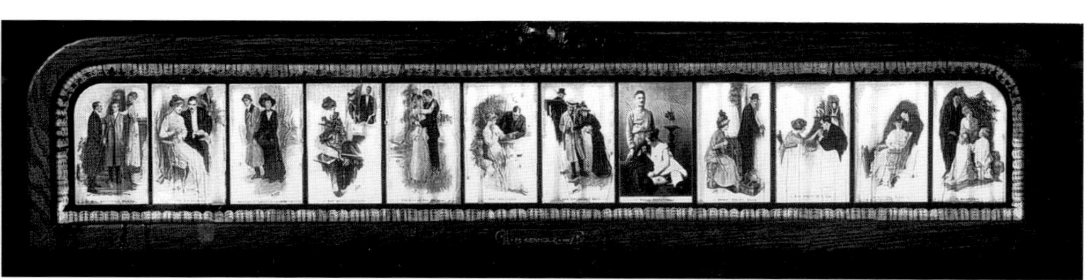

*The Marriage Icon,* published 1972
Oak frame and plexiglass with photo-offset printed on Arches paper, photograph and nylon lace on black Arches paper; hand colored with watercolor and polyester resin
Greatest extension: .321 x 1.321 x .032
(12 5/8 x 52 1/2 x 1 1/4)
Inscribed on recto, at lower center, on brass plate: THE MARRIAGE ICON / #23 KIENHOLZ © 1972; on verso, middle, on printed tag: EDWARD KIENHOLZ THE MARRIAGE ICON / EDITION 75 EK72–2034 / © COPYRIGHT 1972 GEMINI G.E.L. / (Gemini chop)
Gift of Gemini G.E.L.
1981.5.205

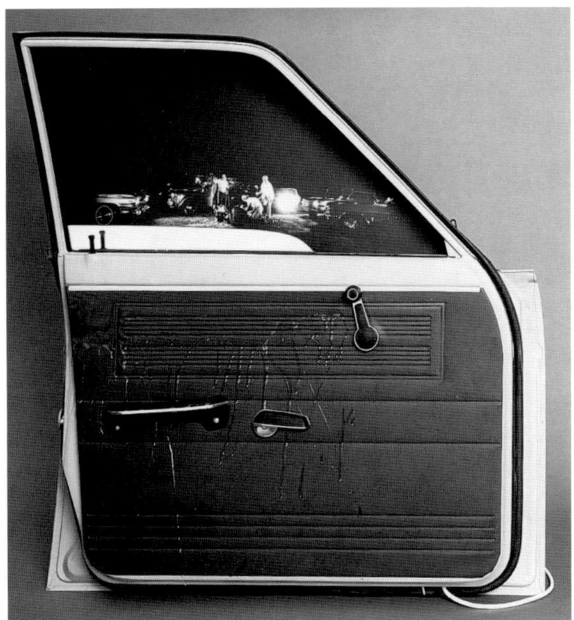

Edward Kienholz
American, born 1927

*Sawdy*, published 1971
Various materials including car door, mirrored window, automotive lacquer, polyester resin, silkprint, fluorescent light, and galvanized sheet metal
1.003 x .914 x .178 ($39^1/_2$ x 36 x 7)
Inscribed inside edge of door on tag: (Gemini chop) TITLE SAWDY / OBJECT NO EK71–2024 / BODY STYLE 70 DATSUN / LIGHT BULB F15T8-CW / EDITION #13 / AUTHORIZED: KIENHOLZ / © COPYRIGHT GEMINI G.E.L. 1971
Gift of Gemini G.E.L.
1981.5.115

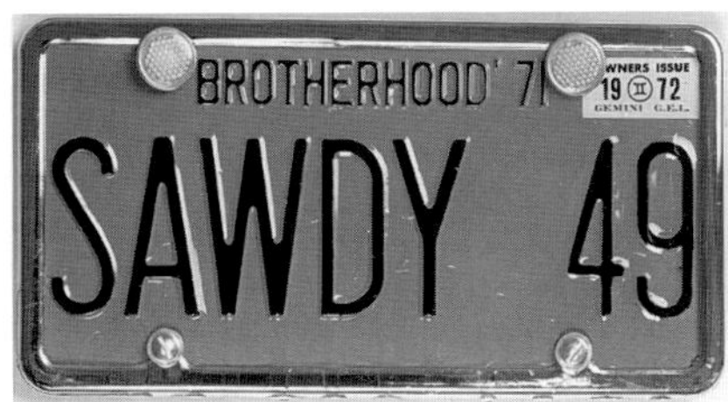


*Souvenir License Plate for Sawdy*, published 1972
Die stamped painted license plate with printed sticker, chrome frame, plastic reflectors, and polyester resin, .159 x .310 ($6^1/_4$ x $12^1/_8$)
Gift of Gemini G.E.L.
1991.74.134

**The Tin TV's Series**

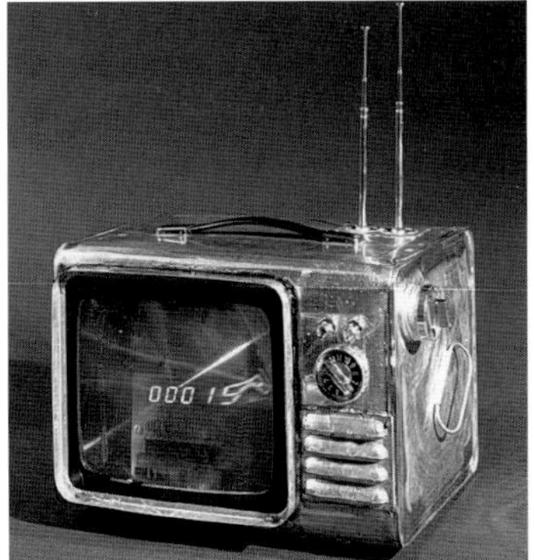

*The Billionaire Deluxe*, published 1977
Various materials including metal, Fresnel lens system, light bulb, solid state electronic counter, .279 x .384 x .356 (11 x $15^1/_8$ x 14)
Inscribed on verso on brass plate: GEMINI (Gemini chop) G.E.L. / MODEL THE BILLIONAIRE MODEL NO / EK 76–2038 / VOLTS 110–220 CYCLES 50/60 LAMP 25 WATTS / KIENHOLZ GEMINI / III / © COPYRIGHT GEMINI G.E.L. 1977
Gift of Gemini G.E.L.
1981.5.132

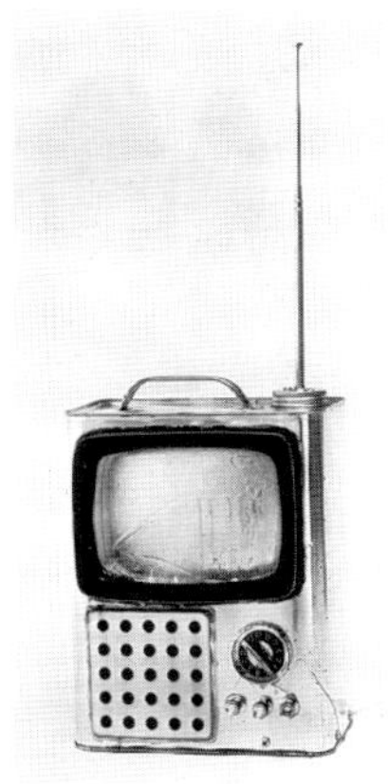

*The Econo-Can*, published 1977
Various materials including metal with Fresnel lens system
Greatest extensions (excluding extended antenna and electrical cord):
.305 x .219 x .216 (12 x 8⅝ x 8½)
Inscribed on verso on brass plate: GEMINI G.E.L. / MODEL THE ECONO-CAN MODEL NO. EK76–2040 / VOLTS O CYCLES O LAMP O WATTS / KIENHOLZ GEMINI II / © COPYRIGHT GEMINI G.E.L. 1977
Gift of Gemini G.E.L.
1981.5.207

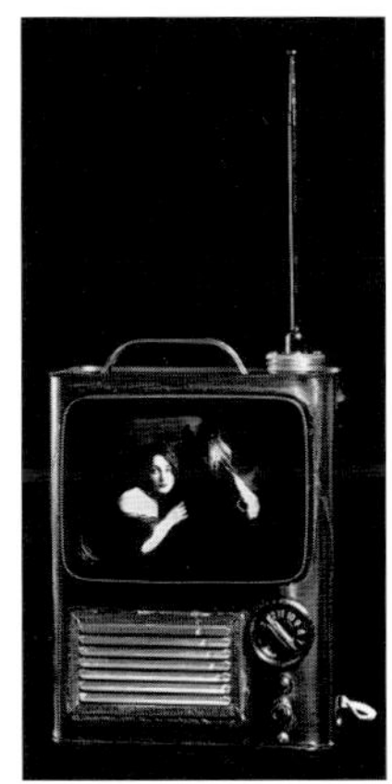

*The Opti-Can Royale*, published 1977
Various materials including metal, Fresnel lens system, light bulb, and set of six photographs (insert images are unattached to piece)
Greatest extension (excluding extended antenna and electrical cord):
.318 x .225 x .216 (12½ x 8⅞ x 8½)
Inscribed on verso on brass tag: GEMINI G.E.L. / MODEL THE OPTI-CAN ROYALE MODEL NO. EK76–2039 / VOLTS 110 CYCLES 50/60 LAMP 15 WATTS / KIENHOLZ GEMINI II/ © COPYRIGHT GEMINI G.E.L. 1977
Gift of Gemini G.E.L.
1981.5.206

## MOÏSE KISLING
*See* JACQUES LIPCHITZ

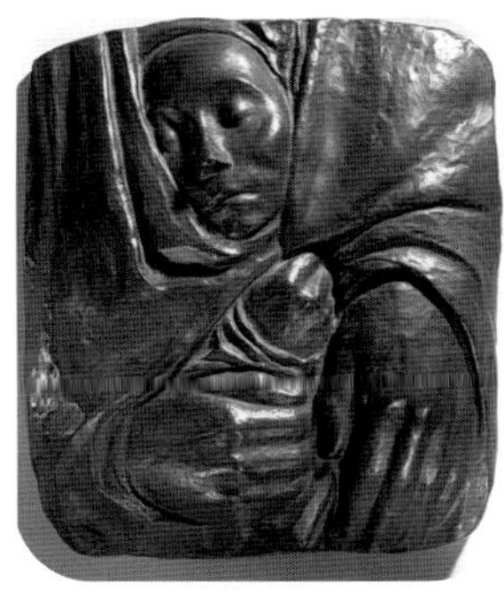

## KÄTHE KOLLWITZ
German, 1867–1945

*In God's Hands*, 1935/1936
Bronze, .355 x .318 x .086
(14 x 12½ x 3⅝)
Inscribed on right edge: KOLLWITZ; foundry mark on bottom edge: H NOACK / BERLIN FRIEDENAU; on right edge: H NOACK / BERLIN FRIEDENAU
Gift of Mr. and Mrs. Hans W. Weigert in memory of Lili B. Weigert
1977.3.1

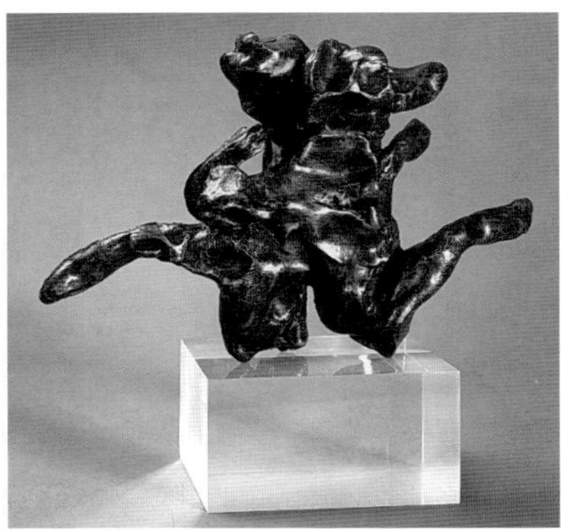

## WILLEM DE KOONING
American, born 1904

*Untitled*, published 1972
Cast pewter, .165 x .279 x .060
(6½ x 11 x 2⅜)
Gift of Gemini G.E.L.
1981.5.107

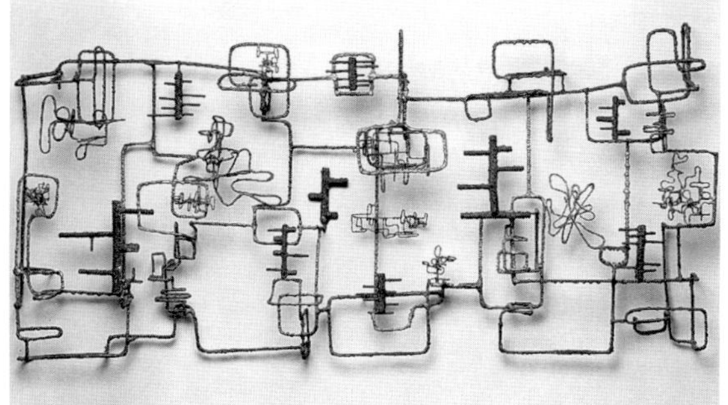

Ibram Lassaw
American, born 1913

*Rhiannon,* 1954
Wire and metal, .965 x 2.106 x .330
(38 x 83 x 13)
Inscribed at bottom lower right, on front:
IBRAM LASSAW 1954
Gift of Enid A. Haupt
1977.47.8

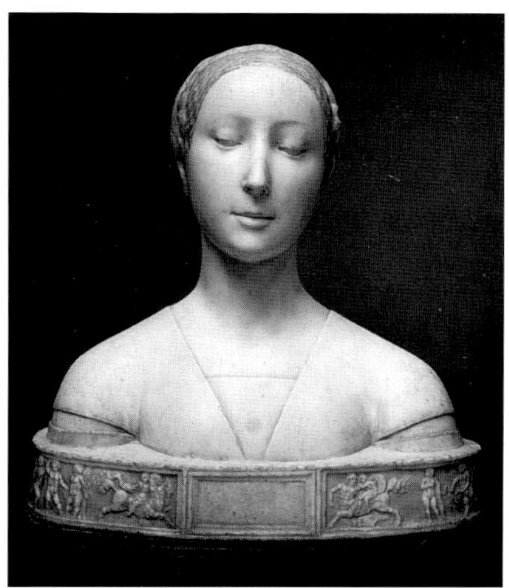

Francesco Laurana
Lombard-Neapolitan, c. 1420/1430–c. 1502

*A Princess of the House of Aragon,* c. 1475
Marble, .444 x .452 x .221
(17 1/2 x 17 3/4 x 8 5/8)
Andrew W. Mellon Collection
1937.1.119

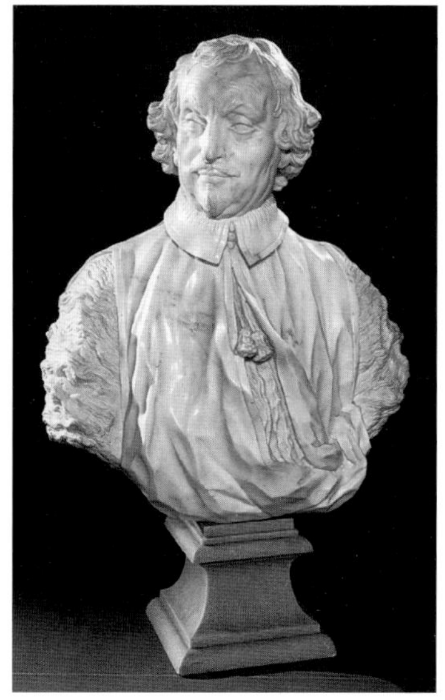

Attributed to Giusto Le Court
Venetian, 1627–1679

*A Venetian Ecclesiastic,* third quarter 17th century
Marble, .755 x .641 x .327
(29 3/4 x 25 1/4 x 12 7/8)
Ruth and Vernon Taylor Fund
1978.42.1

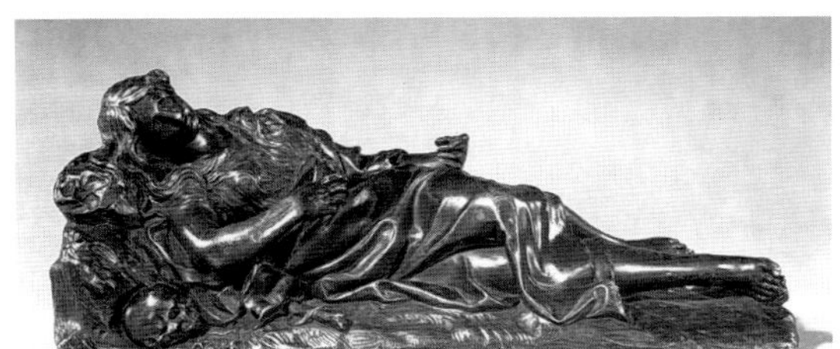

## NICOLAS LEGENDRE
French, 1619–1671

*The Penitent Magdalen,* 1664, cast probably before 1709
Bronze, .185 x .495 x .199
(7 3/8 x 19 1/2 x 8)
Andrew W. Mellon Fund
1971.6.1

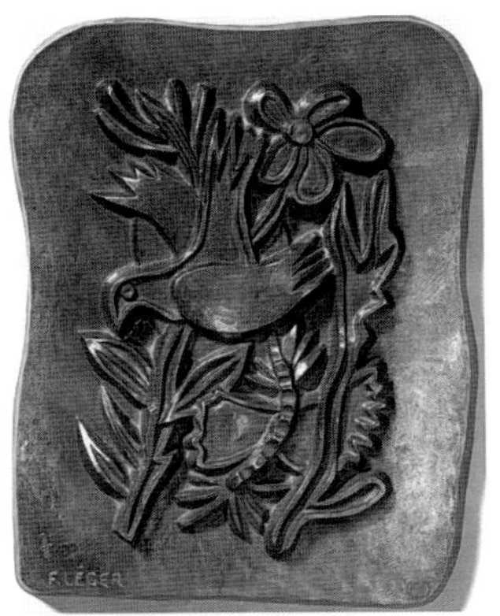


## FERNAND LÉGER
French, 1881–1955

*Bird among Flowers,* c. 1950/1952
Bronze, .439 x .369 x .051
(17 1/4 x 14 1/2 x 2)
Inscribed at lower left: 7/8 / F. LÉGER; foundry mark at lower right: CIRE / C.VALSUANI / PERDUE
Collection of Mr. and Mrs. Paul Mellon
1983.1.55

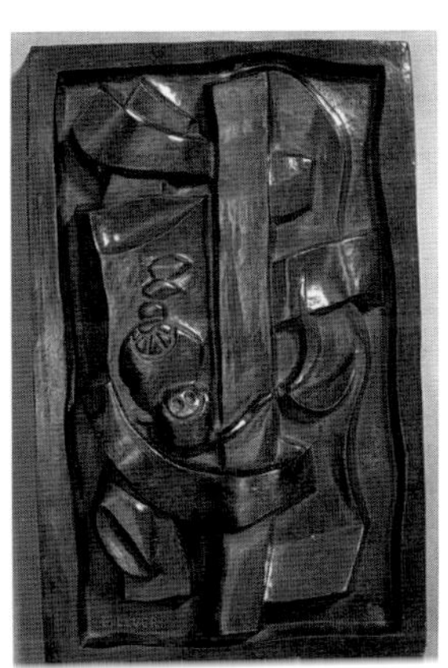

*Composition with Fruit,* c. 1950/1952
Bronze, .621 x .400 x .114
(24 1/2 x 15 3/4 x 4 1/2)
Inscribed at lower left: F. LÉGER; at lower right: 1/8
Collection of Mr. and Mrs. Paul Mellon
1983.1.54

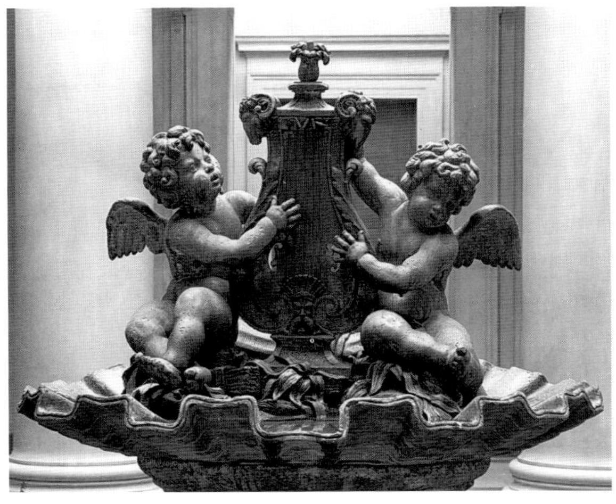

## PIERRE LEGROS I
French, 1629–1714

*Cherubs Playing with a Lyre,* 1672–1673
Lead, traces of gilding, 1.090 x 1.500
(43 x 59)
Andrew W. Mellon Collection
1940.1.16

*See also:* JEAN-BAPTISTE TUBY I, *Cherubs Playing with a Swan,* 1940.1.15

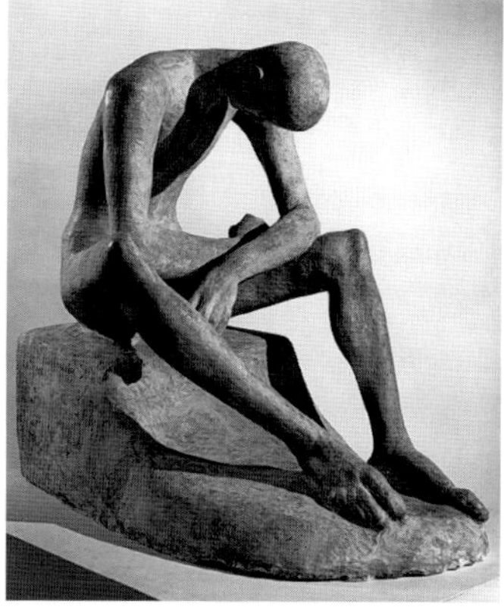

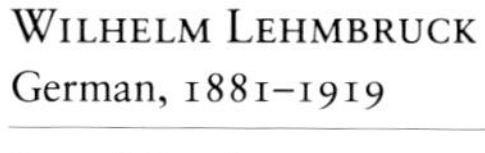

## Wilhelm Lehmbruck
German, 1881–1919

*Seated Youth,* 1917
Composite tinted plaster
1.032 x .762 x 1.155 (40 5/8 x 30 x 45)
Inscribed on side of base under figure's right hip: W. LEHMBRUCK / 1917
Andrew W. Mellon Fund
1974.49.1

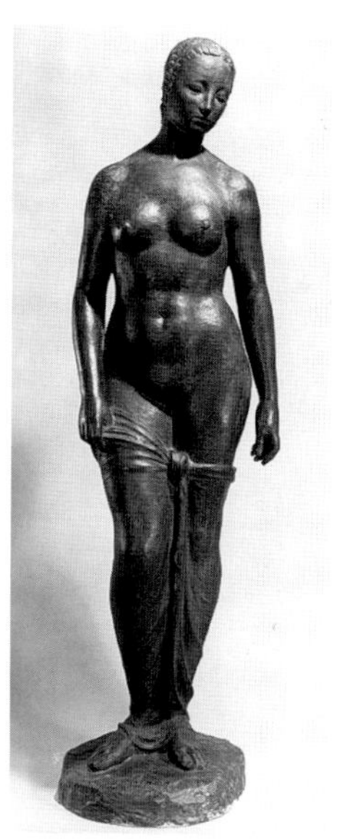

*Standing Woman,* 1910
Bronze, 1.912 x .540 x .399
(75 1/4 x 21 1/4 x 15 3/4)
Inscribed on top of base next to right foot: W. LEHMBRUCK. 1910 / PARIS
Ailsa Mellon Bruce Fund
1965.5.1

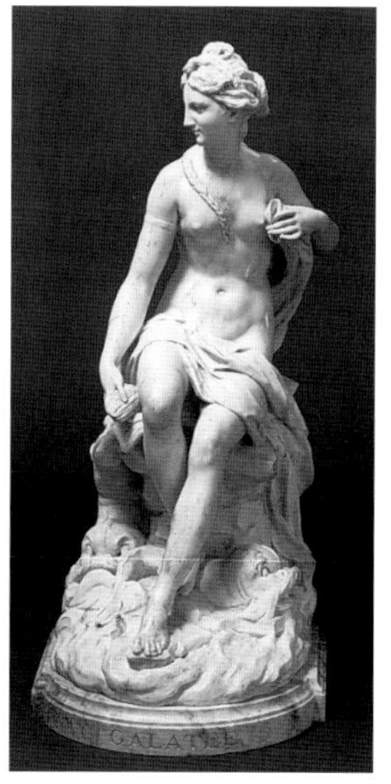

## Robert Le Lorrain
French, 1666–1743

*Galatea,* 1701
Marble, without base: .751 x .377 x .451
(29 1/2 x 14 3/4 x 17 3/4)
Inscribed on front of base: GALATEE; on back of base: ROBERT LE LORRAIN SCULPT. 1701
Samuel H. Kress Collection
1952.5.105

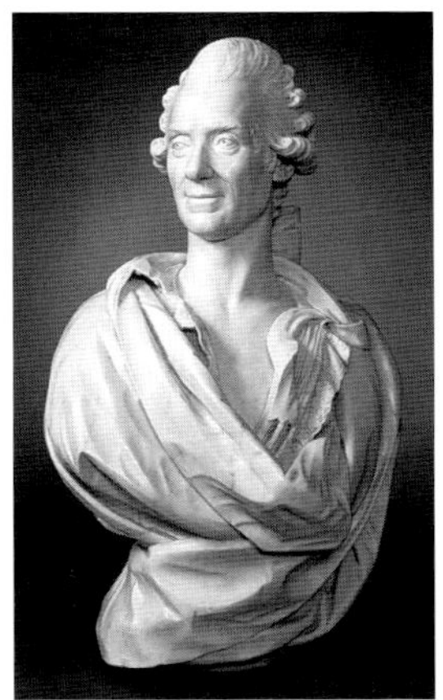

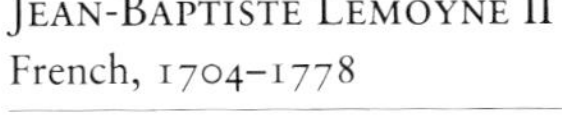

## JEAN-BAPTISTE LEMOYNE II
French, 1704–1778

*Jules-David Cromot, Baron du Bourg,* c. 1757
Marble, .797 x .483 x .419
(31 3/8 x 19 x 16 1/2)
Gift of Camille de Nuchoze, direct descendant, and her husband, John Hadley Cox
1985.39.1

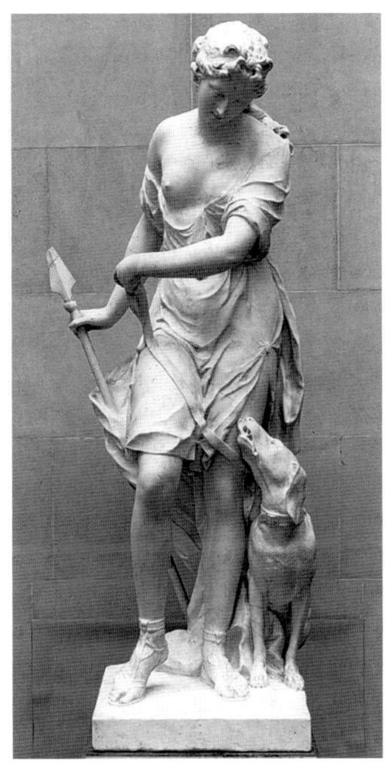

## JEAN-LOUIS LEMOYNE
French, 1666–1755

*A Companion of Diana,* 1724
Marble, 1.825 x .765 x .578
(71 3/4 x 30 1/8 x 22 3/4)
Inscribed on left side of pedestal: J.L. LEMOYNE • PARISINVS • FECIT • / 1724
Widener Collection
1942.9.133

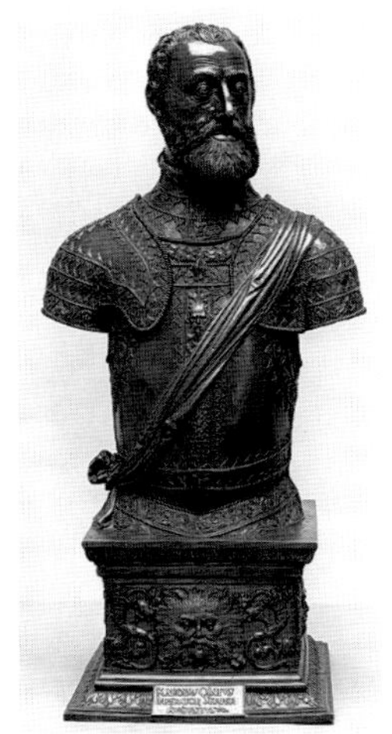

## LEONE LEONI
Milanese, 1509–1590

*Emperor Charles V,* c. 1555
Bronze, including base:
1.090 x .560 x .421 (43 1/8 x 22 x 16 1/2)
Inscribed on front of base: KAROLVS QINTVS / IMPERATOR SEMPER / AVGVSTVS
Samuel H. Kress Collection
1952.5.104

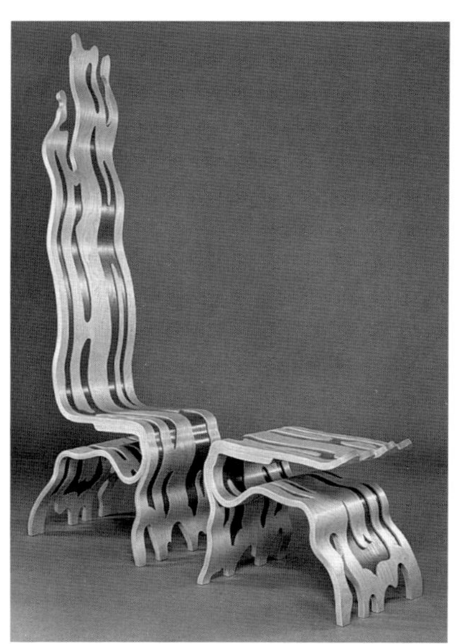

## ROY LICHTENSTEIN
American, born 1923

*Brushstroke Chair, Wood,* 1987
Blue paint on white birch veneer
1.795 x .457 x .692 ($70^{3}/_{4}$ x 18 x $27^{1}/_{4}$)
Inscribed beneath seat: RF LICHTENSTEIN / '88 / NGA / PROOF
Gift of Graphicstudio/University of South Florida and the Artist
1988.55.1

*Brushstroke Ottoman, Wood,* 1987
Blue paint on white birch veneer
.527 x .451 x .610 ($20^{3}/_{4}$ x $17^{3}/_{4}$ x 24)
Inscribed on underside: RF LICHTENSTEIN / '88 / NGA / PROOF
Gift of Graphicstudio/University of South Florida and the Artist
1988.55.2

*Modern Head Relief,* published 1970
Solid brass, .610 x .451 x .019 (24 x $17^{3}/_{4}$ x $^{3}/_{4}$)
Inscribed on verso, lower center, on brass plate: 33/100 RF LICHTENSTEIN '70 / © (Gemini chop)
Gift of Mr. and Mrs. Roger P. Sonnabend
1986.90.19

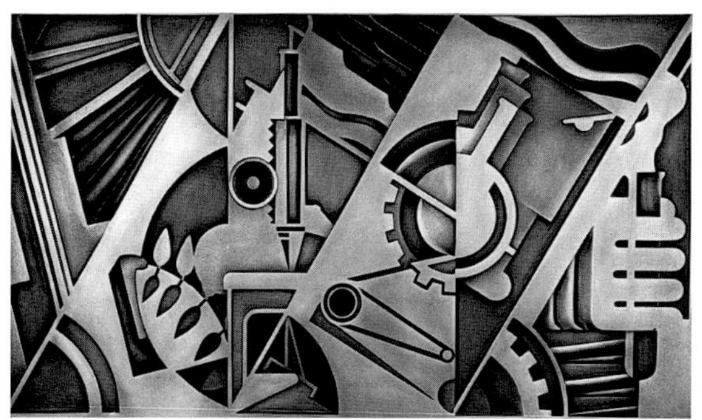

*Peace Through Chemistry Bronze,* published 1970
Bronze, .692 x 1.175 x .032 ($27^{1}/_{4}$ x $46^{1}/_{4}$ x $1^{1}/_{4}$)
Gift of Gemini G.E.L.
1981.5.280

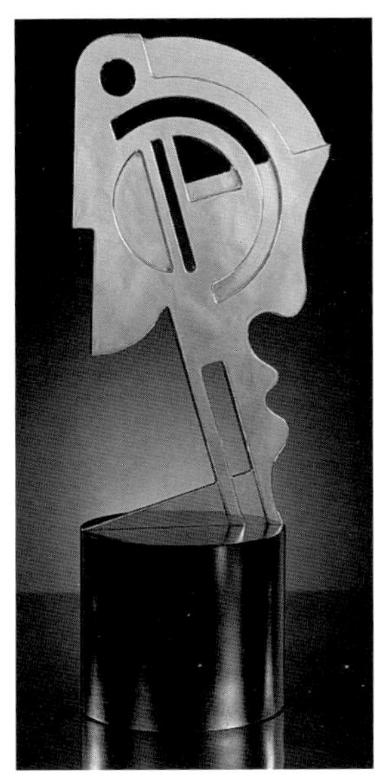

*Study for "Untitled Head II,"* 1970
Aluminum and wood, .559 x .302 x .025 (22 x 11 7/8 x 1)
Inscribed inside base on brass plate: RF LICHTENSTEIN / '70 / PROTO.
Gift of Gemini G.E.L. and the Artist, in Honor of the 50th Anniversary of the National Gallery of Art
1990.104.16

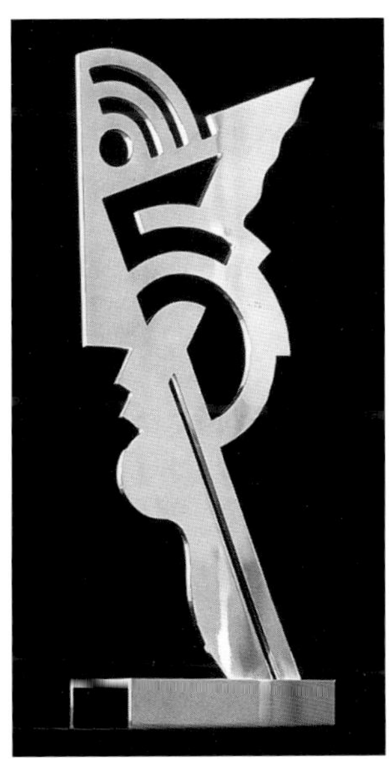

*Untitled Head I,* published 1970
Solid brass on a brass-plated steel base
.651 x .260 x .010 (25 5/8 x 10 1/4 x 3/8)
Inscribed on copper plate inside base: R. LICHTENSTEIN / 15/75 '70 / (Gemini chop and copyright)
Gift of Gemini G.E.L.
1981.5.266

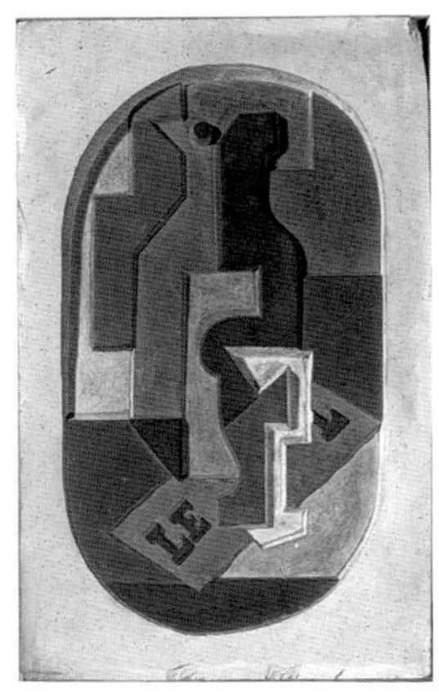

## JACQUES LIPCHITZ
## (CHAIM JACOB LIPCHITZ)
French, 1891–1973

*Bas-Relief, I,* 1918
Stone, polychromed, .557 x .357 x .044 (22 x 14 x 3/4)
Adolph Caspar Miller Fund
1977.29.1

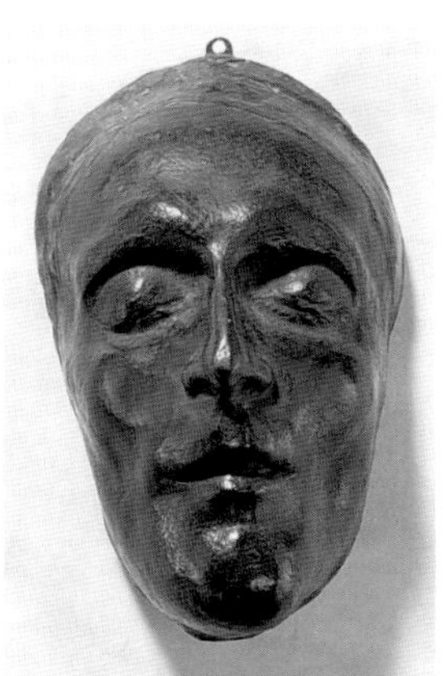

JACQUES LIPCHITZ
(CHAIM JACOB LIPCHITZ)
French, 1891–1973
and MOÏSE KISLING
French, 1891–1953
and CONRAD MORICAND
French, active 20th century

*Death Mask of Amedeo Modigliani,* 1920
Bronze, .222 x .151 x .115
(8 3/4 x 6 x 4 1/2)
Chester Dale Collection
1963.10.237

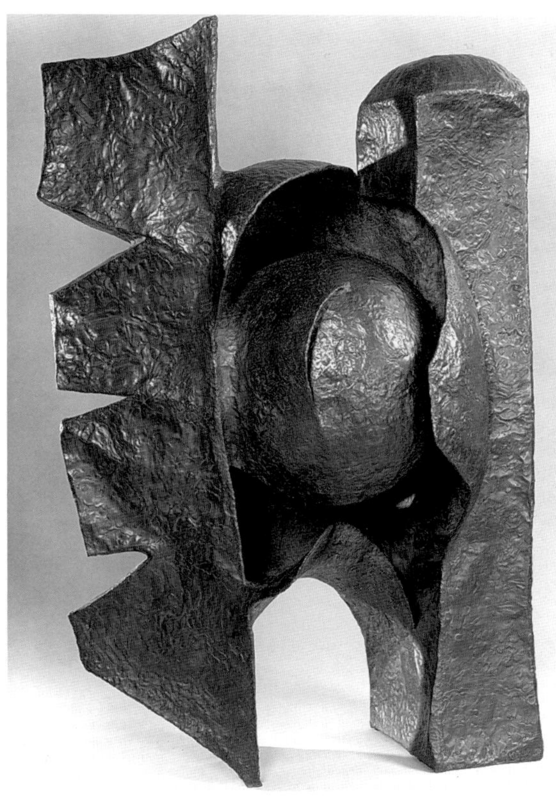

SEYMOUR LIPTON
American, 1903–1986

*Gateway,* 1964
Nickel silver on Monel
1.930 x 1.498 x .889 (76 x 59 x 35)
Gift of Seymour Lipton
1986.75.43

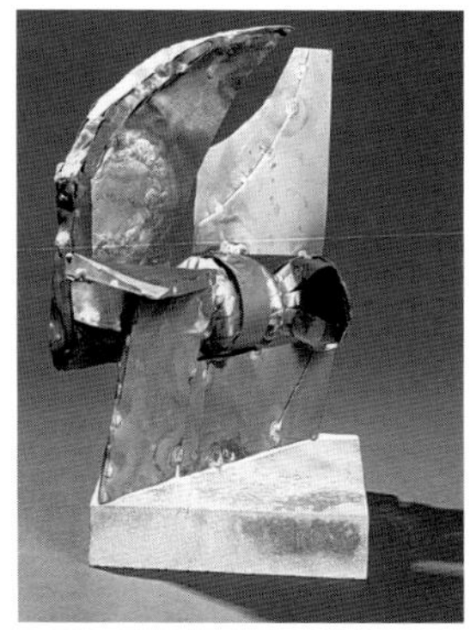

*Maquette for "Sailing,"* 1976
Monel, welded, .286 x .254 x .127
(11 1/4 x 10 x 5)
Gift of Seymour Lipton
1986.75.3

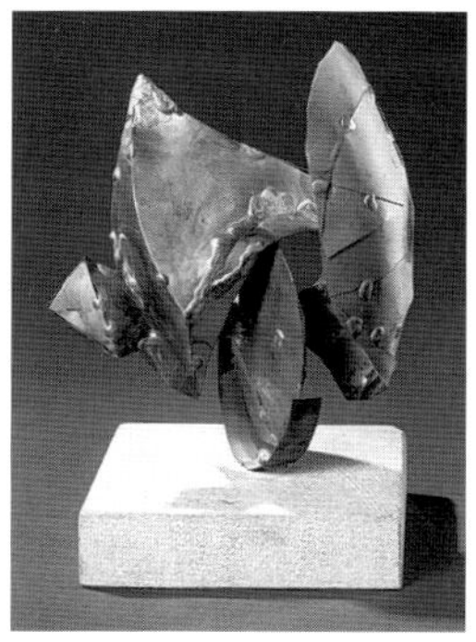

*Maquette for "Thorn Mill,"* 1975
Monel, welded, .216 x .178 x .114
($8^1/_2$ x 7 x $4^1/_2$)
Gift of Seymour Lipton
1986.75.2

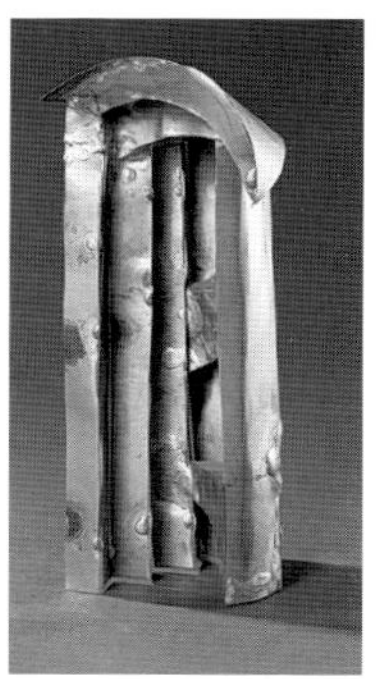

*Maquette for "Threshold,"* 1981
Monel, welded, .294 x .134 x .132
($11^5/_8$ x $5^1/_4$ x $5^1/_4$)
Gift of Seymour Lipton
1986.75.1

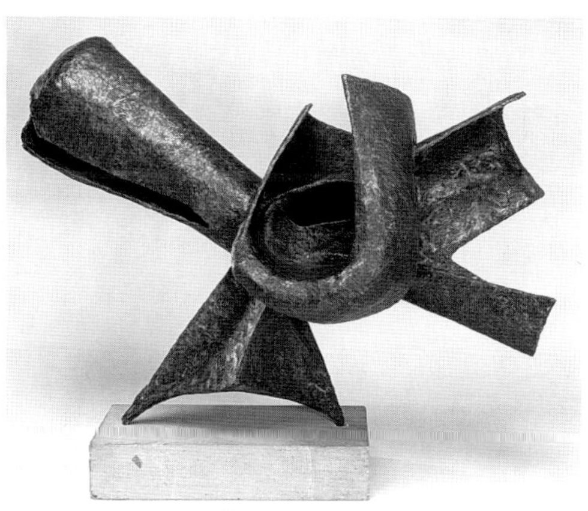

*Sower,* 1960
Nickel silver on Monel
.673 x 1.118 x .356 ($26^1/_2$ x 44 x 14)
Ailsa Mellon Bruce Fund
1987.35.1

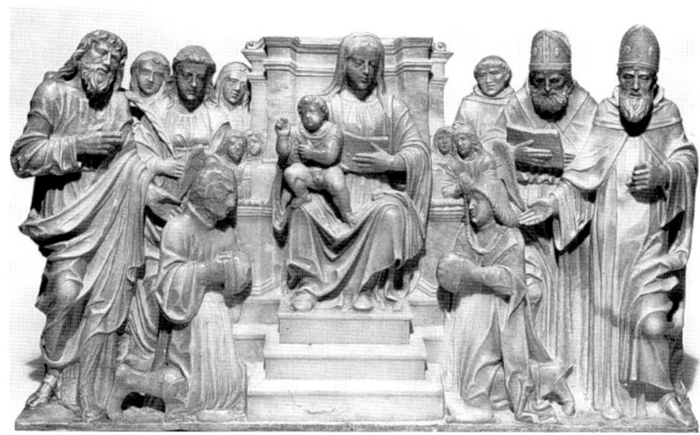

## Lombard 16th Century

*Madonna and Child with Saints and Donors,* early 16th century
Marble, .550 x .910 ($21^1/_2$ x 36)
Samuel H. Kress Collection
1939.1.336

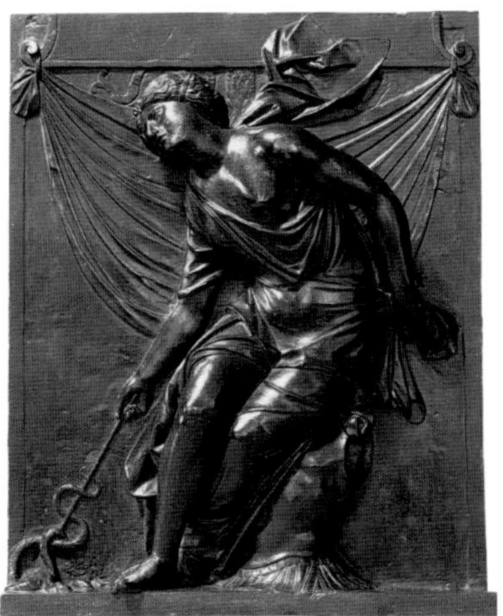

ANTONIO LOMBARDO
Venetian, c. 1458–1516

*Peace Establishing Her Reign,* 1512
Bronze, .406 x .339 x .076
(16 x 13 3/8 x 3)
Ailsa Mellon Bruce Fund
1972.12.1

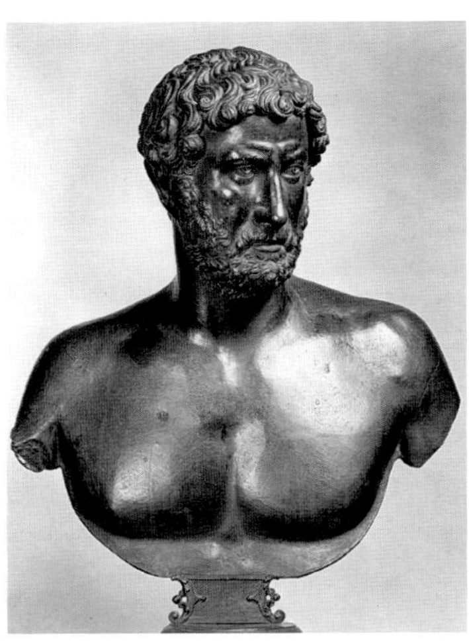

LODOVICO LOMBARDO
Venetian, 1507/1508–1575

*The Emperor Hadrian,* c. 1550
Bronze, .727 x .638 x .411
(28 5/8 x 25 1/8 x 16 1/4)
Gift of Stanley Mortimer
1945.16.1

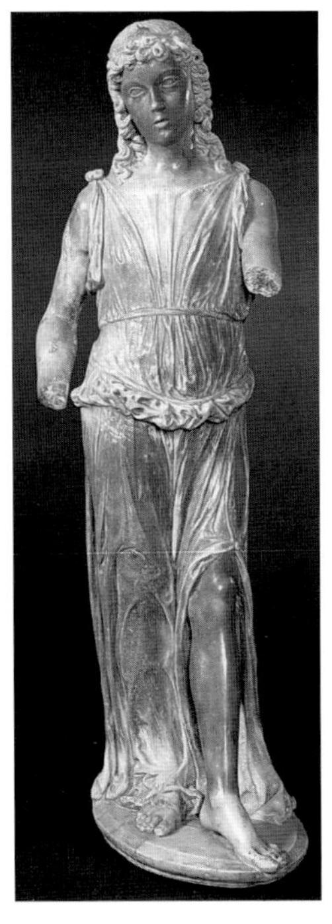

PIETRO LOMBARDO
Venetian, c. 1435–1515

*Allegorical Figure,* c. 1485
Marble, .860 x .280 x .300
(33 7/8 x 11 x 11 3/4)
Samuel H. Kress Collection
1943.4.72

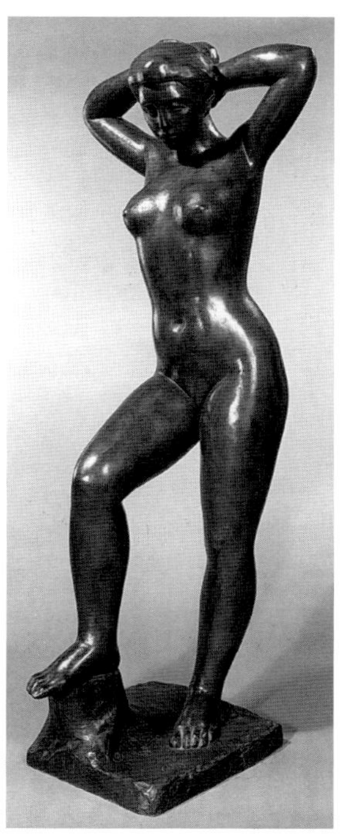

## Aristide Maillol

French, 1861–1944

*Bather with Raised Arms,* 1930
Bronze, 1.575 x .661 x .601
(62 x 26 1/4 x 23 5/8)
Inscribed on top of base in front of left foot: AM (monogram); foundry mark on rear edge of base: ALEXIS RUDIER / FONDEUR, PARIS
Ailsa Mellon Bruce Fund
1967.15.1

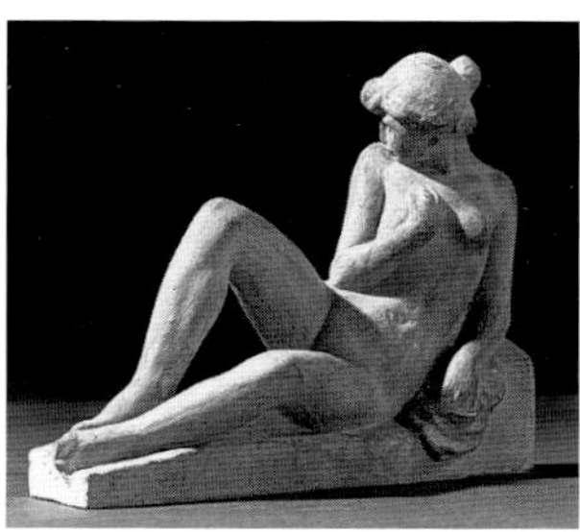

*Modesty,* c. 1900
Terra cotta, .159 x .210 (6 1/4 x 8 1/4)
Inscribed on right side of base below left arm: M (monogram)
Collection of Mr. and Mrs. Paul Mellon
1983.1.56

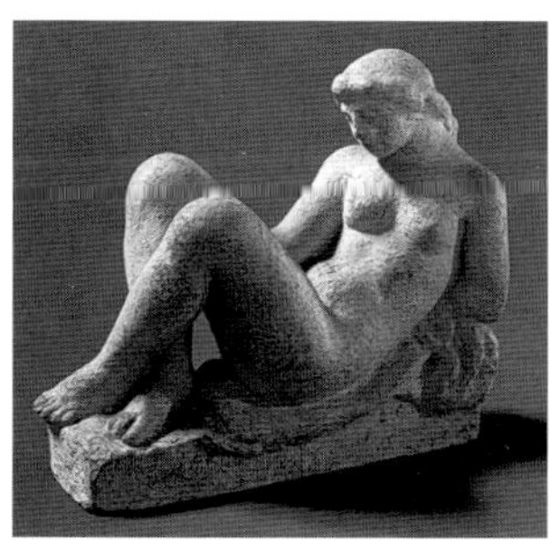

*Reclining Nude,* c. 1900
Terra cotta, .159 x .178 (6 1/4 x 7)
Inscribed on base at rear: (initials)
Collection of Mr. and Mrs. Paul Mellon
1983.1.57

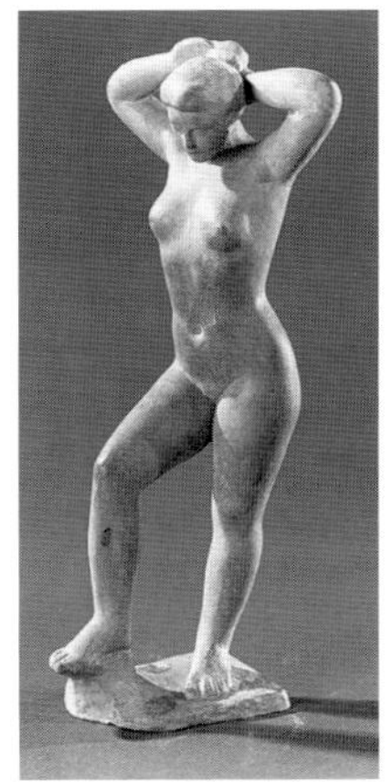

Aristide Maillol
French, 1861–1944

*Rosita*, c. 1890/1899
Terra cotta, height: .260 (10 1/4)
Inscribed on top of base by left foot: AM (monogram)
Collection of Mr. and Mrs. Paul Mellon
1983.1.58

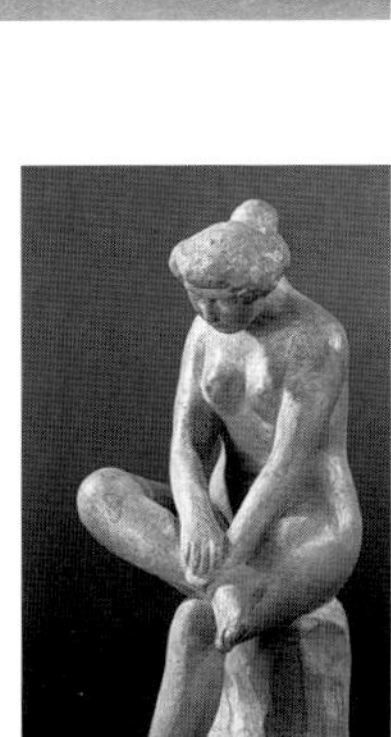

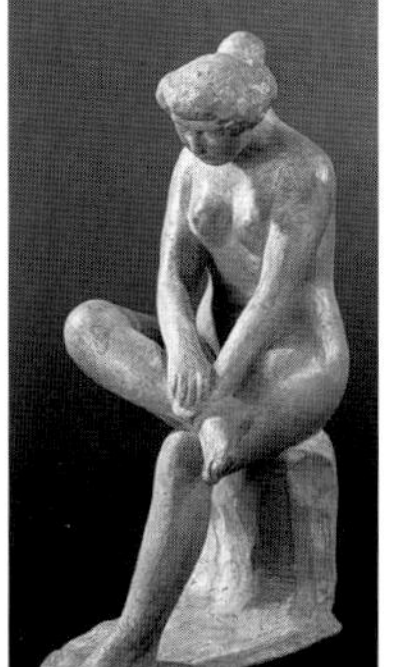

*Seated Woman*, c. 1900
Terra cotta, height: .216 (8 1/2)
Collection of Mr. and Mrs. Paul Mellon
1983.1.59

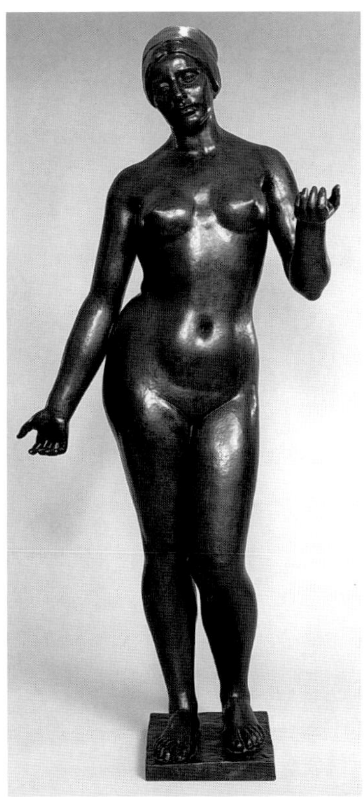

*Summer*, 1910
Bronze, 1.630 x .737 x .332 (64 1/8 x 29 x 13)
Inscribed on top of base in rear right corner: AM (monogram); foundry mark on rear edge of base: .ALEXIS RUDIER. / .FONDEUR.PARIS.
Ailsa Mellon Bruce Fund
1967.5.1

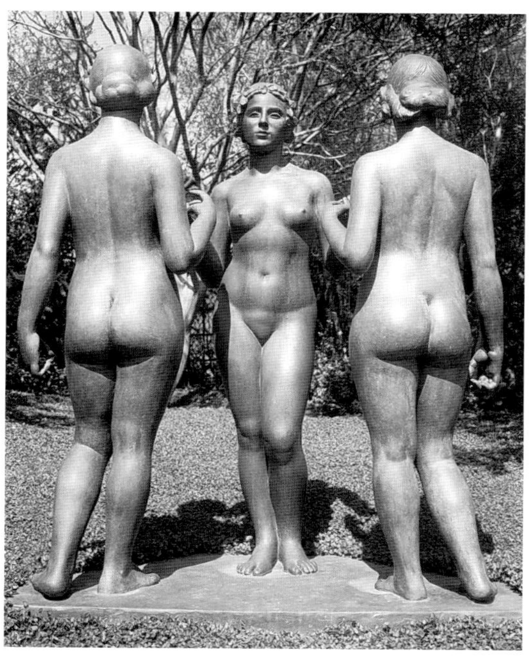

*The Three Nymphs*, 1930–1938
Lead, 1.575 x 1.457 x .800
(62 x $57^3/_8$ x $31^1/_2$)
Inscribed on top of base in front of figure with right arm by her side: AM (monogram); foundry mark on angled side of base by figure with left arm by her side: .GEORGES RUDIER. / .FONDEUR.PARIS.
Gift (Partial and Promised) of Lucille Ellis Simon, in Honor of the 50th Anniversary of the National Gallery of Art
1991.39.1

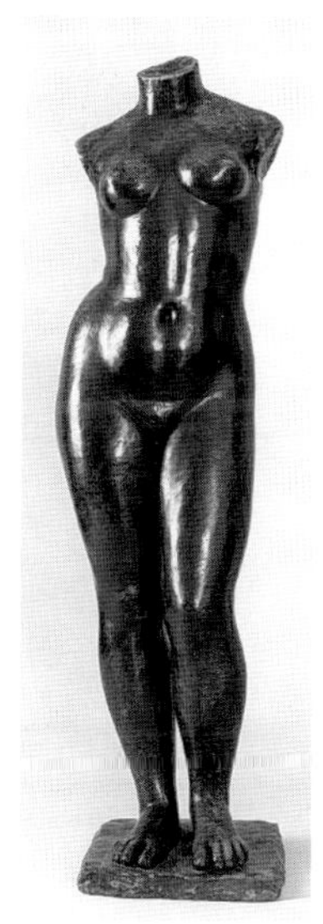

*Torso of Venus*, probably c. 1918/1928
Bronze, height: 1.553 ($61^1/_8$); at base: .381 x .362 (15 x $14^1/_4$)
Inscribed on top of base next to left foot: AM (monogram) 1/6; foundry mark on rear edge of base: ALEXIS RUDIER. / .FONDEUR.PARIS.
Gift of June P. Carey
1984.27.1

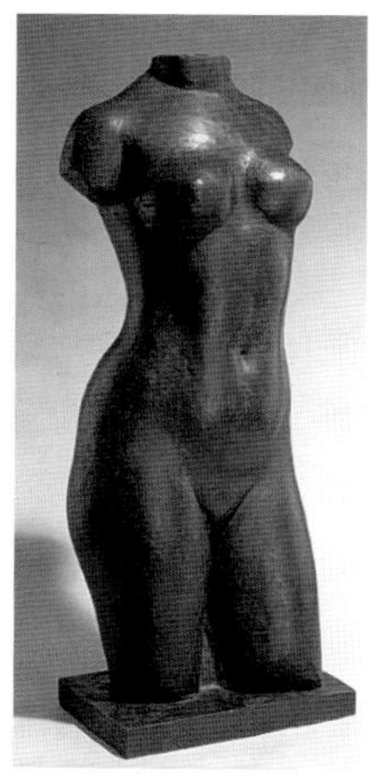

*Torso of a Young Woman*, c. 1930
Bronze, .898 x .403 x .273
($35^3/_8$ x $15^7/_8$ x $10^3/_4$)
Inscribed on top of base behind left leg: M (monogram); foundry mark on rear edge of base: CIRE / C.VALSUANI / PERDUE
Collection of Mr. and Mrs. Paul Mellon
1983.1.60

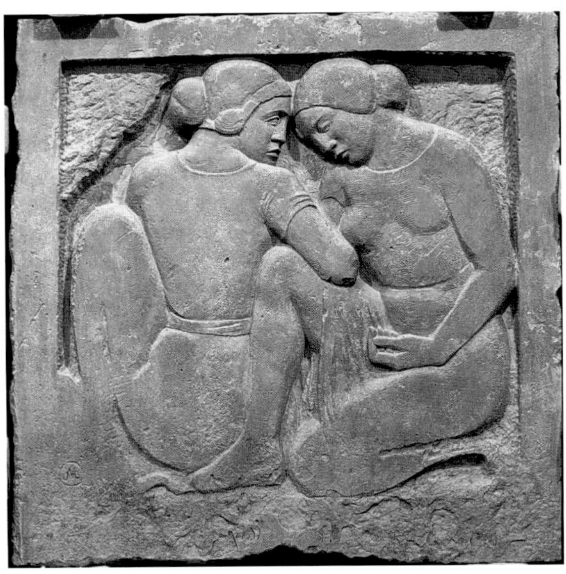

ARISTIDE MAILLOL
French, 1861–1944

*Two Young Girls,* c. 1930
Stone, 1.219 x 1.270 (48 x 50)
Inscribed at lower left: M (monogram)
Collection of Mr. and Mrs. Paul Mellon
1983.1.61

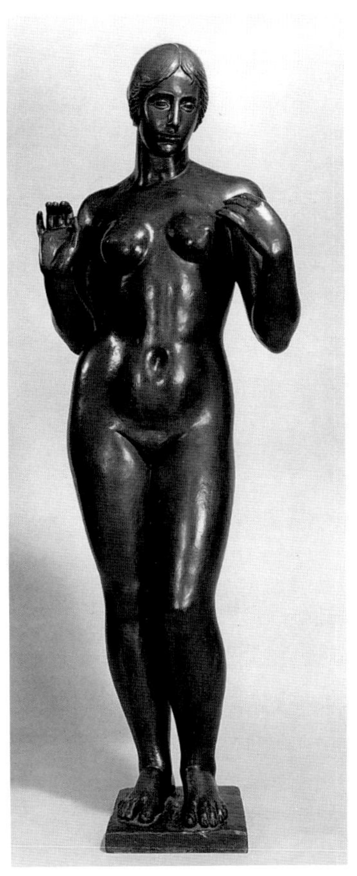

*Venus,* 1918/1928
Bronze, 1.755 x .602 x .423
(69 1/8 x 23 3/4 x 16 5/8)
Inscribed on top of base in rear left corner: AM (monogram); foundry mark on rear edge of base: ALEXIS RUDIER / FONDEUR PARIS
Ailsa Mellon Bruce Fund
1965.4.1

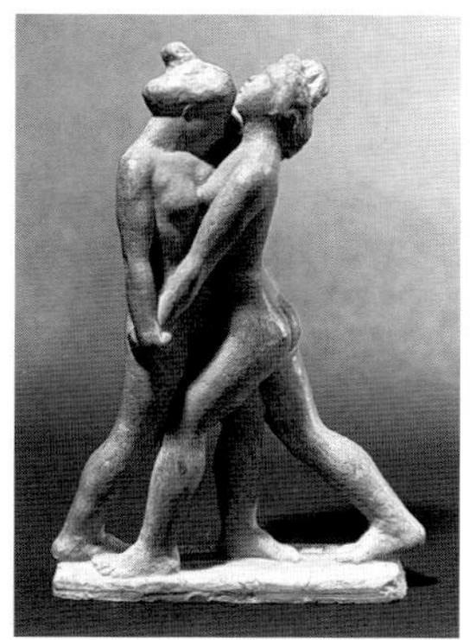

*Women Wrestlers,* 1900
Terra cotta, height: .184 (7 1/4)
Collection of Mr. and Mrs. Paul Mellon
1983.1.62

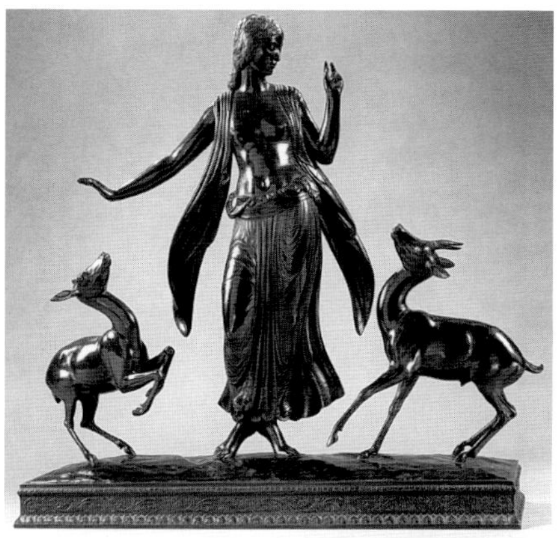

Paul Manship
American, 1885–1966

*Dancer and Gazelles,* 1916
Bronze, .826 x .883 x .285
(32 1/2 x 34 3/4 x 11 1/4)
Inscribed on top of base near dancer's right foot: PAUL MANSHIP / © 1916; foundry mark on top of base in rear right corner: ROMAN BRONZE WORKS•N.Y.
Gift of Mrs. Houghton P. Metcalf
1977.48.1

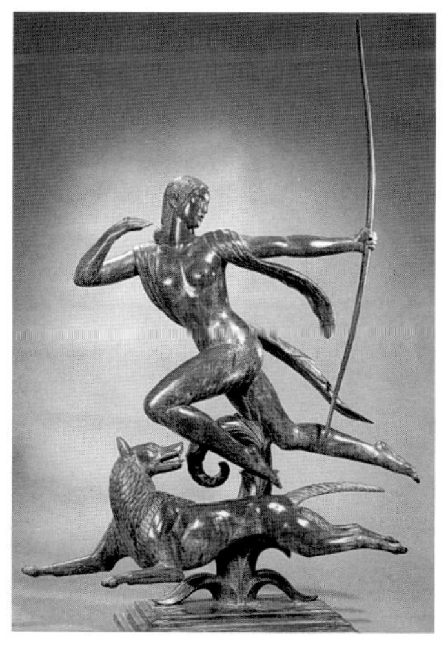

*Diana and a Hound,* 1925
Bronze, 1.647 x 1.099 x .492
(64 7/8 x 43 1/4 x 19 3/8)
Inscribed on top of base, front: PAUL MANSHIP•SCULPTOR• / •©•1925•; foundry mark on right side of base, on edge of lowest "step": ALEXIS RUDIER. / FONDEUR PARIS.
Gift of Mrs. Houghton P. Metcalf
1977.48.2

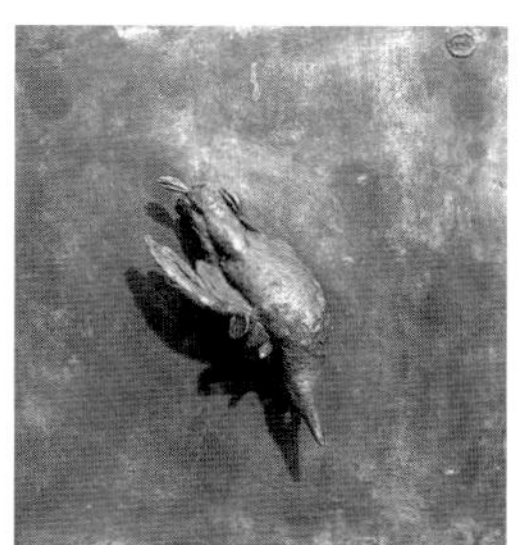

Giacomo Manzù
Italian, 1908–1991

*Dead Bird,* 1962
Bronze, .473 x .469 x .112
(18 5/8 x 18 1/2 x 4 3/8)
Signature with foundry mark in circle at upper right: MANZU / NFMM
Collection of Mr. and Mrs. Paul Mellon
1983.1.67

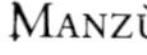


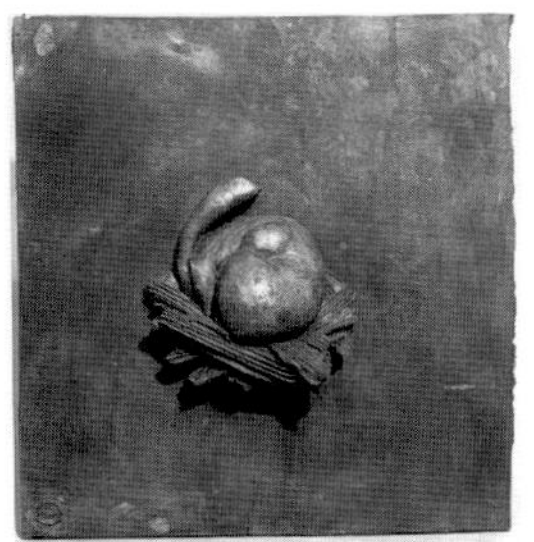

## Giacomo Manzù
Italian, 1908–1991

*Dormouse*, 1962
Bronze, .470 x .469 x .105
($18^{1}/_{2}$ x $18^{1}/_{2}$ x $4^{1}/_{8}$)
Signature with foundry mark in circle at lower left: MANZU / NFMM
Collection of Mr. and Mrs. Paul Mellon
1983.1.68

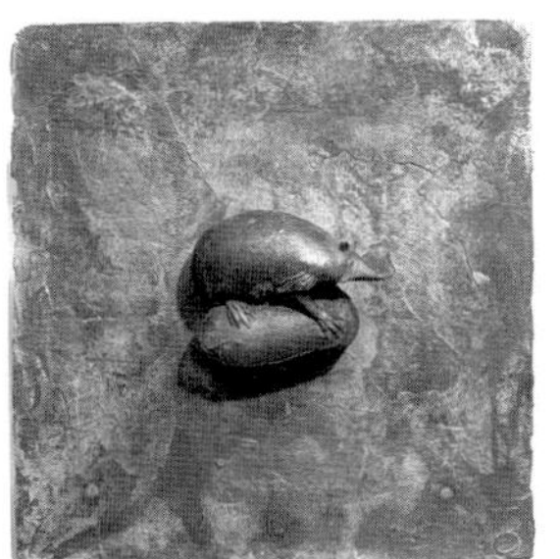

*Hedgehog*, 1962
Bronze, .498 x .497 x .092
($19^{5}/_{8}$ x $19^{5}/_{8}$ x $3^{5}/_{8}$)
Signature with foundry mark in circle at lower right: MANZÙ / NFMM
Collection of Mr. and Mrs. Paul Mellon
1983.1.69

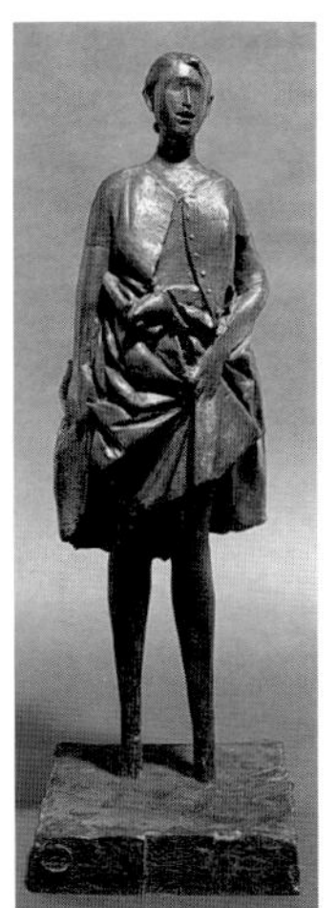

*Model Undressing II*, 1965
Bronze, .638 x .210 x .207
($25^{1}/_{8}$ x $8^{1}/_{4}$ x $8^{1}/_{8}$)
Signature with foundry mark in circle on front edge of base: MANZÙ / NFMM
Collection of Mr. and Mrs. Paul Mellon
1983.1.65

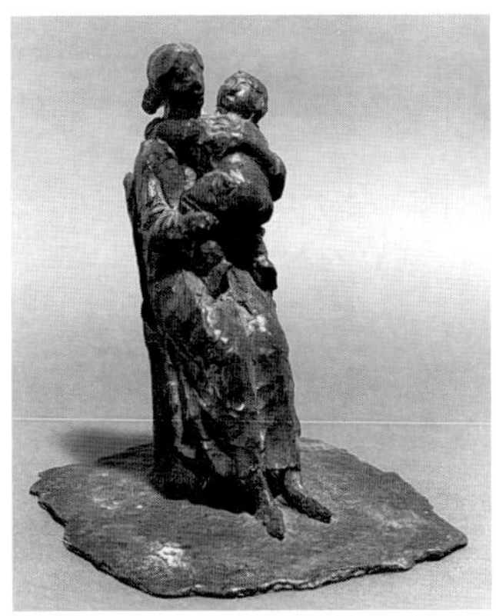

*Mother and Child*, 1956
Bronze, .330 x .276 x .327
(13 x $10^{7}/_{8}$ x $12^{7}/_{8}$)
Signature with foundry mark on bottom back of chair: FONDERIA MAF MILANO / MANZU
Collection of Mr. and Mrs. Paul Mellon
1983.1.66

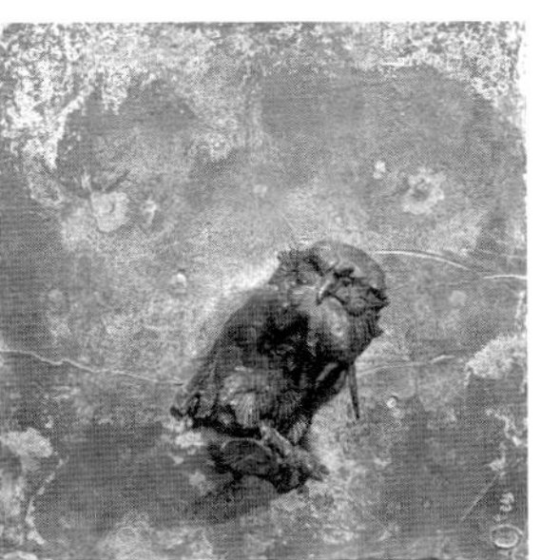

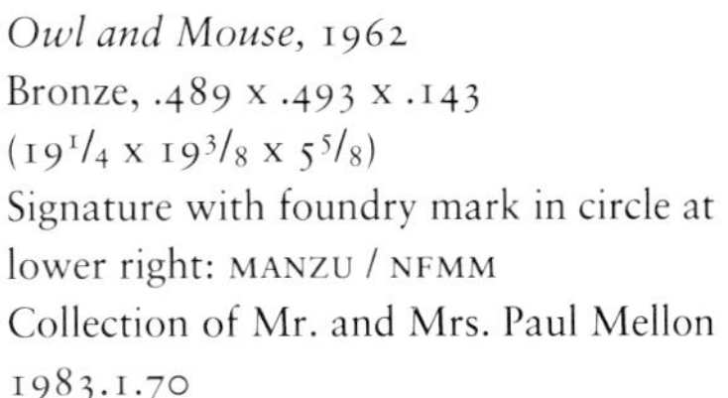

*Owl and Mouse,* 1962
Bronze, .489 x .493 x .143
(19 1/4 x 19 3/8 x 5 5/8)
Signature with foundry mark in circle at lower right: MANZU / NFMM
Collection of Mr. and Mrs. Paul Mellon
1983.1.70

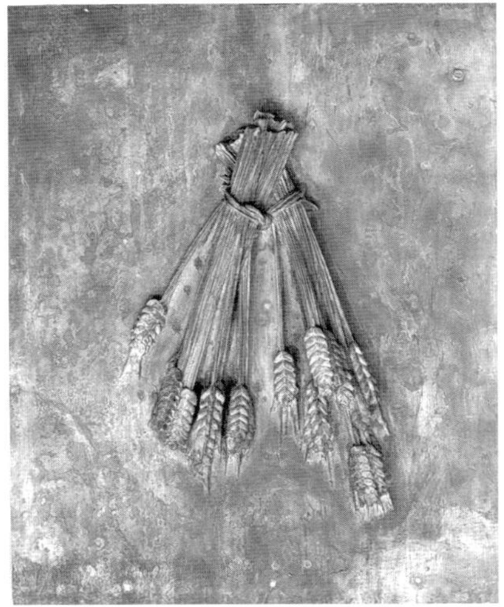

*Sheaves of Wheat,* 1960
Bronze, 1.574 x 1.308 x .127
(62 x 51 1/2 x 5)
Signature with foundry mark in circle at upper right: MANZU / NFMM
Collection of Mr. and Mrs. Paul Mellon
1983.1.63

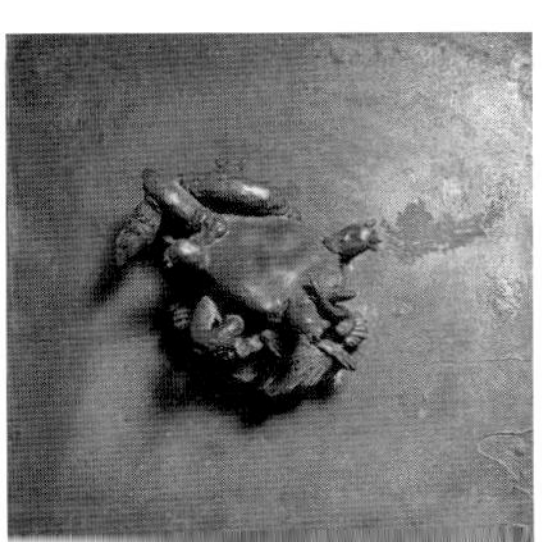

*Turtle Seizing a Snake,* 1962
Bronze, .451 x .479 x .109
(17 3/4 x 18 7/8 x 4 1/4)
Signature with foundry mark in circle at lower right: MANZÙ / NFMM
Gift of Alexandre P. Rosenberg
1983.21.1

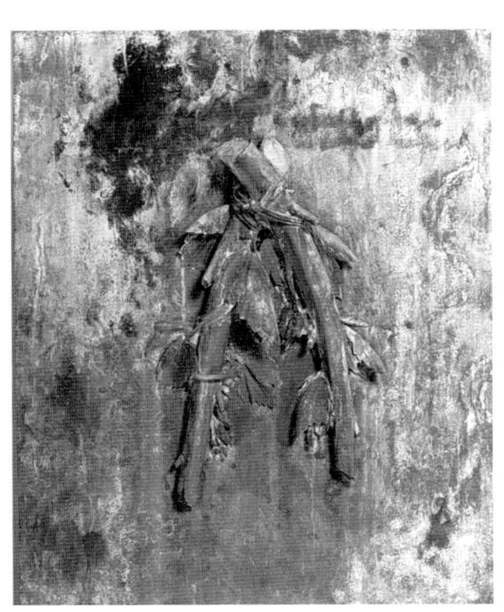

*Vine Branches,* 1960
Bronze, 1.574 x 1.358 x .153
(62 x 53 1/2 x 6)
Signature with foundry mark in circle at lower right: MANZÙ / NFM[M]
Collection of Mr. and Mrs. Paul Mellon
1983.1.64

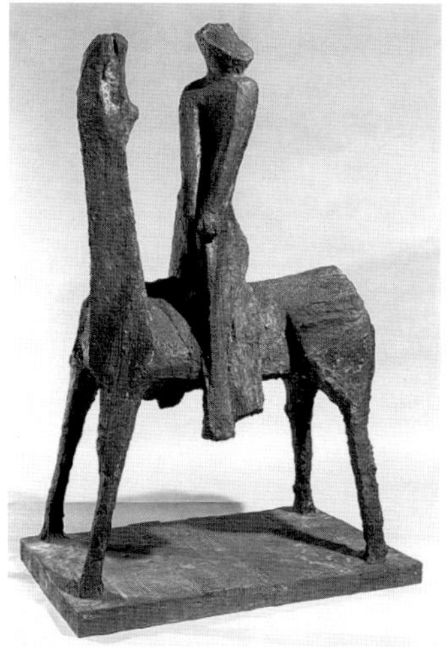

Marino Marini
Italian, 1901–1980

*The Concept of the Rider (L'Idea del Cavaliere)*, 1952–1954
Bronze, 2.146 x 1.391 x .927
(84 1/2 x 54 3/4 x 36 1/2)
Inscribed on top of base between back legs of horse: M.M / 1/3
Collection of Mr. and Mrs. Paul Mellon
1985.64.68

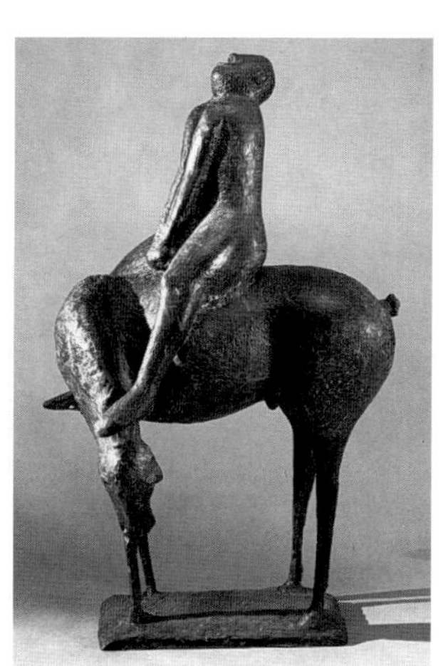

*Horseman*, 1947
Bronze, .991 x .470 x .660
(39 x 18 1/2 x 26)
Inscribed on top of base between back legs of horse: MM 5/6
Gift of Enid A. Haupt
1977.47.9

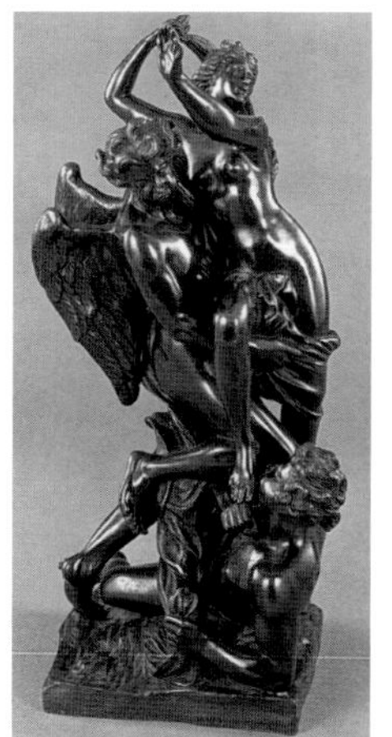

Gaspard Marsy II
French, 1624–1681
and Anselme Flamen
French, 1647–1717

*Boreas and Orithyia (Allegory of Air)*, 1677/1687, bronze reduction made and cast c. 1693–1716
Bronze, .533 x .272 x .245
(21 x 10 3/4 x 9 5/8)
Gift of Asbjorn R. Lunde
1986.74.2

*See also:* François Girardon, *Pluto and Persephone (Allegory of Fire)*, 1986.74.1

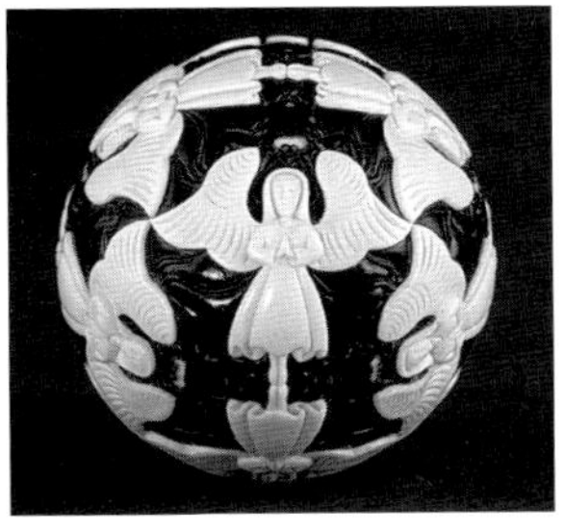

Masatoshi, after M. C. Escher
Japanese

*Heaven and Hell,* 1962
Carved ivory sphere with black lacquer, diameter: .051 (2)
Cornelius Van S. Roosevelt Collection
1974.28.81

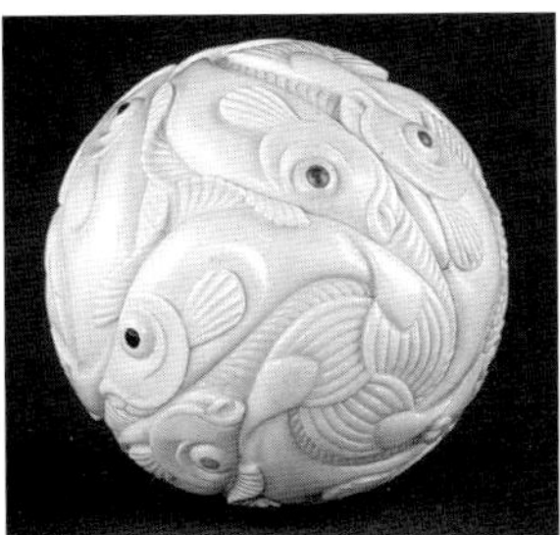

*Sphere with Fish,* 1962
Carved ivory sphere with inlay, diameter: .053 ($2^1/_8$)
Cornelius Van S. Roosevelt Collection
1974.28.80

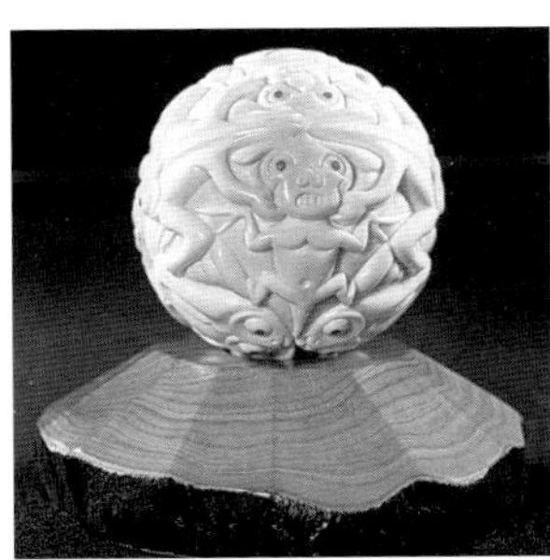

*Three Elements,* 1963/1964
Carved ivory sphere with inlay, diameter: .053 ($2^1/_8$)
Cornelius Van S. Roosevelt Collection
1974.28.79

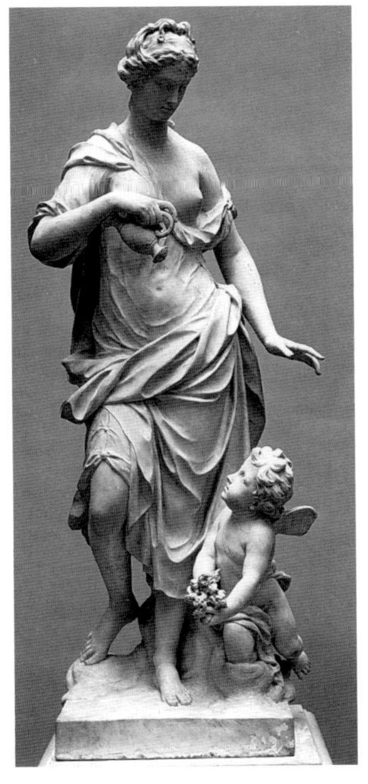

Benoît Massou
French, 1633–1684
and Anselme Flamen
French, 1647–1717
and Nicolas Rebillé
French, active 1732–1751

*A Garden Allegory: The Dew and Zephyr Cultivating Flowers,* 1683/1732
Marble, 1.805 x .772 x .673
(71 x $30^1/_2$ x $26^5/_8$)
Samuel H. Kress Collection
1952.5.106

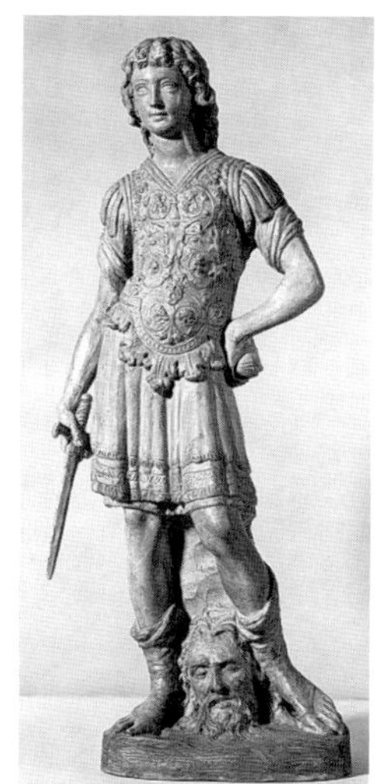

Master of the David and Saint John Statuettes
Florentine, active late 15th–early 16th century

*David,* late 15th or early 16th century
Terra cotta, .500 x .174 x .140
(19 3/4 x 6 7/8 x 5 1/2)
Samuel H. Kress Collection
1943.4.81

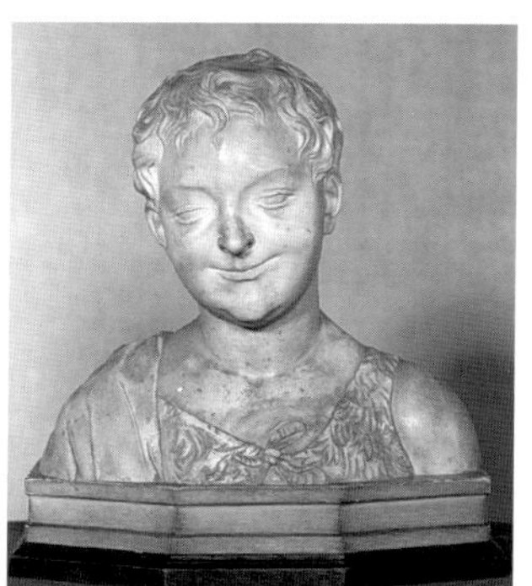

Master of the Marble Madonnas
Florentine (?), active c. 1470/1500

*The Young Saint John the Baptist,*
c. 1470/1500
Marble, .267 x .292 x .162
(10 1/2 x 11 1/2 x 6 3/8)
Widener Collection
1942.9.134

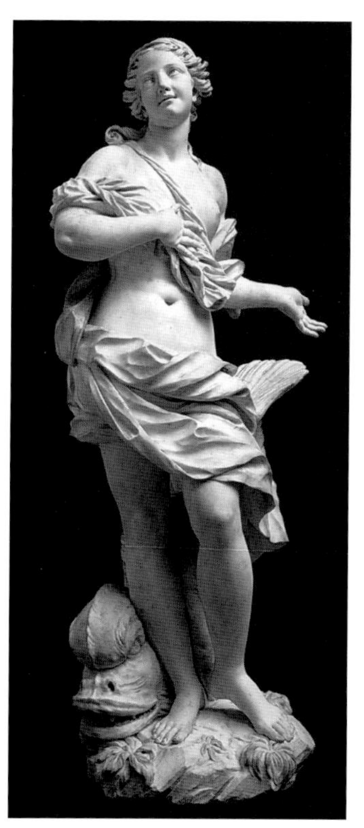

Attributed to Giuseppe Mazzuoli
Italian, 1644–1725

*A Nereid,* c. 1705/1715
Marble, 2.042 x .916 x .603
(80 1/4 x 36 x 23 3/4)
Samuel H. Kress Collection
1952.5.92

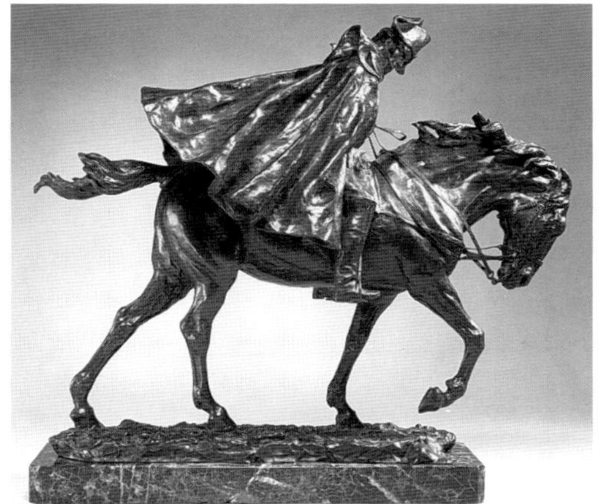

## JEAN-LOUIS-ERNEST MEISSONIER
French, 1815–1891

*A Horseman in a Storm*, c. 1880,
cast after 1893
Bronze, .472 x .593 x .239
(18 5/8 x 23 3/8 x 9 7/8)
Inscribed on ground on proper left side: MEISSONIER; foundry mark on proper right side of base at rear: SIOT DECAUVILLE / .PARIS.; behind left rear hoof of horse, in circle: 31
Collection of Mr. and Mrs. Paul Mellon
1980.44.10

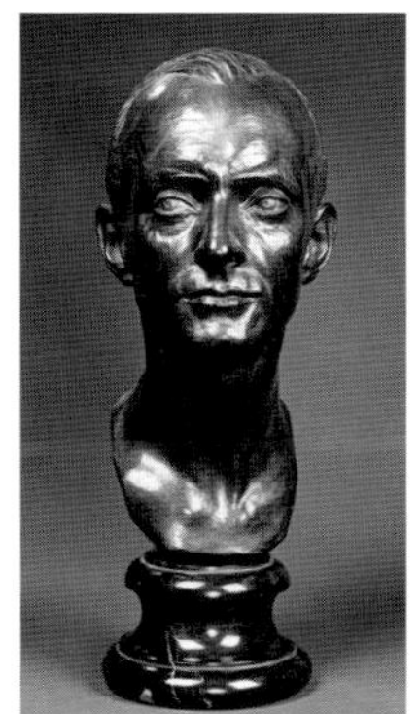

## FAUSTA VITTORIA MENGARINI
Italian, 1893–1952

*David E. Finley*, 1930
Bronze, .311 x .183 x .222
(12 1/4 x 7 1/4 x 8 3/4)
Inscribed on left side of truncation: FAUSTA- / VITTORIA MENGARINI; on right side of truncation: NEW YORK / 1930; foundry mark on back edge: CELLINI BRONZE WORKS, N.Y.
Gift of David E. Finley
1981.101.1

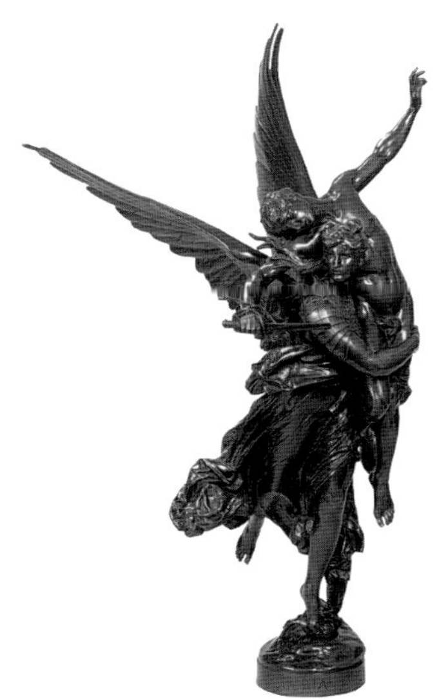

## MARIUS-JEAN-ANTONIN MERCIÉ
French, 1845–1916

*Gloria Victis!*, c. 1874
Bronze, with base: 1.400 x .841 x .673
(55 1/8 x 33 1/8 x 26 1/2)
Inscribed on top of base near left foot: A. MERCIÉ; around front edge of circular base: GLORIA VICTIS; foundry mark around rear edge of circular base: F. BARBEDIENNE, FONDEUR
Andrew W. Mellon Fund
1985.52.1

## CLAUDE MICHEL, CALLED CLODION
*See* CLODION

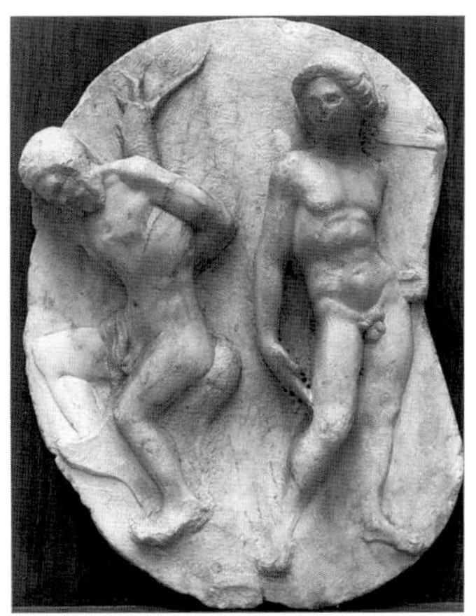

### Follower of Michelangelo Buonarroti, After the Antique

*Apollo and Marsyas*, c. 1495/1535
Marble, .412 x .314 (16 1/4 x 12 3/8)
Samuel H. Kress Collection
1961.1.5

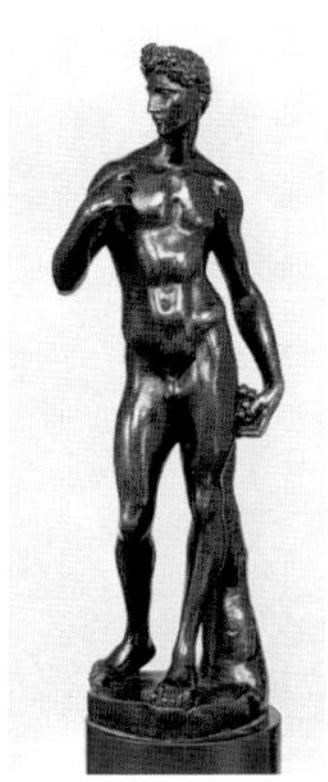

### After Michelangelo Buonarroti

*Bacchus*, 16th/19th century
Bronze, with self-base: .181 x .063 x .055
(7 1/8 x 2 1/2 x 2 3/16)
Samuel H. Kress Collection
1957.14.26

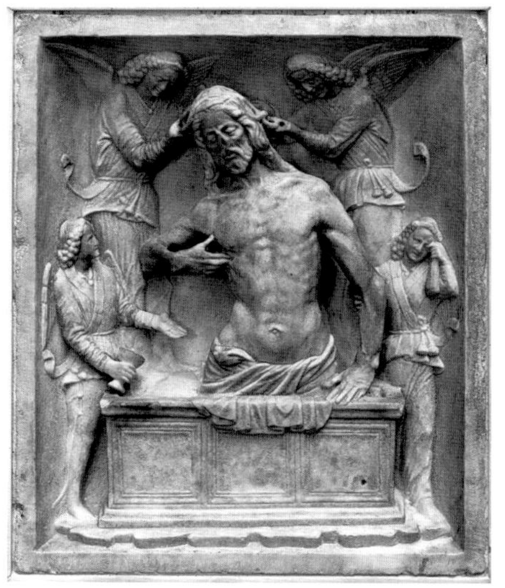

### Milanese 16th Century

*The Man of Sorrows*, early 16th century
Marble, .295 x .254 (11 5/8 x 10)
Samuel H. Kress Collection
1961.9.94

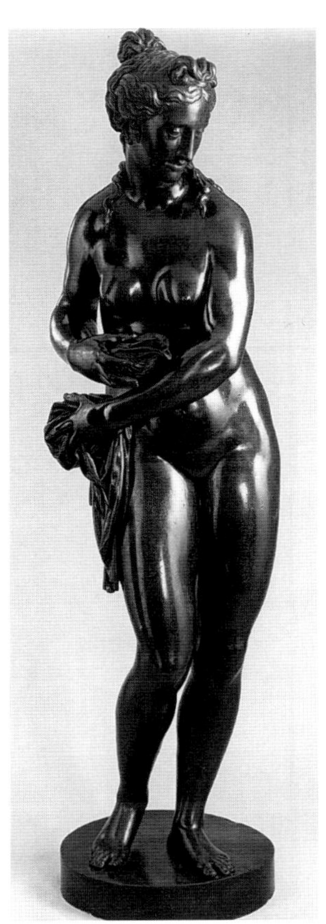

MILANESE 16TH CENTURY

*Venus*, c. 1580/1590, model attributed to Francesco Brambilla the Younger, 1530–1599
Bronze, 1.660 x .440 x .337
($65^{1}/_{2}$ x $17^{1}/_{4}$ x $13^{1}/_{4}$)
Andrew W. Mellon Collection
1937.1.132

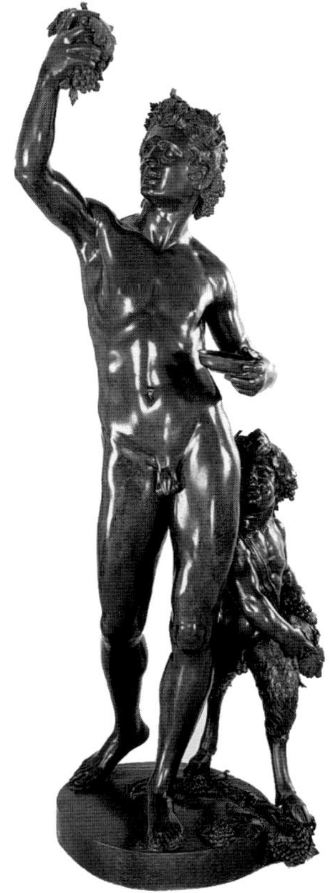

PROBABLY MILANESE 16TH CENTURY

*Bacchus and a Faun*, c. 1580/1600
Bronze, 1.815 x .760 x .652
($71^{1}/_{2}$ x 30 x $25^{5}/_{8}$)
Andrew W. Mellon Collection
1937.1.133

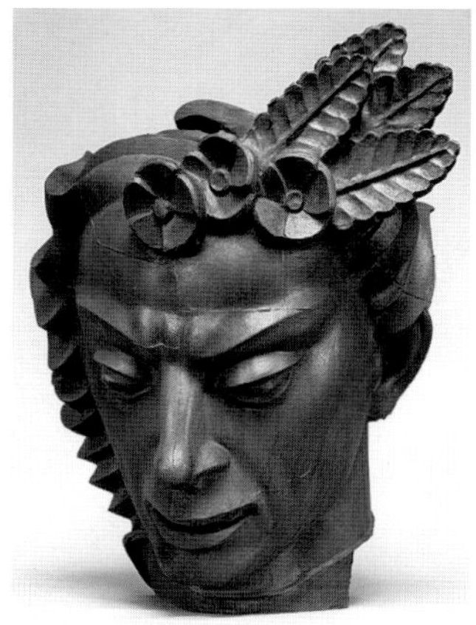

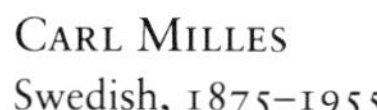

## CARL MILLES
Swedish, 1875–1955

*Head of Orpheus,* 1936
Iron, 1.016 x .559 (40 x 22)
Rosenwald Collection
1964.8.3

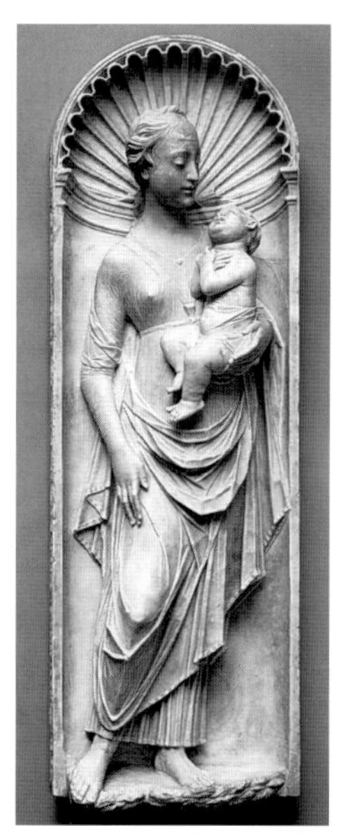

## MINO DA FIESOLE
Florentine, 1429–1484

*Charity,* 1475/1480
Marble, 1.260 x .430 ($49\frac{3}{4}$ x 17)
Andrew W. Mellon Collection
1937.1.117

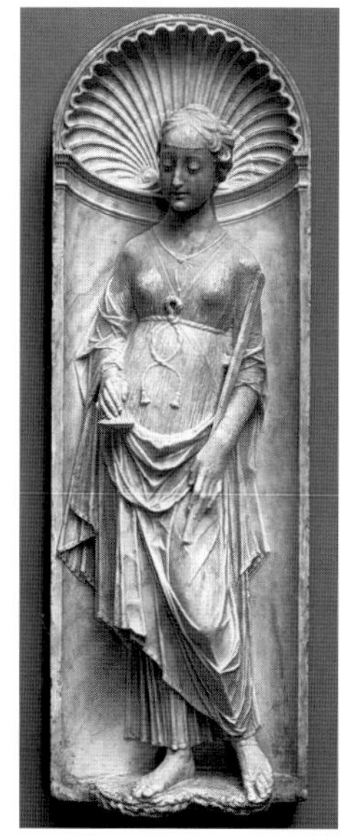

*Faith,* 1475/1480
Marble, 1.260 x .430 ($49\frac{3}{4}$ x 17)
Andrew W. Mellon Collection
1937.1.118

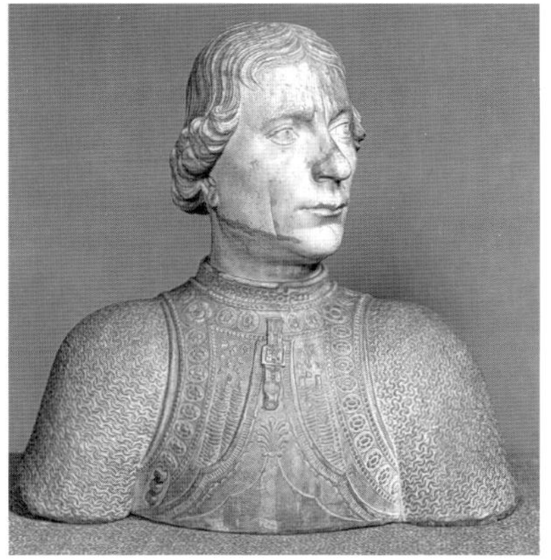

*Astorgio Manfredi,* 1455
Marble, .515 x .542 x .277
($20^{1}/_{4}$ x $21^{1}/_{4}$ x $10^{7}/_{8}$)
Inscribed on bottom and inside of base:
ASTORGIVS•MANFREDVS• / SECVDVS•[sic] FAVENTIE•DOMINVS• / ANNO•XLII•ETATIS• SVE• / 1455 / OPVS•NINI
Widener Collection
1942.9.135

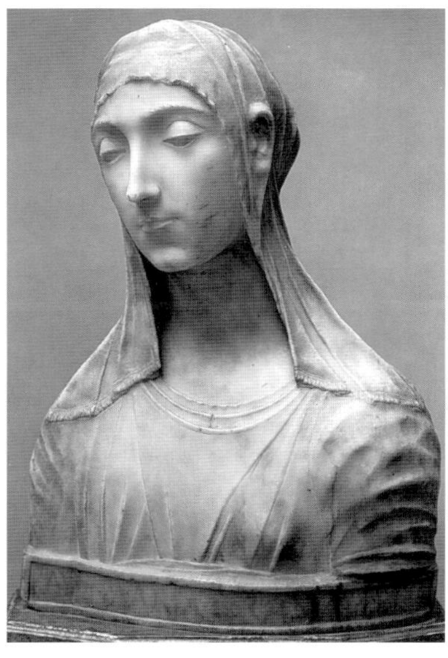

*The Virgin Annunciate,* c. 1455/1460
Marble, .510 x .370 x .136
(20 x $14^{1}/_{2}$ x $5^{3}/_{8}$)
Inscribed on front of base (faint): AVE MARIA GRATIA PLENA
Samuel H. Kress Collection
1943.4.71

## After Mino da Fiesole

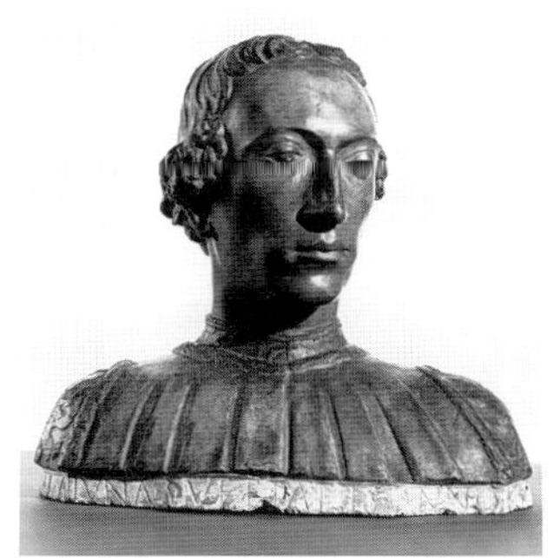

*Rinaldo della Luna,* late 19th century
Cement, .333 x .407 x .181
(13 x 16 x $7^{1}/_{8}$)
Falsely signed and dated, on receding strip around bottom: RINALDO DELLA LVNA• SVE•ETATIS•ANNO XXVII• OPVS•MINI NE MCCCCIXI
Samuel H. Kress Collection
1943.4.80

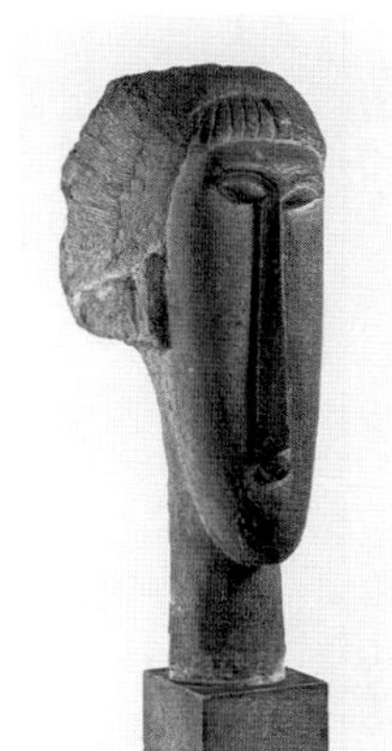

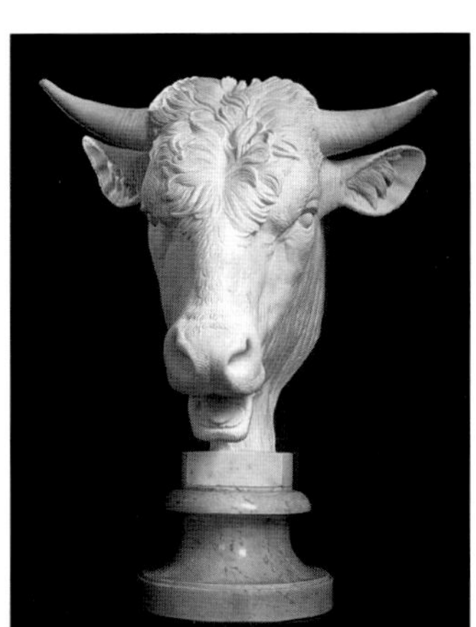

Amedeo Modigliani
Italian, 1884–1920

*Head of a Woman,* 1910/1911
Limestone, .652 x .190 x .248
(25 3/4 x 7 1/2 x 9 3/4)
Chester Dale Collection
1963.10.241

Gaetano Monti
Milanese, 1776–1847

*Head of a Bull,* 1824
Marble, .710 x .705 x .689
(28 x 27 3/4 x 27 1/8)
Inscribed on right side of truncation:
MONTI / DI MILANO / FECE 1824
C. Michael Paul Memorial Fund
1981.63.1

Henry Moore
British, 1898–1986

*Knife Edge Mirror Two Piece,* 1977/1978
Bronze, 5.345 x 7.211 x 3.631
(210 1/2 x 284 x 143)
Foundry mark on flatter side of larger segment, at lower right corner: MORRIS / SINGER / FOUNDERS / LONDON
Gift of The Morris and Gwendolyn Cafritz Foundation
1978.43.1

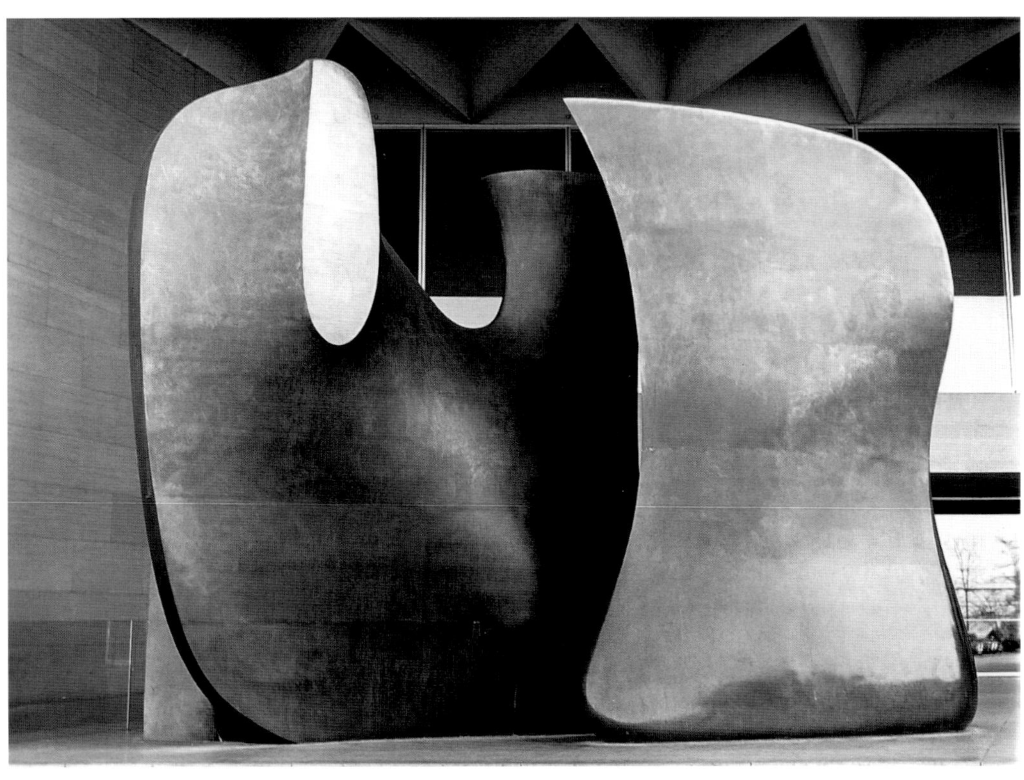

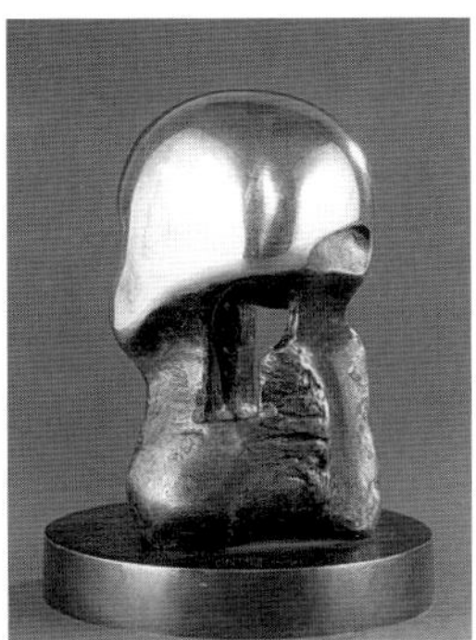

*Maquette for "Atom Piece,"* 1964
Bronze, .147 x .098 (5 3/4 x 3 7/8)
Inscribed on lower side, in script:
MOORE 5/12
Gift of Mr. and Mrs. Harry Brooks, in Honor of the 50th Anniversary of the National Gallery of Art
1991.55.1

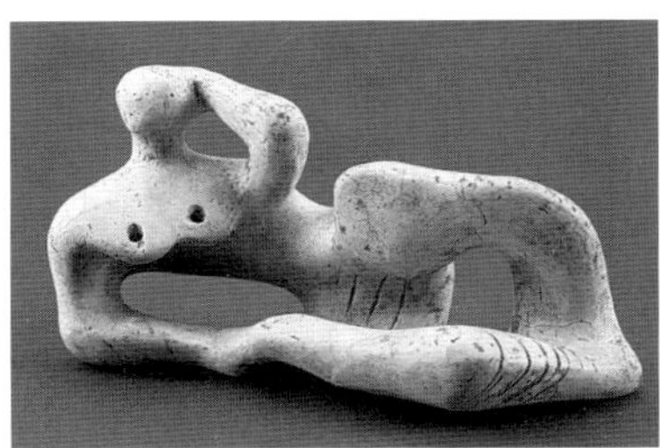

*Sketch-Model for Reclining Figure,* 1946
Terra cotta, .083 x .168 x .072
(3 1/4 x 6 5/8 x 2 7/8)
Given in memory of Frederick Zimmermann by his wife, Dorothy Zimmermann
1985.18.3

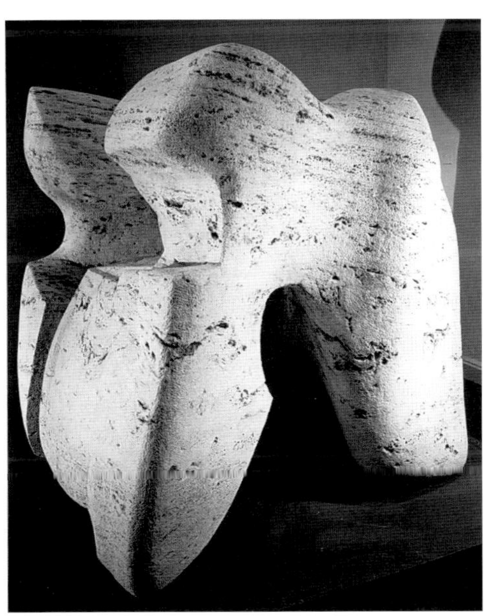

*Stone Memorial,* 1961/1969
Roman travertine, 1.517 x 1.749 x 1.708
(59 3/4 x 68 7/8 x 67 1/4)
Collection of Mr. and Mrs. Paul Mellon
1983.1.71

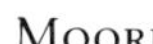

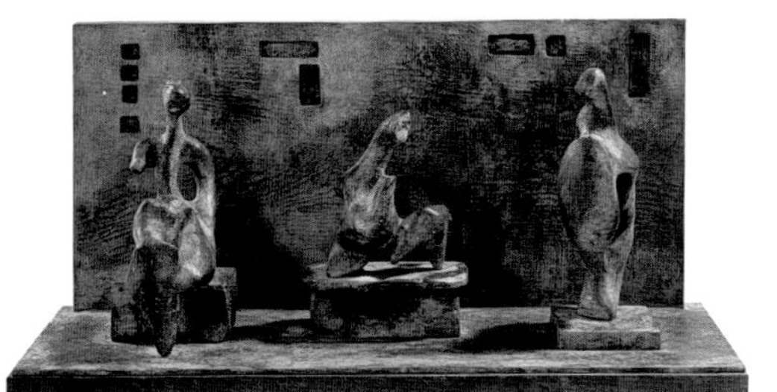

HENRY MOORE
British, 1898–1986

*Three Motives Against Wall, Number 1,* 1958/1959
Bronze, .505 x 1.074 x .437
(19 7/8 x 42 1/4 x 17 1/4)
Gift of Enid A. Haupt
1977.47.10

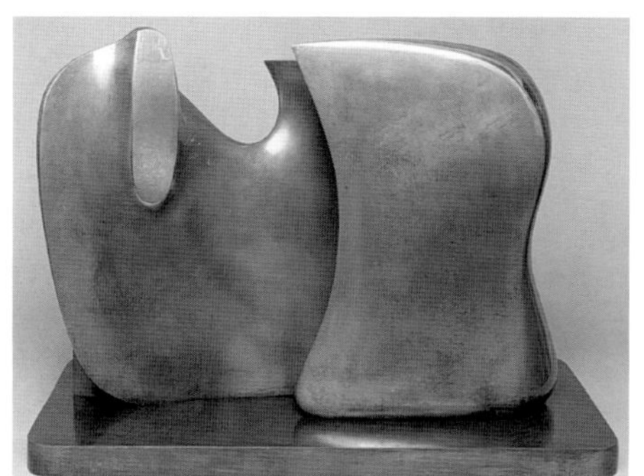

*Two Piece Mirror Knife Edge,* 1976
Bronze, .476 x .685 x .359
(18 3/4 x 27 x 14 1/8)
Inscribed on top of base in rear left corner: MOORE; foundry mark on rear edge of base: H. NOACK BERLIN
Adolph Caspar Miller Fund
1978.13.1

Plaster maquette for 1978.13.1 is HENRY MOORE, *Two Piece Mirror Knife Edge,* 1978.43.2

CONRAD MORICAND
*See* JACQUES LIPCHITZ

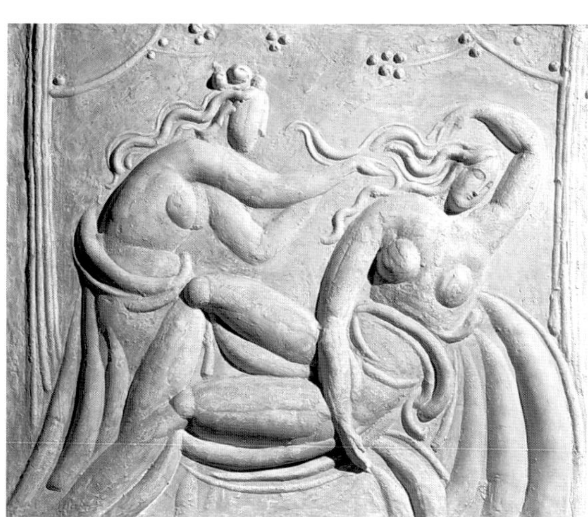

ELIE NADELMAN
American, 1882–1946

*Two Nudes,* c. 1911
Plaster, 1.215 x 1.492 x .096
(47 7/8 x 58 3/4 x 3 3/4)
Gift of Robert P. and Arlene R. Kogod
1975.79.1

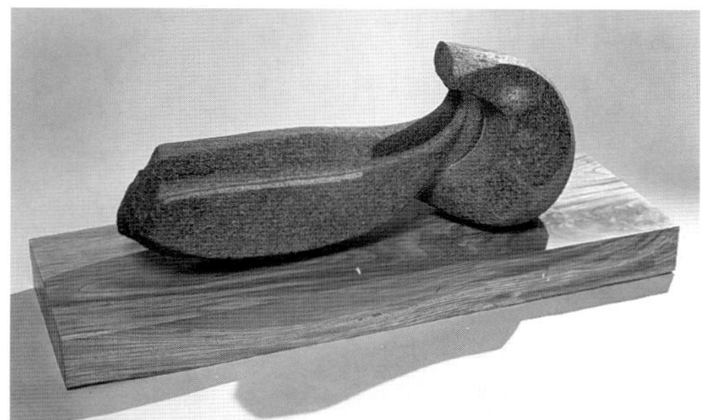

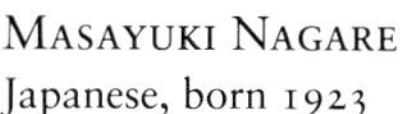

### Masayuki Nagare
Japanese, born 1923

*Breakers (The Wave),* 1963
Aji granite, .260 x .673 x .225
(10 1/4 x 26 1/2 x 8 7/8)
Inscribed on lower center of one longitudinal side: NAGARE (in Japanese) 63
Gift of Mr. and Mrs. Ralph F. Colin
1974.115.1

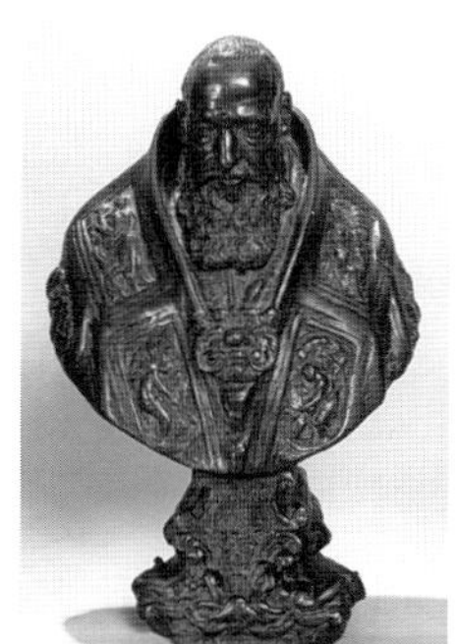

### Probably Neapolitan
19th/20th Century

*Paul III (Farnese), Pope*
Bronze, .299 x .210 x .157
(11 3/4 x 8 1/4 x 6 1/8)
Inscribed on front of base: PAOLO / III / FARNESE
Gift of Asbjorn R. Lunde
1975.6.1

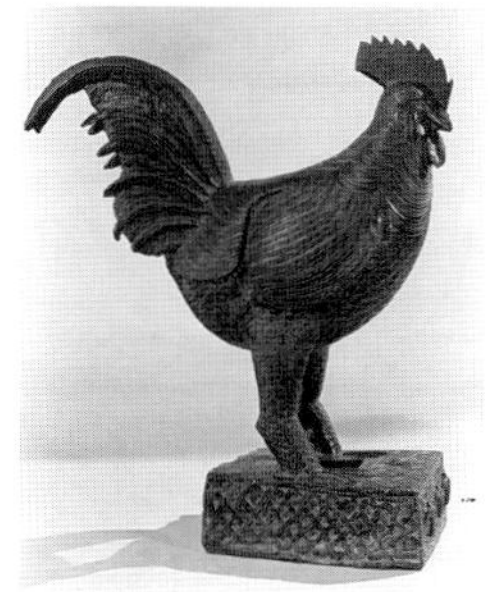

### Nigerian, Court of Benin

*Fowl,* mid-18th century
Brass with cast iron supports, with base:
.523 x .180 x .469 (20 1/2 x 7 x 18 3/8)
Gift of Mr. and Mrs. Winston F. C. Guest
1955.10.1

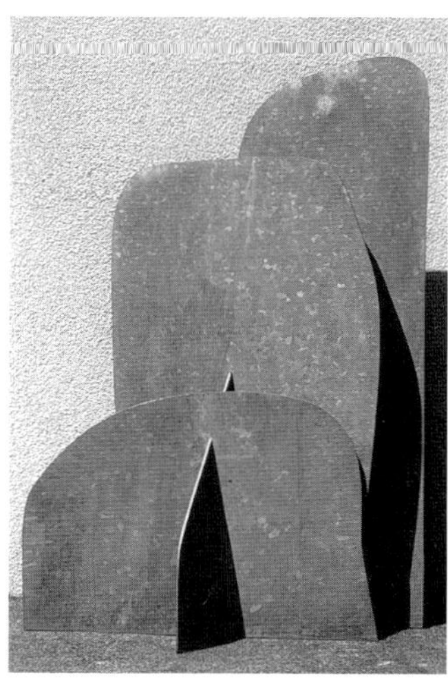

### Isamu Noguchi
American, 1904–1988

*Cloud Mountain,* published 1983
Galvanized steel, 1.772 x 1.251 x .718
(69 3/4 x 49 1/4 x 28 1/4)
Inscribed on base: I.N. '82; on middle segment, at lower left, on metal plate: ISAMU NOGUCHI CLOUD MOUNTAIN DI / PUBLISHED BY GEMINI G.E.L. (Gemini Chop) © ISAMU NOGUCHI FOUNDATION 1983 IN82–2089
Gift of Mr. and Mrs. Roger P. Sonnabend
1986.90.23

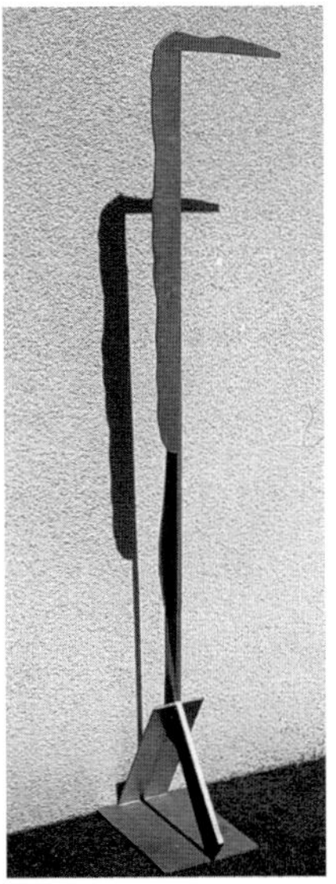

ISAMU NOGUCHI
American, 1904–1988

*Giacometti's Shadow,* published 1983
Galvanized steel, 1.975 x .419 x .432 (77¾ x 16½ x 17)
Inscribed on front of base: I.N. '82; at bottom of front panel on metal plate: ISAMU NOGUCHI / GIACOMETTI'S SHADOW DI / PUBLISHED BY GEMINI G.E.L. (Gemini Chop) © ISAMU NOGUCHI FOUNDATION 1983 IN82–2094
Gift of Mr. and Mrs. Roger P. Sonnabend
1986.90.24

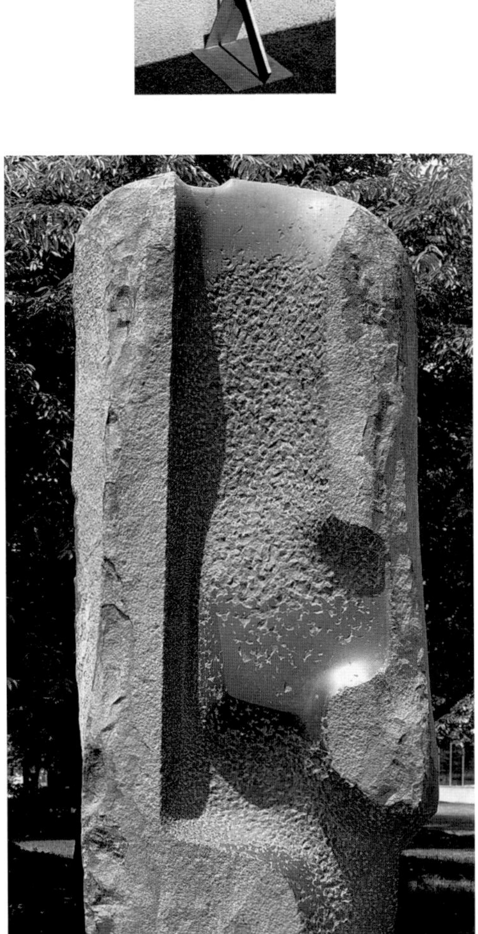

*Great Rock of Inner Seeking,* 1974
Basalt, 3.248 x 1.584 x .889 (127⅞ x 62⅜ x 35)
Inscribed on back at bottom: I.N. / 74
Gift of Arthur M. Sackler, M.D. and Mortimer D. Sackler, M.D.
1976.58.1

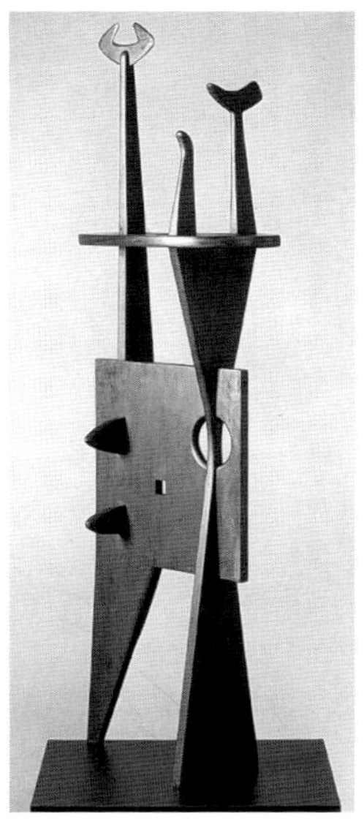

*Untitled*, 1945
Wood, painted, 1.270 x .482 x .235
($50 \times 19 \times 9^{1}/_{4}$)
Gift (Partial and Promised) of Robert P. and Arlene R. Kogod, in Honor of the 50th Anniversary of the National Gallery of Art
1991.45.1

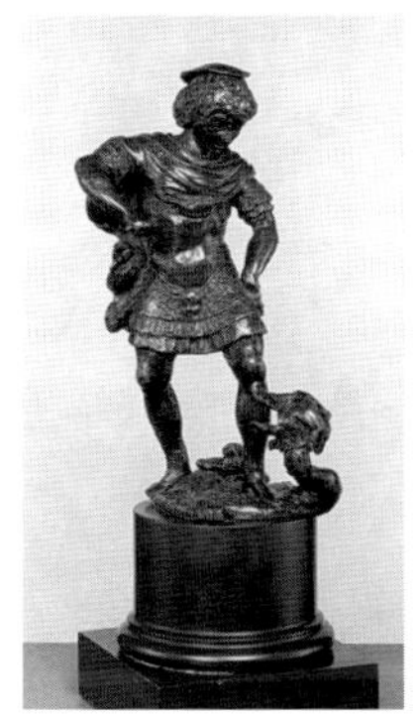

## Probably North Italian 15th Century

*Saint George and the Dragon*
Bronze, .132 x .068 x .055
($5^{3}/_{16} \times 2^{15}/_{16} \times 2^{1}/_{8}$)
Samuel H. Kress Collection
1957.14.16

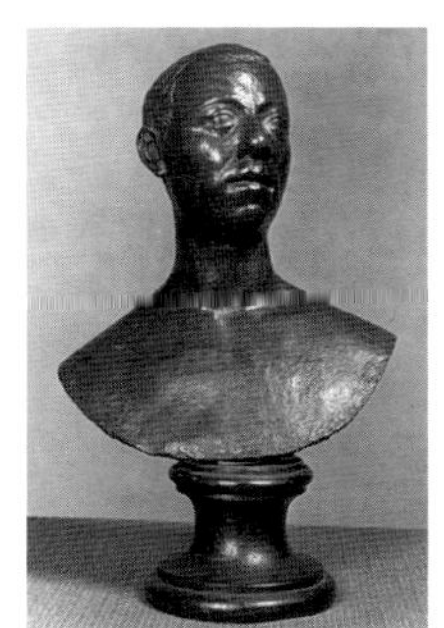

## North Italian 16th Century

*Bust of a Man*, first half 16th century
Bronze, .202 x .175 x .095
($7^{15}/_{16} \times 6^{7}/_{8} \times 3^{11}/_{16}$)
Widener Collection
1942.9.136

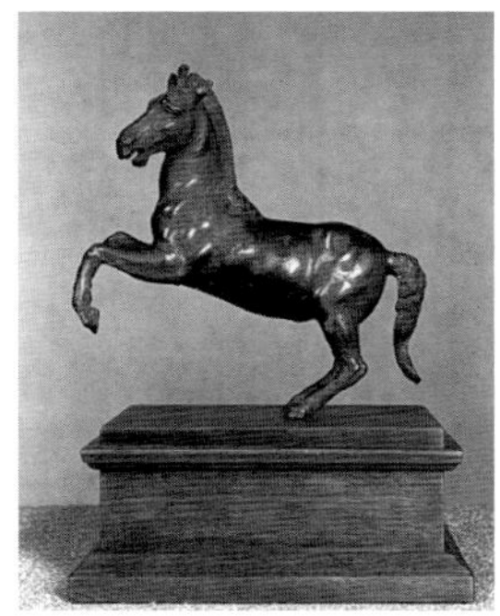

## North Italian 16th Century

*Rearing Horse*
Bronze, .202 x .230 x .070
($8 \times 9^{1}/_{8} \times 2^{3}/_{4}$)
Widener Collection
1942.9.122

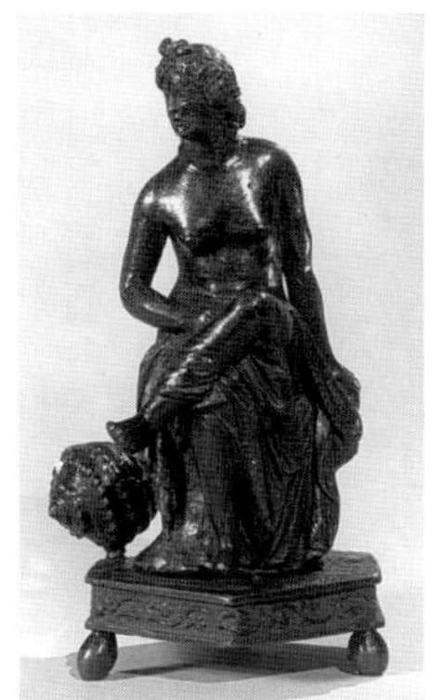

## North Italian 16th Century

*Seated Female Figure,* early 16th century
Bronze, .190 x .132 x .133
($7^1/_2$ x $5^3/_{16}$ x $5^1/_4$)
Widener Collection
1942.9.138

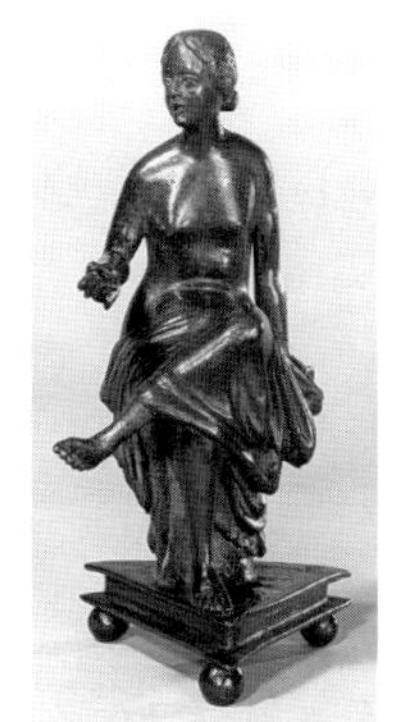

## North Italian 16th Century

*A Seated Nymph,* early 16th century
Bronze, .217 x .131 x .126
($8^5/_8$ x $5^1/_4$ x 5)
Samuel H. Kress Collection
1957.14.21

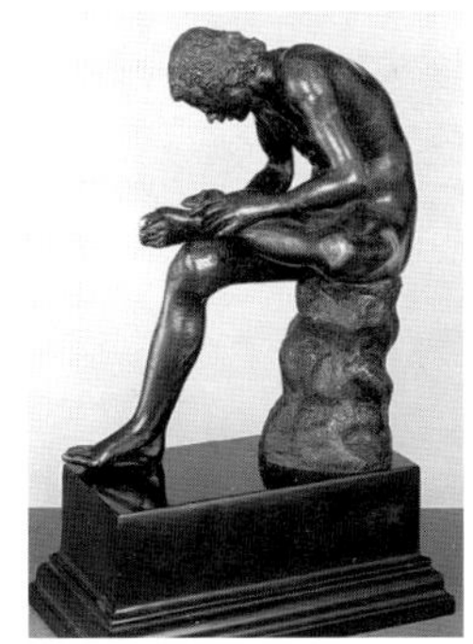

## North Italian 16th Century

*The Spinario,* first quarter 16th century
Bronze, .147 x .096 x .126
($5^{13}/_{16}$ x $3^3/_4$ x 5)
Samuel H. Kress Collection
1957.14.14

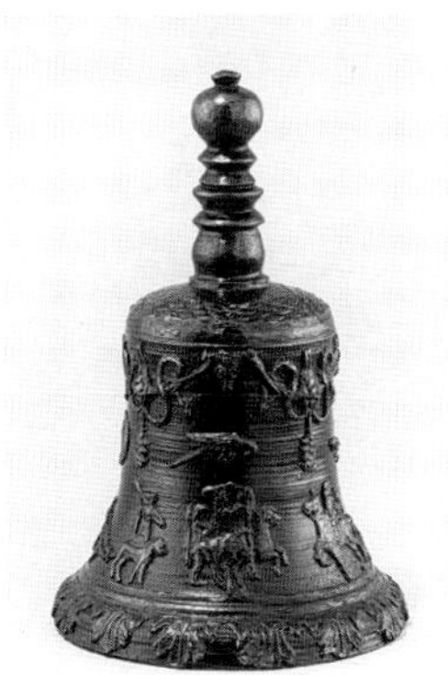

## North Italian 16th Century

*Table-Bell,* early 16th century
Bronze, .140 x .096 ($5^1/_2$ x $3^{13}/_{16}$)
Inscribed on basket: (?) MARTIVS
Samuel H. Kress Collection
1957.14.114

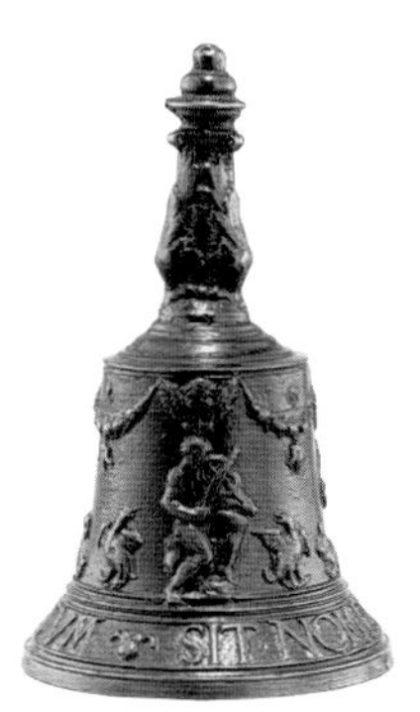


## North Italian 16th Century

*Table-Bell (Orpheus)*, early 16th century
Bronze, .120 x .073 ($4^3/_4$ x $2^7/_8$)
Inscribed around lip: SIT NOMEN DOMINI BENEDICTVM
Samuel H. Kress Collection
1957.14.117

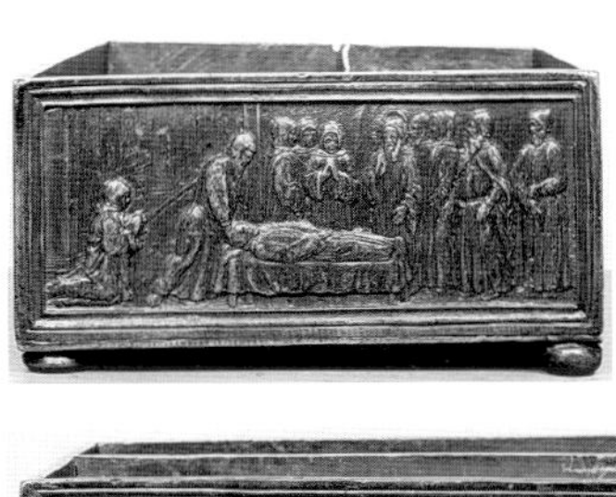

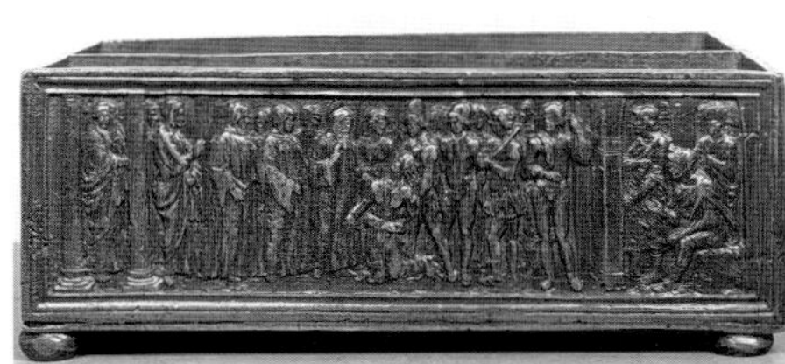

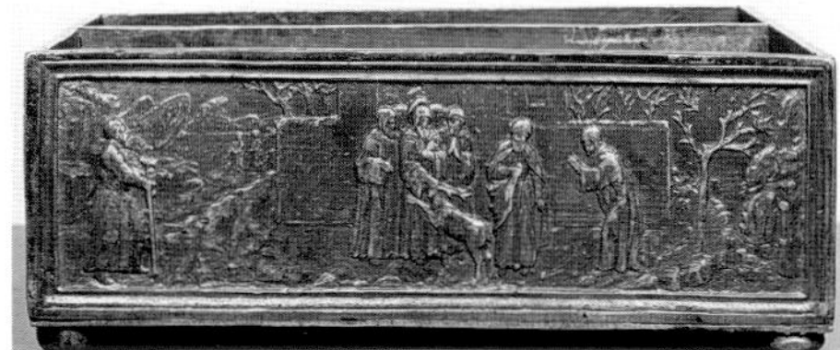

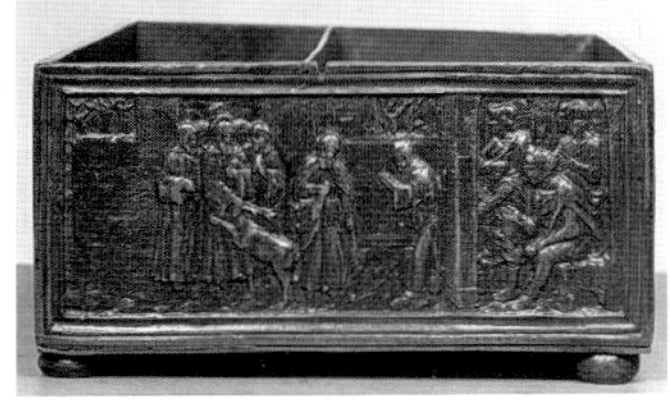

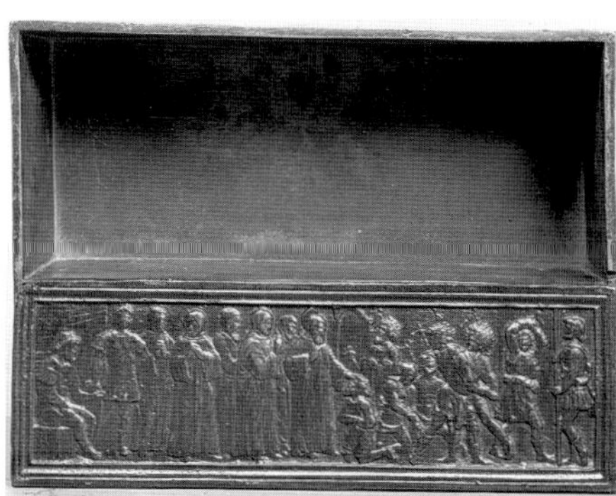

## North Italian (Mantuan?) 16th Century

*Writing Casket with Scenes from the Life of Saint Simeon of Podirolo*, c. 1500
Bronze, .076 x .189 x .138
(3 x $7^7/_{16}$ x $5^7/_{16}$)
Samuel H. Kress Collection
1957.14.60

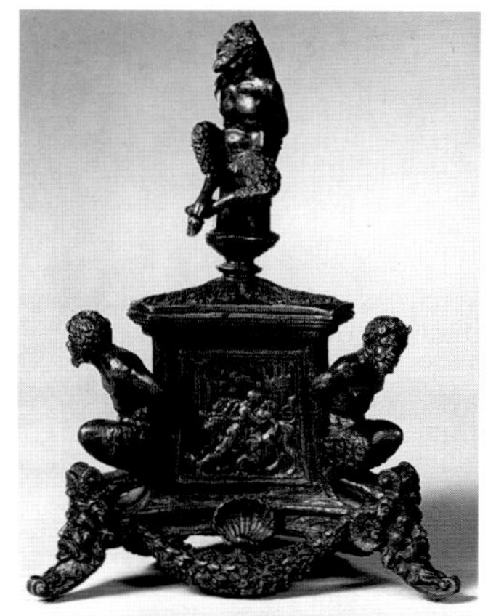

North Italian (Paduan?)
16th Century

*Inkstand with Bound Satyrs and Three Labors of Hercules,* c. 1530/1540
Bronze, .249 x .190 x .160
($9^{3}/_{4}$ x $7^{1}/_{2}$ x $6^{3}/_{8}$)
Widener Collection
1942.9.140

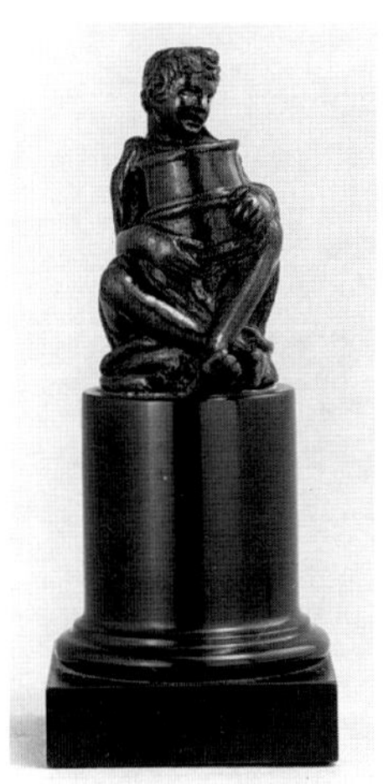

North Italian (Paduan?)
16th Century

*Seated Boy Holding a Jar (an Inkwell ?),* first half 16th century
Bronze, .063 x .037 x .055
($2^{1}/_{2}$ x $1^{1}/_{2}$ x $2^{3}/_{16}$)
Samuel H. Kress Collection
1957.14.34

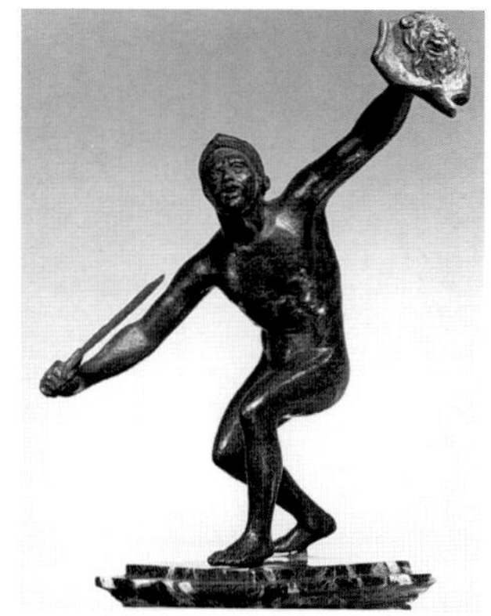

North Italian (Paduan?)
16th Century

*A Warrior,* c. 1500/1525
Bronze, .173 x .137 x .107
($6^{13}/_{16}$ x $5^{3}/_{8}$ x $4^{1}/_{4}$)
Widener Collection
1942.9.137

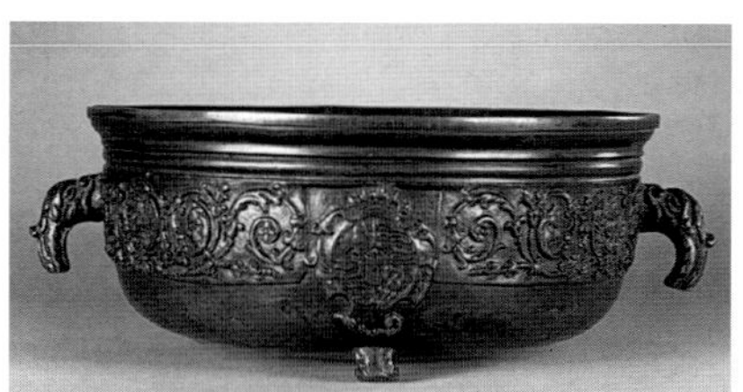

North Italian 16th or
17th Century

*Bowl with a Shield of Arms*
Bronze, height: .101 (4); diameter: .279 (11)
Gift of Ruth Blumka in memory of her daughter Vicki Blumka, through the continued friendship of Douglas Lewis
1991.70.1

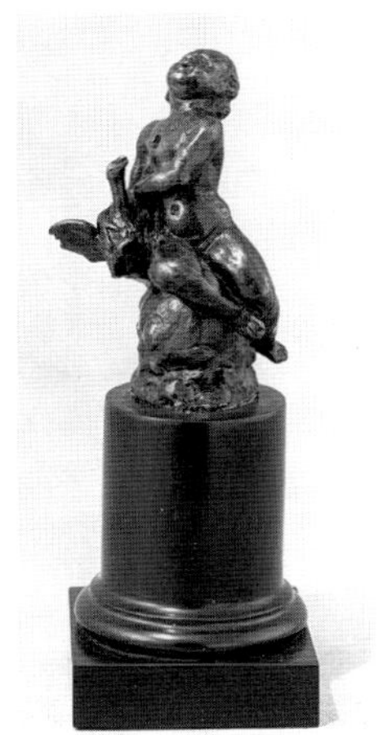

## North Italian 16th or 17th Century

*Child Clasping a Bird,* late 16th or early 17th century
Bronze, .076 x .052 x .037
(3 x $2^{1}/_{16}$ x $1^{1}/_{2}$)
Samuel H. Kress Collection
1957.14.49

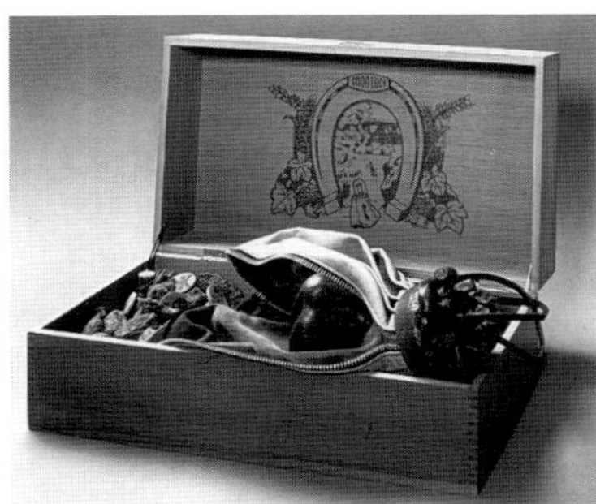

## Claes Oldenburg
American, born 1929

*Double-Nose/Purse/Punching Bag/Ashtray,* published 1970
Cowhide, reversible zipper, bronze, redwood box (with screenprinted image inside lid), redwood chips, stamped wooden discs, and deerskin-covered book
.276 x .527 x .213 ($10^{7}/_{8}$ x $20^{3}/_{4}$ x $8^{3}/_{8}$)
Gift of Gemini G.E.L.
1981.5.120

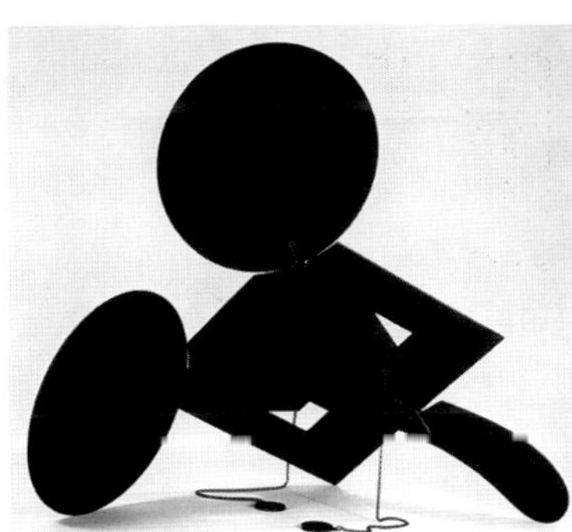

*Geometric Mouse—Scale C,* published 1971
Black anodized aluminum with steel pins
Greatest extension: .660 x .520
(26 x $20^{1}/_{2}$)
Inscribed on discs attached to chains: CO–111/120; © 1971 CLAES OLDENBURG / PRODUCED BY GEMINI G.E.L. (Gemini chop)
Gift of Gemini G.E.L.
1981.5.227

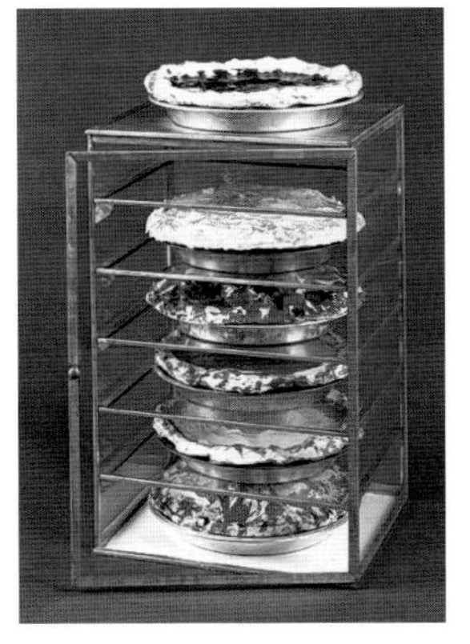

*Glass Case with Pies (Assorted Pies in a Case),* 1962
Mixed media, .476 x .311 x .276
($18^{3}/_{4}$ x $12^{1}/_{4}$ x $10^{7}/_{8}$)
Gift of Leo Castelli, in Honor of the 50th Anniversary of the National Gallery of Art
1991.54.1

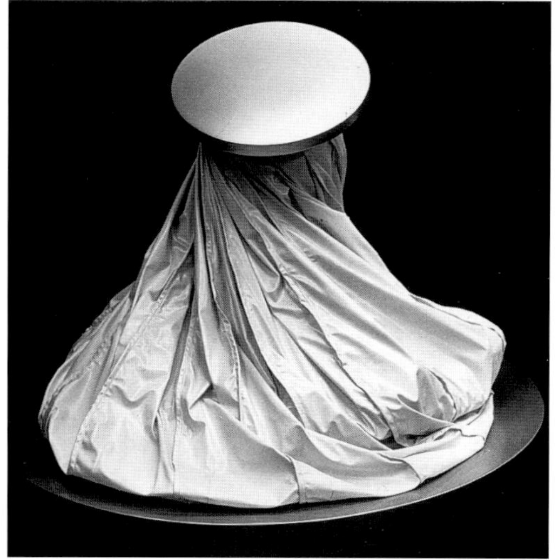

Claes Oldenburg
American, born 1929

*Ice Bag—Scale B,* published 1971
Programmed kinetic sculpture, yellow nylon material, fiberglass, and mechanical movement, diameter: 1.219 (48), rising to: 1.016 (40)
Gift of Gemini G.E.L.
1981.5.139

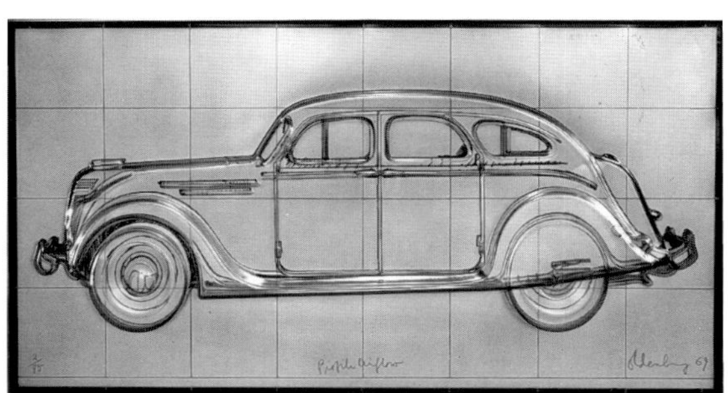

*Profile Airflow,* published 1969
Molded polyurethane over 2-color lithograph (aluminum) on Special Arjomari paper, .851 x 1.664 (33 1/2 x 65 1/2)
Inscribed at lower right: OLDENBURG 69; at lower left: 2/75; at bottom center: PROFILE AIRFLOW
Gift of Gemini G.E.L.
1981.5.70

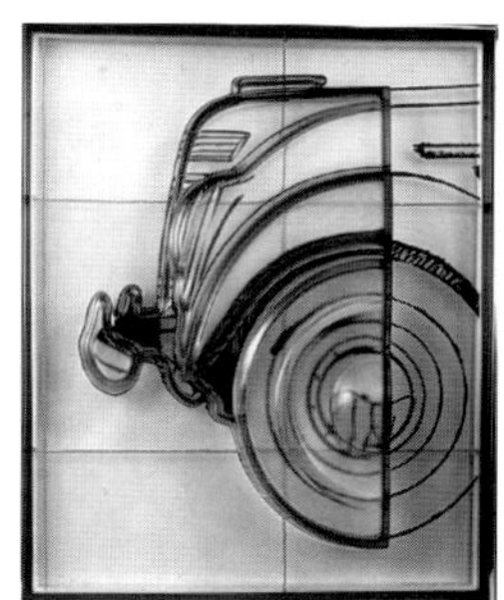

*Profile Airflow—Test Mold, Front End,* published 1972
Molded polyurethane relief over 1-color screenprint on plexiglass installed in welded aluminum frame
.470 x .397 x .102 (18 1/2 x 15 5/8 x 4)
Inscribed at lower left: CO.GEM.I; at lower right: © COPYRIGHT CLAES OLDENBURG 1972
Gift of Gemini G.E.L.
1991.74.181

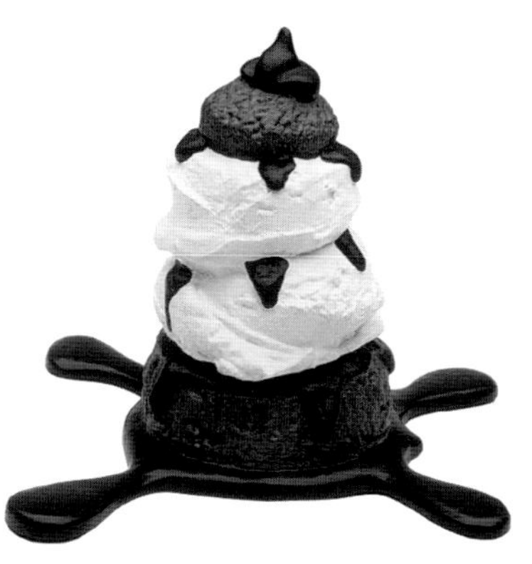

*Profiterole,* published 1990
Painted cast bronze, .146 x .203 x .219 (5 3/4 x 8 x 8 5/8)
Inscribed on bottom, center: SP3 / CO. '89 / PROFITEROLE
Gift of Gemini G.E.L. and the Artist, in Honor of the 50th Anniversary of the National Gallery of Art
1990.104.17

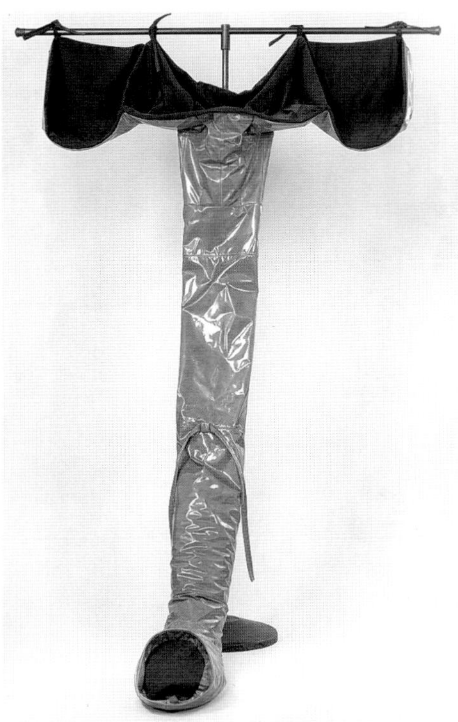

*Soft Drainpipe—Red (Hot) Version,* 1967
Vinyl, styrofoam, canvas, metal
3.048 x 1.524 x 1.143 (120 x 60 x 45)
Robert and Jane Meyerhoff Collection, Gift in Honor of the 50th Anniversary of the National Gallery of Art
1990.75.1

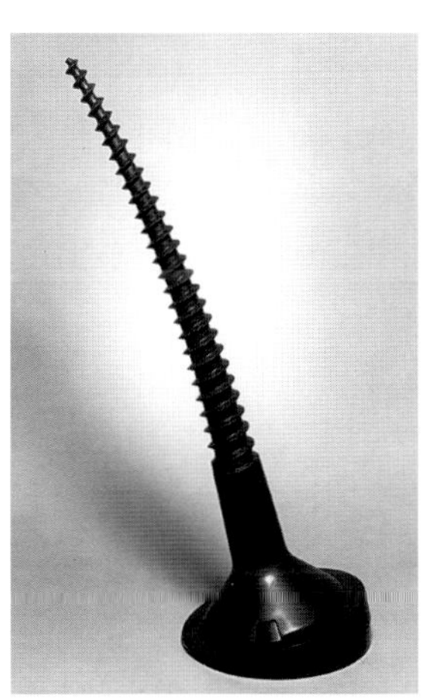

*Soft Screw,* published 1976
Cast elastomeric urethane with a mahogany base, 1.213 x .372 (47 3/4 x 14 5/8)
Gift of Gemini G.E.L.
1981.5.133

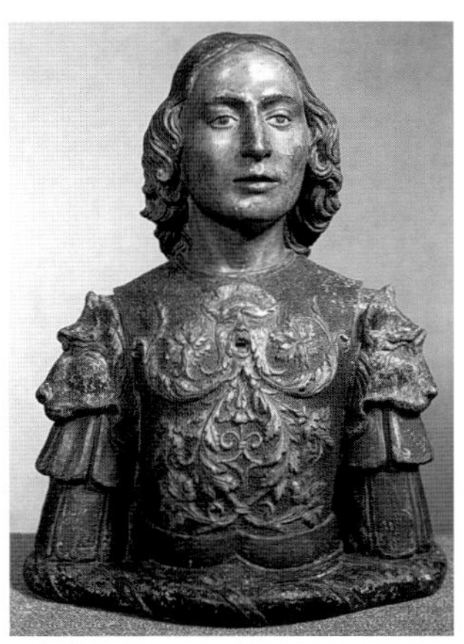

## Vincenzo Onofri

Bolognese, active c. 1503/1524

*Portrait of a Nobleman,* c. 1500
Terra cotta, painted and gilt
.630 x .500 x .290 (24 5/8 x 19 5/8 x 11 3/8)
Widener Collection
1942.9.106

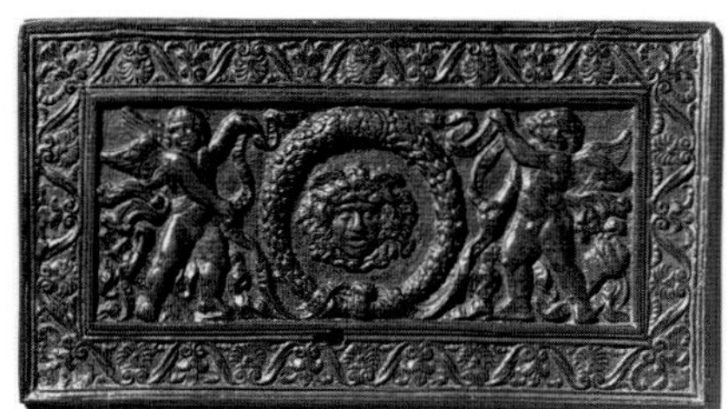

## PADUAN 15TH CENTURY

*Cover of a Writing Casket: Geniuses with Wreath and Medusa Head,* c. 1500
Bronze, .106 x .198 ($4^{3}/_{16}$ x $7^{13}/_{16}$)
Widener Collection
1942.9.149.a

## PADUAN 15TH CENTURY

*End Panel of a Writing Casket: Medusa Head, Garland and Bucrania,* c. 1500
Bronze, .062 x .100 ($2^{7}/_{16}$ x $3^{15}/_{16}$)
Widener Collection
1942.9.149.c

## PADUAN 15TH CENTURY

*Front of a Writing Casket: Centaurs and Nymphs with Cornucopiae and Bust,* c. 1500
Bronze, .062 x .194 ($2^{7}/_{16}$ x $7^{5}/_{8}$)
Widener Collection
1942.9.149.b

## PADUAN 15TH OR 16TH CENTURY

*Box in the Form of a Crab,* late 15th or early 16th century
Bronze, .048 x .171 x .093 ($1^{7}/_{8}$ x $6^{3}/_{4}$ x $3^{11}/_{16}$)
Samuel H. Kress Collection
1957.14.86

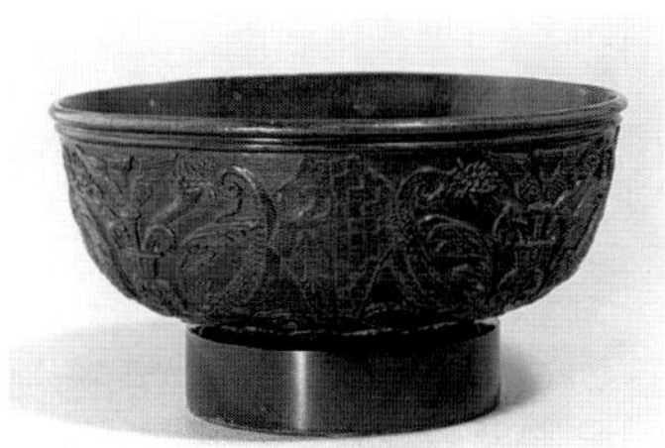

## PADUAN OR VENETIAN 15TH OR 16TH CENTURY

*Bowl,* late 15th or early 16th century
Bronze, .075 x .196 (3 x $7^{3}/_{4}$)
Samuel H. Kress Collection
1957.14.95

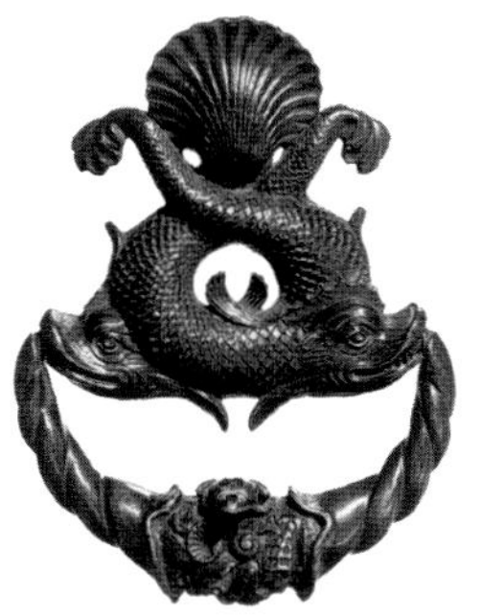

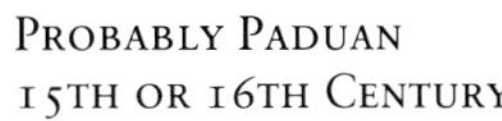

## PROBABLY PADUAN 15TH OR 16TH CENTURY

*Door Knocker,* late 15th or early 16th century
Bronze, .205 x .160 (8 1/8 x 6 3/8)
Samuel H. Kress Collection
1957.14.119

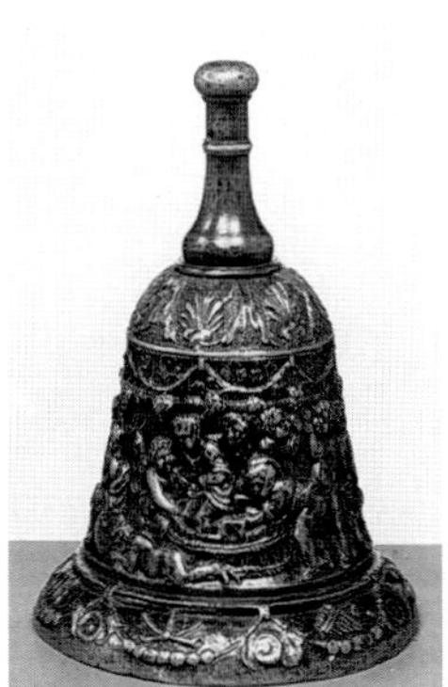

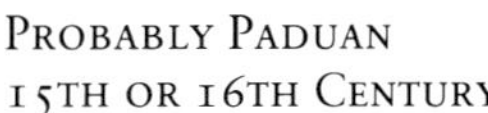

## PROBABLY PADUAN 15TH OR 16TH CENTURY

*Table-Bell,* late 15th or early 16th century
Bronze, .132 x .091 (5 3/16 x 3 9/16)
Samuel H. Kress Collection
1957.14.116

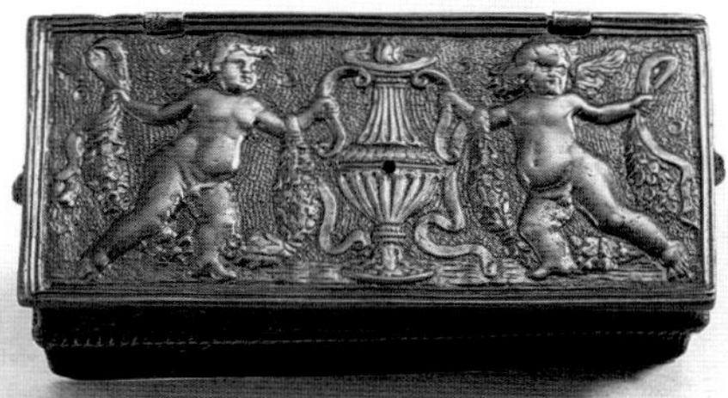

## PADUAN 16TH CENTURY

*Box,* c. 1500
Bronze, .047 x .172 x .075
(1 7/8 x 6 3/4 x 2 15/16)
Samuel H. Kress Collection
1957.14.64

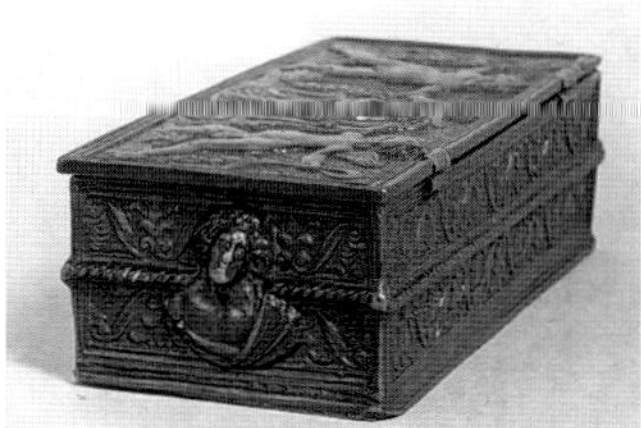

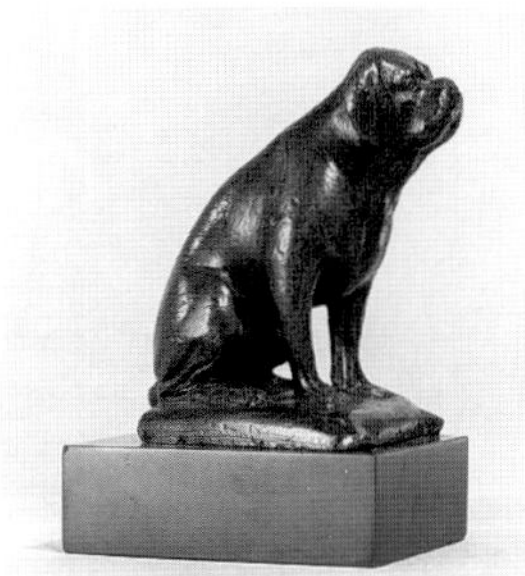

## Paduan 16th Century

*A Dog*
Bronze, .091 x .057 x .072
($3\frac{9}{16}$ x $2\frac{1}{4}$ x $2\frac{13}{16}$)
Samuel H. Kress Collection
1957.14.79

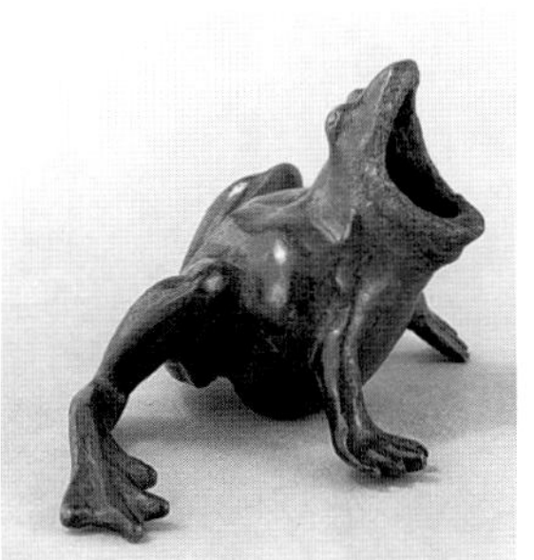

## Paduan 16th Century

*A Frog*, early 16th century
Bronze, .071 x .146 x .077
($2\frac{13}{16}$ x $5\frac{3}{4}$ x $3\frac{1}{16}$)
Samuel H. Kress Collection
1957.14.92

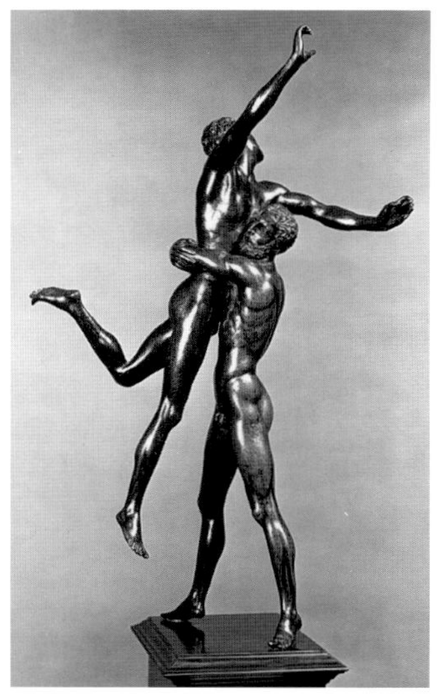

## Paduan 16th Century

*Hercules and Antaeus*, c. 1525
Bronze, .380 x .120 x .265
(15 x $4\frac{3}{4}$ x $10\frac{1}{2}$)
Widener Collection
1942.9.119

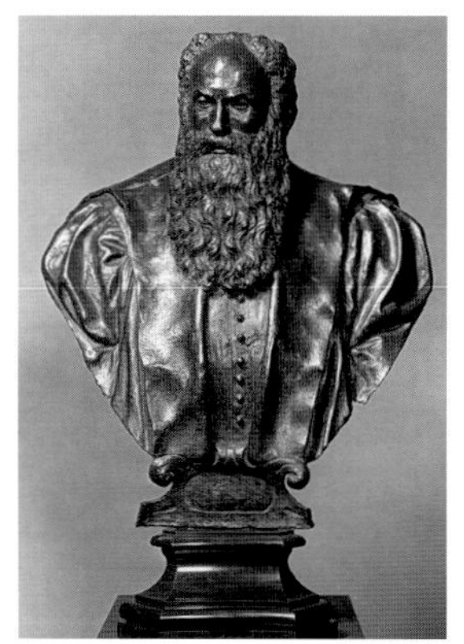

## Paduan 16th Century

*A Jurist*, c. 1550
Bronze, .820 x .715 x .343
($32\frac{1}{4}$ x $28\frac{1}{8}$ x $13\frac{1}{2}$)
Widener Collection
1942.9.145

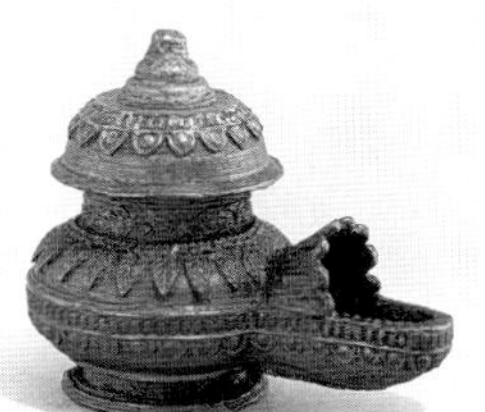

## PADUAN 16TH CENTURY

*Lamp*, early 16th century
Bronze, .090 x .118 x .073
($3^{9}/_{16}$ x $4^{11}/_{16}$ x $1^{7}/_{8}$)
Samuel H. Kress Collection
1957.14.67

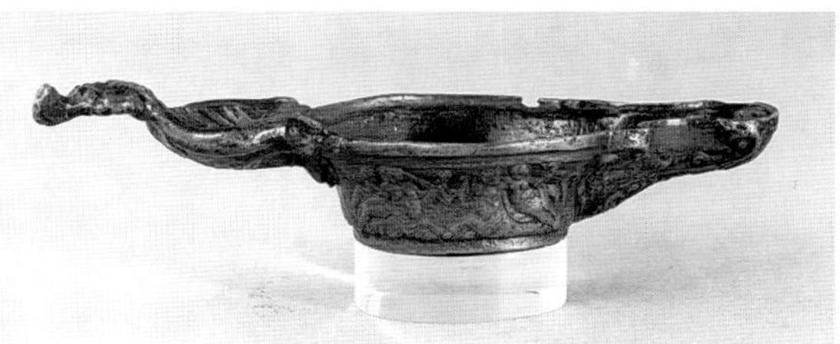

## PADUAN 16TH CENTURY

*Lamp*, early 16th century
Bronze, .033 x .149 x .055
($1^{5}/_{16}$ x $5^{1}/_{8}$ x $2^{3}/_{16}$)
Inscribed beneath base: CIC.IOMS
Samuel H. Kress Collection
1957.14.69

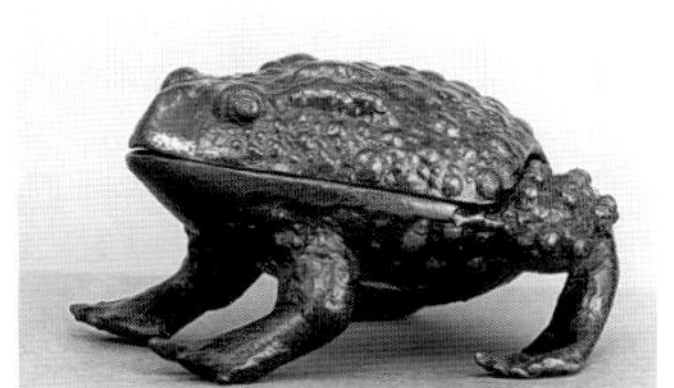

## PADUAN 16TH CENTURY

*A Large Toad*
Bronze, .068 x .128 x .108
($2^{7}/_{8}$ x 5 x $4^{1}/_{4}$)
Samuel H. Kress Collection
1957.14.91

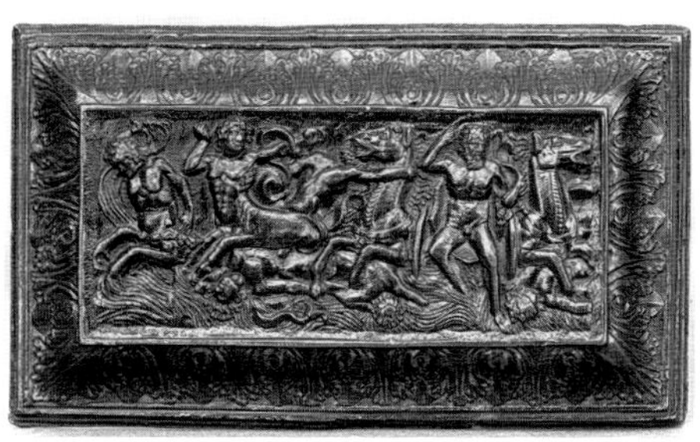

## PADUAN 16TH CENTURY

*Lid of a Box*, c. 1500
Bronze, length by width: .213 x .122
($8^{3}/_{8}$ x $4^{7}/_{8}$)
Samuel H. Kress Collection
1957.14.65

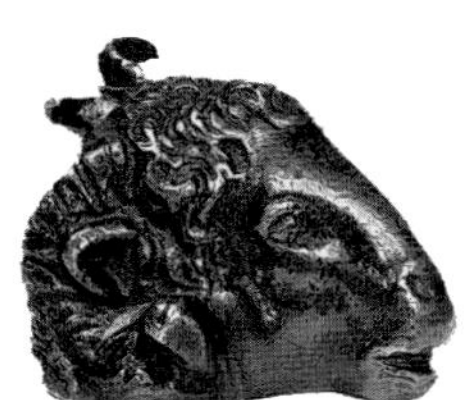

## PADUAN 16TH CENTURY

*A Ram's Head*, early 16th century
Bronze, .044 x .060 x .063
($1^{15}/_{16}$ x $2^{3}/_{8}$ x $2^{1}/_{2}$)
Samuel H. Kress Collection
1957.14.80

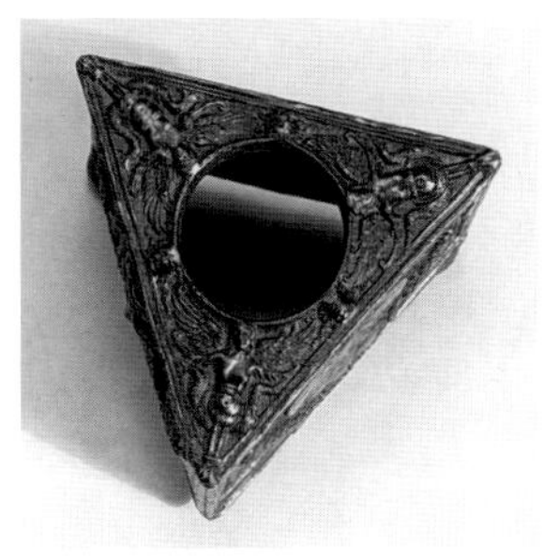

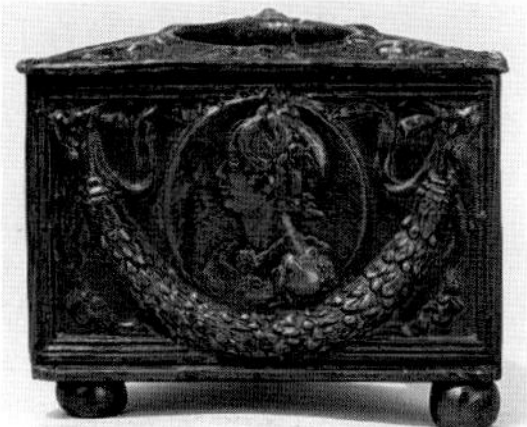

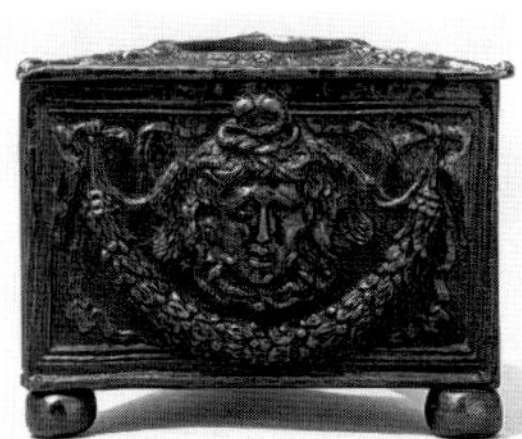

## Paduan 16th Century

*Sand-Box*, c. 1500
Bronze, .080 x .106 x .094
(3 1/8 x 4 3/16 x 3 11/16)
Samuel H. Kress Collection
1957.14.62

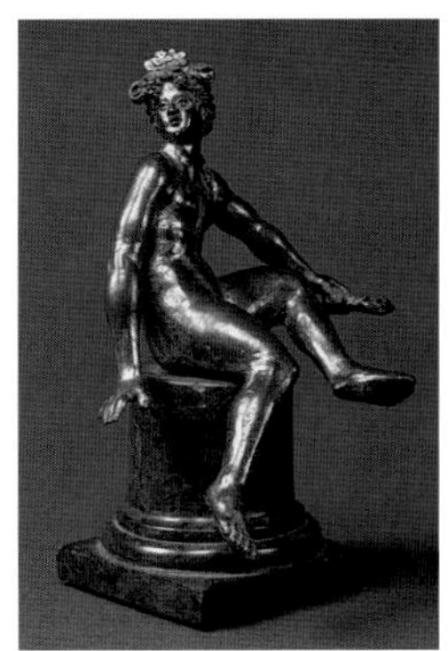

## Paduan 16th Century

*Seated Bacchante*, c. 1500/1525
Gilt bronze, .137 x .117 x .092
(5 3/8 x 4 5/8 x 3 5/8)
Ailsa Mellon Bruce Fund
1985.24.1

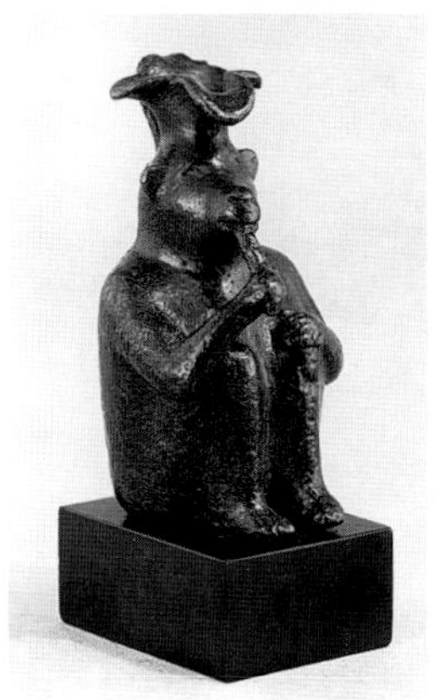

## Paduan 16th Century

*Small Vase in the Form of a Monkey*, early 16th century
Bronze, .076 x .045 x .047
(3 x 1 13/16 x 1 7/8)
Samuel H. Kress Collection
1957.14.82

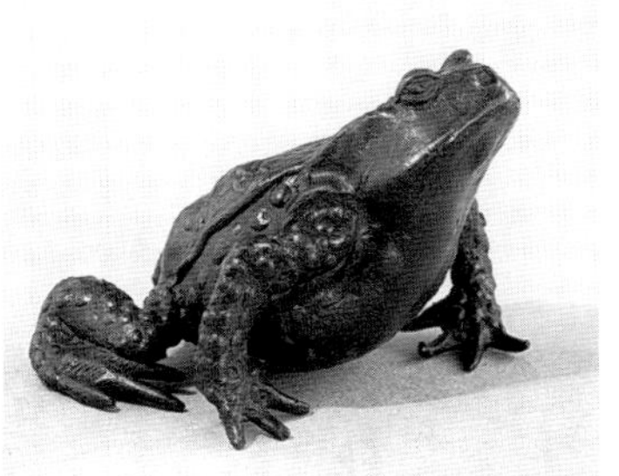

## Paduan 16th Century

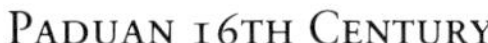

*A Toad,* early 16th century
Bronze, .061 x .079 x .080
($2^{7}/_{16}$ x $3^{1}/_{16}$ x $3^{1}/_{8}$)
Samuel H. Kress Collection
1957.14.90

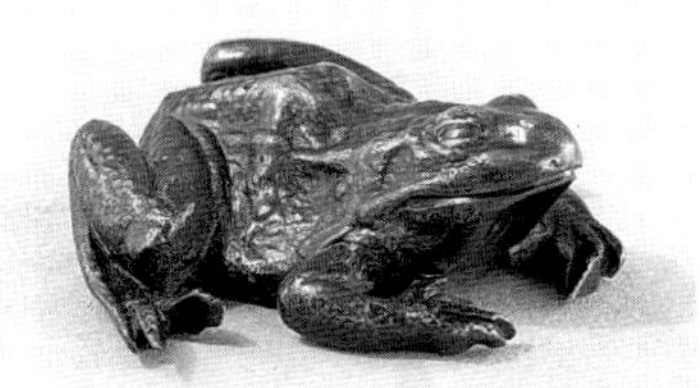

## Paduan 16th Century

*A Toad*
Bronze, .023 x .065 x .059
($^{15}/_{16}$ x $2^{9}/_{16}$ x $2^{3}/_{8}$)
Samuel H. Kress Collection
1957.14.93

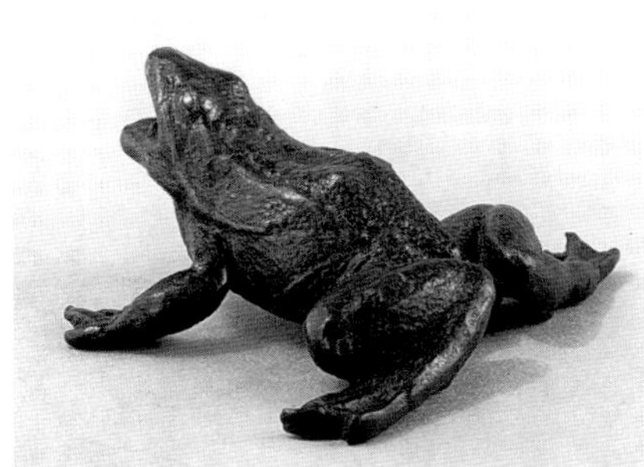

## Paduan 16th Century

*A Toad,* early 16th century
Bronze, .046 x .105 x .090
($1^{13}/_{16}$ x $4^{1}/_{8}$ x $3^{9}/_{16}$)
Samuel H. Kress Collection
1957.14.94

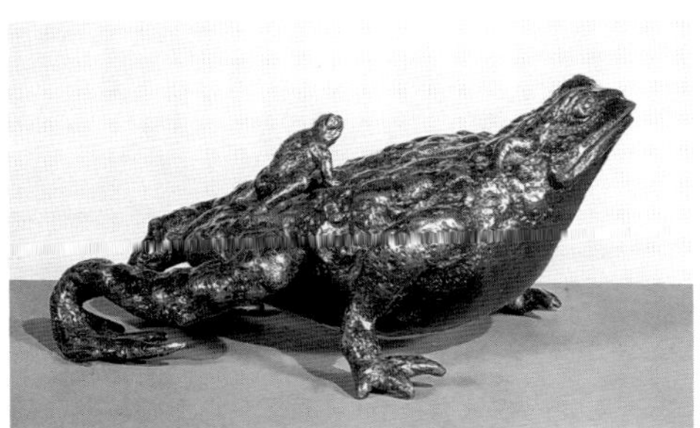

## Paduan 16th Century

*A Toad with a Toad,* early 16th century
Bronze, .060 x .131 x .086
($2^{3}/_{8}$ x $5^{1}/_{8}$ x $3^{3}/_{8}$)
Samuel H. Kress Collection
1957.14.88

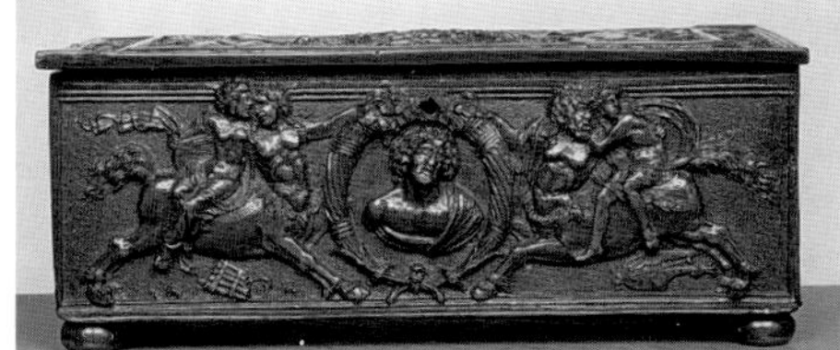

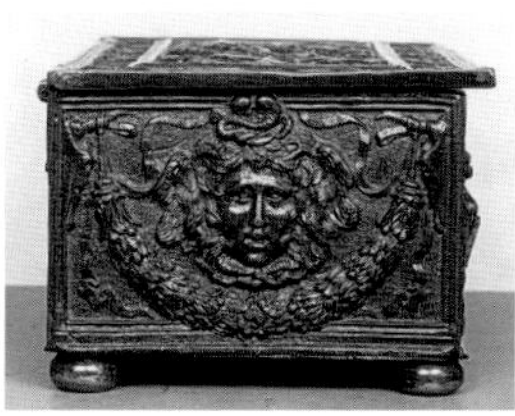

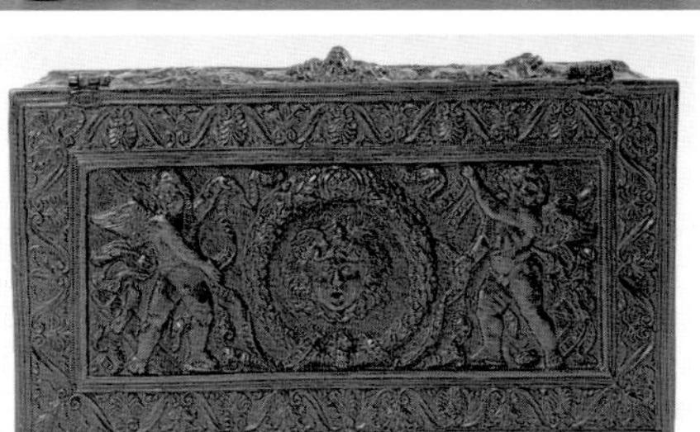

PADUAN 16TH CENTURY

*Writing Casket*, c. 1500
Bronze, .078 x .203 x .120
($3^{1}/_{16}$ x 8 x $4^{3}/_{4}$)
Samuel H. Kress Collection
1957.14.61

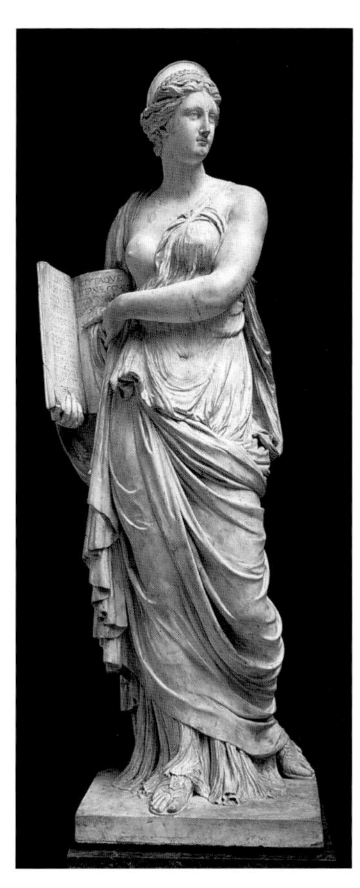

AUGUSTIN PAJOU
French, 1730–1809

*Calliope*, c. 1763
Marble, 1.580 x .608 x .461
($62^{1}/_{8}$ x $23^{7}/_{8}$ x $18^{1}/_{8}$)
Inscribed on book: CALLIOPE REGI / NA,HOMINVM, / DIVVMQVE VO / LVPTAS / CARMINIS HE / ROI NVMERIS / FVLGENTIA / SIGNIS / AGMINA,BEL / LANTVMQVE / ANIMOS,ET / PRLÆIA CAN / TO, / INCLYTAQVE / ÆTERNÆ COMMI / TTO. NOMINA / FAMÆ
Samuel H. Kress Collection
1952.5.107

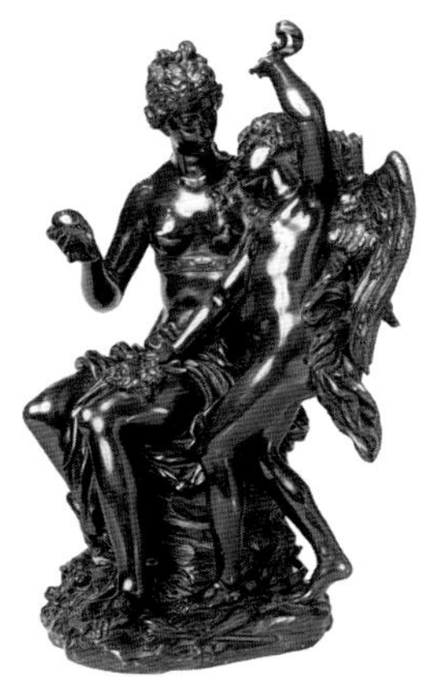

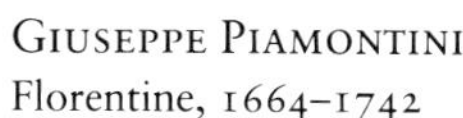

### Giuseppe Piamontini
Florentine, 1664–1742

*Venus and Cupid,* 1711/1724
Bronze, .370 x .254 x .220
(14 5/8 x 10 x 8 5/8)
Ailsa Mellon Bruce Fund
1974.18.2

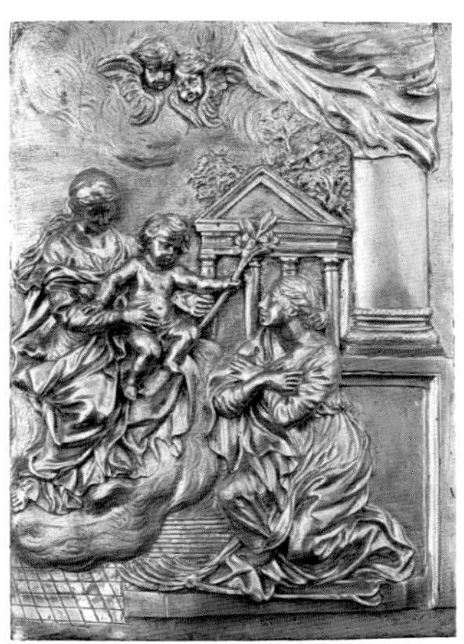

### Pietro da Cortona
Roman, 1596–1669

*The Virgin and Child Appearing to Saint Martina,* c. 1650
Gilt bronze, .508 x .381 (20 x 15)
Gift of David Edward Finley and Margaret Eustis Finley
1984.6.1

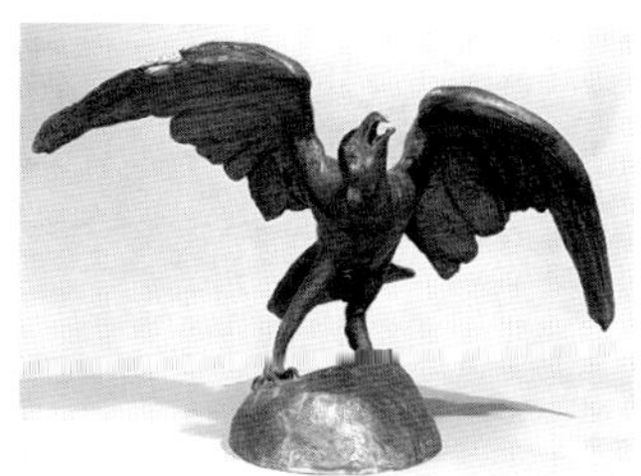

### Gustave Pimienta
French, 1888–1982

*Eagle,* 1962 and 1966
Bronze, 1.020 x 1.652 x 1.024
(40 1/8 x 65 x 40 1/4)
Inscribed on edge of base below right claw: GUSTAVE PIMIENTA / EPREUVE NO 1/5 1966; foundry mark: CIRE / C. VALSUANI / PERDUE
Gift of Gustave Pimienta
1968.23.1

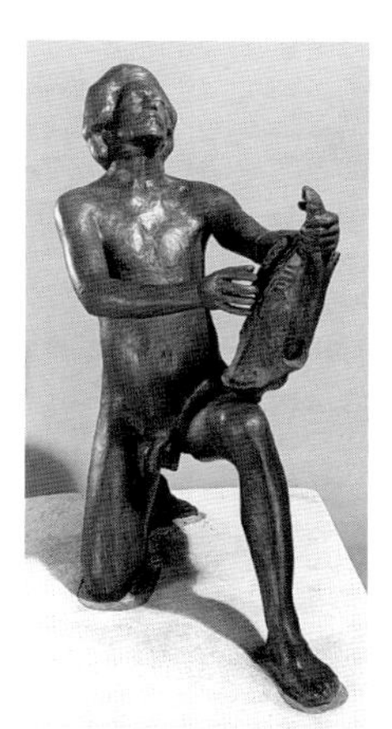

*Orpheus,* 1938 and 1966
Bronze, 1.201 x .630 x 1.030
(47 1/4 x 24 3/4 x 40 1/2)
Foundry mark on side of right foot: CIRE / M PAST[ORI] / PERDUE
Gift of Gustave Pimienta
1968.23.2

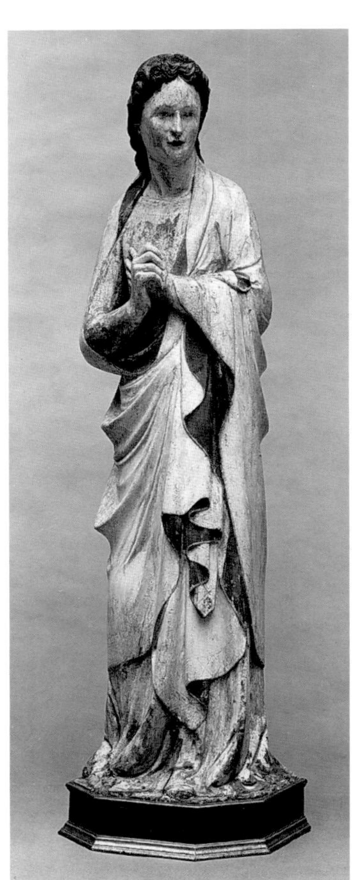

### Pisan 14th Century

*The Archangel Gabriel,* c. 1325/1350
Wood, polychromed and gilt
1.594 x .473 x .360 ($62^{3}/_{4}$ x $18^{5}/_{8}$ x $14^{1}/_{8}$)
Samuel H. Kress Collection
1961.9.97

### Pisan 14th Century

*The Virgin Annunciate,* c. 1325/1350
Wood, polychromed and gilt
1.623 x .538 x .399 ($63^{7}/_{8}$ x $21^{1}/_{8}$ x $15^{3}/_{4}$)
Samuel H. Kress Collection
1961.9.98

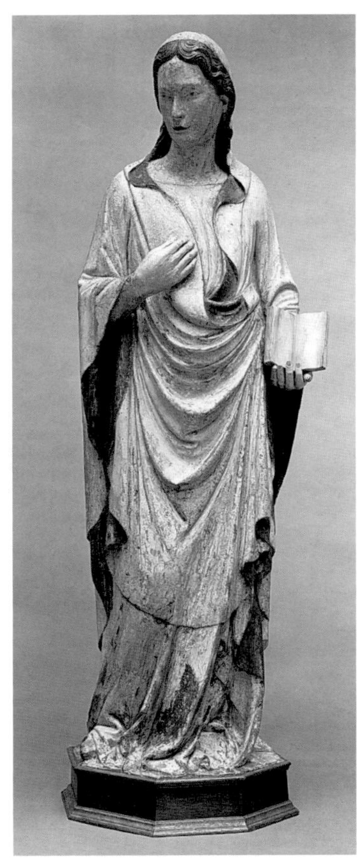

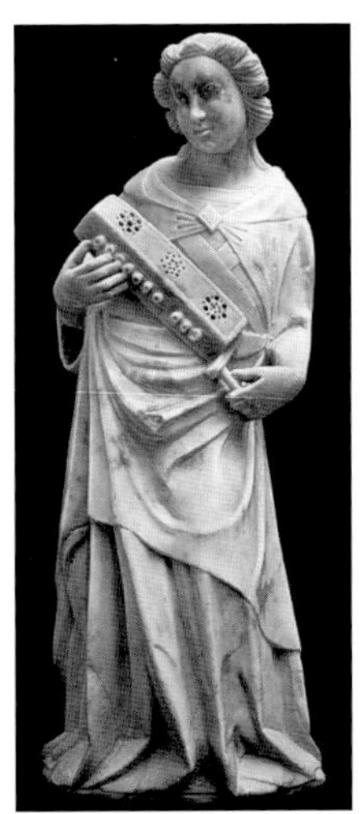

### Possibly Pisan 14th Century

*Angel with Symphonia,* c. 1350/1370
Marble, .538 x .215 x .178
($21^{1}/_{8}$ x $8^{3}/_{8}$ x 7)
Samuel H. Kress Collection
1960.5.14

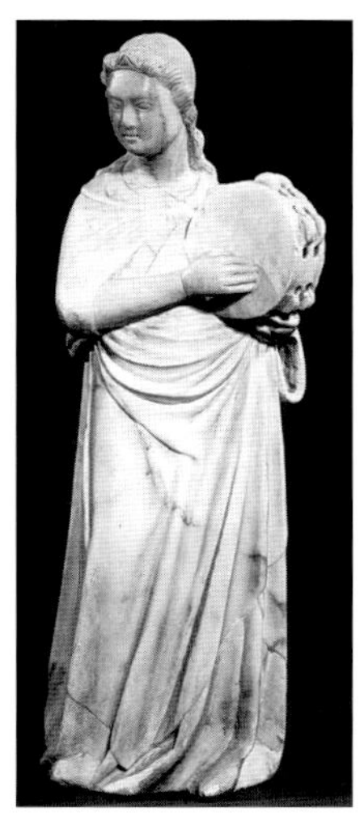

## Possibly Pisan 14th Century

*Angel with Tambourine*, c. 1350/1370
Marble, .542 x .218 x .226
($21^{1}/_{4}$ x $8^{1}/_{2}$ x $8^{7}/_{8}$)
Samuel H. Kress Collection
1960.5.15

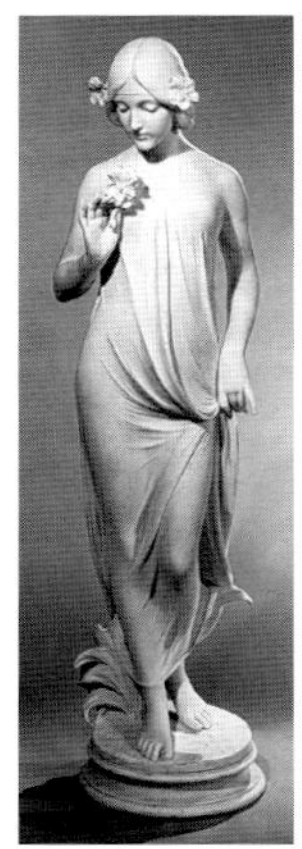

## Pittaluga

Italian, active 1915

*Nymph of the Fields*, 1915
Marble, 1.693 x .490 x .495
($66^{5}/_{8}$ x $19^{1}/_{4}$ x $19^{1}/_{2}$)
Inscribed on edge of base under left foot:
PITTA[LU]GA
Gift of the Honorable W. S. Stuckey, Jr.
1975.101.1

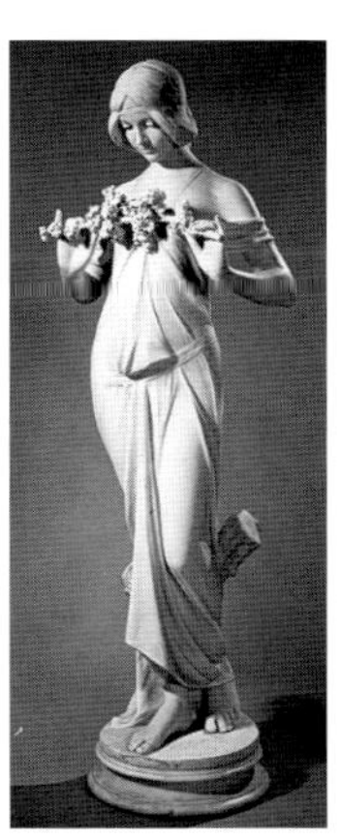

*Nymph of the Woods*, 1915
Marble, 1.683 x .583 x .508
($66^{1}/_{4}$ x 23 x 20)
Inscribed on edge of base under left foot:
PITTALUGA
Gift of the Honorable W. S. Stuckey, Jr.
1975.101.2

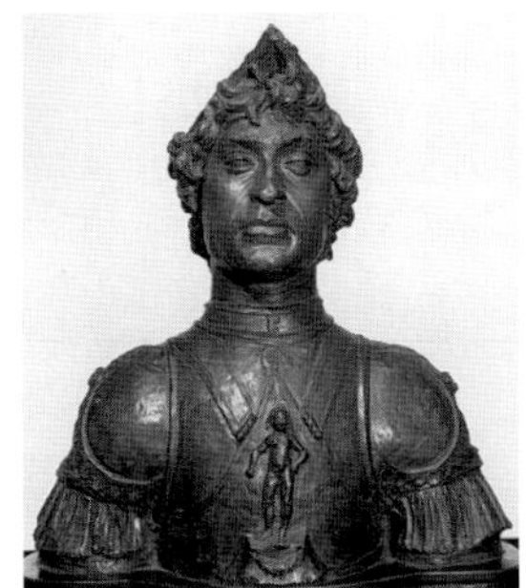

### Imitator of Antonio del Pollaiuolo

*Bust of a Warrior,* 1850/1870
Terra cotta, .623 x .550 x .259
(24 5/8 x 21 3/4 x 10 1/4)
Samuel H. Kress Collection
1943.4.74

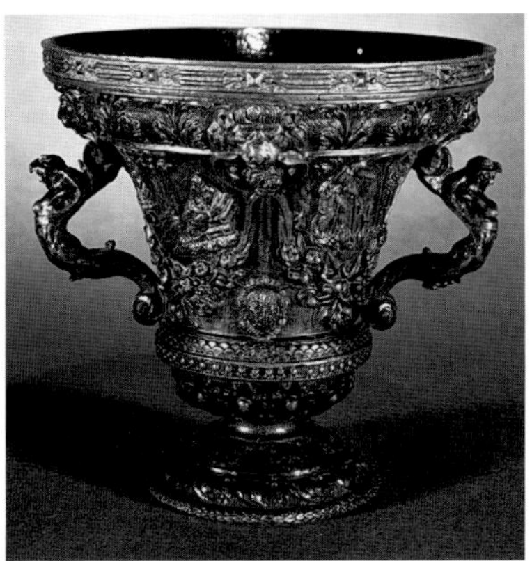

### Circle of Guglielmo della Porta
Italian

*Cup with Allegorical Scenes and Shields of Este Arms,* 1560s
Bronze, .130 x .146 x .139
(5 1/8 x 5 3/4 x 5 1/2)
Widener Collection
1942.9.132

### Jean Pougny
*See* Ivan Puni

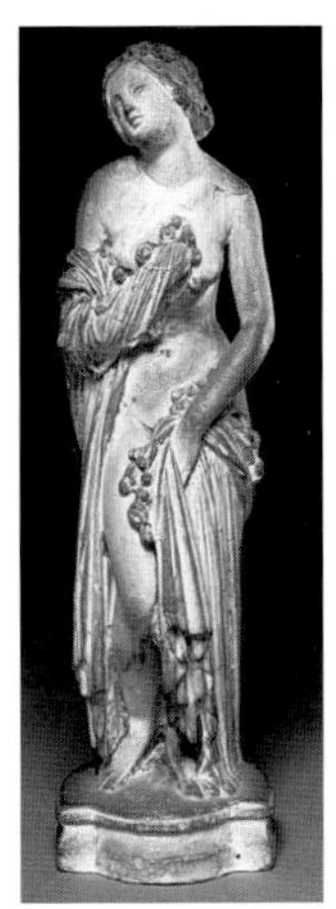

### Jean-Jacques Pradier (called James)
French, 1792–1852

*Chloris Caressed by Zephyr,* model 1847
Plaster, .295 x .083 x .078
(11 5/8 x 3 1/4 x 3 1/8)
Inscribed on right side of base: J PRADIER
Gift of Esther J. Willcox and Esther W. Putnam
1981.55.1

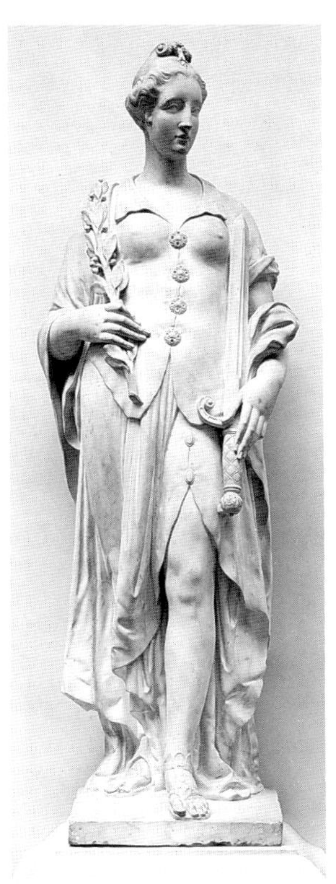

Barthélemy Prieur
French, 1536–1611

*Justice*, 1610
Marble, with base: 1.815 x .643 x .492
(71 1/2 x 25 1/4 x 19 1/2)
Samuel H. Kress Collection
1943.4.86

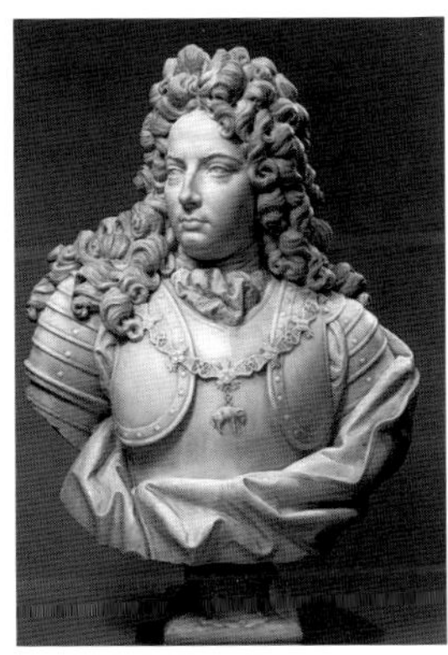

Jacques Prou II
French, 1655–1706

*Charles, Duc de Berry*
Marble, .793 x .677 x .420
(26 1/4 x 26 5/8 x 16 1/2)
Ailsa Mellon Bruce Fund
1967.14.1

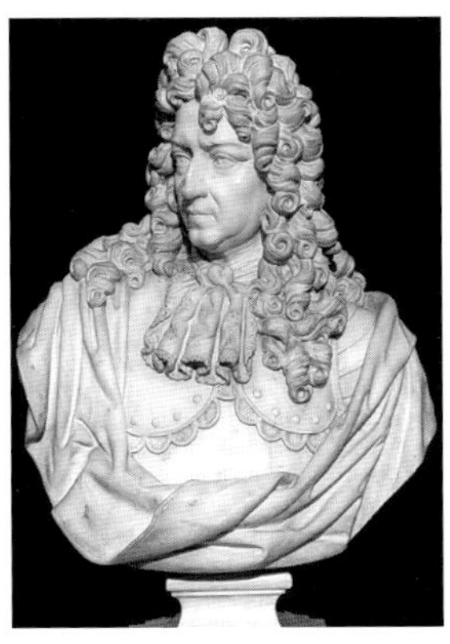

*Philippe, Duc D'Orleans*
Marble, .916 x .693 x .464
(36 x 27 1/8 x 18 1/4)
Samuel H. Kress Collection
1943.4.88

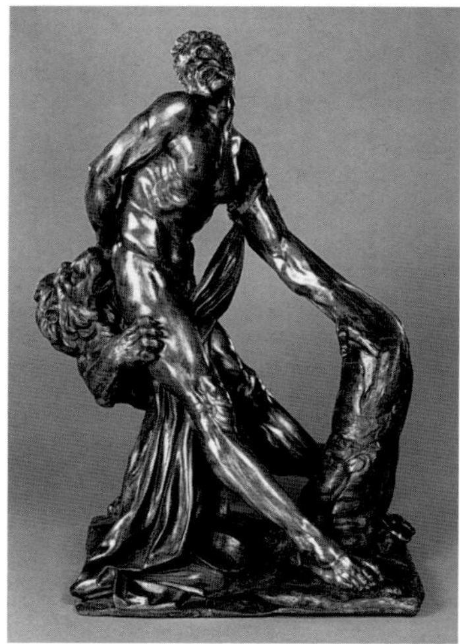

PIERRE PUGET
French, 1620–1694

*Milo of Croton,* marble original 1670–1682, bronze reduction late 17th/early 18th century
Bronze, .616 x .470 x .381 (24 1/4 x 18 1/2 x 15)
Andrew W. Mellon Fund
1985.51.1

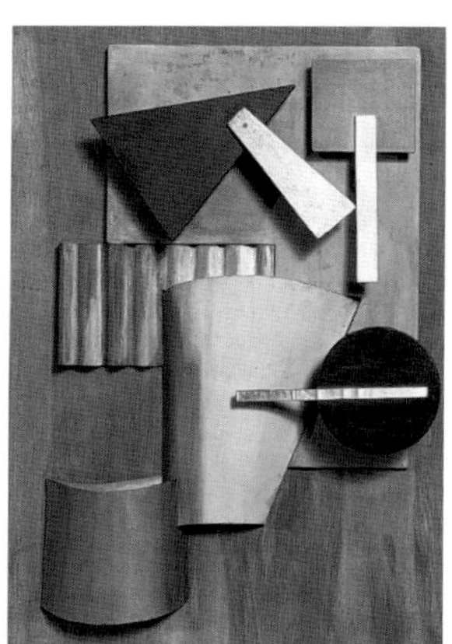

IVAN PUNI (JEAN POUGNY)
Russian, 1894–1956

*Suprematist Construction Montage,* 1915/1916
Painted wood, metal and cardboard
.698 x .487 x .070 (27 1/2 x 19 1/8 x 2 3/4)
Andrew W. Mellon Fund
1976.70.1

MARTIN PURYEAR
American, born 1941

*Lever No. 3,* 1989
Wood, carved and painted
2.146 x 4.115 x .330 (84 1/2 x 162 x 13)
Gift of the Collectors Committee
1989.71.1

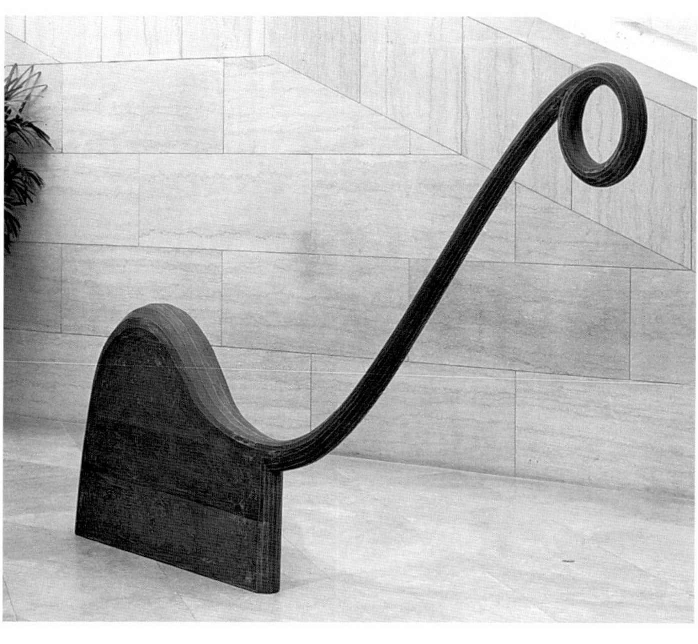

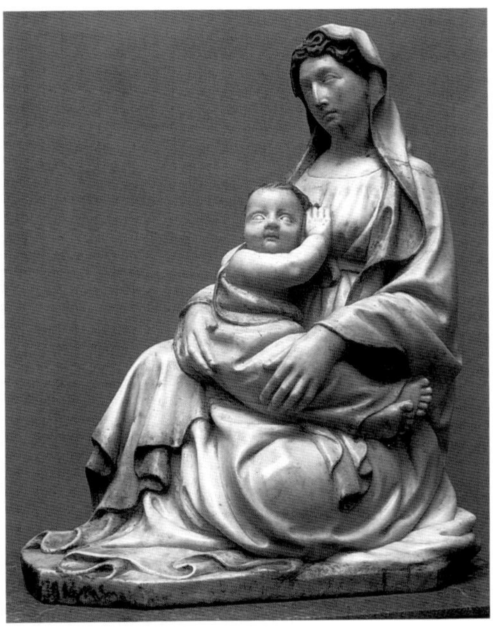

Jacopo della Quercia
Sienese, 1371/1374–1438

*Madonna of Humility*, c. 1400
Marble, traces of gilding
.584 x .488 x .283 (22 7/8 x 19 1/4 x 11 1/8)
Samuel H. Kress Collection
1960.5.2

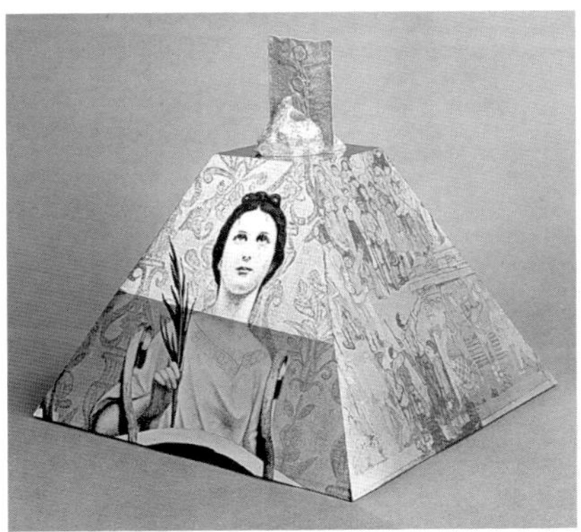

Robert Rauschenberg
American, born 1925

*Araucan Mastaba*, 1985–1986
Sterling silver, lapis lazuli, screenprinted enamel and hand-applied acrylic on polished natural aluminum with plywood substructure, overall dimensions: .524 x .559 x .559 (20 5/8 x 22 x 22); base: .359 x .559 x .559 (14 1/8 x 22 x 22); envelope: .165 x .115 x .019 (6 1/2 x 4 1/4 x 1/4); lapis lazuli: .076 x .102 x .127 (3 x 4 x 5)
Inscribed on lower edge of one side of pyramid: RAUSCHENBERG NGA PROOF 86
Gift of Graphicstudio/University of South Florida and the Artist
1991.75.216

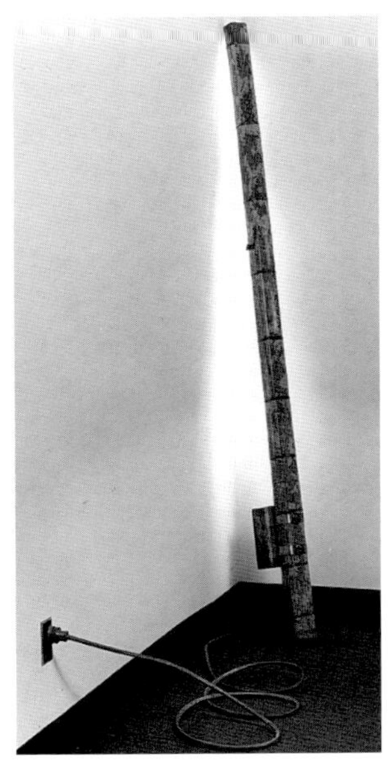

*Bamhue*, 1986–1987
Square bamboo, neon lights, brass electrical box and fittings, brass electrical cable, 2.286 x .102 x .273 (90 x 4 x 10 3/4); electrical cable: 4.572 (180)
Inscribed on bamboo near bottom: (Gemini chop) RAUSCHENBERG
Gift of Graphicstudio/University of South Florida and the Artist
1991.75.217

ROBERT RAUSCHENBERG
American, born 1925

**Bones and Unions Series**

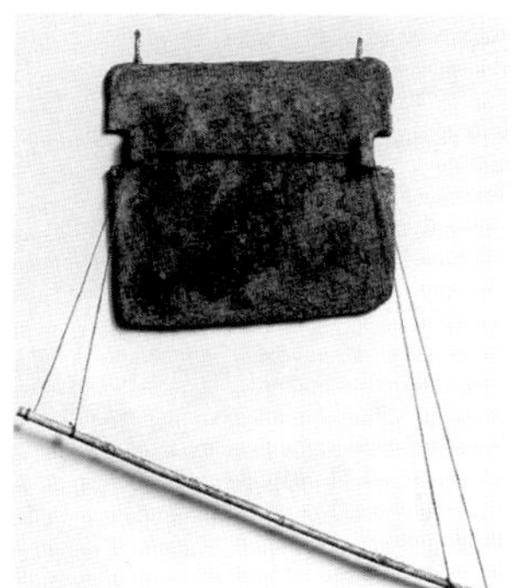

*Ally*, published 1975
Rag-mud, rope, dyed string, and bamboo
Greatest extension: 1.143 x 1.245 x .089
(45 x 49 x 3 1/2)
Inscribed on verso, lower right: '75 /
RAUSCHENBERG GEMINI II
Gift of Gemini G.E.L.
1981.5.240

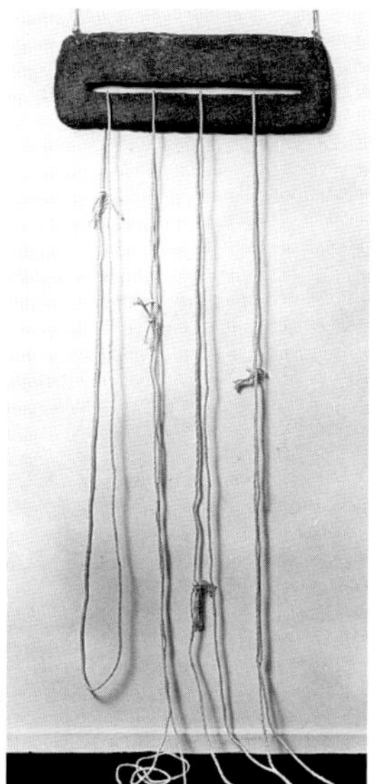

*Ballot*, published 1975
Rag-mud and rope, 1.829 x .711 x .038
(72 x 28 x 1 1/2)
Inscribed on verso, lower right:
RAUSCHENBERG GEMINI II 75
Gift of Gemini G.E.L.
1990.27.47

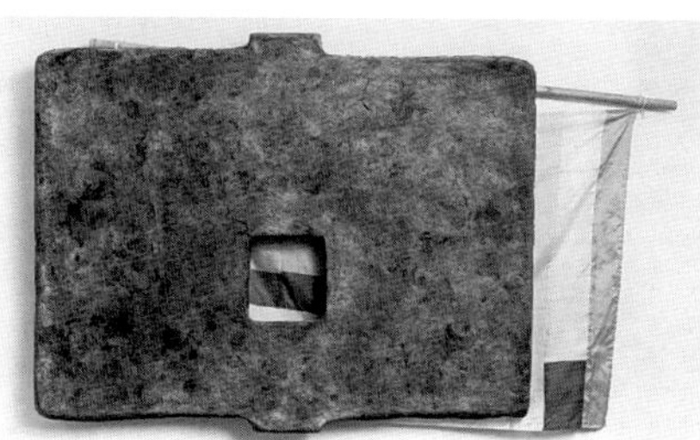

*Capitol*, published 1975
Rag-mud, bamboo, silk, string, glass, and teakwood, .864 x 1.359 x .102
(34 x 53 1/2 x 4)
Inscribed on verso, lower right:
RAUSCHENBERG GEMINI II / 75
Gift of Gemini G.E.L.
1981.5.83

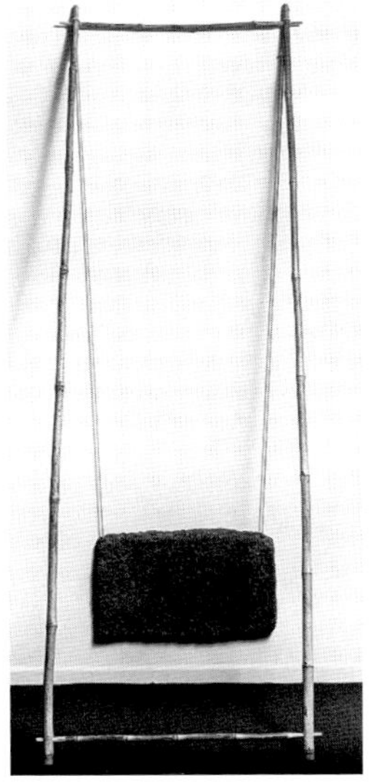

*Charter*, published 1975
Rag-mud, rope, and bamboo
2.057 x .749 x .597 (81 x 29 1/2 x 23 1/2)
(variable)
Inscribed on verso, lower right:
RAUSCHENBERG GEMINI II 75
Gift of Gemini G.E.L.
1991.74.274

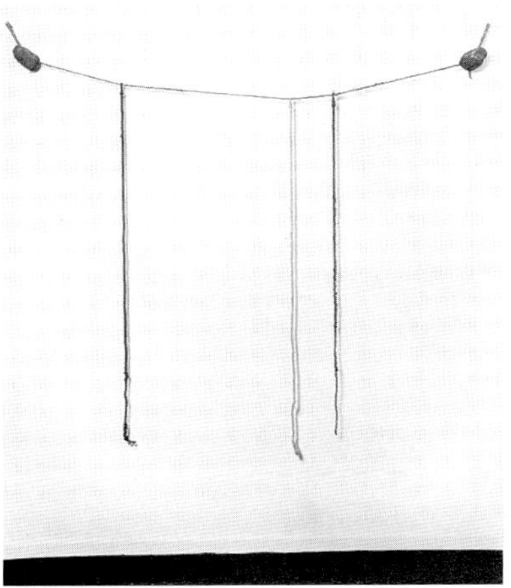

*Junction*, published 1975
Mud and rope, 1.905 x 1.778 x .089
(75 x 70 x 3 1/2)
Inscribed on ball attached by rope:
GEMINI I / RAUSCHENBERG / 75
Gift of Gemini G.E.L.
1991.74.273

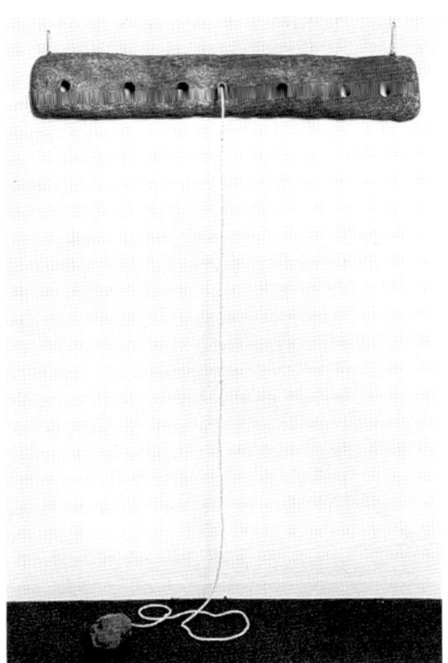

*Quorum*, published 1975
Rag-mud, rope, bamboo, and mud
1.626 x 1.143 x .114 (64 x 45 x 4 1/2)
(variable)
Inscribed on ball attached by rope: 75 /
RAUSCHENBERG / GEMINI / I
Gift of Gemini G.E.L.
1991.74.275

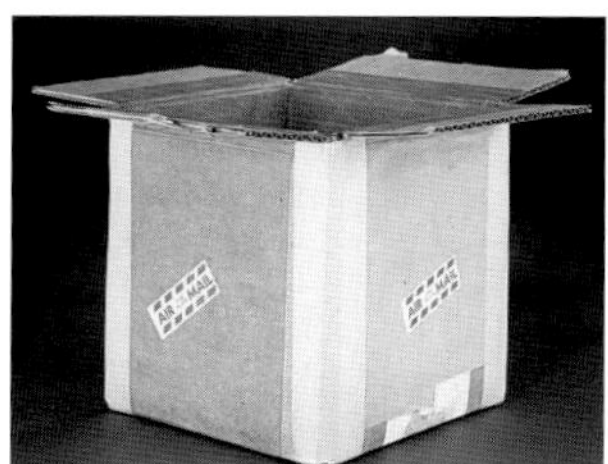

## Robert Rauschenberg
American, born 1925

*Cardbird Box I*, published 1971
Offset lithography, cardboard, and wood
.228 x .310 x .266 (9 x 12 1/8 x 10 1/2)
Inscribed inside bottom at edge:
RAUSCHENBERG 4/20 71
Gift of Benjamin B. Smith
1985.47.178

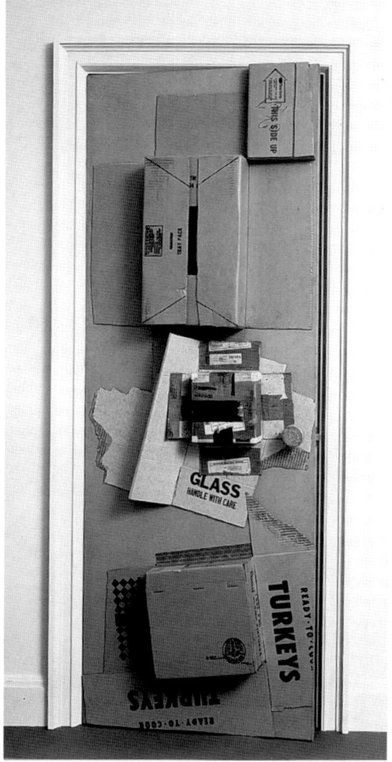


*Cardbird Door* (recto), published 1971
Cardboard, paper, tape, wood, metal, offset lithography, and screenprint
2.032 x .762 x .279 (80 x 30 x 11)
Gift of Gemini G.E.L.
1981.5.123

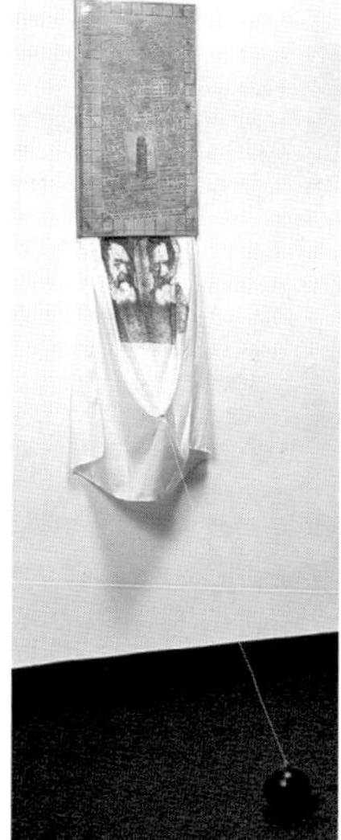

*Fifth-Force*, 1986
Bronze, Xerox transfer on silk, thread, shot, 2.115 x .381 x 1.143
(83 1/4 x 15 x 45)
Inscribed on right edge on brass plate:
RAUSCHENBERG 86; stamped: RR '86
N.G.A. PROOF (Graphicstudio chop)
Gift of Graphicstudio/University of South Florida and the Artist in Honor of the 50th Anniversary of the National Gallery of Art
1990.72.7

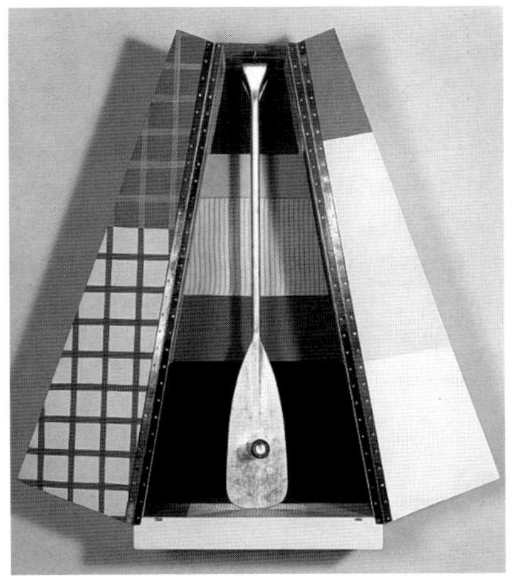

*Publicon—Station I,* published 1978
Wood, collage, fabric, paddle, light bulbs, plexiglass, paint, gold leaf, closed: 1.499 x .762 x .305 (59 x 30 x 12); variable when open
Inscribed underneath on plaque: RAUSCHENBERG 78 PROTOTYPE / (Gemini chop) PUBLICON-STATION I / © 1978 GEMINI G.E.L. / RR78–2042
Gift of Gemini G.E.L.
1981.5.267

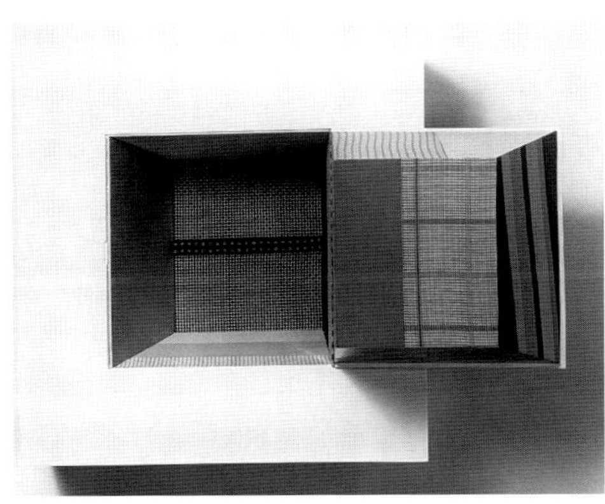

*Publicon—Station II,* published 1978
Wood construction coated with automotive acrylic lacquer, collaged silk and cotton fabrics, closed: .914 x .914 x .356 (36 x 36 x 14); variable when open
Inscribed on back on plaque: RAUSCHENBERG 78 PROTOTYPE / (Gemini chop) PUBLICON-STATION II / © GEMINI G.E.L. / RR78–2044
Gift of Gemini G.E.L.
1981.5.268

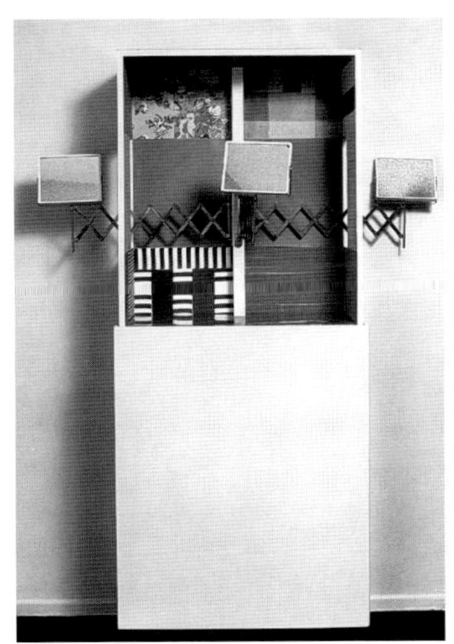

*Publicon—Station III,* published 1978
Wood construction with automotive acrylic lacquer, silk and cotton fabrics, mirror extenders, baked epoxy enamel over polished aluminum, closed: .927 x .787 x .381 ($36^1/_2$ x 31 x 15); variable when open
Inscribed on back on plaque: RAUSCHENBERG 78 PROTOTYPE / (Gemini chop) PUBLICON-STATION III / © 1978 GEMINI G.E.L. / RR78–2047
Gift of Gemini G.E.L.
1981.5.269

## Robert Rauschenberg
American, born 1925

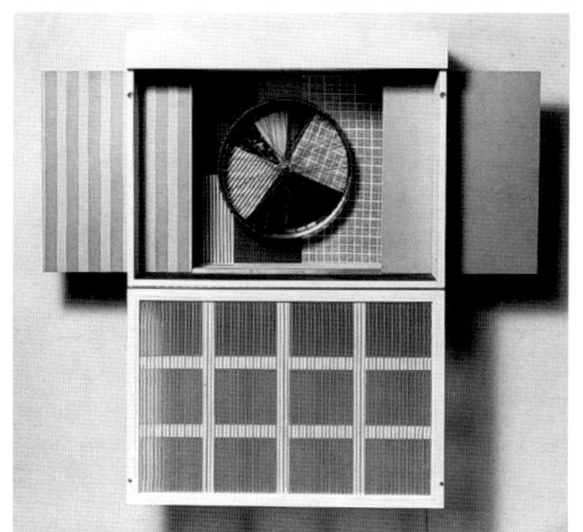

*Publicon—Station IV,* published 1978
Wood construction, automotive acrylic lacquer, collaged silk, cotton fabrics, bicycle wheel, baked epoxy enamel over aluminum, plexiglass, light bulb, closed: .711 x .914 x .330 (28 x 36 x 13); variable when open
Inscribed on back on plaque: RAUSCHENBERG 78 PROTOTYPE / (Gemini chop) PUBLICON-STATION IV / © 1978 GEMINI G.E.L. / RR78–2046
Gift of Gemini G.E.L.
1981.5.270

---

*Publicon—Station V,* published 1978
Wood construction, automotive acrylic lacquer, collaged silk, cotton fabrics, brick, baked epoxy enamel over polished aluminum, plexiglass, light bulb, closed: .457 x .914 x .203 (18 x 36 x 8); variable when open
Inscribed on back on plaque: RAUSCHENBERG 78 PROTOTYPE / (Gemini chop) PUBLICON-STATION V / © 1978 GEMINI G.E.L. / RR78–2045
Gift of Gemini G.E.L.
1981.5.271

---

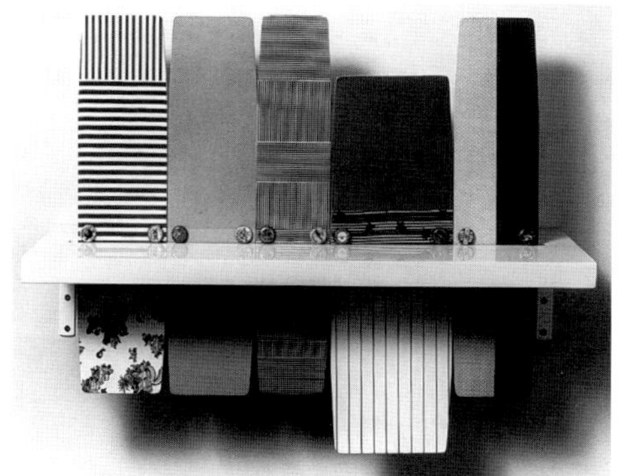

*Publicon—Station VI,* published 1978
Wood construction, automotive acrylic lacquer, collaged silk and cotton fabrics, bottle caps, .610 x .914 x .305 (24 x 36 x 12)
Inscribed under shelf on plaque: RAUSCHENBERG 78 PROTOTYPE / (Gemini chop) PUBLICON-STATION VI / © 1978 GEMINI G.E.L. / RR78–2043
Gift of Gemini G.E.L.
1981.5.272

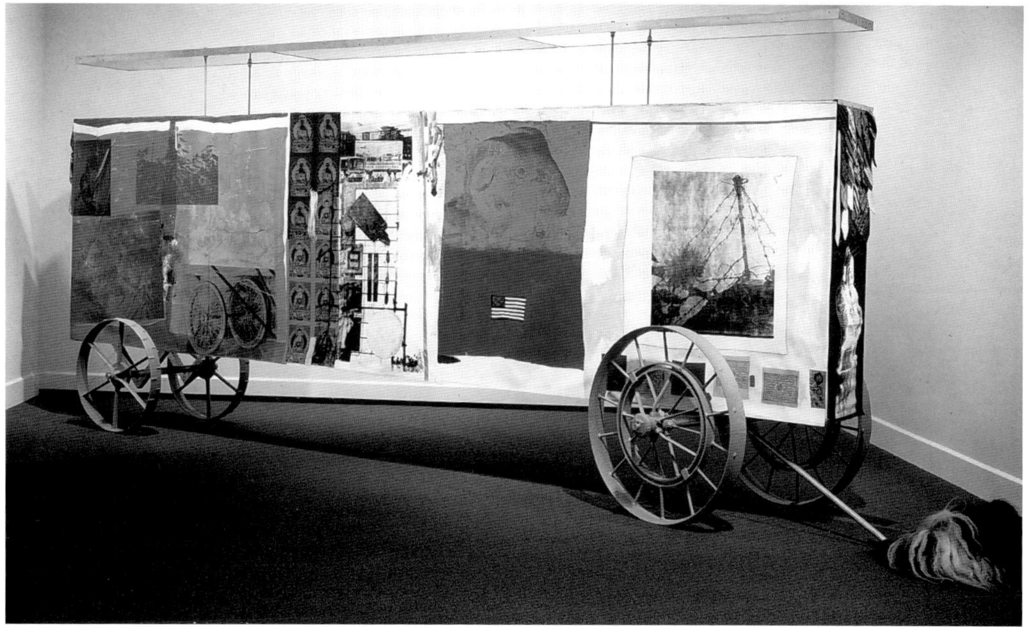

*Sino-Trolley*/ROCI CHINA, 1986
(Rauschenberg Overseas Culture Interchange)
Acrylic and fabric collages on fabric laminated paper mounted on aluminum support with objects
2.185 x 5.869 x 1.397 (86 x 231 x 55)
Gift of the Robert Rauschenberg Foundation
1991.76.4

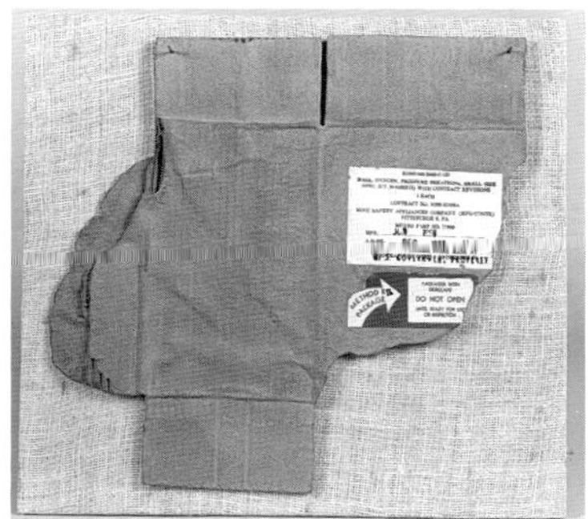

*Tampa Clay Piece 1*, 1972
Clay and fiberglass, .368 x .394 x .019 (14 1/2 x 15 1/2 x 3/4)
Gift of Graphicstudio/University of South Florida and the Artist
1986.26.96

Prototype for 1986.26.96 is ROBERT RAUSCHENBERG, *Tampa Clay Piece 1*, 1985.48.31

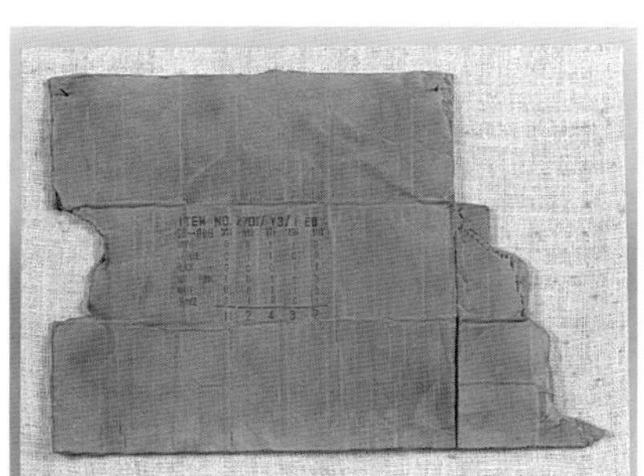

*Tampa Clay Piece 2*, 1972
Clay and fiberglass, .394 x .597 x .019 (15 1/2 x 23 1/2 x 3/4)
Gift of Graphicstudio/University of South Florida and the Artist
1986.26.97

Prototype for 1986.26.97 is ROBERT RAUSCHENBERG, *Tampa Clay Piece 2*, 1985.48.32

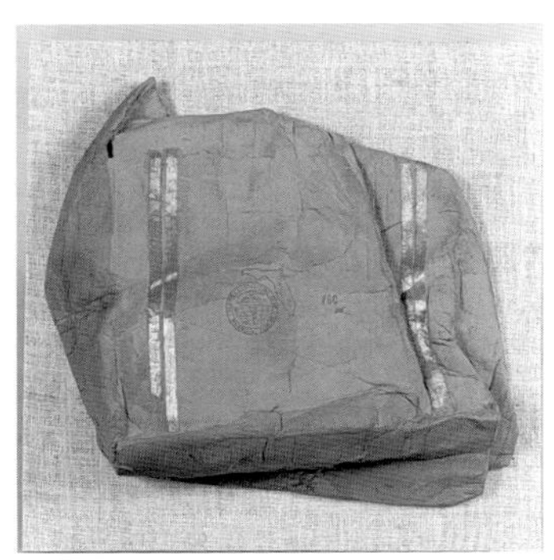

ROBERT RAUSCHENBERG
American, born 1925

*Tampa Clay Piece 3*, 1972
Clay and fiberglass, .495 x .610 x .140 ($19^{1}/_{2}$ x 24 x $5^{1}/_{2}$)
Gift of Graphicstudio/University of South Florida and the Artist
1986.26.98

Prototype for 1986.26.98 is ROBERT RAUSCHENBERG, *Tampa Clay Piece 3*, 1985.48.33

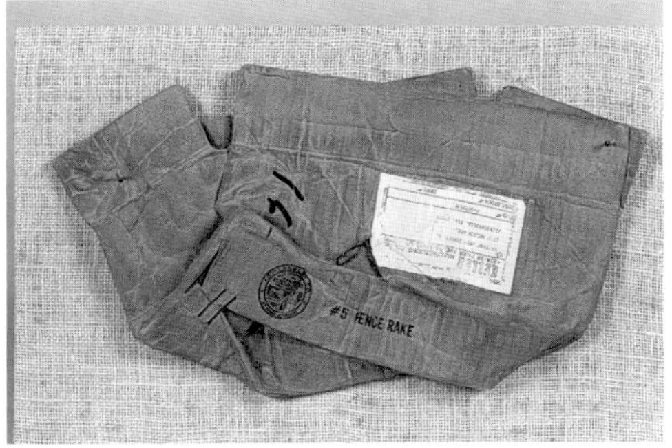


*Tampa Clay Piece 4*, 1972
Clay and fiberglass, .241 x .432 x .038 ($9^{1}/_{2}$ x 17 x $1^{1}/_{2}$)
Gift of Graphicstudio/University of South Florida and the Artist
1986.26.107

Prototype for 1986.26.107 is ROBERT RAUSCHENBERG, *Tampa Clay Piece 4*, 1985.48.34

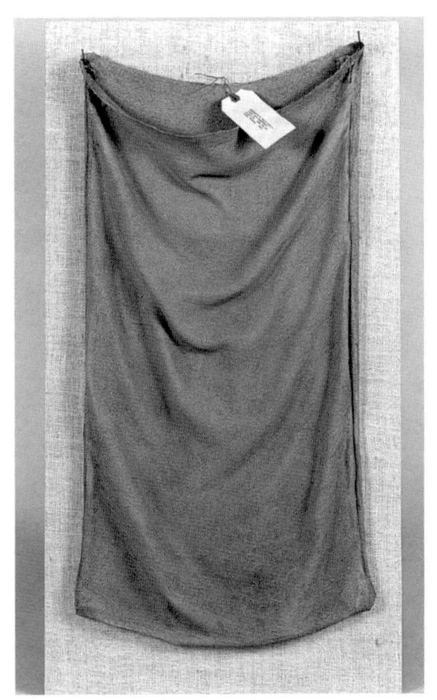

*Tampa Clay Piece 5*, 1972
Clay and fiberglass, .864 x .457 x .076 (34 x 18 x 3)
Gift of Graphicstudio/University of South Florida and the Artist
1986.26.108

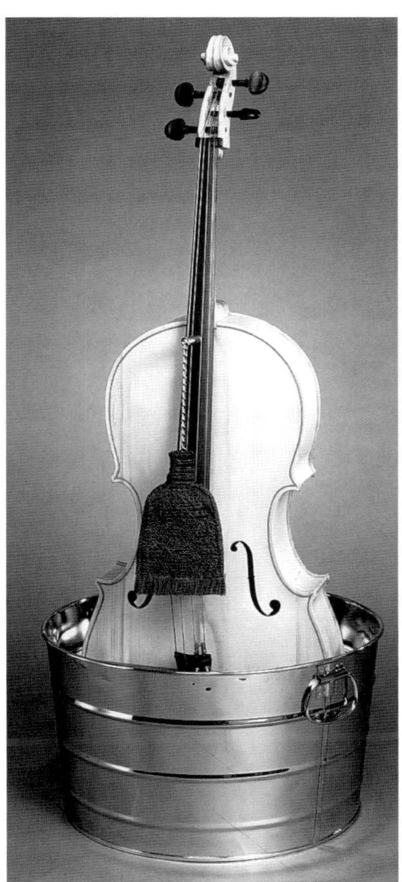

*Tibetan Garden Song*, 1985–1986
Commercially manufactured cello, chrome-plated washtub, glycerin, Chinese scrollmaker's brush, mirrored plexiglass, height: 1.092 (43); diameter: .464 ($18^{1}/_{4}$)
Inscribed on side of cello: RAUSCHENBERG / NGA PROOF 86
Gift of Graphicstudio/University of South Florida and the Artist
1991.75.215

NICOLAS REBILLÉ
*See* BENOÎT MASSOU

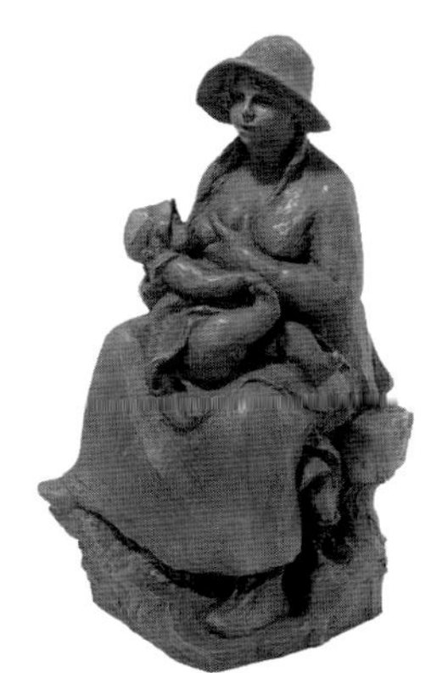

AUGUSTE RENOIR
French, 1841–1919

*Maternity: Madame Renoir and Son*, c. 1916
Terra cotta, .511 x .248 x .324 ($20^{1}/_{8}$ x $9^{3}/_{4}$ x $12^{3}/_{4}$)
Inscribed on back in center, underlined: RENOIR
Collection of Mr. and Mrs. Paul Mellon
1983.1.72

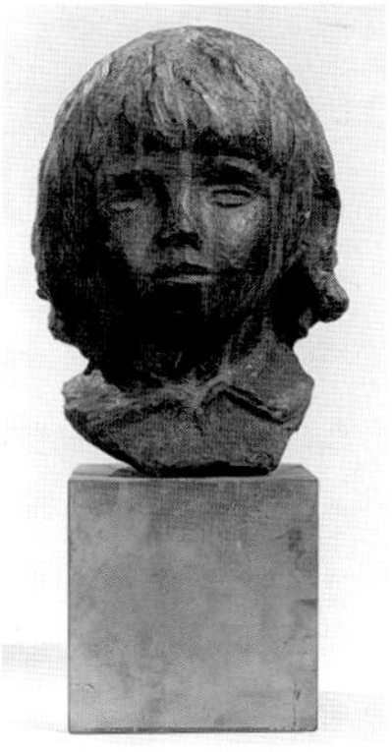

## Auguste Renoir
French, 1841–1919

*Claude Renoir ("Coco"),* c. 1908
Bronze, .264 x .196 x .191
($10^{3}/_{8}$ x $7^{3}/_{4}$ x $7^{1}/_{8}$)
Inscribed on right edge: RENOIR.; on back edge: NO. 3/30; foundry mark on back edge: CIRE / C. VALSUANI / PERDUE
Gift of Margaret Seligman Lewisohn in memory of her husband, Sam A. Lewisohn
1954.8.2

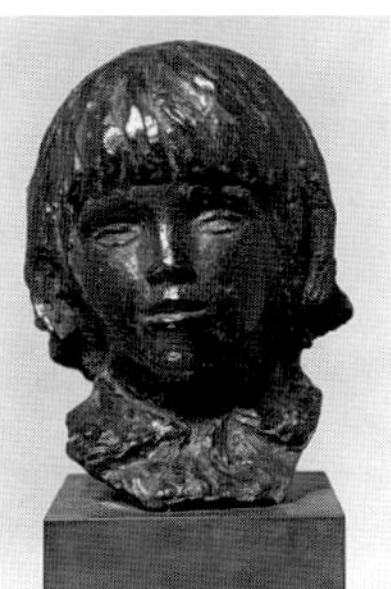

*Claude Renoir ("Coco"),* 1908
Bronze, .264 x .204 x .194
($10^{3}/_{8}$ x 8 x $7^{5}/_{8}$)
Inscribed on right edge: RENOIR; on back edge: 9/30; foundry mark on back edge: CIRE / C. VALSUANI / PERDUE
Chester Dale Collection
1963.10.242

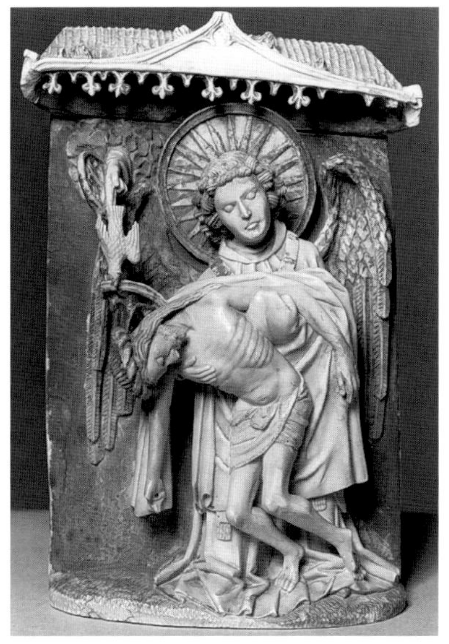

## Rhenish or South Netherlandish 15th Century

*The Dead Christ Supported by an Angel (The Trinity),* c. 1440
Alabaster, polychromed and gilt
.311 x .226 x .098 ($12^{1}/_{4}$ x $8^{7}/_{8}$ x $3^{7}/_{8}$)
Gift of Mrs. Ralph Harman Booth
1942.11.3

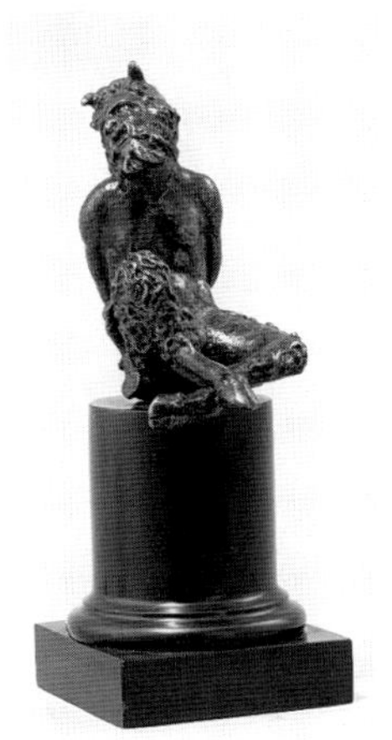

## Andrea Riccio (Andrea Briosco), called Riccio

Paduan, 1470–1532

*Bound Satyr*
Bronze, .073 x .045 x .073
($2\frac{7}{8}$ x $1\frac{13}{16}$ x $2\frac{7}{8}$)
Samuel H. Kress Collection
1957.14.33

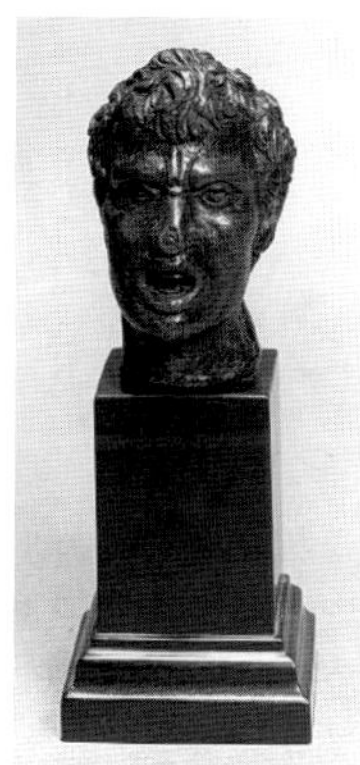

*Bust of a Man (Vulcan?)*
Bronze, .051 x .038 x .043
($2\frac{1}{4}$ x $1\frac{7}{16}$ x $1\frac{11}{16}$)
Samuel H. Kress Collection
1957.14.56

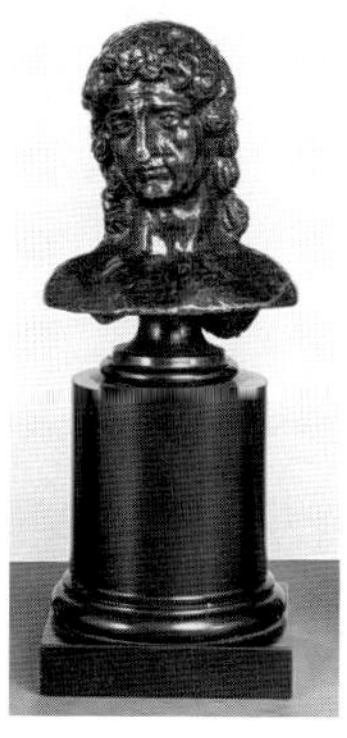

*Bust of a Youth (Saint John?)*
Bronze, .079 x .067 x .049
($3\frac{1}{8}$ x $2\frac{5}{8}$ x $1\frac{15}{16}$)
Samuel H. Kress Collection
1957.14.55

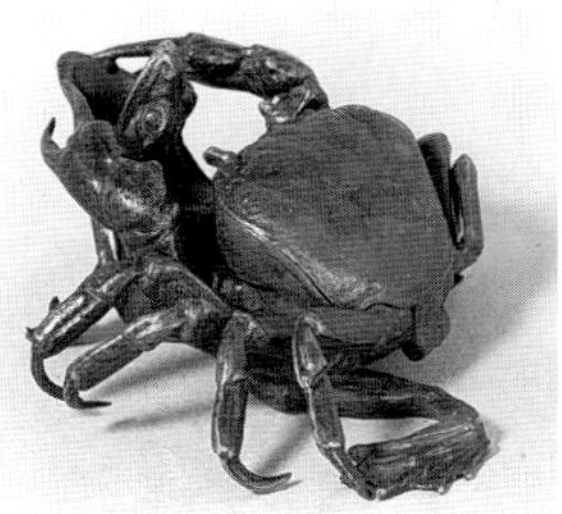

*A Crab on a Toad*
Bronze, .050 x .113 x .100
(2 x $4\frac{7}{16}$ x $3\frac{15}{16}$)
Samuel H. Kress Collection
1957.14.87

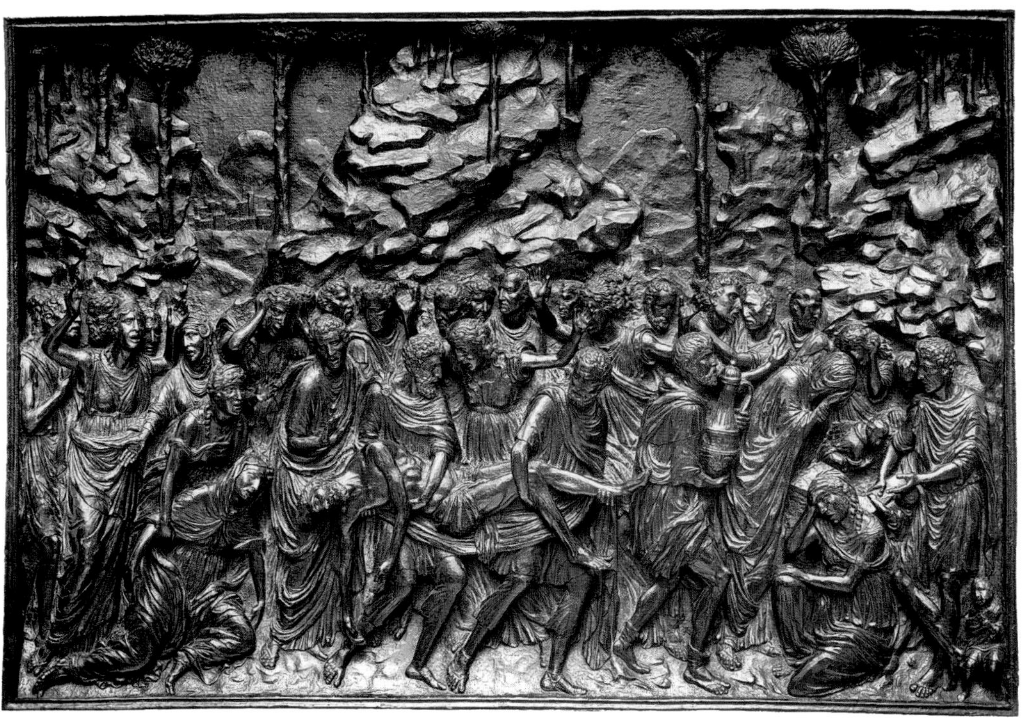

Andrea Riccio (Andrea Briosco), called Riccio
Paduan, 1470–1532

*The Entombment*
Bronze, .504 x .755 (19 7/8 x 29 3/4)
Inscribed at right, on urn, artist's name in retrograde: AERDNA
Samuel H. Kress Collection
1957.14.11

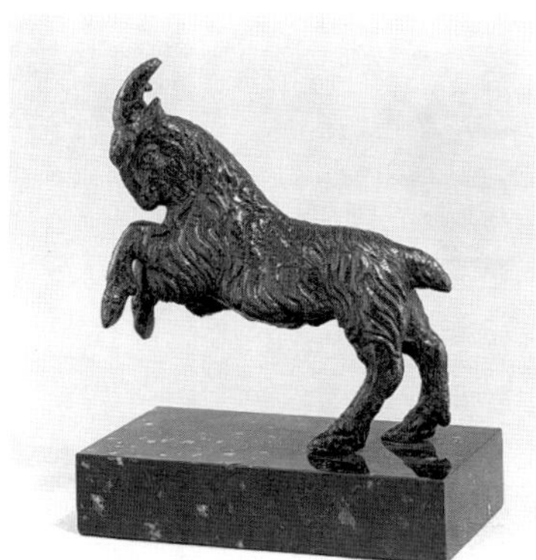

*A Goat*
Bronze, .098 x .092 x .026
(3 7/8 x 3 5/8 x 1)
Samuel H. Kress Collection
1957.14.77

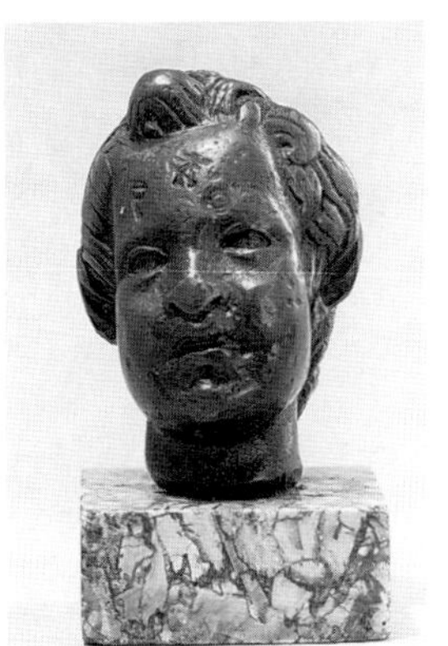

*Head of a Faun*
Bronze, .059 x .042 x .048
(2 5/16 x 1 5/8 x 1 7/8)
Marks on forehead: P * O (?)
Samuel H. Kress Collection
1957.14.57

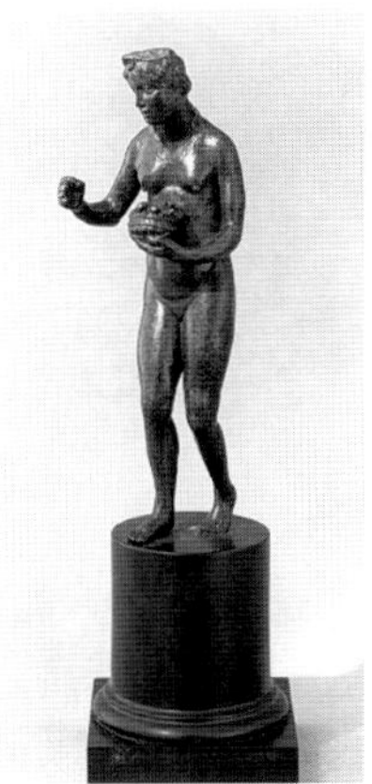

*Pomona*
Bronze, .164 x .055 x .048
($6\frac{7}{16}$ x $2\frac{3}{16}$ x $1\frac{7}{8}$)
Samuel H. Kress Collection
1957.14.20

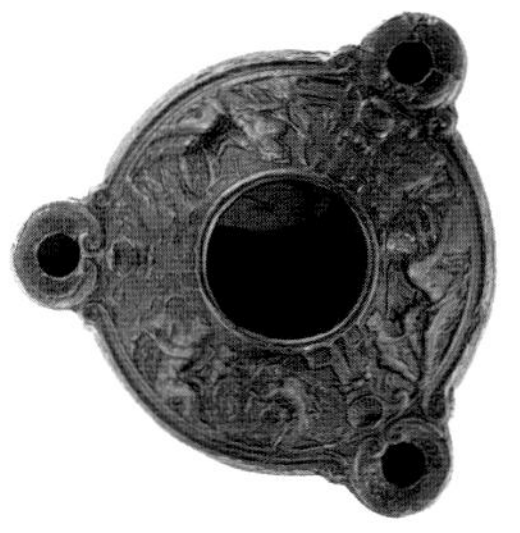

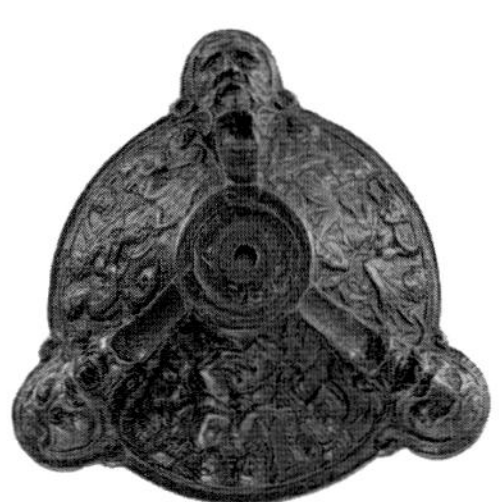

*Three Wick Lamp with Bacchic Scenes,*
c. 1500
Bronze, .050 x .108 x .110
(2 x $4\frac{1}{4}$ x $4\frac{5}{16}$)
Samuel H. Kress Collection
1957.14.66

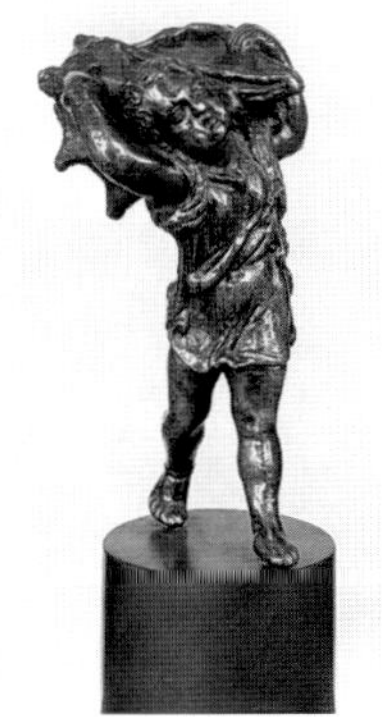

WORKSHOP OF ANDREA RICCIO
(ANDREA BRIOSCO), CALLED RICCIO
Paduan

*Inkwell in the Form of a Child Carrying a Shell*
Bronze, .116 x .037 x .039
($4\frac{5}{8}$ x $1\frac{7}{16}$ x $1\frac{9}{16}$)
Samuel H. Kress Collection
1957.14.35

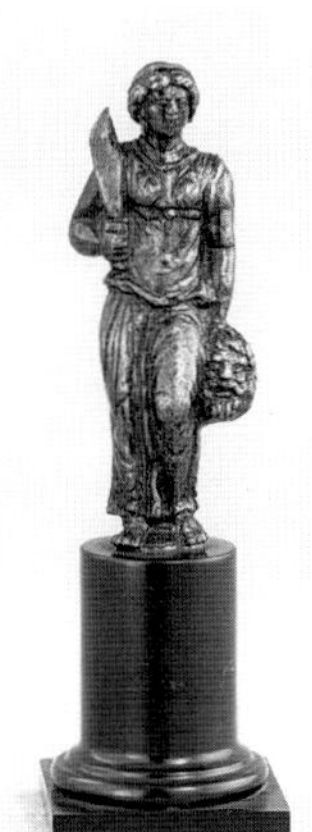

WORKSHOP OF ANDREA RICCIO
(ANDREA BRIOSCO), CALLED RICCIO
Paduan

*Judith with the Head of Holofernes*
Bronze, .065 x .028 x .015
($2\frac{5}{8}$ x $1\frac{1}{8}$ x $\frac{5}{8}$)
Samuel H. Kress Collection
1957.14.18

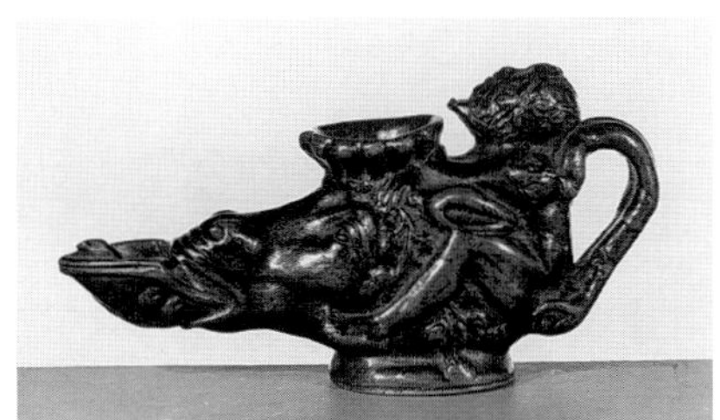

Workshop of Andrea Riccio (Andrea Briosco), called Riccio
Paduan

*Lamp in the Form of an Ass' Head*
Bronze, .069 x .137 x .036
(2 3/4 x 5 3/8 x 1 7/16)
Samuel H. Kress Collection
1957.14.68

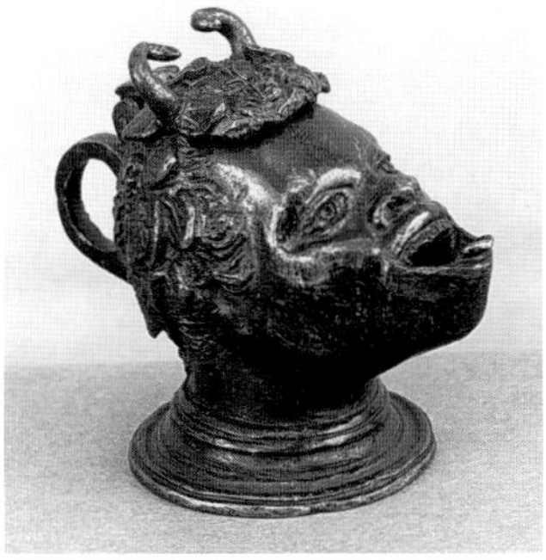

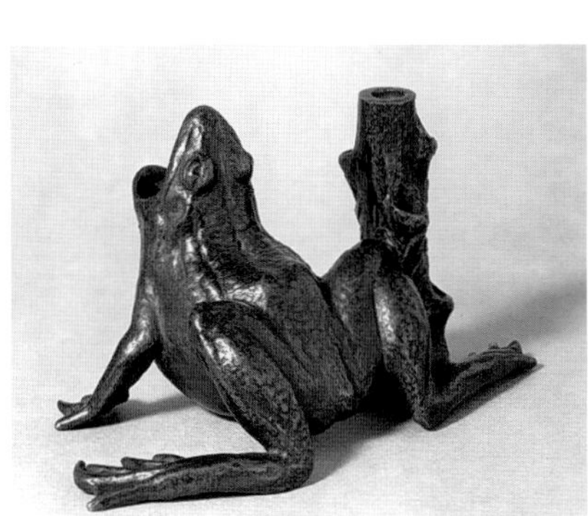

Workshop of Andrea Riccio (Andrea Briosco), called Riccio
Paduan

*Lamp in the Form of a Satyr's Head*
Bronze with copper plate on base
.078 x .059 x .102 (3 1/16 x 2 3/8 x 4 1/16)
Inscribed on copper plate on base: (two undecipherable symbols)
Samuel H. Kress Collection
1957.14.58

Attributed to Workshop of Andrea Riccio (Andrea Briosco), called Riccio
Paduan

*Inkwell in the Form of a Frog beside a Tree Stump*
Bronze, .074 x .142 x .082
(2 7/8 x 5 9/16 x 3 1/4)
Samuel H. Kress Collection
1957.14.89

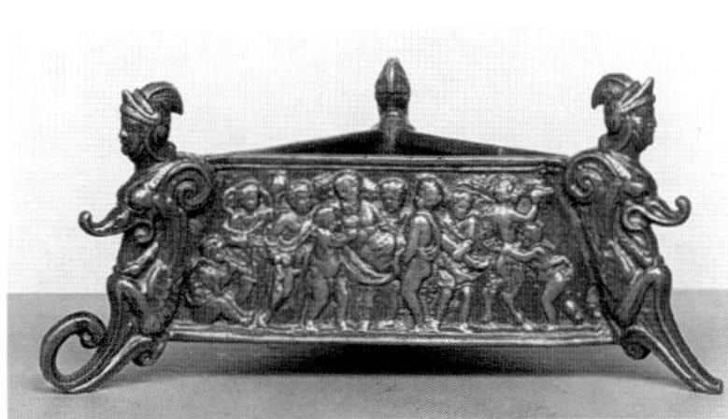

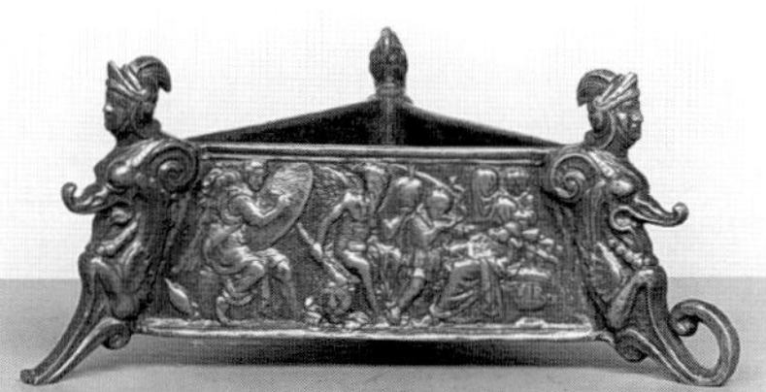

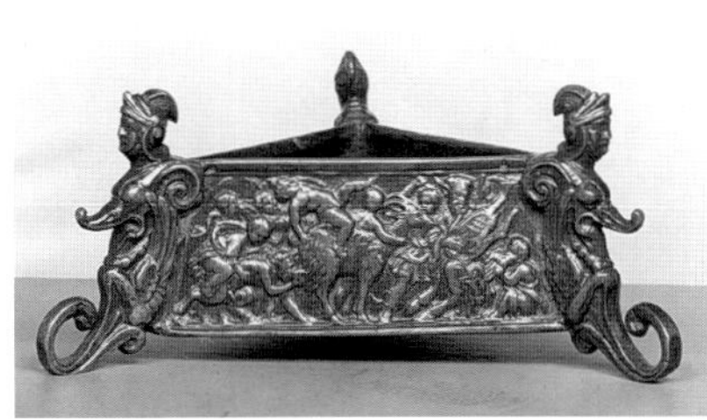

Follower of Andrea Riccio (Andrea Briosco), called Riccio
Paduan

*Sand-Box (Triangular)*, c. 1525/1540
Bronze, .074 x .170 (2 15/16 x 6 11/16)
Inscribed on side with Victory, at lower right on vase: VIR
Samuel H. Kress Collection
1957.14.63

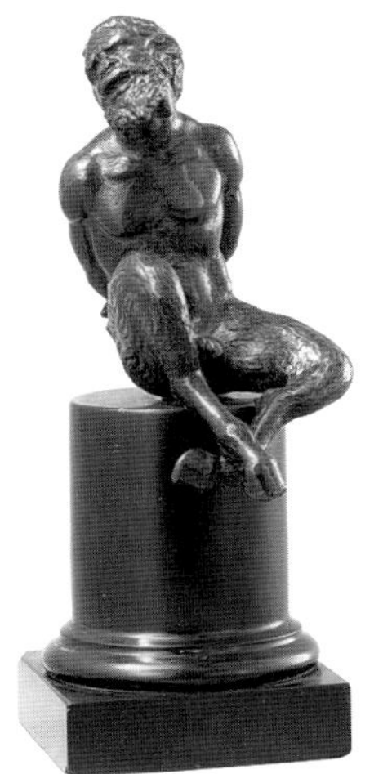

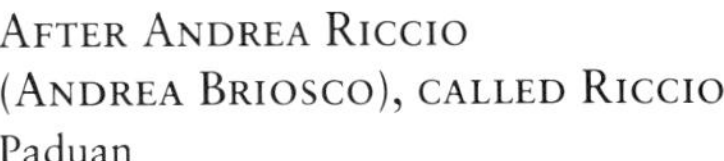

AFTER ANDREA RICCIO
(ANDREA BRIOSCO), CALLED RICCIO
Paduan

*Bound Satyr*
Bronze, .089 x .056 x .064
(3 1/2 x 2 3/16 x 2 9/16)
Samuel H. Kress Collection
1957.14.32

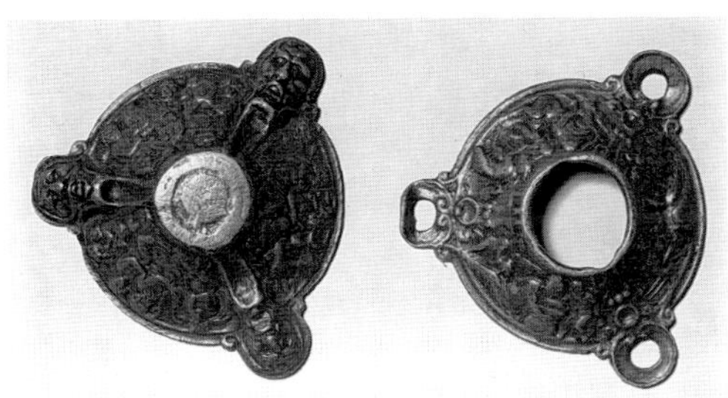

AFTER ANDREA RICCIO
(ANDREA BRIOSCO), CALLED RICCIO
Paduan

*Lamp in Two Parts*, c. 1800/1899
Gilt bronze, outer lip of cup to opposite circumference, lower portion: .103 (4 1/16), upper portion: .105 (4 1/8); depth, lower portion: .023 (7/8), upper portion: .029 (1 1/8)
Widener Collection
1942.9.150.b and a

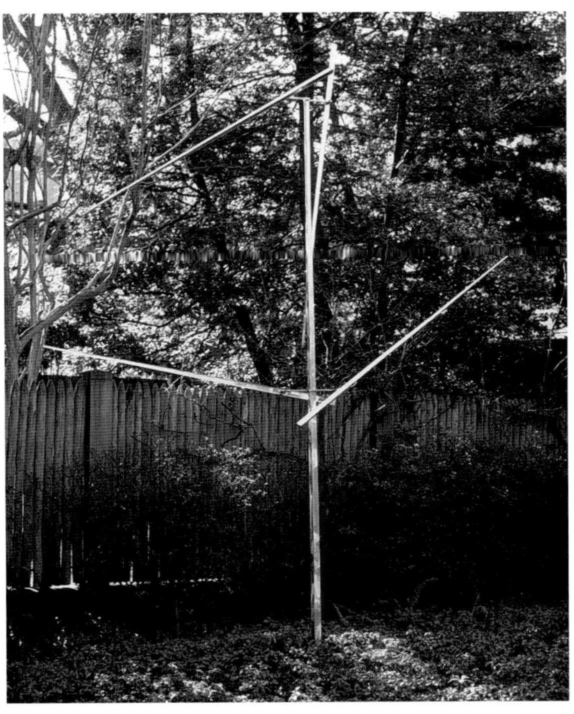

GEORGE RICKEY
American, born 1907

*Divided Square Oblique II*, 1981
Stainless steel, 3.505 x 2.083 x .305
(138 x 82 x 12)
Gift of Mr. and Mrs. William A. Nitze, in Honor of the 50th Anniversary of the National Gallery of Art
1991.93.1

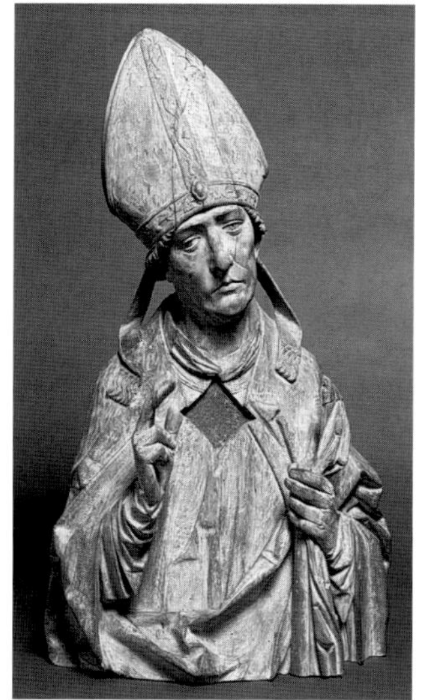

Tilman Riemenschneider
German, c. 1460–1531

*Saint Burchard of Würzburg,* c. 1510/1523
Linden wood, painted, .823 x .472 x .302 (32 3/8 x 18 1/2 x 11 7/8)
Samuel H. Kress Collection
1961.1.1

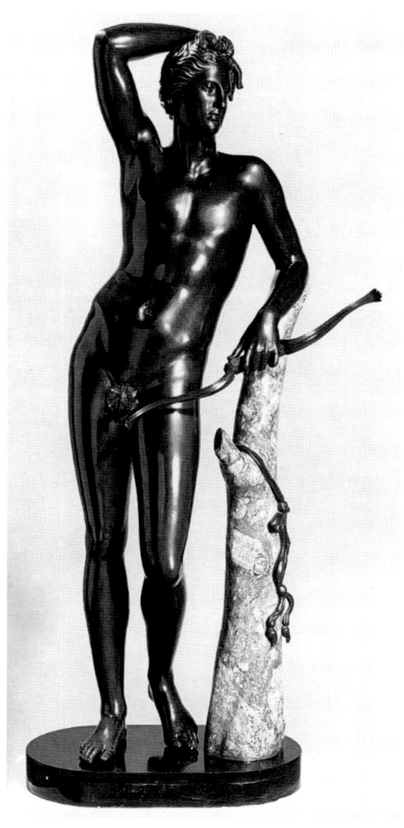

Attributed to Francesco Righetti
Roman, 1749–1819

*Apollino of the Villa Medici,* c. 1775/1819
Bronze, 1.400 x .497 x .340 (55 x 19 1/2 x 13 3/8)
Samuel H. Kress Collection
1952.5.94

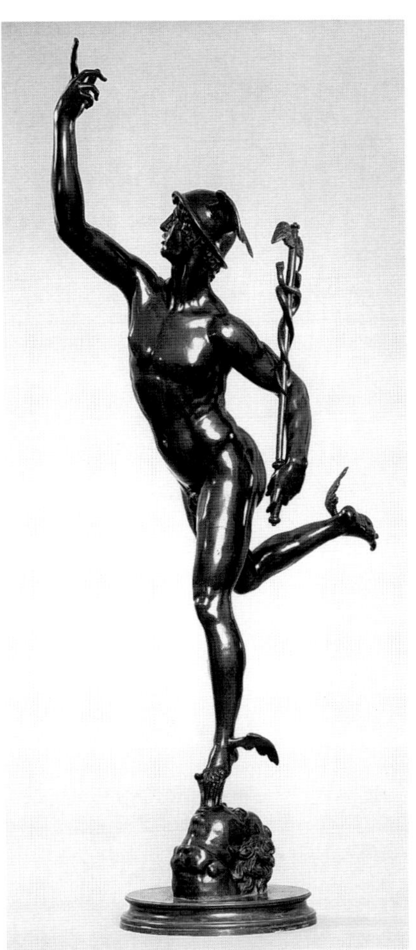

ATTRIBUTED TO
FRANCESCO RIGHETTI,
AFTER GIOVANNI BOLOGNA
Roman, 1749–1819

*Mercury*, c. 1780/1800
Bronze, 1.770 x .485 x .949
(69 5/8 x 19 x 37 1/4)
Andrew W. Mellon Collection
1937.1.131

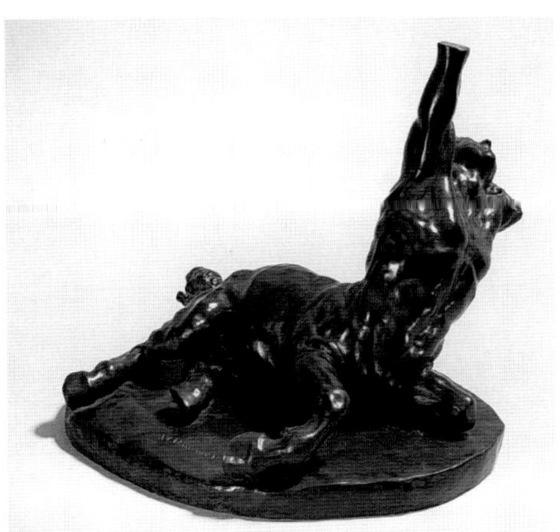

WILLIAM RIMMER
American, 1816–1879

*Dying Centaur*, c. 1869, cast 1967
Bronze, .654 x .651 x .546
(25 3/4 x 25 5/8 x 21 1/2)
Inscribed on top of base: W. RIMMER;
foundry mark on edge of base by centaur's
tail: © / CAST BY KENNEDY GALLERIES INC.
1967 / #2/15
Gift of the Avalon Foundation
1968.2.1

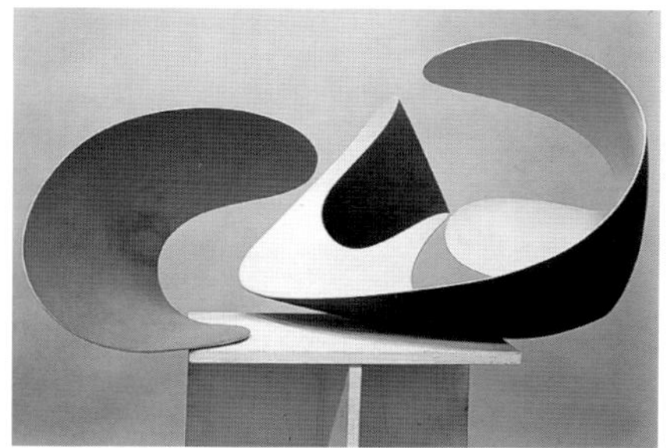

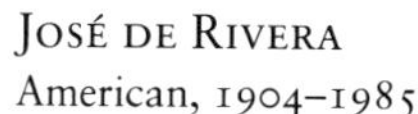

JOSÉ DE RIVERA
American, 1904–1985

*Black, Yellow, Red,* 1942
Aluminum, painted, .473 x .998 x .471
($18\frac{5}{8}$ x $39\frac{1}{4}$ x $18\frac{1}{2}$)
Gift of Mr. and Mrs. Burton Tremaine
1977.75.8

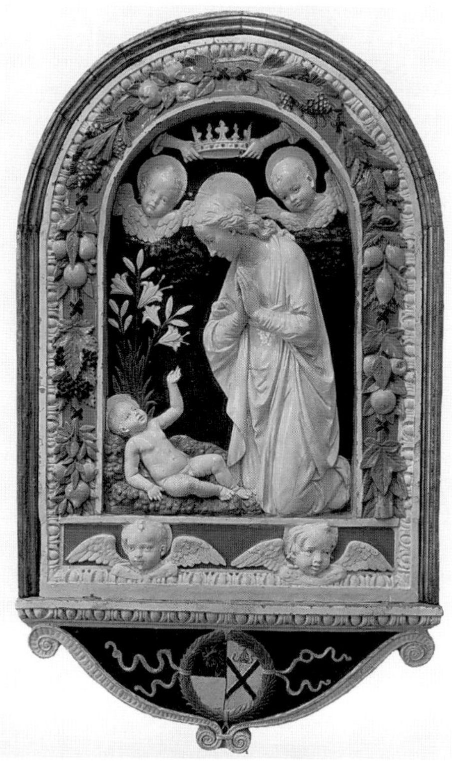

ANDREA DELLA ROBBIA
Florentine, 1435–1525

*The Adoration of the Child,* after 1477
Glazed terra cotta, 1.278 x .774
($50\frac{3}{8}$ x $30\frac{1}{2}$)
Samuel H. Kress Collection
1961.1.2

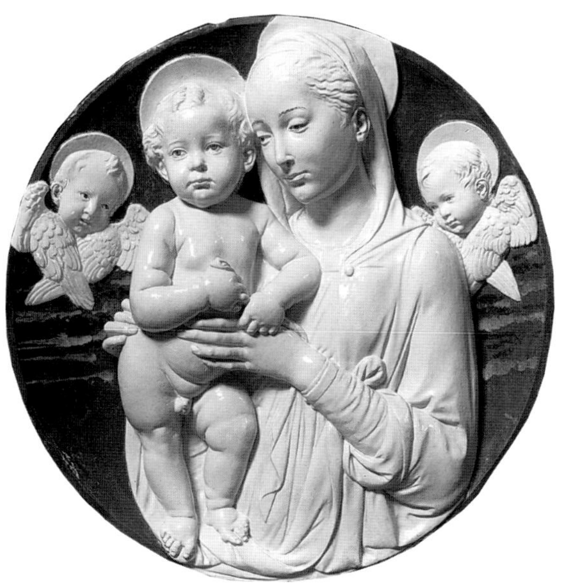

*Madonna and Child with Cherubim,*
c. 1485
Glazed terra cotta, diameter: .547 ($21\frac{1}{2}$)
Andrew W. Mellon Collection
1937.1.122

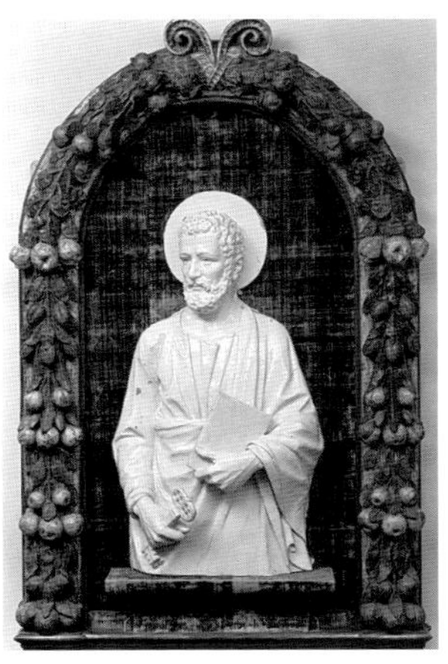

*Saint Peter*, c. 1480
Glazed terra cotta, .950 x .550
(37 1/2 x 21 1/2)
Samuel H. Kress Collection
1939.1.329

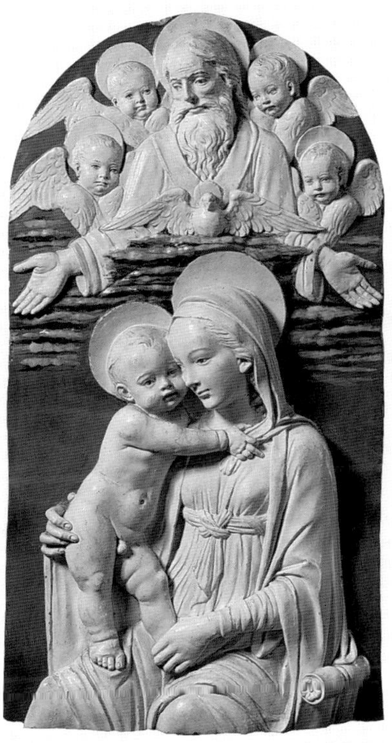

Studio of Andrea della Robbia
Florentine

*Madonna and Child with God the Father and Cherubim*, 1480/1490
Glazed terra cotta, .900 x .480
(35 1/2 x 19)
Andrew W. Mellon Collection
1937.1.123

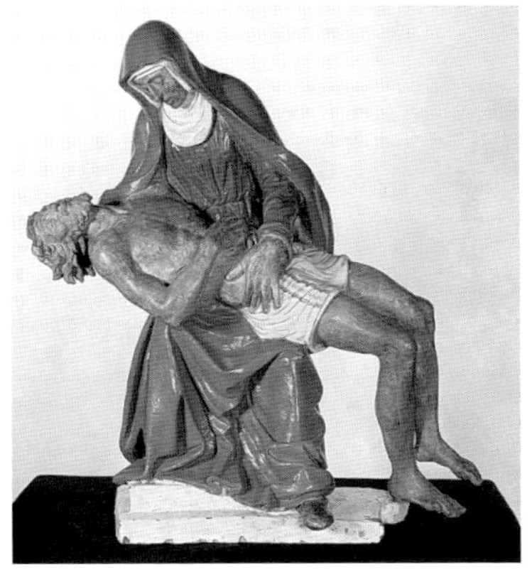

Giovanni della Robbia
Florentine, 1469–1529/1530

*Pietà*, c. 1510/1520
Glazed terra cotta, .720 x .440 x .327
(28 1/2 x 17 1/2 x 12 7/8)
Samuel H. Kress Collection
1943.4.70

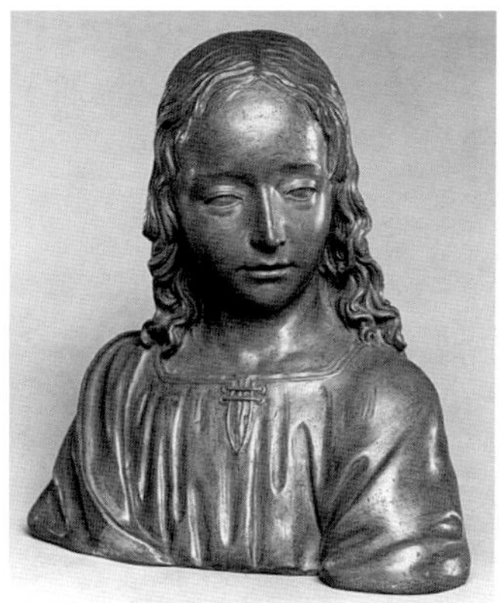

Giovanni della Robbia
Florentine, 1469–1529/1530

*The Young Christ (?)*, c. 1500/1510
Terra cotta, .376 x .369 x .182
($14^{7}/_{8}$ x $14^{5}/_{8}$ x $7^{1}/_{4}$)
Samuel H. Kress Collection
1943.4.73

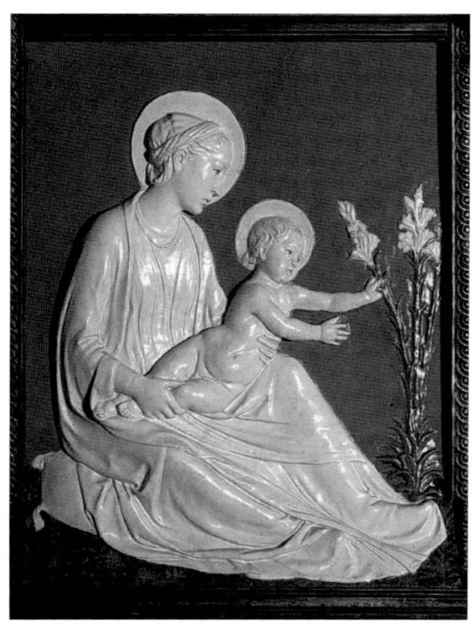

Luca della Robbia
Florentine, c. 1400–1482

*Madonna and Child*, c. 1475
Glazed terra cotta, .483 x .389
(19 x $15^{1}/_{4}$)
Widener Collection
1942.9.141

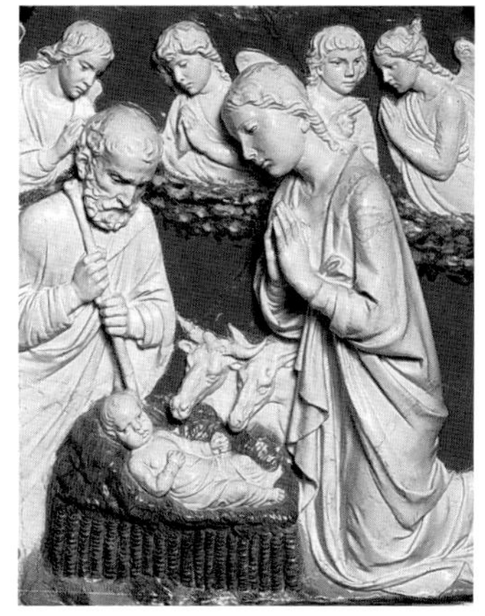

*The Nativity*, c. 1460
Glazed terra cotta, .565 x .479
($22^{1}/_{4}$ x $18^{7}/_{8}$)
Samuel H. Kress Collection
1961.1.3

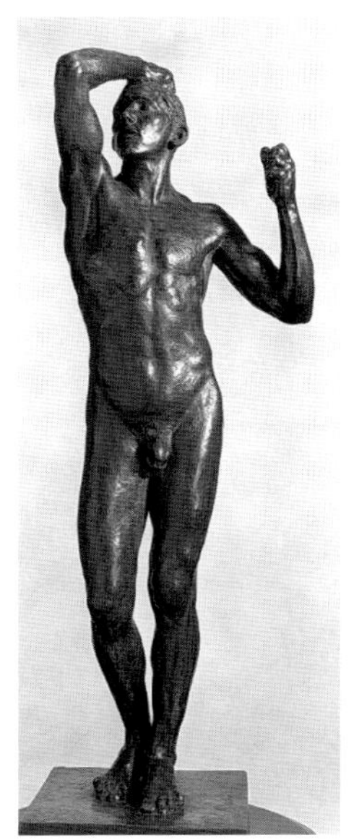

Auguste Rodin
French, 1840–1917

*The Age of Bronze,* late 1890s
Bronze, 1.041 x .355 x .219
(41 x 14 x 8 5/8)
Inscribed on top of base by left foot: RODIN; inside base near left foot: A. RODIN
Gift of Mrs. John W. Simpson
1942.5.10

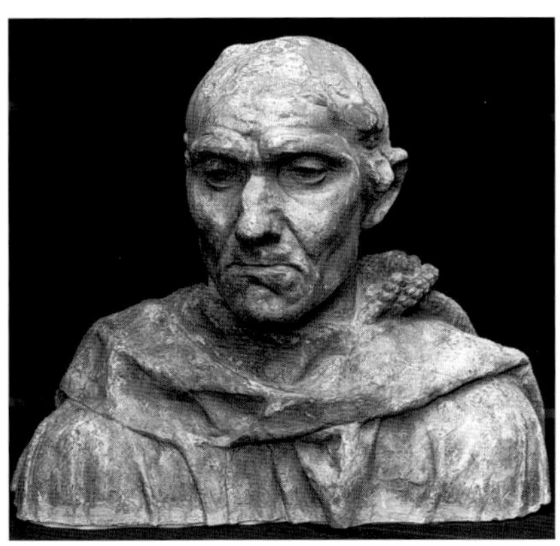

*Jean d'Aire,* c. 1887
Plaster, lacquered, .476 x .584 x .400
(18 3/4 x 23 x 15 3/4)
Gift of the B. G. Cantor Art Foundation
1984.85.1

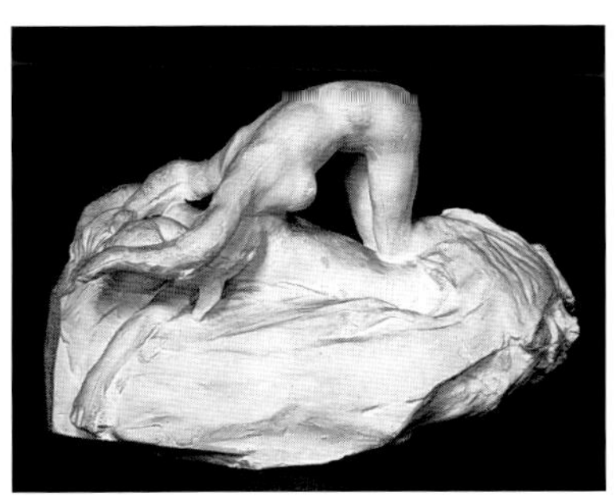

*Aurora and Tithonus,* 1907
Plaster, greatest extension: .266 (10 1/2)
Inscribed on left side: L'AURORE SE LEVE DE LA / COUCHE DU BEAU TYPHON [sic] / METAMORPHOSE / D'OVIDE; on back: HOMMAGE MME KATE SIMPSON / A RODIN / 1907
Gift of Mrs. John W. Simpson
1942.5.20

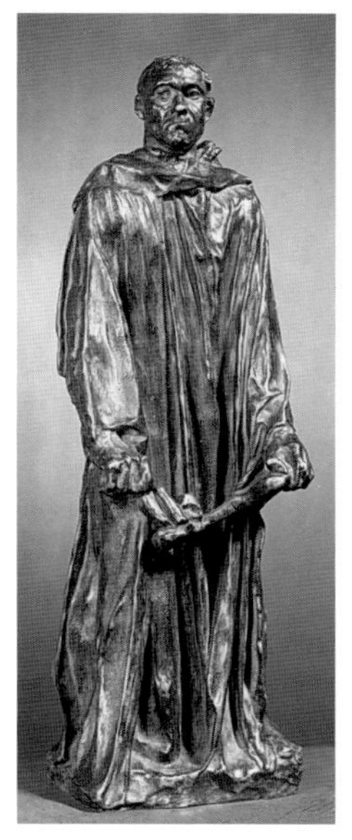

Auguste Rodin
French, 1840–1917

*A Burgher of Calais,* late 1890s
Bronze, .470 x .160 x .140
(18 1/2 x 6 1/4 x 5 1/2)
Inscribed on back of base: A. RODIN
Gift of Mrs. John W. Simpson
1942.5.13

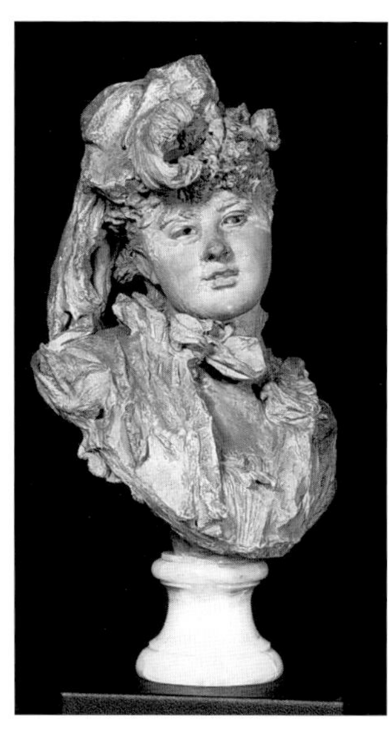

*Bust of a Woman,* c. 1865
Terra cotta and tinted plaster
.489 x .356 x .336 (19 1/4 x 14 1/8 x 10 5/8)
Inscribed on back: OFFERT À MADAME & / MONSIEUR J.W. SIMPSON / A. RODIN / 1908 / TERRE-CUITE ORIGINALE FAITE / EN 1875
Gift of Mrs. John W. Simpson
1942.5.3

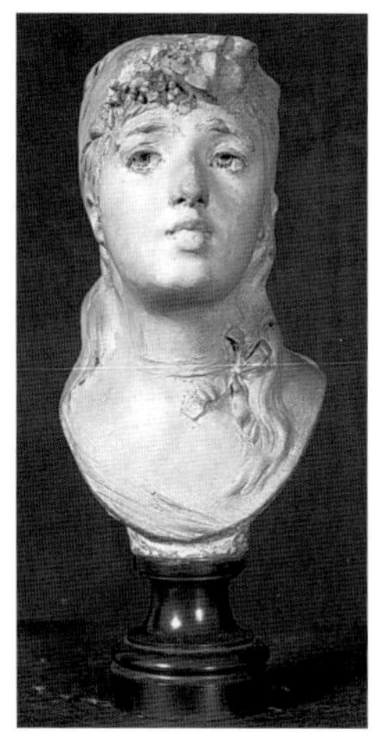

*Bust of a Young Girl,* 1868
Terra cotta, .311 x .165 x .174
(12 1/4 x 6 1/2 x 6 7/8)
Inscribed on back: BUSTE.FAIT.EN.1868 / RETROUVÉ.OFFERT.A.MME K. SIMPSON / EN 1908 / A. RODIN
Gift of Mrs. John W. Simpson
1942.5.4

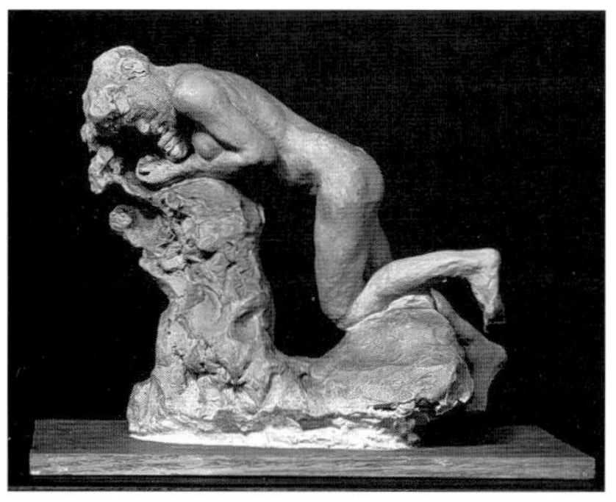

*Eve Eating the Apple*, c. 1885
Terra cotta, .230 x .273 x .156
($9^{1}/_{8}$ x $10^{3}/_{4}$ x $6^{1}/_{4}$)
Inscribed on base, below left leg: A. RODIN
Gift of Mrs. John W. Simpson
1942.5.7

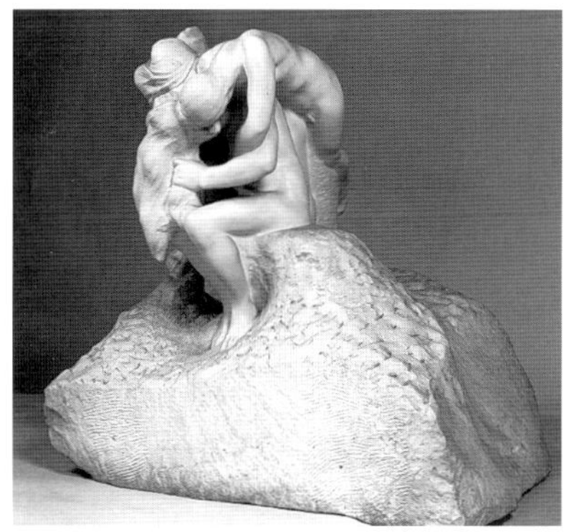

*The Evil Spirits*, 1899
Marble, .712 x .757 x .590
(28 x $29^{3}/_{4}$ x $23^{1}/_{4}$)
Inscribed on left side of base: A RODIN
Gift of Mrs. John W. Simpson
1942.5.17

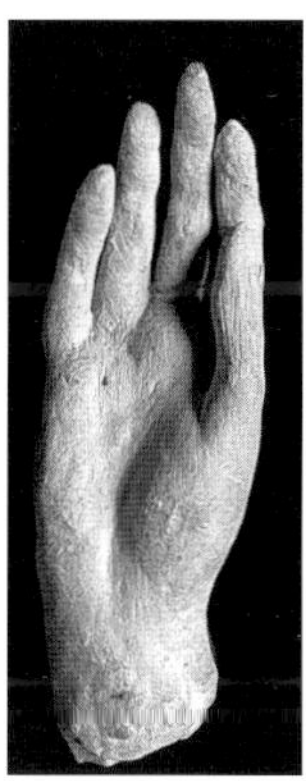

*Female Hand (Pianist)*, 1880s
Terra cotta, greatest extension: .133 ($5^{1}/_{4}$)
Inscribed on wrist: RODIN
Gift of Mrs. John W. Simpson
1942.5.8

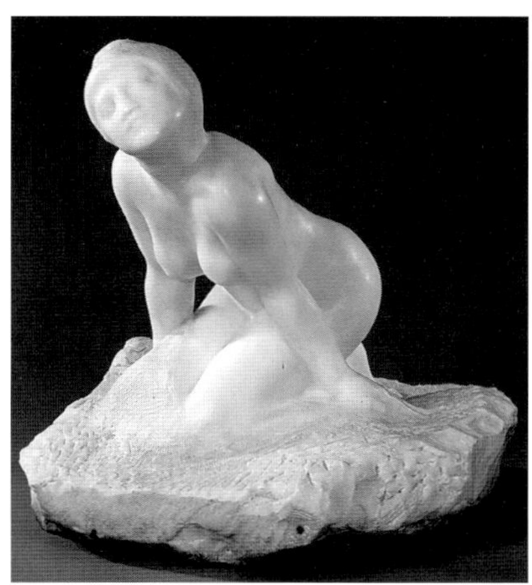

*Figure of a Woman "The Sphinx"*
Marble, .590 x .621 x .583
($23^{1}/_{4}$ x $24^{1}/_{2}$ x 23)
Inscribed on edge of base near right arm:
A. RODIN
Gift of Eugene and Agnes E. Meyer
1967.13.6

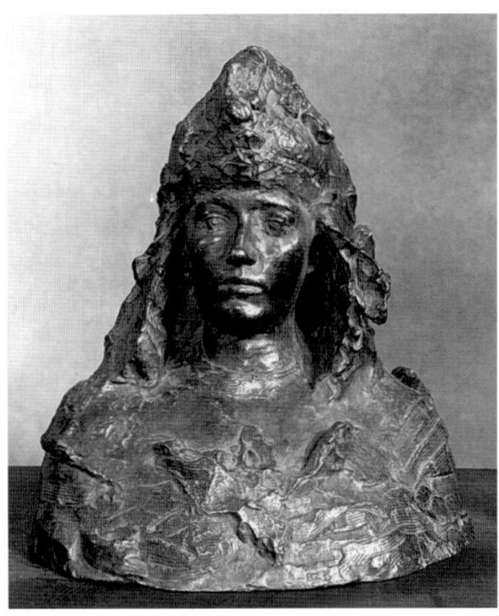

Auguste Rodin
French, 1840–1917

*La France*, c. 1904/1905
Bronze, .495 x .485 x .353
($19^{1}/_{2}$ x 18 x $13^{7}/_{8}$)
Inscribed on left shoulder: A RODIN
Gift of Mrs. John W. Simpson
1942.5.9

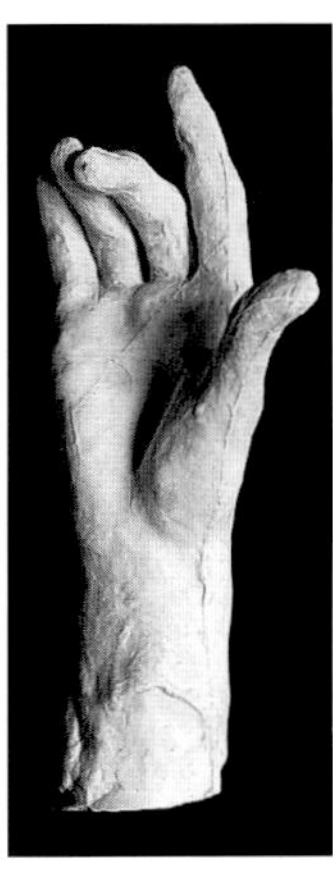

*Hand of a Pianist*
Plaster, greatest extension: .102 (4)
Gift of Mrs. John W. Simpson
1942.5.26

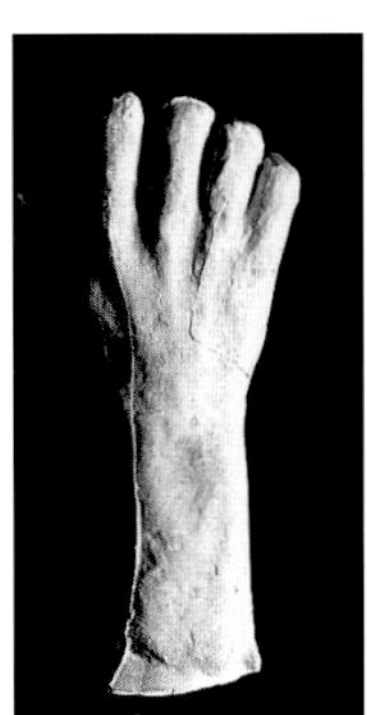

*Hand of a Pianist*
Plaster, greatest extension: .080 ($3^{1}/_{8}$)
Gift of Mrs. John W. Simpson
1942.5.27

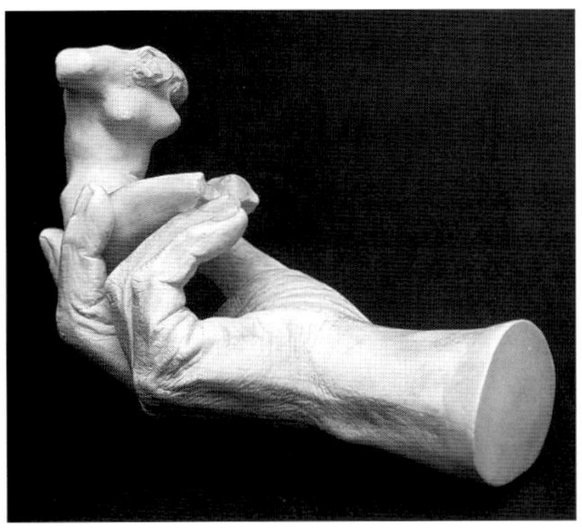

*Hand of Rodin with Female Figure,* 1917
Plaster, greatest extension: .247 (9)
Gift of Mrs. John W. Simpson
1942.5.22

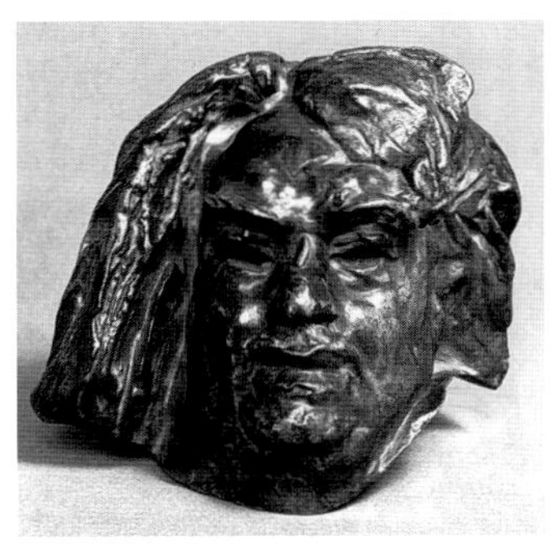

*Head of Balzac,* 1897
Bronze, .165 x .211 x .183
($6^1/_2$ x $8^3/_8$ x $7^1/_4$)
Inscribed on back: A. RODIN
Gift of Mrs. John W. Simpson
1942.5.14

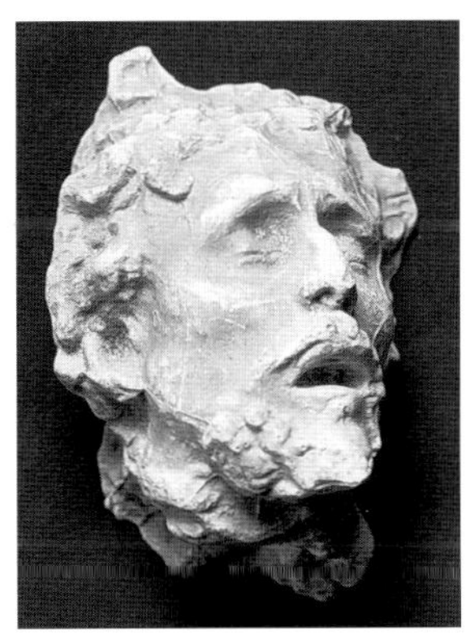

*Head of Saint John the Baptist,* 1907
Plaster, greatest extension: .067 ($2^5/_8$)
Inscribed on back: EN SOUVENIR DE PARIS / L'AN 1907 / A MONSIEUR J.W. / SIMPSON DE / NEW YORK EN GRANDE SYM / PATHIE / A RODIN
Gift of Mrs. John W. Simpson
1942.5.25

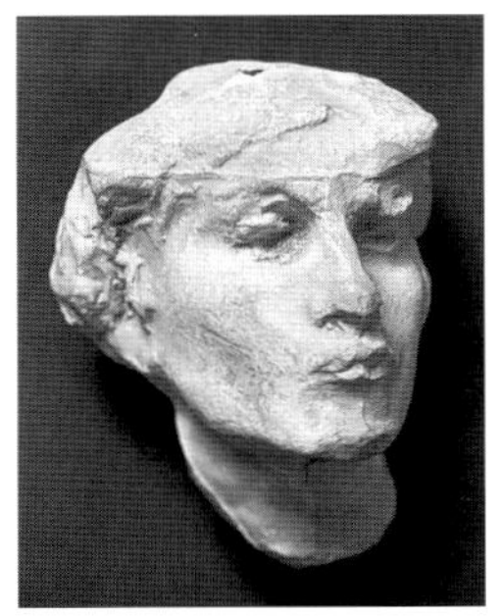

*Head of a Woman,* 1880s
Plaster, .062 x .046 x .051
($2^1/_2$ x $1^3/_4$ x 2)
Gift of Mrs. John W. Simpson
1942.5.24

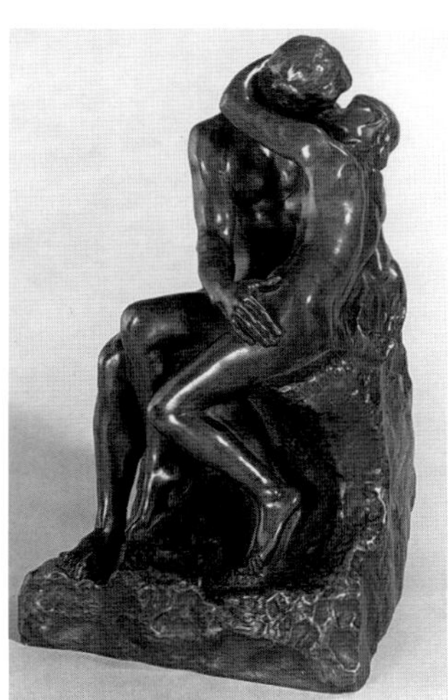

## Auguste Rodin

French, 1840–1917

*The Kiss*, invented 1880/1887, cast 1902
Bronze, .247 x .158 x .174 (9 3/4 x 6 1/4 x 6 7/8)
Inscribed on base next to woman's hip: RODIN; on right side of base: HOMMAGE À MADAME / KATE SIMPSON / EN SOUVENIR DES HEURES / D'ATELIER SEPT 1902 / A. RODIN; foundry mark on left side of base: F. BARBEDIENNE, FONDEUR; on right side of base: RÉDUCTION MECHANIQUE / A. COLLAS / BREVETÉ
Gift of Mrs. John W. Simpson
1942.5.15

*Left Hand*
Plaster, greatest extension: .042 (1 5/8)
Gift of Mrs. John W. Simpson
1942.5.29

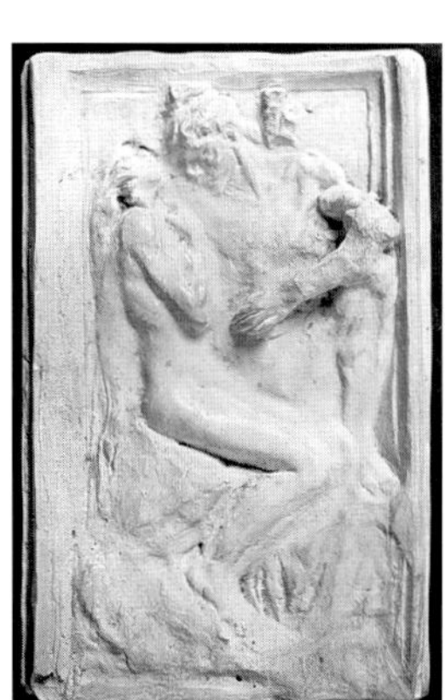

*The Lovers*, 1880–1897
Plaster, .111 x .075 (4 3/8 x 2 7/8)
Gift of Mrs. John W. Simpson
1942.5.23

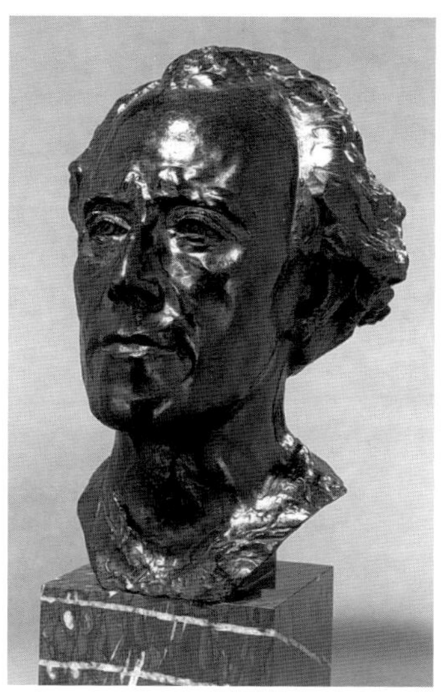

*Gustav Mahler,* 1909
Bronze, .346 x .245 x .247
(13 5/8 x 9 5/8 x 9 3/4)
Inscribed on left shoulder: A. RODIN; on plate soldered inside right front: A. RODIN; foundry mark on rear edge: ALEXIS RUDIER / FONDEUR PARIS
Gift of Lotte Walter Lindt
1972.78.1

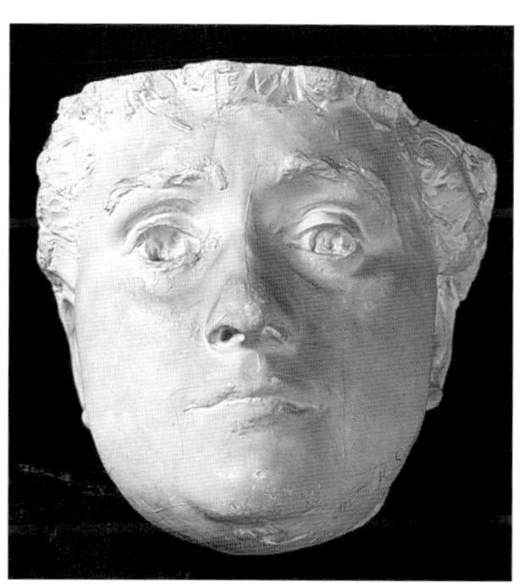

*Mask of Mrs. Simpson,* 1909
Plaster, .178 x .195 x .153 (7 x 7 3/4 x 6)
Inscribed on left side of face: MME. K SIMPSON ESQUISSE POUR LE PORTRAIT / 12 SEPTEMBRE 1909 / A. RODIN
Gift of Mrs. John W. Simpson
1942.5.21

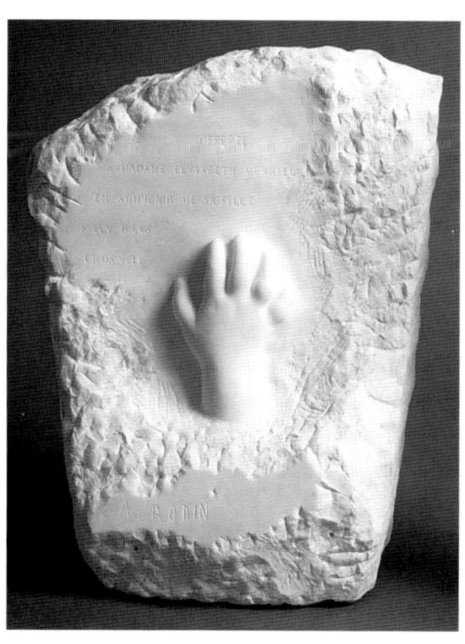

*Memorial Relief (Hand of Child),* c. 1905
Marble, .408 x .327 x .149
(16 x 12 7/8 x 5 7/8)
Inscribed across bottom: A. RODIN; across top: OFFERTE / A MADAME ELYSABETH MERRILL / EN SOUVENIR DE SA FILLE / SALLY HICKS / CROSWELL
Gift of Elizabeth Merrill Furness
1982.6.1

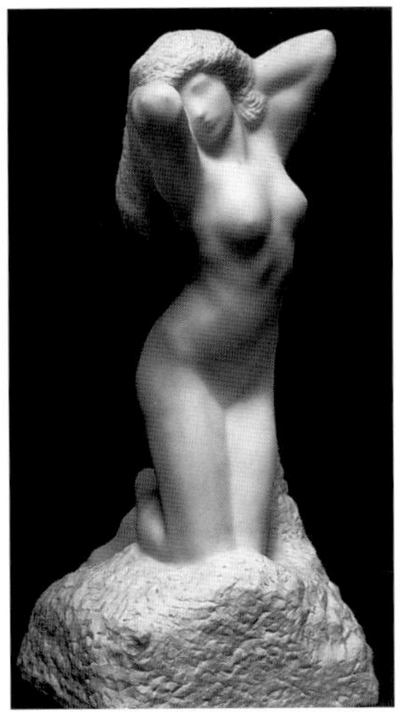

Auguste Rodin
French, 1840–1917

*Morning,* 1906
Marble, .604 x .287 x .333
(23 3/4 x 11 1/4 x 13 1/8)
Inscribed on right side of base: A. RODIN 1906; at right front corner, near figure's left knee: A R (partial signature, with "R" incomplete)
Gift of Mrs. John W. Simpson
1942.5.18

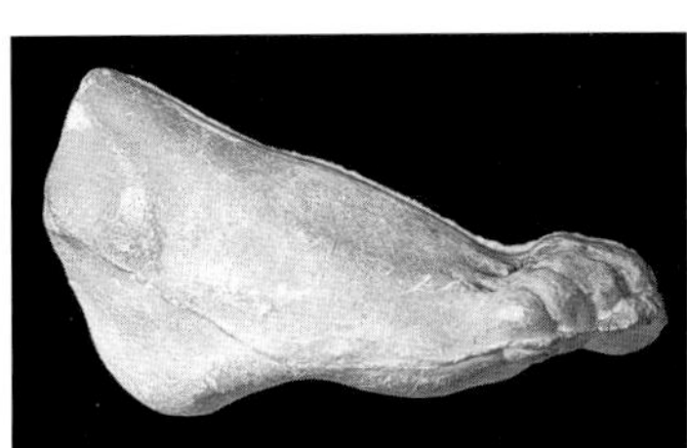

*Right Foot*
Plaster, greatest extension: .069 (2 3/4)
Gift of Mrs. John W. Simpson
1942.5.30

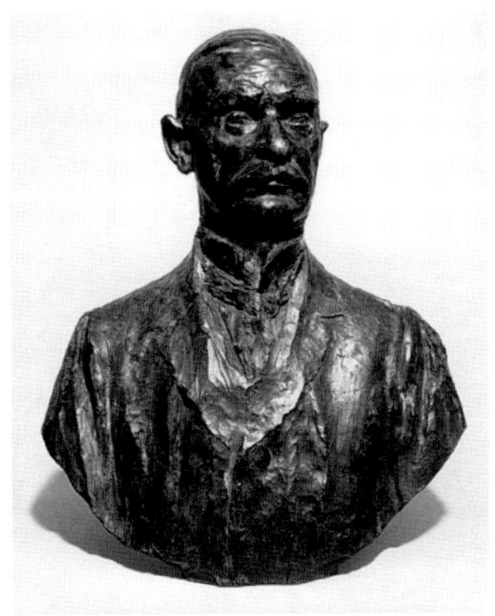

*Thomas Fortune Ryan,* 1909
Bronze, .607 x .523 x .310
(23 7/8 x 20 5/8 x 12 1/4)
Inscribed on front truncation of left arm: A. RODIN
Gift of Mrs. John Barry Ryan
1974.29.1

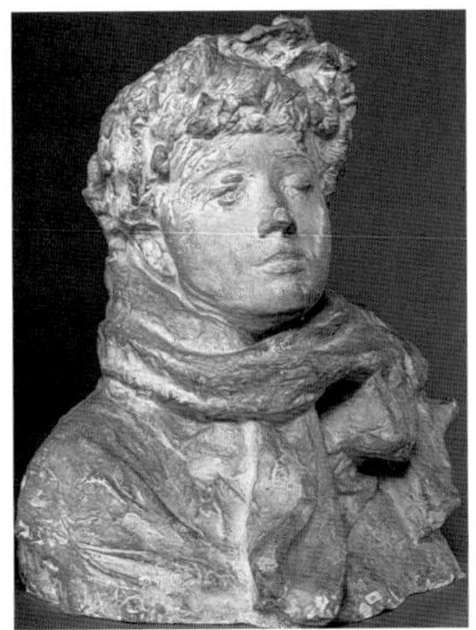

*Lady Sackville,* 1913/1914
Plaster, .457 x .476 x .375
(18 x 18 3/4 x 14 3/4)
Inscribed on red wax seal on lower back edge: HG
Gift of the B. Gerald Cantor Art Foundation
1988.54.1

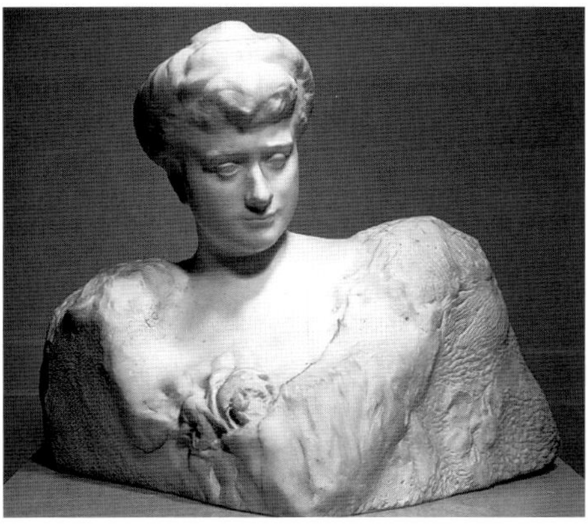

*Mrs. John W. Simpson*, 1901/1903
Marble, .554 x .690 x .415
(21 3/4 x 27 1/8 x 16 3/8)
Inscribed on side of base under left shoulder: A RODIN / 1903
Gift of Mrs. John W. Simpson
1942.5.16

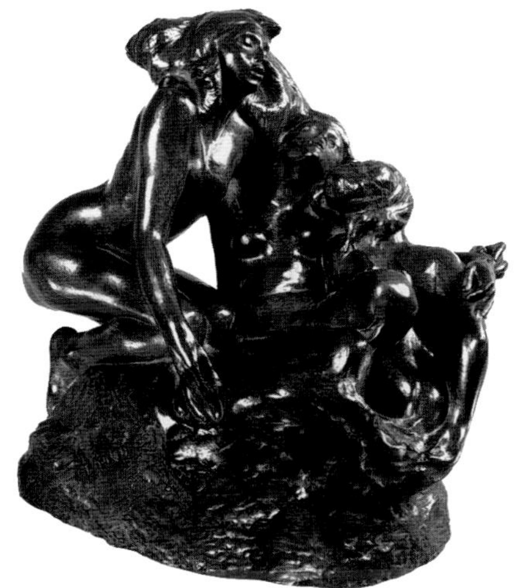

*The Sirens*, c. 1888
Bronze, .432 x .458 x .318
(17 x 18 x 12 1/2)
Inscribed on edge of base below uppermost siren: A. RODIN; on plate soldered inside base: A. RODIN; foundry mark on back of base: ALEXIS RUDIER / FONDEUR. PARIS.
Gift of David Baron in memory of his wife, Mary F. Baron
1978.71.1

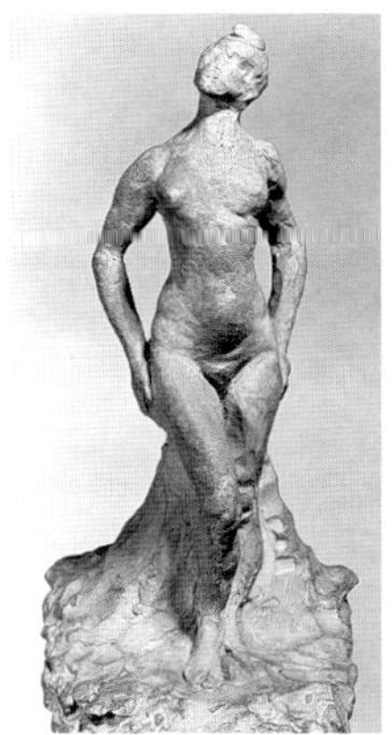

*Statuette of a Woman*, 1880s
Terra cotta, .350 x .172 x .187
(13 3/4 x 6 3/4 x 7 3/8)
Inscribed on side of base below right hip: RODIN
Gift of Mrs. John W. Simpson
1942.5.5

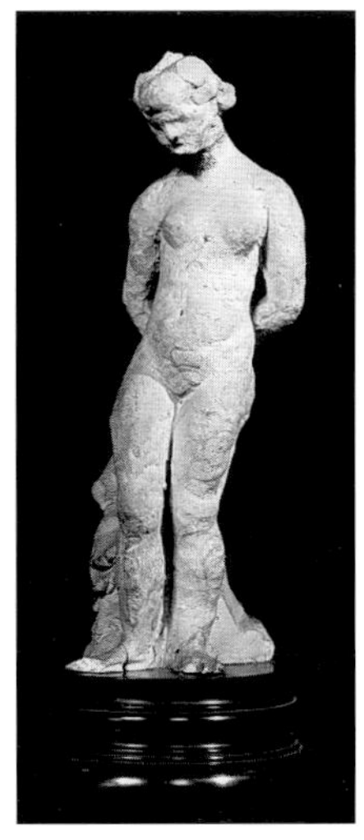

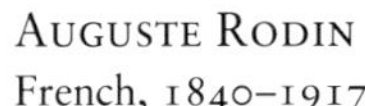

Auguste Rodin
French, 1840–1917

*Statuette of a Woman*, 1880s
Terra cotta, .324 x .102 x .116
($12\frac{3}{4}$ x 4 x $4\frac{1}{2}$)
Inscribed behind left leg: RODIN
Gift of Mrs. John W. Simpson
1942.5.6

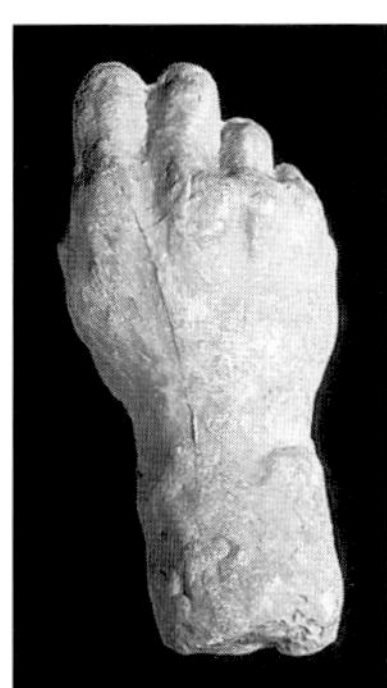

*Study for a Hand of a Burgher of Calais*, 1886
Plaster, greatest extension: .064 ($2\frac{1}{2}$)
Gift of Mrs. John W. Simpson
1942.5.28

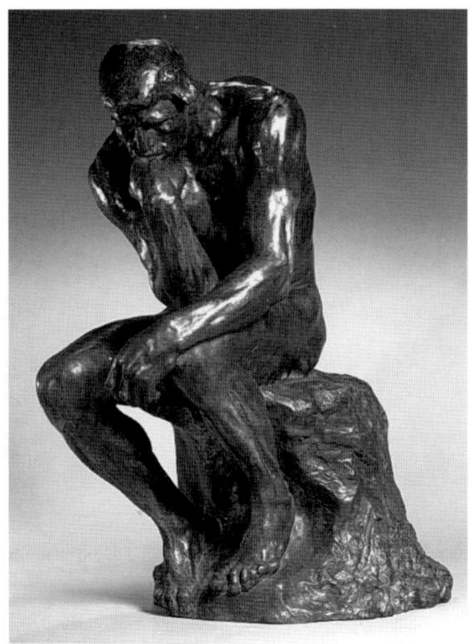

*The Thinker*, 1880
Bronze, .715 x .364 x .595
($28\frac{1}{8}$ x $14\frac{3}{8}$ x $23\frac{1}{2}$)
Inscribed on side of base below left hip:
A. RODIN
Gift of Mrs. John W. Simpson
1942.5.12

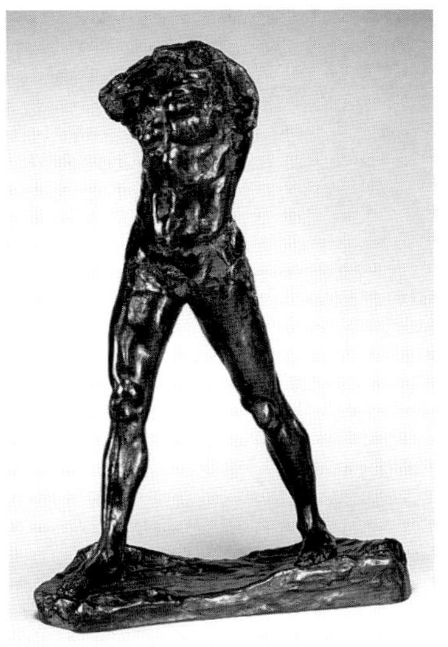

*The Walking Man,* probably c. 1900
Bronze, .845 x .426 x .555
($33^{1}/_{4}$ x $16^{3}/_{4}$ x $21^{7}/_{8}$)
Inscribed on top of base between feet: A. RODIN; inside of base on ball of left foot: A. RODIN; inside edge of base behind right foot: A. RODIN
Gift of Mrs. John W. Simpson
1942.5.11

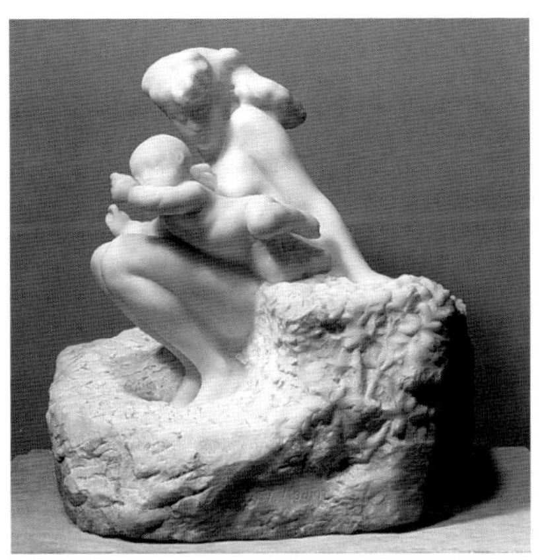

*Young Woman and Winged Child,* c. 1885
Marble, .432 x .444 x .331
(17 x $17^{1}/_{2}$ x 13)
Inscribed on lower side of base beneath child's feet: A. RODIN
Gift of Mrs. John W. Simpson
1942.5.19

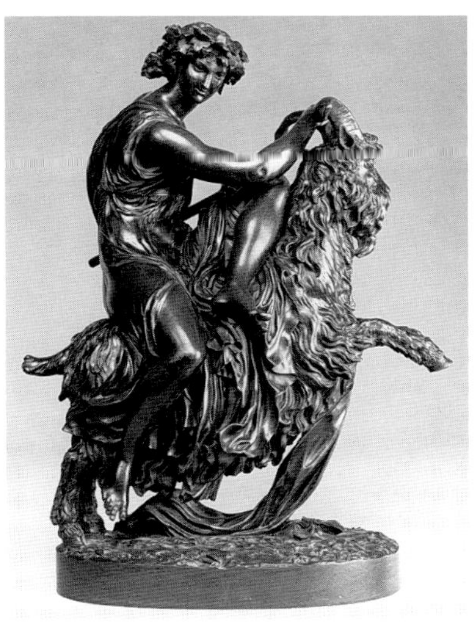

## Phillipe-Laurent Roland
French, 1746–1816

*Bacchante with a Goat,* 1796, cast 1798
Bronze, height: .414 ($16^{5}/_{16}$); integral base, length: .267 ($10^{1}/_{2}$); width: .152 (6)
Inscribed on rear edge of base, in script: ROLAND SCULPT / CISEL PAR L JEANNEST
Gift of Mr. and Mrs. John R. Gaines, in Honor of the 50th Anniversary of the National Gallery of Art
1989.92.1

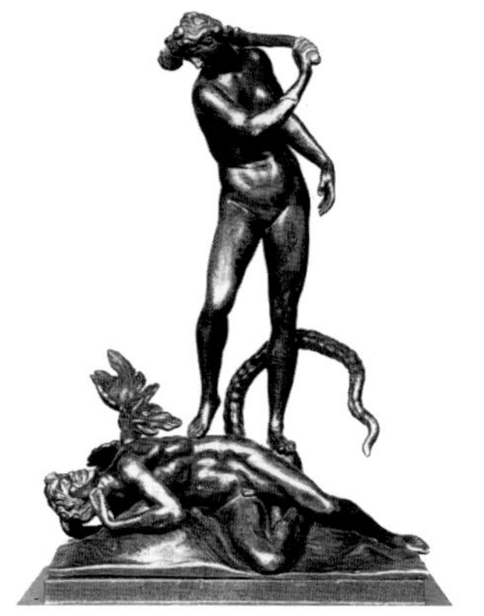

## Roman 16th/17th Century

*Virtue Overcoming Vice,* late 16th or early 17th century
Bronze, .243 x .272 x .090
(9 5/8 x 10 3/4 x 3 1/2)
Widener Collection
1942.9.107

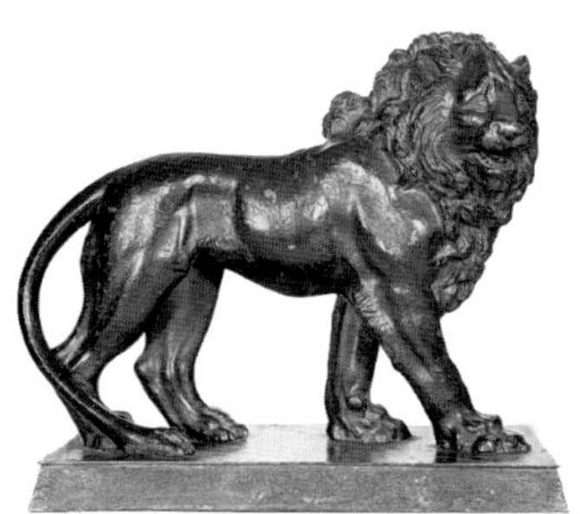

## Roman 18th/19th Century

*Lion,* c. 1780/1855
Bronze, .321 x .419 x .118
(12 5/8 x 16 1/2 x 4 5/8)
Samuel H. Kress Collection
1957.14.7

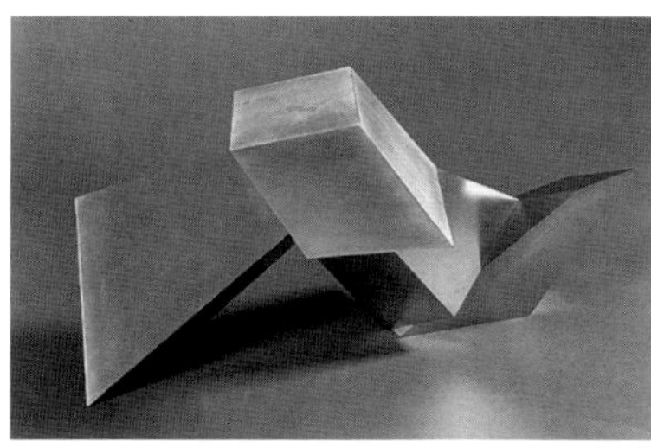

## James Rosati
American, 1912–1988

*Untitled,* 1971
Zinc, .378 x .838 x .368
(14 7/8 x 33 x 14 1/2)
Gift of James Rosati in memory of William C. Seitz
1977.49.1

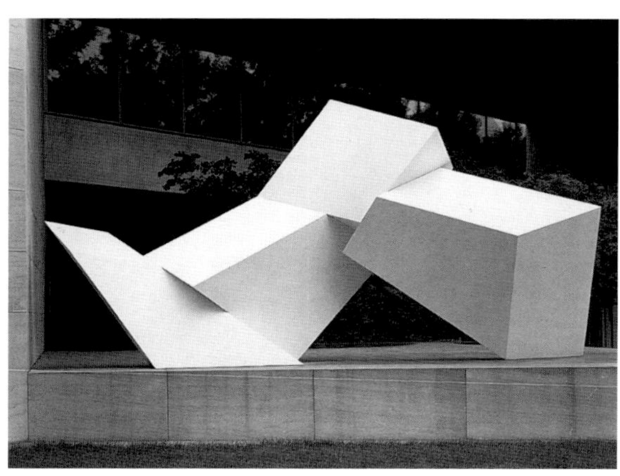

*Untitled,* 1971/1977
Aluminum, painted
2.882 x 6.335 x 2.711
(113 1/2 x 249 1/2 x 106 3/4)
Inscribed on end face at bottom edge: ROSATI 1977; foundry mark below inscription: WORK EXECUTED BY / LIPPINCOTT / NORTH HAVEN CONN
Gift of the Collectors Committee based on model given by the artist in memory of William C. Seitz
1978.24.1

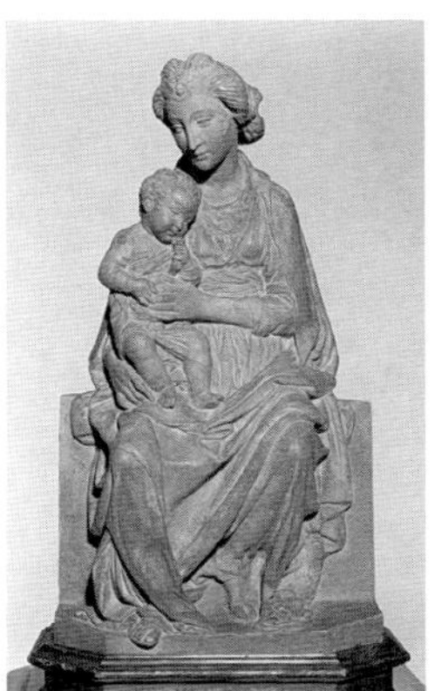

ANTONIO ROSSELLINO
*See* BERNARDO ROSSELLINO

ANTONIO ROSSELLINO
Florentine, 1427–1479

*Madonna and Child*, c. 1475
Plaster, .470 x .265 x .124
($18^{1}/_{2}$ x $10^{1}/_{2}$ x $4^{7}/_{8}$)
Andrew W. Mellon Collection
1937.1.125

*Madonna and Child*, c. 1475/1478
Marble, .840 x .560 (33 x 22)
Inscribed on lower center, in garland:
Y H S
Samuel H. Kress Collection
1939.1.327

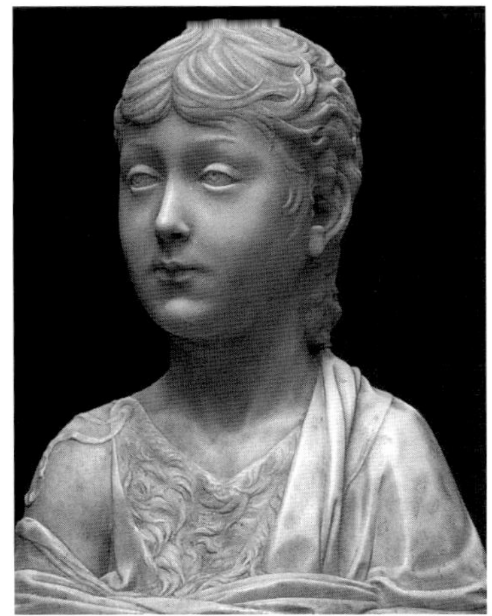

*The Young Saint John the Baptist*, c. 1455
Marble, .397 x .336 x .178
($15^{1}/_{2}$ x $13^{1}/_{8}$ x 7)
Widener Collection
1942.9.142

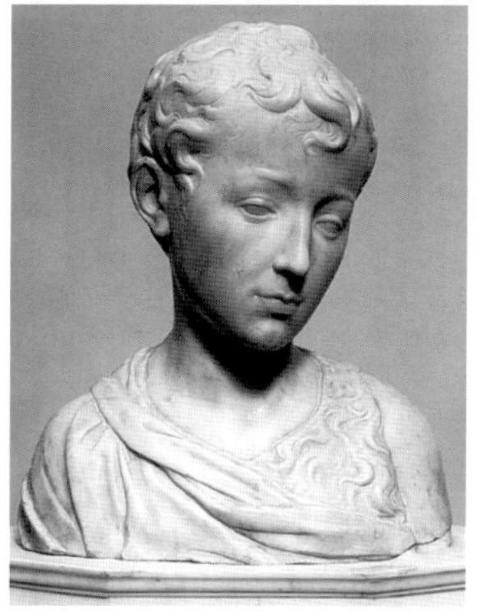

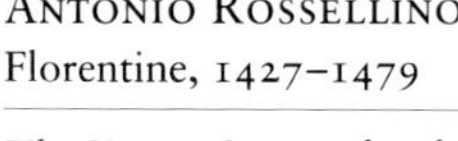

Antonio Rossellino
Florentine, 1427–1479

*The Young Saint John the Baptist*, c. 1470
Marble, .347 x .298 x .161
(13 5/8 x 11 3/4 x 6 1/4)
Samuel H. Kress Collection
1943.4.79

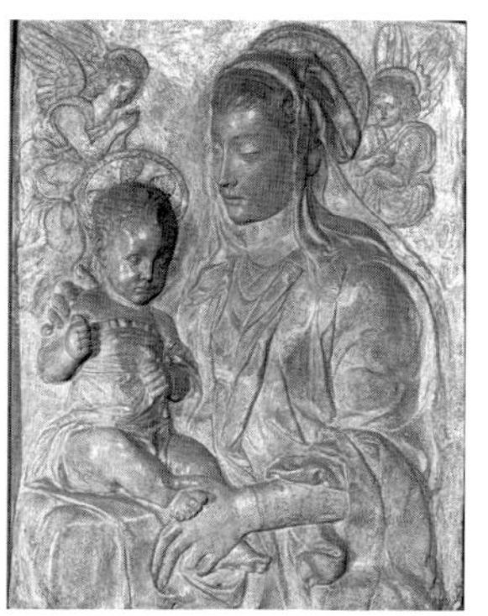

After Antonio Rossellino
Florentine

*Madonna and Child with Angels*, c. 1470
Stucco, .698 x .553 (27 1/2 x 21 3/4)
Samuel H. Kress Collection
1943.4.78

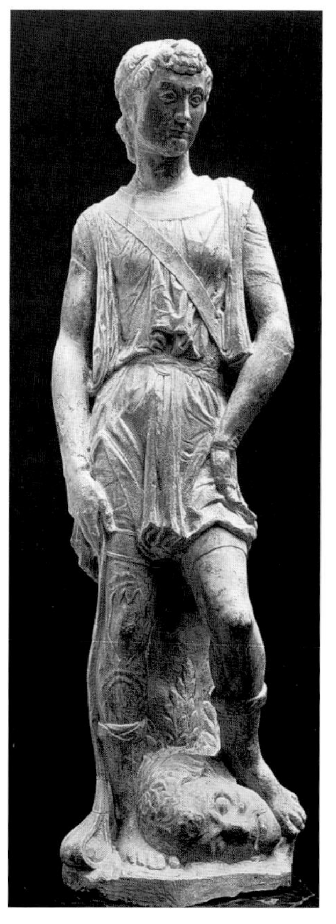

Bernardo Rossellino
Florentine, 1409–1464
or Antonio Rossellino
Florentine, 1427–1479

*The David of the Casa Martelli*,
c. 1461/1479
Marble, 1.646 x .504 x .424
(64 3/4 x 19 3/4 x 16 5/8)
Widener Collection
1942.9.115

## AUGUSTUS SAINT-GAUDENS
American, 1848–1907

*Charles Stewart Butler and Lawrence Smith Butler,* 1880–1881
Plaster, .622 x .902 ($24^{1}/_{2}$ x $35^{1}/_{2}$)
Inscribed at upper right with monogram: FE / ASTG / CIT; at center right: LAWRENCE• SMITH•BVTLER•IN•HIS•SIXTH• / YEAR; at lower right: MODELLED•BY•AVGVSTVS• SAINT-G[AV]DENS•NE[W] / YORK•OCTOBER• EIGHTEEN•HVNDRED•AND / EIGHTY— MARCH•EIGHTEEN•HVNDRED•AND• EIGHTY•ONE; at upper left, written twice in ribbon decoration: DABIT DEVS HIS QVOQVE FINEM; at center left: CHARLES• STEWART•BVTLER•IN•HIS•FOVRTH• / YEAR; at lower left: TO•MY•FRIEND• PRESCOTT•HALL•BVTLER•SW [in monogram] / SIXTH•OF•IVLY•EIGHTEEN•HVNDRED•AND• / EIGHTY—MARCH•TWENTY• SIXTH• EIGHTEEN•HVNDRED•AND•EIGHTY• ONE; on verso, middle: CAST FOR / MR. WHITE
Avalon Fund and Margaret Bouton Memorial Fund
1990.31.1

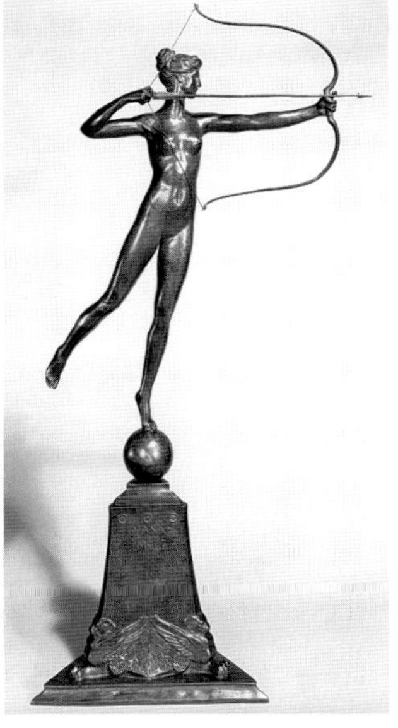

*Diana of the Tower,* 1899
Bronze, .966 x .485 x .289
(38 x $19^{1}/_{8}$ x $11^{3}/_{8}$)
Inscribed on front of pedestal: •DIANA• / OF THE• / TOWER•; on top of base, near back: AVGVSTVS / SAINTGAVDENS / MDCCCXCIX; in circle: •COPYRIGHT• / •BY• AVGVSTVS• / SAINT-GAVDENS /•M• / DCCCXC / •III•, foundry mark on top of base near back, in circle: E. GRUET / JEUNE / FONDEUR / 44BIS AVENUE DE CHATILLON .PARIS.
Pepita Milmore Memorial Fund
1975.12.1

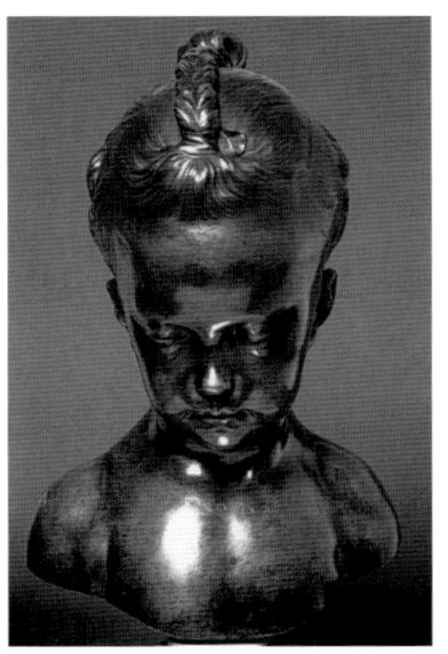

## JACQUES-FRANÇOIS-JOSEPH SALY
French, 1717–1776

*Bust of a Little Girl,* 1774
Bronze, .370 x .252 x .197
($14^{1}/_{2}$ x $9^{7}/_{8}$ x $7^{3}/_{4}$)
Widener Collection
1942.9.128

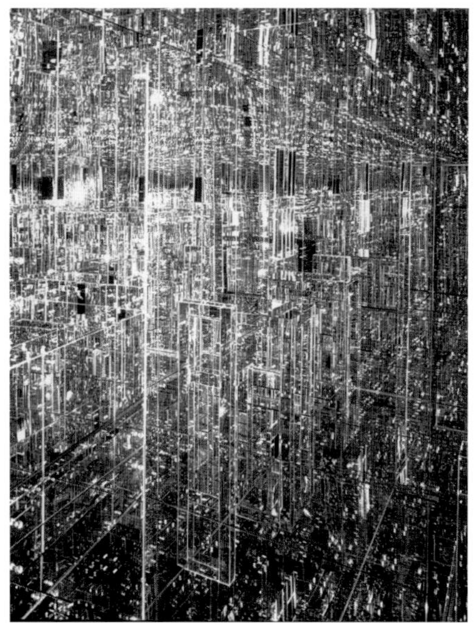

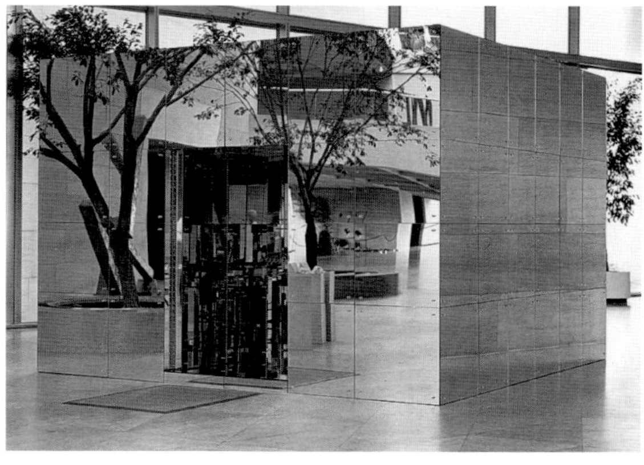

LUCAS SAMARAS
American, born 1936

*Mirrored Cell,* 1969–1988
Mirror over wood, 2.743 x 3.991 x 3.876
(108 x $157^{1}/_{8}$ x $152^{5}/_{8}$)
Gift of the Collectors Committee
1989.73.1

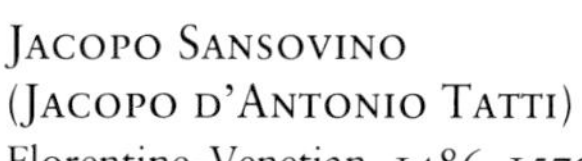

JACOPO SANSOVINO
(JACOPO D'ANTONIO TATTI)
Florentine-Venetian, 1486–1570

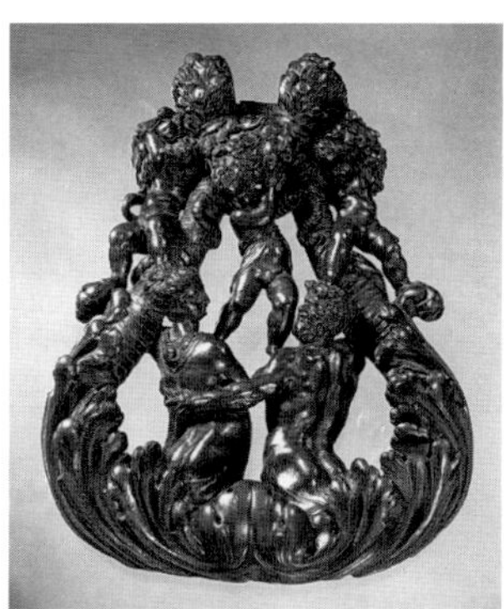

*Door Knocker with Nereid, Triton, and Putti,* c. 1550
Bronze, .356 x .288 x .085
(14 x $11^{3}/_{8}$ x $3^{3}/_{8}$)
Pepita Milmore Memorial Fund
1979.10.1

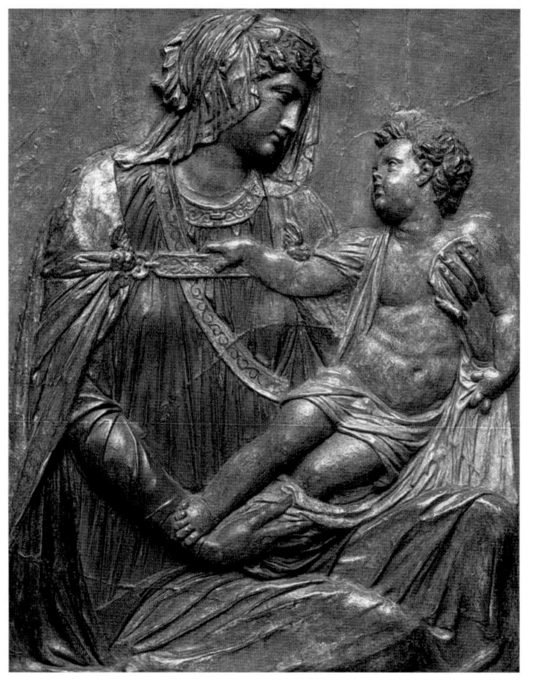

*Madonna and Child,* c. 1550
Papier mâché and stucco, painted and gilt
1.194 x .956 (47 x $37^{5}/_{8}$)
Samuel H. Kress Collection
1961.1.6

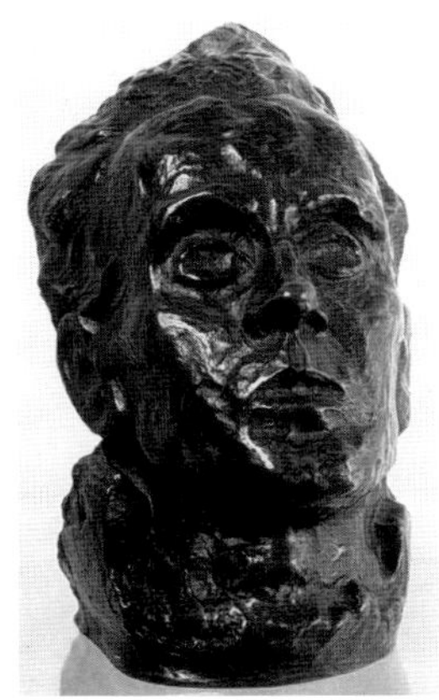

Egon Schiele
Austrian, 1890–1918

*Self-Portrait*, c. 1917, cast c. 1925–1928
Bronze, .276 x .165 x .232
(10 7/8 x 6 1/2 x 9 1/8)
Gift of Mr. and Mrs. Leonard Lauder, in Honor of the 50th Anniversary of the National Gallery of Art
1991.36.1

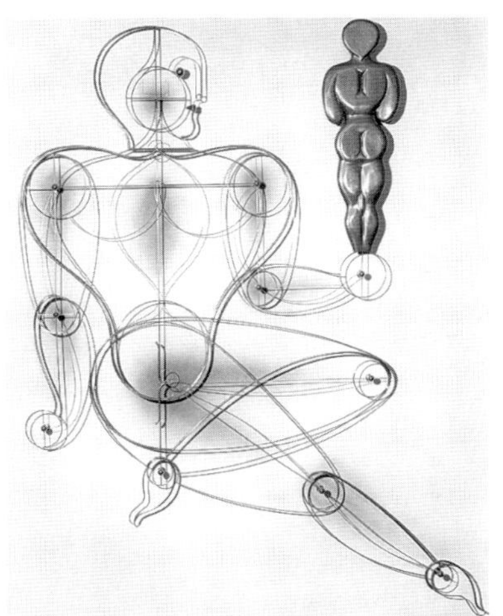

Oskar Schlemmer
German, 1888–1943

*Homo*, 1931 and 1968
Wire and metal, 2.930 x 2.381 x .124
(115 3/8 x 93 3/4 x 4 7/8)
Gift of Enid A. Haupt
1977.47.11

George Segal
American, born 1924

*The Dancers*, 1971 and 1982
Bronze with white patina
1.790 x 2.692 x 1.803 (70 1/2 x 106 x 71)
Gift of the Collectors Committee
1983.78.1

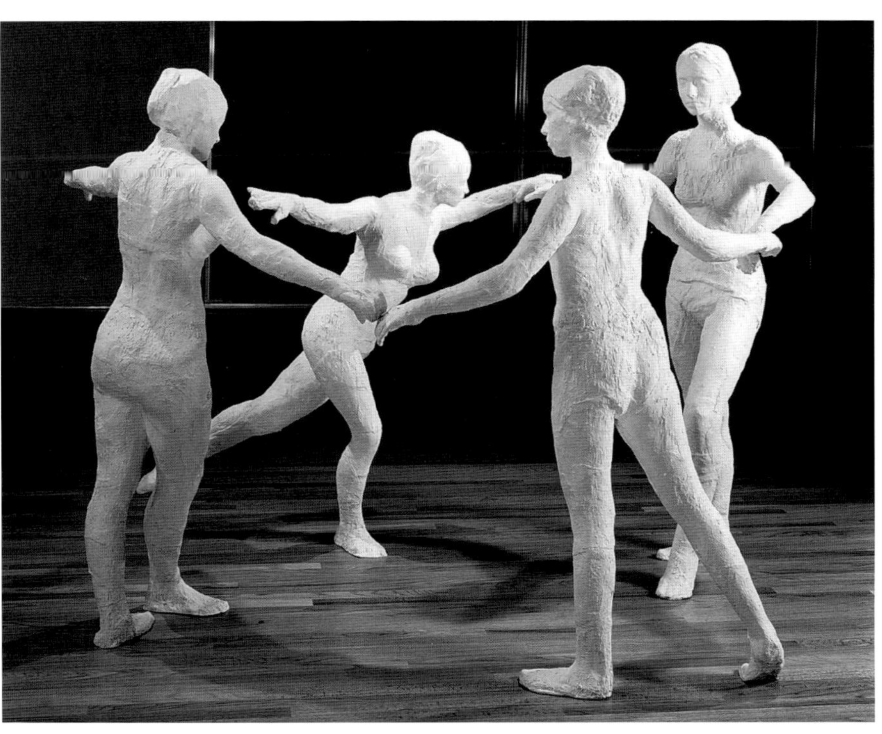

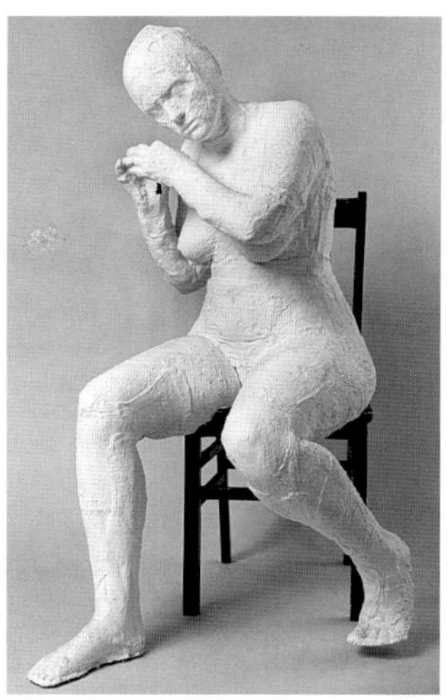

GEORGE SEGAL
American, born 1924

*Girl Putting on an Earring,* 1967
Plaster and mixed media
1.309 x .724 x .959 ($51^{5}/_{8}$ x $28^{1}/_{2}$ x $37^{3}/_{4}$)
Ailsa Mellon Bruce Fund
1971.66.13

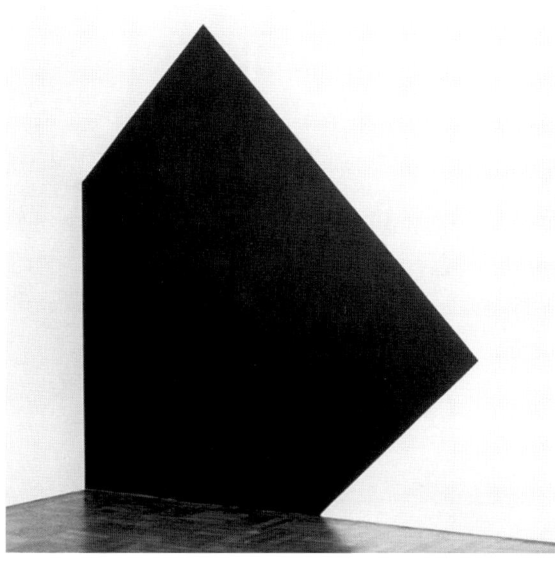

RICHARD SERRA
American, born 1939

*Left Square Into Left Corner,*
published 1981
Paintstik on $^{1}/_{8}$ inch aluminum
2.718 x 2.642 (107 x 104)
Gift of Mr. and Mrs. Roger P. Sonnabend
1986.90.33

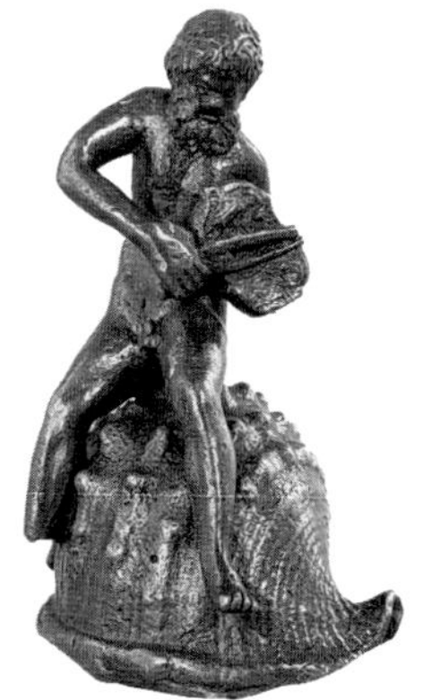

SEVERO DA RAVENNA
Paduan, active 1496–in or before 1543

*Arion Seated on a Shell*
Bronze, .086 x .053 x .042
($3^{7}/_{16}$ x $2^{1}/_{8}$ x $1^{11}/_{16}$)
Samuel H. Kress Collection
1957.14.19

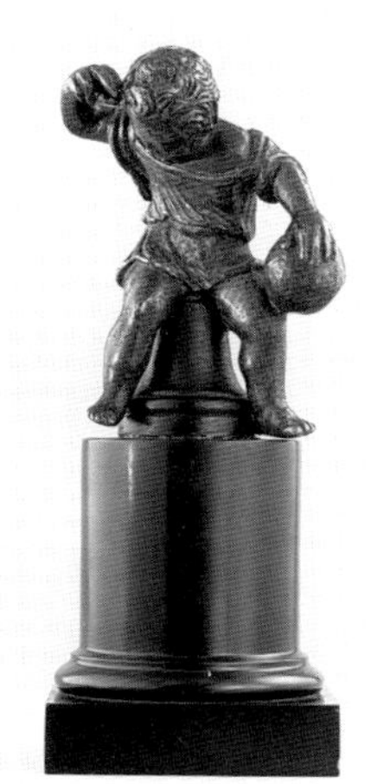

*The Christ Child,* 16th century
Bronze, .089 x .073 x .068
(3 1/2 x 2 7/8 x 2 11/16)
Samuel H. Kress Collection
1957.14.53

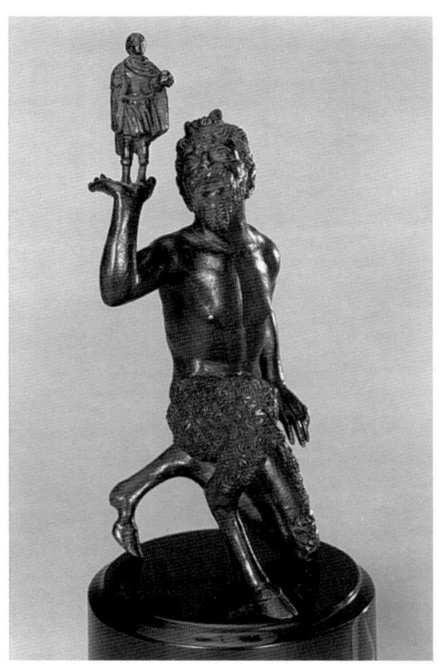

*Kneeling Satyr Supporting the Figure of an Emperor,* c. 1500
Bronze, .238 x .124 x .113
(9 3/8 x 4 7/8 x 4 1/2)
Pepita Milmore Memorial Fund
1985.12.1

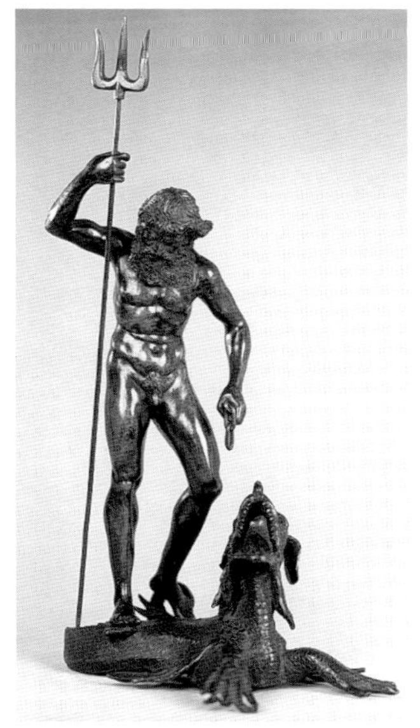

*Neptune on a Sea Monster*
Bronze, .456 x .267 x .200
(17 7/8 x 10 1/2 x 7 7/8)
Widener Collection
1942.9.104

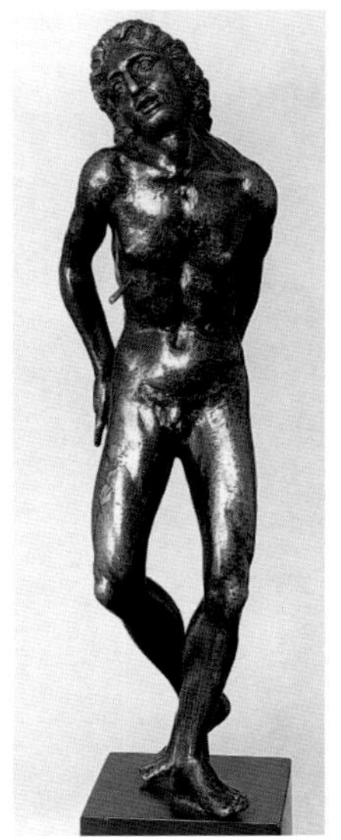

Severo da Ravenna
Paduan, active 1496–in or before 1543

*Saint Sebastian*
Bronze, .246 x .077 x .058
(9 3/4 x 3 1/8 x 2 3/8)
Samuel H. Kress Collection
1957.14.17

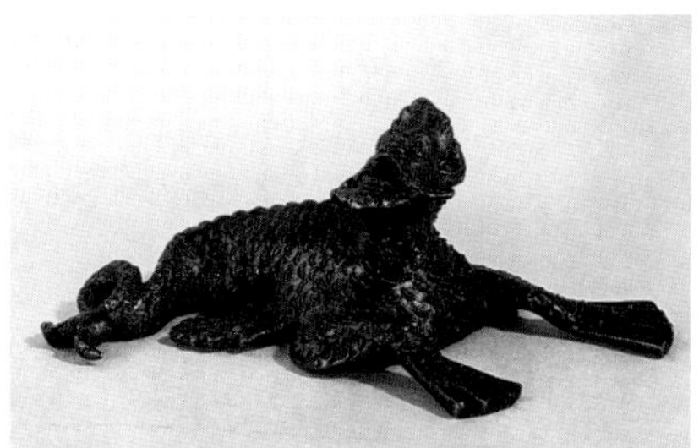

Workshop of Severo da Ravenna
Paduan

*A Sea Monster*
Bronze, .045 x .133 x .088
(1 3/4 x 5 1/4 x 3 1/2)
Samuel H. Kress Collection
1957.14.74

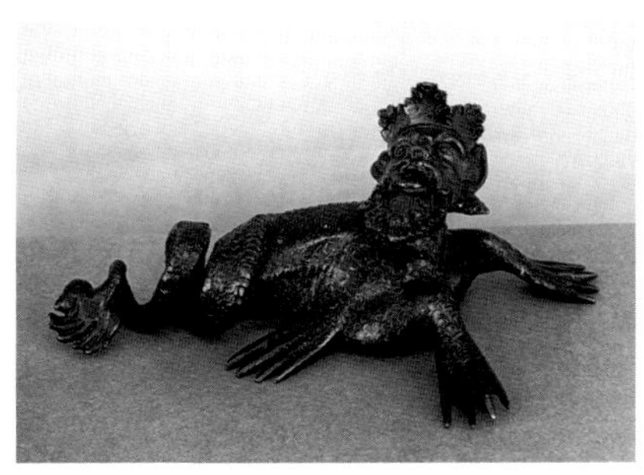

Workshop of Severo da Ravenna
Paduan

*A Sea Monster*
Bronze, .089 x .226 x .136
(3 1/2 x 9 x 5 3/8)
Samuel H. Kress Collection
1957.14.75

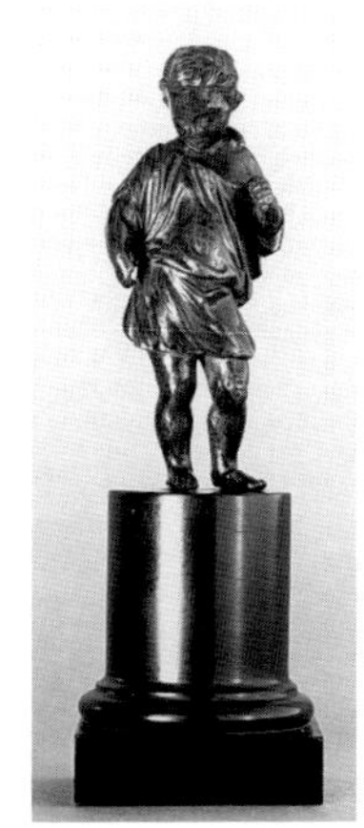

Attributed to Workshop of Severo da Ravenna
Paduan

*Standing Boy,* early 16th century
Bronze, .096 x .042 x .029
(3 3/4 x 1 11/16 x 1 1/8)
Samuel H. Kress Collection
1957.14.45

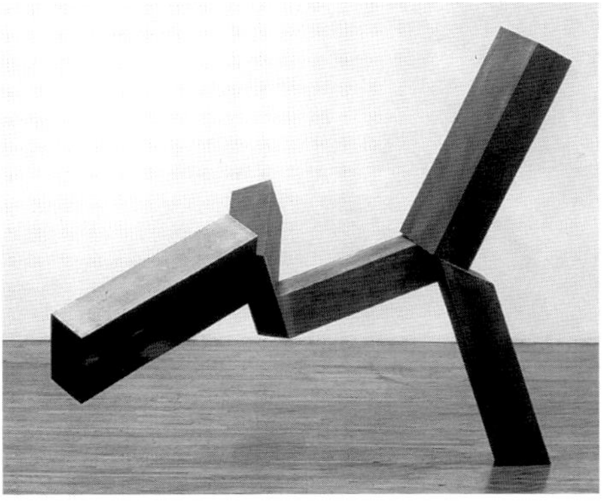

JOEL SHAPIRO
American, born 1941

*Untitled,* 1989
Bronze, 1.651 x 1.956 x 1.587
(65 x 77 x 62 1/2)
Gift of the Collectors Committee
1990.29.1

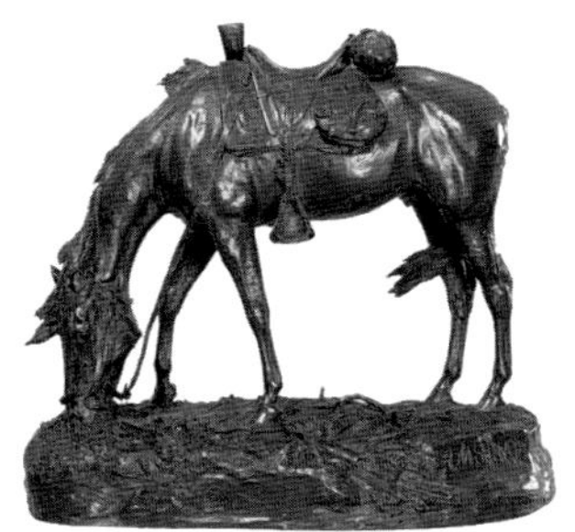

HENRY MERWIN SHRADY
American, 1871–1922

*The Empty Saddle,* 1900
Bronze, .279 x .326 x .165
(11 x 12 7/8 x 6 1/2)
Inscribed on side of base below rear left hoof: H M SHRADY; beneath, in clover leaf: H M S F; on side of base below rear right hoof: COPYRIGHT 1900 [sic] / THEODORE B. STARR; foundry mark inside base: CIRE PERDUE C / ROMAN BRONZE WKS. / N.Y. / E.W. (in circle) / 2 (in circle)
Gift of Joseph Ternbach
1971.1.1

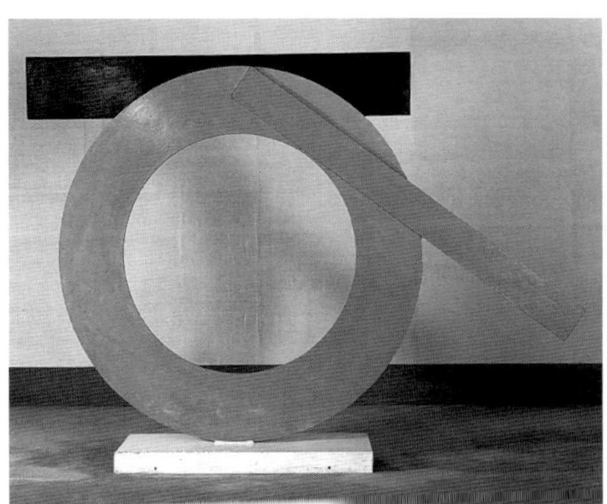

DAVID SMITH
American, 1906–1965

*Circle I,* 1962
Steel, painted, 2.006 x 2.736 x .457
(79 x 107 3/4 x 18)
Inscribed on top of base: DAVID SMITH CI.I 10-17-62
Ailsa Mellon Bruce Fund
1977.60.1

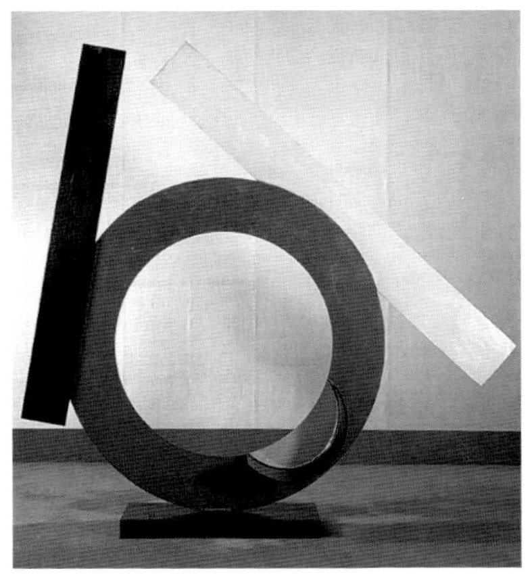

*Circle II,* 1962
Steel, painted, 2.679 x 2.812 x .600
(105 1/2 x 110 3/4 x 23 5/8)
Inscribed on top of base: DAVID SMITH CI.II 10-20-62
Ailsa Mellon Bruce Fund
1977.60.2

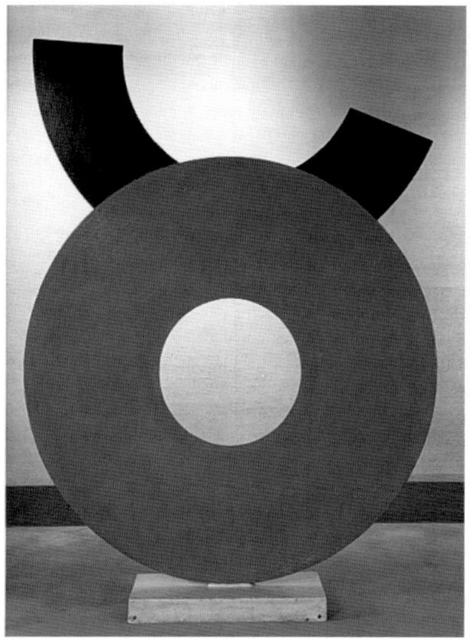

DAVID SMITH
American, 1906–1965

*Circle III*, 1962
Steel, painted, 2.425 x 1.828 x .457
(95 1/2 x 72 x 18)
Inscribed on top of base: DAVID SMITH CI.III 10-22-62
Ailsa Mellon Bruce Fund
1977.60.3

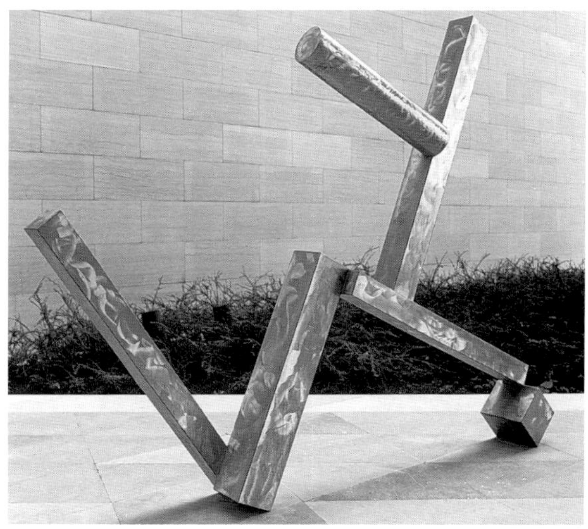

*Cubi XXVI*, 1965
Steel, 3.034 x 3.834 x .656
(119 1/2 x 151 x 25 7/8)
Inscribed on top of bar projecting from cube: DAVID SMITH / JANUARY 12 1965 / CUBI XXVI
Ailsa Mellon Bruce Fund
1978.14.1

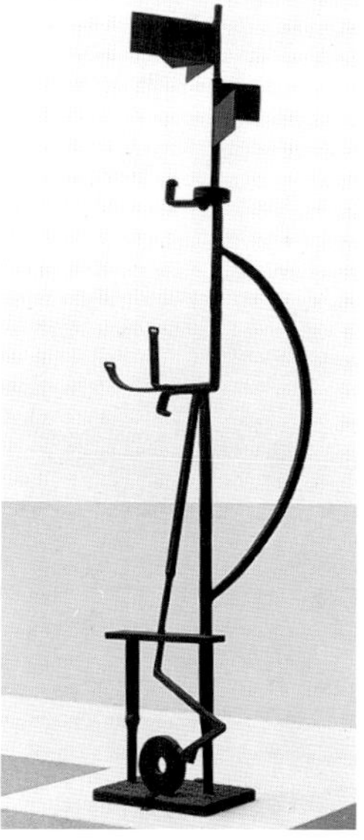

*Sentinel I*, 1956
Steel, 2.276 x .429 x .575
(89 5/8 x 16 7/8 x 22 5/8)
Inscribed on top bar, back: DAVID SMITH / SENTINEL / 10-20-56
Gift of the Collectors Committee
1979.51.1

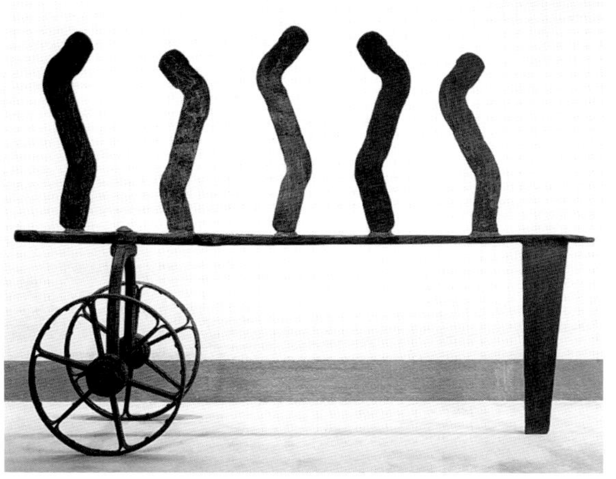

*Voltri VII*, 1962
Iron, 2.158 x 3.116 x 1.105
(85 x 122 x 43 1/2)
Inscribed on horizontal bar projecting above wheels: DAVID SMITH 1962; on horizontal bar, top center: VOLTRI-VII
Ailsa Mellon Bruce Fund
1977.60.4

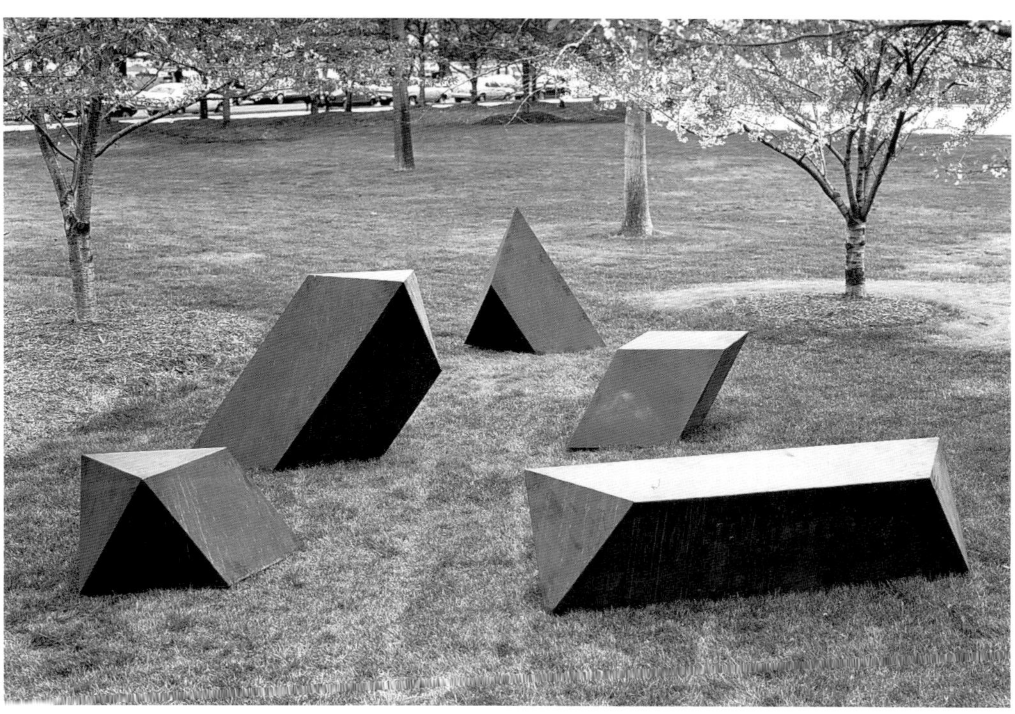

TONY SMITH
American, 1912–1980

*Wandering Rocks*, 1967
Stainless steel, five elements, dimensions variable
Gift of the Collectors Committee
1981.53.1

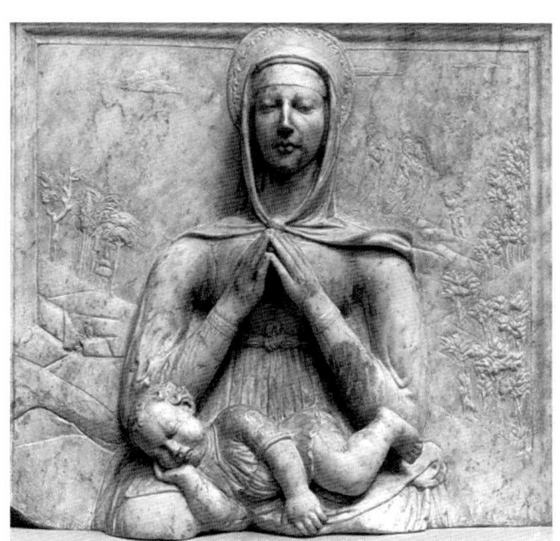

CRISTOFORO SOLARI
Lombard, active 1489–1527

*Madonna and Child*, c. 1489
Marble, .502 x .560 (19 3/4 x 22)
Samuel H. Kress Collection
1960.5.3

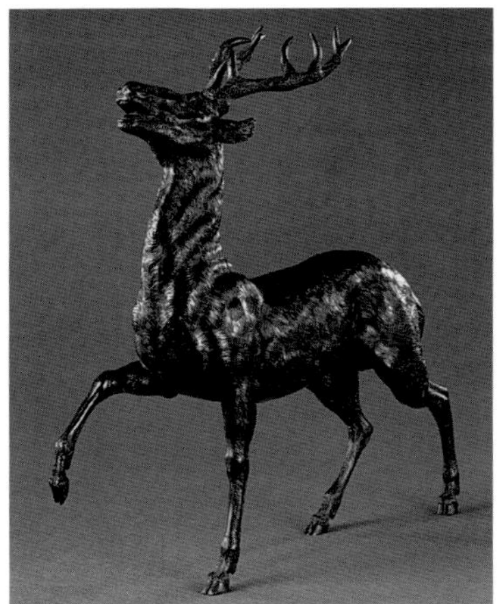

### South German (Nuremberg) 16th Century

*Striding Stag*, c. 1590/1599
Bronze, .281 x .290 x .068
(11 1/8 x 11 3/8 x 2 3/4)
Gift of Asbjorn R. Lunde, in Honor of the 50th Anniversary of the National Gallery of Art
1991.18.1

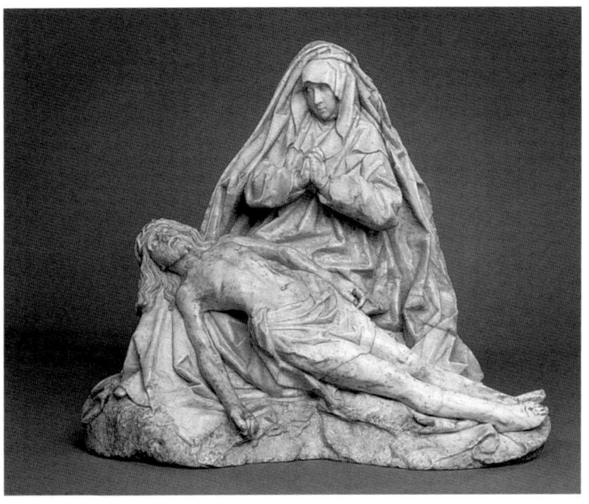

### South Netherlandish 15th Century

*Pietà*, c. 1450/1475
Alabaster, .420 x .500 x .235
(16 5/8 x 19 3/4 x 9 1/4)
Patrons' Permanent Fund
1990.13.1

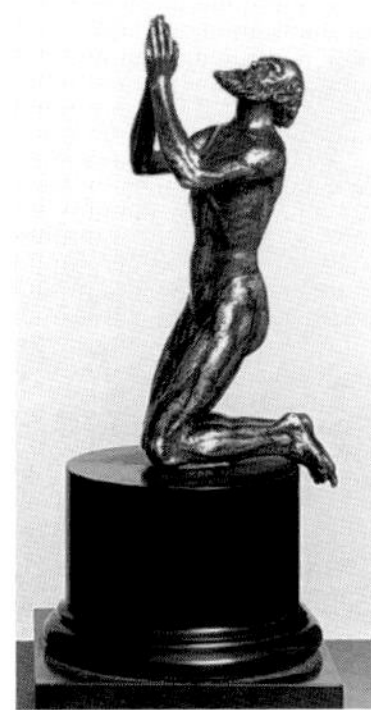

### Spanish 16th Century

*Kneeling Supplicant*
Gilt bronze, .103 x .032 x .061
(4 1/16 x 1 1/4 x 2 7/16)
Samuel H. Kress Collection
1957.14.27

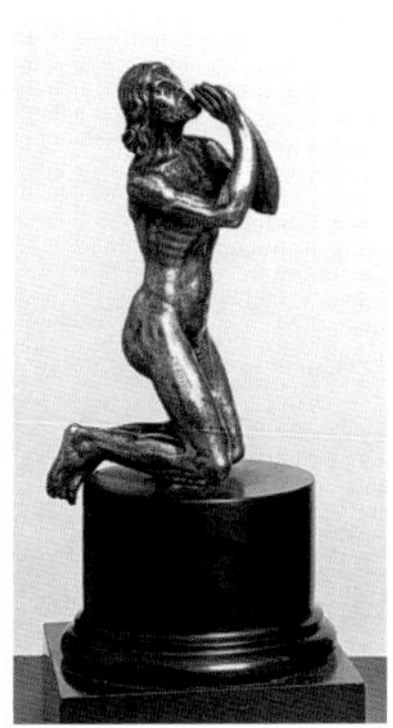

### Spanish 16th Century

*Kneeling Supplicant*
Gilt bronze, .098 x .032 x .040
(3 13/16 x 1 1/4 x 1 9/16)
Samuel H. Kress Collection
1957.14.28

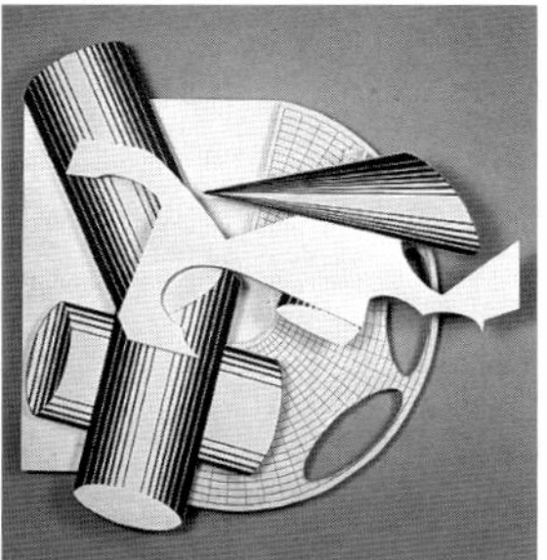

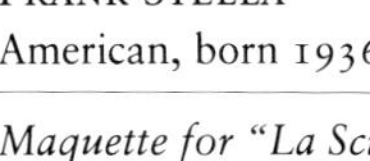

FRANK STELLA
American, born 1936

*Maquette for "La Scienza della Fiacca,"* 1983
Black ink and lithograph on paper glued to sheets of foamcore, .921 x .959 x .162 ($36^{1}/_{4}$ x $37^{3}/_{4}$ x $6^{3}/_{8}$)
Gift of Lawrence Rubin
1988.58.1

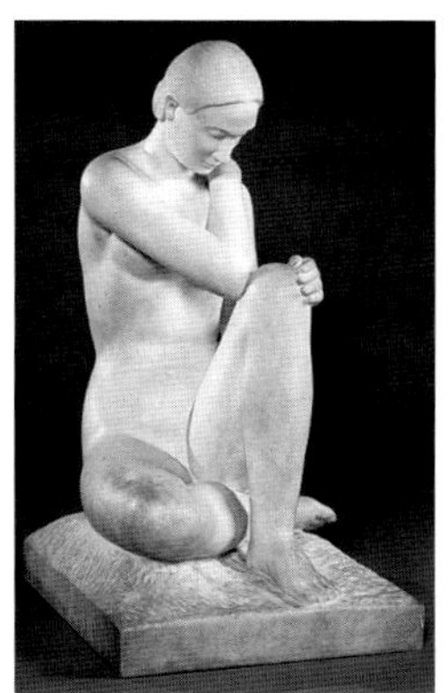

MAURICE STERNE
American, 1877/1878–1957

*Sitting Figure,* 1932
Marble, .579 x .322 x .411 ($22^{3}/_{4}$ x $12^{5}/_{8}$ x $16^{1}/_{8}$)
Inscribed on underside of base: MAURICE STERNE / FIRST VERSION / 1932
Gift of Lauson H. Stone and Marshall H. Stone
1969.4.1

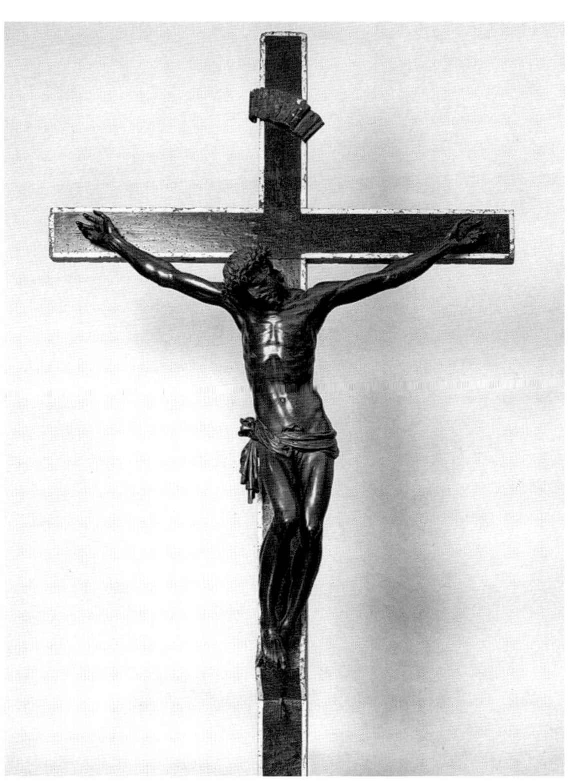

PIETRO TACCA
Florentine, 1577–1640

*The Pistoia Crucifix,* c. 1600/1616
Bronze, corpus: .869 x .790 x .206 ($34^{1}/_{4}$ x $31^{1}/_{8}$ x $8^{1}/_{8}$); cross: 1.669 x .901 ($65^{3}/_{4}$ x $35^{1}/_{2}$)
Inscribed on banner, at top of cross: INRI
Ailsa Mellon Bruce Fund
1973.9.1

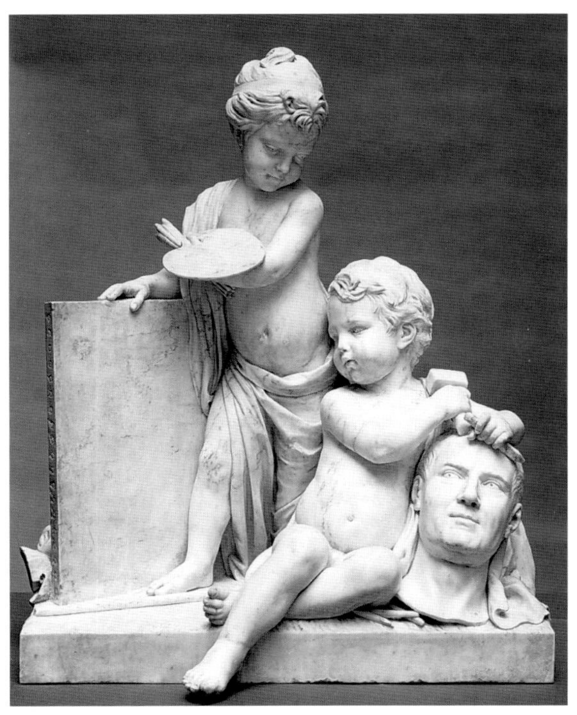

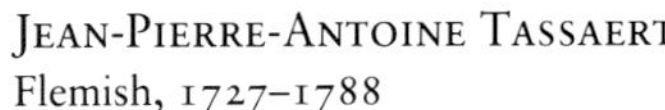

JEAN-PIERRE-ANTOINE TASSAERT
Flemish, 1727–1788

*Painting and Sculpture,* 1774/1778
Marble, .983 x .872 x .638
($38^{5}/_{8}$ x $34^{1}/_{4}$ x $25^{1}/_{8}$)
Samuel H. Kress Collection
1952.5.110

*See also:* CLAUDE MICHEL, CALLED CLODION, *Poetry and Music,* 1952.5.98

JACOPO D'ANTONIO TATTI
*See* JACOPO SANSOVINO

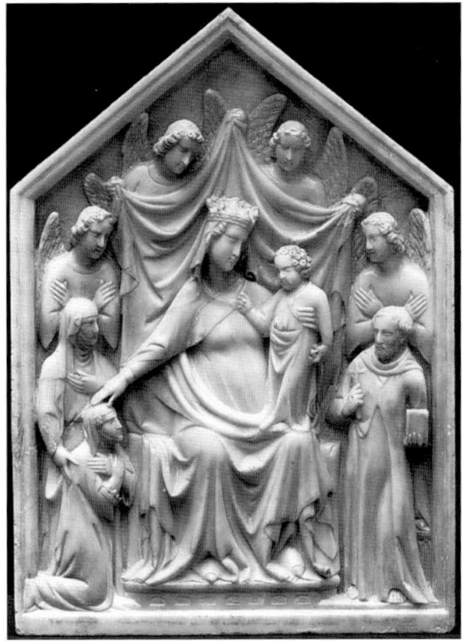

TINO DA CAMAINO
Tuscan, c. 1285–1337

*Madonna and Child with Queen Sancia, Saints and Angels,* c. 1335
Marble with traces of bolus for gilding on angel's wings, .514 x .378 x .085
($20^{1}/_{4}$ x $14^{7}/_{8}$ x $3^{3}/_{8}$)
Samuel H. Kress Collection
1960.5.1

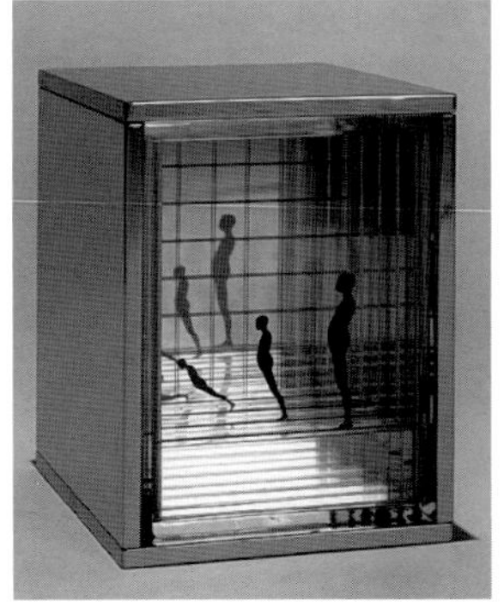

ERNEST TINO TROVA
American, born 1927

*Falling Man,* 1970
Bronze, plexiglass, paint, mirror
.144 x .115 x .140 ($5^{5}/_{8}$ x $4^{1}/_{2}$ x $5^{1}/_{2}$)
Gift of Mr. and Mrs. Burton Tremaine
1977.75.9

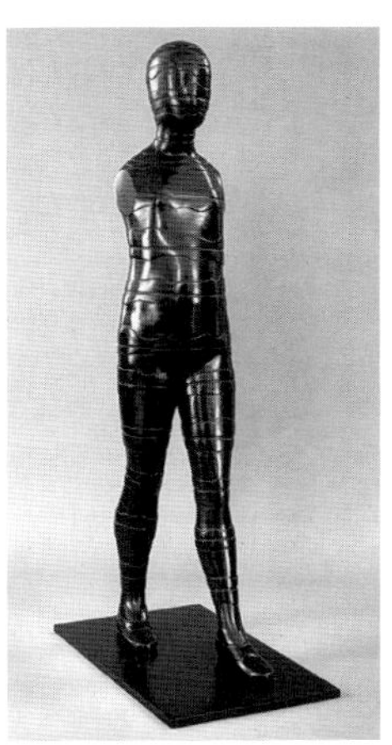

*Walking Man*, 1970
Bronze, 1.498 x .457 x .768
(59 x 18 x 30¼)
Gift of Enid A. Haupt
1977.47.12

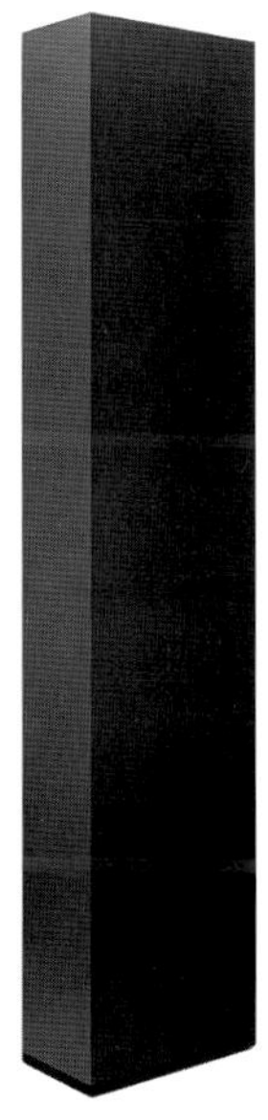

ANNE DEAN TRUITT
American, born 1921

*Mid-Day*, 1972
Acrylic on wood, 3.053 x .650 x .344
(120¼ x 25⅝ x 13⅝)
Inscribed on bottom: TRUITT / 12 AUG '72
Gift of Harry and Margery Kahn
1975.44.1

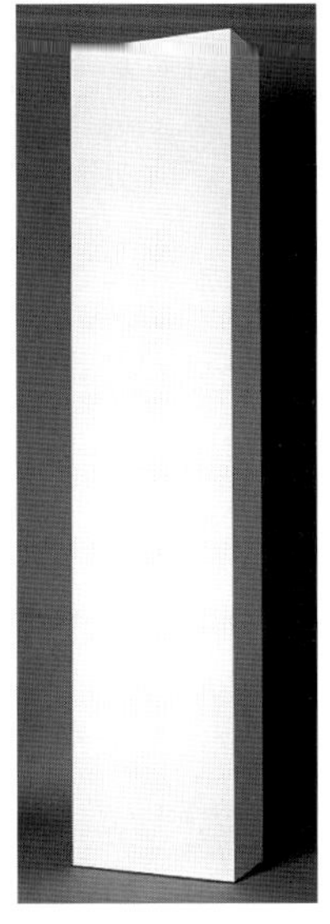

*Spume (Light Grey)*, 1972
Wood, painted, 3.050 x .649 x .344
(120⅛ x 25⅝ x 13⅝)
Inscribed on bottom: TRUITT / 8 AUG '72
Gift of friends of Anne Truitt
1973.12.1

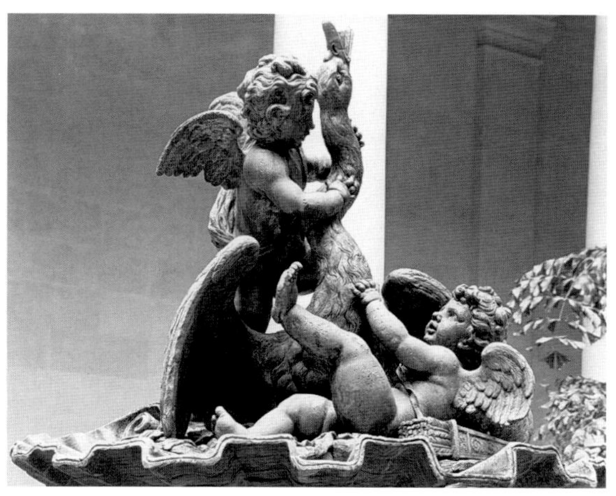

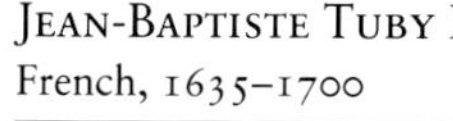

Jean-Baptiste Tuby I
French, 1635–1700

*Cherubs Playing with a Swan,* 1672–1673
Lead, traces of gilding, 1.19 x 1.50
(47 x 59)
Andrew W. Mellon Collection
1940.1.15

*See also:* Pierre Legros I, *Cherubs Playing with a Lyre,* 1940.1.16

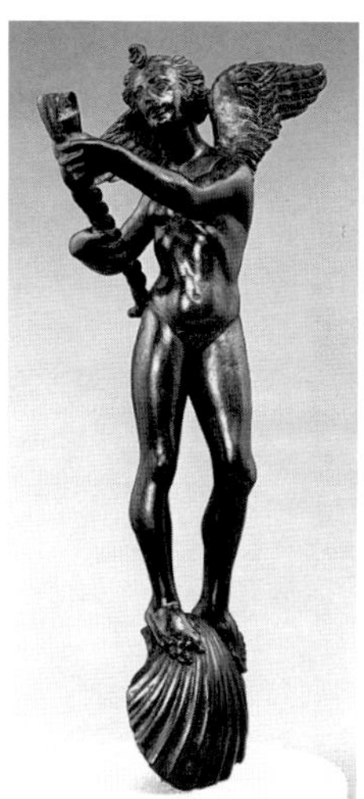

Lorenzo di Pietro,
called Vecchietta
Sienese, c. 1412–1480

*Winged Figure Holding a Torch,* 1470s
Bronze, .465 x .177 x .210
($17^{7}/_{8}$ x $6^{7}/_{8}$ x $8^{1}/_{4}$)
Samuel H. Kress Collection
1957.14.9

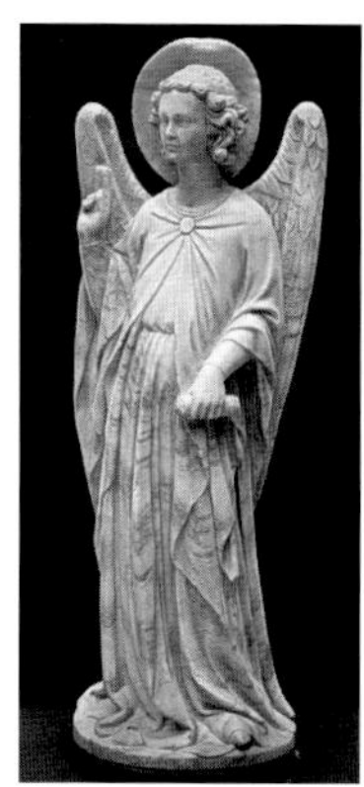

Venetian 14th Century

*Angel of the Annunciation,* c. 1340
Marble, .616 x .229 x .181
($24^{1}/_{4}$ x 9 x $7^{1}/_{8}$)
Samuel H. Kress Collection
1960.5.10

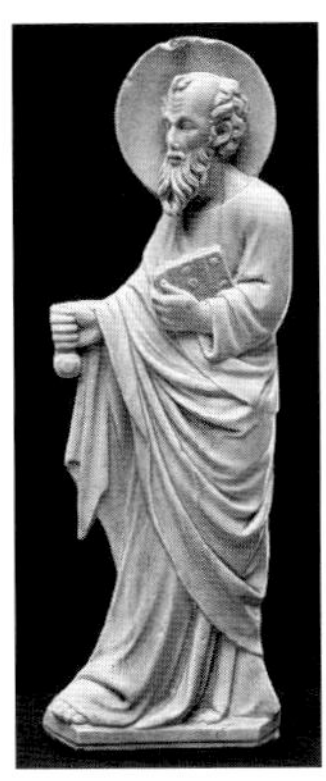

## VENETIAN 14TH CENTURY

*Saint Paul,* c. 1340
Marble, .602 x .215 x .089
($23\frac{5}{8}$ x $8\frac{3}{8}$ x $3\frac{1}{8}$)
Samuel H. Kress Collection
1960.5.13

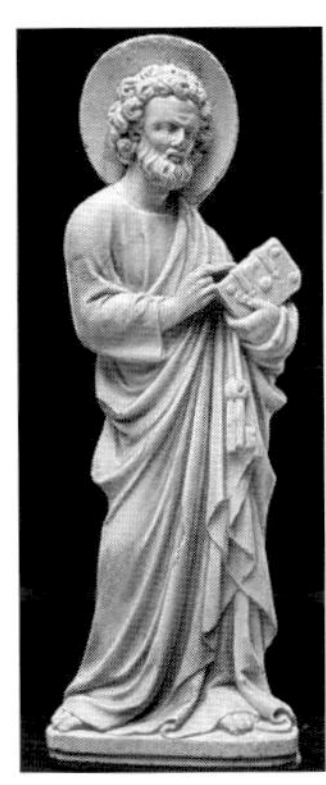

## VENETIAN 14TH CENTURY

*Saint Peter,* c. 1340
Marble, .618 x .218 x .089
($24\frac{1}{4}$ x $8\frac{1}{2}$ x $3\frac{1}{8}$)
Samuel H. Kress Collection
1960.5.12

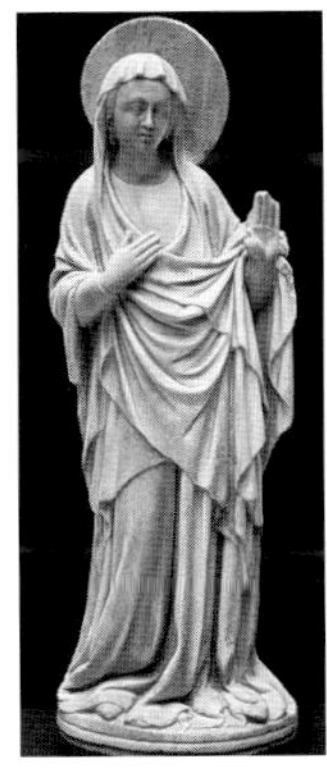

## VENETIAN 14TH CENTURY

*Virgin of the Annunciation,* c. 1340
Marble, .613 x .213 x .153
($24\frac{1}{8}$ x $8\frac{3}{8}$ x 6)
Samuel H. Kress Collection
1960.5.11

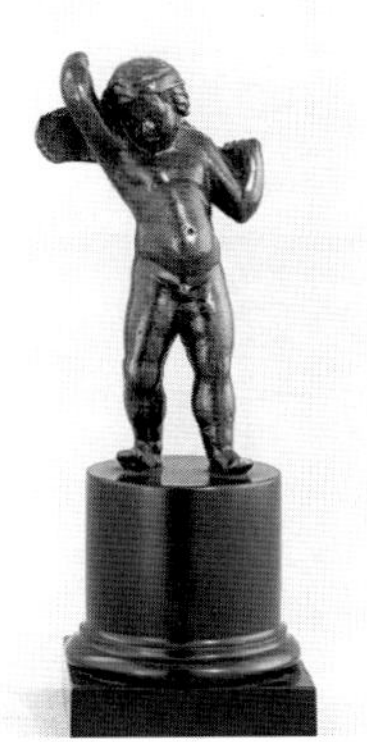

## VENETIAN 15TH CENTURY

*Winged Boy with Hands Raised,* late 15th century
Bronze, .105 x .059 x .036
($4\frac{1}{8}$ x $2\frac{3}{8}$ x $1\frac{7}{16}$)
Samuel H. Kress Collection
1957.14.38

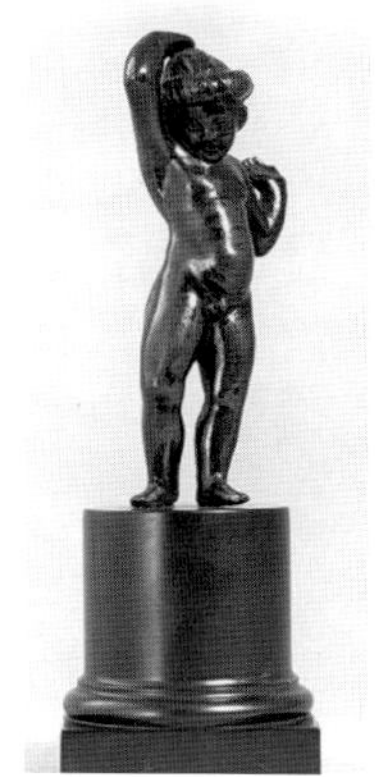

VENETIAN 15TH CENTURY

*Wreathed Boy with Hands Raised,* late 15th century
Bronze, .111 x .054 x .029
(4 1/8 x 2 1/8 x 1 1/8)
Samuel H. Kress Collection
1957.14.39

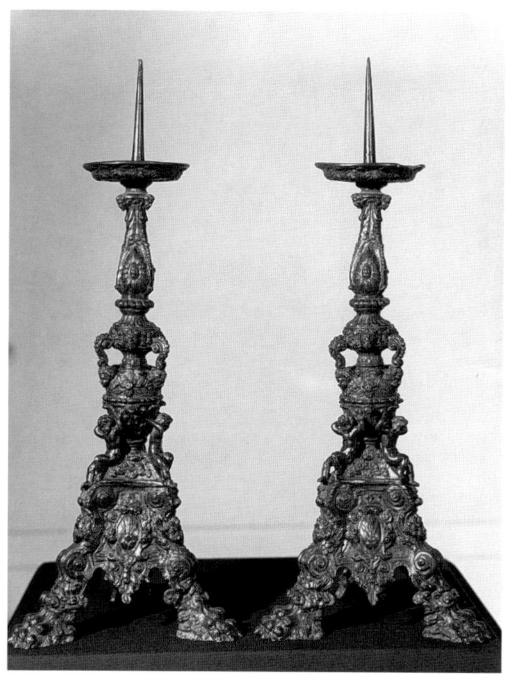

VENETIAN 16TH CENTURY

*Altar-Candlestick with Shield of Arms of the Garzoni of Venice,* third quarter 16th century
Bronze, .572 x .241 x .205
(22 1/2 x 9 1/2 x 8)
Samuel H. Kress Collection
1957.14.71

*Altar-Candlestick with Shield of Arms of the Garzoni of Venice,* third quarter 16th century
Bronze, .572 x .241 x .205
(22 1/2 x 9 1/2 x 8)
Samuel H. Kress Collection
1957.14.70

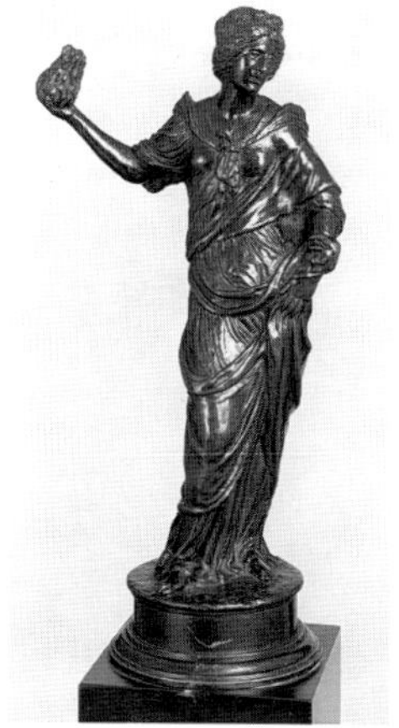

VENETIAN 16TH CENTURY

*Charity,* c. 1530
Bronze, .208 x .105 x .072
(8 1/4 x 4 1/8 x 2 7/8)
Samuel H. Kress Collection
1957.14.29

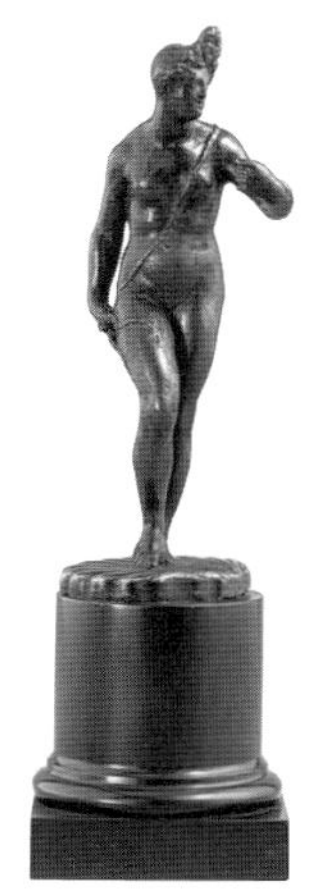

## Venetian 16th Century

*Fortuna,* second half 16th century
Bronze, .134 x .051 x .045
($5^{1}/_{4}$ x 2 x $1^{13}/_{16}$)
Samuel H. Kress Collection
1957.14.23

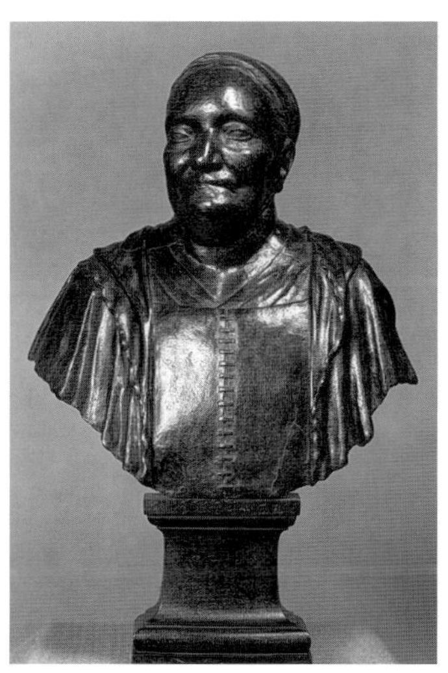

## Venetian 16th Century

*Agnesina Badoer Giustinian,* c. 1542
Bronze, .528 x .495 x .270
($20^{3}/_{4}$ x $19^{3}/_{8}$ x $10^{5}/_{8}$)
Widener Collection
1942.9.146

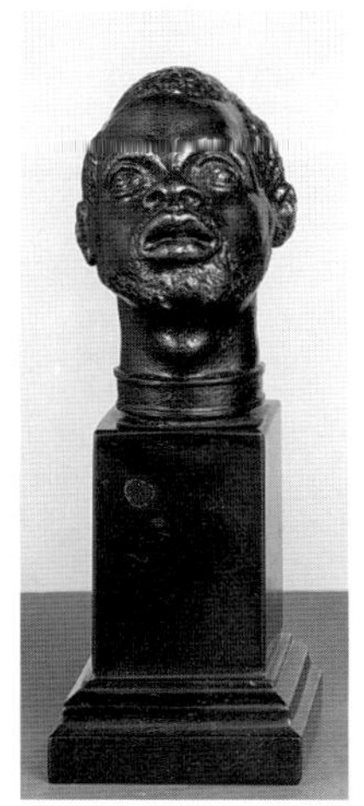

## Venetian 16th Century

*Head of a Moor,* second half 16th century
Iron, .057 x .037 x .046
($2^{1}/_{4}$ x $1^{7}/_{16}$ x $1^{13}/_{16}$)
Samuel H. Kress Collection
1957.14.54

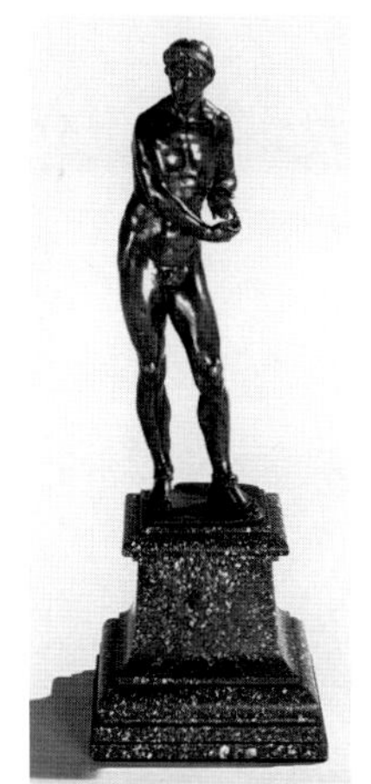

## Venetian 16th Century

*Mercury,* second half 16th century
Bronze, .204 x .055 x .045
(8 1/8 x 2 1/4 x 1 7/8)
Widener Collection
1942.9.117

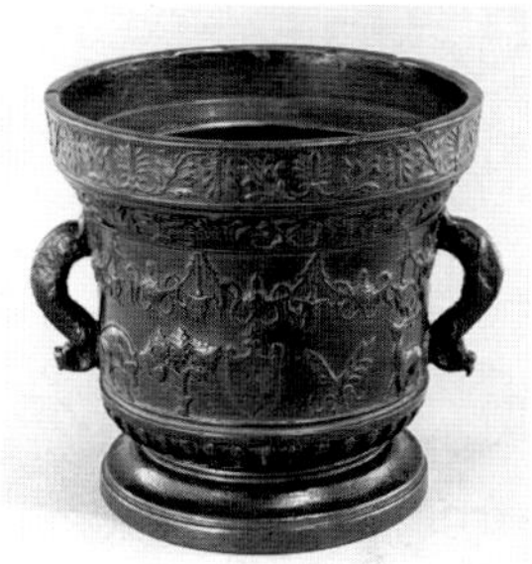

## Probably Venetian 16th Century

*Mortar*
Bronze, .150 x .186 (5 7/8 x 7 5/16)
Samuel H. Kress Collection
1957.14.97

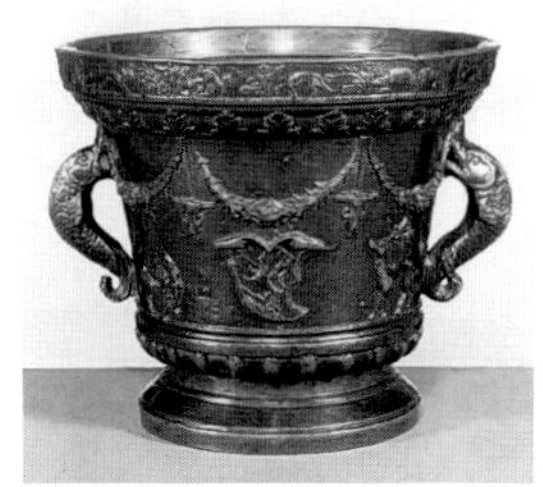

## Probably Venetian 16th Century

*Mortar with Shields of Badoer Arms*
Bronze, .134 x .168 (5 5/16 x 6 5/8)
Samuel H. Kress Collection
1957.14.103

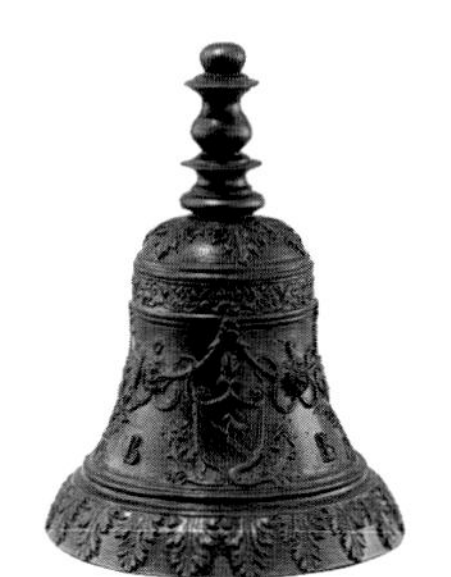

## Probably Venetian 16th Century

*Table-Bell*
Bronze, .131 x .102 (5 3/16 x 4)
Inscribed to left and right of each shield: B
Samuel H. Kress Collection
1957.14.112

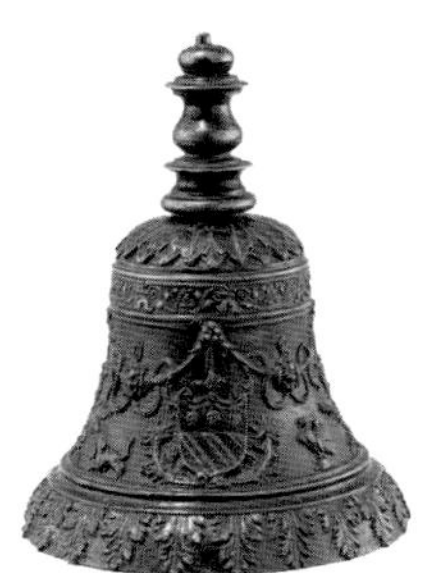

## PROBABLY VENETIAN 16TH CENTURY

*Table-Bell*
Bronze, .133 x .110 (5 1/4 x 4 5/16)
Samuel H. Kress Collection
1957.14.115

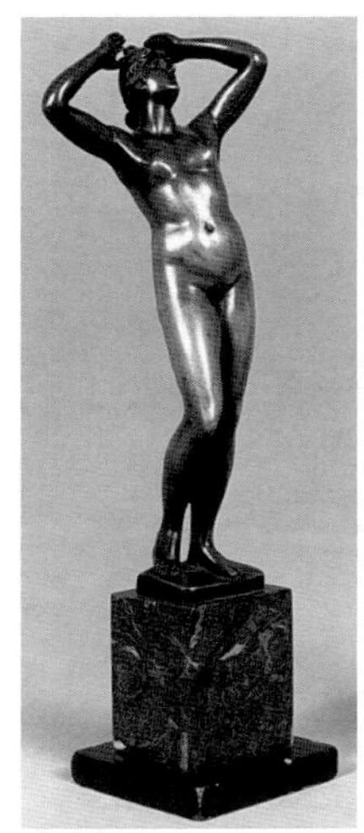

## STYLE OF VENICE OR PADUA 16TH CENTURY

*Female Figure with Raised Arms (a Niobid?)*, c. 1520/1530
Bronze, .248 x .098 x .076 (9 3/4 x 3 7/8 x 3)
Gift of Asbjorn R. Lunde
1985.65.1

## VENETO-ISLAMIC 16TH CENTURY

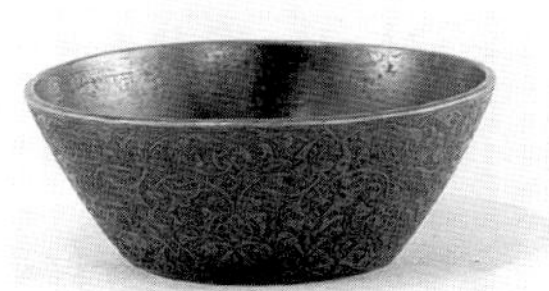

*Bowl*, mid-16th century
Bronze, .052 x .142 (2 1/16 x 5 5/8)
Inscribed in interior: (signature of the maker, Hatim, in Arabic)
Samuel H. Kress Collection
1957.14.96

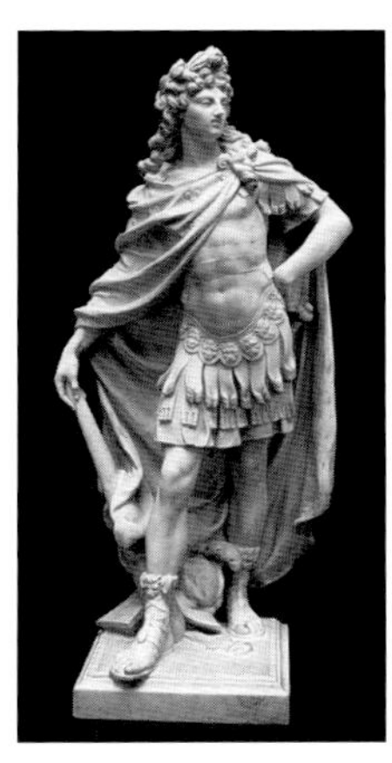

## C. VERONA
Italian, active late 19th century

*Louis XIV*, probably c. 1875/1900
Marble, .975 x .492 x .356 (38 3/8 x 19 3/8 x 14)
Falsely signed and dated, on rear edge of base: DES IARDINS.1675
Samuel H. Kress Collection
1961.1.4

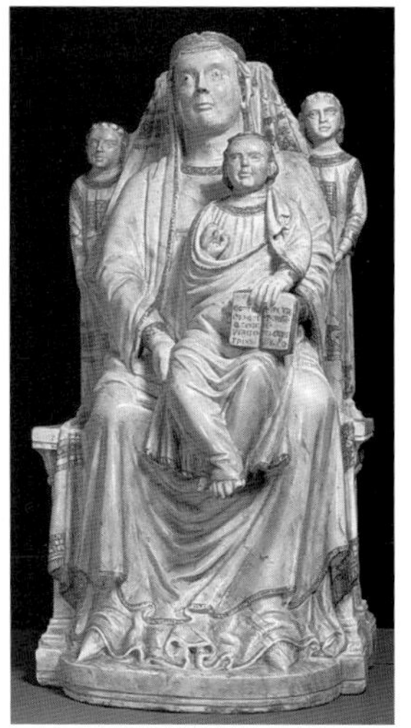

## VERONESE 14TH CENTURY

*Madonna and Child with Two Angels,* 1321
Marble, .895 x .464 x .388
(35¹/₄ x 18¹/₄ x 15¹/₄)
Inscribed on book: CONTINET•IN GER / MIO•CELV̄•TERRĀ• / Q̄•REGENTĒ• / VIRGO• DEI•GENI / TRIX•••M̊CCC•X̊XI
Samuel H. Kress Collection
1961.9.95

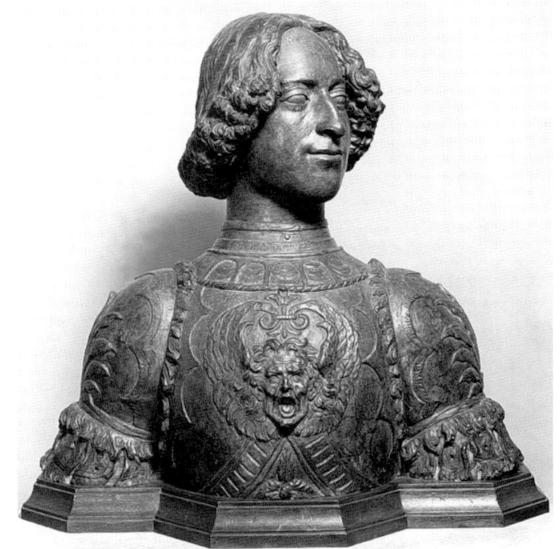

## ANDREA DEL VERROCCHIO
Florentine, 1435–1488

*Giuliano de' Medici,* c. 1475/1478
Terra cotta, .610 x .660 x .283
(24 x 26 x 11¹/₈)
Andrew W. Mellon Collection
1937.1.127

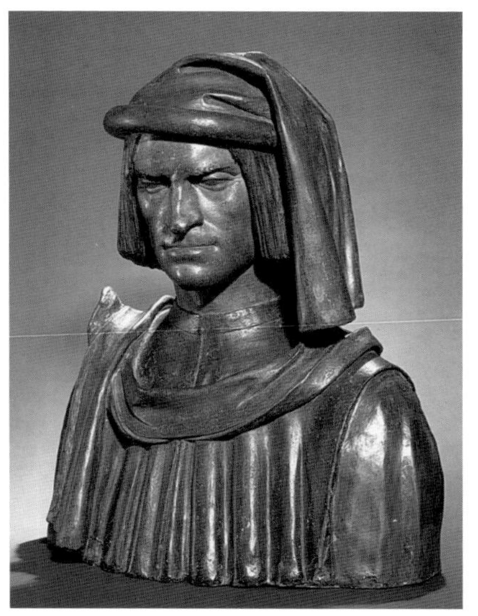

*Lorenzo de' Medici,* c. 1478
Terra cotta, painted, .658 x .591 x .327
(25⁷/₈ x 23¹/₄ x 12⁷/₈)
Samuel H. Kress Collection
1943.4.92

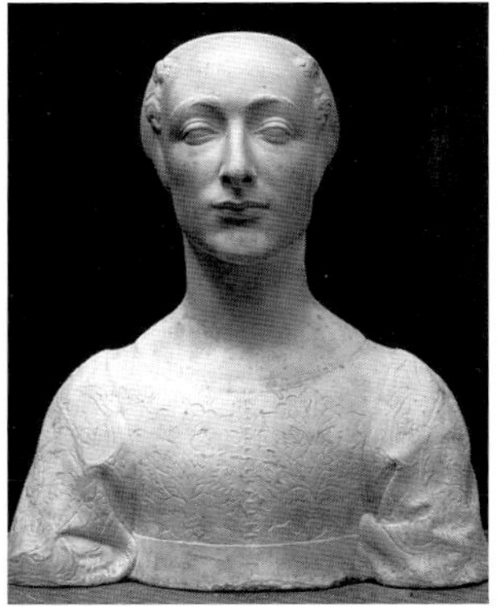

*A Lady of the Vespucci Family (?)*, c. 1475/1480
Marble, .530 x .488 x .199
($20^7/_8$ x $19^1/_8$ x $7^3/_4$)
Samuel H. Kress Collection
1939.1.326

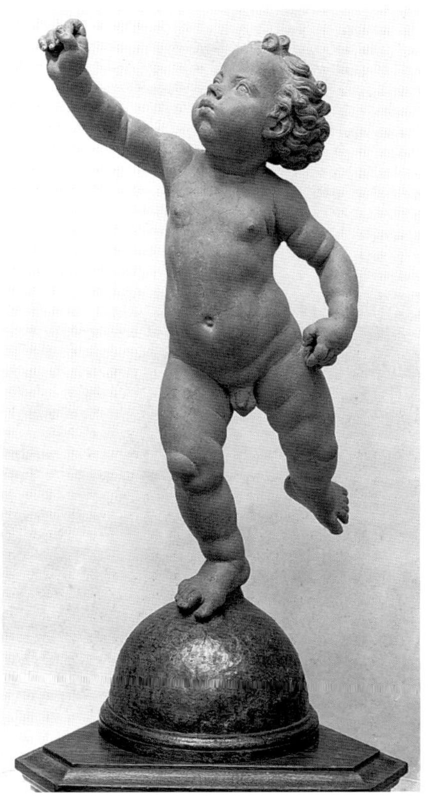

*Putto Poised on a Globe*, probably 1480
Unbaked clay, .750 x .383 x .230
($29^1/_2$ x 15 x $11^3/_4$)
Andrew W. Mellon Collection
1937.1.128

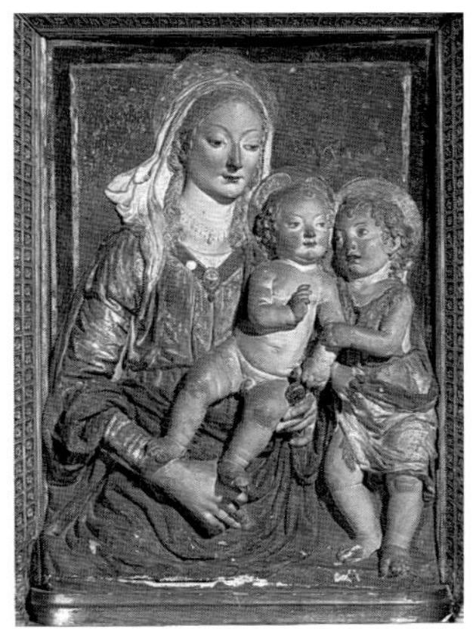

Follower of
Andrea del Verrocchio
Florentine

*Virgin and Child with Saint John*
Terra cotta, painted, .757 x .572
($29^3/_4$ x $22^1/_2$)
Widener Collection
1942.9.147

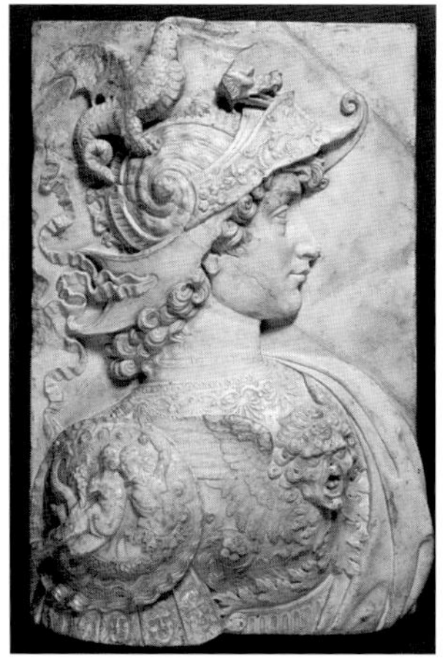

After Andrea del Verrocchio
Florentine

*Alexander the Great*, c. 1480
Marble, .559 x .367 (21 x 14 1/2)
Gift of Therese K. Straus
1956.2.1

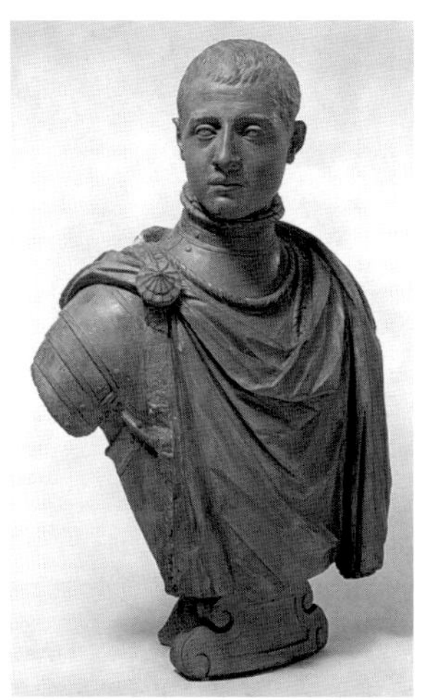

Alessandro Vittoria
Venetian, 1525–1608

*A Gentleman of the Zorzi Family*, 1570/1580
Terra cotta, .902 x .616 x .323 (35 1/2 x 24 1/4 x 12 3/4)
Inscribed on truncated right side of chest: •A•V•F•
Samuel H. Kress Collection
1961.9.106

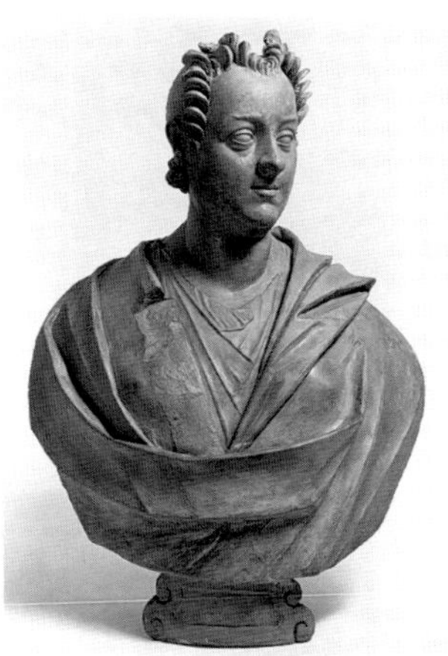

*A Lady of the Zorzi Family*, 1570/1580
Terra cotta, .810 x .590 x .331 (31 7/8 x 23 1/4 x 13)
On truncation of left arm: •ALEXAN• VICTORIA•F•
Samuel H. Kress Collection
1961.9.107

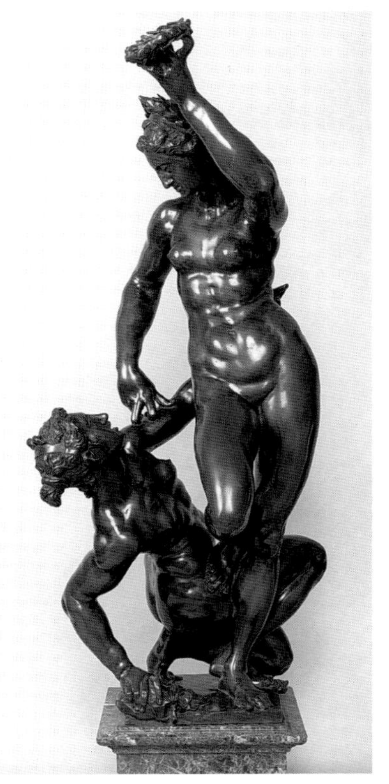

ADRIAEN DE VRIES
Netherlandish, c. 1545–1626

*Empire Triumphant over Avarice,* 1610
Bronze, .773 x .348 x .318
($30^{3}/_{8}$ x $13^{5}/_{8}$ x $12^{1}/_{2}$)
Inscribed on back of base: ADRIANVS•
FRIES•FE 1610
Widener Collection
1942.9.148

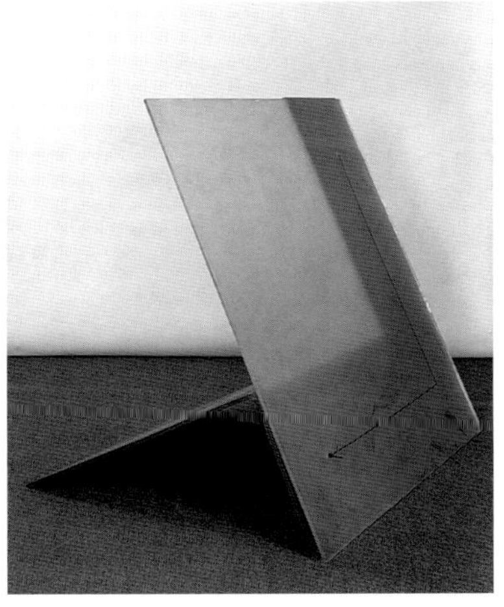

CHRISTOPHER WILMARTH
American, 1943–1987

*Clearing,* 1972
Etched plate glass and steel, with cable
1.353 x 1.524 x 1.181 ($53^{1}/_{4}$ x 60 x $46^{1}/_{2}$)
Gift of Rose and Charles F. Gibbs
1985.66.1

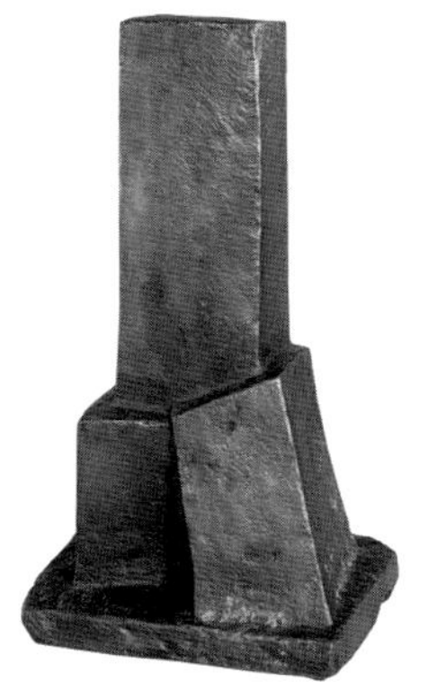

FRITZ WOTRUBA
Austrian, 1907–1975

*Torso,* 1968/1969
Bronze, .634 x .390 x .254
(25 x $15^{3}/_{8}$ x 10)
Foundry mark inside hollow cast at
bottom edge: GUSS A. ZOTTL WIEN ZW
(monogram)
Gift of Z-Bank of Vienna
1984.54.1

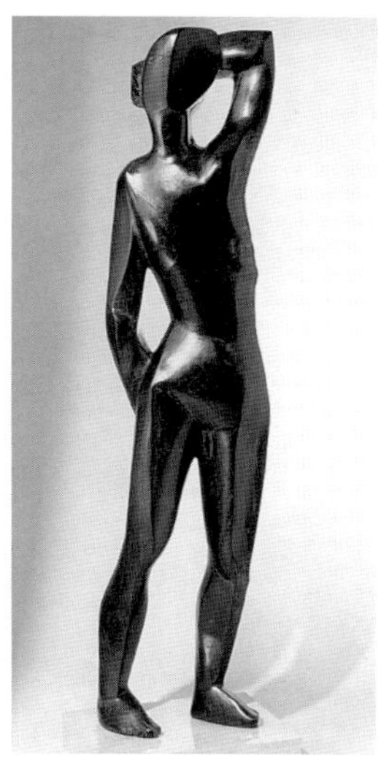

OSSIP ZADKINE
French, 1890–1967

*Le Jouvenceau*, 1961
Ebony, 1.070 x .267 x .152
($42^1/_8$ x $10^1/_2$ x 6)
Inscribed on lower back side of right leg:
OZ 1961
Gift (Partial and Promised) of Mr. and Mrs. Nathan L. Halpern, in Honor of the 50th Anniversary of the National Gallery of Art
1991.53.1

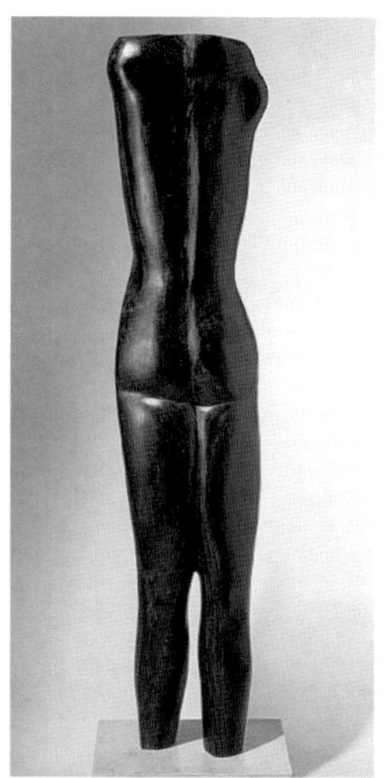

*Torso*, 1963
Ebony, 1.060 x .254 x .165
($41^3/_4$ x 10 x $6^1/_2$)
Inscribed on lower side of left leg:
O ZADKIN
Gift (Partial and Promised) of Mr. and Mrs. Nathan L. Halpern, in Honor of the 50th Anniversary of the National Gallery of Art
1991.53.2

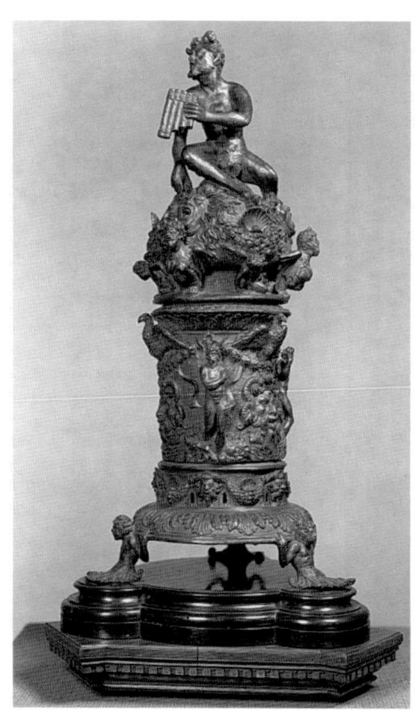

ATTRIBUTED TO AGOSTINO ZOPPO
Paduan, c. 1520–1572

*Incense Burner*
Bronze, leg to leg: .520 x .260
($20^1/_2$ x $10^1/_4$); diameter of round base:
.187 ($7^3/_8$)
Widener Collection
1942.9.139

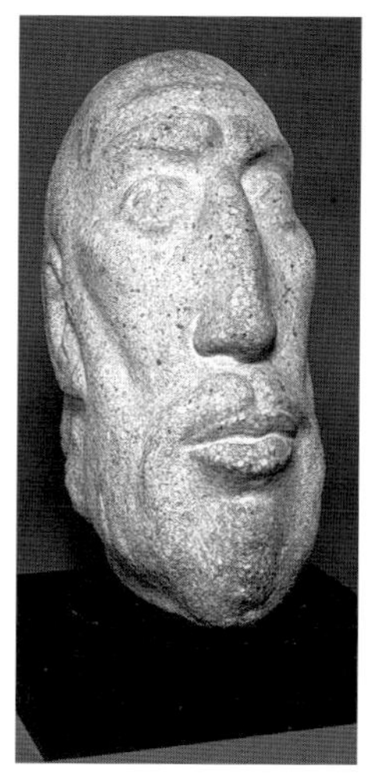

WILLIAM ZORACH
American, 1887–1966

*Man of Judah*, 1950
Granite, .426 x .194 x .345
($16^3/_4$ x $7^5/_8$ x $13^5/_8$)
Inscribed on left edge of neck: ZORACH
Gift of Tessim Zorach and Dahlov Ipcar
1979.52.1

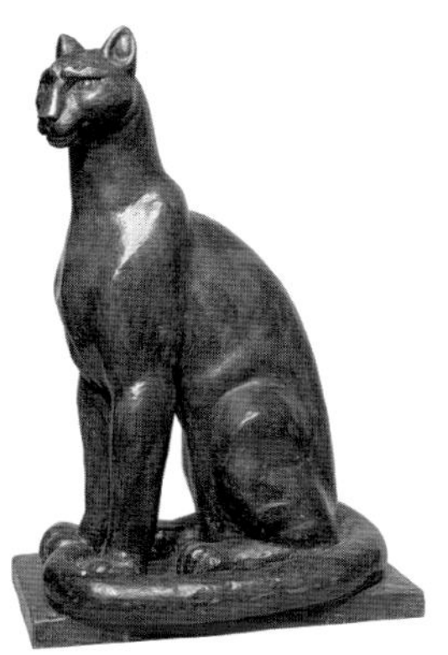

*Puma (looking left)*, 1948
Bronze, .939 x .423 x .642
(37 x $16^5/_8$ x $25^1/_4$)
Inscribed on top of base, rear left corner:
WILLIAM ZORACH. 1948–2/6
Gift of Eric M. Wunsch
1971.33.1

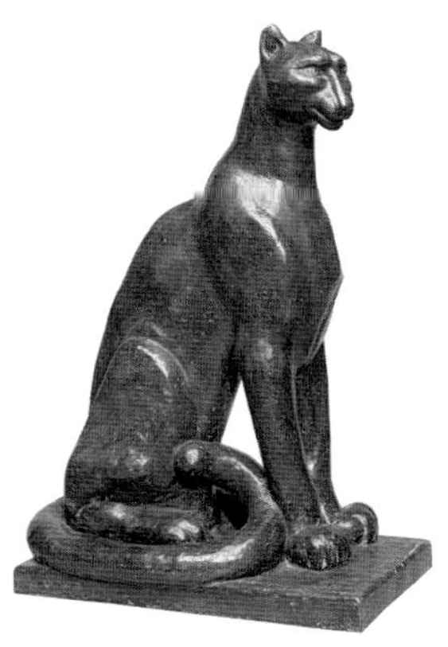

*Puma (looking right)*, 1948
Bronze, .936 x .384 x .683
($36^7/_8$ x $15^1/_8$ x $26^7/_8$)
Inscribed on top of base, front left corner:
WILLIAM ZORACH 2/6 / 1948
Gift of Eric M. Wunsch
1971.33.2

# CHANGES IN ATTRIBUTION, TITLES, AND NOMENCLATURE

Since publication of National Gallery of Art, *Summary Catalogue of European Paintings and Sculpture*, 1965/1968 and
Carolyn C. Wilson, *Renaissance Small Bronze Sculpture and Associated Decorative Arts at the National Gallery of Art*, 1983
(arranged alphabetically by former attribution)

| Formerly | Currently |
|---|---|
| A-9<br>GIOVANNI ANTONIO AMADEO<br>*Lodovico Sforza, called il Moro* | 1937.1.120<br>BENEDETTO BRIOSCO<br>*Lodovico Sforza, Duke of Bari* |
| A-10<br>GIOVANNI ANTONIO AMADEO<br>*Gian Galeazzo Sforza* | 1937.1.121<br>WORKSHOP OF BENEDETTO BRIOSCO<br>*Gian Galeazzo Maria Sforza, Duke of Milan* |
| A-25<br>GIOVANNI ANTONIO AMADEO<br>*Kneeling Angel* | 1939.1.321<br>WORKSHOP OF GIOVANNI ANTONIO AMADEO<br>*Kneeling Angel* |
| A-52<br>GIOVANNI ANTONIO AMADEO<br>*Filippo Maria Visconti* | 1943.4.77<br>IMITATOR OF BENEDETTO BRIOSCO<br>*Filippo Maria Visconti* |
| A-96<br>BACCIO BANDINELLI<br>*Samson Slaying the Philistine* | 1942.9.102<br>GERMAN 16TH CENTURY<br>*Samson Slaying the Philistine* |
| A-50<br>BENEDETTO DA MAIANO<br>*Bust of a Florentine Statesman* | 1943.4.75<br>FLORENTINE 16TH CENTURY<br>*A Gentleman* |
| A-99<br>BENEDETTO DA MAIANO<br>*Pietro Talani* | 1942.9.105<br>GIOVANNI BASTIANINI<br>*Pietro Talani* |
| A-1668<br>BENIN STYLE<br>*Bronze Cock* | 1955.10.1<br>NIGERIAN, COURT OF BENIN<br>*Fowl* |
| A-62<br>GIAN LORENZO BERNINI<br>*Louis XIV* | 1943.4.87<br>AFTER GIAN LORENZO BERNINI<br>*Louis XIV* |
| A-1616<br>SCHOOL OF GIAN LORENZO BERNINI<br>*Thetis* | 1952.5.92<br>ATTRIBUTED TO GIUSEPPE MAZZUOLI<br>*A Nereid* |
| A-1704<br>BERNHARD A. BÖHMER<br>*Death Mask of Ernst Barlach* | 1962.7.1<br>BERNHARD A. BÖHMER<br>*Death Mask of Ernst Barlach ?* |

| Formerly | Currently |
| --- | --- |
| A-20<br>Giovanni Bologna<br>*Mercury* | 1937.1.131<br>Attributed to Francesco Righetti, after Giovanni Bologna<br>*Mercury* |
| A-115<br>Giovanni Bologna<br>*Hercules Carrying the Erymanthian Boar* | 1942.9.121<br>After Giovanni Bologna, called Giambologna<br>*Hercules Carrying the Erymanthian Boar* |
| A-1618<br>Elia Candido<br>*Apollo of Lycia* | 1952.5.94<br>Attributed to Francesco Righetti<br>*Apollino of the Villa Medici* |
| A-101<br>Benvenuto Cellini<br>*Virtue Overcoming Vice* | 1942.9.107<br>Roman 16th/17th Century<br>*Virtue Overcoming Vice* |
| A-179<br>Circle of Vincenzo Danti<br>*Bacchus* | 1957.14.26<br>After Michelangelo Buonarroti<br>*Bacchus* |
| A-1598<br>Honoré Daumier<br>*The Laughing Man* | 1951.17.1<br>Imitator of Honoré Daumier<br>*The Laughing Man* |
| A-1599<br>Honoré Daumier<br>*Man in a Tall Hat* | 1951.17.2<br>Imitator of Honoré Daumier<br>*Man in a Tall Hat* |
| A-1638<br>Honoré Daumier<br>*Man of Affairs* | 1953.8.1<br>Imitator of Honoré Daumier<br>*The Man of Affairs* |
| A-1639<br>Honoré Daumier<br>*The Dandy* | 1953.8.2<br>Imitator of Honoré Daumier<br>*The Dandy* |
| A-1641<br>Honoré Daumier<br>*The Stroller* | 1954.13.2<br>Imitator of Honoré Daumier<br>*The Stroller* |
| A-1642<br>Honoré Daumier<br>*The Lover* | 1954.13.3<br>Imitator of Honoré Daumier<br>*The Lover* |
| A-1697<br>Honoré Daumier<br>*The Confidant* | 1958.8.1<br>Imitator of Honoré Daumier<br>*The Confidant* |
| A-1698<br>Honoré Daumier<br>*The Representative* | 1958.8.2<br>Imitator of Honoré Daumier<br>*The Representative* |
| A-1702<br>Honoré Daumier<br>*The Small Shopkeeper* | 1961.17.1<br>Imitator of Honoré Daumier<br>*The Small Shopkeeper* |

| Formerly | Currently |
|---|---|
| A-1703<br>Honoré Daumier<br>*The Visitor* | 1961.17.2<br>Imitator of Honoré Daumier<br>*The Visitor* |
| A-1715<br>Honoré Daumier<br>*The Jolly Good Fellow* | 1964.8.1<br>Imitator of Honoré Daumier<br>*The Jolly Good Fellow* |
| A-1716<br>Honoré Daumier<br>*The Listener* | 1964.8.2<br>Imitator of Honoré Daumier<br>*The Listener* |
| A-3<br>Desiderio da Settignano<br>*Madonna and Child* | 1937.1.114<br>Florentine 19th Century<br>*Madonna and Child* |
| A-4<br>Desiderio da Settignano<br>*The Young Christ with Saint John the Baptist* | 1937.1.115<br>Style of Desiderio da Settignano<br>*Christ with Saint John the Baptist as Children* |
| A-30<br>Desiderio da Settignano<br>*Bust of a Lady* | 1939.1.326<br>Andrea del Verrocchio<br>*A Lady of the Vespucci Family (?)* |
| A-106<br>Desiderio da Settignano<br>*Marietta Strozzi* | 1942.9.112<br>Desiderio da Settignano<br>*"Marietta Strozzi"* |
| A-148<br>Desiderio da Settignano<br>*The Christ Child* | 1943.4.94<br>Desiderio da Settignano<br>*The Christ Child (?)* |
| A-1624<br>Desiderio da Settignano<br>*Tabernacle* | 1952.5.100<br>Desiderio da Settignano<br>*Ciborium for the Sacrament* |
| A-1651<br>Martin Desjardins<br>*Louis XIV* | 1961.1.4<br>C. Verona<br>*Louis XIV* |
| A-1<br>Donatello<br>*Madonna and Child* | 1937.1.112<br>Florentine 15th Century<br>*Madonna and Child* |
| A-19<br>Donatello<br>*Saint John the Baptist* | 1937.1.130<br>Benedetto da Maiano<br>*Saint John the Baptist* |
| A-108<br>Donatello<br>*Cupid* | 1942.9.114<br>Attributed to Lucas Faydherbe<br>*Cupid (?)* |
| A-109<br>Donatello<br>*The David of the Casa Martelli* | 1942.9.115<br>Bernardo or Antonio Rossellino<br>*The David of the Casa Martelli* |
| A-150<br>English School<br>*The Holy Trinity* | 1953.2.1<br>English or Spanish 14th Century<br>*The Holy Trinity* |

Attribution

| Formerly | Currently |
|---|---|
| A-110<br>Étienne-Maurice Falconet<br>*Madame de Pompadour as the Venus of the Doves* | 1952.5.101<br>Étienne-Maurice Falconet<br>*Venus of the Doves* |
| A-128<br>Tommaso Fiamberti<br>*The Young Saint John the Baptist* | 1942.9.134<br>Master of the Marble Madonnas<br>*The Young Saint John the Baptist* |
| A-1652<br>Tommaso Fiamberti<br>*Madonna and Child* | 1960.5.9<br>Florentine 19th Century, after the Master of the Marble Madonnas<br>*Madonna and Child* |
| A-194<br>Flemish 16th Century<br>*Handle in the Form of Three Winged Children* | 1957.14.41<br>Flemish 16th Century<br>*Three Cupids* |
| A-125<br>Florentine School<br>*Architectural Plaque: Putti Bearing Inscribed Tablet* | 1942.9.131<br>Benedetto da Rovezzano<br>*Relief from an Altar or Tabernacle* |
| A-153<br>Florentine School<br>*Lion* | 1957.14.7<br>Roman 18th/19th Century<br>*Lion* |
| A-23<br>Annibale Fontana<br>*The Adoration of the Shepherds* | 1939.1.319<br>After Annibale Fontana<br>*The Adoration of the Shepherds* |
| A-1653<br>Attributed to Francesco di Giorgio<br>*Winged Figure with Cornucopia* | 1957.14.9<br>Lorenzo di Pietro, called Vecchietta<br>*Winged Figure Holding a Torch* |
| A-113<br>Francesco da Sant'Agata<br>*Hercules and Antaeus* | 1942.9.119<br>Paduan 16th Century<br>*Hercules and Antaeus* |
| A-143<br>Franco-Flemish<br>*Pietà* | 1942.11.2<br>German or Netherlandish 15th Century<br>*Pietà* |
| A-1626<br>Franco-Portugese School<br>*Saint Barbara* | 1952.5.102<br>Probably French or Belgian 19th Century<br>*Saint Barbara* |
| A-193<br>German, probably Nuremberg, first half 16th Century<br>*Seated Boy Holding a Bird* | 1957.14.40<br>German 16th Century (possibly Nuremberg)<br>*A Child with a Crow* |
| A-231<br>German, possibly Nuremberg, second quarter 16th Century<br>*Hound Scratching its Left Ear* | 1957.14.78<br>German 16th Century (possibly Nuremberg)<br>*A Dog Scratching* |

## Attribution

| Formerly | Currently |
|---|---|
| A-147<br>Lorenzo Ghiberti<br>*Madonna and Child* | 1943.4.93<br>Florentine 15th Century<br>*Madonna and Child* |
| A-1663<br>Giovanni di Turino<br>*Madonna and Child* | 1961.9.103<br>Circle of Giovanni di Turino<br>*Madonna and Child* |
| A-142<br>Greek 4th Century B.C.<br>*Head of a Youth* | 1942.11.1<br>Probably Hellenistic School, Egypt<br>*Head of a Youth (Dionysus or a Follower?)* |
| A-117<br>Jean-Antoine Houdon<br>*Alexandre Brongniard* | 1942.9.123<br>Jean-Antoine Houdon<br>*Alexandre Brongniart* |
| A-118<br>Jean-Antoine Houdon<br>*Louise Brongniard* | 1942.9.124<br>Jean-Antoine Houdon<br>*Louise Brongniart* |
| A-177<br>Italo-Netherlandish or Italo-French, 16th Century<br>*Woman Cutting Her Nails* | 1957.14.24<br>Probably French (possibly Barthélemy Prieur) 17th Century<br>*Woman Cutting Her Nails* |
| A-1706<br>Moïse Kisling<br>*Death Mask of Amedeo Modigliani* | 1963.10.237<br>Jacques Lipchitz (Chaim Jacob Lipchitz), Moïse Kisling, and Conrad Moricand<br>*Death Mask of Amedeo Modigliani* |
| A-42<br>Pierre Legros<br>*Cherubs Playing with a Lyre* | 1940.1.16<br>Pierre Legros I<br>*Cherubs Playing with a Lyre* |
| A-1630<br>Robert Le Lorrain<br>*The Dew* | 1952.5.106<br>Benoît Massou, Anselme Flamen, and Nicolas Rebillé<br>*A Garden Allegory: The Dew and Zephyr Cultivating Flowers* |
| A-127<br>Jean-Louis Lemoyne<br>*Diana* | 1942.9.133<br>Jean-Louis Lemoyne<br>*A Companion of Diana* |
| A-59<br>Leone Leoni<br>*Giovanni Capponi* | 1943.4.84<br>Attributed to Giovanni Battista Caccini<br>*Giovanni Capponi* |
| A-163<br>Attributed to Leone Leoni<br>*A Member of the Order of Santiago* | 1948.15.1<br>Florentine or Neapolitan 16th Century<br>*Don Pedro Alvarez de Toledo* |
| A-1614<br>Lombard School<br>*The Adoration of the Magi* | 1952.5.90<br>Benedetto Briosco and Tommasso Cazzaniga<br>*The Adoration of the Magi* |

| Formerly | Currently |
|---|---|
| A-1615<br>LOMBARD SCHOOL<br>*The Flight into Egypt* | 1952.5.91<br>BENEDETTO BRIOSCO AND TOMMASSO CAZZANIGA<br>*The Flight into Egypt* |
| A-47<br>PIETRO LOMBARDO<br>*A Singing Angel* | 1943.4.72<br>PIETRO LOMBARDO<br>*Allegorical Figure* |
| A-1654<br>MASTER OF THE MASCOLI ALTAR<br>*Angel of the Annunciation* | 1960.5.10<br>VENETIAN 14TH CENTURY<br>*Angel of the Annunciation* |
| A-1655<br>MASTER OF THE MASCOLI ALTAR<br>*Virgin of the Annunciation* | 1960.5.11<br>VENETIAN 14TH CENTURY<br>*Virgin of the Annunciation* |
| A-1656<br>MASTER OF THE MASCOLI ALTAR<br>*Saint Peter* | 1960.5.12<br>VENETIAN 14TH CENTURY<br>*Saint Peter* |
| A-1657<br>MASTER OF THE MASCOLI ALTAR<br>*Saint Paul* | 1960.5.13<br>VENETIAN 14TH CENTURY<br>*Saint Paul* |
| A-1658<br>ATTRIBUTED TO MICHELANGELO<br>*Apollo and Marsyas* | 1961.1.5<br>FOLLOWER OF MICHELANGELO BUONARROTI, AFTER THE ANTIQUE<br>*Apollo and Marsyas* |
| A-15<br>MINO DA FIESOLE<br>*Madonna and Child* | 1937.1.126<br>ITALIAN 19TH CENTURY<br>*Madonna and Child* |
| A-1632<br>NINO PISANO<br>*The Archangel Gabriel* | 1961.9.97<br>PISAN 14TH CENTURY<br>*The Archangel Gabriel* |
| A-1633<br>NINO PISANO<br>*The Virgin Annunciate* | 1961.9.98<br>PISAN 14TH CENTURY<br>*The Virgin Annunciate* |
| A-169<br>NORTH ITALIAN, POSSIBLY FERRARESE, 15TH OR 16TH CENTURY<br>*Saint George* | 1957.14.16<br>PROBABLY NORTH ITALIAN 15TH CENTURY<br>*Saint George and the Dragon* |
| A-168<br>ATTRIBUTED TO NORTH ITALIAN, 15TH OR 16TH CENTURY<br>*A Dancing Faun* | 1957.14.15<br>PROBABLY ITALIAN 15TH CENTURY<br>*A Dancing Faun* |
| A-131<br>NORTH ITALIAN, POSSIBLY LEONE LEONI<br>*A Warrior* | 1942.9.137<br>NORTH ITALIAN (PADUAN?) 16TH CENTURY<br>*A Warrior* |
| A-1659<br>ORCAGNA<br>*Angel with Hurdy-Gurdy* | 1960.5.14<br>POSSIBLY PISAN 14TH CENTURY<br>*Angel with Symphonia* |

| Formerly | Currently |
|---|---|
| A-1660<br>ORCAGNA<br>*Angel with Tambourine* | 1960.5.15<br>POSSIBLY PISAN 14TH CENTURY<br>*Angel with Tambourine* |
| A-61<br>GERMAIN PILON<br>*Allegory of Victory* | 1943.4.86<br>BARTHÉLEMY PRIEUR<br>*Justice* |
| A-1765<br>GUGLIELMO DELLA PORTA<br>*Paul III* | 1975.6.1<br>PROBABLY NEAPOLITAN 19TH/20TH CENTURY<br>*Paul III (Farnese), Pope* |
| A-40<br>PYRGOTELES<br>*Madonna and Child with Saints* | 1939.1.336<br>LOMBARD 16TH CENTURY<br>*Madonna and Child with Saints and Donors* |
| A-1640<br>AUGUSTE RENOIR<br>*Coco* | 1954.8.2<br>AUGUSTE RENOIR<br>*Claude Renoir ("Coco")* |
| A-1711<br>AUGUSTE RENOIR<br>*Coco* | 1963.10.242<br>AUGUSTE RENOIR<br>*Claude Renoir ("Coco")* |
| A-143<br>MIDDLE RHENISH SCHOOL<br>*Pietà* | 1942.11.2<br>GERMAN OR NETHERLANDISH 15TH CENTURY<br>*Pietà* |
| A-144<br>UPPER RHENISH SCHOOL<br>*The Dead Christ Supported by an Angel (The Trinity)* | 1942.11.3<br>RHENISH OR SOUTH NETHERLANDISH 15TH CENTURY<br>*The Dead Christ Supported by an Angel (The Trinity)* |
| A-13<br>ANDREA DELLA ROBBIA<br>*The Virgin in Adoration* | 1937.1.124<br>ITALIAN 19TH CENTURY<br>*The Virgin in Adoration* |
| A-11<br>STUDIO OF ANDREA DELLA ROBBIA<br>*Madonna and Child with Cherubim* | 1937.1.122<br>ANDREA DELLA ROBBIA<br>*Madonna and Child with Cherubim* |
| A-83<br>AUGUSTE RODIN<br>*Woman and Child* | 1942.5.19<br>AUGUSTE RODIN<br>*Young Woman and Winged Child* |
| A-87<br>AUGUSTE RODIN<br>*Study for "The Lovers," Gates of Hell* | 1942.5.23<br>AUGUSTE RODIN<br>*The Lovers* |
| A-89<br>AUGUSTE RODIN<br>*Study for "St. John the Baptist," Gates of Hell* | 1942.5.25<br>AUGUSTE RODIN<br>*Head of Saint John the Baptist* |

| Formerly | Currently |
|---|---|
| A-21<br>Jacopo Sansovino<br>*Venus Anadyomene* | 1937.1.132<br>Milanese 16th Century<br>*Venus* |
| A-22<br>Jacopo Sansovino<br>*Bacchus and a Young Faun* | 1937.1.133<br>Probably Milanese 16th Century<br>*Bacchus and a Faun* |
| A-138<br>Jacopo Sansovino<br>*Pietro Aretino* | 1942.9.145<br>Paduan 16th Century<br>*A Jurist* |
| A-1645a<br>Jacopo Sansovino<br>*Andiron with Figure of Mars* | 1961.9.100<br>Circle of Tiziano Aspetti<br>*Andiron with Figure of Mars* |
| A-1645b<br>Jacopo Sansovino<br>*Andiron with Figure of Venus* | 1961.9.101<br>Circle of Girolamo Campagna<br>*Andiron with Figure of Venus* |
| A-170<br>Attributed to Severo da Ravenna<br>*Saint Sebastian* | 1957.14.17<br>Severo da Ravenna<br>*Saint Sebastian* |
| A-155<br>Sienese School, Late 15th Century<br>*The Capitoline Wolf* | 1957.14.8<br>Central Italian (Roman?) 15th or 16th Century<br>*The She-Wolf Suckling Romulus and Remus* |
| A-66<br>Cristoforo Solari<br>*The Man of Sorrows* | 1961.9.94<br>Milanese 16th Century<br>*The Man of Sorrows* |
| A-184<br>South German, first half 16th Century<br>*Female Nude (Lucretia?)* | 1957.14.31<br>German 16th Century (Southern)<br>*Venus* |
| A-41<br>Jean Baptiste Tubi<br>*Cherubs Playing with a Swan* | 1940.1.15<br>Jean-Baptiste Tuby I<br>*Cherubs Playing with a Swan* |
| A-203<br>Venetian<br>*Cupid on a Dolphin* | 1957.14.50<br>Workshop of Francesco Fanelli<br>*Cupid on a Dolphin* |
| A-137a<br>Venetian School, 17th Century<br>*Andiron Representing Jupiter* | 1942.9.143<br>Italian 17th/19th Century<br>*Andiron with Figure of Jupiter* |
| A-137b<br>Venetian School, 17th Century<br>*Andiron Representing Juno* | 1942.9.144<br>Italian 17th/19th Century<br>*Andiron with Figure of Juno* |
| A-139<br>Venetian School, 16th Century<br>*Portrait of an Old Woman* | 1942.9.146<br>Venetian 16th Century<br>*Agnesina Badoer Giustinian* |

| Formerly | Currently |
|---|---|
| A-37<br>Andrea del Verrocchio<br>*The Adoration of the Shepherds* | 1939.1.333<br>Francesco di Simone Ferrucci<br>*The Adoration of the Shepherds* |
| A-1669<br>Andrea del Verrocchio<br>*Alexander the Great* | 1956.2.1<br>After Andrea del Verrocchio<br>*Alexander the Great* |
| A-60<br>Alessandro Vittoria<br>*Jacopo Contarini* | 1943.4.85<br>Attributed to Jacopo Albarelli<br>*A Knight of Santiago* |
| A-1666<br>Alessandro Vittoria<br>*Portrait of a Young Knight* | 1961.9.106<br>Alessandro Vittoria<br>*A Gentleman of the Zorzi Family* |
| A-1667<br>Alessandro Vittoria<br>*Andriana Palma, Wife of Palma Giovane* | 1961.9.107<br>Alessandro Vittoria<br>*A Lady of the Zorzi Family* |
| A-141<br>Adriaen de Vries<br>*Virtue and Vice* | 1942.9.148<br>Adriaen de Vries<br>*Empire Triumphant Over Avarice* |

# CONCORDANCE OF OLD AND NEW ACCESSION NUMBERS

| Old | New | Artist and Title |
|---|---|---|
| A-1 | 1937.1.112 | FLORENTINE 15TH CENTURY<br>*Madonna and Child* |
| A-2 | 1937.1.113 | DESIDERIO DA SETTIGNANO<br>*A Little Boy* |
| A-3 | 1937.1.114 | FLORENTINE 19TH CENTURY<br>*Madonna and Child* |
| A-4 | 1937.1.115 | STYLE OF DESIDERIO DA SETTIGNANO<br>*Christ with Saint John the Baptist as Children* |
| A-5 | 1937.1.116 | AGOSTINO DI DUCCIO<br>*Madonna and Child* |
| A-6 | 1937.1.117 | MINO DA FIESOLE<br>*Charity* |
| A-7 | 1937.1.118 | MINO DA FIESOLE<br>*Faith* |
| A-8 | 1937.1.119 | FRANCESCO LAURANA<br>*A Princess of the House of Aragon* |
| A-9 | 1937.1.120 | BENEDETTO BRIOSCO<br>*Lodovico Sforza, Duke of Bari* |
| A-10 | 1937.1.121 | WORKSHOP OF BENEDETTO BRIOSCO<br>*Gian Galeazzo Maria Sforza, Duke of Milan* |
| A-11 | 1937.1.122 | ANDREA DELLA ROBBIA<br>*Madonna and Child with Cherubim* |
| A-12 | 1937.1.123 | STUDIO OF ANDREA DELLA ROBBIA<br>*Madonna and Child with God the Father and Cherubim* |
| A-13 | 1937.1.124 | ITALIAN 19TH CENTURY<br>*The Virgin in Adoration* |
| A-14 | 1937.1.125 | ANTONIO ROSSELLINO<br>*Madonna and Child* |
| A-15 | 1937.1.126 | ITALIAN 19TH CENTURY<br>*Madonna and Child* |
| A-16 | 1937.1.127 | ANDREA DEL VERROCCHIO<br>*Giuliano de' Medici* |
| A-17 | 1937.1.128 | ANDREA DEL VERROCCHIO<br>*Putto Poised on a Globe* |
| A-18 | 1937.1.129 | GIOVANNI BASTIANINI<br>*Portrait of a Lady, "Giovanna Albizzi"* |
| A-19 | 1937.1.130 | BENEDETTO DA MAIANO<br>*Saint John the Baptist* |
| A-20 | 1937.1.131 | ATTRIBUTED TO FRANCESCO RIGHETTI, AFTER GIOVANNI BOLOGNA<br>*Mercury* |
| A-21 | 1937.1.132 | MILANESE 16TH CENTURY<br>*Venus* |
| A-22 | 1937.1.133 | PROBABLY MILANESE 16TH CENTURY<br>*Bacchus and a Faun* |
| A-23 | 1939.1.319 | AFTER ANNIBALE FONTANA<br>*The Adoration of the Shepherds* |
| A-24 | 1939.1.320 | GIOVANNI ANTONIO AMADEO<br>*Kneeling Angel* |
| A-25 | 1939.1.321 | WORKSHOP OF GIOVANNI ANTONIO AMADEO<br>*Kneeling Angel* |
| A-30 | 1939.1.326 | ANDREA DEL VERROCCHIO<br>*A Lady of the Vespucci Family (?)* |
| A-31 | 1939.1.327 | ANTONIO ROSSELLINO<br>*Madonna and Child* |

| Old | New | Artist and Title |
|---|---|---|
| A-32 | 1939.1.328 | Domenico Gagini<br>*The Nativity* |
| A-33 | 1939.1.329 | Andrea della Robbia<br>*Saint Peter* |
| A-37 | 1939.1.333 | Francesco di Simone Ferrucci<br>*The Adoration of the Shepherds* |
| A-40 | 1939.1.336 | Lombard 16th Century<br>*Madonna and Child with Saints and Donors* |
| A-41 | 1940.1.15 | Jean-Baptiste Tuby I<br>*Cherubs Playing with a Swan* |
| A-42 | 1940.1.16 | Pierre Legros I<br>*Cherubs Playing with a Lyre* |
| A-43 | 1940.2.2 | Claude Michel, called Clodion<br>*Monumental Urn* |
| A-44 | 1940.2.3 | Claude Michel, called Clodion<br>*Monumental Urn* |
| A-45 | 1943.4.70 | Giovanni della Robbia<br>*Pietà* |
| A-46 | 1943.4.71 | Mino da Fiesole<br>*The Virgin Annunciate* |
| A-47 | 1943.4.72 | Pietro Lombardo<br>*Allegorical Figure* |
| A-48 | 1943.4.73 | Giovanni della Robbia<br>*The Young Christ (?)* |
| A-49 | 1943.4.74 | Imitator of Antonio del Pollaiuolo<br>*Bust of a Warrior* |
| A-50 | 1943.4.75 | Florentine 16th Century<br>*A Gentleman* |
| A-51 | 1943.4.76 | Matteo Civitali<br>*Saint Sebastian* |
| A-52 | 1943.4.77 | Imitator of Benedetto Briosco<br>*Filippo Maria Visconti* |
| A-53 | 1943.4.78 | After Antonio Rossellino<br>*Madonna and Child with Angels* |
| A-54 | 1943.4.79 | Antonio Rossellino<br>*The Young Saint John the Baptist* |
| A-55 | 1943.4.80 | After Mino da Fiesole<br>*Rinaldo della Luna* |
| A-56 | 1943.4.81 | Master of the David and Saint John Statuettes<br>*David* |
| A-57 | 1943.4.82 | Italian 20th Century<br>*Madonna Adoring the Child* |
| A-58 | 1943.4.83 | Style of Desiderio da Settignano<br>*Saint John the Baptist* |
| A-59 | 1943.4.84 | Attributed to Giovanni Battista Caccini<br>*Giovanni Capponi* |
| A-60 | 1943.4.85 | Attributed to Jacopo Albarelli<br>*A Knight of Santiago* |
| A-61 | 1943.4.86 | Barthélemy Prieur<br>*Justice* |
| A-62 | 1943.4.87 | After Gian Lorenzo Bernini<br>*Louis XIV* |
| A-63 | 1943.4.88 | Jacques Prou II<br>*Philippe, Duc D'Orleans* |
| A-64 | 1943.4.89 | Jean-Baptiste Carpeaux<br>*Neapolitan Fisherboy* |
| A-65 | 1943.4.90 | Jean-Baptiste Carpeaux<br>*Girl with a Shell* |
| A-66 | 1961.9.94 | Milanese 16th Century<br>*The Man of Sorrows* |
| A-67 | 1942.5.3 | Auguste Rodin<br>*Bust of a Woman* |
| A-68 | 1942.5.4 | Auguste Rodin<br>*Bust of a Young Girl* |
| A-69 | 1942.5.5 | Auguste Rodin<br>*Statuette of a Woman* |
| A-70 | 1942.5.6 | Auguste Rodin<br>*Statuette of a Woman* |
| A-71 | 1942.5.7 | Auguste Rodin<br>*Eve Eating the Apple* |
| A-72 | 1942.5.8 | Auguste Rodin<br>*Female Hand (Pianist)* |
| A-73 | 1942.5.9 | Auguste Rodin<br>*La France* |

| Old | New | Artist and Title |
|---|---|---|
| A-74 | 1942.5.10 | AUGUSTE RODIN<br>*The Age of Bronze* |
| A-75 | 1942.5.11 | AUGUSTE RODIN<br>*The Walking Man* |
| A-76 | 1942.5.12 | AUGUSTE RODIN<br>*The Thinker* |
| A-77 | 1942.5.13 | AUGUSTE RODIN<br>*A Burgher of Calais* |
| A-78 | 1942.5.14 | AUGUSTE RODIN<br>*Head of Balzac* |
| A-79 | 1942.5.15 | AUGUSTE RODIN<br>*The Kiss* |
| A-80 | 1942.5.16 | AUGUSTE RODIN<br>*Mrs. John W. Simpson* |
| A-81 | 1942.5.17 | AUGUSTE RODIN<br>*The Evil Spirits* |
| A-82 | 1942.5.18 | AUGUSTE RODIN<br>*Morning* |
| A-83 | 1942.5.19 | AUGUSTE RODIN<br>*Young Woman and Winged Child* |
| A-84 | 1942.5.20 | AUGUSTE RODIN<br>*Aurora and Tithonus* |
| A-85 | 1942.5.21 | AUGUSTE RODIN<br>*Mask of Mrs. Simpson* |
| A-86 | 1942.5.22 | AUGUSTE RODIN<br>*Hand of Rodin with Female Figure* |
| A-87 | 1942.5.23 | AUGUSTE RODIN<br>*The Lovers* |
| A-88 | 1942.5.24 | AUGUSTE RODIN<br>*Head of a Woman* |
| A-89 | 1942.5.25 | AUGUSTE RODIN<br>*Head of Saint John the Baptist* |
| A-90 | 1942.5.26 | AUGUSTE RODIN<br>*Hand of a Pianist* |
| A-91 | 1942.5.27 | AUGUSTE RODIN<br>*Hand of a Pianist* |
| A-92 | 1942.5.28 | AUGUSTE RODIN<br>*Study for a Hand of a Burgher of Calais* |
| A-93 | 1942.5.29 | AUGUSTE RODIN<br>*Left Hand* |
| A-94 | 1942.5.30 | AUGUSTE RODIN<br>*Right Foot* |
| A-95 | 1942.5.31 | CLAUDE MICHEL, CALLED CLODION<br>*Satyrs at Play* |
| A-96 | 1942.9.102 | GERMAN 16TH CENTURY<br>*Samson Slaying the Philistine* |
| A-97 | 1942.9.103 | AFTER BARTOLOMEO BELLANO<br>*David* |
| A-98 | 1942.9.104 | SEVERO DA RAVENNA<br>*Neptune on a Sea Monster* |
| A-99 | 1942.9.105 | GIOVANNI BASTIANINI<br>*Pietro Talani* |
| A-100 | 1942.9.106 | VINCENZO ONOFRI<br>*Portrait of a Nobleman* |
| A-101 | 1942.9.107 | ROMAN 16TH/17TH CENTURY<br>*Virtue Overcoming Vice* |
| A-102 | 1942.9.108 | FRENCH 19TH CENTURY, AFTER JEAN-HONORÉ FRAGONARD<br>*Bacchanal* |
| A-103 | 1942.9.109 | CLAUDE MICHEL, CALLED CLODION<br>*Faun Family* |
| A-104 | 1942.9.110 | ANTOINE COYSEVOX<br>*Louis II de Bourbon, Prince de Condé* |
| A-105 | 1942.9.111 | VINCENZO DANTI<br>*The Descent from the Cross* |
| A-106 | 1942.9.112 | DESIDERIO DA SETTIGNANO<br>*"Marietta Strozzi"* |
| A-107 | 1942.9.113 | DESIDERIO DA SETTIGNANO<br>*Saint Jerome in the Desert* |
| A-108 | 1942.9.114 | ATTRIBUTED TO LUCAS FAYDHERBE<br>*Cupid (?)* |
| A-109 | 1942.9.115 | BERNARDO ROSSELLINO OR ANTONIO ROSSELLINO<br>*The David of the Casa Martelli* |

| Old | New | Artist and Title |
|---|---|---|
| A-110 | 1942.9.116 | Étienne-Maurice Falconet<br>*The Punishment of Cupid* |
| A-111 | 1942.9.117 | Venetian 16th Century<br>*Mercury* |
| A-112 | 1942.9.118 | Florentine 16th Century<br>*Brunaccino Rinaldi* |
| A-113 | 1942.9.119 | Paduan 16th Century<br>*Hercules and Antaeus* |
| A-114 | 1942.9.120 | German 17th Century<br>*A Dancing Faun* |
| A-115 | 1942.9.121 | After Giovanni Bologna, called Giambologna<br>*Hercules Carrying the Erymanthian Boar* |
| A-116 | 1942.9.122 | North Italian 16th Century<br>*Rearing Horse* |
| A-117 | 1942.9.123 | Jean-Antoine Houdon<br>*Alexandre Brongniart* |
| A-118 | 1942.9.124 | Jean-Antoine Houdon<br>*Louise Brongniart* |
| A-119 | 1942.9.125 | Imitator of Jean-Antoine Houdon<br>*Alexandre Brongniart* |
| A-120 | 1942.9.126 | Imitator of Jean-Antoine Houdon<br>*Louise Brongniart* |
| A-121 | 1942.9.127 | Jean-Antoine Houdon<br>*Voltaire* |
| A-122 | 1942.9.128 | Jacques-François-Joseph Saly<br>*Bust of a Little Girl* |
| A-123 | 1942.9.129 | Giovanni Battista Foggini<br>*Ferdinando II de' Medici, Grand Duke of Tuscany* |
| A-124 | 1942.9.130 | Giovanni Battista Foggini<br>*Vittoria della Rovere, Wife of Ferdinando II* |
| A-125 | 1942.9.131 | Benedetto da Rovezzano<br>*Relief from an Altar or Tabernacle* |
| A-126 | 1942.9.132 | Circle of Guglielmo della Porta<br>*Cup with Allegorical Scenes and Shields of Este Arms* |
| A-127 | 1942.9.133 | Jean-Louis Lemoyne<br>*A Companion of Diana* |
| A-128 | 1942.9.134 | Master of the Marble Madonnas<br>*The Young Saint John the Baptist* |
| A-129 | 1942.9.135 | Mino da Fiesole<br>*Astorgio Manfredi* |
| A-130 | 1942.9.136 | North Italian 16th Century<br>*Bust of a Man* |
| A-131 | 1942.9.137 | North Italian (Paduan?) 16th Century<br>*A Warrior* |
| A-132 | 1942.9.138 | North Italian 16th Century<br>*Seated Female Figure* |
| A-133 | 1942.9.139 | Attributed to Agostino Zoppo<br>*Incense Burner* |
| A-134 | 1942.9.140 | North Italian (Paduan?) 16th Century<br>*Inkstand with Bound Satyrs and Three Labors of Hercules* |
| A-135 | 1942.9.141 | Luca della Robbia<br>*Madonna and Child* |
| A-136 | 1942.9.142 | Antonio Rossellino<br>*The Young Saint John the Baptist* |
| A-137 | 1942.9.143 | Italian 17th/19th Century<br>*Andiron with Figure of Jupiter* |
| A-137 | 1942.9.144 | Italian 17th/19th Century<br>*Andiron with Figure of Juno* |
| A-138 | 1942.9.145 | Paduan 16th Century<br>*A Jurist* |
| A-139 | 1942.9.146 | Venetian 16th Century<br>*Agnesina Badoer Giustinian* |
| A-140 | 1942.9.147 | Follower of Andrea del Verrocchio<br>*Virgin and Child with Saint John* |
| A-141 | 1942.9.148 | Adriaen di Vries<br>*Empire Triumphant over Avarice* |

| Old | New | Artist and Title |
|---|---|---|
| A-142 | 1942.11.1 | PROBABLY HELLENISTIC SCHOOL, EGYPT<br>*Head of a Youth (Dionysos or a Follower?)* |
| A-143 | 1942.11.2 | GERMAN OR NETHERLANDISH 15TH CENTURY<br>*Pietà* |
| A-144 | 1942.11.3 | RHENISH OR SOUTH NETHERLANDISH 15TH CENTURY<br>*The Dead Christ Supported by an Angel (The Trinity)* |
| A-145 | 1942.12.1 | CLAUDE MICHEL, CALLED CLODION<br>*The Surprise* |
| A-146 | 1943.4.92 | ANDREA DEL VERROCCHIO<br>*Lorenzo de' Medici* |
| A-147 | 1943.4.93 | FLORENTINE 15TH CENTURY<br>*Madonna and Child* |
| A-148 | 1943.4.94 | DESIDERIO DA SETTIGNANO<br>*The Christ Child (?)* |
| A-150 | 1953.2.1 | ENGLISH OR SPANISH 14TH CENTURY<br>*The Holy Trinity* |
| A-151 | 1953.2.2 | ENGLISH 14TH OR 15TH CENTURY<br>*Saint George and the Dragon* |
| A-152 | 1961.1.1 | TILMAN RIEMENSCHNEIDER<br>*Saint Burchard of Würzburg* |
| A-153 | 1957.14.7 | ROMAN 18TH/19TH CENTURY<br>*Lion* |
| A-154 | 1961.9.95 | VERONESE 14TH CENTURY<br>*Madonna and Child with Two Angels* |
| A-155 | 1957.14.8 | CENTRAL ITALIAN (ROMAN?) 15TH OR 16TH CENTURY<br>*The She-Wolf Suckling Romulus and Remus* |
| A-156 | 1960.5.1 | TINO DA CAMAINO<br>*Madonna and Child with Queen Sancia, Saints and Angels* |
| A-157 | 1960.5.2 | JACOPO DELLA QUERCIA<br>*Madonna of Humility* |
| A-158 | 1960.5.3 | CRISTOFORO SOLARI<br>*Madonna and Child* |
| A-159 | 1961.1.2 | ANDREA DELLA ROBBIA<br>*The Adoration of the Child* |
| A-160 | 1945.16.1 | LODOVICO LOMBARDO<br>*The Emperor Hadrian* |
| A-161 | 1961.9.96 | FLORENTINE 19TH CENTURY<br>*Madonna with the Sleeping Child* |
| A-162 | 1961.1.3 | LUCA DELLA ROBBIA<br>*The Nativity* |
| A-163 | 1948.15.1 | FLORENTINE OR NEAPOLITAN 16TH CENTURY<br>*Don Pedro Alvarez de Toledo (1484-1553)* |
| A-164 | 1957.14.11 | ANDREA RICCIO (ANDREA BRIOSCO), CALLED RICCIO<br>*The Entombment* |
| A-165 | 1957.14.12 | FRANCESCO DI GIORGIO MARTINI<br>*Saint Jerome* |
| A-166 | 1957.14.13 | IMITATOR OF DESIDERIO DA SETTIGNANO<br>*Saint John the Baptist* |
| A-167 | 1957.14.14 | NORTH ITALIAN 16TH CENTURY<br>*The Spinario* |
| A-168 | 1957.14.15 | PROBABLY ITALIAN 15TH CENTURY<br>*A Dancing Faun* |
| A-169 | 1957.14.16 | PROBABLY NORTH ITALIAN 15TH CENTURY<br>*Saint George and the Dragon* |
| A-170 | 1957.14.17 | SEVERO DA RAVENNA<br>*Saint Sebastian* |
| A-171 | 1957.14.18 | WORKSHOP OF ANDREA RICCIO (ANDREA BRIOSCO), CALLED RICCIO<br>*Judith with the Head of Holofernes* |
| A-172 | 1957.14.19 | SEVERO DA RAVENNA<br>*Arion Seated on a Shell* |
| A-173 | 1957.14.20 | ANDREA RICCIO (ANDREA BRIOSCO), CALLED RICCIO<br>*Pomona* |
| A-174 | 1957.14.21 | NORTH ITALIAN 16TH CENTURY<br>*A Seated Nymph* |

| Old | New | Artist and Title |
|---|---|---|
| A-176 | 1957.14.23 | VENETIAN 16TH CENTURY<br>*Fortuna* |
| A-177 | 1957.14.24 | PROBABLY FRENCH (POSSIBLY BARTHÉLEMY PRIEUR) 17TH CENTURY<br>*Woman Cutting Her Nails* |
| A-178 | 1957.14.25 | POSSIBLY FLORENTINE 16TH CENTURY<br>*Male Nude with Raised Left Arm* |
| A-179 | 1957.14.26 | AFTER MICHELANGELO BUONARROTI<br>*Bacchus* |
| A-180 | 1957.14.27 | SPANISH 16TH CENTURY<br>*Kneeling Supplicant* |
| A-181 | 1957.14.28 | SPANISH 16TH CENTURY<br>*Kneeling Supplicant* |
| A-182 | 1957.14.29 | VENETIAN 16TH CENTURY<br>*Charity* |
| A-183 | 1957.14.30 | PROBABLY FRENCH 19TH CENTURY<br>*The Virgin of the Annunciation* |
| A-184 | 1957.14.31 | GERMAN 16TH CENTURY (SOUTHERN)<br>*Venus* |
| A-185 | 1957.14.32 | AFTER ANDREA RICCIO (ANDREA BRIOSCO), CALLED RICCIO<br>*Bound Satyr* |
| A-186 | 1957.14.33 | ANDREA RICCIO (ANDREA BRIOSCO), CALLED RICCIO<br>*Bound Satyr* |
| A-187 | 1957.14.34 | NORTH ITALIAN (PADUAN?) 16TH CENTURY<br>*Seated Boy Holding a Jar (an Inkwell ?)* |
| A-188 | 1957.14.35 | WORKSHOP OF ANDREA RICCIO (ANDREA BRIOSCO), CALLED RICCIO<br>*Inkwell in the Form of a Child Carrying a Shell* |
| A-189 | 1957.14.36 | ITALIAN 15TH OR 16TH CENTURY<br>*Cupid with Raised Arms* |
| A-190 | 1957.14.37 | ITALIAN 15TH CENTURY<br>*Cupid* |
| A-191 | 1957.14.38 | VENETIAN 15TH CENTURY<br>*Winged Boy with Hands Raised* |
| A-192 | 1957.14.39 | VENETIAN 15TH CENTURY<br>*Wreathed Boy with Hands Raised* |
| A-193 | 1957.14.40 | GERMAN 16TH CENTURY (POSSIBLY NUREMBERG)<br>*A Child with a Crow* |
| A-194 | 1957.14.41 | FLEMISH 16TH CENTURY<br>*Three Cupids* |
| A-195 | 1957.14.42 | ATTRIBUTED TO A FOLLOWER OF PETER FLÖTNER<br>*A Child on a Dolphin* |
| A-196 | 1957.14.43 | GERMAN 16TH CENTURY (POSSIBLY SOUTHERN)<br>*A Child with a Puppy* |
| A-197 | 1957.14.44 | ITALIAN 16TH CENTURY<br>*A Child Standing* |
| A-198 | 1957.14.45 | ATTRIBUTED TO WORKSHOP OF SEVERO DA RAVENNA<br>*Standing Boy* |
| A-199 | 1957.14.46 | ITALIAN 16TH CENTURY<br>*A Child Standing* |
| A-200 | 1957.14.47 | ITALIAN 16TH CENTURY<br>*A Triton* |
| A-201 | 1957.14.48 | ITALIAN 16TH CENTURY<br>*Standing Child with Raised Left Arm* |
| A-202 | 1957.14.49 | NORTH ITALIAN 16TH OR 17TH CENTURY<br>*Child Clasping a Bird* |
| A-203 | 1957.14.50 | WORKSHOP OF FRANCESCO FANELLI<br>*Cupid on a Dolphin* |
| A-204 | 1957.14.51 | HELLENISTIC OR ROMAN 2D CENTURY B.C.–1ST CENTURY A.D.<br>*Winged Child Carrying a Torch* |
| A-205 | 1957.14.52 | HELLENISTIC OR ROMAN 2D CENTURY B.C.–1ST CENTURY A.D.<br>*Striding Cupid* |
| A-206 | 1957.14.53 | SEVERO DA RAVENNA<br>*The Christ Child* |

| Old | New | Artist and Title |
|---|---|---|
| A-207 | 1957.14.54 | VENETIAN 16TH CENTURY<br>*Head of a Moor* |
| A-208 | 1957.14.55 | ANDREA RICCIO (ANDREA BRIOSCO), CALLED RICCIO<br>*Bust of a Youth (Saint John?)* |
| A-209 | 1957.14.56 | ANDREA RICCIO (ANDREA BRIOSCO), CALLED RICCIO<br>*Bust of a Man (Vulcan?)* |
| A-210 | 1957.14.57 | ANDREA RICCIO (ANDREA BRIOSCO), CALLED RICCIO<br>*Head of a Faun* |
| A-211 | 1957.14.58 | WORKSHOP OF ANDREA RICCIO (ANDREA BRIOSCO), CALLED RICCIO<br>*Lamp in the Form of a Satyr's Head* |
| A-213 | 1957.14.60 | NORTH ITALIAN (MANTUAN?) 16TH CENTURY<br>*Writing Casket with Scenes from the Life of Saint Simeon of Podirolo* |
| A-214 | 1957.14.61 | PADUAN 16TH CENTURY<br>*Writing Casket* |
| A-215 | 1957.14.62 | PADUAN 16TH CENTURY<br>*Sand-Box* |
| A-216 | 1957.14.63 | FOLLOWER OF ANDREA RICCIO (ANDREA BRIOSCO), CALLED RICCIO<br>*Sand-Box (Triangular)* |
| A-217 | 1957.14.64 | PADUAN 16TH CENTURY<br>*Box* |
| A-218 | 1957.14.65 | PADUAN 16TH CENTURY<br>*Lid of a Box* |
| A-219 | 1957.14.66 | ANDREA RICCIO (ANDREA BRIOSCO), CALLED RICCIO<br>*Three Wick Lamp with Bacchic Scenes* |
| A-220 | 1957.14.67 | PADUAN 16TH CENTURY<br>*Lamp* |
| A-221 | 1957.14.68 | WORKSHOP OF ANDREA RICCIO (ANDREA BRIOSCO), CALLED RICCIO<br>*Lamp in the Form of an Ass' Head* |
| A-222 | 1957.14.69 | PADUAN 16TH CENTURY<br>*Lamp* |
| A-223 | 1957.14.70 | VENETIAN 16TH CENTURY<br>*Altar-Candlestick with Shield of Arms of the Garzoni of Venice* |
| A-224 | 1957.14.71 | VENETIAN 16TH CENTURY<br>*Altar-Candlestick with Shield of Arms of the Garzoni of Venice* |
| A-225 | 1957.14.72 | FLORENTINE 15TH CENTURY<br>*Romulus and Remus Suckled by a She-Wolf* |
| A-226 | 1957.14.73 | CENTRAL OR NORTH ITALIAN 16TH CENTURY<br>*Pacing Female Panther* |
| A-227 | 1957.14.74 | WORKSHOP OF SEVERO DA RAVENNA<br>*A Sea Monster* |
| A-228 | 1957.14.75 | WORKSHOP OF SEVERO DA RAVENNA<br>*A Sea Monster* |
| A-229 | 1957.14.76 | PROBABLY ITALIAN 16TH/19TH CENTURY<br>*Object with Sphinx Head (Furniture Mount?)* |
| A-230 | 1957.14.77 | ANDREA RICCIO (ANDREA BRIOSCO), CALLED RICCIO<br>*A Goat* |
| A-231 | 1957.14.78 | GERMAN 16TH CENTURY (POSSIBLY NUREMBERG)<br>*A Dog Scratching* |
| A-232 | 1957.14.79 | PADUAN 16TH CENTURY<br>*A Dog* |
| A-233 | 1957.14.80 | PADUAN 16TH CENTURY<br>*A Ram's Head* |
| A-234 | 1957.14.81 | GERMAN 16TH CENTURY<br>*A Bear* |
| A-235 | 1957.14.82 | PADUAN 16TH CENTURY<br>*Small Vase in the Form of a Monkey* |
| A-236 | 1957.14.83 | ITALIAN 16TH CENTURY<br>*A Cock* |
| A-237 | 1957.14.84 | ITALIAN 16TH CENTURY<br>*A Crow* |
| A-238 | 1957.14.85 | CASPAR GRAS<br>*A Crow* |

| Old | New | Artist and Title |
|---|---|---|
| A-239 | 1957.14.86 | Paduan 15th or 16th Century<br>*Box in the Form of a Crab* |
| A-240 | 1957.14.87 | Andrea Riccio (Andrea Briosco), called Riccio<br>*A Crab on a Toad* |
| A-241 | 1957.14.88 | Paduan 16th Century<br>*A Toad with a Toad* |
| A-242 | 1957.14.89 | Attributed to Workshop of Andrea Riccio (Andrea Briosco), called Riccio<br>*Inkwell in the Form of a Frog beside a Tree Stump* |
| A-243 | 1957.14.90 | Paduan 16th Century<br>*A Toad* |
| A-244 | 1957.14.91 | Paduan 16th Century<br>*A Large Toad* |
| A-245 | 1957.14.92 | Paduan 16th Century<br>*A Frog* |
| A-246 | 1957.14.93 | Paduan 16th Century<br>*A Toad* |
| A-247 | 1957.14.94 | Paduan 16th Century<br>*A Toad* |
| A-248 | 1957.14.95 | Paduan or Venetian 15th or 16th Century<br>*Bowl* |
| A-249 | 1957.14.96 | Veneto-Islamic 16th Century<br>*Bowl* |
| A-250 | 1957.14.97 | Probably Venetian 16th Century<br>*Mortar* |
| A-251 | 1957.14.98 | Italian 16th Century<br>*Mortar* |
| A-252 | 1957.14.99 | Italian 16th Century<br>*Mortar* |
| A-253 | 1957.14.100.a | Italian 16th Century<br>*Mortar with Rope-Shaped Handle* |
| A-253 | 1957.14.100.b | Italian 16th Century<br>*Pestle* |
| A-254 | 1957.14.101 | Italian 16th Century<br>*Mortar* |
| A-255 | 1957.14.102 | Italian 16th Century<br>*Mortar* |
| A-256 | 1957.14.103 | Probably Venetian 16th Century<br>*Mortar with Shields of Badoer Arms* |
| A-257 | 1957.14.104 | Italian 16th Century<br>*Mortar* |
| A-258 | 1957.14.105 | Italian 16th Century<br>*Mortar* |
| A-259 | 1957.14.106 | Italian 16th Century<br>*Mortar* |
| A-260 | 1957.14.107 | Italian 16th Century<br>*Mortar* |
| A-261 | 1957.14.108 | Italian 16th Century<br>*Mortar* |
| A-262 | 1957.14.109 | Italian 16th Century<br>*Mortar* |
| A-263 | 1957.14.110 | Giovanni I Alberghetti<br>*Table-Bell with Portrait of Lodovico Maria Sforza, 1451–1508, called Il Moro, 7th Duke of Milan 1494–1508* |
| A-264 | 1957.14.111 | Italian 16th Century<br>*Table-Bell* |
| A-265 | 1957.14.112 | Probably Venetian 16th Century<br>*Table-Bell* |
| A-266 | 1957.14.113 | Italian 16th Century<br>*Table-Bell* |
| A-267 | 1957.14.114 | North Italian 16th Century<br>*Table-Bell* |
| A-268 | 1957.14.115 | Probably Venetian 16th Century<br>*Table-Bell* |
| A-269 | 1957.14.116 | Probably Paduan 15th or 16th Century<br>*Table-Bell* |
| A-270 | 1957.14.117 | North Italian 16th Century<br>*Table-Bell (Orpheus)* |
| A-271 | 1957.14.118 | Flemish 16th Century<br>*Table-Bell* |

| Old | New | Artist and Title |
|---|---|---|
| A-272 | 1957.14.119 | PROBABLY PADUAN 15TH OR 16TH CENTURY<br>*Door Knocker* |
| A-273 | 1957.14.120 | ITALIAN 16TH CENTURY<br>*Door Knocker* |
| A-274 | 1957.14.121 | ITALIAN 16TH CENTURY<br>*Door Knocker* |
| A-275 | 1957.14.122 | ITALIAN 16TH CENTURY<br>*Door Knocker* |
| A-400 | 1957.14.247 | FRANCESCO DI GIORGIO MARTINI<br>*Saint Sebastian* |
| A-401 | 1957.14.248 | FRANCESCO DI GIORGIO MARTINI<br>*Saint John the Baptist* |
| A-1471 | 1942.9.149.a | PADUAN 15TH CENTURY<br>*Cover of a Writing Casket: Geniuses with Wreath and Medusa Head* |
| A-1471 | 1942.9.149.b | PADUAN 15TH CENTURY<br>*Front of a Writing Casket: Centaurs and Nymphs with Cornucopiae and Bust* |
| A-1471 | 1942.9.149.c | PADUAN 15TH CENTURY<br>*End Panel of a Writing Casket: Medusa Head, Garland and Bucrania* |
| A-1472 | 1942.9.150.a | AFTER ANDREA RICCIO (ANDREA BRIOSCO), CALLED RICCIO<br>*Lamp in Two Parts* |
| A-1472 | 1942.9.150.b | AFTER ANDREA RICCIO (ANDREA BRIOSCO), CALLED RICCIO<br>*Lamp in Two Parts* |
| A-1598 | 1951.17.1 | IMITATOR OF HONORÉ DAUMIER<br>*The Laughing Man* |
| A-1599 | 1951.17.2 | IMITATOR OF HONORÉ DAUMIER<br>*Man in a Tall Hat* |
| A-1600 | 1951.17.3 | HONORÉ DAUMIER<br>*Ratapoil* |
| A-1601 | 1951.17.4 | HONORÉ DAUMIER<br>*Hippolyte-Abraham (?) Dubois* |
| A-1602 | 1951.17.5 | HONORÉ DAUMIER<br>*Antoine-Maurice-Apollinaire, Comte D'Argout* |
| A-1603 | 1951.17.6 | HONORÉ DAUMIER<br>*François-Dominique-Reynaud, Comte de Montlosier* |
| A-1604 | 1951.17.7 | HONORÉ DAUMIER<br>*Laurent Cunin, Called Cunin-Gridaine* |
| A-1605 | 1951.17.8 | HONORÉ DAUMIER<br>*Jacques-Antoine-Adrien, Baron Delort* |
| A-1606 | 1951.17.9 | HONORÉ DAUMIER<br>*Charles-Guillaume Etienne* |
| A-1607 | 1951.17.10 | HONORÉ DAUMIER<br>*Joachim-Antoine-Joseph Gaudry* |
| A-1608 | 1951.17.11 | HONORÉ DAUMIER<br>*François-Pierre-Guillaume Guizot* |
| A-1609 | 1951.17.12 | HONORÉ DAUMIER<br>*Père Jean-Marie Harlé* |
| A-1610 | 1951.17.13 | HONORÉ DAUMIER<br>*Jacques Lefebvre* |
| A-1611 | 1951.17.14 | HONORÉ DAUMIER<br>*Alexandre-Simon Pataille* |
| A-1612 | 1951.17.15 | HONORÉ DAUMIER<br>*Nicolas Soult (?)* |
| A-1613 | 1952.5.89 | ITALIAN 16TH CENTURY<br>*Eagle* |
| A-1614 | 1952.5.90 | BENEDETTO BRIOSCO AND TOMMASSO CAZZANIGA<br>*The Adoration of the Magi* |
| A-1615 | 1952.5.91 | BENEDETTO BRIOSCO AND TOMMASSO CAZZANIGA<br>*The Flight into Egypt* |
| A-1616 | 1952.5.92 | ATTRIBUTED TO GIUSEPPE MAZZUOLI<br>*A Nereid* |
| A-1617 | 1952.5.93 | EDMÉ BOUCHARDON<br>*Cupid* |
| A-1618 | 1952.5.94 | ATTRIBUTED TO FRANCESCO RIGHETTI<br>*Apollino of the Villa Medici* |

| Old | New | Artist and Title |
|---|---|---|
| A-1619 | 1952.5.95 | French 19th Century<br>*Bacchant* |
| A-1620 | 1952.5.96 | French 19th Century<br>*Bacchante* |
| A-1621 | 1952.5.97 | French 19th Century<br>*Bacchante* |
| A-1622 | 1952.5.98 | Claude Michel, called Clodion<br>*Poetry and Music* |
| A-1623 | 1952.5.99 | Claude Michel, called Clodion<br>*A Vestal* |
| A-1624 | 1952.5.100 | Desiderio da Settignano<br>*Ciborium for the Sacrament* |
| A-1625 | 1952.5.101 | Étienne-Maurice Falconet<br>*Venus of the Doves* |
| A-1626 | 1952.5.102 | Probably French or Belgian 19th Century<br>*Saint Barbara* |
| A-1627 | 1952.5.103 | Jean-Antoine Houdon<br>*Giuseppe Balsamo, Comte di Cagliostro* |
| A-1628 | 1952.5.104 | Leone Leoni<br>*Emperor Charles V* |
| A-1629 | 1952.5.105 | Robert Le Lorrain<br>*Galatea* |
| A-1630 | 1952.5.106 | Benoît Massou, Anselme Flamen, and Nicolas Rebillé<br>*A Garden Allegory: The Dew and Zephyr Cultivating Flowers* |
| A-1631 | 1952.5.107 | Augustin Pajou<br>*Calliope* |
| A-1632 | 1961.9.97 | Pisan 14th Century<br>*The Archangel Gabriel* |
| A-1633 | 1961.9.98 | Pisan 14th Century<br>*The Virgin Annunciate* |
| A-1636 | 1952.5.110 | Jean-Pierre-Antoine Tassaert<br>*Painting and Sculpture* |
| A-1637 | 1952.13.1 | Florentine 15th Century<br>*An Old Man* |
| A-1638 | 1953.8.1 | Imitator of Honoré Daumier<br>*The Man of Affairs* |
| A-1639 | 1953.8.2 | Imitator of Honoré Daumier<br>*The Dandy* |
| A-1640 | 1954.8.2 | Auguste Renoir<br>*Claude Renoir ("Coco")* |
| A-1641 | 1954.13.2 | Imitator of Honoré Daumier<br>*The Stroller* |
| A-1642 | 1954.13.3 | Imitator of Honoré Daumier<br>*The Lover* |
| A-1643 | 1960.5.4 | Giovanni di Balduccio<br>*Charity* |
| A-1644 | 1961.9.99 | French 14th Century<br>*Virgin and Child* |
| A-1645 | 1961.9.100 | Circle of Tiziano Aspetti<br>*Andiron with Figure of Mars* |
| A-1645 | 1961.9.101 | Circle of Girolamo Campagna<br>*Andiron with Figure of Venus* |
| A-1646 | 1961.9.102 | Gian Lorenzo Bernini<br>*Monsignor Francesco Barberini* |
| A-1647 | 1960.5.5 | Bonino da Campione<br>*Justice* |
| A-1648 | 1960.5.6 | Bonino da Campione<br>*Prudence* |
| A-1649 | 1960.5.7 | Antoine Coysevox<br>*Louis of France, The Grand Dauphin* |
| A-1650 | 1960.5.8 | French 18th Century<br>*Louis, Duc de Bourgogne* |
| A-1651 | 1961.1.4 | C. Verona<br>*Louis XIV* |
| A-1652 | 1960.5.9 | Florentine 19th Century, after the Master of the Marble Madonnas<br>*Madonna and Child* |
| A-1653 | 1957.14.9 | Lorenzo di Pietro, called Vecchietta<br>*Winged Figure Holding a Torch* |

| Old | New | Artist and Title |
|---|---|---|
| A-1654 | 1960.5.10 | Venetian 14th Century<br>*Angel of the Annunciation* |
| A-1655 | 1960.5.11 | Venetian 14th Century<br>*Virgin of the Annunciation* |
| A-1656 | 1960.5.12 | Venetian 14th Century<br>*Saint Peter* |
| A-1657 | 1960.5.13 | Venetian 14th Century<br>*Saint Paul* |
| A-1658 | 1961.1.5 | Follower of Michelangelo Buonarroti, After the Antique<br>*Apollo and Marsyas* |
| A-1659 | 1960.5.14 | Possibly Pisan 14th Century<br>*Angel with Symphonia* |
| A-1660 | 1960.5.15 | Possibly Pisan 14th Century<br>*Angel with Tambourine* |
| A-1661 | 1960.5.16 | Benedetto da Maiano<br>*Madonna and Child* |
| A-1662 | 1961.1.6 | Jacopo Sansovino (Jacopo d' Antonio Tatti)<br>*Madonna and Child* |
| A-1663 | 1961.9.103 | Circle of Giovanni di Turino<br>*Madonna and Child* |
| A-1664 | 1961.9.104 | Italian 17th Century<br>*Chiaro da Verrazano* |
| A-1665 | 1961.9.105 | Italian 17th Century<br>*Giovanni da Verrazano* |
| A-1666 | 1961.9.106 | Alessandro Vittoria<br>*A Gentleman of the Zorzi Family* |
| A-1667 | 1961.9.107 | Alessandro Vittoria<br>*A Lady of the Zorzi Family* |
| A-1668 | 1955.10.1 | Nigerian, Court of Benin<br>*Fowl* |
| A-1669 | 1956.2.1 | After Andrea del Verrocchio<br>*Alexander the Great* |
| A-1670 | 1956.14.2 | Jules Dalou<br>*Alphonse Legros* |
| A-1671 | 1957.1.1 | Jean-Antoine Houdon<br>*Diana* |
| A-1673 | 1943.3.1 | Honoré Daumier<br>*Joseph, Baron de Podenas* |
| A-1674 | 1943.3.2 | Honoré Daumier<br>*Benjamin Delessert* |
| A-1675 | 1943.3.3 | Honoré Daumier<br>*Jean-Claude Fulchiron* |
| A-1676 | 1943.3.4 | Honoré Daumier<br>*Auguste-Hilarion, Comte de Kératry* |
| A-1677 | 1943.3.5 | Honoré Daumier<br>*Félix Barthe* |
| A-1678 | 1943.3.6 | Honoré Daumier<br>*Pierre-Paul Royer-Collard* |
| A-1679 | 1943.3.7 | Honoré Daumier<br>*Auguste-Hippolyte Ganneron* |
| A-1680 | 1943.3.8 | Honoré Daumier<br>*Dr. Clément-François-Victor-Gabriel Prunelle* |
| A-1681 | 1943.3.9 | Honoré Daumier<br>*Jean-Pons-Guillaume Viennet* |
| A-1682 | 1943.3.10 | Honoré Daumier<br>*André-Marie-Jean-Jacques Dupin Âiné* |
| A-1683 | 1943.3.11 | Honoré Daumier<br>*Jean-Marie Fruchard* |
| A-1684 | 1943.3.12 | Honoré Daumier<br>*Le Rieur Edenté (Toothless Laughter, Charles Philipon?)* |
| A-1685 | 1943.3.13 | Honoré Daumier<br>*Pelet de la Lozère (?)* |
| A-1686 | 1943.3.14 | Honoré Daumier<br>*Jean-Auguste Chevandier de Valdrome* |
| A-1687 | 1943.3.15 | Honoré Daumier<br>*Jean-Charles Persil* |
| A-1688 | 1943.3.16 | Honoré Daumier<br>*Alexandre (?) Lecomte* |
| A-1689 | 1943.3.17 | Honoré Daumier<br>*Antoine Odier* |

| Old | New | Artist and Title |
|---|---|---|
| A-1690 | 1943.3.18 | Honoré Daumier<br>*Charles-Malo-François, Comte de Lameth* |
| A-1691 | 1943.3.19 | Honoré Daumier<br>*Horace-François, Comte Sébastiani* |
| A-1692 | 1943.3.20 | Honoré Daumier<br>*Girod de l'Ain (or Admiral Verhuel?)* |
| A-1693 | 1943.3.21 | Honoré Daumier<br>*Charles-Léonard Gallois (?)* |
| A-1694 | 1943.3.22 | Honoré Daumier<br>*Claude Baillot* |
| A-1695 | 1943.3.23 | Honoré Daumier<br>*Alfred-Frédéric-Pierre, Comte de Falloux* |
| A-1696 | 1943.3.24 | Honoré Daumier<br>*Jean Vatout* |
| A-1697 | 1958.8.1 | Imitator of Honoré Daumier<br>*The Confidant* |
| A-1698 | 1958.8.2 | Imitator of Honoré Daumier<br>*The Representative* |
| A-1699 | 1959.7.1 | Italian 16th Century<br>*Mercury* |
| A-1700 | 1960.2.2 | Sir Jacob Epstein<br>*An American Soldier* |
| A-1701 | 1960.10.1 | Florentine 16th Century<br>*Farnese Hercules* |
| A-1702 | 1961.17.1 | Imitator of Honoré Daumier<br>*The Small Shopkeeper* |
| A-1703 | 1961.17.2 | Imitator of Honoré Daumier<br>*The Visitor* |
| A-1704 | 1962.7.1 | Bernhard A. Böhmer<br>*Death Mask of Ernst Barlach ?* |
| A-1705 | 1963.10.236 | Charles Despiau<br>*Maud Dale* |
| A-1706 | 1963.10.237 | Jacques Lipchitz (Chaim Jacob Lipchitz), Moïse Kisling, and Conrad Moricand<br>*Death Mask of Amedeo Modigliani* |
| A-1707 | 1963.10.238 | Paul Gauguin<br>*Père Paillard* |
| A-1708 | 1963.10.239.a | Paul Gauguin<br>*Pair of Wooden Shoes* |
| A-1708 | 1963.10.239.b | Paul Gauguin<br>*Pair of Wooden Shoes* |
| A-1709 | 1963.10.240 | Jean-Antoine Houdon<br>*Voltaire* |
| A-1710 | 1963.10.241 | Amedeo Modigliani<br>*Head of a Woman* |
| A-1711 | 1963.10.242 | Auguste Renoir<br>*Claude Renoir ("Coco")* |
| A-1715 | 1964.8.1 | Imitator of Honoré Daumier<br>*The Jolly Good Fellow* |
| A-1716 | 1964.8.2 | Imitator of Honoré Daumier<br>*The Listener* |
| A-1717 | 1964.8.3 | Carl Milles<br>*Head of Orpheus* |
| A-1718 | 1943.3.25 | Honoré Daumier<br>*The Refugees* |
| A-1719 | 1964.8.4 | Ethiopian 18th or 19th Century<br>*The Nativity* |
| A-1720 | 1965.4.1 | Aristide Maillol<br>*Venus* |
| A-1721 | 1965.5.1 | Wilhelm Lehmbruck<br>*Standing Woman* |
| A-1722 | 1967.5.1 | Aristide Maillol<br>*Summer* |
| A-1723 | 1967.14.1 | Jacques Prou II<br>*Charles, Duc de Berry* |
| A-1724 | 1967.15.1 | Aristide Maillol<br>*Bather with Raised Arms* |
| A-1725 | 1967.13.2 | Antoine-Louis Barye<br>*Tiger Seizing a Gazelle* |

| Old | New | Artist and Title |
|---|---|---|
| A-1726 | 1967.13.3 | Constantin Brancusi<br>*Bird in Space* |
| A-1727 | 1967.13.4 | Constantin Brancusi<br>*Agnes E. Meyer* |
| A-1728 | 1967.13.5 | Charles Despiau<br>*Agnes E. Meyer* |
| A-1729 | 1967.13.6 | Auguste Rodin<br>*Figure of a Woman "The Sphinx"* |
| A-1730 | 1968.2.1 | William Rimmer<br>*Dying Centaur* |
| A-1732 | 1969.4.1 | Maurice Sterne<br>*Sitting Figure* |
| A-1733 | 1968.23.1 | Gustave Pimienta<br>*Eagle* |
| A-1734 | 1968.23.2 | Gustave Pimienta<br>*Orpheus* |
| A-1735 | 1969.10.2 | Charles Despiau<br>*Head of a Woman* |
| A-1736 | 1970.7.1 | Alessandro Algardi<br>*Saint Matthew* |
| A-1737 | 1970.30.1 | Paul Gauguin<br>*Eve* |
| A-1738 | 1972.78.1 | Auguste Rodin<br>*Gustav Mahler* |
| A-1739 | 1971.1.1 | Henry Merwin Shrady<br>*The Empty Saddle* |
| A-1740 | 1971.6.1 | Nicolas Legendre<br>*The Penitent Magdalen* |
| A-1741 | 1971.5.1 | After Martin van den Bogaert, called Desjardins<br>*The Grand Dauphin* |
| A-1742 | 1971.5.2 | After Martin van den Bogaert, called Desjardins<br>*Louis XIV* |
| A-1743 | 1971.33.1 | William Zorach<br>*Puma (looking left)* |
| A-1744 | 1971.33.2 | William Zorach<br>*Puma (looking right)* |
| A-1745 | 1969.9.1 | Possibly Hellenistic or Roman 2d Century B.C. –1st Century A.D.<br>*Torso of Aphrodite* |
| A-1746 | 1971.66.10 | Alexander Archipenko<br>*Woman Combing Her Hair* |
| A-1747 | 1971.66.11 | Jean Arp (Hans Arp)<br>*Grande Sculpture Classique* |
| A-1748 | 1971.66.12 | Raymond Duchamp-Villon<br>*Torso of a Young Man* |
| A-1749 | 1971.66.13 | George Segal<br>*Girl Putting on an Earring* |
| A-1750 | 1972.12.1 | Antonio Lombardo<br>*Peace Establishing Her Reign* |
| A-1751 | 1972.24.1 | François Coudray<br>*Saint Sebastian* |
| A-1752 | 1973.2.3 | Sir Jacob Epstein<br>*Princess Menen* |
| A-1753 | 1973.9.1 | Pietro Tacca<br>*The Pistoia Crucifix* |
| A-1754 | 1973.12.1 | Anne Dean Truitt<br>*Spume (Light Grey)* |
| A-1755 | 1974.8.1 | After the Antique, 19th/20th Century<br>*Hercules Slaying Lichas* |
| A-1756 | 1974.18.1 | Giovanni Battista Foggini<br>*Bacchus and Ariadne* |
| A-1757 | 1974.18.2 | Giuseppe Piamontini<br>*Venus and Cupid* |
| A-1758 | 1973.27.1 | Alberto Giacometti<br>*The Invisible Object (Hands Holding the Void)* |
| A-1759 | 1974.29.1 | Auguste Rodin<br>*Thomas Fortune Ryan* |
| A-1760 | 1977.28.1 | Alfredo Halegua<br>*America* |
| A-1761 | 1974.49.1 | Wilhelm Lehmbruck<br>*Seated Youth* |
| A-1762 | 1974.89.1 | James Garrison Hagan<br>*Column IV* |
| A-1763 | 1974.115.1 | Masayuki Nagare<br>*Breakers (The Wave)* |

| Old | New | Artist and Title |
|---|---|---|
| A-1764 | 1975.11.1 | Pierre-Jean David d'Angers<br>*Thomas Jefferson* |
| A-1765 | 1975.6.1 | Probably Neapolitan, 19th/20th Century<br>*Paul III (Farnese), Pope* |
| A-1766 | 1975.12.1 | Augustus Saint-Gaudens<br>*Diana of the Tower* |
| A-1767 | 1975.44.1 | Anne Dean Truitt<br>*Mid-Day* |
| A-1768 | 1975.43.1 | Sir Jacob Epstein<br>*Meum Lindsell-Stewart* |
| A-1769 | 1975.79.1 | Elie Nadelman<br>*Two Nudes* |
| A-1770 | 1975.80.1 | Lila Pell Katzen<br>*Antecedent* |
| A-1771 | 1975.100.2 | Larry Bell<br>*Chrome and Glass Construction* |
| A-1772 | 1975.101.1 | Pittaluga<br>*Nymph of the Fields* |
| A-1773 | 1975.101.2 | Pittaluga<br>*Nymph of the Woods* |
| A-1774 | 1976.10.1 | Claude Michel, called Clodion<br>*Model for "Poetry and Music"* |
| A-1775 | 1976.3.1 | Johannes Götz<br>*Boy Balancing on a Ball* |
| A-1776 | 1976.28.1 | Louis-Simon Boizot<br>*Louis XVI* |
| A-1777 | 1976.58.1 | Isamu Noguchi<br>*Great Rock of Inner Seeking* |
| A-1778 | 1977.3.1 | Käthe Kollwitz<br>*In God's Hands* |
| A-1779 | 1976.70.1 | Ivan Puni (Jean Pougny)<br>*Suprematist Construction Montage* |
| A-1780 | 1977.27.1 | Pierre-Jean David d'Angers<br>*Ambroise Paré* |
| A-1781 | 1977.20.1 | Jean Arp (Hans Arp)<br>*The Forest* |
| A-1782 | 1977.29.1 | Jacques Lipchitz (Chaim Jacob Lipchitz)<br>*Bas-Relief, I* |
| A-1783 | 1977.48.1 | Paul Manship<br>*Dancer and Gazelles* |
| A-1784 | 1977.48.2 | Paul Manship<br>*Diana and a Hound* |
| A-1785 | 1977.58.1 | Albert-Ernest Carrier-Belleuse<br>*The Abduction of Hippodamia* |
| A-1786 | 1977.59.1 | Claude Michel, called Clodion<br>*Silenus Crowned by Nymphs* |
| A-1787 | 1977.47.1 | Reginald Butler<br>*Girl* |
| A-1788 | 1977.47.2 | Alberto Giacometti<br>*The Chariot* |
| A-1789 | 1977.47.3 | Alberto Giacometti<br>*The City Square* |
| A-1790 | 1977.47.4 | Alberto Giacometti<br>*The Forest* |
| A-1791 | 1977.47.5 | Alberto Giacometti<br>*Kneeling Woman* |
| A-1792 | 1977.47.6 | Alberto Giacometti<br>*Standing Woman* |
| A-1793 | 1977.47.7 | Alberto Giacometti<br>*Walking Man II* |
| A-1794 | 1977.47.8 | Ibram Lassaw<br>*Rhiannon* |
| A-1795 | 1977.47.9 | Marino Marini<br>*Horseman* |
| A-1796 | 1977.47.10 | Henry Moore<br>*Three Motives Against Wall, Number 1* |
| A-1797 | 1977.47.11 | Oskar Schlemmer<br>*Homo* |
| A-1798 | 1977.47.12 | Ernest Tino Trova<br>*Walking Man* |
| A-1799 | 1977.76.1 | Alexander Calder<br>*Untitled* |
| A-1800 | 1977.60.1 | David Smith<br>*Circle I* |

| Old | New | Artist and Title |
|---|---|---|
| A-1801 | 1977.60.2 | DAVID SMITH<br>*Circle II* |
| A-1802 | 1977.60.3 | DAVID SMITH<br>*Circle III* |
| A-1803 | 1977.49.1 | JAMES ROSATI<br>*Untitled* |
| A-1804 | 1977.60.4 | DAVID SMITH<br>*Voltri VII* |
| A-1805 | 1975.114.1 | ALEXANDER CALDER<br>*Model for East Building Mobile* |
| A-1806 | 1977.75.6 | JEAN ARP (HANS ARP)<br>*Mirr* |
| A-1807 | 1977.75.7 | MARY CALLERY<br>*Amity* |
| A-1808 | 1977.75.8 | JOSÉ DE RIVERA<br>*Black, Yellow, Red* |
| A-1809 | 1977.75.9 | ERNEST TINO TROVA<br>*Falling Man* |
| A-1810 | 1977.64.1 | HERBERT FERBER<br>*Homage to Piranesi V* |
| A-1811 | 1977.65.1 | MICHAEL BOLUS<br>*Sculpture Number 2* |
| A-1812 | 1978.13.1 | HENRY MOORE<br>*Two Piece Mirror Knife Edge* |
| A-1813 | 1978.14.1 | DAVID SMITH<br>*Cubi XXVI* |
| A-1814 | 1978.24.1 | JAMES ROSATI<br>*Untitled* |
| A-1815 | 1978.43.1 | HENRY MOORE<br>*Knife Edge Mirror Two Piece* |
| A-1816 | 1978.22.1 | AFTER JEAN ARP (HANS ARP)<br>*Oriforme* |
| A-1817 | 1978.21.1 | ANTHONY CARO<br>*National Gallery Ledge Piece* |
| A-1818 | 1978.42.1 | ATTRIBUTED TO GIUSTO LE COURT<br>*A Venetian Ecclesiastic* |
| A-1819 | 1978.71.1 | AUGUSTE RODIN<br>*The Sirens* |
| A-1820 | 1979.10.1 | JACOPO SANSOVINO (JACOPO D'ANTONIO TATTI)<br>*Doorknocker with Nereid, Triton, and Putti* |
| A-1821 | 1979.52.1 | WILLIAM ZORACH<br>*Man of Judah* |
| A-1822 | 1979.51.1 | DAVID SMITH<br>*Sentinel I* |
| A-1823 | 1979.30.1 | MAX ERNST<br>*Capricorn* |
| A-1830 | 1980.44.1 | ANTOINE-LOUIS BARYE<br>*Charles VII Victorious on Horseback* |
| A-1831 | 1980.44.2 | ANTOINE-LOUIS BARYE<br>*Gaston de Foix on Horseback* |
| A-1832 | 1980.44.3 | ANTOINE-LOUIS BARYE<br>*General Bonaparte on Horseback* |
| A-1833 | 1980.44.4 | ANTOINE-LOUIS BARYE<br>*Horse Attacked by a Tiger* |
| A-1834 | 1980.44.5 | ANTOINE-LOUIS BARYE<br>*Two Bears Wrestling* |
| A-1835 | 1980.44.6 | AUGUST-NICOLAS CAIN<br>*Crowing Rooster* |
| A-1836 | 1980.44.7 | THÉODORE GERICAULT<br>*Flayed Horse I* |
| A-1837 | 1980.44.8 | THÉODORE GERICAULT<br>*Flayed Horse II* |
| A-1838 | 1980.44.9 | THÉODORE GERICAULT<br>*Flayed Horse III* |
| A-1839 | 1980.44.10 | JEAN-LOUIS-ERNEST MEISSONIER<br>*A Horseman in a Storm* |
| A-1840 | 1981.55.1 | JEAN-JACQUES PRADIER (CALLED JAMES)<br>*Chloris Caressed by Zephyr* |
| A-1842 | 1980.74.1 | CESAR BALDACCINI, CALLED CESAR<br>*Homage to Brancusi* |
| A-1843 | 1980.75.1 | CONSTANTIN BRANCUSI<br>*Maiastra (Bird Before It Flew)* |
| A-1844 | 1981.63.1 | GAETANO MONTI<br>*Head of a Bull* |

| Old | New | Artist and Title |
|---|---|---|
| A-1845 | 1981.53.1 | TONY SMITH<br>*Wandering Rocks* |
| A-1852 | 1982.6.1 | AUGUSTE RODIN<br>*Memorial Relief (Hand of Child)* |
| A-1853 | 1982.33.2 | BRUCE CONNER<br>*Camera Obscura* |
| A-1854 | 1982.33.3 | JOSEPH CORNELL<br>*La Ricordanza* |
| A-1855 | 1982.54.1 | JOSEPH CORNELL<br>*Untitled (Medici Prince)* |
| A-1856 | 1982.77.1 | SIR JACOB EPSTEIN<br>*George Bernard Shaw* |
| A-1857 | 1942.9.2520 | ITALIAN 18TH CENTURY<br>*Andiron: Apollo with the Serpent* |
| A-1858 | 1942.9.2521 | ITALIAN 18TH CENTURY<br>*Andiron: Vulcan with His Anvil* |
| A-1859 | 1983.1.49 | ALEXANDER CALDER<br>*Obus* |
| A-1860 | 1983.1.50 | MARY CALLERY<br>*Epoque de Rennes* |
| A-1861 | 1983.1.51 | JULES DALOU<br>*Mother and Child* |
| A-1862 | 1983.1.52 | JO DAVIDSON<br>*Ailsa Mellon Bruce* |
| A-1863 | 1983.1.53 | CHARLES DESPIAU<br>*Adolescent Girl* |
| A-1864 | 1983.1.54 | FERNAND LÉGER<br>*Composition with Fruit* |
| A-1865 | 1983.1.55 | FERNAND LÉGER<br>*Bird among Flowers* |
| A-1866 | 1983.1.56 | ARISTIDE MAILLOL<br>*Modesty* |
| A-1867 | 1983.1.57 | ARISTIDE MAILLOL<br>*Reclining Nude* |
| A-1868 | 1983.1.58 | ARISTIDE MAILLOL<br>*Rosita* |
| A-1869 | 1983.1.59 | ARISTIDE MAILLOL<br>*Seated Woman* |

| Old | New | Artist and Title |
|---|---|---|
| A-1870 | 1983.1.60 | ARISTIDE MAILLOL<br>*Torso of a Young Woman* |
| A-1871 | 1983.1.61 | ARISTIDE MAILLOL<br>*Two Young Girls* |
| A-1872 | 1983.1.62 | ARISTIDE MAILLOL<br>*Women Wrestlers* |
| A-1873 | 1983.1.63 | GIACOMO MANZÙ<br>*Sheaves of Wheat* |
| A-1874 | 1983.1.64 | GIACOMO MANZÙ<br>*Vine Branches* |
| A-1875 | 1983.1.65 | GIACOMO MANZÙ<br>*Model Undressing II* |
| A-1876 | 1983.1.66 | GIACOMO MANZÙ<br>*Mother and Child* |
| A-1877 | 1983.1.67 | GIACOMO MANZÙ<br>*Dead Bird* |
| A-1878 | 1983.1.68 | GIACOMO MANZÙ<br>*Dormouse* |
| A-1879 | 1983.1.69 | GIACOMO MANZÙ<br>*Hedgehog* |
| A-1880 | 1983.1.70 | GIACOMO MANZÙ<br>*Owl and Mouse* |
| A-1881 | 1983.1.71 | HENRY MOORE<br>*Stone Memorial* |
| A-1882 | 1983.1.72 | AUGUSTE RENOIR<br>*Maternity: Madame Renoir and Son* |
| B-31805 | 1981.5.70 | CLAES OLDENBURG<br>*Profile Airflow* |
| B-31818 | 1981.5.83 | ROBERT RAUSCHENBERG<br>*Capitol* |
| B-33832 | 1981.5.103 | JASPER JOHNS<br>*Flag* |
| B-33833 | 1981.5.104 | JASPER JOHNS<br>*0 through 9* |
| B-33838 | 1981.5.107 | WILLEM DE KOONING<br>*Untitled* |
| B-33846 | 1981.5.115 | EDWARD KIENHOLZ<br>*Sawdy* |
| B-33851 | 1981.5.120 | CLAES OLDENBURG<br>*Double-Nose/Purse/Punching Bag/Ashtray* |

| Old | New | Artist and Title |
|---|---|---|
| B-33854 | 1981.5.123 | Robert Rauschenberg<br>*Cardbird Door* (recto) |
| B-33863 | 1981.5.132 | Edward Kienholz<br>*The Billionaire Deluxe* |
| B-33864 | 1981.5.133 | Claes Oldenburg<br>*Soft Screw* |
| B-33865 | 1981.5.134 | Mark Di Suvero<br>*T'ang* |
| B-33880 | 1981.5.139 | Claes Oldenburg<br>*Ice Bag—Scale B* |
| B-33881 | 1981.5.267 | Robert Rauschenberg<br>*Publicon—Station I* |
| B-33882 | 1981.5.268 | Robert Rauschenberg<br>*Publicon—Station II* |
| B-33883 | 1981.5.269 | Robert Rauschenberg<br>*Publicon—Station III* |
| B-33884 | 1981.5.270 | Robert Rauschenberg<br>*Publicon—Station IV* |
| B-33885 | 1981.5.271 | Robert Rauschenberg<br>*Publicon—Station V* |
| B-33886 | 1981.5.272 | Robert Rauschenberg<br>*Publicon—Station VI* |
| B-33953 | 1981.5.205 | Edward Kienholz<br>*The Marriage Icon* |
| B-33954 | 1981.5.206 | Edward Kienholz<br>*The Opti-Can Royale* |
| B-33955 | 1981.5.207 | Edward Kienholz<br>*The Econo-Can* |
| B-33975 | 1981.5.227 | Claes Oldenburg<br>*Geometric Mouse—Scale C* |
| B-33988 | 1981.5.240 | Robert Rauschenberg<br>*Ally* |
| B-34790 | 1981.5.266 | Roy Lichtenstein<br>*Untitled Head I* |
| B-34827 | 1974.28.79 | Masatoshi, after<br>M.C. Escher<br>*Three Elements* |
| B-34828 | 1974.28.80 | Masatoshi, after<br>M.C. Escher<br>*Sphere with Fish* |
| B-34829 | 1974.28.81 | Masatoshi, after<br>M.C. Escher<br>*Heaven and Hell* |
| B-34830 | 1974.28.82 | M.C. Escher<br>*Three Elements* |
| B-34831 | 1981.5.273 | Edward Kienholz<br>*The Block Head* |
| B-34836 | 1981.5.278 | Edward Kienholz<br>*The Jerry Can Standard* |
| B-34837 | 1981.5.279 | Ellsworth Kelly<br>*Mirrored Concorde* |
| B-34838 | 1981.5.280 | Roy Lichtenstein<br>*Peace Through Chemistry Bronze* |
| SA-1 | 1942.8.43 | Jo Davidson<br>*Andrew W. Mellon* |
| SA-2 | 1941.13.1 | Jo Davidson<br>*Andrew W. Mellon* |
| SA-3 | 1949.15.1 | Possibly Egyptian<br>Ptolemaic Period<br>332–30 B.C.<br>*Male Head* |
| SA-4 | 1954.21.1 | Walker Hancock<br>*Andrew W. Mellon* |
| SA-7 | 1981.101.1 | Fausta Vittoria Mengarini<br>*David E. Finley* |

# INDEX OF TITLES

Portraits are alphabetized under the sitter's surname.

## A

# B

# C

# D

# E

# H



# I

# M

# N

# P

# Q



# R

# S

# U



# V